CW00944385

THE ARCHAEOBOTANY OF AŞVAN

ENVIRONMENT & CULTIVATION IN EASTERN ANATOLIA

FROM THE CHALCOLITHIC TO THE MEDIEVAL PERIOD

Mark Nesbitt, Jennifer Bates,
Gordon Hillman & Stephen Mitchell

BRITISH INSTITUTE AT ANKARA
Monograph 33
2017

Published by
British Institute at Ankara
10 Carlton House Terrace, London SW1Y 5AH
www.biaa.ac.uk

ISBN 978 1 898249 17 7

Typeset by Gina Coulthard
Printed by Short Run Press Ltd, Exeter

Preface & acknowledgements

Gordon Hillman collecting wild einkorn near Can Hasan in June 1971 (photo Nicholas Mitchell).

More than 40 years have passed since David French, Director of the British Institute at Ankara from 1968 to 1994, directed rescue excavations and an innovative project in environmental archaeology at Aşvan in eastern Turkey. Research on the flora, cultivars and archaeobotany of the Aşvan region played a very large role in the project, but the publication has taken many years of collaboration, and there have been unforeseen delays in bringing this work to a conclusion. Many debts need to be acknowledged in its preparation.

The excavations at the Aşvan sites, which ran from 1968 to 1973, were largely financed by the British Institute at Ankara (BIAA; then the British Institute of Archaeology at Ankara) itself, and by additional grants from the British Academy. Full details of the financial support provided to the project may be found in French 1973a: 72. The fieldwork for the project, which included systematic collection of contemporary flora as well the collection and initial classification of archaeobotanical material from the archaeological sites, was initiated by Gordon Hillman and carried out by student teams under his direction: Nick Ball, Pat Bean, Anne Martin and David Midmore. George Willcox, then a postgraduate student at University College London, was part of the botanical team in 1972 and made a study of the charcoal finds in 1973. Hillman's work on Aşvan was carried out while he was a research fellow of the BIAA from 1970 to 1975, before he returned to the UK to hold academic positions, first at the University of Wales Cardiff (now the University of Cardiff) and then at the Institute of Archaeology, University College London. Mark Nesbitt took over responsibility for publishing the archaeobotanical material in 1985 after completing a master's degree in archaeobotany with Hillman at the Institute of Archaeology, University College London. He spent extended periods as a postdoctoral researcher at the BIAA between 1987 and 1999, working on Aşvan as well as other material from Turkish and Near Eastern sites, before taking up a position at Kew Gardens in 1999. A number of other factors complicated and delayed this study, which began more than a decade after the excavations ended. The archaeobotanical material had been split between the BIAA's archaeobotany laboratory in Ankara and museum stores in Elazığ. In many cases, samples had been subdivided and partly sorted by other hands, requiring considerable detective work in reconstruction. Although there are full records of the excavations, memories about specific details relating to the fieldwork are not as fresh as they once were. Nonetheless, the richness of the material, covering a 5,000-year time span, is a tribute to the original excavation and recovery strategy.

Mark Nesbitt is grateful to David French and Gordon Hillman for entrusting him with the material for publication, to the BIAA for funding his research and to Gülgün Kazan, Yaprak Eran, David French, David Shankland and Roger Matthews for support and encouragement in Ankara. The General Directorate of Antiquities and Museums in Ankara provided the necessary research permissions and the staff of Elazığ Museum gave practical assistance. Bay Turgay Sunguroğlu, a long-standing friend of the Aşvan excavations, was kind enough to take Nesbitt to visit the new village of Aşvan. Antonio Sagona and the late Sven Helms provided information about the Early Bronze Age levels at the Aşvan sites. Particular thanks are due to Anne-Dawn Sykes (formerly Sutton) and to Jane Goddard for the line drawings of the botanical material, to Catherine Longford and Simone Riehl for archaeobotanical advice, to Jim Coulton for advice in the preparation of the publication and to Delwen Samuel for support throughout the study period. The detailed input of the anonymous referees into the manuscript is also much appreciated.

Jennifer Bates of the McDonald Institute for Archaeological Research, University of Cambridge, who was recruited to the team in 2014 as she was concluding a doctoral thesis on the archaeobotany of the Indus Valley civilisation, has enlarged and updated Nesbitt's manuscript. Stephen Mitchell, who directed the excavations at Aşvan Kale from 1970–1972 and who has contributed information on the sites and the regional archaeology, was awarded a British Academy/Leverhulme small grant to complete the publication, which covered Jennifer Bates' expenses during the first four months of 2015. The volume also includes three groundbreaking studies by Gordon Hillman which were originally published in the main preliminary report of the Aşvan project.

The BIAA is grateful to two other organisations, which have supported this publication. The Stanley Smith Horticultural Trust made an award of £5,000 in 2010 to cover publication costs of the volume, at a moment when this seemed imminent. The Trust has generously allowed the BIAA to retain the grant during the following years, when the volume was delayed, and we are grateful to it that the award can now be put to its proper use. The trustees continued to see the Aşvan publication as a priority, and and we especially appreciate their patience in this regard. In 2011 the Robert Kiln Charitable Trust awarded the BIAA £2,000 to support its archaeobotanical work, and this has been used to fund the production of additional illustrations for this volume, which have been prepared by Jennifer Bates.

All the authors owe a large and specific debt to the BIAA Monographs Editor, Tamar Hodos, Bristol University, whose experience and personal knowledge have been indispensable in bringing a complicated academic project to its final conclusion.

Mark Nesbitt, Jennifer Bates & Stephen Mitchell
January 2017

Contents

List of figures

Chapter 5

List of tables

Foreword

This volume contains the final publication of the archaeobotanical remains recovered from four sites at the village of Aşvan in eastern Turkey, which were excavated between 1968 and 1973. The botanical material was collected between 1969 and 1972. As an interval of more than 40 years has passed between the excavations and their publication, this foreword is designed to place the Aşvan project in its context, and to explain the circumstances in which this publication has been produced.

During the 1960s Turkey east of the river Euphrates was virtually uncharted terrain for archaeologists. Excavation permits were almost exclusively restricted to Turkish scholars and most fieldwork was concentrated on Iron Age Urartian sites around Lake Van. An exploratory British venture into this territory was the planned excavation of the Urartian site of Kayalıdere in the province of Muş by Seton Lloyd and Charles Burney, which began in 1965. In the following year there was a long delay in the renewal of the dig permit. The excavation was eventually resumed, but all prospects of future work were definitively aborted after a major earthquake struck the region on 19 August 1966 and destroyed the village of Kayalıdere (Burney 1966; see http://biaa.ac.uk/research/item/name/mus-excavation).

Another east Anatolian excavation during this period had a more direct influence on the Aşvan project. This was the joint Turkish-American dig directed by Halet Çambel and Robert Braidwood at Çayönü, an early Neolithic site located northwest of Diyarbakır. The primary objective of the work at Çayönü was to investigate the origins of animal and plant domestication in northern Mesopotamia, and the excavators paid particular attention to animal bone and plant remains. Study of the botanical material was carried out by the Dutch scholar Willem van Zeist, who was responsible for much groundbreaking work on the arcaheobotany of the Near East at this period (Van Zeist 1972). Domestication and the origins of agriculture became an important focus for archaeological and anthropological research in the late 1960s and early 1970s, and were also the subject of a British Academy major research project on the early history of agriculture, carried out in the Department of Archaeology at the University of Cambridge under the direction of Eric Higgs.

The practical and theoretical approaches of these projects were a major influence on David French, who had been appointed Director of the British Institute at Ankara (BIAA) in 1968. In the same year the BIAA was invited by the Turkish authorities to participate in rescue excavations in the Keban region, which was due to be flooded by the construction of Turkey's first major hydro-electric dam in the upper Euphrates basin. French began work in 1968 at the large mound beside the village of Aşvan. During the 1969 season, French developed a more ambitious strategy to conduct a diachronic environmental study of the Aşvan region by means of the simultaneous excavation of four sites in the village's territory, covering a chronological range from the Chalcolithic to the Medieval period, and including a detailed investigation of the modern village and its environment (http://biaa.ac.uk/research/item/name/the-asvan-project). This programme was carried out between 1970 and 1972. In 1973 work was restricted to the excavations at Taşkun Kale and Taşkun Mevkii, as the waters of the Keban lake rose to submerge the lower-lying sites of Aşvan Kale and Çayboyu. Further details of the excavations and research related to them are discussed in the first chapter of this report.

Four aspects of the Aşvan project were both novel and important in the context of Near Eastern archaeology of the 1960s and 1970s. First, this was the earliest systematic attempt in the Near East to bring an environmental archaeological approach to such a long time period, with particular emphasis on relatively recent historical periods rather than on the origins of human sedentarisation. Second, the excavations applied very high standards of material recovery. This involved not only carefully recorded stratigraphical excavation, but also consistent standards of recovery by the use of sieves: dry-sieving for animal bone, pottery and other non-organic materials; water-sieving and flotation for botanical remains, mostly in the form of carbonised seeds and other plant remains, and wood charcoal. The pioneering use of water-sieving is described in more detail in chapter 2. Third, the approach to the study of Aşvan's environment was dominated by environmental botanical research, both into the cereals and pulses which provided the major food staples and into other plants as critical proxy evidence for the ancient climate, water availability and soil conditions. Fourth, agricultural and domestic practices in the contemporary village, which were still largely unmechanised around 1970, were recorded in detail to provide a template of processes and activities against which the much more sparsely attested ancient record could be assessed. Ethnographic enquiries in the village also served as a means of reconstructing a base-line of agricultural activity around 1938, before any tractors or agricultural machinery were available to the villagers (French 1973b; Mitchell 1998).

French's decision to approach the Aşvan sites from the perspective of their environmental history was partly the product of his own training and experience as a prehistoric archaeologist. At the time when the Aşvan project began he was also directing the excavation of the early Neolithic settlement at Can Hasan III, in the southeast corner of the Konya province, a site which was expected to throw light on the origins of domestication in central Anatolia. Regrettably, as with the publication of the Aşvan project up till now, although the stratigraphy, architecture and artefacts from Can Hasan have been published, the final report on the animal bones, botanical remains and other detailed aspects of this site is still work in progress (http://biaa.ac.uk/research/item/name/can-hasan-excavations).

However, the critical impulse which transformed the work at Aşvan from a relatively conventional excavation to an innovatory and groundbreaking project was the arrival of Gordon Hillman. Hillman, like most archaeobotanists at that period, had a primary interest in cereals and crop domestication, but had been trained as a field botanist. Immediately the focus was turned on the regional flora. He and other members of the botanical team systematically collected plant specimens and seeds from the village territory and further afield, including the mountainous terrain north of Aşvan around Çemişgezek and the lake basin of Hazar Göl south of Elazığ. These still constitute the core of the botanical reference collection housed at the British Institute at Ankara. This exploratory reconnaissance was undertaken at a time when only the first two volumes of Peter Davis' monumental *Flora of Turkey* were available for reference. Environmental archaeologists in the 1960s and 1970s regularly took note of geology, geomorphology and soil types in compiling a picture of the ecological niche which their sites occupied. Hillman's work redirected attention to the whole range of plant life associated with human settlements, including naturally occurring weeds and those that spread in the wake of human activity, as well as the food crops that were already a regular object of research for archaeobotanists (Willcox 2009). The influence of this approach went beyond the botanical team. Many regular archaeologists, including the project director David French, found themselves viewing the landscapes of Anatolia with different eyes. The weeds occurring at contemporary Aşvan, and the carbonised weed seeds recovered from the archaeological sites, also provided an important clue to prevailing environmental conditions at the time of their growth. One important aspect of weed seeds was that they could provide vital proxy evidence for ancient weather, soil and irrigation conditions. They thus supplement the very limited information which is available from ancient pollen samples in eastern Anatolia (Van Zeist 1968).

Hillman's second methodological approach was to identify, record and analyse the human activities relating to cultivated plants, especially cereals, in the 20th-century village. The information that he collected was partly based on observation of conditions around 1970, but also depended on interviews with the older generation of villagers to establish local conditions and practices across the previous generation, back to 1938, for which cadastral surveys of the village and its territory were available (Hillman 1973a, reprinted here as appendix 4). Even as late as 1970 the village of Aşvan was a largely self-sufficient community, with low dependency on external markets, including the regional centre at Elazığ. Despite the introduction of a few tractors owned by wealthier villagers in the 1960s and the use of simple threshing machinery, the agriculture was almost entirely unmechanised. Most of the agricultural processes, from sowing, through harvesting, threshing and winnowing, grain storage, milling and bread-making, were at a technological level that could have been, and often certainly was, replicated in Medieval or earlier times. Data and samples were collected in the modern village in the expectation that these could be correlated with samples found in the archaeological record. This research also provided an indispensable opportunity to record the actual organisation of human activity relating to food production and other aspects of domestic life. Matina Weinstein carried out a participant observation study of village families in the summer of 1972, which not only provided a diary of the largely unseen and often monotonous daily routine of 'women's work', but also noted the impact of these routine activities, including fuel collection, bread-making and waste disposal, within the physical space of a house, its courtyard and the village fields (Weinstein 1973).

One of the most time-consuming chores undertaken by the women of a household was sorting weed seeds from the harvested grain, to ensure that a clean product was taken to the village's single mill, where most of it was turned into coarse flour used for bread-making, or cracked, boiled and dried to make *bulgur*. Village women thus required no special training to sort the archaeological samples that were recovered from the excavations by water-sieving and flotation. The local workforce used during the Aşvan project was thus made up of the men, who were employed to do the digging on site, and the women, who operated the dry-sieves beside the trenches, separating pottery, glass, bone and other finds or who worked through the floated deposits, after these were dry, making the preliminary division into carbonised cereal husks and seeds, weed seeds, charcoal fragments and other flotsam and jetsam. This too provided another insight into the place and role of mostly younger, unmarried women in the village community.

During the period of the excavations, research into the archaeobotany of Aşvan was largely confined to these contemporary ethnographical studies. This state of research is reflected in the series of preliminary reports, written by team members, which makes up the bulk of the 1973 edition of the journal *Anatolian Studies* (volume 23). Hillman wrote three articles for this volume, to explain the work that had been done, and to set out the most important methodological objectives for the project (Hillman 1973a; 1973b; 1973c).

The first paper, 'Agricultural resources and settlement in the Aşvan region', provides the background to the next two papers, outlining the distribution of agricultural assets in the mid 20th century and factors that could influence agricultural systems, and notes the location of the ancient settlements within this modern landscape. The second paper, 'Agricultural productivity and past population potential at Aşvan', models the upper population limits that could have been based on Aşvan's territory, as well as land management systems and agricultural productivity based on the agricultural resources outlined in the previous paper. Hillman's final paper in the volume, 'Crop husbandry and food production: modern basis for the interpretation of plant remains', proved to be the first step in an important aspect of his subsequent research: the use of ethnographic analogies to inform archaeobotanical analysis. In this paper he outlines the importance of using these analogies to create holistic, quantified models of past economies. The study reviews the ways in which plants were used and how assemblages of botanical material correspond to the various processing stages of food crops, especially cereals. They reflect the diverse ways in which a settlement's inhabitants interacted with plants, covering the spectrum from initial cultivation to the final deposition of plant remains in their archaeological contexts.

The relevance of these preliminary studies to this final report on the Aşvan archaeobotany is self-evident, and we have accordingly decided to reprint them as appendixes to this volume. The methodological approach developed by Hillman at Aşvan created a foundation on which much of his own later work and that of other archaeobotanists has been based. In 1981 Hillman published a full discussion of his approach to reconstructing ancient crop husbandry from carbonised crops remains (Hillman 1981) and this was followed by two detailed studies of the processing of glume wheats and free-threshing wheats with particular reference to the Near Eastern evidence (Hillman 1984b; 1985). All three papers repeatedly cite and draw on the Aşvan research (for a full bibliography of Hillman's work, compiled by Mark Nesbitt, see www.homepages.ucl.ac.uk/~tcrndfu/hillman.htm).

The processing of most of the archaeological material from the Aşvan sites lagged far behind the ethnographic study of the contemporary village. Hillman's pupil, George Willcox, undertook a study of the charcoal remains, recovered up to the final 1973 season, and this was published in 1974 (Willcox 1974). Willcox's study included charcoal that had been hand-collected from burnt levels in the trenches, as well as the more fragmentary material recovered by flotation. The only substantive report on the remaining carbonised material recovered by flotation from the site appeared in 1988. It provides a first account of the millet which occurred in Hellenistic and later levels and appears to have been a new introduction to the repertoire of cereals grown at Aşvan in the historical period (Nesbitt, Summers 1988; see section 5.3 in this report).

Hillman, who had other commitments connected to excavations in northwest Europe and the Middle East, including the Epipalaeolithic site of Abu Hureyra in northern Syria (Hillman 2000), entrusted the publication of the Aşvan material to his pupil Mark Nesbitt, now Curator of the Economic Botany Collection at the Royal Botanic Gardens, Kew. Nesbitt has carried out all the primary research on the flots and other carbonised deposits from the Aşvan sites, established the criteria for distinguishing between the cereal remains and paid special attention to identifying the weed seeds. He completed a first draft of chapter 1 on the archaeology of the Aşvan sites and chapter 2 on the methodology, sample selection and recovery methods, including the statistical tabulations. Nesbitt prepared the text for chapter 3, which contains the catalogue and discussion of wild and domesticated plant species present at Aşvan, and 50% of chapter 4, dealing with sample composition and site formation. This includes the economic analysis based on the ratio of different grain types present in the samples, the discussions of dung fuel and the development of new cereal cultivars after the Chalcolithic period, and a comparative evaluation of the archaeobotany of the four Aşvan sites. He also completed about 60% of chapter 5 on plant husbandry and land use. The drawings of seeds by the illustrators Anne-Dawn Suttton and Jane Goddard were also made under his supervision (see Goddard, Nesbitt 1997 for the approach and principles used). When in 2014 it became clear that Nesbitt was not in a position to finish the work on his own, Tamar Hodos of Bristol University, the Monographs Editor for the British Institute at Ankara, made an assessment of the manuscript and materials that had been prepared up to this date to establish how much further work would be needed to complete it. With this in mind, she approached Jennifer Bates of the University of Cambridge, who was in the final stage of completing a PhD thesis on the macrobotanical and phytolith analysis of Indus civilisation villages, with special reference to subsistence agriculture, and was available to take the project forward. In the early months of 2015, following consultation with Nesbitt and drawing on his notes, Bates revised and completed chapters 4 and 5, and drafted chapter 6, which sets out the botanical evidence for climate variation, and chapter 7, which outlines the main conclusions and sets out an agenda for further research. Stephen Mitchell, who participated in the Aşvan project from 1970, and was site director of the excavations at Aşvan Kale itself, has provided further information about the excavations and the methodologies for material recovery used at the sites. With the close support of the two main authors he has also revised the manuscript as a whole in preparation for the final publication.

This report, as may be seen, has had a lengthy genesis and is a collaborative product. The authors hope that it does justice to the inspiration and creative energy that Gordon Hillman brought to its origins. David French, the overall director of the Aşvan project, established the central principle that a systematic record of the resources and activities of the contemporary settlement should provide a template against which the archaeological record of previous habitation could be assessed and measured. This approach was not confined to archaeobotany but extended also to cover animal husbandry, village architecture and settlement layout, communications systems, water management, geomorphology and land use. Inevitably, the record of a contemporary settlement, based on repeated observation, is in most respects far more extensive and detailed than any possible account of an archaeological site. The excavations at Aşvan, as at almost all ancient sites, only extended to a small fraction of the original settlements and could only recover material that had survived, usually broken, degraded or otherwise transformed from its original state, into modern times. It is accordingly difficult to make direct comparisons between conditions of the distant past and those of the present day.

The survival of botanical remains on the majority of sites, which are not favoured by exceptional preservation conditions, depends on the chance that seeds and other parts of plants have been charred and that the carbonised material has not been crushed or pulverised to the point that identification is no longer possible. Under these conditions, the material, and in particular carbonised cereal remains, can provide especially detailed information about the ways in which they were used and exploited if the find context can be identified, either within the life-cycle of the crop, from harvest to consumption and the generation of waste products, or spatially within ancient structures (see section 4.1). The archaeology of the Aşvan sites produced few high-quality assured contexts. The principle exception to this generalisation were the burnt ruins of a late Hellenistic house at Aşvan Kale, containing several cooking ovens and items of furniture, including a loom, various bronze and pottery vessels, as well as a hoard of silver coins which was concealed in a coarse-ware pot and stashed into one of the walls around 66/65 BC (McNicoll 1973; Mitchell 1980: 40). These find circumstances allow more detailed analysis of the food crops than is possible in any of the other deposits on the Aşvan sites. The heavily grain-rich samples are characteristic of late-stage cereal processing, as would be expected at a location where food was being made and consumed. Other finds include seeds of bitter vetch (*Vicia ervilia*), nigella and chickpea, all probably for culinary use. However, it is important to notice that most of the batches recovered from the Medieval levels also seem to have derived from primary food production or from cooking accidents (see section 4.3.3.2), and this shows that the specific identification of the find-spot within or near a building is not an essential prerequisite for deducing the nature of the archaeobotanical deposit. The actual composition of the seeds and other remains within a batch can also indicate where this batch fitted into the chain of food production and consumption. However, it is not always possible to draw conclusions even from plentiful deposits. The earliest Aşvan site at Çayboyu, dating to the Chalcolithic period, produced rich deposits of carbonised grain, but virtually no architecture. In the absence of a close definition of the find context, the interpretation of the samples, which contained significant proportions of hulled barley, hulled wheat and free-threshing wheat mixed with one another, remains enigmatic (see section 4.3.1.2).

Find circumstances and the element of luck and chance, that are part of all excavations, set limits to the scope of the argument in any archaeological research project. The excavations at Aşvan produced results that are typical for many archaeological sites. It was much more unusual to encounter ancient structures complete with the furniture and products of daily life, and direct indications of the activities that took place in them, than to uncover the ruins of buildings that had been emptied, and thus contained only the sporadic waste products of daily life. Nevertheless, in these circumstances, the use of flotation and wet-sieving comes into its own as a means of recovering carbonised botanical material. Material can be gathered from each and every soil deposit, as far as these have been selected for sampling, and the contents usually represent a random but specific cross section of charred seed and other charred plant material that was present in the settlement at that moment. This sample retains its evidential value for reconstructing both the environment of the ancient settlement and the cultivation and consumption practices of its inhabitants. The primary objective of this report has been to identify and analyse the archaeobotanical material in as much detail as possible to reconstruct the environment and cultivation practices of the people of the Aşvan sites from their earliest recorded settlements to the present day.

1. The Aşvan sites

1.1 Introduction

The British Institute of Archaeology at Ankara (BIAA) conducted rescue excavations between 1968 and 1973 in advance of construction of the Keban dam at four sites near the village of Aşvan in Elazığ province, in eastern Turkey (fig. 1). Aşvan, which was located about 35km north-northwest of the provincial capital Elazığ, was on the south bank of the Murat river, the largest eastern tributary of the Euphrates (Turkish: Fırat nehri), and part of the large basin due to be flooded by the Keban dam. This was the first of Turkey's major hydro-electrical engineering projects on the Euphrates. Members of the Architecture Faculty of the Middle East Technical University in Ankara were the first to respond to the threatened disappearance of the region's archaeological heritage by undertaking a short survey of standing monuments in 1966, and this was published in the following year (*Doomed by the Dam* 1967). In 1967 Robert Whallon from the University of Michigan and Sönmez Kantman from Istanbul University surveyed prehistoric sites in the area that was to be flooded, paying particular attention to the Aşvan area itself and to the Altınova valley east of Elazığ. Their identification number for Aşvan was N52/4, and they also reported and identified the neighbouring sites of Taşkun Kale (N52/2), Taşkun Mevkii (N52/1) and Çayboyu (N52/9) (Whallon 1979). In spring 1968 Turkish and non-Turkish excavation teams were invited to conduct rescue excavations at sites of particular importance (*1968 Summer Work* 1970: 5–7). The newly appointed Director of the British Institute at Ankara, David French, opted for the large sugar-loaf mound at Aşvan, whose pottery suggested an occupation sequence between the Early Bronze Age and the Medieval period (fig. 2). The Assistant Director of the BIAA, Richard Harper, chose to work at the late Roman fort site of Pağnik, on the west bank of the Euphrates.

During 1968 and 1969 excavations were confined to Aşvan Kale itself, adjoining the modern village (French 1970; 1971a). In 1970 the project strategy changed. Between 1970 and 1973 excavations were also carried out at three further sites: Taşkun Kale and Taşkun Mevkii, which lay on higher ground about 3km south of the river, and Çayboyu, about 1km upstream and east of the village.

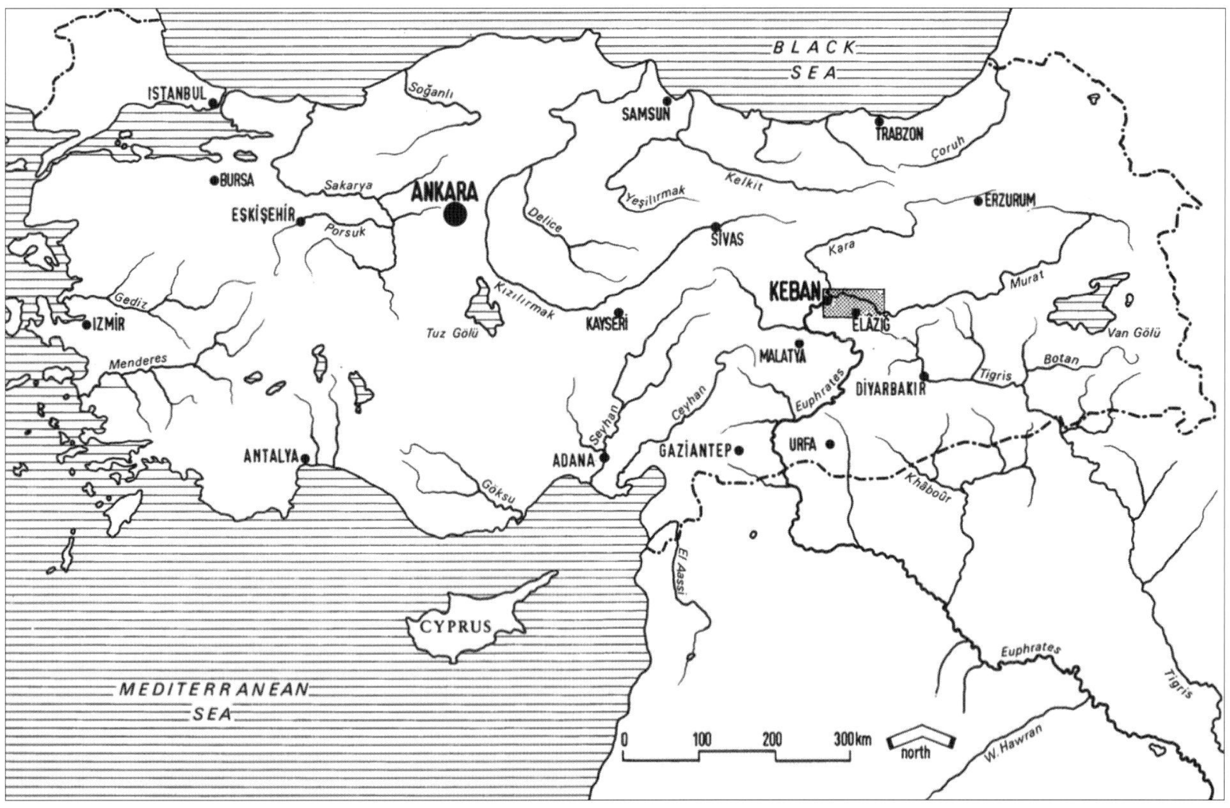

Fig. 1. Turkey and the Keban area (French 1973b: fig. 1).

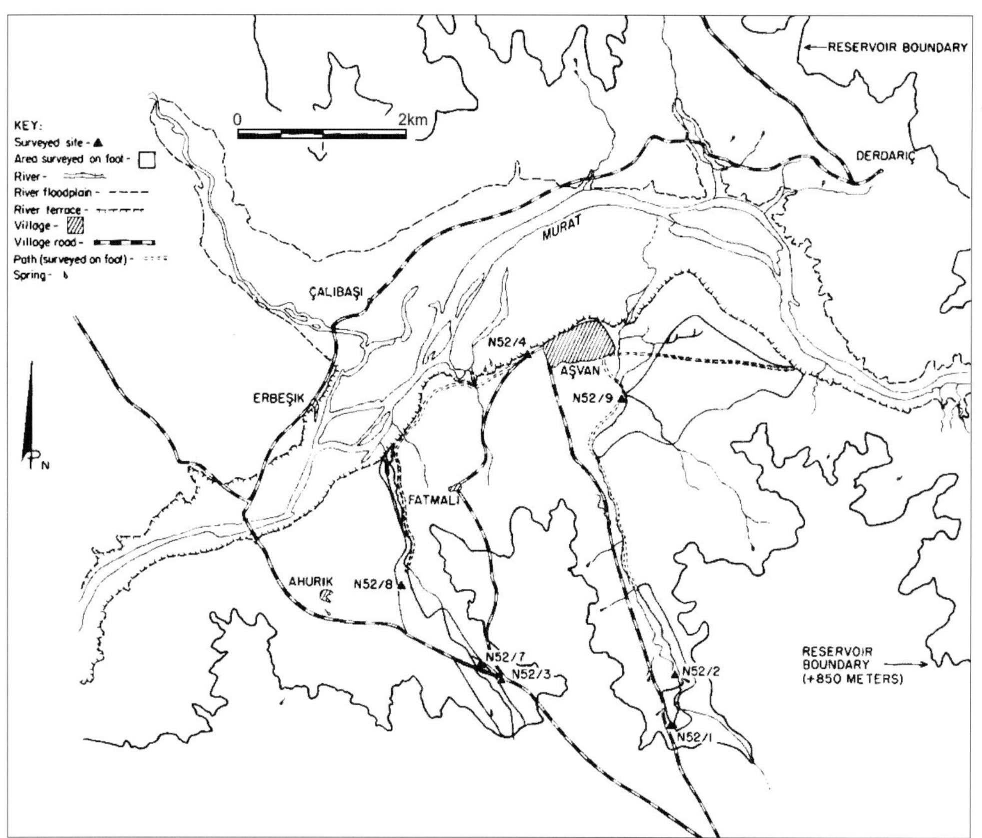

Fig. 2. Map of the Aşvan region before flooding, showing the archaeological sites and the projected dam reservoir boundary at 850m a.s.l. (Whallon 1979: fig. 3).

Survey no.	*Site name*	*5th mill.*	*4th mill.*	*3rd mill.*	*2nd mill.*	*1st mill.*	*AD 1st mill.*	*AD 2nd mill.*
N51/1	**Taşkun Mevkii**		X	X	?			
N52/2	**Taşkun Kale**			X		X	X	X
N52/3	**Kurupınar**	X	X					
N52/4	**Aşvan Kale**			X		X	X	X
N52/7	**Fatmalı**			X				
N52/8	Ahurik						?	
N52/9	**Çayboyu**		X					

Table 1. Archaeological sites and periods in the Aşvan region (modified after Mitchell 1998: 86). Excavated sites are in bold type.

This ensured that the chronological coverage of settlements explored during the Aşvan project extended back to the Chalcolithic period (Çayboyu), to earlier (Taşkun Mevkii) and later phases of the Early Bronze Age (Taşkun Kale, Aşvan Kale) and to the Late Bronze Age (Aşvan Kale), and also included several phases of historical occupation at Taşkun Kale and Aşvan Kale between the first century BC and the 14th century AD. In addition, a range of other interrelated research activities was added to the excavations to create a project which accommodated wider objectives in environmental archaeology (French 1972; 1973c). We show the periods that were represented at Aşvan and the sites in its immediate neighbourhood in a simplified diagram (table 1).

The prehistoric archaeology of the upper Euphrates region as a whole has been documented by Whallon and Kantman's 1967 survey (Whallon, Kantman 1969; Whallon 1979), by the rescue excavations, including those at Aşvan, which took place during the Keban project and by the long-term excavation of the large site of Arslantepe (Frangipane 2011), which lies close to the modern city of Malatya on the west bank of the Euphrates, around 60km as the crow flies southwest of Keban.

The specific objective of the excavation of the Aşvan sites was to investigate the settlement pattern and agricultural economy of their catchment area, covering about 50km^2 on the southern side of the Murat river, in which Aşvan Kale appeared to be the most important settlement site (fig. 3). The excavations were therefore matched by botanical, geomorphological and ethnographic work, which collected data relating to the modern environment. This was a pioneering interdisciplinary research strategy, designed to gather information about the basis for modern subsistence at Aşvan, which could then be used as a benchmark against which to assess any evidence that could be recovered from the ancient settlements. A volume entitled *Aşvan 1968–1972: an interim report*, containing preliminary site reports and several studies related to the environmental project, appeared in 1973, edited by the project's director, David French (French 1973a). Of the sites, Çayboyu and Aşvan Kale are now permanently flooded by the dam, Taşkun Mevkii is at the edge of the lake, crowned by modern buildings, and Taşkun Kale was reported in 2003 as almost entirely submerged.

The excavations took place at a time of great interest in innovative methodologies, linked to the 'New Archaeology' of the 1960s (French 1973c). In addition to Gordon Hillman's archaeobotanical studies, work on the contemporary village and its territory included study of sheep and goat mandibles, designed among other things to establish the relationship between the age at which animals were slaughtered to the economic exploitation of the flocks (Payne 1973). There was a full-scale examination of the architecture of contemporary Aşvan, concerned with the design and functions of individual houses and with the layout of the village as a whole (Hall et al. 1973). Agricultural tools were collected and classified in relation to their functions and the community's needs (Williams 1973a) and there was an ethnographic analysis of household activities, especially relating to food storage and preparation (Weinstein 1973).

The Aşvan sites were some of the first excavations at which large-scale flotation and wet-sieving was used for the recovery of seeds, charcoal and animal bone. A flotation machine had been developed during the 1969 excavation of Can Hasan III, in central Turkey, in a collaboration between David French, Gordon Hillman and the zooarchaeologist Sebastian Payne (French 1971b; 1972; French et al. 1972). Large volumes of soil were floated from the second season of the Aşvan excavations; in addition, deposits of burnt seeds were hand-collected from the Hellenistic destruction level of Aşvan Kale (see chapter 2.2.1, 2.2.2).

One of the important influences on the research strategy at Aşvan was the University of Cambridge project, inspired and directed by Eric Higgs, which focused on the origins and early phases of plant and animal domestication in a diverse range of environments and locations. However, while sharing many of the Cambridge project's research methods and questions, the Aşvan project had a different objective: to conduct a diachronic study of human exploitation of the region's resources from the early prehistoric

Fig. 3. View of Aşvan Kale and the Murat river from the south.

as black locust (*Robinia pseudoacacia*, a native of North America) and tree-of-heaven (*Ailanthus altissima*, from China). Fruit trees such as the mulberry, pear, peach, apricot, almond, cherry, plum, pomegranate and walnut are also cultivated. Hillman describes their uses (Hillman 1973b: 238–39 = appendix 5). A number of spiny wild trees grow around the village, including oleaster (*Elaeagnus angustifolia*), hackberry (*Celtis tournefortii*), Christ's thorn (*Paliurus spina-christi*), blackberry (*Rubus* sp.), fig, elder (*Sambucus ebulus*) and hawthorn (*Crataegus* sp.), most of which produce edible fruit as well as thorny wood, which is used for fencing and fuel (Willcox 1974: 120–21). In addition to these trees, there are many ruderal herbs and grasses, which colonise disturbed ground and often have a wide geographical distribution.

Cultivated land. In addition to the range of cereal crops that were cultivated in mid-20th-century Aşvan, comprising soft and hard wheats, two- and six-rowed barley, oats, millet and sorghum, many weed species are noted in modern fields in the region. The significance of these is discussed in chapter 4 in the context of interpreting the ancient seeds.

The valley bottom. The unstable sandbanks and mudflats of the flood plain are dominated by spiny or toxic plants. Tamarisk (*Tamarix smyrnensis*) has been periodically a dominant species, heavily exploited for fuel. Smaller herbs include thorny saltwort (*Noaea mucronata*), cocklebur (*Xanthium echinatum*), liquorice (*Glycyrrhiza glabra*) and Camelthorn (*Alhagi pseudalhagi*). These last three species are also common on the similarly disturbed and heavily grazed fallow fields of the region. Small trees such as willow (*Salix* sp.) and, less commonly, the chaste-tree (*Vitex agnus-castus*) grow on the unstable riverbanks. Reed (*Phragmites australis*) is common and frequently used for roofing.

Upland grazing. The steeper, non-cultivable hillsides are heavily grazed. Grasses and herbs resistant to grazing, such as *Aegilops triuncialis* and *Ae. umbellata*, *Euphorbia* sp. and *Astragalus* sp., are accordingly important and these grasses become dominant by mid summer. There are a few spiny shrubs, including hawthorn and Christ's thorn, and wild almond grows nearby in the region (*Amygdalus* sp.). Willcox records the presence of a small area of relict forest of oak (*Quercus brantii*) on an inaccessible, north-facing outcrop of rock some 8km south of Aşvan Kale (Willcox 1974: 122).

Woodland. All of the above classes of habitat are heavily under the influence of humans and their grazing animals. An artificial climax vegetation is imposed on the area by the disturbance of grazing and cultivation. For the nature of the vegetation in the past, when human activities were less intense, it is necessary to examine 'primary' habitats where something closer to a natural climax vegetation has formed. Two of the nearest such habitats to the Aşvan region are the screes of the limestone ranges of Çemişgezek, some 17km to the north of Aşvan, and the oak woodland on the northern shore of Hazar Gölü, 55km southeast of Aşvan. The road from Elazığ to Çemişgezek, north of the Murat, runs through the limestone foothills of the Munzur mountain ranges. The limestone scree slopes are too stony for cultivation and are lightly covered with numerous patches of oak scrub. The oak species collected in this area by the Aşvan project botanists include *Quercus brantii*, *Q. infectoria* subsp. *boissieri* and *Q. libanii*, with *Q. robur* subsp. *pedunculiflora* and *Q. petraea* subsp. *pinnatiloba* recorded from the higher hills to the north. Other common trees and shrubs include *Jasminum fruticans*, *Juniperus oxycedrus*, *Rhus coriaria*, *Pistacia eurycarpa*, *Pyrus syriaca*, *Celtis tournefortii*, *Crataegus* sp., *Sambucus* sp. and *Cotinus* sp. Wild grape vine (*Vitis vinifera* ssp. *sylvestris*), *Frangula alnus* and *Platanus orientalis* also grow by stream edges. In mid summer grasses dominate the understory, including abundant wild einkorn, goatgrasses (*Aegilops* sp.) and wild rye (*Secale* sp.). The woodlands that border the northeastern edge of Hazar Göl are much denser. This area, at 1,300m, is a little more elevated than the Çemişgezek woodlands (ca 1,100m) and the rainfall on these south-facing slopes some 70km further south is most unlikely to be higher than there. It seems most likely that the increased density of vegetation is due to these woodlands being better protected from over-grazing. Again, oak is the dominant tree, in quite dense patches. In mid summer the dominant grass species is *Triticum boeticum*. Other wild grasses include *Aegilops* spp., *Hordeum bulbosum*, *Bromus* spp., *Arrhenatherum* spp., *Avena* spp. and *Taeniatherum caput-medusae*. In earlier summer, a rich diversity of wild pulses is present (as doubtless also at Çemişgezek): wild pea, vetches and vetchling. Wild chickpeas and lentils grow nearby in more open, disturbed areas, such as young forest plantations. The pulses typically mature in mid June, the cereals and other grasses in mid to late July. Clearly these woodlands are rich in the wild cereals, pulses and fruits that were an important part of the diet for hunter-gathers, and at least for fruit, until recent times. Oak trees may have been an important source of fodder in the past, as they are today in southeastern Turkey (Mason, Nesbitt 2009).

1.3. The archaeological context

1.3.1. The current state of knowledge

Whallon and Kantman's 1967 survey of the Keban sites broke new ground in the archaeological investigation of eastern Turkey (Whallon, Kantman 1969; Whallon 1979: 168–71, fig.66). Up to that date, survey and excavation of prehistoric sites east of the Euphrates had been restricted to excavation and fieldwork on the Urartian strongholds, mostly conducted by archaeologists from Istanbul University, around Lake Van and at earlier Neolithic settlements in northern Mesopotamia, notably Robert Braidwood and Halet Çambel's excavation of the site of Çayönü, near Diyarbakır. Whallon and Kantman were respectively pupils of Braidwood and Çambel, and the approach and methods applied to the Keban reservoir survey were inspired by Braidwood and Çambel's work (Braidwood et al. 1974). The final report includes valuable observations on the region's climate, vegetation, fauna and mineral resources (Whallon 1979: 5–10). From an archaeological viewpoint this survey was only marginally concerned with sites of the historical period. The subsequent excavations in the Keban project also focused on major sites of the Early Bronze Age, including Korucutepe, Norşuntepe and Tepecik, which were all large settlements in the Altınova, east of Elazığ, and the prehistoric settlements at Pulur and Hanibrahimşah, which were closer to Aşvan. Most of the published reports on these excavations, notably the work of Cathérine Marro relating to the Early Bronze Age (Marro 1997; 2005), have concentrated on the ceramics. As far as archaeobotany is concerned, special mention should be made of the report on the American-Dutch excavation at Korucutepe, which includes a discussion of carbonised botanical samples, dating between the fourth and second millennia BC, obtained by flotation from Korucutepe and the neighbouring site of Tepecik (Van Zeist, Bakker-Heeres in Van Loon 1975: 225–57).

Since the flooding of the Keban basin, attention has turned to the regions south of the Euphrates gorge, which have been flooded by the Karakaya, Atatürk, Birecik and Karkamış dams, a region which extends almost to the modern Syrian border (Özdoğan 1977). Northern Syria has also become one of the best-studied regions of the Near East. A comparative understanding of the Keban region comes from these regional projects and from the excavations at the large site of Arslantepe near Malatya.

The level of investigation of economy and settlement patterns in eastern Anatolia varies considerably according to period. Because of the wealth of evidence available, and because of its relevance to the active debate concerning the interaction between prehistoric Transcaucasian and Mesopotamian cultures, most attention has been given to the Late Uruk and Early Bronze Age periods (Rothman 2003; Smith, Rubinson 2003). There have been few attempts to integrate archaeological and historical sources of later periods, except at a very local level in the interpretation of individual sites. Most broader surveys of the Hellenistic and Roman periods have concentrated on military affairs and political history. It should be noted, however, that there has been an upsurge of environmental research on the Byzantine period, which relies heavily on pollen records from central and eastern Anatolia. This has generated the hypothesis that climate change between the Roman and Medieval periods may have had an appreciable impact on the region's history (Haldon et al. 2014).

1.3.2. Contexts and perspectives

For the purposes of this report, we have treated the archaeology of the Aşvan sites at four levels:

1. Excavated contexts ('loci'). This is concerned with the detailed archaeology of rooms, pits, ovens and the other elements of the sites, and especially the contexts which yielded plant remains. These contexts are mainly treated in the site-by-site analysis (chapter 4.3). The discussions draw on the site excavation reports and additionally on study of the excavation notebooks for Aşvan Kale.

2. The Malatya/Elazığ region. We present a short survey of regional settlement patterns, the chronological framework and the evidence for internal and external influences (section 1.3.3). This draws primarily on Whallon's survey work carried out in 1967 (Whallon and Kantman 1969; Whallon 1979), reports on the other Keban excavations and the long-running Italian excavations at Arslantepe. Arslantepe is important for its long sequence, large-area excavations and well-developed chronology based on numerous radiocarbon dates. It has also yielded well-preserved plant remains. A survey of the Malatya plain, although raising questions about the periodisation of some of Whallon's sites, has identified a similar pattern to that of the Keban region for settlement in the Early Bronze Age (Conti, Persiani 1993), indicating an intensification of the settlement density, which was represented by few sites in Early Bronze Age I and many more in the Early Bronze Age II– III.

3. The Aşvan sites. The summary accounts of the archaeology of each site (see section 1.3.4) are based on the preliminary reports published in *Anatolian Studies* 1969–1974 and the final excavation monographs: Aşvan Kale (Early Bronze Age levels) and Taşkun Mevkii (Sagona 1994), Medieval Taşkun Kale (McNicoll 1983) and post-Bronze Age Aşvan Kale (Mitchell 1980). We have also referred to Stephen Mitchell's retrospective overview of the Aşvan project (Mitchell 1998).

4. The Anatolian/Mesopotamian context. We also offer a brief investigation of how settlement patterns in northern Mesopotamia (northern Syria and Iraq) and the Euphrates valley in Turkey compare to those of the study region (see section 1.3.3). In particular, this includes a comparison with the area around Kurban Höyük, 150km south of Aşvan on the Euphrates, the nearest ancient settlement area to be surveyed in comparable detail (Wilkinson 1990).

1.3.3. The archaeology of the Keban region

The Keban dam was the first of the large dams to be built on the Euphrates. Since the Murat, the largest eastern tributary of the upper Euphrates, joined the main river about 7km north of the dam, this resulted in the flooding of the Euphrates for 50km north of the dam and along a 100km length of the Murat river valley. The lake formed by the dam is mostly narrow, hemmed in by deep rock valleys. No archaeological sites were found in these valleys during survey period.

The Murat valley widens in two places, where archaeological and modern settlement was concentrated. The Aşvan region, covering about 115km^2, contains 11 archaeological sites, all relatively small (see fig. 2). The largest of these, Aşvan Kale, covered about 0.9ha in total. The other point at which the Murat valley broadens is in the Altınova plain, a well-defined area of thick and fertile alluvial soil. Archaeological survey has located 36 sites, of which by far the largest, covering 8.2ha, is Norşuntepe. The Altınova plain contains other relatively large sites, including Tepecik (3.4ha), Değirmen Tepe (2.0ha) and Körtepe (1.7ha).

1.3.3.1. Early settlement. The region has been settled by farmers since the Pre-Pottery Neolithic, as evidenced by the excavations at Cafer Höyük on the Euphrates, not far downstream from the Keban dam (De Moulins 1997), and by unexcavated sites such as Boytepe in the Altınova plain (Özdoğan 2004). Occupation in the Pottery Neolithic, Halafian and Ubaid periods is present, but is too scanty to provide a clear impression of settlement patterns. Late Ubaid levels (period VIII, ending ca 4000 BC) are present at Arslantepe (Balossi-Restelli 2012).

Period VII at Arslantepe is termed by the excavators 'Local Late Chalcolithic', and is chronologically assigned to the Middle Uruk period (4000–3400 BC). Large buildings of a ceremonial or religious nature are found at the top of the mound, and the material finds include mass-produced bowls and a small number of sealings (Frangipane 2001). The pottery tradition is indigenous, with few links to Mesopotamia. It is likely that phases I and II at Çayboyu belong to this local Late Chalcolithic period.

1.3.3.2. Late Uruk (3350–3000 BC). The latter part of the Late Chalcolithic period, the Late Uruk, is well represented in the Keban region. Whallon and Kantman's survey identified a relatively large number of small or medium-sized sites. The pottery shows strong affiliations to Uruk sites in Syro-Mesopotamia. At Arslantepe the monumental public and storage buildings of the Late Uruk period (VIA) show continuities with the preceding phase VII, but the wheelmade light-coloured pottery is markedly different. Although this pottery clearly shows similarities to Syro-Mesopotamian wares, the range of shapes differs from that found at Uruk sites (Frangipane 2000). Thousands of sealings were also found.

Although Whallon's survey did not identify the marked hierarchical site structure which developed in the Keban area in the Early and Late Bronze Ages, there is clearly a strong external influence from Mesopotamia, and some evidence for centralisation that might have affected agricultural practice. This is supported by the survey at Kurban, which observed an intermediate level of occupation with a marked settlement hierarchy and strong Uruk influence. In the Aşvan region, the upper (phase II) levels of Çayboyu are Late Uruk.

Late Uruk pottery is part of a phenomenon – the Uruk expansion – of much-debated significance in greater Mesopotamia (Akkermans, Schwartz 2003: 181–210). In northern Syria a large number of sites dating to the Middle and Late Uruk periods (3600–3000 BC) have architecture, pottery and written records typical of southern Mesopotamia, and this points to the conclusion that these sites housed colonists from that region. In southeastern Turkey, some sites, such as Hassek and Hacınebi, housed colonists, while others, such as Kurban and Arslantepe, show Uruk influence rather than a population influx. At Arslantepe the public buildings combine local architectural forms with Uruk-influenced administrative activity, as evidenced by the thousands of clay sealings, mass-produced bowls and storerooms (Frangipane 2003).

1.3.3.3. Early Bronze Age I (3000–2700 BC). There is a striking change in settlements and pottery at the beginning of the Early Bronze Age. At Arslantepe the Late Uruk phase VIA was burnt, briefly abandoned and replaced by wattle-and-daub huts and handmade Red-Black Burnished Pottery. Very similar architecture and pottery is found at the Aşvan site of Taşkun Mevkii. Whallon's survey, identifying this as a 'Chalcolithic–Early Bronze Age transitional phase', records a collapse in settlement density, with a reduction to seven sites covering a total of 3.4ha. The region around Kurban likewise shows a decreased settlement area, with an increased number of sites, suggesting dispersal of populations into the countryside. The Altınova plain site of Korucutepe was abandoned after the Late Chalcolithic and reoccupied in the Early Bronze Age IIa, perhaps because of the upheavals that may have accompanied the arrival of new cultural influences from Transcaucasia (Van Loon 1980: 272).

The Red-Black Burnished Pottery of eastern Anatolia has long been recognised as having strong affinities with that of Transcaucasia, where the Early Bronze Age sites likewise have wattle-and-daub buildings. The flimsy nature of the structures, the relatively abrupt appearance of a complete package of material culture (the 'Kura-Araxes complex') and its eventual spread as far south as the Levant (where the pottery is known as Khirbet Kerak Ware) have all led archaeologists to propose that the Kura-

Araxes complex was brought by pastoralists travelling south from Transcaucasia (in particular eastern Georgia), possibly in several waves (Rothman 2003). It is not known why these dispersals occurred. Antonio Sagona suggests the movements of culture or population may have been linked to changes in vegetation at the time (see Sagona 1994), but there is no evidence for environmental change or population pressure in Transcaucasia. The export of metal tools and weapons from the Caucasus and eastern Anatolia may have assisted the spread of this culture to the Levant (Kelly-Buccellati 1979; Russell 1980: 55).

The origins of the Kura-Araxes have more recently been questioned in the light of new archaeological evidence from Sos Höyük in northeastern Turkey and radiocarbon dates from Transcaucasia. In essence, small quantities of Red-Black Burnished Pottery appear in the uppermost levels of Arslantepe VII (ca 3500–3350 BC) and VIA (Frangipane 2000), and in large quantities in the earliest level (VA) of Sos Höyük (Sagona, Sagona 2000: 58–65), an archaeological site situated about half way between Arslantepe and Georgia, dated to about 3400 BC. Radiocarbon dates are sparse for Transcaucasia, but the earliest sites with Red-Black Burnished Pottery appear to date to 3350 BC (Palumbi 2003). This raises the question of whether the Kura-Araxes complex in fact arose in Transcaucasia or whether it had a different or wider area of origin, possibly encompassing northeastern Anatolia (Kiguradze 2003). However, some elements of Transcaucasian culture, including wattle-and-daub architecture and monochrome burnished pottery, do appear earlier in eastern Georgia than elsewhere.

Several Early Bronze Age I levels have been excavated in the Keban region, but none of these sites show the curious reversal present at Arslantepe. Here, the arrival of the Kura-Araxes culture in phase VIB1 was followed by a fire and a distinctive new phase VIB2, in which the architecture reverted to mudbrick and pottery was again mainly wheelmade. In contrast to the Late Uruk city, the site remained a small village without a centralised administrative system. This may represent reoccupation by the site's previous inhabitants or co-existence between two groups (Frangipane 2000). This alternation in occupation, combined with evidence of contemporary sites with Transcaucasian and Syro-Mesopotamian affiliations (Arslantepe VIB2 and Norşuntepe 30-25, respectively), has led Marro to propose that the Syro-Mesopotamian sedentary culture co-existed with Transcaucasian pastoralists (Marro 2005).

1.3.3.4. Early Bronze Age II–III (2700–2000 BC). Early Bronze Age II was a period of dense occupation in the Keban region, with 35 sites recorded by Whallon in EBA I and EBA II (probably mainly dating to the later period), covering 46.1ha. In contrast to the Late Uruk period, this appears to have been the indigenous development of a complex society, which produced a local style of eastern Anatolian pottery and less evidence for outside influences. In the Altınova a clear hierarchy of size existed, with two large, six middle-sized and 16 small sites. Whallon suggests that the geographical pattern of sites corresponds closely to modern settlement patterns based on 'markets', with a hierarchy of centres and market areas (Whallon 1979). Settlement around Kurban in the EBA II and EBA III periods is also dense, with the central site of Kurban Höyük reaching an extent of 30ha.

Early Bronze Age III (2500–2000 BC) was a period of contraction, and only seven sites were recorded in the Keban area. This decline may be linked to a wider pattern of change across Anatolia at the end of the Early Bronze Age II, with evidence of destruction by fire at some sites and little continuity in occupation between EBA II and EBA III sites (Bryce 1999: 10). In Early Bronze Age III, there is, however, architectural evidence of centralisation. Large central halls, perhaps with religious functions, appear at Korucutepe and Norşuntepe. The large storehouse-palace at Norşuntepe may have exerted control over the entire Altınova (Van Loon 1980: 274–75). Aşvan Kale and Taşkun Kale provided material covering the Early Bronze Age II and III, but only from small-scale step-trenches.

In some parts of the Near East there is large-scale abandonment of archaeological sites at the end of the Early Bronze Age, which has hypothetically but speculatively been explained by an increase in aridity ca 2200 BC (Kuzucuoğlu, Marro 2007). At Kurban Höyük the main mound was abandoned around 2100 BC, and although the number of settlements increased, the overall settlement area fell by two-thirds (Wilkinson 1990: 102–05). This reduction and dispersal of population in the Kurban region during the Early Bronze Age/Middle Bronze Age transition differs from the evidence of the Keban region, where a decrease in settlement numbers appears to have occurred earlier, at the beginning of EBA III.

1.3.3.5. Middle Bronze Age (2000–1600 BC). Nineteen Middle Bronze Age sites were found in the Keban region (covering 20.2ha), including one unexcavated site near Aşvan. In the Middle Bronze Age II (1800–1600 BC) at Korucutepe the pottery shows clear central Anatolian influence, whereas in the later phase I it has more distinctively local forms (Griffin 1980: 75–76). The first half of the Middle Bronze Age is the period of the Assyrian trading colonies of central Turkey, responsible for trade in metals and textiles that passed through southeastern Turkey, perhaps thus accounting for the strength of central Anatolian influence.

1.3.3.6. Late Bronze Age (1600–1200 BC). Settlement in the Keban area reached a peak in the Late Bronze Age: 27 sites, covering a total of 56ha. Although survey identified Late Bronze Age pottery at Taşkun Kale, Taşkun Mevkii and Çayboyu, only Aşvan Kale produced any excavated remains. As in the Early Bronze Age I–II, there is a marked hierarchy in the Altınova sites. By contrast, only one Late Bronze Age site was found in the Kurban region. It is unclear why the regional settlement patterns are so different from one another.

The Late Bronze Age spans the Hittite Old Kingdom (1600–1400 BC) and the Hittite Empire (1400–1200 BC). The land of Isuwa, which included the Keban region and was important for its copper mines, came under the control of the Hittite Empire in about 1400 BC (MacQueen 1986: 50). The Late Bronze Age pottery from the Keban sites shows strong affinities with central Anatolian wares, and, especially in phase II (1400–1200 BC), with wares from Tarsus and Syria, perhaps reflecting the influence of the Hittite vice-regal kingdoms in Syria, which were established ca 1400 BC (Van Loon 1980: 276).

1.3.3.7. Iron Age (1200-600 BC). Whallon divides the Iron Age into two periods: Early (1200–800 BC) and Middle (800–600 BC) (Whallon 1979: 48–49). His survey did not record definite Iron Age occupation in the Aşvan region, and only modest occupation at 11 sites in the Altınova plain. At Korucutepe and other mounds in the Altınova the end of the Late Bronze Age was marked by catastrophic fires, which may be related to the widespread destruction across Anatolia after the collapse of the Hittite Empire in about 1200 BC. Although the Early Iron Age period (1200–800 BC) at Korucutepe directly follows Late Bronze Age II, with some evidence of cultural continuity in reuse of buildings, settlement was on a small scale and apparently unplanned (Köroğlu 2003). Around Norşuntepe, which has an excavated sequence for the whole of the Iron Age, the Early Iron Age occupation consists of scattered farmsteads (Müller 2005).

Iron Age ceramics – handmade grooved ware – are strikingly different from Late Bronze Age pottery, representing the disappearance of the centralised Hittite civilisation (Winn 1980: 155–56; Müller 2005). This 'new' type of pottery and associated architectural changes have been interpreted as evidence for migration. However, the pottery is similar to wheelmade grooved pottery in the Late Bronze Age levels and appears to be of local origin (Müller 2005). In the Middle Iron Age (800–600 BC) an official building was erected at Norşuntepe, probably by an Urartian king (Müller 2005). In this period the pottery shows close affinities with that found in the Urartian heartlands further east.

In the context of the vigorous Iron Age states of western and central Anatolia, the relatively low occupation density of the Keban region in the Iron Age is puzzling. Occupation in the Kurban area is medium rather than low density.

1.3.3.8. Classical, Hellenistic and Roman periods (600 BC to AD 300). Whallon did not attempt to collect and identify Hellenistic or Roman pottery during his survey, so we lack local evidence for the Keban region (Whallon 1979: 274). In classical antiquity Aşvan lay within the region of Sophene, coming loosely under the control of Seleukid, Cappadocian and Armenian dynasts after the death of Alexander the Great. The destruction of the Hellenistic houses at Aşvan Kale by fire is likely to be the result of a known Roman military campaign in Sophene, carried out in 66 BC. Contemporary Hellenistic buildings, probably of a religious nature, were excavated at Taşkun Kale.

After about AD 75 there was a substantial Roman presence along the Upper Euphrates (Mitchell 1980: 8–12; Mitford 2017). The Keban region lay to the east of the Roman frontier, thus coming under the control of allies of Rome, rather than under direct Roman administration. However, the substantial Hellenistic and Roman architecture present at Aşvan Kale suggests reasonable stability and the likelihood of extensive settlement. This is supported by relatively dense settlement in the Kurban region, where Hellenistic and Roman pottery was identified in the survey and occupation reached a peak in the Late Roman/Byzantine period (AD 225–625), when there was marked evidence for site hierarchy (Wilkinson 1990).

A recent survey of the Roman economy in Asia Minor cautions that 'the study of the economy of Roman Asia Minor is still in its infancy' and that 'there was an enormous degree of variation between the provincial societies of the Roman empire' (Mitchell, Katsari 2005: xvii), but studies of Roman land use as well as food production and consumption in western and central Anatolia are relevant to interpreting the Aşvan plant remains (Mitchell 2015). In central Anatolia settlement was sparse and sometimes semi-nomadic in the Hellenistic period. Under the Roman Empire, settlement became denser, with numerous villages (Mitchell 1993: 148). Although Aşvan lay beyond the Empire's eastern frontier, its situation and material culture were sufficiently similar to those of the adjacent Roman provinces to allow the suggestion that similar economic and political forces may have been at work during the Roman period: relative peace, good roads and wide-ranging interregional trade connections. The needs of the large Roman army on the eastern frontier may have stimulated production and trade (Mitchell 1993: 241–42). Mitchell suggests that in central Anatolia arable cultivation reached a peak of intensity during the Roman Empire that was unmatched until the 20th century (Mitchell 1993: 245). This may have led to over-exploitation. A recent study of the archaeobotanical data from the central Anatolian settlement at Gordion concludes that the intensive exploitation of *Triticum aestivum* in the Roman period combined with over-grazing may have led to soil erosion and significant environmental degradation (Marston, Miller 2014).

1.3.3.9. Byzantine and Islamic periods (AD 300-1400). While not approaching the peaks of the Early Bronze Age II or the Late Bronze Age, the 16 settlements identified by Whallon of the Byzantine and Seljuk periods, covering a total of 25.7ha, represent substantial occupation in the Keban region. In the Kurban region very dense settlement in the Early Byzantine period (fourth to seventh century AD, generally now defined as the late Roman period or as late antiquity) parallels that in northern Syria, the Konya plain and Turkey's southern coast (Whittow 2003; Baird 2004). It is likely that there was similarly dense occupation during this period in the Keban region. In the Kurban area, as elsewhere in Syria and Turkey, there appears to be a hiatus in occupation in the seventh century, which may be explained by the recurrence of plague through the sixth and seventh centuries, or by the wars between the Roman and Sassanid Empires, or the repeated Arab invasions, followed by modest occupation in Medieval times (see Haldon et al. 2014 for a recent discussion of these issues in the light of environmental evidence).

The period from the Arab conquests to AD 1400 saw abrupt political changes in this border zone. At first, Byzantine and Arab forces vied for control, with Byzantine forces recapturing much of southeastern Turkey in the tenth century. After the Byzantine defeat at the Battle of Manzikert in 1071, the Byzantine Empire lost control of central and eastern Anatolia to Turkic dynasties.

The effects of the arrival of Turkic pastoralists in the region, from the 11th century, and of political instability remain unclear, though they were unlikely to have favoured agricultural settlements (Redford 1998: 30). Between the 11th and 13th centuries Aşvan Kale and Taşkun Kale were important centres for pottery production. The Ilkhanid occupation of AD 1300–1350 probably led to the construction of the castle on Taşkun Kale and the probable *medrese* (Islamic religious school) at Aşvan Kale. The Christian population of Aşvan Kale may have been moved to Taşkun Kale, returning to Aşvan Kale at the end of the Ilkhanid occupation. Occupation perhaps continued on the top and sides of the mound until the 16th century and persisted at the foot of the mound up to the moment when the village was abandoned in 1973.

1.3.4. The archaeology of the Aşvan sites

1.3.4.1. Excavation methodology. The strategy adopted for digging the Aşvan sites combined excavation of extensive areas of selected structures with the recovery of chronological sequences through the excavation of smaller areas (French 1973b: 82–88).

Area excavation took place on Taşkun Kale, where about 1,200m^2 of the castle and 450m^2 of the church were exposed, and on Aşvan Kale, where about 900m^2 was excavated on top of the mound. The chronological sequence at the two sites which had large area excavations was extended by a step-trench (40m^2) on the northern side of Aşvan Kale and a sondage at Taşkun Kale (trench S9, 4m^2). The trenches excavated at Çayboyu (4m^2) and Taşkun Mevkii (200m^2) covered much smaller areas and were designed to cover earlier chronological periods than those explored by the area excavations.

This approach led to the recovery of a long sequence of settlements from about 4000 BC ('Local Late Chalcolithic') to about AD 1500 (Medieval III), covering about 5,500 years (see table 2). However, there are two significant gaps in the sequence. The first is from the Middle Bronze Age to the Iron Age (2000–600 BC), a period which is represented only by a small quantity of Late Bronze Age material from Aşvan Kale, and the second is the Byzantine period, between ca AD 700–1050, again represented by some minor remains only. In fact, Whallon's survey of the Aşvan region failed to find any second millennium sites, and first millennium BC occupation was identified only at Aşvan Kale and Taşkun Kale (French 1973b: 77). It is uncertain whether further excavation at any of the Aşvan sites would have filled these chronological gaps. From an archaeobotanical point of view it is regrettable that the excavated Roman building was a religious structure and was almost completely clean of finds. In general, the recovery of plant remains has been problematic at Roman sites in the Near East. Refuse at larger urban sites was often efficiently dumped away from the main areas of occupation and the focus of most classical archaeologists on public buildings has led to a neglect of contexts with rich archaeobotanical remains.

Another important aspect of the excavation methodology was the attention given to the recovery of material finds. Extensive dry-sieving was carried out at all four sites, ensuring recovery of large amounts of animal bone, and all the soil from Çayboyu and many deposits from Taşkun Mevkii and Aşvan Kale were processed through a flotation machine (see chapter 2.2 for details).

1.3.4.2. Çayboyu. Çayboyu is a low mound close to Aşvan Kale, about 80m across at its maximum extent and rising ca 2m high above the current ground level (Aksoy, Diamant 1973).

Regional periodisation	*Arslantepe period*	*Aşvan period*	*Number of botanical samples*	*Aşvan occupation*	*Aşvan dates (cal. BC/AD)*	*Regional/political affiliation*	*Keban settlement sites (area ha) Whallon 1979*	*Cyclical intensity of settlement*
Medieval 1100–1500		Medieval III b–c		AK: domestic house	?1335–1500		Ottoman–recent 32 (25.2)	
		Medieval IIIa	1 2 1	AK: *medrese* TK: castle (*kale*) TK: church	1275–1335	Ilkanid occupation (1300–1350)		
		Medieval II	19	AK: workshops, kilns, pits	1100–1200	Seljuk		
		Medieval I	2	AK: building fragments	?900–1100	Byzantine		
Byzantine 300-1100		Byzantine		TK: church	300–500	Byzantine	Byzantine–Selcuk 16 (15.4)	High
Roman 50-300		Roman	2	AK: Roman temple	AD 0–100	Roman		High
Classical/ Hellenistic 600 BC to AD 50		Hellenistic II	27	AK: domestic rooms, two-storey TK: temple fragments	100–66 BC	Cappadocian kings		High
		Hellenistic I		AK: fragments of non-domestic building	?200–100	Seleukid		High
Iron Age 1200–600	III–II	Iron Age		None	None	Local, then Urartu	11 (11.1)	Low
Late Bronze Age 1650–1200	IV (LB II) VB (LB I)	Late Bronze Age	2	AK: pits from small trench		Central Anatolia (Hittite); northern Syria (Hittite)	27 (32.9)	High
Middle Bronze Age 2000–1650	VA	Middle Bronze Age			None	Central Anatolia	19 (15.3)	Medium

Early Bronze Age III 2500–2000	VID	Early Bronze Age III	10	AK: small trench *TK: small trench*		Local east Anatolian, but increased links to Syro-Mesopotamia	7 (9.5)	Low
Early Bronze Age II 2700–2500	VIC	Early Bronze Age II		AK: small trench TK: small trench		Local east Anatolian		High
Early Bronze Age I 3000–2700	VIB2 VIB1	Early Bronze Age I	12	TM: phases 4 (old-est) to 1 Phase 2: bins and pits Phase 3: wattle-and-daub buildings		Transcaucasian (Red-Black Burnished Pottery)	EBA I–II 35 (31.1)	Low
Late Uruk 3350–3000	VIA	Late Uruk	0			Syro-Mesopotamian (Wheel-made Light-coloured Ware)	14 (12.8)	Medium
Local Late Chalcolithic 4000–3350	VII	Local Late Chalcolithic	20	ÇB: phases I & II Building fragments in small trench	None	Local, but links to Ubaid culture of Mesopotamia		

Table 2. Summary overview of the archaeological context of the Aşvan sites. Aşvan occupation: italics = no seeds; AK = Aşvan Kale; ÇB = Çayboyu; TM = Taşkun Mevkii; TK = Taşkun Kale.

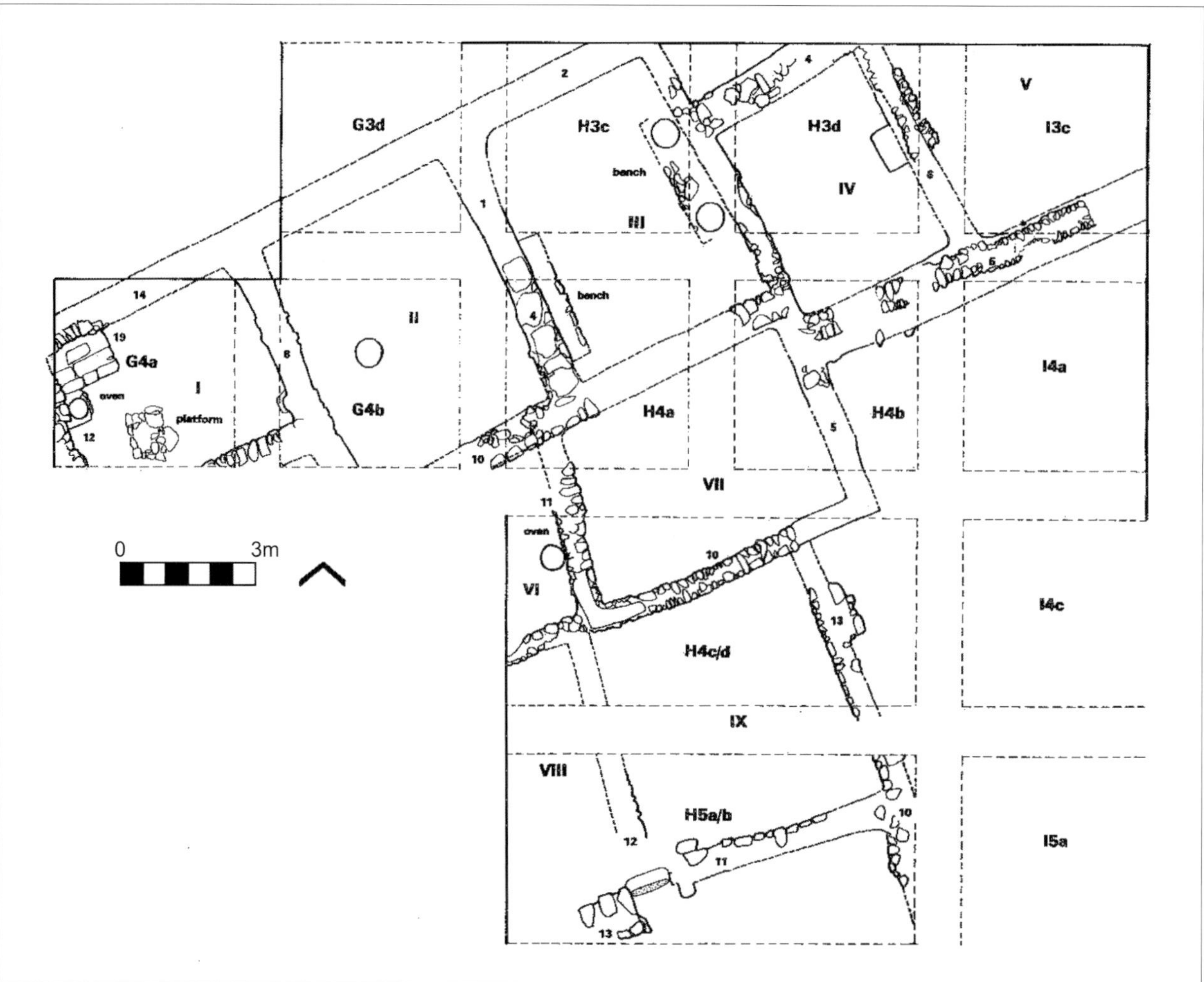

Fig. 7. Late Hellenistic house at Aşvan Kale (Mitchell 1980: fig. 11).

The stratigraphy spans the period from the later part of the Early Bronze Age (ca 2800–2300 BC) to the late Medieval period. Numerous botanical samples were recovered from this settlement sequence. Four phases at the site produced significant architectural remains.

1. Hellenistic II (dating to 100–66 BC). Remains of nine rooms were found (numbered on fig. 7), part of an L-shaped building with a courtyard in the southwestern corner of the excavated area. Traces of two burnt levels were found in rooms I–V, the upper level probably the remains of a burnt second storey. Rooms I–II and V contained ovens; rooms I and IV contained mudbrick benches, perhaps associated with food production. Rooms VIII and IX contained few finds, and were perhaps used for storage or stabling. Interpreted by the excavator as the remains of the dwelling of a well-off family, the building contained much pottery, bronze vessels, remains of a loom and coins, allowing the destruction of the building to be ascribed to Roman military action known to have occurred in 66 BC. Twenty-seven botanical samples were recovered from this phase, all but one burnt in situ during the destruction fire.

2. Roman? A roofed rectangular hall, perhaps a temple, and perhaps dating to the first century AD, contained few finds apart from significant quantities of fragmented animal bone, perhaps relating to butchery on site. Although this was the most substantial structure excavated on the mound, it provided only two archaeobotanical samples.

3. Medieval II. A large building was found, divided into five rooms (fig. 8), and dated by coins to the 11th to 13th century. To the south were pits (the source of many botanical samples) and pottery kilns. The building was probably used as a pottery workshop, in association with the nearby kilns.

4. Medieval III. A large domed building, probably a *medrese* (Islamic religious school) was built and briefly used during a period of Ilkhanid occupation in the first half of the 14th century. It was then dismantled and replaced by small domestic buildings of 14th- to 16th-century date.

Aside from the Hellenistic burnt level and the Medieval pits, the richest sources of plant remains were the flotation samples from the step-trench down the side of the mound. As noted by Harry Russell (Mitchell 1980: 69), many of the excavated layers here contained run-off, and so analysis has been restricted to samples which we judge to come from more secure contexts. Although no structures were found, there were tiplines, surfaces and pits, all evidence of soil that has stayed in situ since deposition (cf. Sagona 1994: fig 13). The pottery is of Early Bronze Age II–III period, dating from 2800–2300 BC (Sagona 1994). It is unclear to what extent the excavated deposits form a continuous sequence over this time, and no attempt has been made to periodise the samples more precisely.

1.3.4.5. Taşkun Kale. Taşkun Kale lies some 4km south of Aşvan Kale and is, as its name suggests, dominated by the ruins of a Medieval castle, with a church some 120m to the southwest. The mound is about 150m long and wide, and about 18–20m high, although occupation probably spread over an area of up to 10ha. In addition to the very abundant Medieval remains, Whallon records a small quantity of Early Bronze Age and Hittite sherds on the surface (Whallon 1979:

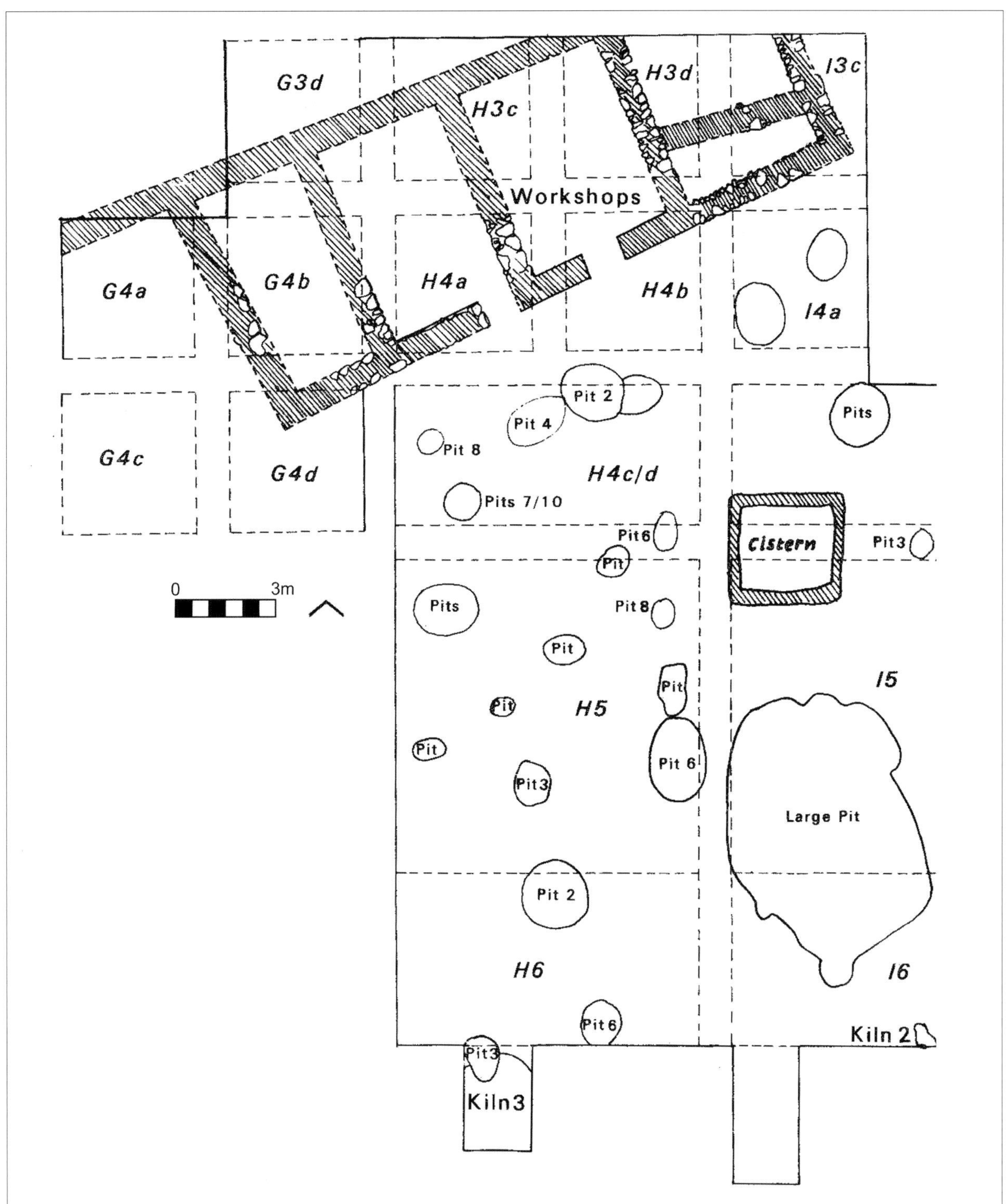

Fig. 8. Medieval workshops, pits and kilns at Aşvan Kale (Mitchell 1980: fig. 16).

164–65), but apart from a small sounding in trench S9 the relatively shallow excavations did not encounter levels of these periods. The deep trench revealed a rectangular mudbrick building with Red-Black Burnished Pottery dating to the Early Bronze Age II–III (Sagona 1994: 11–12). Three main architectural levels were excavated at Taşkun Kale.

1. Late Hellenistic? A square building, perhaps a temple, and perhaps a predecessor of the similar style of building found at Aşvan Kale.

2. Byzantine. A church was built immediately on top of the Hellenistic levels, in the fourth to sixth century. It continued in use to the 11th century and was then replaced in the 13th century by a smaller building, which remained in use until the 14th century. A clay oven in an adjacent room yielded a botanical sample (fig. 9).

3. Late Medieval. A 14th-century castle, excavated in its entirety, was probably occupied for some 50 years during the Ilkhanid occupation of eastern Anatolia (fig. 10). It was contemporary with the Medieval III *medrese* on Aşvan Kale and the second church on Taşkun Kale. The excavators suggest that under Ilkhanid rule a Muslim population may have been established on Aşvan Kale, while the majority Christian population was settled around Taşkun Kale, under the supervision of an Ilkhanid garrison in the castle (McNicoll 1983: 190–91). The site was abandoned after the Ilkhanid occupation ended in about AD 1350.

Flotation produced two samples of botanical material from the castle and one from the church.

1.3.5. Summary: cycles of expansion and contraction

Since the 1960s regional surveys in different parts of the Near East and Aegean have noted evidence for cycles of what Mark Whittow has termed 'intensification and abatement': varying degrees of exploitation of the landscape, invariably linked to different patterns of settlement (Whittow 2003). In some areas, such as Jordan and central Anatolia, this is represented by an alternating cycle of sedentarisation and nomadisation. Interpreting these patterns in terms of population is difficult: a dispersed population may be as large as one concentrated in a few centres.

Table 2 (see section 1.3.4.1) summarises the overall pattern of settlement. The term 'high-density' implies a large settlement area, very often combined with evidence for site hierarchies. There is little evidence for site hierarchies in areas of low-density settlement. Taking into account evidence from Whallon's survey, the survey around Kurban Höyük and excavated sites, the table incorporates a tentative pattern of cyclical intensification and abatement between the Late Uruk and Byzantine periods. There is insufficient historical or archaeological evidence to model settlement intensity in the Medieval period.

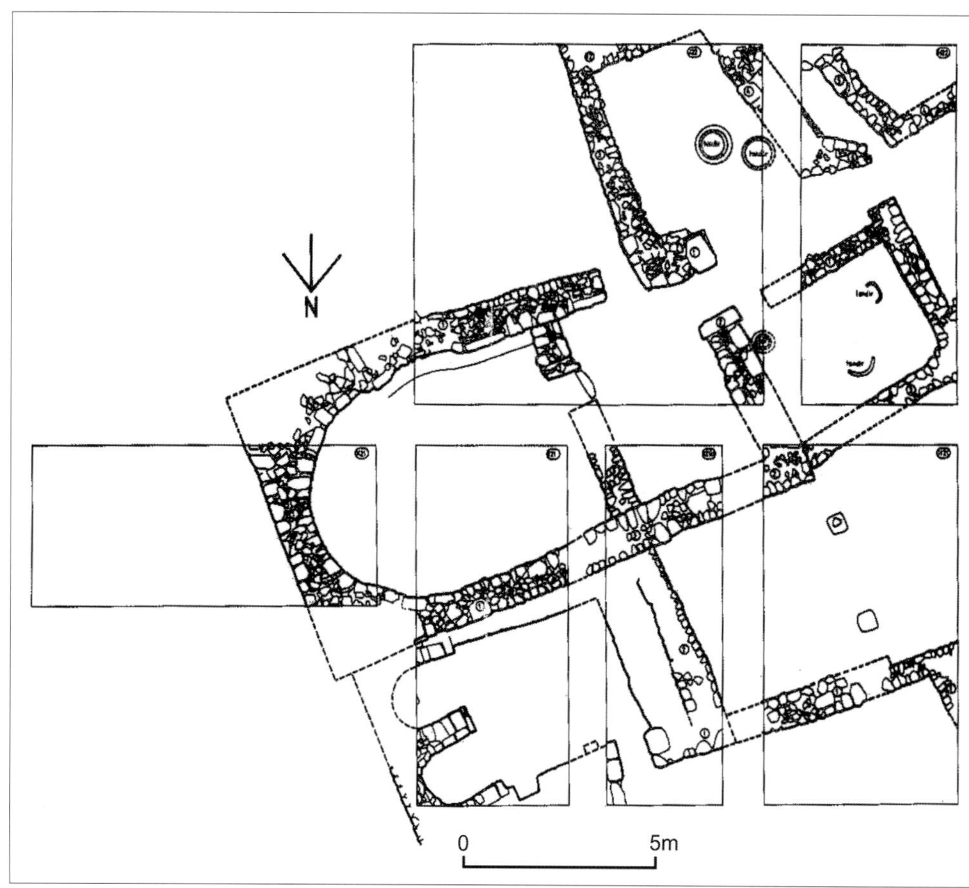

Fig. 9. Church with adjacent rooms at Taşkun Kale (McNicoll 1983: fig. 14).

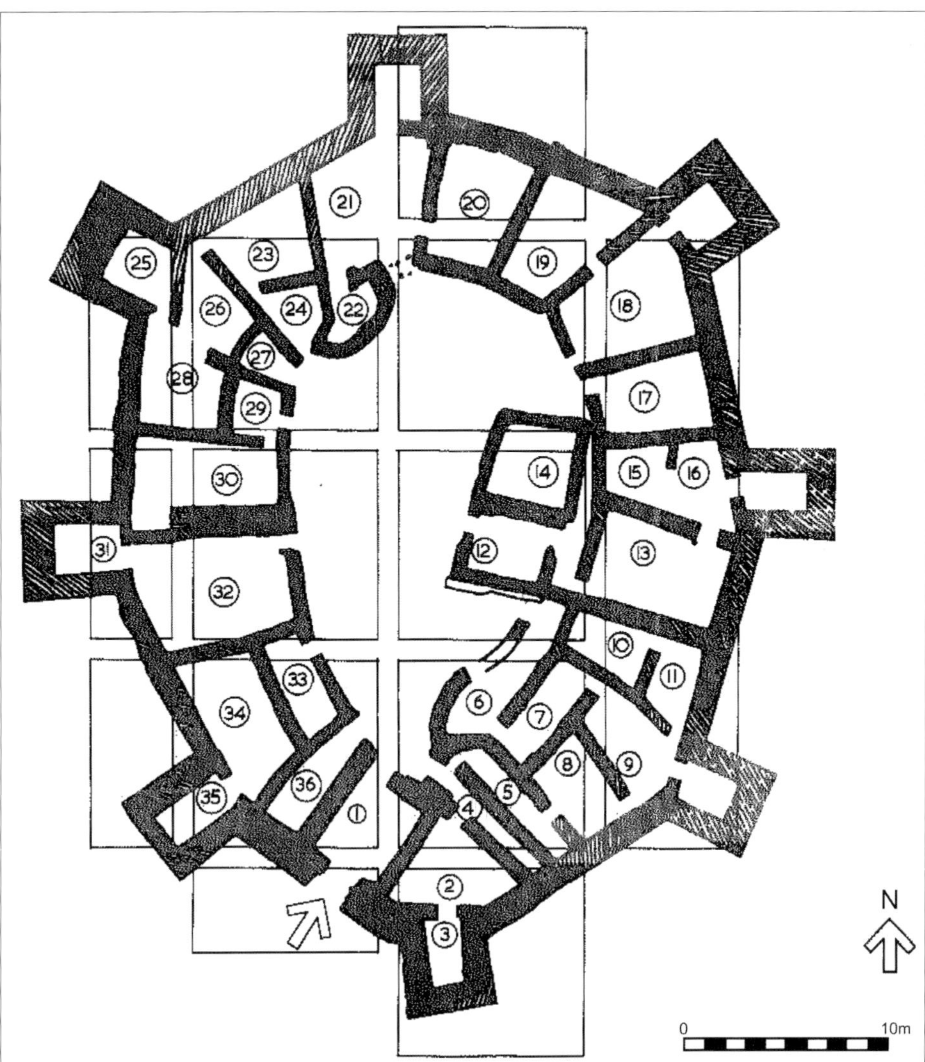

Fig. 10. Taşkun Kale castle (McNicoll 1983: fig. 4a).

1.4. Research questions

Archaeobotanical samples can be used to address a wide range of questions about agricultural strategy, land use, environment and human choices. Plants are affected by both climatic/environmental constraints and human actions, including factors such as water availability, ecological niche and annual cycle predictability, on the one hand, and cultural elements such as taste, labour organisation, perception and trade, on the other. Rather than simply presenting a quantified list of the species present on a site, the study of charred plant remains can provide insights into the choices and decision-making of a settlement's inhabitants and on the interplay between people and their natural and cultural situations. Based on the archaeological background, which has been outlined above, and the long chronology provided by the Aşvan sites, this report follows several lines of enquiry.

1. Can the plant remains be interpreted in the light of ethnographic models such as those developed by Gordon Hillman at Aşvan? Can samples be grouped according to their post-harvest treatment, for instance by classification as cleaned grain or waste fractions. How has the range of crops and wild plants present at the Aşvan sites been affected by crop processing and subsequent deposition processes?

2. Do changes in plant use, particularly the range of crops cultivated and the ways in which they were cultivated, reflect changes in settlement and economy? Is there evidence that greater intensity or centralisation of settlement led farmers to seek greater productivity or more robust and reliable methods of crop production? Were new crops introduced as a result of contact with or migration from other regions?

3. Are climatic fluctuations, seen in other proxies, reflected in the cropping choices and agricultural strategies observed at the sites? Were certain species chosen in response to periods of aridity. Do other mitigating methods such as irrigation present themselves in the archaeobotanical record?

4. How were plants used? For example, is there evidence for use as food or medicines? How does the presence of plants at Aşvan fit with the history of plant use as recorded in other sources?

5. How do the Aşvan sites fit into the broader environmental and settlement history of southeastern Turkey?

2. Methodologies of material recovery and sampling

2.1. Introduction

The Aşvan sites were excavated during a significant period in the development of archaeobotany as a discipline. This period saw the introduction of flotation, or 'water-sieving' as it was described by David French (1971b), as a method for extracting representative charred archaeobotanical samples from soil.

The first part of this chapter provides an account of the role that the Aşvan project played in the development of flotation techniques. The rest of the chapter develops a model of one of the two main sequences that affect the composition of archaeobotanical samples: the journey followed by carbonised seeds and other plant remains from the excavated soil units to the laboratory bench. The other of these sequences, from field to soil, via harvesting, crop processing and burning, will be discussed in chapter 4.

2.2. Flotation

2.2.1. A history of flotation and the role of the Aşvan project

The desirability of collecting archaeobotanical samples from Aşvan Kale was clear from the start of the excavations in 1968. During the long excavation season of 1969, the discovery of archaeobotanical samples in situ in the burnt remains of the Hellenistic level underlined the urgency of devising an appropriate recovery method. Some concentrated samples, for instance botanical material in storage pots, could simply be collected by hand, but charred vegetal material that was enveloped in the soil matrix could not be recovered manually. Already in 1969 some of these soil units were simply collected in their entirety and stored so that the botanical material could be recovered by flotation the following year. During the autumn of 1969, the Aşvan project director, David French, guided by advice from Sebastian Payne and other team members, undertook an experiment in water-sieving at the prehistoric site of Can Hasan, and the prototype water sieve, designed to extract botanical materials by flotation, was introduced to Aşvan in 1970.

Flotation is an environmental recovery method aimed at separating organic remains from soil units by exploiting the difference in density between organic and inorganic materials (Pearsall 1989). Flotation produces a representative sample of all size ranges of macrobotanical remains thereby allowing the flotation samples to be quantified and analysed statistically as well as presenting robust data about the presence of species, as is not possible when seeds are recovered by hand sorting. A telling example of this can be seen at the site of Ali Kosh in southwestern Iran, as the excavators learned by experience. Their final report includes the observation that 'our preliminary report on the 1961 season states confidently that "plant remains were scarce at Ali Kosh". Nothing could be further from the truth. The mound is filled with seeds from top to bottom. All that was "scarce" in 1961 was our ability to find them' (Hole et al. 1969: 24). The impact of the new recovery techniques led to Patty Jo Watson's judgement that 'it is no great exaggeration to say that the widespread and large-scale use of (flotation) has amounted to a revolution in recovery of data' (Watson 1976: 79).

Deborah Pearsall provides an excellent summary of the two parallel pathways in the development of flotation techniques in New World and the Old World archaeology. She notes that the machine flotation system developed at the British Institute at Ankara (BIAA) sites of Can Hasan III and Aşvan (outlined in French 1971b), played a crucial role in the Old World context (Pearsall 1989). The system, the original form of which is described below in section 2.2.1, has since been adapted. It applies the principle of flushing water from underneath to break up the soil and float the buoyant, lightly-charred botanical elements, and then to wash them gently into a fine mesh or flotation box. The process developed at Can Hasan III and Aşvan was soon noticed (Limp 1974) and 'widely adopted' (Pearsall 1989: 22), for example in Tom Jacobsen's excavations at the Franchthi Cave in Greece (Diamant 1979; the archaeobotany was published in Hansen 1991). A comparable system was developed for the Siraf excavations in the Persian Gulf (Williams 1973b) and for the Shell Mound Archaeological Project (SMAP; Watson 1976). The Siraf tanks were less specialised and easier to construct than the BIAA system, and it was this variant that has been adopted by the majority of excavations using a water-sieving flotation machine (Pearsall 1989; Jennifer Bates, personal observation). Rather than the specially constructed tank of the BIAA system, large oil drums, with modifications for the plumbing systems, are used as the main water tank. Siraf-type tanks have been used at Stobi in Yugoslavia (Davis, Wesolowsky 1975). A hybrid system was adopted at Gordion in Turkey during the 1988–1989 excavations (archaeobotany published in Miller 2010). The second development that has had a big impact was the SMAP-style of tank, a New World variation of a water-sieving machine, which the developer described as being based on the BIAA system (Watson 1976). However, rather than relying on the flow pressure of water falling from elevated tanks, this system uses water driven by pumps and regulated by valves. The use of pumps to drive water is now a common element of most flotation systems. Both the Siraf-type and the SMAP tanks have been used at Çatalhöyük (Hastorf 1996). The simplicity of the Siraf drum and the machine-pumped water system of the SMAP tanks are often now combined, for example in the Kilise Tepe excavations in southern Turkey (Bending 2007) and the FRAGSUS project excavations on Malta (Jennifer Bates, personal communication).

As well as introducing a new method for collecting archaeobotanical remains, one of the biggest influences worldwide of the BIAA system has been the use of flotation to enable 'major bulk sieving for excavations, rather than as a device to recover botanical materials' (Pearsall 1989: 22). Payne has discussed the impact of bulk sieving on artefact and bone recovery, referencing the Aşvan sites alongside French's other influential excavation, Can Hasan III. The use of flotation tanks as part of sieving strategies has remained important for obtaining environmental samples, not only of botanical remains but also of smaller bones, shells and even small finds caught in the heavy residue (Payne 1972).

One technical innovation that has not survived the test of time is the elutriator. This part of the BIAA system is described in more detail below, but was essentially included in the Aşvan/Can Hasan III design to 'meet the problem of the mesh-clogging properties of the fine silt and clay held in suspension in the water leaving the main box' (French 1971b: 63). At Can Hasan III and Aşvan this device was difficult to use (French 1971b) although subsequent attempts at Nichoria in Greece were successful in creating silt-free samples (Aschenbrenner, Cooke 1978). However, in general, 'most versions of the water sieve omit the elutriator, relying instead on hand rinsing or adjustment of the water flow to minimise silt in the light fraction' (Pearsall 1989: 28–29).

2.2.2. The flotation system at Aşvan

The system used at Aşvan in the early 1970s has been described in French 1971b and Weaver 1971, but, since flotation techniques have changed since that time (see section 2.2.1), we here provide information about how the Aşvan samples were processed in the field.

Figure 11 shows a cut-away diagram of the flotation system without the elutriator (French 1971b: fig. 1). Water is pumped from a reservoir into two elevated tanks. It flows down from these into the bottom of the main box, a

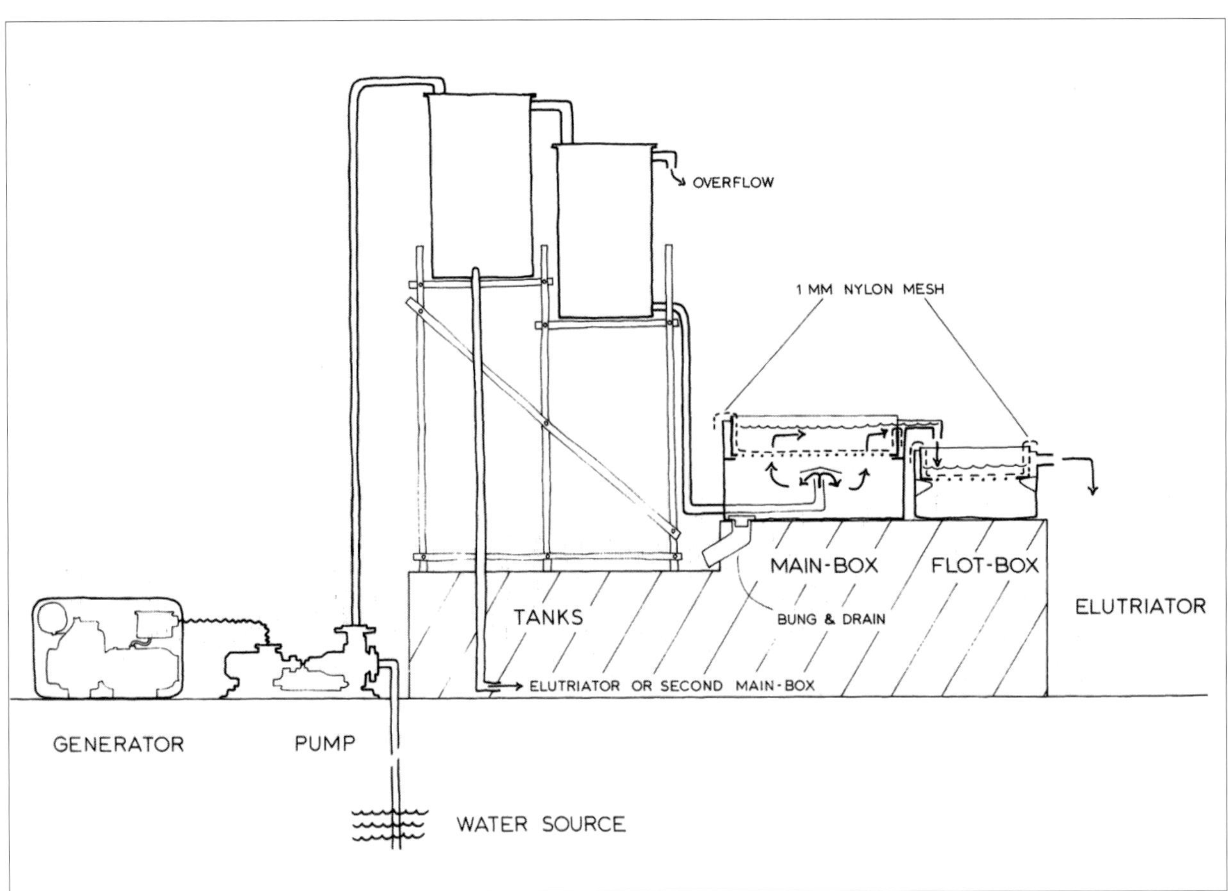

Fig. 11. Cut-away schematic diagram of the flotation tanks at Aşvan (French 1971b: fig. 1).

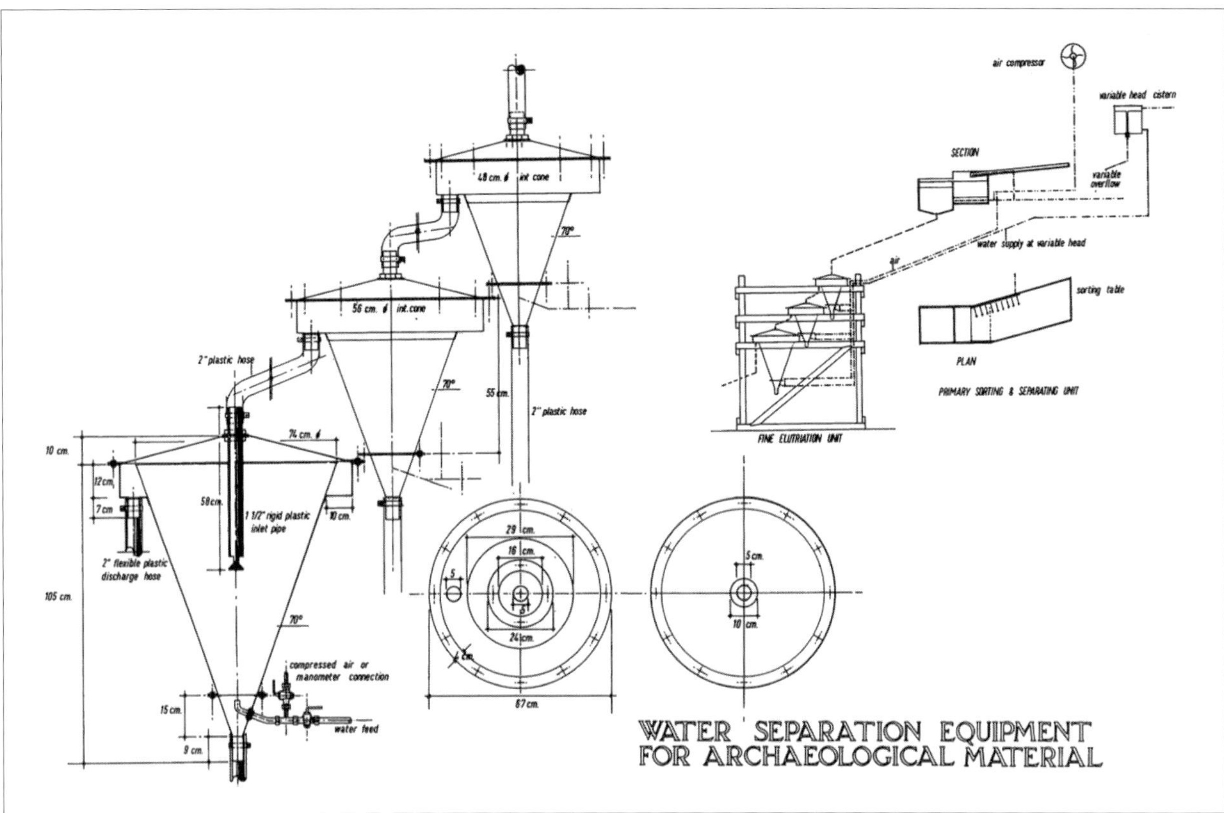

Fig. 12. Cut-away schematic diagram of the elutriator at Aşvan (Weaver 1971: fig. 1).

square, smooth iron tank in which there is a removable sieve. This is used to hold the heavy residue. The water, mainly forced by gravity into the main box, breaks up the soil placed in the sieve, allowing the soil to sink through the mesh. The heavy residue (artefacts, bone, pottery and non-floating botanicals) is caught in the removable sieve while the lighter botanical remains float. These are then sluiced by the water flow into the flot box, a small, smooth, round tank supporting a nylon 1mm mesh.

The holes of this 1 × 1mm mesh had a diagonal length of 1.4mm, and the elutriator was introduced to collect seeds that were smaller than 1mm or 1.4mm in the elutriator's finer meshes of 0.335m and 0.18mm (fig. 12; Weaver 1971). The design of the elutriator was based on devices designed for the size classification of particles in the mining industry and aimed to separate particles based on their density by adjusting the rate at which water moved in a column. It was also thought that the elutriator could be used to collect archaeological pollen. However, wave action, a build-up of sludge, the low volume of water it could handle and the issue of modern pollen contamination (French 1971b) meant that the affectionately nicknamed *şey* (Turkish for 'thing') was only rarely attached to the flotation device (Weaver 1971: 67). It proved unsuitable for processing large soil deposits.

It was clear in any case that seeds smaller than 1mm were being collected in the flot box mesh. This was due to silt clogging in the flot box, the large quantity of material collected in the mesh and the fact that the mesh was immersed in water. Seeds were less likely to fall through the silt during flotation and thus came to rest on the mesh once it was lifted out of the flot box. Mark Nesbitt, during his analysis of the samples for this volume, found that the elutriator samples contained few seeds and suggests that the 1mm meshes achieved similar recovery standards to those achieved by today's flotation machines which do without a 'flot-box', but use a 0.5mm or 0.3mm sieve. In order to maintain consistency between the samples, the small number of elutriator samples collected at Aşvan were not included in the analysis.

Seeds were sorted from the heavy residues which were collected in the 1mm mesh and amalgamated with the light flotation fractions on site. Some sorting of samples into charcoal and seeds took place at the sites, but wherever possible all samples have since been resorted so as to ensure accurate and systematic recording. This particularly applies to subsampling during the analysis.

Between 1970 and 1973 water-sieving was carried out at the site under the supervision of David Williams and Gordon Hillman, with assistance from Nick Ball, Pat Bean, Anne Martin and David Midmore (figs 13 and 14).

Before the water-sieving programme at Aşvan began in 1970, all botanical samples were collected by hand. The implications of this for the analysis are noted in section 2.3.

Fig. 13. The water sieve in operation for the Taşkun Mevkii samples, drawing water from the small stream flowing past Taşkun Kale (from BIAA slide archives, slide Aşvan 1970 18b).

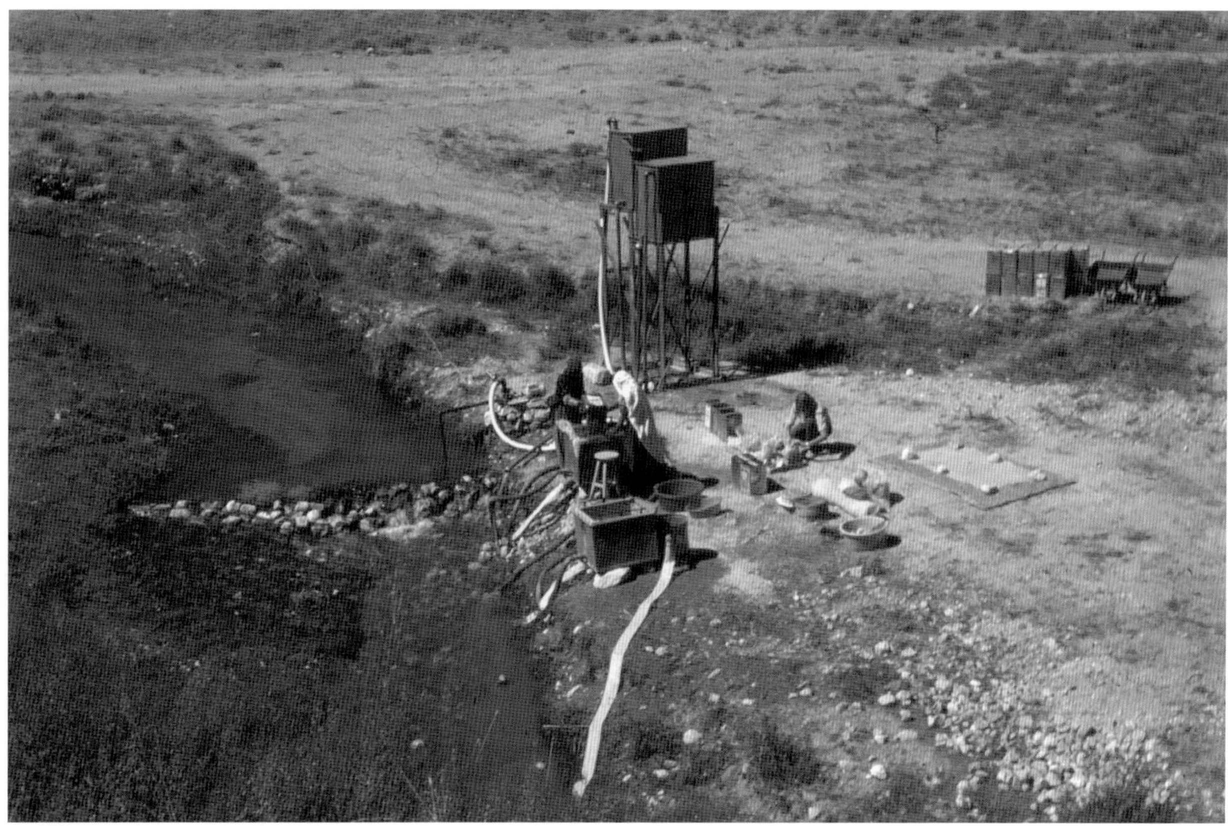

Fig. 14. The water sieve in operation for the Taşkun Mevkii samples, drawing water from the small stream flowing past Taşkun Kale (from BIAA slide archives, slide Aşvan 1970 18).

2.3. The sampling strategy

Circumstances determined that different sampling strategies were adopted at the four excavated sites in the Aşvan project. The trench at Çayboyu was so small that three-quarters of the excavated soil could be water-sieved. Taşkun Kale and Taşkun Mevkii were remote from the excavation headquarters and had difficult access to water. Moreover, a large-scale area excavation was adopted at Taşkun Kale, which was designed to expose architectural units and was less appropriate for fine-grained material recovery. Accordingly, priority was given to limited water-sieving at the Early Bronze Age site of Taşkun Mevkii. More systematic sampling was carried out at Aşvan Kale. Soil for flotation was taken from representative fill types throughout the trenches, including floors and occupation levels, destruction deposits and pits, all of which could potentially supply evidence of food processing or storage that could add to the story of the Aşvan sites' use of plant remains. As well as this, additional contexts, such as storage jar and pot fills, were sampled because they were thought especially likely to contain seed remains. The contexts were chosen on a basis of visual inspection of the trenches, especially when charred material could be readily visually identified in the soil during excavation, and the archaeologists' interpretation of the find contexts. These sampling strategies have to be taken into account in the analysis of the batches (see chapter 4 for more analysis).

2.3.1. Sample recording

All samples are identified in this volume by a two-letter site code: Aşvan Kale is AK, Çayboyu is ÇB, Taşkun Mevkii is TM and Taşkun Kale is TK. On each site the archaeological trenches were laid out and excavated in a grid of 10m squares. These squares were often subdivided into four 5m squares. They are labelled by a square number (for example J11), sometimes with a suffix to indicate the subdivision from which the sample originated (for example H4cd, indicating the southern half of H4). Within the squares the context codes were made up of two parts: a three or four digit number which was assigned to a particular area of the trench, and may have encompassed several overlying stratigraphic units, and a decimal number which recorded individual soil units (for example 1902.4). In some cases, particularly where more than one sample was collected from a single unit, there is an additional sample number (for example 1502.4 sample 2). Samples are also occasionally encountered bearing the same number but with different compositions. Sample numbers in these cases had not been applied at the time of excavation and were given an MN (= Mark Nesbitt) number during analysis (for example 714.8 MN 4). This system enables samples to be traced back to the original references in the excavation reports and notebooks held in the Aşvan site archives at the British Institute at Ankara. Section drawings were made of all the baulks of all the excavated trenches and provide the basic data on which the stratigraphic relations within the excavations were established and recorded. The trench notebooks contain descriptions, made on site, of the nature and composition of all the excavated soil units. With the exception of a single notebook from Çayboyu, all these records are preserved in the British Institute at Ankara.

2.3.2. Çayboyu

A total of 41 samples were collected from the small trench at Çayboyu, all but one (sample 8) processed by flotation. A total of 18,954 litres of soil was floated, representing about 75% of the excavated volume of soil.

The site notebook from Çayboyu is no longer available, and the preliminary reports and the three drawn sections of the trench are the only sources of information about the excavation itself. Twenty of the samples were selected for examination. The other samples were excluded on the following grounds.

Missing: samples 6, 9, 37.

Poor context (section cleanings): 19, 21, 26.

Stratigraphy unknown. Two samples appear to be in a different numbering scheme to the rest: 38, 39.

Poor flotation. Some samples (mainly those from the lowest levels of the trench) are full of earth and modern plant material, and are therefore very time-consuming to sort, with a low yield in charred material: 29, 30, 33, 35, 36.

Post-excavation mixing. At an unknown date an attempt was made to sort the Aşvan samples. No records survive, but in most cases it was possible to reunite the various bags of samples and resort them, at a considerable cost in time. However, the sample boxes 10 and 28 were so mixed that they had to be excluded. Their general composition is, however, similar to the rest of the Çayboyu samples.

For these reasons 15 samples were excluded. Out of the remainder, two samples were analysed from each of the excavator's subsamples, whenever this was possible. All the samples that were not analysed were similar to the rest, and were very rich in cereals and chaff.

2.3.3. Taşkun Mevkii

In 1970 and 1971 flotation was restricted to the burnt level in phase 3. All 11 flotation samples that were recovered and one hand-collected sample (from a pot, TM 101.24) have been analysed for this report.

2.3.4. Aşvan Kale

No flotation was carried out during the 1968 and 1969 excavations at Aşvan Kalc, but conspicuous deposits of charred seeds were collected by hand. Most of these samples were very small and have neither been studied in detail nor included in this analysis. We have, however, checked them to ensure that no items of special interest are present. However, large samples were collected in 1969 from the Hellenistic burnt level, including some extensive soil units which were subsequently floated in 1970. Twenty-seven samples in total were obtained from the Hellenistic burnt level. The other thirty-five samples were from pits, *tandirs* and 'fill' in the non-Hellenistic (usually Medieval) levels. No explicit sampling strategy was used, although it appears from excavation notes that the aim was to sample as many of the pits and ovens as possible. Given that life on an ancient settlement mound commonly involved both the digging and filling of numerous pits for storage, building materials and refuse disposal, there is a clear risk that soil from one part of the mound (perhaps an area of earlier deposits) could be redeposited into later structures. This occurred less often in the case of small pits, which were no doubt swiftly filled by the accumulation of everyday rubbish, but was frequent in the case of large pits which had outlived their original usefulness and needed to be deliberately back-filled. The oak-gall deposits from Hellenistic H3c 606.6 and Medieval I6 3101.24 provide an example of this. The large Hellenistic deposit is in situ and well dated. The one fragment of oak-gall in the Medieval pit originally appeared to be a separate find, as trench I6 is more than 20m away from trench H3. However, the pit also contained a Medieval II sherd that joined a sherd from trench H3, and this confirms the likelihood that seeds, as well as sherds, moved across the mound (Stephen Mitchell, personal communication). This issue of cross-contamination will be returned to in more detail in chapter 4 in relation to all sites.

A number of the samples from Aşvan Kale, mostly from pits close to the surface of the mound, were not assigned to a period by the excavator. These samples share various characteristics: the seeds are exceptionally well preserved with, for example, thick clumps of hairs on the rachises, they are very rich in chaff and weed seeds, and the seeds are dark brown in colour, compared with ancient seeds which are usually black. Even without knowledge of the excavator's doubts, these seeds could have been classified as of dubious antiquity. They appear to result from refuse disposal on the mound by the pre-modern or recent inhabitants of Aşvan village and are clearly the remains of the waste fractions from the threshing and cleaning of grain or of burnt field stubble. The samples are: F5a 2206.2 1; I3c 806.14; I5 1813.1 3; I5 1813.2 4; I6 3102.7 samples 4, 11, 12, 14; I6 3102.7 10.

2.3.5. Taşkun Kale

Only three samples were recovered at Taşkun Kale, two from the castle and one from the church area. Despite the presence of an extensive burnt level in the southern part of the castle, no botanical remains were recovered from this for analysis. The omission of sampling at Taşkun Kale derived from the circumstances of the excavation. Two factors militated against the collection of botanical samples. The site was extensive, and more than 3km from the excavation headquarters, and there was limited provision for floating soil deposits near the site. The transport of bulky soil samples proved impractical in the 1970 and 1971 seasons. Priority at this time was given to the more numerous samples from Taşkun Mevkii. Moreover, the final excavations in 1973 were completed in haste as the waters of the dam advanced, and even dry-sieving was abandoned in the race to record the site's main architectural features.

2.4. Quantification issues

There are no standard quantification practices in archaeobotany. Quantification techniques are instead chosen according to the nature of the remains and the research questions that are being asked (Popper 1988; Pearsall 1989). This chapter will not summarise all the quantification techniques used in this volume. The procedures that we have adopted will be outlined in more detail at suitable points relevant to the analysis in chapters 4 and 5. However, it is important here to explain the methodologies used to deal with the fragmentary nature of the material.

Subsampling was one of the first quantification issues to be addressed. Although most samples were small enough to be sorted in their entirety, a few large batches had to be subsampled. In these cases the sample was chosen by using a riffle box, and the resulting identifications, following standard practice, were multiplied up to 100%. The process is discussed in more detail in Van der Veen and Fieller 1982 and Toll 1988. The scoresheets presented in appendix 1 indicate the amounts subsampled.

The cereals presented a specific quantification problem. The bulk of the cereal grain fragments was too large to allow all the material to be identified or counted. Large quantities were weighed and converted to whole grain equivalents using an average 1,000-grain weight for wheat and barley (9.19g), derived from the figures given in table 3. Because the 1,000-grain weights vary from sample to sample this will lead in some cases to under- or over-representation of grain numbers. In table 3 the numbers of whole grain equivalents have been allocated to the different wheat and barley species according to the proportions of identifiable whole grains. Fragments of two species of wild grass grains were also converted on a similar basis to the domesticated cereals, using the average 1,000-grain weights of 1.88g for *Lolium* spp. and 1.86g for *Stipa* spp. In cases where only a few pieces of grain were present in a sample they have been identified, counted and converted to whole grain equivalents on the basis that two fragments equal one grain. The advantage of converting fragmented grains to whole grain equivalents is that more realistic chaff/grain ratios can be worked out. The disadvantage is that taxa may not be present in the grain

	Taxon	*Period*	*Site*	*Sample*	*N*	*1,000-seed weight*
Cereals	Hordeum vulgare (hulled)	Chalcolithic	ÇB	1	194	8.76
			ÇB	5	69	9.28
			ÇB	8	280	9.68
			ÇB	12	700	8.39
			ÇB	14	529	7.66
		EBA	TM	101.23	1,113	7.23
			TM	101.24	1,397	8.14
			TM	101.24	460	8.30
			AK	1204.12	122	7.95
		Hellenistic	AK	728.14	586	9.40
			AK	12.14	79	11.39
			AK	111.4	49	9.80
			AK	1507.23	233	8.33
			AK	1507.27	337	7.95
		Medieval II	AK	712.7	93	11.18
			AK	1501.8	123	10.65
	Hordeum vulgare (hulled - rounded type)	EBA	TM	101.23	49	2.24
			TM	103.6	51	3.73
	Triticum monococcum	Chalcolithic	ÇB	1	24	10.00
			ÇB	1	26	8.46
			ÇB	5	26	8.85
			ÇB	12	31	11.29
			ÇB	13	100	10.60
			ÇB	14	39	9.74
		EBA	TM	101.24	74	9.73
	Triticum dicoccum (two-grained)		TM	101.24	349	9.51
			ÇB	1	206	9.17
			ÇB	2	88	6.82
			ÇB	3	201	9.25
			ÇB	4	130	9.92
			ÇB	5	405	6.77
			ÇB	8	92	11.09
			ÇB	12	280	11.00
			ÇB	14	280	9.46
	Triticum dicoccum (one-grained)		ÇB	5	102	5.59
			ÇB	13	100	11.00
	Triticum durum/aestivum		TM	503.14	158	7.53
			TM	503.15	59	7.12
			TM	503.16	58	9.48
			TM	101.23	58	4.83
			TM	101.24	205	7.22
			TM	103.6	798	8.85
			ÇB	1	93	9.14
			ÇB	4	71	10.28

Table 3. 1,000-grain weights of grains and seeds from the Aşvan sites. Well-preserved material was chosen for measurement.

Taxon		*Period*	*Site*	*Sample*	*N*	*1,000-seed weight*
			ÇB	12	132	10.38
			ÇB	14	146	7.60
			ÇB	13	100	10.60
		EBA	AK	1015.3	100	10.80
			AK	1016.1	103	10.10
			AK	1016.6	265	10.45
			AK	1017.2	549	10.55
			AK	1204.3	21	9.52
			AK	1204.11	25	8.80
		LBA	AK	508.4	28	8.00
		Hellenistic	AK	606.6/MN2	100	8.10
			AK	726.24	43	12.30
			AK	1507.23	50	8.20
			AK	1507.27/35	32	7.81
		Medieval I	AK	1501.30	66	8.94
			AK	1502.4	50	9.40
		Medieval II	AK	1501.8	37	11.08
			AK	1501.15	27	11.90
Pulses						
	Vicia ervilia		ÇB	22	20	6.50
	Lens culinaris		ÇB	3	15	5.33
	Lens culinaris		ÇB	22	52	5.96
	Pisum sativum		ÇB	13	36	16.11
	Pisum sativum		ÇB	15	19	15.26
Wild plants						
	Aegilops		ÇB	2	208	0.91
	Aegilops		ÇB	3	221	0.90
	Lolium		TM	101.23	224	1.83
	Lolium		TM	101.24	347	1.93
	Pistacia		TM	101.23	9	15.56
	Stipa		ÇB	2	49	1.84
	Stipa		ÇB	3	69	1.88
	Stipa		TM	101.23	26	1.42
	Triticum boeoticum		ÇB	5	57	4.21

Table 3 (continued). 1,000-grain weights of grains and seeds from the Aşvan sites. Well-preserved material was chosen for measurement.

fragments in the same proportions as in the whole grains. This bias was demonstrated in Neolithic grain samples from Höyücek in Turkey (Martinoli, Nesbitt 2003) in which wild einkorn wheat (*Triticum boeoticum*) was heavily over-represented in mixed einkorn and domesticated emmer (*T. dicoccum*) grain fragments, because its grains are narrower and thus more fragile. It was, however, impractical in the Aşvan material to control this bias by sorting subsamples of the grain fragments.

The cereal chaff was also quantified. Glume bases and spikelet forks were scored separately, but the figures are amalgamated in the scoresheets and presented as glume base equivalents (that is one spikelet fork = two glume bases). Identification of glume wheat chaff was carried out on spikelet forks rather than glume bases, because identification criteria are more easily visible on spikelet forks. As with grains, this will lead to under-representation of einkorn, because einkorn's slender spikelet forks are more prone to break into glume bases. In samples containing large numbers of spikelet forks, samples of 100 specimens were identified and then used to convert the total number of spikelet forks and glume bases into species numbers in the summary scoresheets. For free-threshing cereals each rachis segment was scored as a single segment even if it comprised several segments joined together. In practice all but three segments were single.

3. The Aşvan seeds: catalogue and discussion

3.1. Introduction

The range of seeds at the Aşvan sites includes planted crops, weeds and useful wild species. In order to understand how humans and plants interacted at Aşvan it is necessary to examine each species individually. This chapter outlines the identification methodology and nomenclature, and then presents a catalogue of the plants identified from the samples at the four sites. They are classified as cereals, cereal chaff, pulses, fruits, other crops (including fibre and oilseeds), useful wild plants, weeds and unidentified materials. The seed counts are given in appendix 1.

3.2. Identification methodology and nomenclature

Botanical names follow the *Flora of Turkey* (Davis 1965–1985; Davis et al. 1988; Güner 2001), except for some updated family names (for example Poaceae for Gramineae), and information on taxonomy and distribution of plants is also derived from *Flora of Turkey* except where otherwise stated. Identifications have been established not only by morphological comparison but also by excluding species which on the basis of their modern distribution are unlikely to have grown in the Elazığ region in the past. The work of Willem Van Zeist and J.A.H. Bakker-Heeres (Van Zeist, Bakker-Heeres 1982; 1984a; 1984b; 1985) and Simone Riehl (1999) has provided most of the identification criteria, and this volume does not the repeat their detailed descriptions.

3.3. Seed counts

Appendix 1 gives the seed counts from all four sites. This provides the basis for the analysis in chapters 4, 5 and 6.

3.4. Domesticated cereals

Measurements of grains were made following Van Zeist's definition of length, breadth and thickness, always excluding the protruding embryo from the grain length (fig. 15). All measurements were made using a microscope graticule.

3.4.1. Wheats: Triticum

3.4.1.1. Candidate species. A remarkably diverse range of wild and domesticated wheat is (or was in the recent past) found in Turkey. This is attributable to three factors. First, all four wild species of wheat are found within the Fertile Crescent in southeastern Anatolia: diploid wild einkorn, *Triticum boeoticum* Boiss., and its sibling species *T. urartu* Thum., and tetraploid wild emmer, *T. dicoccoides* (Koern.) Schweinf., and its sibling species *T. araraticum* Jakubz. Second, southeastern Anatolia is a centre of origin for wheat domestication. DNA evidence points to the region as the location of both einkorn and emmer domestication (Heun et al. 1997; Özkan et al. 2002; Luo et al. 2007). Although a recent study has suggested that the picture may be more complicated for einkorn (Kilian et al. 2007), wheat cultivation is likely to have occurred in the region for 10,000 years or more, allowing ample time for the emergence of new forms. Third, the rugged topography of the country, which has isolated farming communities, has led both to the evolution and survival of new forms.

Detailed studies of Turkish wheats were carried out in his 1927–1929 expeditions by P.M. Zhukovsky (1933), during and after the 1930s by Mirza Gökgöl (1935; 1939; 1941; 1955) and in the 1940s and 1950s by Osman Tosun (1953). These studies show a far wider range of species and within-species diversity than that observable in the late 20th century. Einkorn (*Triticum monococcum* L.), the only domesticated diploid wheat, now grows in northern Turkey between Thrace and Kastamonu, but was previously also cultivated in central Anatolia. Among the domesticated tetraploid wheats, macaroni wheat (*Triticum durum* Desf.) dominated Mediterranean parts of Turkey then and now. Rivet wheat (*T. turgidum* L.) was common in parts of Black Sea and Mediterranean Turkey, and Polish wheat (*T. polonicum* L.) occurred near Adana. *T. carthlicum* Nevski, another free-threshing wheat that looks very similar to bread wheat, but is tetraploid, has been recorded in north-eastern Anatolia. Mark Nesbitt noted it growing near Lake Van in 1990. Hulled emmer wheat (*T. dicoccum* [Schrank]

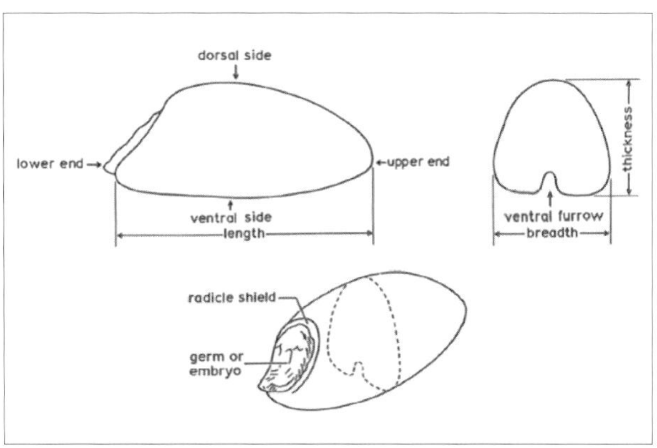

Fig. 15. Method for measuring cereal grains (Van Zeist 1968–1970: 48).

Schübl.) still grows in the Pontic mountains, from Kastamonu province eastwards to Kars. Bread wheat (*T. aestivum* L.) was and is dominant among the hexaploid wheats, and compact forms like club wheat (*T. compactum* Host.) remain important.

At Elazığ bread wheat and compact wheat were predominant cereals in the 1930s, but rivet and macaroni wheat were also present (Gökgöl 1939: 620–22). Gordon Hillman's collections from around Aşvan in the period 1970–1973 comprise 15 bread wheat (*T. aestivum*) and 22 macaroni wheat (*T. durum*) samples.

This evidence for wheat distribution in the 20th century shows that its cultivation in Elazığ has changed substantially over the last 5,000 years. In particular, einkorn and emmer, which had been cultivated over much of the country, are now restricted to north-central and north-eastern Turkey. It is possible that other wheats that are now relatively rare and localised were previously more widespread. The presence of tetraploid wheats (*T. durum*) in this highland area in the 20th century is a useful reminder that both tetraploid and hexaploid wheats have traditionally been grown throughout Turkey, with higher proportions of tetraploid wheats in Mediterranean areas and hexaploid wheats in upland areas. However, except at the highest altitudes, it is not possible to make assumptions about what wheat was grown on ecological grounds.

Great morphological variation is also present within landraces, and this raises the question of whether subtle distinctions between different forms – even at species level – might be visible in archaeological material. In this volume, however, the aim has been only to distinguish wheats at basic levels: between diploid, tetraploid and hexaploid forms, and between hulled and free-threshing types. In particular, no effort has been made to divide the archaeobotanical remains of tetraploid hulled wheat grains and chaff into the classes now described as emmer wheat and 'new' glume wheat; these are simply referred to as *Tricitum dicoccum* or emmer wheat throughout.

3.4.1.2. Grain morphology. Domesticated einkorn: *Triticum monococcum*. Most forms of einkorn have, as their name suggests, only one grain in in the lower floret of each spikelet. However, a few current forms contain both one- and two-grained spikelets in each spike, and two-grained einkorn caryopses have been identified at prehistoric sites including Nea Nikomedeia (ca 5470 BC) in Greece (Van Zeist, Bottema 1971), at Bronze Age Troy in northwestern Turkey (Riehl 1999) and at Jericho (Pre-Pottery Neolithic B, 9900–9500 BC) in the southern Levant (Hopf 1983: 581).

One-grained einkorn (fig. 16) was identified by its strongly convex ventral face (in lateral view), by the presence of pressure grooves on the flanks at the embryo end, by lateral compression (higher than wide, reflected in thickness: breadth indices ranging from 97 to 162) and by the presence of a terminal protrusion. This last characteristic has proved to be an excellent criterion for separating modern one-grained einkorn from terminal emmer grains, from which the protrusion is absent. The einkorn grains are generally widest just above the middle in dorsal view and pointed at both ends, resulting in their characteristic spindle shape. Their width varies considerably. The dorsal ridge is generally straight and central, highest near to the embryo. The upper part of the matt dorsal flanks has usually fallen off. The ventral flanks are rounded in cross-section with no flattening. Two-grained einkorn is also spindle shaped in dorsal view, but has flattened ventral surfaces. None was found at Aşvan.

Grains intermediate between wild and domesticated einkorn were classified as *T. boeoticum/monococcum*.

Domesticated emmer: *Triticum dicoccum*. Emmer was the commonest wheat grain in the Çayboyu samples; a few grains appear in the Taşkun Mevkii samples, but none at all in the Aşvan Kale or Taşkun Kale material. The emmer grains are highly distinctive, but different from modern Turkish grains (possibly reflecting the presence of 'new' glume wheat). Three features usefully separate them from free-threshing wheat grains: longitudinal pressure creases all over the dorsal flanks, deeper grooves on the dorsal and ventral flanks at the embryo end (a feature of modern emmer) and a widest point close to the distal end (not a typical feature of modern emmer). Classic features of emmer, to be noted on most of the grains, are the distinct,

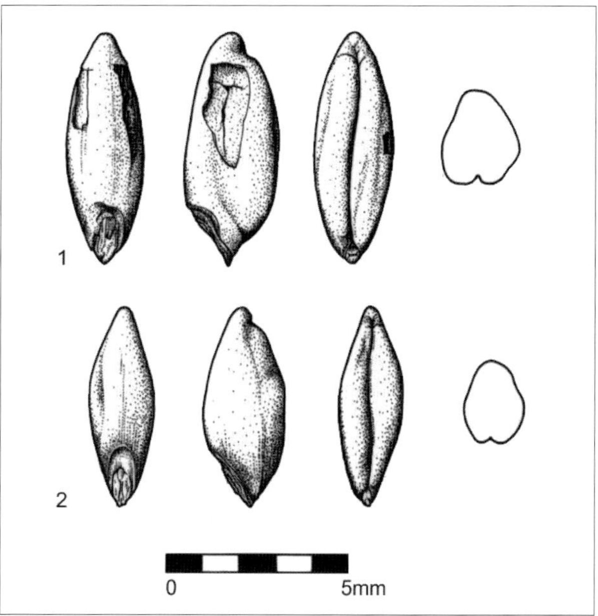

*Fig. 16. Grain from one-grained spikelet, einkorn wheat (*T. monococcum*): (1) ÇB 10.2; (2) TM 101.24.*

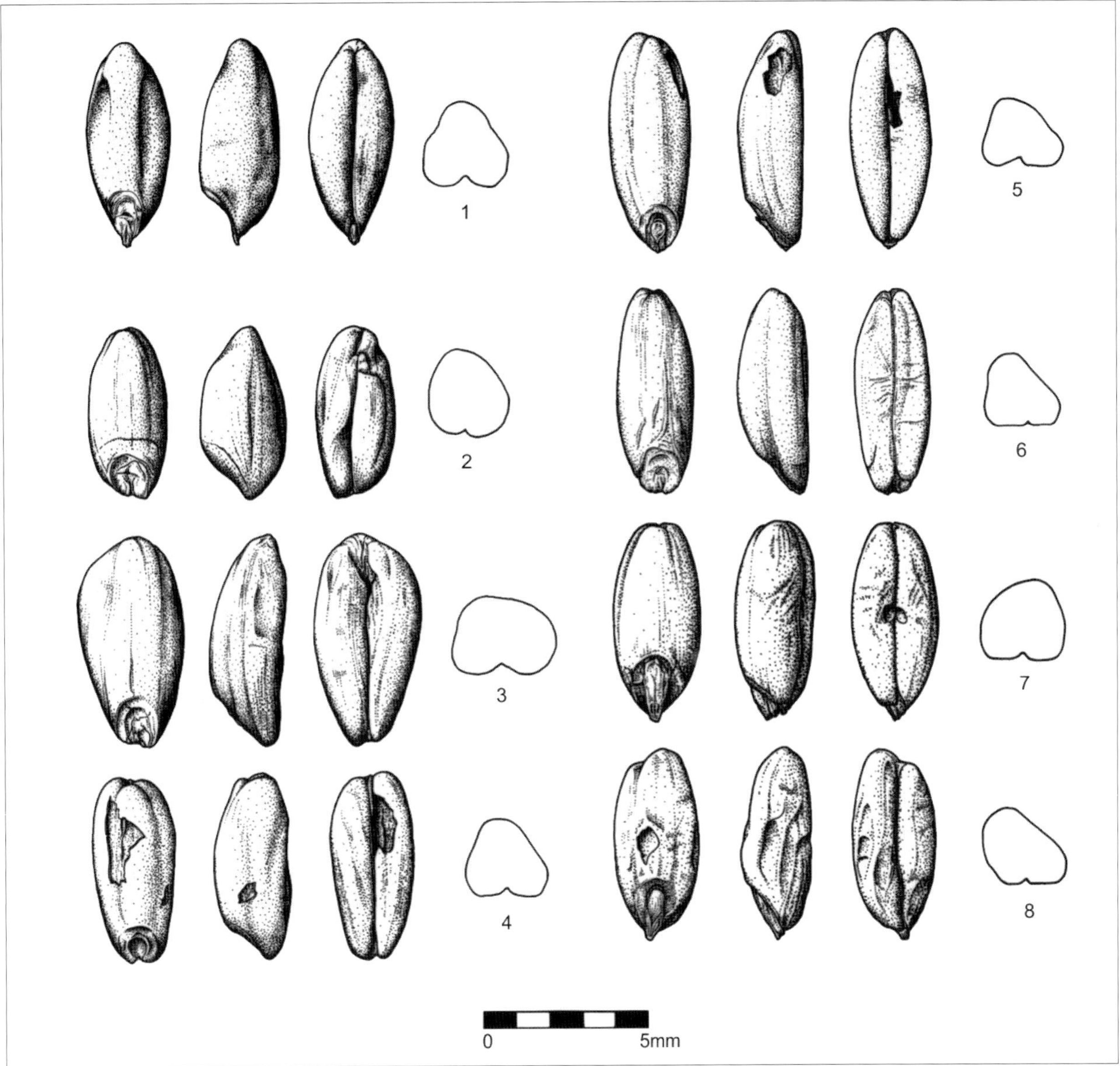

*Fig. 17. Grain from emmer wheat (*T. dicoccum*):(1) one-grained spikelet, ÇB 10.2 s. 1; (2) one-grained spikelet, TM 101.24; (3) two-grained spikelet, ÇB 10.7; (4 and 5) two-grained spikelet, ÇB 10.2; (6) two-grained spikelet, TM 101.24; (7 and 8) two-grained spikelet, AK 1502.10.*

skewed ridge and a long, slender shape. In transverse section the grains are rounded to triangular (depending on how strongly ridged the grains are); in dorsal view the grains are usually very blunt, but sometimes more rounded; in lateral view the grains are usually pointed, sometimes rounded. There is sometimes a hint of distal protuberance, but never as prominent as in einkorn. The highest point of the back is around the middle. The ventral face is usually strongly flattened, but some have rounded flanks in transverse section. These are so similar in shape to the normal emmer grains in all other respects that this is clearly just part of normal variation in grain shape. Naked wheat grains are much more often rounded than glume wheats (fig. 17).

Some very small grains are present, but their shape and proportions are exactly the same as those of the larger grains and quite unlike wild emmer. As with all the other cereals at these sites, there is great variation in grain size.

In emmer the terminal spikelet is usually large, contains one grain and is rotated at 90 degrees to the spike. The distinctive spikelet fork that results is described in section 3.4.1.4. Terminal grains closely resemble grains from one-seeded einkorn. It is important to try and separate these because otherwise emmer grains may be miscounted as einkorn.

Picking out grains derived from one-grained glume wheat seeds in the Aşvan samples was relatively simple, as they could be diagnosed by the pressure grooves and convex ventral face. The next step, of separating one-grained emmer from einkorn was more difficult in the mixed samples from Çayboyu. Modern einkorn always has a protuberance on the end of the grain, never found in modern one-grained emmer. That all the ancient grains lacking such a protuberance are widest in their upper half, and have a blunt or rounded but never pointed end in dorsal view, strongly supports the view that they are emmer rather than einkorn.

The grains in other respects share some characteristics with einkorn. In general, there is much variation in shape and this also applies to the ventral flanks: these vary from openly rounded to tightly rounded to slightly flattened (although not as much as in classic two-grained emmer). Although most of the grains are rounded, when a ridge occurs it is central and straight, and the highest point of the back is right above the embryo. In side view most of the grains have pointed distal ends.

Free-threshing macaroni and bread wheat: *Triticum durum* and *Triticum aestivum.* Most archaeobotanists currently accept that free-threshing wheat grains cannot be identified to ploidy, let alone species level, on the basis of grain shape (Hillman et al. 1996). Identifications of grain in the literature as bread wheat (*Triticum aestivum*) simply refer to the naked wheats as a whole; identifications of club wheat (*T. compactum*) can be taken to mean that unusually compact grains are present. There are two free-threshing wheat species with distinctive, very long grains: Polish wheat (*T. polonicum*) and Khorasan wheat (*T. turanicum* Jakubz.). Neither is represented at the Aşvan sites.

Free-threshing wheats are easily distinguished from emmer by their shorter, wider (i.e. more compact) proportions and by the grain being widest at the point closest to the embryo. In dorsal view the resulting shape is quite distinct from emmer. The flanks of the ventral furrow are almost always rounded, but they are occasionally flattened as in modern grains. There are no pressure creases on the surface of the grains, which are in general more rounded than those of emmer. In dorsal view the grains are usually blunt to curved; the grains are highest near the embryo, sometimes with a 'humped' appearance. The ventral side is slightly convex in lateral view. These observations hold true for the Aşvan free-threshing wheats fig. 18).

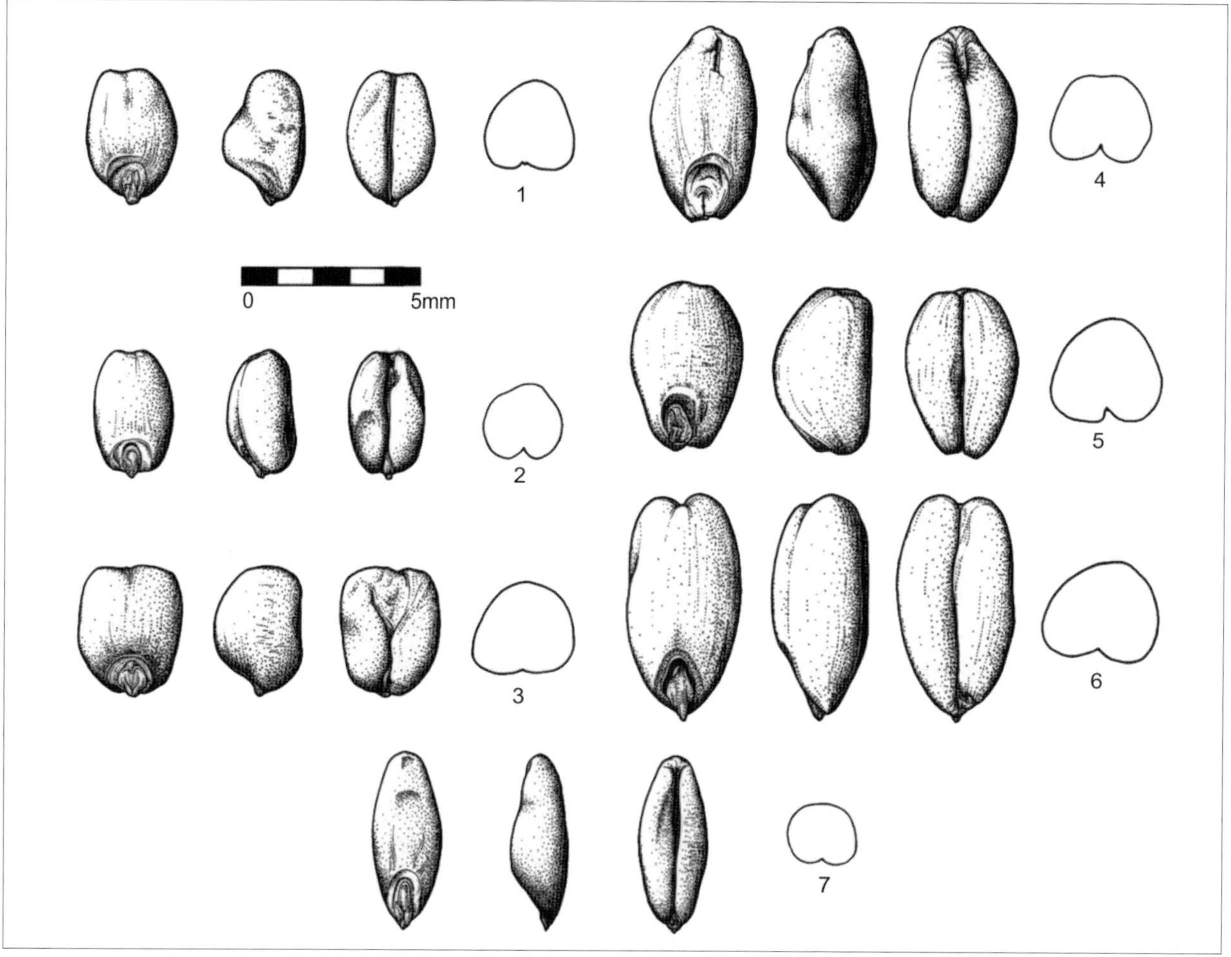

*Fig. 18. Free-threshing wheat (*T. durum/T. aestivum*): (1) ÇB 10.2; (2) TM 103.6; (3 and 4) TM 101.24; (5 and 6) AK 1502.10; (7) TM 101.24.*

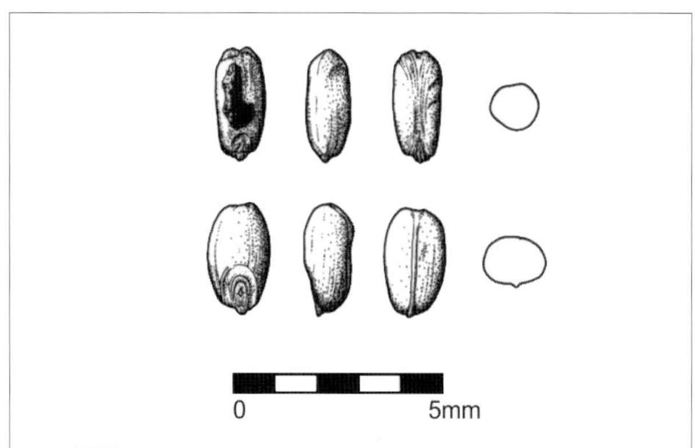

*Fig. 19. Free-threshing wheat runt grains (*T. durum/ T. aestivum*): ÇB 10.2.*

The size of the grains is highly variable. Some very small grains are, however, very similar in shape (although more often with tight, rounded flanks than open). One unusual small type, rarely found, is illustrated in figure 19. These tiny caryopses (length 2–3mm) were clearly of naked wheat (there is no glume wheat or wild grass grain with characteristics anything like this) and have no parallel in the modern reference material. They may derive from rare cases of third florets becoming fertile but not fully developed.

Grains intermediate between emmer and free-threshing wheat were classified as *Triticum dicoccum/T. durum/T. aestivum*.

3.4.1.3. Grain size. The use of grain size and resulting ratios in the identification of cereals is complicated by the effects of charring (Boardman, Jones 1990). While these vary according to different charring regimes, the results reported by Romuald Kosina (1980) are typical: for free-threshing wheat a length reduction of 12–17%, breadth increase of 22–29% and thickness increase of 6–22%.

This leads to the question: how do the measurements of modern (uncharred) grains, shown in table 4, and ancient (charred) grains, shown in table 5, compare?

The length of modern einkorn is consistent with the ancient, taking into account charring, but the lower thickness and breadth suggest either that einkorn responds differently to charring than the *T. aestivum* used in Kosina's (1980) experiment or that ancient einkorn is slimmer. Emmer grains are likewise consistent in length, but with slimmer thickness and breadth. The grains of free-threshing wheat (average length 3.7–4.9mm in the samples reported in table 5) are about one-third shorter than the modern grains of both durum and aestivum, which average 6.2–7.4mm in length. The exceptional shortness of ancient grains is only partly reflected in slimmer thickness and breadth. They also have a much lower length to breadth ratio, reflecting their compact form. Overall, it would appear that free-threshing wheat grains were more compact in antiquity.

3.4.1.4 Chaff. 3.4.1.4.1. Hulled wheat chaff: qualitative characteristics. Two types of spikelet fork were distinguished. The less common form is characterised by a gracile appearance, with narrow glumes and spikelet width, a relative upper scar width (ratio A) at the higher end of the range and smooth glume bases with a distinctive, almost glossy appearance. The glume arms rise smoothly out of the sides of the fork and are slightly curved. All of these are characteristics of einkorn (fig. 20.1–2).

The majority of the spikelet forks in each sample have wide glume and very variable scar widths, and usually display veins (of varying prominence) on the glumes. The rigid, straight glume arms rise rather abruptly out of the fork (the 'knick', described by Jacomet 1987: 62). These are all characteristic of emmer (fig. 20.3).

In all the cases where spikelet forks have well-preserved scars these are of the 'torn-type' typical of domesticated wheats.

Several distinguishing characteristics found useful in other studies were not applicable here. The angle at which the glumes rise from the rachis has been reported as rising straight up in einkorn, but protruding at an angle in emmer (Jacomet 2006). In the Aşvan material the angles were found to be highly variable in both einkorn and emmer.

The primary keel of modern domesticated emmer is much less prominent than in einkorn and wild emmer. However, all the spikelet forks in the Aşvan material have very prominent primary keels. The form of emmer with a pronounced primary keel has been identified by as 'new-type emmer' or 'new glume wheat' (Jones et al. 2000a). It was not possible to reassess all the Aşvan spikelet forks according to these criteria, but a small trial, reported below, was applied to the material from ÇB 13.

The spikelet forks of hexaploid hulled wheat, spelt (*Triticum spelta* L.), from the British Institute at Ankara (BIAA) reference collection were also examined. The most distinctive feature of spelt spikelets is the mode of rachis

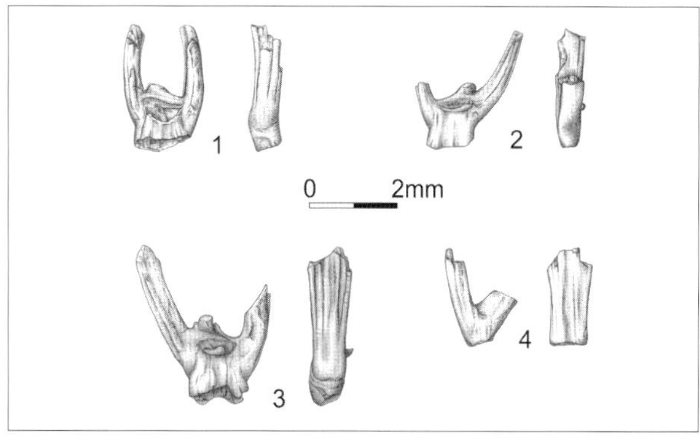

*Fig. 20. Chaff. Hulled wheat spikelet forks from ÇB 13: (1 and 2) Einkorn (*T. monococcum*); (3) Emmer (*T. dicoccum*); (4) Emmer (*T. dicoccum*) – terminal spikelet.*

Accession	*Number Counted*	*Length*	*Breadth*	*Thickness*	*L:B*	*L:T*	*T:B*
Einkorn (*T. monococcum*) one-grained spikelet							
CER70	10	6.6 (7.07) 7.6	2.3 (2.45) 2.7	3.2 (3.35) 3.5	256 (289) 310	129 (137) 143	129 (137) 143
RMN458	10	5.9 (6.59) 7.0	2.0 (2.35) 2.7	3.1 (3.31) 3.5	232(284) 348	126 (142) 168	126 (142) 168
RMN461	10	6.0 (6.78) 7.4	1.6 (2.04) 2.5	2.7 (2.98) 3.4	281 (337) 414	122 (148) 174	122 (148) 174
RMN1000	10	6.2 (7.33) 8.0	1.8 (2.50) 3.1	2.7 (3.44) 3.9	257 (297) 344	125 (139) 153	125 (139) 153
RMN1013	10	5.9 (6.46) 7.1	1.6 (2.07) 2.3	2.1 (2.97) 3.4	276 (316) 390	109 (144) 180	109 (144) 180
RMN1014	10	5.5 (6.03) 7.0	2.0 (2.16) 2.3	2.8 (3.10) 2.3	258 (279) 300	135 (144) 160	135 (144) 160
Emmer (*T. dicoccum*) two-grained spikelet							
RMN1136	25	5.6 (6.63) 7.3	2.3 (2.80) 3.1	2.1 (2.56) 2.9	180 (239) 308	84 (92) 105	84 (92) 105
RMN1161	25	6.0 (6.74) 7.4	2.5 (2.89) 3.3	2.1 (2.62) 3.1	209 (234) 257	85 (91) 98	85 (91) 98
Emmer (*T. dicoccum*) one-grained spikelet							
RMN1136 (terminal)	10	5.5 (6.05) 6.4	2.1 (2.44) 2.8	2.2 (2.41) 2.7	213 (250) 285	90 (99) 107	90 (99) 107
RMN1161 (not terminal)	10	5.9 (6.43) 7.0	2.5 (2.74) 3.1	2.7 (2.91) 3.1	222 (235) 264	87 (107) 115	97 (107) 115
RMN1161 (terminal)	10	5.4 (6.26) 6.8	2.0 (2.58) 2.8	2.1 (2.64) 2.9	199 (244) 304	95 (102) 105	95 (102) 105
Macaroni wheat (*T. durum*)							
B+B2	25	5.8 (6.71) 7.6	2.8 (3.24) 3.8	2.5 (2.95) 3.4	192 (208) 225	81 (90) 97	81 (90) 97
GCH1816	25	5.7 (6.49) 7.3	2.7 (3.07) 3.3	2.3 (2.75) 3.0	200 (212) 227	84 (90) 95	84 (90) 95
RMN429	25	6.0 (7.27) 8.0	2.9 (3.43) 3.7	2.7 (3.22) 3.5	197 (212) 232	81 (94) 101	81 (94) 101
RMN453a	25	6.3 (7.40) 8.3	2.9 (3.40) 3.9	2.7 (3.08) 3.6	203 (218) 243	80 (91) 103	80 (91) 103
(*T. turgidum*)							
CER36	25	5.6 (6.68) 7.2	3.3 (3.67) 3.9	3.2 (3.64) 4.1	158 (182) 197	87 (99) 110	87 (99) 110
Bread wheat (*T. aestivum*)							
GCH1807	25	6.4 (6.86) 7.6	2.5 (2.93) 2.4	2.3 (2.61) 2.9	217 (235) 263	79 (89) 101	79 (89) 101
GCH1832	25	5.5 (6.18) 6.7	2.8 (3.06) 3.3	2.5 (2.86) 3.1	189 (202) 217	88 (93) 103	88 (93) 103
RMN417a	25	5.7 (6.60) 7.1	2.7 (3.15) 3.5	2.4 (3.08) 3.3	199 (209) 225	91 (98) 105	91 (98) 105
RMN1509a	25	5.2 (6.19) 6.8	2.5 (3.31) 3.6	2.4 (3.29) 3.6	175 (187) 211	89 (100) 116	89 (100) 116
Club wheat (*T. compactum*)							
RMN1289	14	4.9 (5.89) 6.4	2.2 (2.71) 3.3	2.4 (2.96) 3.3	174 (219) 254	87 (110) 129	87 (110) 129
RMN2712b	25	5.3 (6.30) 7.0	2.6 (3.11) 3.4	2.2 (2.89) 3.3	177 (203) 219	69 (93) 103	69 (93) 103

Table 4. Measurements of modern (uncharred) wheat grains.

Sample	*Period*	*Number counted*	*Length*	*Breadth*	*Thickness*	*L:B*	*T:B*
Einkorn (*T. monococcum*)							
ÇB 13		100	4.3 (5.39) 6.4	1.3 (2.14) 2.78	1.9 (2.50) 3.0	191 (256) 396	97 (118) 162
Emmer (*T. dicoccum*) two-grained							
ÇB 13		100	3.8 (5.64) 6.8	1.6 (2.60) 3.6	1.3 (2.10) 3.29	160 (220) 323	49 (81) 121
Emmer (*T. dicoccum*) one-grained							
ÇB 13		42	3.5 (4.87) 6.4	1.7 (2.40) 3.1	1.7 (2.33) 2.9	159 (204) 283	84 (97) 109
Naked Wheat (*T. durum/aestivum*)							
ÇB 13	Chalcolithic	100	2.2 (4.13) 5.3	1.3 (2.84) 3.8	1.2 (2.37) 3.1	97 (146) 193	53 (84) 100
AK 1015.3	EBA	100	5.0 (5.31) 6.5	2.0 (3.13) 3.9	2.0 (2.61) 3.3	132 (172) 248	54 (84) 101
AK 1016.1	EBA	100	4.6 (4.75) 5.0	2.1 (2.88) 3.6	1.8 (2.48) 3.1	133 (167) 229	61 (87) 127
AK 1204.12	EBA	52	2.5 (3.68) 4.1	1.7 (2.38) 3.4	1.5 (2.07) 2.8	115 (157) 203	70 (87) 111
AK 606.6	Hellenistic	100	3.6 (4.67) 5.5	2.1 (2.92) 3.7	1.7 (2.32) 2.9	126 (161) 244	65 (80) 109
AK 726.24	Hellenistic	41	4.0 (4.92) 5.6	2.1 (2.87) 3.5	1.7 (2.44) 3.1	135 (173) 220	74 (85) 99
AK 1507.23	Hellenistic .	48	3.6 (4.55) 5.4	2.1 (2.72) 3.4	1.8 (2.28) 3.0	138 (168) 198	70 (84) 107
AK 1502.4	Medieval I	50	3.8 (4.91) 6.6	2.0 (3.26) 3.9	1.3 (2.72) 3.5	110 (153) 234	63 (83) 115

Table 5. Measurements of ancient (charred) wheat grains.

attachment. In emmer and einkorn the top of the rachis segment stays attached to the spikelet after disarticulation, so that it sticks out from the bottom of the spikelet; in spelt the rachis segment is attached at the bottom, so that it remains adpressed to the back of the spikelet. The rachis segment in well-preserved spikelet forks of emmer and einkorn clearly points downwards, even if it has partly broken off. However, if the internode has broken off higher up then the distinction is subtler. In any case, the internode on some spelt spikelets may remain attached in the typical position for emmer.

Six characteristics of modern spelt chaff could be checked in the Aşvan material.

1. The appearance of the glume bases in abaxial ('back') view. In spelt these almost rise separately from the bottom of the spikelet. In emmer and einkorn they are clearly joined to each other by a wide belt of tissue with an unbroken surface. In spelt a large inverted V-shaped scar rises up the abaxial side; it would be highly unusual for an emmer or einkorn rachis to tear off in this way. This feature may explain why spelt spikelet forks tend to disarticulate more readily into separate glume bases (Helbaek 1952: 101).

2. A view from the bottom of the broken surface of emmer and einkorn tends to be undifferentiated. In spelt this area is the disarticulation point and it looks like what it is – a clearly defined scar.

3. The area below the attachment scar of emmer and einkorn flows smoothly between the glume bases in adaxial view. In spelt it is deeply concave and wrinkled.

4. The rachis segment and the glume sides are far more heavily veined in spelt than in emmer, where the veins are light or even absent. As in bread wheat, this is a characteristic derived from *Aegilops tauschii* Coss., the donor of the DD genome. This venation is clearly visible on published photographs (for instance Jørgensen 1979: 138, fig. 2).

5. Hans Helbaek pointed out that the median portion of the lower part of the glume side appears convex in spelt and concave in emmer and einkorn (Helbaek 1952).

6. The size of the spelt spikelets is considerably larger than those of emmer and einkorn.

According to these qualitative criteria, no spikelet forks of spelt wheat were found in any of the thousands of examples examined from Çayboyu and Taşkun Mevkii.

Quantitative characteristics. Although the separation of the well-preserved forks into einkorn and emmer proved straightforward, a large number were too badly damaged to be assigned with certainty on the basis of appearance alone. They could, however, be measured. Three measurements were taken (fig. 21; cf. Nesbitt 1993). The first was spikelet scar width (USW), equivalent to Helbaek's 'Dimension A', based on measurements of examples at Hacılar, where the emmer and einkorn spikelet forks were separated on the basis of USW. However, this clear separation is doubtless due to the fact that at this site the emmer spikelets were 'extremely short and wide'. At Beycesultan, Helbaek was not able to obtain a clear separation with this character alone. The second measurement was glume width (GW) at the level of the same scar. This is very similar to Helbaek's 'Dimension B', although in the Aşvan case the measurements were taken across the glume base at the level of the suture in the upper articulation scar, whereas Helbaek measured this just above the suture. No significant difference in width results from this. At both Hacılar and Beycesultan this measurement alone was enough to give good separation of the spikelet forks (Helbaek 1970).

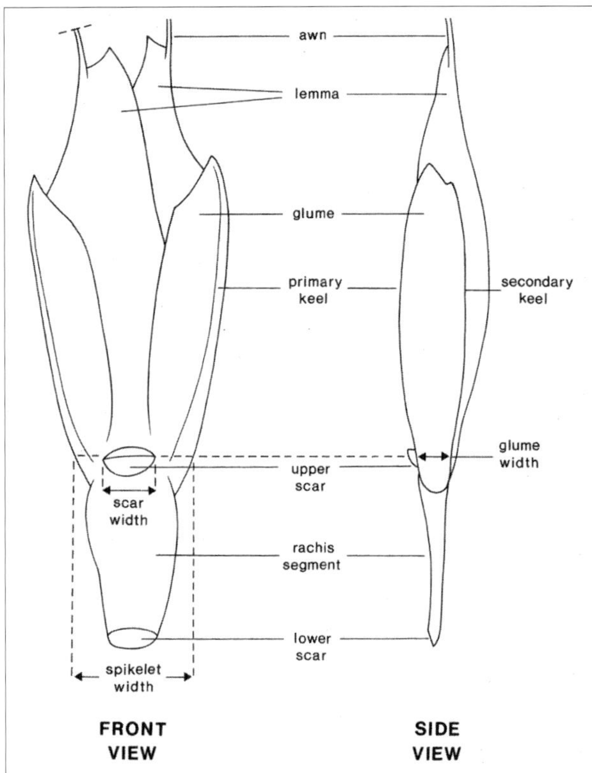

Fig. 21. Diagram of hulled wheat spikelet showing measurement points (indicated by arrows).

Trials on securely identified Aşvan material showed that the glume width of einkorn forks was in the 0.51–0.7mm range, while that of emmer was 0.77–1.18mm. However, spikelet scar widths with ranges of 0.73–0.92mm and 0.84–0.97mm respectively could not readily be separated, and so the spikelet width (SSW) was also measured. The ratio of scar width (USW) to spikelet width (SSW) multiplied by 100 produces values which give a clearer separation of einkorn from emmer, with ranges of 44–53 for einkorn and 39–48 for emmer. Spikelet forks with a scar ratio in the emmer range also had glume widths above 0.7mm, which confirms the usefulness of glume width as a criterion for separation.

A sample of the material from Taşkun Mevkii (TM 101.24) illustrates the identification process. One hundred spikelet forks were sorted using qualitative

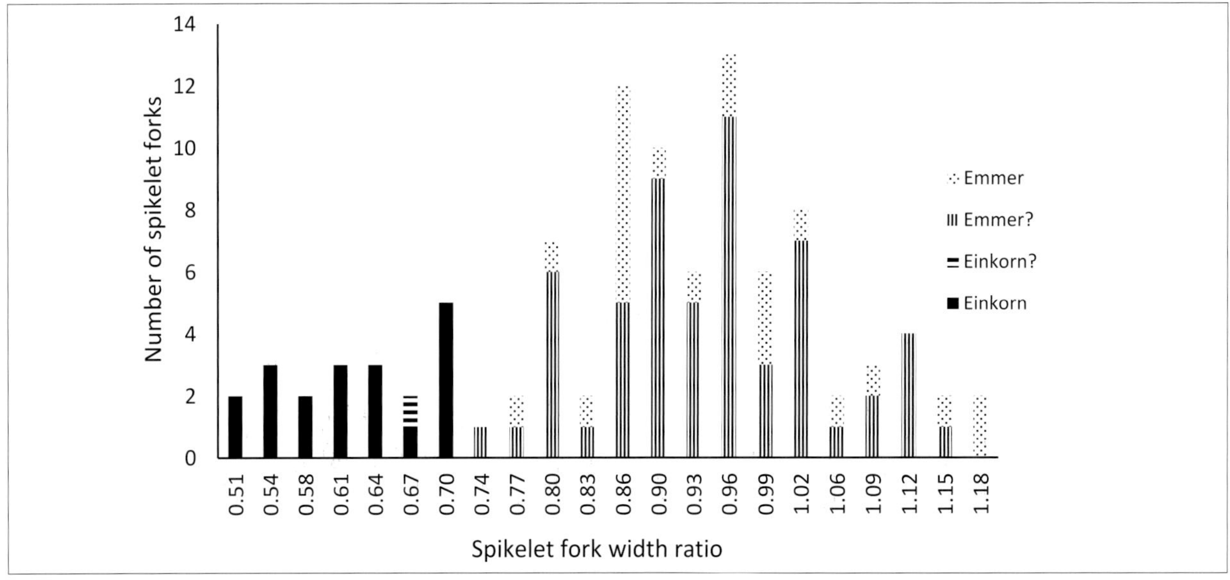

Fig. 22. Measurements of 100 spikelets from sample TM 101.24: glume width. The chart shows the spikelet forks identified with certainty on the basis of qualitative characteristics and the spikelet forks whose tentative identification has been confirmed by measurements and ratios. All the emmer forks have a glume width of 0.74mm or more.

criteria: 23 were securely identified as emmer, 19 as einkorn. All the spikelet forks were then measured. When glume width was plotted, it formed a bimodal curve consistent with the good separation at 0.7–0.77mm (fig. 22). Less well-preserved spikelet forks that had been tentatively identified as einkorn or emmer were then plotted onto the chart; the measurements in all cases confirmed the identification.

Apart from focusing on glume width, the other measurements and ratios were tested against the Aşvan material. No separation was achieved by measuring the relative scar width (USW/SSW; fig. 23); but the grains could be partially distinguished by upper scar width (fig. 24).

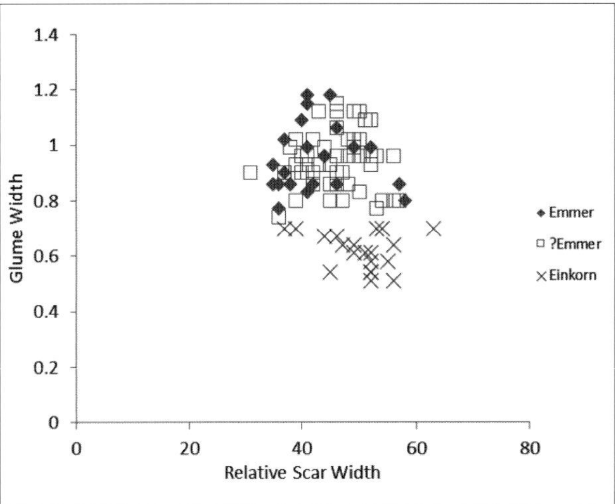

Fig. 23. Measurements of 100 spikelets from sample TM 101.24: relative scar width. Note that relative scar width does not separate einkorn and emmer.

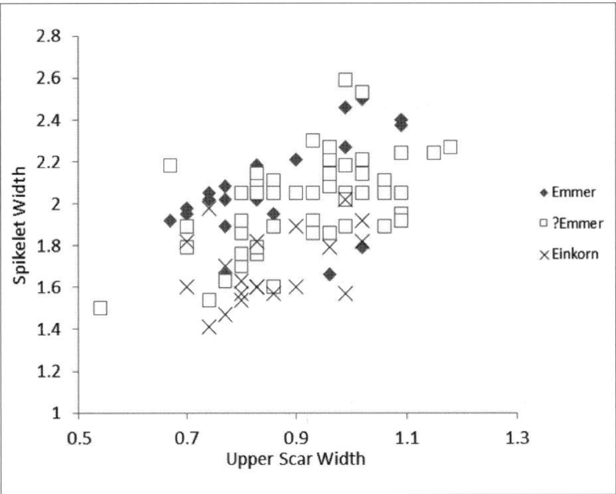

Fig. 24. Measurements of 100 spikelets from sample TM 101.24: upper scar width. The upper scar width only partially separates einkorn and emmer; emmer spikelets are wider than einkorn spikelets but there is considerable overlap between the types.

The 100 spikelet forks measured from ÇB 13 were reassessed using the criteria for new-type glume wheat (Jones et al. 2000a). The highly robust primary keel was the easiest character to spot, and enabled 82 forks to be assigned to a 'new-type' group. Overall these spikelet forks appear larger than the others. A scan of the other samples, although these were not measured again, provides a similar impression: that the 'new glume wheat' is the dominant form at Çayboyu and Taşkun Mevkii.

3.4.1.4.2. Free-threshing wheat chaff. Until the 1980s, it was thought that free-threshing wheat rachises could not be identified to species or ploidy level, but since then research by Hillman (2001) and Stephanie Jacomet (2006) has identified a number of characteristics for identifying wheats at ploidy level.

Four of the characteristics that are relevant to the separation of tetraploid free-threshing wheat, usually *T. durum* in the Near East, from hexaploid free-threshing wheat (*T. aestivum*) are described by Jacomet (2006).

1. Straight versus curved edges on the rachis segment. Tetraploid wheat (*T. durum*) usually has straight edges, with the widest point at the top. This character is variable in modern Turkish material and the Aşvan samples, and some tetraploid rachises have a slightly curved shape, although this is never as pronounced as in hexaploid wheat. Hexaploid (*T. aestivum*) rachises invariably have curving edges, with the widest point above the middle.

2. Pad-shaped thickening just below the glume attachment. Pads are usually present in *T. durum*, but, contrary to Jacomet's (2006) findings on her European material, these have also been noted by Nesbitt on some modern Turkish *T. aestivum*.

3. Remains of the glumes adhering to the rachis. This is often the case with *T. durum*, and does not usually occur with *T. aestivum*.

4. Longitudinal striations on the rachis segment. This is a very useful characteristic. *T. aestivum* has longitudinal striations along the front edge of the rachis segment. As Hillman (2001) points out, this character is derived from one of *T. aestivum*'s wild ancestors, *Aegilops tauschii*, and is absent in the tetraploid wheats (*T. durum*).

As well as looking at the commoner free-threshing wheats of the *durum* and the *aestivum* group, the tetraploid wheats, *T. turgidum* (rivet wheat) and *T. turgidum* subsp. *carthlicum*, were also examined to see if their characteristics would allow them to be distinguished to species level or, if not, whether they could be grouped at ploidy level with *T. durum* or *T. aestivum*.

The main differences between rivet wheat and *durum* are a squarer spike, relatively shorter glumes and soft grains, but these do not leave any traces on the rachis. The spike is often laxer than on *T. durum*, so the internode segments are longer. Mid-spike rachis segments from the one batch of rivet wheat in the BIAA collection measure 2.6–3.2mm wide. The internodes are wider than those of *T. durum*, typically 1.3–2.9mm. There is a very distinct decrease in internode width up the spike. Overall these internodes would be recognisable as tetraploid.

The most striking features of the internodes of *T. carthlicum* are their length (4mm in the BIAA reference material from Turkey), narrow width (1.3–1.6mm) and markedly shield-shaped appearance, with pronounced narrowing in the lower half. The rachis is also thin (minimum thickness 0.3mm, maximum thickness 0.7mm). There is no veining on the internode. The glume bases grade smoothly into the rachis, as in *T. durum*. This suggests that they belong to the tetraploid group.

Based on these criteria, seven rachis segments from the Aşvan sites could be identified at ploidy level: six hexaploid and one tetraploid (table 6; fig. 25). Three were too badly damaged for identification.

3.4.2. Barley: Hordeum vulgare

3.4.2.1. Candidate species. There are four candidates for grains that fall into the size range of domesticated barley. The first three are the main domesticated forms, now usually considered to be one species, *Hordeum vulgare*. Hulled barley can be either two-row (*Hordeum vulgare* subsp. *distichum*) or six-row (*H. vulgare* subsp. *vulgare*); naked barley is almost always six-row (*H. vulgare* subsp. *vulgare* var. *nudum*). The fourth candidate is the wild ancestor of the crop, the two-rowed, brittle-rachised *H. spontaneum* C. Koch. Thus the barley remains were assessed for the three characteristics: wild versus domesticated status, naked versus hulled and two-row versus six-row.

Hillman's modern barley collections from the Aşvan region are dominated by two-row hulled barley, with just one specimen of six-row hulled barley.

3.4.2.2. Grain morphology and size. Virtually all of the Aşvan barley grains that were in reasonably good condition could clearly be identified as hulled. Patches of lemma or palea still adhere to the well-preserved grains. Grains are also angular in cross-section and lack the fine transverse wrinkling often found on the dorsal side of naked barley grains.

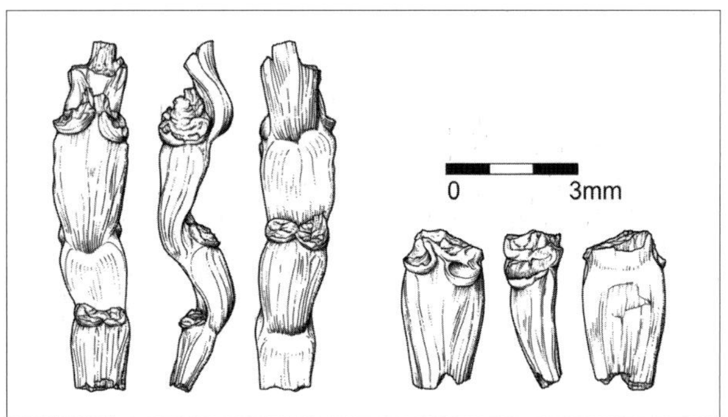

*Fig. 25. Hexaploid free-threshing wheat rachises (*T. aestivum*): AK 718.8.*

Most wild barleys have smaller and proportionately narrower grains. Distinguishing the seeds of *H. vulgare* subsp. *spontaneum* and two-row domesticated barley has proved a difficult problem for archaeobotanists. In contrast to the other cereals, the grains of the wild ancestor of barley are similar in size to those of the cultivated crop. *H. vulgare* subsp. *spontaneum* has perhaps the largest caryopses of any Near Eastern grass, usually at least 8mm long, but a little narrower and considerably thinner than those of *H. vulgare* subsp. *vulgare* (table 7).

Apart from the dimensions, three differences are visible in comparisons between modern grains of *H. spontaneum* and Turkish hulled two-row barley

1. The ventral furrow of domesticated barley is deep and narrow at the bottom, only widening at the top. Furrows of *H. spontaneum* widen from the bottom upwards.

2. The back of *H. spontaneum* grains are usually markedly concave, sometimes with a median ridge. The backs of domesticated two-row grains are usually slightly convex with a median ridge.

3. A ventral/dorsal view of domesticated barley shows that the sides of the grain widen to a definite midpoint, while in *H. spontaneum* the sides curve more gently.

H. spontaneum was collected on a grassy hillside near Aşvan (accession number GCH 1801) and has been observed among large stands of wild einkorn and emmer in oak parkland by Hazar Göl (Nesbitt, personal observation). In contrast to wild einkorn, which is a common weed, it was not found in segetal or ruderal contexts at Aşvan. The occurrence of *H. spontaneum* cannot be definitively excluded, but it was not a common plant in the Aşvan region.

Distinguishing two- and six-row barley is problematic. Six-row barley has three fertile florets at each node. The two lateral spikelets jut out at an angle, forced apart by the central spikelet. The grains borne in the lateral spikelets are thus usually twisted, both in the ventral groove and in the overall shape of the grain. The lateral spikelets are also smaller than the central one. The central spikelet has a slightly larger grain with a straight ventral furrow (fig. 26).

Table 8 and figure 26 show the proportions of straight and twisted barley grains in the Aşvan samples. A high proportion of grains was too damaged to ascertain whether twisting was due to lateral status or to deformation caused by charring. The ratio of twisted to straight grains (T:S) was calculated: a six-row barley (two twisted grains, one straight at each node) would have a ratio of 2:1 or 2; a two-row barley would (in principle) have a ratio of 0:1 or close to zero.

Sample	Identification	Description	Rachis shape	Glume crease	Pad height	Striations	Length	Min. width	Max. width	Min. thickness	Max. thickness
ÇB 38	Tetraploid		Str.	A	H	A	1.31	1.22	1.86	0.45	0.96
ÇB 13	Hexaploid	Lower part of rachis broken	Sh.	(G)	L	P	–	–	1.44	–	0.74
ÇB 17	Hexaploid	Lower part of rachis broken	(Sh.)	P	L	P	–	–	1.86	–	1.12
ÇB 32	Hexaploid		Sh.	P	L	P	1.89	1.18	1.47	0.48	0.8
TM 101.21	Hexaploid	Badly abraded, lower part or rachis missing	Sh.	P	L	–	–	–	–	–	0.64
TM 101.23	Hexaploid	Lower part of rachis broken	–	P	L	–	–	–	–	–	1.15
ÇB 2	cf. Hexaploid	Badly abraded, but clear shape	Sh.	(P)	L	–	0.86	0.93	1.25	0.35	0.42
ÇB 2	Naked wheat	Glume bases abraded off	–	–	–	–	1.06	1.18	1.41	0.54	1.06
ÇB 27	Naked wheat	Badly abraded, lower part or rachis missing	–	–	–	–	–	–	–	–	–
TM 101.23	Naked wheat	Badly abraded, lower part or rachis missing	–	–	–	–	–	–	–	–	–
ÇB 2	Indet. wheat – basal or sub-basal		–	–	–	–	1.44	0.7	1.06	0.42	0.67
TM 101.21	cf. tetraploid – first sub-basal	Very prominent glume pads	–	–	–	–	1.6	0.96	1.06	0.51	0.67

Table 6. Measurements of free-threshing wheat chaff. Str. = straight; Sh. = shield; H = high; L = low; A = absent; P = present.

Sample	*Number*	*Length*	*Breadth*	*Thickness*	*L:B*	*T:B*
WILD SPECIES						
H.violaceum						
RMN1422	10	3.7 (4.13) 4.5	1.3 (1.41) 1.5	0.8 (0.92) 1.1	261 (294) 339	57 (65) 71
H.geniculatum						
GCH2515	10	3.5 (3.73) 4.2	1.0 (1.16) 1.4	0.7 (0.82) 1.0	290 (322) 370	63 (70) 74
H.murinum						
[five samples]	15	3.5 (4.57) 5.8	1.1 (1.54) 2.3	0.5 (0.68) 1.1	254 (300) 336	35 (44) 57
DHF70	10	3.9 (4.41) 5.1	1.2 (1.38) 1.6	0.5 (0.70) 1.1	290 (319) 351	35 (50) 74
GCH1803	10	4.0 (4.35) 5.2	1.1 (1.30) 1.6	0.5 (0.58) 0.8	317 (336) 354	37 (44) 53
GCH2505	10	4.7 (5.29) 5.8	1.6 (1.79) 2.0	0.6 (0.78) 0.9	282 (296) 317	38 (43) 48
H.bulbosum						
DHF419	4	6.4 (6.75) 7.0	1.9 (2.03) 2.1	1.1 (1.16) 1.2	309 (333) 368	54 (57) 65
RMN503	10	5.8 (7.11) 7.5	1.6 (1.77) 1.9	0.7 (0.79) 0.9	360 (402) 447	37 (45) 55
RMN 769	5	6.0 (6.49) 6.9	1.7 (1.79) 1.8	1.1 (1.22) 1.3	329 (364) 385	65 (68) 71
RMN1625	8	6.9 (7.41) 7.7	1.6 (1.73) 1.9	0.8 (1.01) 1.2	391 (429) 476	50 (58) 67
H.spontaneum						
GCH1801		6.4 (8.26) 9.1	2.1 (2.58) 2.9	1.0 (1.54) 1.8	250 (321) 386	41 (59) 67
GW96	10	7.7 (8.18) 9.3	2.3 (2.75) 3.4	1.2 (1.64) 2.3	244 (302) 350	50 (59) 70
RMN218	7	8.0 (9.08) 9.4	2.6 (2.71) 2.9	1.6 (1.78) 1.9	310 (336) 355	62 (66) 70
RMN2144	10	9.7 (10.42) 11.8	2.9 (3.13) 3.4	1.3 (1.73) 2.0	309 (334) 358	44 (55) 62
RMN2152	10	8.6 (9.42) 40.0	2.5 (2.73) 3.0	1.1 (1.54) 1.8	309 (346) 366	42 (56) 67
RMN2161	10	7.7 (8.35) 9.1	2.3 (2.53) 2.7	1.3 (1.62) 1.8	317 (330) 349	56 (64) 69
RMN2162	10	9.6 (10.27) 10.9	3.0 (3.16) 3.5	1.5 (1.90) 2.6	280 (326) 354	49 (60) 74
RMN2163	10	8.3 (9.22) 10.2	2.5 (2.96) 3.2	1.5 (1.92) 2.2	285 (313) 351	57 (65) 70
RMN2167	10	8.8 (9.51) 10.0	3.0 (3.28) 3.4	1.9 (2.08) 2.3	270 (290) 302	59 (64) 70
Damascus	?	8.3 (9.20) 10.4	2.5 (2.84) 3.2	1.2 (1.55) 1.8	295 (325) 357	48 (55) 64
PBI	?	8.5 (9.81) 10.6	2.6 (3.29) 3.6	1.7 (2.41) 2.7	260 (303) 353	63 (73) 79
DOMESTICATED SPECIES						
Two-row barley (*H.distichum*)						
CER55	10	7.0 (7.54) 7.8	3.0 (3.10) 3.28	2.0 (2.17) 2.3	231 (243) 256	63 (70) 77
CER58	10	7.2 (7.66) 8.4	2.8 (3.39) 3.9	2.0 (2.41) 2.8	210 (227) 264	63 (71) 77
GCH1814	10	7.4 (8.21) 8.7	3.1 (3.38) 3.6	2.0 (2.40) 2.7	227 (243) 264	65 (71) 80
Six-row barley (*H.vulgare*)						
Straight	19	6.9 (7.87) 8.8	3.0 (3.28) 3.5	2.3 (2.54) 2.8	209 (241) 276	74 (78) 81
Twisted	33	6.4 (7.14) 8.6	2.5 (3.03) 3.3	2.0 (2.39) 2.6	204 (237) 279	74 (79) 82
Average	52	6.4 (7.40) 8.8	2.5 (3.12) 3.49	2.0 (2.45) 2.8	204 (237) 279	74 (78) 82

Table 7. Measurements of contemporary barley grains.

Sample	*Period*	*Straight*	*Twisted*	*Indeterminate*
ÇB 10.2	Late Chalcolithic	80	34	80
ÇB 10.4	Late Chalcolithic	7	4	15
ÇB 10.7	Late Chalcolithic	14	21	10
ÇB 10.9	Late Chalcolithic	99	89	92
ÇB 10.14	Late Chalcolithic	153	93	283
ÇB 11.1	Late Chalcolithic	5	2	10
TM 501.23	Early Bronze Age I	4	1	10
TM 503.12	Early Bronze Age I	7	3	14
TM 503.15	Early Bronze Age I	3	0	8
TM 101.23	Early Bronze Age I	118	314	671
TM 101.24	Early Bronze Age I	199	400	799
TM 101.25	Early Bronze Age I	184	42	532
TM 103.6	Early Bronze Age I	16	21	30
AK 1204.Ia	Early Bronze Age II	8	3	1
AK 1204.2	Early Bronze Age II	7	5	4
AK 1204.3	Early Bronze Age II	7	2	10
AK 1204.10	Early Bronze Age II	3	3	7
AK 1204.11	Early Bronze Age II	16	20	20
AK 1204.12	Early Bronze Age II	36	24	62
AK 507.15	Late Bronze Age	9	2	13
AK 508.4	Late Bronze Age	11	4	4
AK 12.12	Hellenistic	9	5	6
AK 12.14	Hellenistic	19	19	43
AK 111.4	Hellenistic	18	13	18
AK 602.24	Hellenistic	4	0	18
AK 606.6	Hellenistic	4	3	10
AK 728.14	Hellenistic	336	81	258
AK 726.26	Hellenistic	7	6	10
AK 729.18	Hellenistic	12	2	30
AK 807.6	Hellenistic	7	2	11
AK 807.14	Hellenistic	13	6	4
AK 1507.23	Hellenistic	51	37	164
AK 1507.27	Hellenistic	76	11	250
AK 1806.4	Roman	4	3	6
AK 1501.30	Medieval	17	4	33
AK 712.7	Medieval	14	19	60
AK 712.8	Medieval	3	4	16
AK 714.8 MN 1	Medieval	9	17	40
AK 714.8 MN 4	Medieval	25	15	67
AK 1501.8	Medieval	45	15	66
AK 1501.15	Medieval	5	11	9
TK 605.5	Medieval	4	3	3
TK 201.15	Medieval	175	87	48

Period	*No. of samples*	*Overall twisted to straight proportion*
Late Chalcolithic	6	0.68
Early Bronze Age I	7	1.47
Early Bronze Age II/Late Bronze Age	8	0.65
Hellenistic/Roman	13	0.34
Medieval	9	0.59

Values for overall ratios for each phase (not weighted mean)

Table 8. Proportions of straight and twisted barley grains.

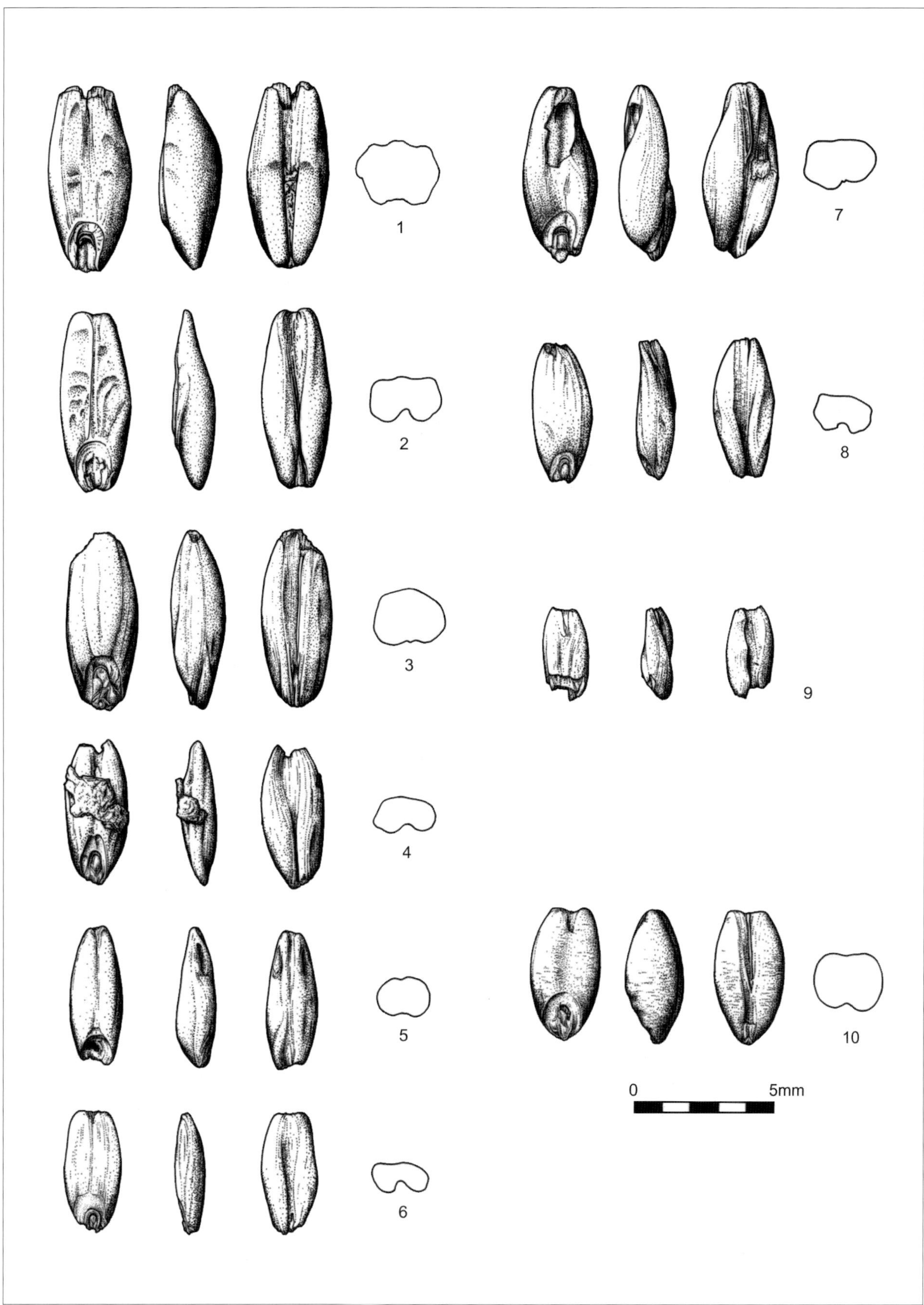

*Fig. 26. Barley grains at the Aşvan sites (*Hordeum vulgare*). Hulled, straight grain: (1 and 2) G2b 1204.3; hulled, twisted grain: (3) G2b 1204.3; (4) TK 201.15; (5) TM 101.24; (6–8) TM 103.6; hulled, twisted runt grain: (9) TM 101.24; naked grain: (10) TM 101.24.*

The ratio between twisted and straight examples (T:S) at Aşvan varies, with ratios in 35 measured samples ranging from 0.14–1.50, with an average in each period varying from 0.34–1.47 (table 8). Only two samples (TM 101.23 and 101.24), both from Early Bronze Age I deposits at Taşkun Mevkii, have ratios close to that of six-row barley; the rest are likely to be mixtures. For example, a T:S ratio of 0.67 would derive from a ratio of one-third six-row plants to two-thirds two-row plants; 0.5 would represent one-quarter six-row plants; and 0.33 one-fifth six-row plants, assuming that the ears of two-row and six-row barley bore the same number of grains. If grain numbers were fewer in two-row barley then ratios would be higher and the proportion of six-row plants would be overestimated. For example, even modelling a 50% reduction in the number of grains on two-row ears, a T:S ratio of 0.5 would only represent a field of one-sixth six-row barley. Overall, the sample ratios point to fields dominated by two-row barley, as they were in the 1960s, but with six-row barley definitely present, whether as admixtures or (certainly in some cases) as a separate crop.

There is great variation in barley grain size (table 9). This may be because lateral spikelets produced smaller grains. In modern Turkish barleys, grains from the lateral spikelets are only slightly smaller than the median grains. However, other forms, described as 'intermedium', have markedly smaller lateral grains. Measurement of the Aşvan grains indicate relatively small average size differences between straight and twisted grains.

An unusual shape was observed in the abundant hulled barley in TM101.23, 101.24, 101.25, 103.6 and 103.7. The proportions vary from 37% from TM103.6 (304 grains, of which 111 are of unusual form) to 2.9% from TM101.23 (320 unusual grains from a total of 11,069). The unusual grains were small with markedly rounded contours (fig. 28, 5–9). However, they were too large – and in particular too broad – to be from any of the smaller-seeded wild barleys. Further evidence for domestication is to be identified in the proportion of twisted grains, which are not found in the wild. Grains of the unusual form in sample TM101.23 were divided into 23 straight, 24 twisted and two indeterminate, suggesting that, like the full-size grains, they derive from a mix of six-row and two-row barley. These have been interpreted as runt grains from domesticated barley and are included as hulled barley in the score-sheets.

3.4.2.3. Chaff. As very few grains of naked barley were found in any of the Aşvan samples, it is unlikely that any of the barley rachises found belong to this form.

Sample	*Period*	*Number counted*	*Length*	*Breadth*	*Thickness*	*L:B*	*T:B*
INDIVIDUAL SAMPLES							
ÇB13 (straight)	Late Chalcolithic	50	4.2 (5.89) 7.5	1.9 (2.70) 3.4	1.1 (2.04) 2.8	174 (219) 273	56 (76) 92
ÇB13 (twisted)	Late Chalcolithic	100	3.1 (4.95) 6.32	1.3 (2.37) 3.1	1.1 (1.80) 2.8	183 (210) 252	58 (76) 116
AK728.14 (straight)	Hellenistic	100	5.1 (6.14) 7.4	1.6 (2.90) 3.7	1.4 (2.27) 3.1	151 (214) 333	51 (79) 138
AK728.14 (twisted)	Hellenistic	47	4.3 (5.95) 6.9	2.0 (2.92) 4.0	1.3 (2.13) 2.7	137 (206) 250	41 (73) 93
TK201.15 (straight)	Medieval	100	3.9 (5.07) 5.9	1.9 (2.43) 3.0	1.2 (1.68) 2.1	176 (209) 248	59 (69) 78
TK201.15 (twisted)	Medieval	50	4.5 (5.16) 6.2	1.9 (2.42) 4.1	1.2 (1.65) 1.95	123 (216) 254	40 (68) 76
TOTAL MEASUREMENTS BY PHASE							
AK (straight)	Early Bronze Age	48	4.8 (6.1) 8.0	2.1 (2.83) 3.7	1.2 (2.05) 3.0	177 (217) 291	53 (72) 87
AK (twisted)	Early Bronze Age	39	3.6 (5.41) 7.2	1.9 (2.46) 3.2	1.0 (1.68) 2.5	179 (221) 270	51 (68) 107
AK (straight)	Hellenistic	184	4.8 (6.08) 7.4	1.6 (2.87) 3.7	1.2 (2.20) 3.1	151 (215) 368	51 (77) 138
AK (twisted)	Hellenistic	101	4.3 (5.82) 6.9	1.9 (2.83) 4.0)	1.3 (2.07) 3.1	137 (208) 250	41 (74) 133
AK (straight)	Medieval	58	4.8 (6.40) 8.0	1.9 (2.66) 4.3	1.2 (1.92) 3.0	171 (210) 276	55 (71) 95
AK (twisted)	Medieval	30	4.8 (6.24) 7.3	2.0 (3.00) 3.62	1.48 (2.21) 2.76	166 (209) 242	65 (74) 89
TK (straight)	Medieval	102	3.9 (5.09) 6.9	1.9 (2.44) 3.0	1.2 (1.69) 2.7	176 (209) 248	59 (69) 78
TK (twisted)	Medieval	52	4.5 (5.18) 6.5	1.9 (2.43) 4.1	1.1 (1.66) 2.6	123 (215) 254	40 (68) 81

Table 9. Size of barley grains.

cultivars of the pea. All the pulse seeds from the Aşvan sites that were relatively spherical or cuboidal-spherical, which have maximum diameters of over about 2.5mm, were classified as *Pisum* (fig. 32). As the testa fragments are invariably smooth, a domesticated species is involved, which could be either be the common *P. sativum* subsp. *sativum* var. *sativum*, cultivated for its edible seeds, or the less common var. *arvense* which grows as a field weed and is also cultivated for fodder.

3.5.5. Indeterminate Fabeae

It has been impossible to assign a number of Fabeae (also termed 'Vicieae') seeds to the species described above or to any of the wild species represented in the BIAA collection. One badly abraded seed was found in a Hellenistic level at Aşvan Kale (H3c 606.6) with dimensions that match archaeological examples of broad bean (*Vicia faba* L.). However, neither the hilum nor radicle survived, so it is not possible to rule out an identification with one of the large-seeded wild vetches. The cotyledons of this seed did, however, bear faint traces of depressions that match those of *V. faba*.

3.6. Fruits

3.6.1. Grape: Vitis vinifera

Two forms of grape vine grow in the Mediterranean area: the wild vine, *Vitis sylvestris* (C.C. Gmelin) Hegi., and the domesticated vine, *V. vinifera*. The wild vine grows in widespread but scattered locations over most of Turkey as a minor component of deciduous and riverine forests. Domesticated vines are grown over most of Turkey, both for table consumption and for wine making.

The two forms can be separated on the basis of flower characters, fruit size and numbers of seeds per fruit, but as these parts of the plant rarely survive in archaeological material, pip characteristics are most often used.

It has been suggested that there are some obvious differences in the shape of wild and domesticated grape pips. Wild grape pips are smaller, shorter and broader, with a body tending towards a spherical or heart shape, with a short beak; domesticated grape pips are larger, longer and more slender, with an oblong or egg-like shape and a longer beak (Stummer 1911). The most frequently used quantitative characteristic for separating pips of the two types of grape has been the breadth to length ratio (breadth/length ×100). In general, therefore, we would expect pips from domesticated grapes to be longer and narrower – i.e. more slender – and thus have a lower index than the plumper pips of wild grape.

Various measurements have been made of modern seeds from Europe but there is a considerable overlap in ratios. Taking the effects of charring into consideration, it has not been possible to develop quantitative criteria that are uniformly applicable to all archaeological sites. Measurements of reference material demonstrate the differences in size and the degree of overlap (table 10).

In the case of these two populations, the stalk length of wild and domesticated grapes expressed as a percentage of body length is not very different, but in absolute terms the stalk length of wild grapes is shorter (table 11). The wild pips are smaller, but size alone is not necessarily a reliable indicator. A.M. Negrul (1960, cited by Janushevitch et al. 1985: 120) has shown that the length of cultivated grape pips is related to the diameter of the grape. Thus a variety selected for small grape size might well have small pips.

The results of the studies summarised above are generally rather unsatisfactory, and it was decided that it was easiest simply to make a subjective evaluation of the pips by comparison with modern reference material and

		Seed	
	Length	*Breadth*	*Thickness*
V. sylvestris SP137 (n = 25)			
Minimum	3.95	3.05	2.24
Maximum	5.38	3.9	2.9
Average	4.58	3.46	2.6
V. vinifera RMN907 (n = 25)			
Minimum	5.47	3.57	2.62
Maximum	6.9	5.14	3.19
Average	6.33	4.24	2.96

Table 10. Measurements of modern grape pip reference material.

		Stalk	
	Length	*%*	*B:L*
V. sylvestris SP137 (n = 25)			
Minimum	10	65	62
Maximum	21	84	91
Average	17	75	76
V. vinifera RMN907 (n = 25)			
Minimum	14	53	51
Maximum	23	94	84
Average	19	66	70

Table 11. Grape stalk length as a percentage of body length of modern reference material.

drawings. In practice the pips from Aşvan fall clearly into three groups: domesticated, wild and under-developed domesticated pips.

Virtually all of the Aşvan grape pips from the Early Bronze Age onwards have been confidently assigned to domesticated *V. vinifera* subsp. *Vinifera*. Most of the pips have long stalks (0.71–1.71mm; 14–33% of pip length) and elongated bodies. This is perhaps the most reliable characteristic of the domesticated type. The furrow at the bottom of the pip is also often deeper in cultivated populations, and this is very clear on many of the Aşvan specimens (fig. 33).

The Chalcolithic pips were too fragmentary to allow comparison. There is some limited evidence for grape domestication in the fourth millennium BC, and it is therefore not possible to assign these to wild/domesticated status purely on the basis of age (Miller 2008).

The Roman pips are larger than the rest, but their glossy and rather swollen appearance suggests that they had been charred at particularly high temperatures, and that their size was not directly comparable with the Hellenistic and Medieval grapes. The Early Bronze Age grapes, however, did seem to be genuinely smaller. The increased size of later samples may well reflect selection for larger berries.

A few smaller, rounder pips with much shorter stalks of another type were found in three Early Bronze Age and Hellenistic samples. These were separated by eye and measured separately. Their average width/length value was 82 (range 74–92) and stalk lengths were on average 16% of total pip length. Their length and width are on average less than those of the cultivated type, although their thickness is a little greater. In appearance these pips closely match modern wild grapes.

All of these wild-type pips were in the Early Bronze Age levels, which also produced several pips that closely matched the domesticated type. Similar mixtures of morphologically wild- and domesticated-type pips have been reported from the early levels of other sites, such as Sitagroi (Renfrew 1973: 130), and it is tempting to suggest that this is characteristic of the 'primitive' or 'transitional' form of the newly domesticated crop. Greater genetic variability in ancient populations is the most likely explanation for these pips; it has often been suggested that both wild and cultivated vines were in use when these mixtures are found (Hjelmquist 1970; Renfrew 1970). However, it seems unlikely that any village that cultivated the productive and sweeter domesticated vines would trouble to harvest wild vines.

A third kind of grape pip, very small and with long stalks, was measured separately, but classified as cultivated. These small pips were presumably immature; all four were found in Hellenistic samples, and match the under-developed type described by Kroll (1999).

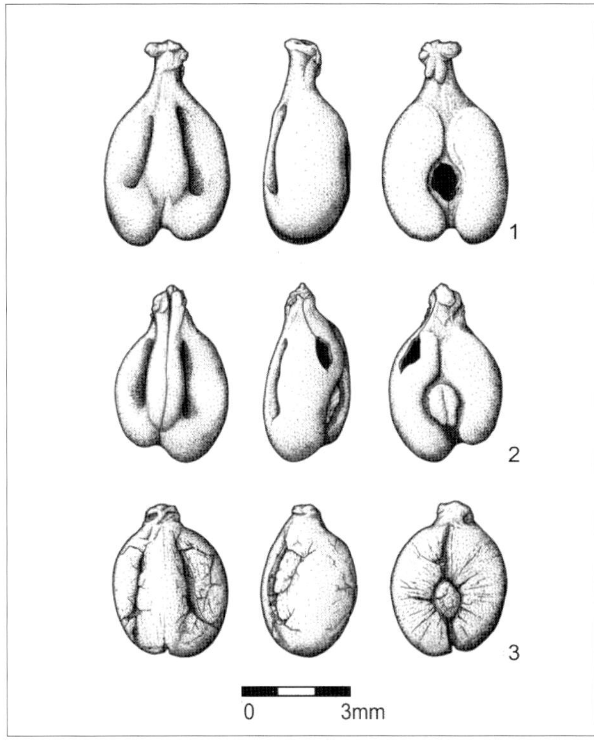

*Fig. 33. Grape pips, domesticated type (*Vitis vinifera*): (1 and 2) AK 1204.11; wild type: (3) AK 606.6.*

Many uncharred grape pips were found in the Medieval samples, sometimes with pieces of flesh attached. As grape pips are very woody, they could well be ancient uncharred remains. Ancient grapes are often reported from late prehistoric periods such as the Iron Age (Kroll 1983: 67). As decay and abrasion has generally removed much of the outer shells of the pips, often leaving only the kernels, they have not been measured. They were recorded separately from the charred pips on the scoresheets.

3.6.2. Almond: Amygdalus communis

Almond shells were found in three Hellenistic samples from Aşvan Kale, probably all part of the same original deposit. As the characteristics of the stone are important in identifying fresh material of this genus, the *Flora of Turkey* gives detailed descriptions of the modern material used as comparison for identification purposes (Davis et al. 1988; Güner 2001).

The Aşvan stones had a distinct keel and the flanks were pitted and clearly grooved. Apart from *A. communis*, three other species are recorded from the Aşvan region: *A. trichamygdalus* (Hand.-Mazz) Woronow, *A. orientalis* Mill. and *A. arabica* Olivier. Of these, only *A. trichamygdalus* is recorded as having a pitted stone. However, this species has 'indistinctly marked grooves' along the keel, whilst the grooves are well developed on the Aşvan specimens, which closely resemble modern *A. communis* shells.

Two reasonably intact stones were found (fig. 34) at Aşvan Kale: AK H3c 606.15 s.18 (length 11mm) and AK H3c 606.15 s.28 (length 14mm, width 21mm).

Sample 21 at Aşvan Kale, which was excavated from the same deposit that contained the intact almonds, included numerous small fragments, which had perhaps been crushed in the collapse of the building when it was burnt. The fragments showed the same pitting and grooving that could be observed on the whole nuts. The fragments weighed 25g. As the complete charred nut in sample 28 weighed about 3.28g (after conservation with a consolidant), the fragments probably represent about eight whole nuts.

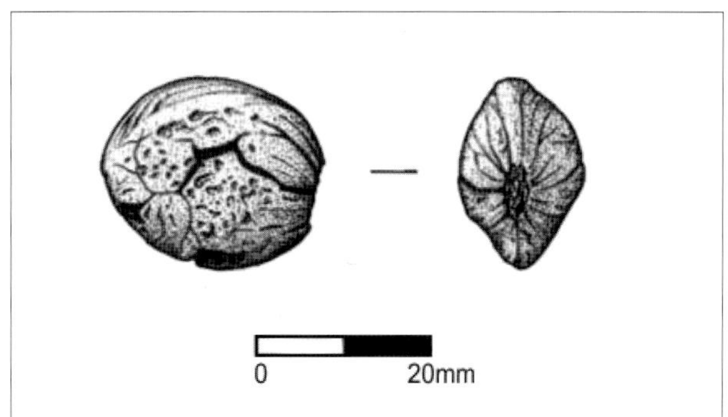

*Fig. 34. Almond stone (*Amygdalus communis*): AK 606.15.*

3.7. Other crops

3.7.1. Flax: Linum usitatissimum

The Aşvan flax seeds are 2.75–3.7mm long, with a distinct hook (fig. 35). They are therefore definitely of the domesticated form. As usual with oil-rich seeds, they are friable and in poor condition. Most seeds are very swollen; on unswollen seeds the breadth is 0.65–0.7mm.

3.7.2. Cotton: Gossypium arboreum/herbaceum

Cotton seeds (fig. 36, table 12), which could not be determined as either *Gossypium arboreum* or *G. herbaceum*, were found in small caches in the Medieval II, IIIa and IIIb period (12th to 14th centuries AD). A thin, usually smooth mesocarp, about 0.1mm thick, covers a thick, smooth endocarp, about 0.4mm thick. The inside is filled by a kernel which is smooth on the surface and has a spongey texture inside. The mesocarp forms a distinct beak at its 'upper' end, which continues as a ridge down the side of the fruit, ending in a small protuberance. The beaks are definitely an integral part of the mesocarp, and are not merely the abraded remains of stalks. Although the mesocarp is usually smooth apart from the ridge, a few specimens have several longitudinal pleats in addition to the ridge. Remains of hairs are present at the base of the fruit.

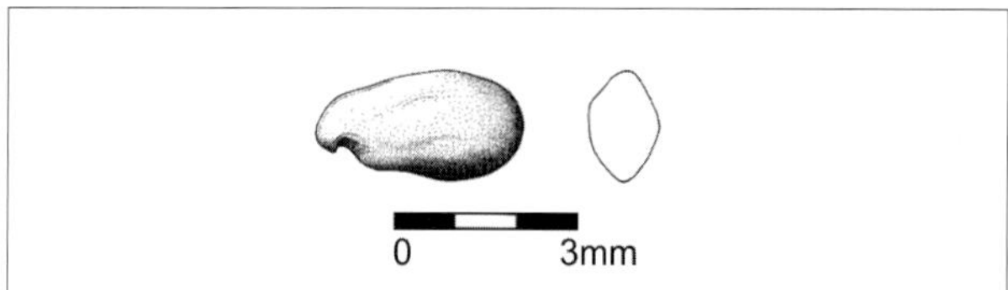

*Fig. 35. Flax (*Linum usitatissimum*): ÇB 10.2.*

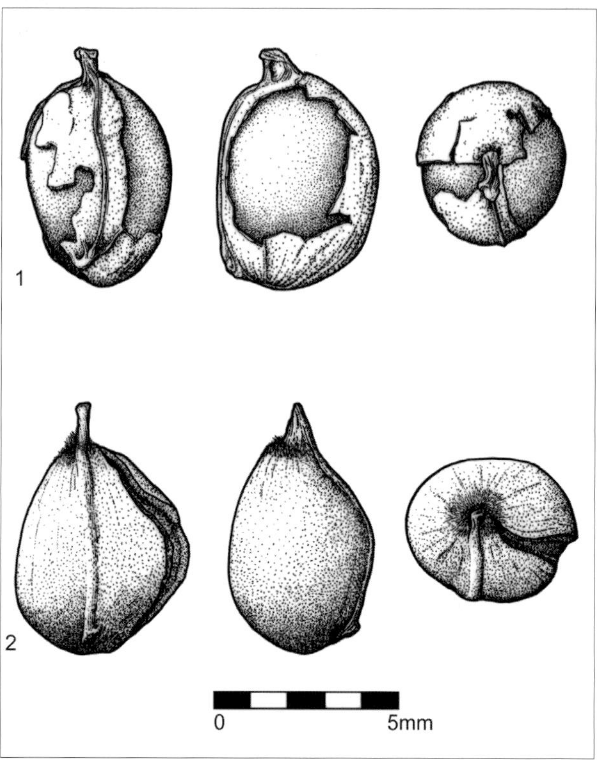

*Fig. 36. Cotton seed (*Gossypium arboreum/herbaceum*): (1) G4cd 1902.4; (2) H3d 714.8.*

AK 1902.4	*Length*	*Breadth*	*Thickness*
Minimum	2.8	2.1	2.1
Maximum	5.1	4.1	5
Average	3.93	2.85	2.97
Standard deviation	1.05	0.75	0.92

Table 12. Measurements of cotton seeds.

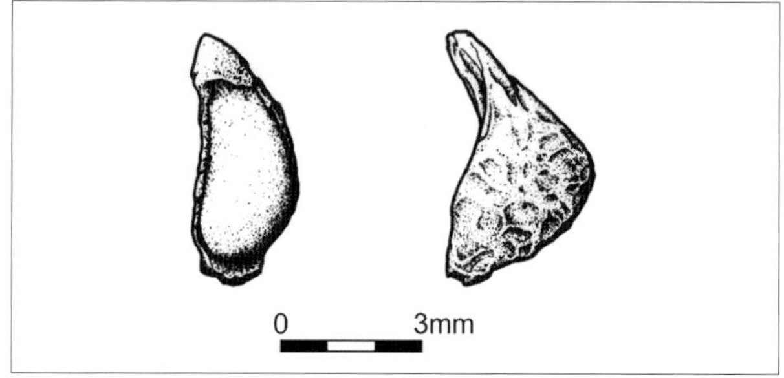

*Fig. 37. Black cumin (*Nigella sativa*): AK 606.15.*

3.7.3. Black cumin: Nigella sativa

Over 2,500 *Nigella sativa* seeds occurred as a more or less pure deposit (mixed only with 150 grains of foxtail millet) in sample AK 606.15 of the Hellenistic level at Aşvan Kale (see fig. 7 M6). The seeds (fig. 37) are 2.5–3mm long and a maximum of 1.1–1.6mm in cross-section. As usual with oil-rich seeds, the seed coat is friable and some seeds have swollen. Less badly affected seeds appear somewhat trigonous in cross-section, with traces of a reticulate seed coat. A number of weed species occur in southeastern Turkey. *N. oxypetala* Boiss. and *N. latisecta* P.H. Davis belong to subsection *Nigellastrum* with flattened ovate seeds entirely unlike the Aşvan specimens (Dadandi et al. 2009; Heiss et al. 2011). *N. segetalis* M. Bieb. has smooth seeds. In terms of shape and texture *N. arvensis* L. is the most similar wild species but has a papillate surface rather than the reticulate surface of *N. sativa*. The size and shape of the Aşvan seeds closely resemble those found in a flask at the Hittite site of Boyalı (Salih et al. 2009). Comparison with reference material and other archaeological finds, and the large number of seeds found in a cache at Aşvan, strongly support identification as the domesticated form of black cumin, *N. sativa*.

3.8. Useful wild plants

3.8.1. Hackberry: Celtis

Hackberry stones, like the seeds of many of the Boraginaceae, are highly silicaceous and it is difficult to distinguish charred ancient specimens from modern intrusive examples. However, virtually all of the Aşvan hackberries have the desiccated remains of flesh on their exteriors and the interior contents are powdery and white, rather than charred. This suggests that the Aşvan hackberries are probably of recent origin. The Aşvan stones are reticulate and 5–7mm in diameter.

3.8.2. Hawthorn: Crataegus

A narrow pyrene was found, from a multi-pyrenate species such as *C. orientalis* M. Bieb. However, without more examples it is determined only as *Crataegus* Tourn. ex L.

3.8.3. Terebinth: Pistacia

Terebinth nuts occur mainly as fragments (fig. 38). The most likely candidates for the Aşvan region are *P. terebinthus* L., *P. eurycarpa* Yaltirik and *P. khinjuk* Stocks. Typical measurements are: height 3.5–4.5mm; width 4.5–5mm; thickness 3.5mm. These measurements most closely match *P. terebinthus*, the most abundant species in the region. The nuts of fresh *P. eurycarpa* are also wider than they are thick, but measure 6–7mm thick and 7–9mm wide. This is too large, even allowing for the effects of charring. The nuts of *P. khinjuk* are never wider than they are thick, and are closer in size to the ancient nuts at 5–7mm thick and 4–6mm wide. Some nuts in some populations of *P. terebinthus* are wider than they are thick, and their measurements of 4–6mm thick and 4–5.5mm wide are consistent with the Aşvan nuts.

3.8.4. Wild plum: Prunus

A fragment of a compressed wild *Prunus* L. *sensu stricto* was found. A number of wild species are candidates, including *P. cerasifera* Ehrh.

3.8.5. Oak gall: Quercus

Oak (*Quercus* sp.) galls have a very distinctive structure consisting of a larval chamber, created by wasps, surrounded by spongy tissue, seen clearly in a modern specimen bought from a Turkish herbalist and in ancient material (fig. 39).

3.9. Weed seeds

3.9.1. Asteraceae

3.9.1.1. Carthamus. The achene from ÇB10.2 is 3.9mm long and 1.9mm in maximum diameter (fig. 40.1). The longitudinal ridging is reminiscent of *Carthamus* sp., but the shape does not match the short, squat achenes of wild species or the thicker achenes of the domesticated *C. tinctorius* L. (Marinova, Riehl 2009). This identification should probably be considered as cf. *Carthamus*.

Two achenes of safflower were identified. The specimen from AK 606.6 measures: length 5.5mm; breadth 3mm; thickness 2.7mm. That from AK 1506.3 measures: length 4.6mm; breadth 2.3mm; depth 1.9mm (fig. 40.2). The relatively slender shape suggests that it belongs to the domesticated species *C. tinctorius*

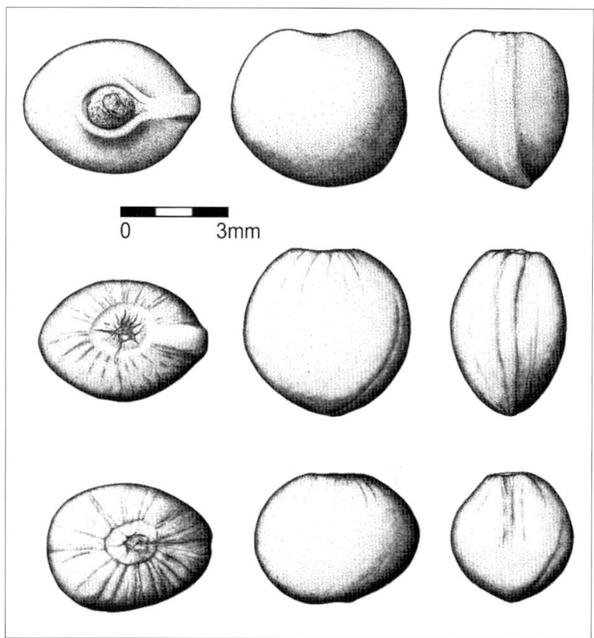

*Fig. 38. Terebinth nuts (*Pistachia terebinthus*): TM 103.6.*

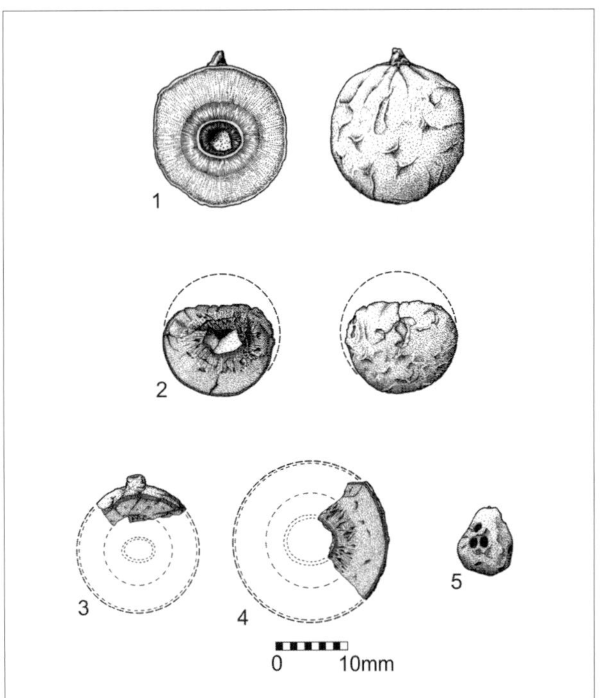

Fig. 39. Oak galls, modern: (1) RMN 330; ancient: (2–5) AK 606.15.

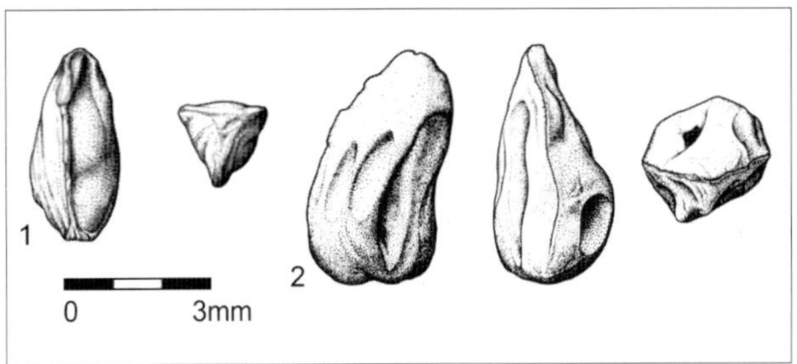

Fig. 40. Carthamus*: (1) ÇB 10.2. 9; (2) AK 1506.3, perhaps* Carthamus tinctorius.

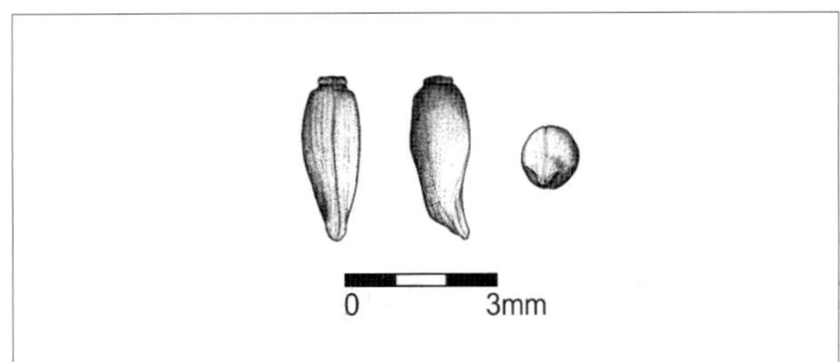

Fig. 41. Centaurea*: ÇB 10.2.*

(Marinova, Riehl, 2009), but the identification remains uncertain given the presence in the Aşvan region of two wild species: *C. persicus* Willd. and *C. glaucus* M. Bieb. Although squatter in shape, these have some overlap with the Aşvan finds. In view of the small number of achenes found, the identification is maintained as *Carthamus* sp.

3.9.1.2. Centaurea. The achene from ÇB 10.2 measure: length 3.1mm; maximum diameter 1.2mm (fig. 41). The constricted, clearly delimited pappus base at the top of the achene and the hooked base are typical of *Centaurea* sp. More than 100 species are present in Turkey, and species-level identification is impossible.

3.9.2. Boraginaceae

Several Boraginaceae seeds have a grey, charred appearance. Dissection of several grey seeds showed a charred ball of endosperm inside, while white seeds have a yellowy, powdery interior. Only grey/black Boraginaceae seeds were included in the scoresheet.

3.9.2.1 Buglossoides arvensis *and* B. tenuiflora. *Buglossoides arvensis* is the more robust seed, with measurements of: length 2.6–3.2mm; breadth 1.6–2.2mm; thickness 1.4–1.8mm (fig. 42.1). The large basal scar is 1.2–1.9mm wide. *B. tenuiflora* has a slender, distinct neck (fig. 42.2). Its measurements are: length 2–2.5mm; breadth 1.4–1.7mm; thickness 1.2–1.8 mm; scar width 0.7–0.9mm. The great variability in size is also obvious in modern reference material. *B. arvensis* is a common weed of fields and steppe throughout Turkey; *B. tenuiflora* is markedly less common. Most *Buglossoides* sp. seeds have a grey, charred appearance, described above.

3.9.3. Brassicaceae

3.9.3.1. Euclidium syriacum. The highly distinctive capsule was found intact with its two seeds, with reticulate nervation on the fruit valves (Van Zeist, Casparie 1984: 207–08). Three capsules in ÇB 3 were measured: (1) length 2.14mm, width 1.63mm; (2) length 2.28mm, width 1.7mm; and (3) length 1.84mm, width 1.33mm. Only one species grows in Turkey: *Euclidium syriacum*.

3.9.3.2. Neslia. The Aşvan finds are all capsules, sometimes intact, sometimes opened (Van Zeist, Bakker-Heeres 1985: 250, 254). The capsules have a distinctive reticulate surface and a maximum diameter of 1.45–2.1mm.

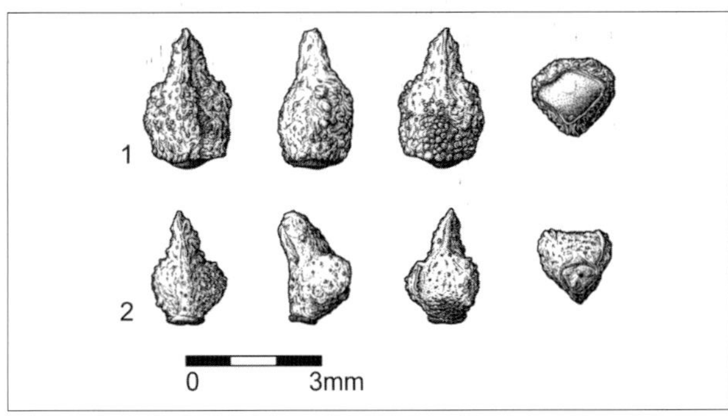

Fig. 42. Buglossoides*: (1)* B. arvensis*; (2)* B. tenuiflora*, TM 101.24.*

3.9.4. Caryophyllaceae

3.9.4.1. Silene. With more than 120 species present in Turkey, *Silene* sp. seeds are hard to specify. Four species were collected from the fields at Aşvan, but the identifications of this herbarium material are also uncertain. The Aşvan archaeological seeds have a distinctive sunken depression in the faces and ridges run in broken lines from the centre to the periphery. The sunken centre is similar to that seen in *S. gallica* L., but that species has a mainly coastal distribution and is not a likely candidate for the Aşvan sites. Seed size is: length 1–1.3mm; breadth 0.7–1mm; thickness 0.8–1mm

3.9.4.2. Vaccaria pyramidata *Medik.* The examples in the modern reference collection are spherical, but in the archaeological material the two halves of the seed have invariably been pushed apart as the centre expanded during charring (fig. 43). Diameter (excluding expanded area) is 1.1mm. Well-preserved material has traces of papillae. *Vaccaria pyramidata* is the only species in this genus and is common in fields throughout Turkey.

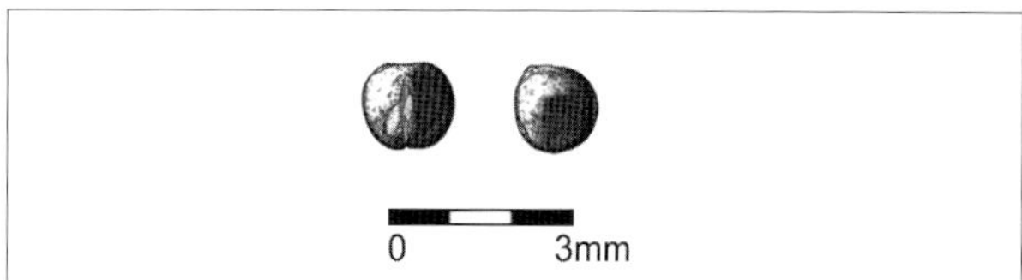

Fig. 43. Vaccaria pyramidata*: TM 101.24.*

3.9.5. Cyperaceae

3.9.5.1. Bolboschoenus glaucus. The trigonous nutlets of this species were previously referred to by archaeobotanists as *Bolboschoenus maritimus* or *Scirpus maritimus*. Recent research has shown that *B. maritimus* is limited to saline habitats, mainly in Europe, and is not the species found at inland archaeological sites in the Near East (Wollstonecroft et al. 2011); this is *B. glaucus*, which has smaller nutlets, usually 2.2–2.5mm long, as compared to 3–4mm long for *B. maritimus*. The Aşvan nutlets are 1.65–2.05mm long and 1.25–1.5mm wide (fig. 44).

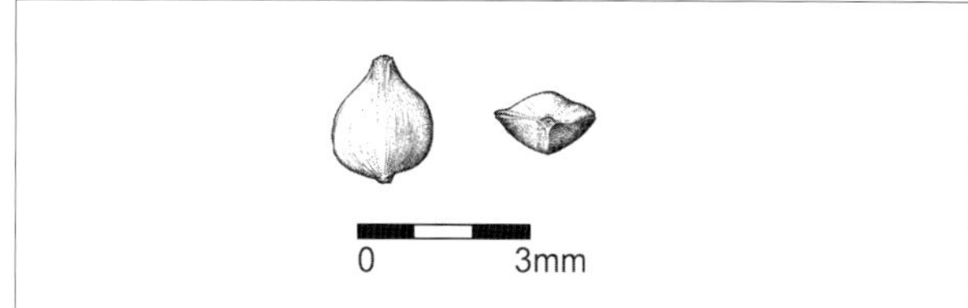

Fig. 44. Bolboschoenus glaucus*: ÇB 10.4.*

3.9.5.2. Carex. The nutlets of *Carex* are similar to those of *Bolboschoenus* but are not trigonous (Van Zeist, Bakker-Heeres 1982: 215–16).

3.9.6. Fabaceae

3.9.6.1. Grass vetchling: Lathyrus *cf.* cicera/sativus. Both of these species have been cultivated in Turkey. *Lathyrus cicera* is also a widespread wild plant and weed, while *L. sativus* has a more restricted wild distribution as a segetal weed. Both species have a very distinctive hatchet-shaped seed, apparently similar in both wild and cultivated material. Differentiating the seeds of the two species is still problematic, but in general *L. cicera* seeds are smaller in all dimensions and less rounded. At Dimini the seeds identified by Kroll (1979) as *L.* cf. *cicera* had a maximum width of 3.5mm, whilst those of *L.* cf. *sativus* had a minimum width of about 2.7mm.

Three grass vetchling seeds were found at Aşvan Kale, all in the Hellenistic level. They were of varying size: heights 3.5mm, 2mm and 4.3mm. Given the small number of seeds, no specific identification has been made. However, considering the prevalence of *L. cicera* as a weed plant of pulse crops in eastern Turkey and that the widths of the Aşvan seeds are all under 3mm, it is likely that they are weed plants of *L. cicera*. One grass vetchling seed was found in the Taşkun Kale samples.

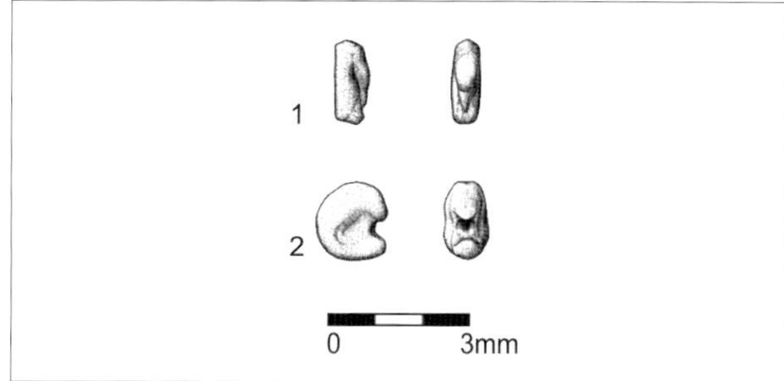

Fig. 45. Trifolieae: (1) ÇB 10.4; (2) 10.2.

3.9.6.2. Trifolieae. These small legume seeds are notoriously difficult to distinguish, particularly in the absence of hilum and testa. During the sorting, the seeds were divided as follows: *Trigonella* L. and some *Astragalus*, markedly oblong and angular in lateral view (fig. 45.1); *Coronilla*, somewhat cylindrical; *Medicago*, flattened, kidney shaped; *Trifolium*, kidney shaped (fig. 45.2). However, these identifications are too insecure to specify on the scoresheet.

3.9.7. Lamiaceae

3.9.7.1. Ajuga *and* Teucrium. The dorsal side of seeds of both genera bears traces of a reticulate pattern. The seed of *Ajuga* is larger and more markedly obovate (as illustrated in Van Zeist, Bakker-Heeres 1985: 259–60). The measurements of *Teucrium* sp. are: length 1.5–1.6mm; breadth 1mm; thickness 0.9–1.1mm (fig. 46). Those of *Ajuga* sp. are: length 2.5mm; breadth 1mm; thickness 0.9mm.

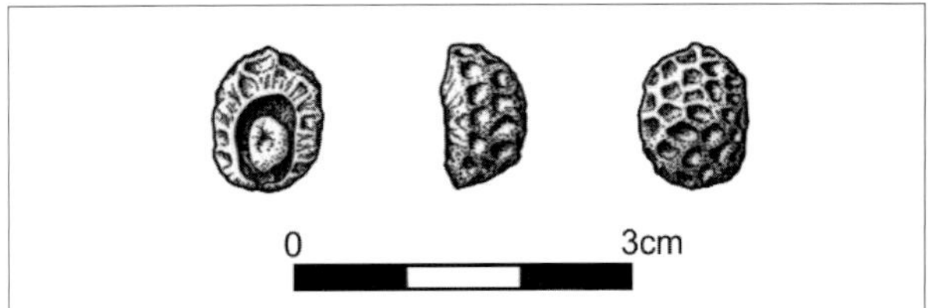

Fig. 46. Teucrium*: ÇB 10.4.*

3.9.7.2. Lallemantia. TM103.6 contained one seed with a rounded dorsal side and two slanted surfaces on the ventral side characteristic of Lamiaceae mericarps. The measurements (length 3mm; breadth 1.05mm) and shape match the *Lallemantia* sp. seeds found in quantity at Bronze Age sites in northern Greece (Jones, Valamoti 2005). They grow there outside their native range and can therefore be interpreted as cultivated oil seeds. In eastern Turkey several species, including *L. canescens* (L.) Fisch. & C.A. Mey., *L. iberica* (M. Bieb.) Fisch. & C.A. Mey. and *L. peltata* (L.) Fisch. & C.A. Mey, grow as annual crop weeds. Of these, *L. iberica* can be used for edible oil, and its use is documented in the Bronze Age at Arkadikio in northern Greece (Valamoti 2009; cf. Megaloudi 2006). However, without a larger number of finds and without species-level identification it is difficult to know whether this was a weed or cultivar at Taşkun Mevkii. The early date of this find suggests that it is most likely to be a wild species.

3.9.8. Liliaceae

3.9.8.1. Bellevallia. Globular seeds with maximum diameter at Aşvan of 1.25-1.5mm. They have a characteristic round hole and channel through the seed, visible in broken specimens (cf. Van Zeist, Bakker-Heeres 1982: 216, 227). Several of the Turkish species are recorded as occurring in fields.

3.9.9. Malvaceae

3.9.9.1. Malva *cf.* neglecta. Seed size is: length 1.3–1.5mm; breadth 0.7–0.8mm; thickness 1.2–1.5mm. *Malva neglecta* is the most widespread species in Turkey, found on steppe and infields, and its seeds are similar in size and rounded shape to the archaeological seeds from Aşvan.

3.9.10. Papaveraceae

3.9.10.1. Fumaria. Nutlets from ÇB 5 are 1.5–1.6mm long. They are rugulose and the apex has two pits usually joined to form a slot. The margin is slightly winged. *Fumaria asepala* Boiss. is the most widespread of five species present in southeastern Turkey and grows in fields.

3.9.11. Poaceae

3.9.11.1. Goatgrass: Aegilops. The Aşvan examples are flattened grains (fig. 47.6) with compressed ventral flanks, similar in texture to *Triticum* sp. grains but differently shaped. *Aegilops* sp. grains are highly variable; the species most often found as a weed in eastern Turkey is *Ae. cylindrica* Host, but an identification to species would only be possible with well-preserved chaff remains.

3.9.11.2. Oats: Avena. The Aşvan oat grains (fig. 47.5) are widest in their upper half. The ventral furrow is usually very tight, but there is a lot of variation and some grains have a shallow V-shaped furrow. While the ventral surface is somewhat flattened, the back is rounded in all views and this is reflected in the cross-section. A particularly useful genus-level character is the sharply V-shaped embryo emplacement, although this is not always visible on the archaeological specimens. Most spikelets have two fertile florets, the grain from the upper being substantially smaller. Occasionally the top, third, floret is fertile and contains even smaller grains. Thus a wide variation in size could be expected in prehistoric samples. Identification of the grains to species was not possible. However, oats are rare in the archaeobotanical record of the Near East and it can be assumed that these occasional records represent wild oats such as *Avena sterilis* L.

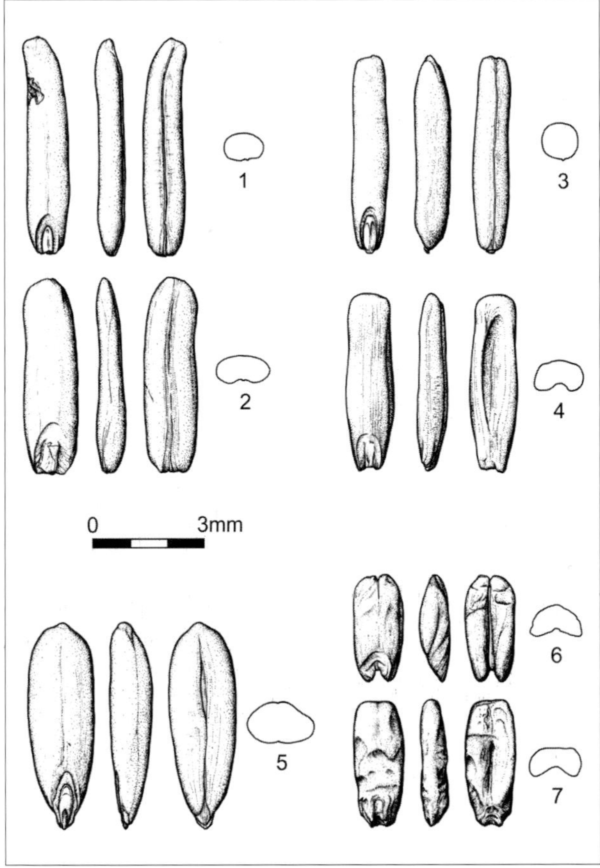

*Fig. 47. Wild grasses: (1 to 3) feathergrass (*Stipa*), ÇB 10.5; (4) ryegrass (*Lolium persicum*), TM 101.25; (5) wild oat (*Avena sp.*), AK 1501.5; (6) goatgrass (*Aegilops sp.*), ÇB 10.7; (7) ryegrass (*Lolium perenne/rigidum*), TM 103.6.*

3.9.11.3. Brome grass: Bromus. The grains of *Bromus* are elongated and flattened, with a long linear hilum usually still visible on charred material. Where the scutellum is visible on Aşvan material it is V-shaped, distinguishing it from the similar grains of *Brachypodium*. Study of modern material has identified two groups: long grained (>10.5mm) belonging to section *Genea* and short-grained (Nesbitt 2006). The Aşvan grains are all broken and no attempt has been made to measure them. There is a large number of candidate species that grow in both ruderal and cultivated habitats, including the following species collected by members of the botanical team at Aşvan: *B. danthoniae* Trin., *B. japonicus* Thunb., *B. sterilis* L., *B. scoparius* L., *B. squarrosus* L. and *B. tectorum* L.

3.9.11.4. Echinochloa. Mark Nesbitt and Geoff Summers (1988) describe the grains of *Echinochloa crus-galli* (L.) P. Beauv. as small, very flat millet grains with a typical thickness to width index of 40–65, a long (70–90%) embryo and high variability in grain width.

3.9.11.5. Wild barley: Hordeum. All the wild species of barley are rather similar in appearance. All have one fertile spikelet and two sterile lateral spikelets on each rachis segment, and therefore the seeds are not dimorphic. The caryopses are flattened, with a rounded (verging on blunt) distal end and a wide, deep furrow. Most of the wild species are small. *Hordeum spontaneum*, however, overlaps with domesticated barley and this creates a problem of identification (see section 3.4.2.2).

Three species can be excluded on ecological grounds. *H. violaceum* Boiss. & Huet is a species of high altitudes (1,600–3,000m) and is therefore an unlikely component of the Aşvan plant remains. *H. marinum* Huds. grows in sand marshes and coastal sands and has not been collected near Aşvan. *H. geniculatum* All. is a species of meadows, steppe and roadsides; a single specimen was collected by Hillman from the grassy slopes of a hill near Aşvan. This has small seeds and a furrow that is narrow for its lowest half, widening slightly towards the top.

The following two species are the most likely to occur in the Aşvan samples. Their morphology was examined and is described below, but no convincing matches were seen in ancient material.

H. murinum: the taxa comprising this species are the most common wild barleys of the Near East, ubiquitous in overgrazed steppe and on roadsides. The narrowly obtri-angular shape of the grain (always widest near the top) is distinctive. The furrow varies: sometimes the ventral cheeks are so flattened that there is barely a furrow between them, and in cross-section the ventral face is a shallow, concave V-shape. If the cheeks are higher then the furrow is clear and always narrow, widening towards the top. The grains are always thin and the upper part of the back is slightly concave. There is a flange on either side of the ventral flanks and the transverse section is very angular. These grains are highly distinctive and should be easily spotted in ancient samples.

H. bulbosum L: this perennial species is common on hillsides throughout Turkey and has been collected in cereal fields. At Aşvan this bulbous species, when found in archaeological contexts, has many sterile spikelets. The grains are quite long, slender and flat. The groove is always clearly defined and very narrow, widening up the grain. The upper part of the back is markedly concave. The grains are widest at about two-thirds of their length and thickest near the embryo. There are flanges on each flank.

3.9.11.6 Ryegrass: Lolium. Ryegrass species in south-eastern Turkey fall into three groups: *Lolium temulentum* L. and the smaller *L. remotum* Schrank. with turgid, swollen grains; *L. persicum* Boiss. & Hohen. with quite large slender, flat seeds (length 4.5–6.5mm); and *L. rigidum* Gaudin and *L. perenne* L. with smaller seeds of a similar shape (length 2.5–4.5mm). Ryegrass seeds have an adhesive lemma and palea with a distinctive punctate appearance and an adpressed rachilla; these often survive threshing and charring. Along the longitudinal lines where the palea and lemma meet on either side of the ventral face there is a sharp fold or crease in the surface of the grain. These are usually visible in charred samples and are another very useful generic character. All *Lolium* sp. grains have rounded, partly blunt ends.

L. perenne and *L. rigidum* have very similar grains, widest in the upper part. In lateral view the back is slightly convex, the front a little more curved (fig. 47.7). The ventral surface is a shallow V-shape in cross-section, with no distinct ventral furrow. There are no ventral cheeks. The maximum length of *L. rigidum* reference material is about 0.5mm longer than that of *L. perenne*. The grains of *L. multiflorum* Lam. are similar, but this is a Mediterranean species that can be discounted at Aşvan.

L. temulentum (darnel) and *L. remotum* have a highly distinctive turgid, swollen appearance. Each spikelet of *L. temulentum* contains between two and eight fertile florets, and this accounts for the variability in size and shape of the seeds. In general, grains from higher up the spikelet are more slender and shorter. The widest point of the grains is variable, but often in the upper half. The furrow is variable: sometimes deep, wide and V-shaped with distinct cheeks, sometimes just V-shaped. The back is curved in cross-section, unlike the rather oblong section of *rigidum*, *persicum* and *perenne*. There is usually a crease on each side of the grain as well as the palea impress. Darnel grains can be best distinguished from barley grains by their more

Site	*Identification*	*Length*	*Breadth*	*Thickness*	*L:B*	*T:B*
ÇB 2	*Aegilops?*	3.05	1.2	0.85	254	71
ÇB 2	*Aegilops?*	2.35	1.25	0.7	188	56
ÇB 2	*Aegilops?*	3.2	1.35	0.8	237	59
ÇB 2	*Aegilops?*	3.15	1	0.9	315	90
ÇB 2	*Aegilops?*	2.15	1	0.85	215	85
ÇB 2	*Aegilops?*	2.5	1.05	0.8	238	76
ÇB 2	*Aegilops?*	2.95	1.55	0.95	190	61
ÇB 2	*Aegilops?*	2.35	1.25	0.85	188	68
ÇB 2	*Aegilops?*	2.4	0.9	0.95	267	106
ÇB 2	*Aegilops?*	2.15	1.2	0.9	179	75
ÇB 40	*Lolium*	2.15	0.95	0.75	226	79
ÇB 40	*Lolium*	2.65	1.3	1	204	77
ÇB 40	*Lolium*	2.85	1.45	0.95	197	66
ÇB 40	*Lolium*	2.9	1.25	0.7	232	56
ÇB 40	*Lolium*	2.5	1.15	0.9	217	78
ÇB 40	*Lolium*	2.35	1.1	0.7	214	64
ÇB 40	*Lolium*	2.5	1.25	0.9	200	72
ÇB 40	*Lolium*	2.95	1.35	1	219	74
ÇB 40	*Lolium*	2.6	1.2	1	217	83
ÇB 40	*Lolium*	2.55	1.1	0.85	232	77
ÇB 40	*Aegilops?*	2.1	1.3	0.9	162	69
ÇB 40	*Aegilops?*	2.55	1.45	0.85	176	59
ÇB 40	*Aegilops?*	2.7	1.35	0.9	200	67
ÇB 40	*Aegilops?*	1.8	1.05	0.8	171	76
ÇB 40	*Aegilops?*	2.65	1.2	0.55	221	46
ÇB 40	*Aegilops?*	2.3	1.15	0.7	200	61
ÇB 40	*Aegilops?*	2.7	1.2	0.85	225	71
ÇB 40	*Aegilops?*	2.35	1.25	0.8	188	64
ÇB 40	*Aegilops?*	2.9	1.35	0.85	215	63
ÇB 40	*Aegilops?*	2.7	1.35	0.9	200	67
TM 101.24	*Lolium*	4.75	1.5	0.9	317	60
TM 101.24	*Lolium*	4	1.25	0.8	320	64
TM 101.24	*Lolium*	4.05	1.3	0.85	312	65
TM 101.24	*Lolium*	4.15	1.45	0.95	286	66
TM 101.24	*Lolium*	4.4	1.4	0.9	314	64
TM 101.24	*Lolium*	4.75	1.35	0.85	352	63
TM 101.24	*Lolium*	3.9	1.25	0.85	312	68
TM 101.24	*Lolium*	4.3	1.2	0.75	358	63

Table 13. Measurements of grains now identified as Lolium.

Site	*Identification*	*Length*	*Breadth*	*Thickness*	*L:B*	*T:B*
TM 101.24	*Lolium*	4.45	1.4	0.9	318	64
TM 101.24	*Lolium*	4.55	1.4	0.85	325	61
TM 101.24	*Aegilops*	2.75	1.25	1.15	220	92
TM 101.24	*Aegilops*	2.85	1.2	0.9	238	75
TM 101.24	*Aegilops*	2.4	0.95	0.95	253	100
TM 101.24	*Aegilops*	2.45	1.25	0.75	196	60
TM 101.24	*Aegilops*	2.25	1.3	0.7	173	54
TM 101.24	*Aegilops*	2.35	1.2	0.9	196	75
TM 101.24	*Aegilops*	2.85	1.7	0.95	168	56
AK	*Lolium*	4.75	1.4	0.75	339	54
AK	*Lolium*	3.95	1.25	1	316	80
AK	*Lolium*	4.15	1.25	1	332	80
AK	*Lolium*	3.35	1.2	0.85	279	71
AK	*Lolium*	5.05	1.75	1.15	289	66
AK	*Lolium*	5.15	1.55	1.25	332	81
AK	*Lolium*	4.4	1.3	0.9	338	69
AK	*Lolium*	4.25	1.15	0.95	370	83
AK	*Lolium*	3.65	1.1	0.55	332	50
AK	*Lolium*	4	1.2	0.75	333	63

Table 13 (continued). Measurements of grains now identified as Lolium.

rounded appearance, the markedly concave upper dorsal side with crinkling at the tip, their relatively greater width and the more curved ventral side in lateral view. The grains of *L. remotum* are very similar in appearance to *L. temulentum*, but smaller. Size alone separates them from *L. temulentum*.

L. persicum is similar in appearance to *L. perenne/rigidum* but much larger (fig. 47.1–4). One accession in the reference collection (GCH 3809) lacks any distinct ventral furrow, resulting in a very shallow V-shaped furrow in cross-section. The other (RMN 945) has a deep but very wide furrow, resulting in a more deeply V-shaped cross-section. As in *perenne/rigidum*, the back is rather rectangular in cross-section, but in lateral view the distal end is blunter. In lateral view the back varies from being slightly concave to slightly convex.

The Aşvan grains from archaeological contexts fall into two groups: small-grained (mostly 1.8–3.2mm long) and large-grained (3.35–5.15mm long).

At first the small-grained form was divided into two groups: grains with flattened ventral cheeks and a distinct ventral groove were named as *Aegilops*; grains without clear ventral cheeks were named as *Lolium*. However, it became clear that the so-called *Aegilops* and the *Lolium* had strikingly similar measurements (table 13) and texture, and close examination showed some typical *Aegilops* grains had adhering fragments of punctate lemma, reliably diagnostic of *Lolium*. All '*Aegilops*' grains have been reassigned to *Lolium*, with the exception of those with the strongly flattened ventral cheeks typical of *Aegilops* (section 3.9.11.1) and of a few grains over 3.5mm long, which have been retained as *Aegilops* (fig. 47.6).

The small-seeded grains are highly variable in shape, more so than seen in reference material, reflecting charring and, doubtless, their position in the spikelet (fig. 47.7). A few are swollen, probably as a result of charring, but many have flattened ventral cheeks; *Lolium remotum* can probably be excluded. The measurements match modern *L. rigidum* and *L. perenne* (uncharred reference material), and these seeds are assigned to that group. The large grains are much more regular in shape: long and narrow with a rectangular cross-section (fig. 47.4). These grains are almost all over 3.5mm long; allowing for the effects of charring, they are a good match for the grains of *L. persicum* (uncharred reference material is 4.4–6.4mm long). The dimensions of the reference material are shown in figure 48 and table 14; this replaces the incorrect graph in Nesbitt 2006: 55.

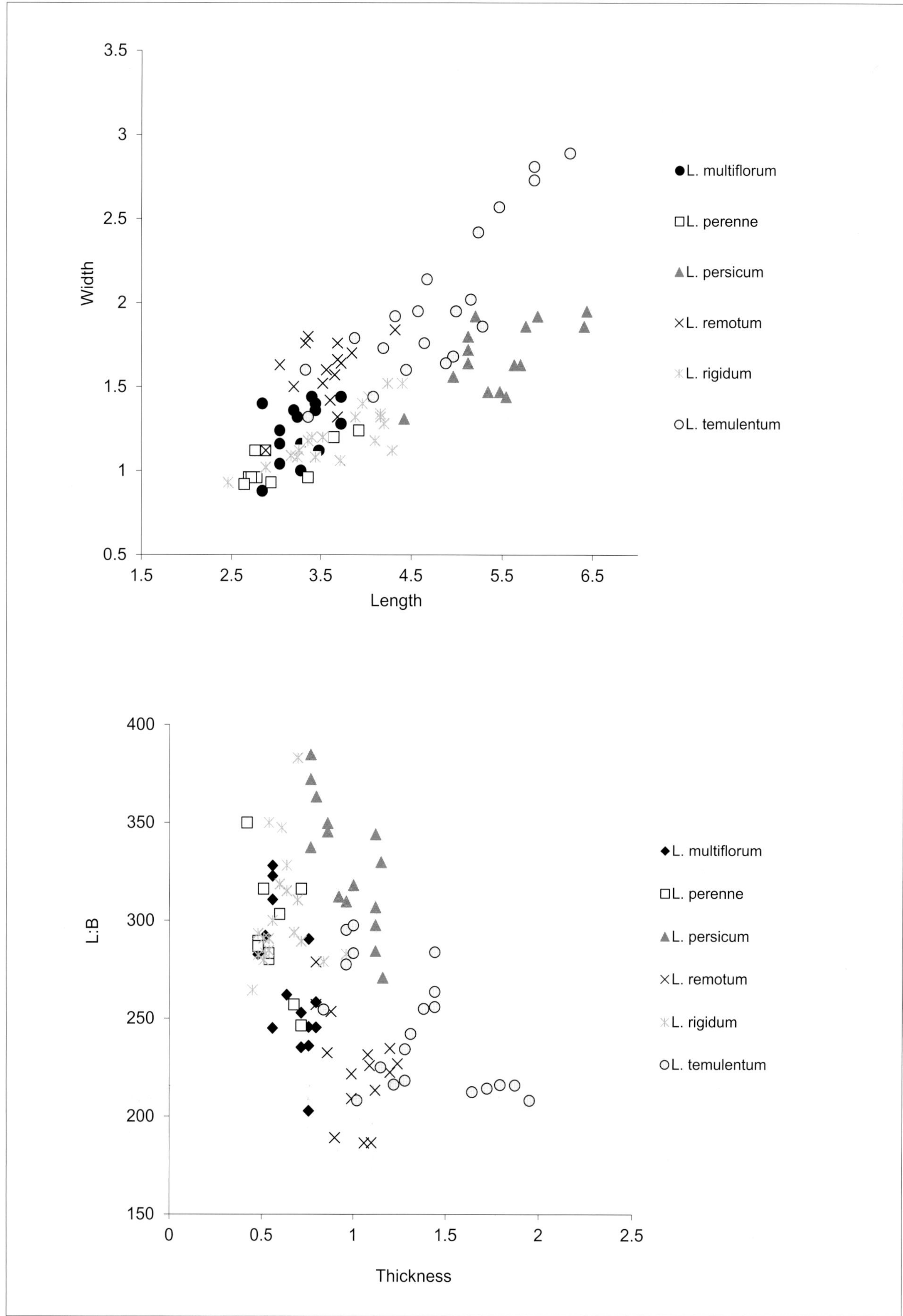

Fig. 48. Scatter plots of modern Lolium *measurements.*

	Length	*Breadth*	*Thickness*	*Length to breadth*	*Thickness to breadth*
L. multiflorum					
RMN4803	3.24	1.32	0.8	245	61
	3.44	1.4	0.76	246	54
	3.72	1.44	0.8	258	56
	3.04	1.16	0.64	262	55
	3.4	1.44	0.76	236	53
RMN4599	3.44	1.36	0.72	253	53
	2.84	1.4	0.76	203	54
	3.72	1.28	0.76	291	59
	3.04	1.24	0.56	245	45
	3.2	1.36	0.72	235	53
GCH7523	3.48	1.12	0.56	311	50
	2.84	0.88	0.56	323	64
	3.28	1	0.56	328	56
	3.28	1.16	0.48	283	41
	3.04	1.04	0.52	292	50
L. perenne					
RMN990	2.69	0.96	0.54	280	56
	2.78	0.96	0.48	290	50
	2.94	0.93	0.51	316	55
	2.72	0.96	0.54	283	56
	3.36	0.96	0.42	350	44
Unnumbered	3.64	1.2	0.6	303	50
	3.92	1.24	0.72	316	58
	2.76	1.12	0.72	246	64
	2.88	1.12	0.68	257	61
	2.64	0.92	0.48	287	52
L. persicum					
GCH3809	5.7	1.63	0.86	350	53
	5.34	1.47	0.8	363	54
	4.42	1.31	0.77	337	59
	5.63	1.63	0.86	345	53
	5.54	1.44	0.77	385	53
RMN945	6.4	1.86	1.12	344	60
	5.76	1.86	0.96	310	52
	5.47	1.47	0.77	372	52
	6.43	1.95	1.15	330	59
	5.89	1.92	1.12	307	58

Table 14. Measurements of modern Lolium *species (individual caryopses).*

	Length	Breadth	Thickness	Length to breadth	Thickness to breadth
RMN2870	4.96	1.56	1	318	64
	5.12	1.64	0.92	312	56
	5.2	1.92	1.16	271	60
	5.12	1.8	1.12	284	62
	5.12	1.72	1.12	298	65
L. remotum					
RMN2111	3.36	1.8	1.1	187	61
	3.6	1.42	0.88	254	62
	2.88	1.12	0.8	257	71
	3.04	1.63	1.06	187	65
	3.84	1.7	1.09	226	64
	3.65	1.57	0.86	232	55
	3.68	1.66	0.99	222	60
	3.2	1.5	1.12	213	75
	3.33	1.76	0.9	189	51
	3.68	1.76	0.99	209	56
NIAB	4.32	1.84	1.2	235	65
	3.52	1.52	1.08	232	71
	3.72	1.64	1.24	227	76
	3.68	1.32	0.8	279	61
	3.56	1.6	1.2	223	75
L. rigidum					
NM943	3.26	1.12	0.51	291	46
	2.46	0.93	0.45	265	48
	3.17	1.09	0.54	291	50
	3.71	1.06	0.54	350	51
	2.88	1.02	0.48	282	47
B1226	4.16	1.34	0.7	310	52
	4.03	1.44	0.51	280	35
	4.1	1.18	0.61	347	52
	4.29	1.12	0.7	383	63
	3.36	1.18	0.54	285	46
RMN4228	3.4	1.2	0.52	283	43
	4.2	1.28	0.64	328	50
	4.16	1.32	0.64	315	48
	3.24	1.08	0.56	300	52
	3.52	1.2	0.48	293	40

Table 14 (continued). Measurements of modern Lolium *species (individual caryopses).*

	Length	*Breadth*	*Thickness*	*Length to breadth*	*Thickness to breadth*
DJS148	3.96	1.4	0.96	283	69
	3.44	1.08	0.6	319	56
	3.88	1.32	0.68	294	52
	4.4	1.52	0.72	289	47
	4.24	1.52	0.84	279	55
L. temulentum					
SP52	6.24	2.89	1.87	216	65
	5.85	2.73	1.72	214	63
	5.46	2.57	1.64	212	64
	5.85	2.81	1.95	208	69
	5.23	2.42	1.79	216	74
GCH2242	4.67	2.14	1.28	218	60
	3.33	1.6	1.02	208	64
	4.57	1.95	1.28	234	66
	3.87	1.79	1.22	216	68
	4.32	1.92	1.15	225	60
RMN697	4.99	1.95	1.44	256	74
	4.64	1.76	1.44	264	82
	5.28	1.86	1.44	284	77
	4.19	1.73	1.31	242	76
	5.15	2.02	1.38	255	68
DJS470	4.44	1.6	0.96	278	60
	4.96	1.68	0.96	295	57
	3.36	1.32	0.84	255	64
	4.88	1.64	1	298	61
	4.08	1.44	1	283	69
Minimum	2.46	0.92	0.42	187	35
Average	4.12	1.52	0.89	278	58
Maximum	6.43	2.89	1.95	385	76

Table 14 (continued). Measurements of modern Lolium *species (individual caryopses).*

3.9.11.7. Wild millet: Setaria viridis/verticillata. The grains of these wild species are flatter (thickness averaging 0.81mm), narrower (length:width 136, compared with 119 for the *Setaria italica*) and with more pointed ends than *S. italica*. Full identification criteria have already been published (Nesbitt, Summers 1988). *S. viridis* grows in disturbed ground; *S. verticillata* is a weed of wet places. The two species cannot be distinguished using caryopsis or floret.

3.9.11.8. Feather grass: Stipa. *Stipa* grains are highly distinctive, being long and slender with a circular cross-section (fig. 47.1–3). Grains of other genera with a circular cross-section are much shorter (Nesbitt 2006: 51). Reference material can be divided into small species, (grains 3.7–4.8mm long) and large species (sections *Stipa* and *Barbatae*, grains 6.8–11mm long). The Aşvan grains (3.45–6.1mm long) match the large group, allowing for charring. Candidate species in the Aşvan region include *S.*

arabica Trin. & Rupr., *S. holosericea* Trin. and *S. ehrenbergiana* Trin. & Rupr., all of which grow on dry mountain slopes. No traces were found of the robust (but not adhesive) lemma and palea.

3.9.11.9. Taeniatherum caput-medusae. The grains are superficially similar to those of *Lolium*, but are larger (in modern material 8.5–14.5mm long) and the grain has deep longitudinal impressions made by the lemma and palea.

3.9.11.10. Wild wheat: Triticum boeoticum. Wild einkorn (*Triticum boeoticum*) is divided into two subspecies: a smaller form with one grain in each spikelet, which grows in the Balkans, Crimea and in western Turkey, and a larger, two-grained, form, which grows in Turkey and eastwards to northern Syria, Iran and Transcaucasia, with isolated appearances in the Balkans and Crimea (Schiemann 1948). As Jack Harlan and Daniel Zohary (1966) have pointed out, over much of its range the species is a weed of disturbed, secondary habitats such as field and road edges, into which it spread as agriculture created these new habitats. As a plant of primary, undisturbed habitats, wild einkorn is at present limited to southeastern Turkey, north-eastern Iraq and western Iran.

In the Elazığ region wild einkorn is found both in the relatively primary habitat of open oak woodlands, for example near Cemişgezek and Hazar Gölü, but also as a common weed of field margins and disturbed ground (for example, there are dense stands on the campus of Fırat University on the outskirts of Elazığ). The four or five lowest spikelets of spikes of wild einkorn collected in this area are typically one-grained, while the upper spikelets are two-grained. Given the variability in the grains and spikelets found in the Aşvan region, grains from both one- and two-grained spikelets could occur in the Aşvan samples.

According to Lennart Johnson (1975: 33) about 90% of the spikelets of *T. urartu* bear two grains of similar size, shape and colour, and are more slender than those of *T. boeoticum*. Studies by Nesbitt of *T. urartu* obtained from the International Center for Agricultural Research in the Dry Areas suggest that this is broadly true. However, as in two-grained *T. boeoticum*, one grain is smaller (but with a lesser size difference), with a squarer cross-section and concave ventral face, and one grain is larger, with a slightly convex ventral face. Both grains are a little longer and slimmer than those of *T. boeoticum*. These differences could probably be used if the seed sample was sufficiently large. Given the rather small number of wild diploid wheat grains in the Aşvan samples, and the current-day prevalence of *T. boeoticum* as a weed in the area, it was decided to classify the grains as *T. boeoticum*.

Wild emmer grains (*T. dicoccoides*) and the related wild Timopheev's wheat (*T. araraticum*) are usually from two-grained spikelets. They are similar to two-grained einkorn, but larger and proportionally longer. All wild wheat grains identified at Aşvan closely match wild einkorn. While it is not possible to exclude wild emmer grains on morphological grounds, the strong ecological preference of wild emmer for undisturbed habitats and the absence of wild emmer from Hillman's plant collections in the Aşvan area, suggest that it was probably not present.

Grain from one-grained spikelets (fig. 49) are usually rather large and can develop in the upper or lower floret, with grains from the lower floret being smaller than those from the upper. In lateral view both sides of the grain have a deep longitudinal groove starting just below the embryo and running to just below the tip. One side is rather concave (this is also visible in transverse section), while the other side is convexly curved. There are also several shallower grooves on the flanks. The tight ventral furrow is visible in central view; in dorsal view the ridge and the grain as a whole are slightly twisted. The grain is very narrow, widest at the middle. The ventral cheeks are rounded in cross-section, with creases but no flattened face.

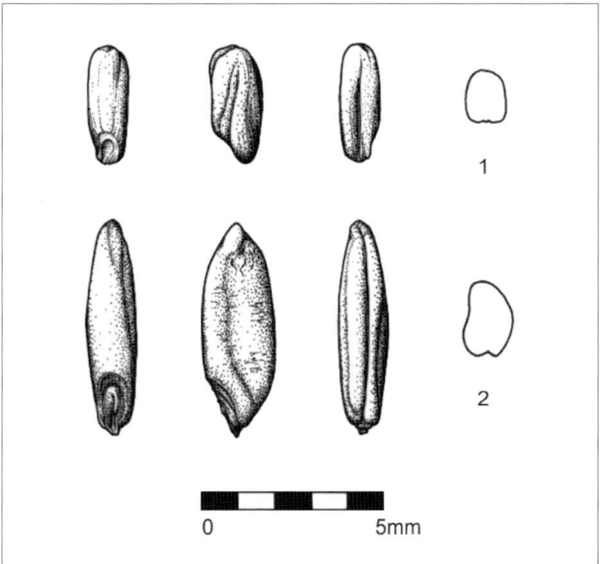

*Fig. 49. Wild einkorn (*triticum boeoticum*): (1) from two-grained spikelet, upper floret, ÇB 10.1; (2) from one-grained spikelet, ÇB 10.2.*

Grains from two-grained spikelets differ according to their floret of origin: the one which develops in the upper floret is larger and pale yellow in colour, with a convex ventral face, superficially similar to caryopses from one-grained spikelets. The grain of the lower floret is small and dark, with a concave ventral face.

In lateral view the ventral face of the grain in the upper floret curves much more gently than in one-grained caryopses, owing to the pressure exerted against the ventral face by the other grain. The grain is wider than that from one-grained spikelets and thus appears even more spindle shaped. At Aşvan no attempt was made to separate grains from one-grained spikelets from those from the upper florets of two-grained spikelets. However, this might be possible with more abundant material.

The small grains from lower florets (fig. 49) have a flat or slightly concave base in lateral view, ending in a point with a gently sloping top. There are several grooves in each side. In ventral view the distal end is gently rounded. The ventral groove is tight and more or less straight, with concave flattened cheeks. The grains have a very distinctive square cross-section with four angled corners. The concave ventral face and sides are clearly visible.

3.9.12. Polygonaceae

3.9.12.1. Polygonum. These are three-sided nutlets with smooth surfaces. At Aşvan they measure: thickness 1.15–1.5mm; width 0.75–1mm (fig. 50; compare to Van Zeist, Bakker-Heeres 1982: 228–29). This is a large genus with 27 species recorded in the *Flora of Turkey*; candidate species in the Aşvan region include *P. cognatum* Meisn., *P. arenastrum* Boreau., *P. pulchellum* Loisel. and *P. bellardii* All., all of which grow in similar habitats including disturbed or cultivated land.

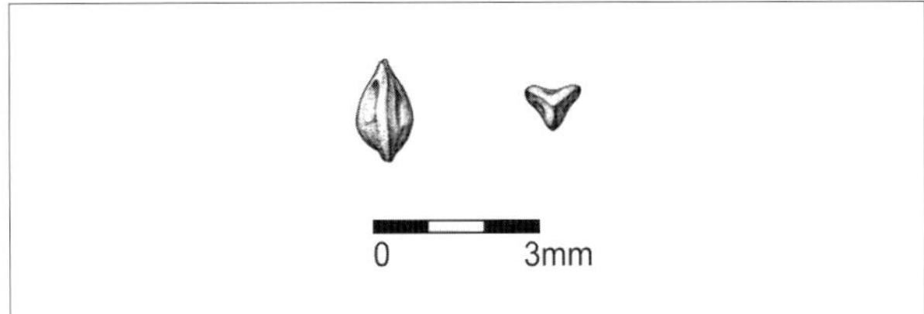

Fig. 50. Polygonum*: AK 1506.3.*

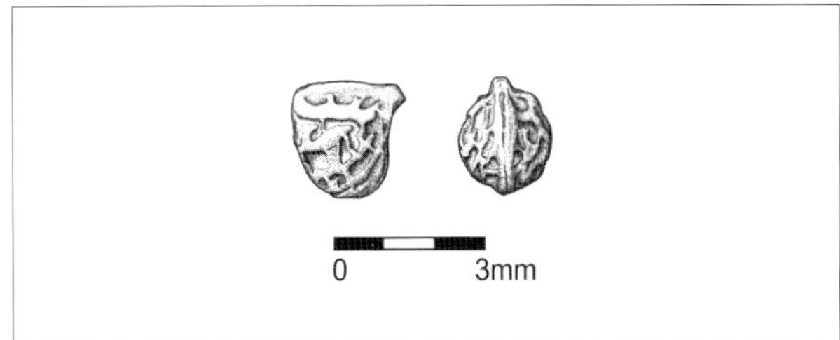

Fig. 51. Adonis *cf.* flammea*: AK 1507.27.*

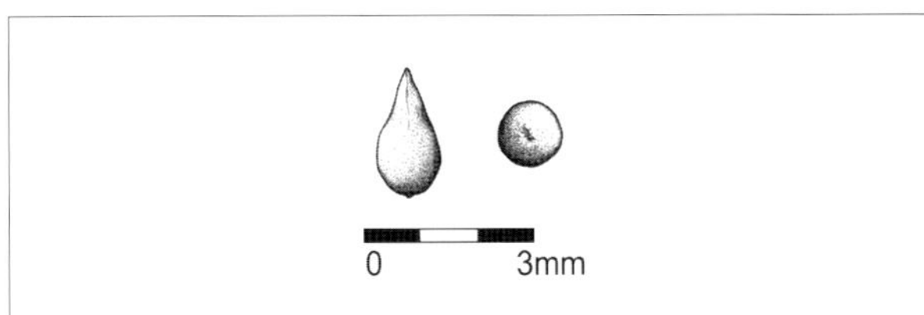

Fig. 52. Thymelaea*: TM 101.24.*

3.9.13. Ranunculaceae

3.9.13.1. Adonis *cf.* flammea. There are two widespread species in fields and steppe in eastern Turkey. Modern *Adonis flammea* achenes are about 3mm long; *A. aestivalis* L. achenes are 4–5mm long. The Aşvan material measures: length 2.1–2.8mm; breadth 1.5–1.9mm; thickness 1.9–2.2mm. This is consistent with *A. flammea* (fig. 51). Both species were collected at Aşvan by Hillman.

3.9.13.2. Ranunculus arvensis. *Ranunculus arvensis* is the most common species in Turkey, found in cereal fields, and was collected twice at Aşvan. The achenes are ca 3.6mm long and bear clear traces of the spines typical of this species.

3.9.13.3. Thalictrum. These are ovoid, ridged achenes. The Aşvan specimens measure: length 2.8–3.6mm; width 1.55–2mm. Candidate species include *T. isopyroides* C.A. Mey, but there are insufficient distribution records in the *Flora of Turkey* to give clear guidance.

3.9.14. Rosaceae

3.9.14.1. Geum. Achenes were found. Candidate species include *G. rivale* L. and the widespread *G. urbanum* L., both recorded from damp wild places.

3.9.15. Rubiaceae

3.9.15.1. Galium. These hemispherical mericarps vary in size from 1.5–3.05mm maximum dimension, with a small number in the range 0.9–1.5mm. There are few traces of surface patterns. There are at least 101 species in Turkey, and *G. verum* L. and *G. incanum* ssp. *elatius* (Boiss.) Ehrend. are commonest in southeastern Turkey. Both species grow on rocky slopes; *G. verum* is also found in fields.

3.9.16. Thymelaeaceae

3.9.16.1. Thymelaea. These are smooth fruits with a rounded base and pointed top, measuring 2–2.2mm in length (fig. 52; cf. Van Zeist, Bakker-Heeres 1984b: 162, 164). The main candidate species is *T. passerina* (L.) Coss. & Germ., found in fallow fields and stony areas.

3.9.17. Apiacaae

3.9.17.1. Coriander: Coriandrum sativum. ÇB 14 contains one mericarp with longitudinal ridges (length 2.6mm; width 2mm) and four inner parts. Coriander grows wild in eastern Turkey and the seeds of wild and domesticated forms are very similar in appearance. In the absence of any cache, and given the Chalcolithic date of these finds, they are interpreted as wild.

3.9.18. Valerianaceae

3.9.18.1. Valerianella. The ovate fruits have a distinctive ringed collar (Van Zeist, Bakker-Heeres 1984b: 162, 164; 1985: 260, 263).

3.10. Unidentified material

3.10.1. Amorphous material

All the Taşkun Mevkii samples contain several cubic centimetres of vesicular charred material, not included in the scoresheet. Three types of material were visible. Firstly, flat surfaces with longitudinal veins were noted. These resembled the leaves of a large grass such as a reed, *Phragmites australis* (Cav.) Trin. The maximum width of the fragments observed was 3.5mm, but they could be broken remains of a larger leaf blade. The veins were approximately 0.12mm apart. The surfaces could be the cast of leaf blades on which this material was resting at the time of charring. Secondly, tangled but recognisably structured plant material was identified and, thirdly, bubbly, vesicular material could be seen. Further identification was not attempted; it is tempting to speculate that these are food remains. It is unlikely that these samples were derived from reed thatching, as the habitat at Taşkun Mevkii was dry and not suitable for reed growth.

3.10.2. Fruit?

Sample ÇB10.16 from Çayboyu contains a fragment of nut or fruit: length 6.6mm; width 4.3mm; thickness 2.2mm. The interior surface is slightly concave, the outer is wrinkled. Neither the texture nor shape correspond to a Fabaceae cotyledon and this is possibly a fragment of a fruit such as hawthorn (*Crataegus* sp.).

3.10.3 Fruit?

ÇB10.5 from Çayboyu contains several fragments of another possible fruit. The best preserved example has a maximum diameter of 10.7mm and a thickness of 5.8mm. The cavities, perhaps for seeds, are 2–3mm long.

3.10.4 Tuber?

There is a small fragment with a 'stalk' that does not resemble a fruit (fig. 53). No identification was attempted.

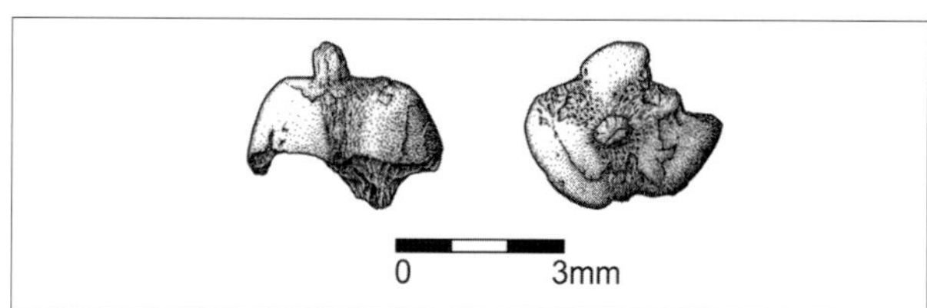

Fig. 53. Tuber?: AK 1501.5.

4. Pathways to preservation: investigating sample composition

4.1. Introduction

There are many pathways by which charred plant remains are first burnt and then incorporated into an archaeological assemblage, and understanding these is crucial to understanding the activities that have led to the formation of the samples and the overall assemblage (for a selection of the literature on this, see Hillman 1981; 1984a; 1984b; 1985; Jones 1983a; 1983b; 1984; Miller 1991; Hubbard, Clapham 1992; Hastorf 1999; Pearsall 1988; 2000; Fuller et al. 2014). Pre-charring events led to the creation of primary products and also by-products. Plant materials arrive at a fire and became carbonised through both deliberate and accidental events, including fuel burning and cooking accidents. Some may be wind-blown inclusions. Botanical assemblages can become mixed before, during or after charring, and there are several ways in which they might be deposited into the archaeological matrix, including being raked out of a fire or an oven, or moved into a waste pit. Post-depositional processes also need to be taken into account before the sample is analysed. The factors that need to be explored include the following.

Planting: farmers make decisions regarding the choice of crop and the relative quantities and proportions of crops that need to be sown according to crop ecology (for example the appropriateness of the climate and the soil), security of yield, the crop's suitability for intended use (for example culinary versus foddering properties), market demand and non-utilitarian cultural factors.

Crop-husbandry: the methods used for sowing, manuring, weeding and irrigating crops may all influence the composition of crops and weeds in a field and therefore have a potential effect on what is brought back to the site.

Crop-processing: in a set of articles (Hillman 1981; 1984a; 1984b; 1985), Gordon Hillman has explored the series of processes from harvest to storage of the product that separates the harvested crop into different components; this work has been followed up by other researchers (for instance Jones 1983a; 1983b; 1984; 1987; Van der Veen 1992; Viklund 1998; Peña-Chocarro 1999; Stevens 2003). These components include the main product, usually grain or seed for field crops, and by-products, for instance parts of the crop which can be used for animal feed or fuel.

Storage: bulk storage of a product is important for two reasons. First, if mixing with the harvest of other fields has not already taken place during crop-processing, it will occur at this stage. Second, if buildings catch fire, it is likely that foodstuffs stored within a structure will be charred in situ.

Uses of product/by-product: The product – in the case of cereal, grain – is likely to undergo further processing when it is prepared for use as food or even as fodder. This may involve removing parts of the product, for example, stripping the bran, and physical modification caused by milling and heating. By-products may have considerable economic importance as construction material, fuel or animal feed, or may be disposed of as refuse. The impact of these uses is critical in determining whether plant remains are likely to come into contact with fire and enter the archaeological record.

Contact with fire/deposition: most plant material does not enter the archaeological record; it is consumed and digested by humans and livestock, burnt to fine ashes as fuel or refuse, or is consumed by micro-organisms and organisms such as mice and ants. Unless unusual conditions of deposition, such as extreme aridity or cold, waterlogging or mineralisation occur, three factors are essential for preservation: plant material must come into contact with fire, it must be charred rather than burnt to ashes and the charred material must be incorporated into the matrix of the settlement mound (see Miller 1991; Hastorf 1999; Pearsall 1988; 2000; Fuller et al. 2014). Common routes that lead to the presence of charred remains are through the burning of crop-processing waste, the cooking of food and the inclusion of seeds in dung used as fuel (Miller 1991). Disentangling these processes is an important step in understanding the presence of seeds in archaeological deposits and thus for understanding why and how they were used on sites.

Post-deposition: natural processes can lead to the movement or even destruction of seeds. Charles Miksicek (1987) discusses the issue of faunal turbation, that is the addition and removal of materials by animals such as ants and rodents, and 'floral turbation' by roots, wind and alluvial action, and natural seed rain. Human action, such as digging that disturbs the soil matrix, is another factor that may affect an assemblage.

Excavation and recovery: mechanical factors such as imprecise excavation techniques, the loss of delicate items during flotation and inadvertent mixing of separate contexts can change the composition of a seed assemblage.

For example, it may prove difficult during sampling of in situ burnt deposits to identify where one deposit ends and another begins.

Although the ways in which each of these steps and processes may affect a seed assemblage are broadly predictable, and have been explored in several ethnographic and experimental studies, the effect of multiple steps and processes, some of them repeated, is hard to calculate and unpredictable. For example, some archaeobotanists have predicted that the use of dung fuel (section 4.2.3) is likely to have a significant impact on the introduction of wild seeds to a site (Miller 1984; 1991; 1998; Miller, Smart 1984; Charles 1998; Charles, Bogaard 2004), but not all sites will necessarily have used dung as a fuel source (Miller 1984; Charles 1998; Fuller et al. 2014). In addition, when dung is used for fuel it may be burnt to ash or the seeds may have been digested by the animal before excretion, and thus will not be fully identifiable (Fuller et al. 2014; Valamoti, Charles 2005). In order to ensure comparability between different samples, a sample-by-sample consideration of the filtering effects of these steps is essential (Van der Veen 1992: 81). This chapter therefore focuses on four questions that have significance for explaining the assemblage composition at the Aşvan sites.

1. To what extent can the batches of material be separated from one another and considered as individual samples? This question is mainly affected by post-depositional disturbance, the recovery methods used during excavation and the archaeological interpretation of the soil deposits. It is considered first because it is fundamental to the interpretation of the overall assemblage.

2. What impact did crop-processing have on the assemblage? How should the samples be classified according to the predictive models of crop processing (Hillman 1981; 1984a; 1984b; 1985; Jones 1983a; 1983b; 1984)?

3. What role did dung fuel play at the Aşvan sites in the creation of the seed assemblage?

4. What other factors, after crop processing, might have affected the make-up of the assemblages? This question also relates to other site-formation processes.

4.2. Methodology

4.2.1. Sample definition

To what extent can each sample be considered individual? This is important for the overall quantification of the plant remains; proportions and particularly ubiquity will be more meaningful if based on samples that result from a wide variety of 'sampling points' of past human activity (see Fuller et al. 2014). Seed assemblages are here considered at the point of deposition, after they have been charred, recognising that mixing can occur at many different stages before deposition, including during cultivation. The focus of this approach is to reunite in the analysis samples that clearly derive from the same seed assemblage, although they have been collected from the site in separate lots. Such assemblages are often divided during recovery when the excavator judges from changes in soil colour and texture that a feature could contain soil derived from different deposition events. Division may also occur when a deposit is extensive, for example when an in situ burnt store spreads across a floor.

The criteria used to decide whether samples should be treated as separate from each other or form one analytical unit were their relative location, the precise archaeological context (for example pot contents versus dispersed materials) and, most importantly, the similarity of the sample composition. Samples were compared using three measures. First, how do the composition of samples affected by crop processing compare with one another, as measured by the chaff:grain ratio of hulled wheats and the proportions of crops, chaff and weed seeds? However, the problem with this approach is that separate deposits resulting from the same processes may have a very similar composition. A second approach is to observe the proportion of hulled wheat in the overall wheat grain assemblage and the proportion of naked wheat in the overall naked grain category (barley, rye and naked wheat). These proportions are likely to vary between different fields or storage locations. The third measure is the presence or absence of particular species in the weed flora. Caution is needed as infrequent weed seeds may not be consistently present; also, subsampling during analysis may lead to rare seeds being missed or over-represented by multiplying up. In view of the uncertainties associated with all three criteria, they were used conservatively, with an assumption that samples are discrete unless this is clearly not the case.

There is also the problem of assemblages that become mixed post-deposition; for example, when two burnt stores spread and mix at their margins. Attempts have been made to identify such cases, but it is not possible to separate them on paper because it is unclear which components belong to which assemblages. However, the identification of such mixed samples is important because of their implication for the assessment of crop purity.

4.2.2. Crop processing

The ethnographic work carried out by Hillman (1981; 1984a; 1984b; 1985) mainly in the modern village of Aşvan and by Glynis Jones (1983a; 1983b; 1984) in Greek villages has demonstrated that the traditional harvest and cleaning of cereals must have been carried out within a narrow framework of technological constraints, which result in a series of by-products from cleaning that have a distinctive composition. Of the numerous steps that make up the full crop-processing sequence, the four that are most likely to generate assemblages of plant remains are: threshing, which generates straw and in some cases chaff; winnowing, which removes light chaff and weed seeds; sieving with a coarse mesh, which removes large chaff and weed seeds; and sieving with a fine mesh, which removes small chaff and weed seeds, and retains the final product, the clean grain. Although crop-processing sequences have been recorded for pulses, these are less informative as the processing is simpler, and the pods of pulses are lighter and tend not to survive burning.

The different compositions of by-products from cereal processing is shown in table 15. They are different for free-threshing cereals (such as durum wheat, bread wheat, barley and rye) and hulled wheats (einkorn, emmer) because of the extra steps needed to break up the spikelets in hulled wheats.

One approach to correlating the archaeobotanical and ethnographic analyses at Near Eastern and Anatolian sites has been through correspondence analysis and/or discriminant analysis, applied by Simone Riehl (1999) to material

	Hulled wheats		**Free-threshing cereals**	
Process	*Effect*	*By-product*	*Effect*	*By-product*
Harvest	Reaping or uprooting, height of harvest affects weed composition	None	Reaping or uprooting, height of harvest affects weed composition	None
Threshing, winnowing and raking	Removes straw, breaks ear into spikelets, wind removes small, light, free weeds	Straw, small, free, light weeds	Removes straw, breaks up ear into light chaff, rachis fragments, loose grain, wind removed light straw and small, free, light weeds	Straw, small, free, light weeds, rachis fragments
Coarse sieving	Sieve allows spikelets to fall through	Large straw nodes, headed weeds	Sieve allows grain to fall through	Large straw nodes, headed weeds, rachis fragments
Fine sieving	Sieve retains spikelets	Loose grain, small, free, heavy weeds, rachis fragments	Sieve retains grains	Tail grain, small, free, heavy weeds, small rachis fragments
Storage	**Clean spikelets**		**Clean grain**	
Pounding	Releases grain from spikelets		N/A	
Winnowing	Wind carries away light contaminants	Remaining light weeds, light chaff	N/A	
Coarse sieving	Sieve allows grain to fall through	Unbroken spikelets, remaining headed weeds, large chaff	N/A	
Fine sieving	Sieve retains grain	Tail grain, small free, remaining heavy weeds, small heavy chaff	N/A	
Hand-picking	Removes seeds and chaff of a similar size and weight to grain	Large, free, heavy weeds, large, heavy chaff	Removes seeds and chaff of a similar size (and weight) to grain	Large, free, heavy weeds, large chaff
	Clean grain		**Clean grain**	

Table 15. Crop-processing stages and by-products (after Hillman 1981; 1984a; 1984b; 1985; Jones 1983a; 1983b; 1984).

collected from the sites of Troy and Kumtepe, by Michael Charles and Amy Bogaard (2004) at Jeitun and by Bogaard and colleagues (2013) at Çatalhöyük. These studies compared the weed seed assemblages with those from Jones' (1984) ethnographic models, classifying the weeds by size (relevant to fine sieving), headedness (relevant to coarse sieving) and weight (relevant to winnowing).

A study of the grain, weed and chaff proportions was carried out for the Aşvan sites (see section 4.3) and compared with the compositions in table 15, using simpler statistical techniques, primarily in the form of ratios. This was complemented by a study of the ratios of chaff elements to grain, and weeds to field crops and cereal grain, and an exploration of the types of weeds found in the assemblages, based on their size, headedness,and aerodynamic properties (following the procedures of Jones 1984; 1987; Van der Veen 1992; Popper 1988).

4.2.3. Dung fuel

Ethnographic studies have shown that in arid and semi-arid regions where wood is scarce, dried dung is commonly used as a fuel source (for example Miller 1984; 1991; 1998; Charles 1998; Miller, Smart 1984; Reddy 1997; 2003) (figs 54–56).

Cow, sheep and goat dung are widely used as fuel in treeless parts of Turkey today and were important fuel resources in Aşvan village in the 1960s (Robert 1961: 115–37 is a classic study based on written evidence from antiquity and from the observations of travellers in the late Ottoman and modern period). Modern studies have shown that dung can contain crop products such as grain, by-products fed to animals or seeds derived from plants eaten while grazing (Miller 1984) which have survived the digestive tract (for discussion, see Valamoti, Charles 2005). Dung used as a fuel can also have chaff added to increase its combustibility (Valamoti, Charles 2005). Naomi Miller and Tristine Smart (1984) noted that the end product of dung-fuel combustion at Malyan in modern Iran was dung fragments containing identifiable burnt seeds and ash.

Fig. 54. Aşvan 1972, making dung cakes: collecting and moulding the dung (photo M. Weinstein).

Fig. 55. Aşvan 1972, making dung cakes: mixing chaff with dung (photo M. Weinstein).

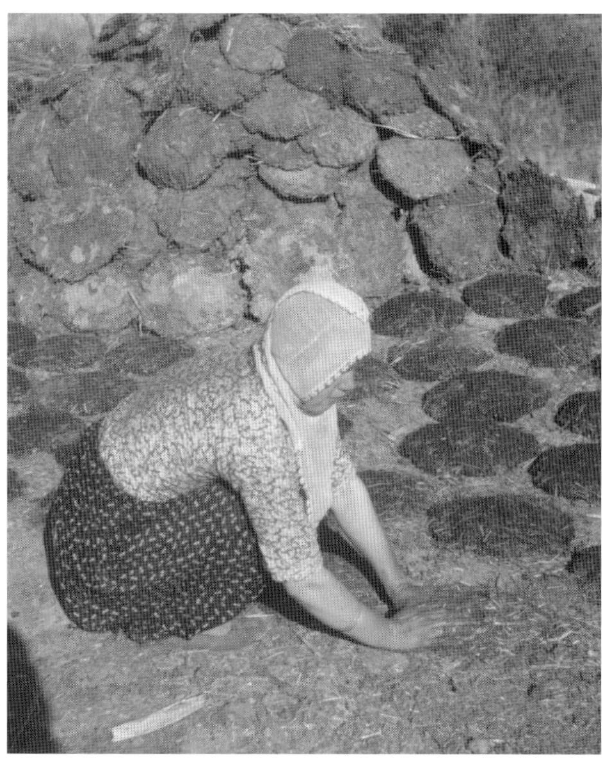

Fig. 56. Aşvan 1972, making dung fuel: shaping flat dung cakes and drying them on a roof (photo M. Weinstein).

Dung fuel was regularly used in all the village households at Aşvan and a description of the processes was recorded in Matina Weinstein's 1972 notebook:

> Dung cakes – the dung is collected from the animal quarters and kneaded with water until soft. The dung is then moulded into hemispherical pieces and thrown into a handful of straw which covers the outside and makes the cake transportable. The cake is then dried on the roof – it is flattened into a flat circle – often finger impressions are left on the surface. The dung cakes are often dried on the side of rocks if they are available (observed in the neighbouring village of Fatmalı). When dry they are peeled off and collected into piles.

As many macrobotanical remains are liable to occur in dung fuel, which is intended for combustion and is therefore likely to enter the archaeological record in a charred condition, a debate has arisen about how to interpret seeds that might have come from burning dung fuel in reconstructing past plant use. Based on her ethnographic study of the modern Iranian village of Malyan, Miller has argued that archaeobotanists must 'consider why material is *not* a fuel residue before attempting other explanations' (Miller 1991: 154). Here she notes that 'most material that becomes carbonised due to ordinary modern household activities has been placed intentionally in the fire' in the form of dung fuel or wood fuel (Miller 1984: 75), and that other pathways to carbonisation, such as the intentional discarding of crop-processing waste, cooking accidents or wind-blown material, are rare and form only a small proportion of the samples she collected. Other researchers have called this conclusion into question. Dorian Fuller and colleagues (2014) note that although dung fuel may have been important in the Near East, it was used much less frequently in the cooler and wetter (and usually more forested) parts of northern Europe and the New World, where animals that produce suitable dung were also relatively scarce. They observe that on the basis of Miller's hypothesis charred seeds from sources other than dung fuel would occur rarely, but that this seems at odds with the facts. Why would the seeds in the Near East come mainly from dung fuel while those in Europe and the New World derive from cooking accidents and crop-processing waste? To provide support for this observation, they note the shift between the Pre-Pottery and Pottery Neolithic periods in the Near East. For assemblages from both periods the same suite of wild seeds is present, although domesticated animals were introduced over the course of the Neolithic period. Since it is implausible that dung fuel was collected from wild animals during the Pre-Pottery Neolithic period, and since current environmental models suggest that wood was widely available, they argue that 'the simplest and most widely acceptable explanation is that charred seeds are derived from burnt waste generated during the regular processing and preparation of food' (Fuller et al. 2014: 187). They conclude that dung burning should not be considered as the single most important route by which seeds enter the archaeological record and that cross-cultural, daily activities like food processing are quantitatively more significant. Whatever the force of these observations, given that dung was until recently a major fuel source alongside wood at Aşvan, consideration must nevertheless be given to the likelihood of dung residue in soil units, as Miller (1991) suggests. The possibility that burnt residue from dung fuel was present in soil units should be taken fully into account in hypothesising the pathways to the preservation of the charred Aşvan assemblages.

Taking an intermediate position, Charles (1998), following earlier work by Miller and Smart (1984), has suggested that there are several criteria that need to be met before dung can be considered as a fuel source. He notes that dung is not a good fuel compared with wood or coal and it is used less frequently or not at all if better fuel sources are available. However, he also notes that dung fuel may be used for specific functions. This has also been noted archaeologically by Carla Lancelotti (2010) for the Indus Civilisation sites of Kanmer and Harappa using a combination of phytolith, faecal spheroid and wood charcoal analyses. Charles (1998) also suggests that dung fuel may be used because it is easy to access and to prepare, while it is clearly less likely to be used in areas where large domesticated herbivores are not available. He also notes that it is only common in semi-arid and arid regions. Applying all these observations to the Aşvan sites, dung fuel has to be seen a potential pathway for seeds to enter the archaeological record: the region is semi-arid, large herbivores were an essential part of the domestic economic environment and the wood charcoal evidence suggests that wood availability began to decline after the Hellenistic period (Willcox 1974).

Based on the work of Miller (1984; 1991; 1998), Miller and Smart (1984), Charles (1998) and Charles and Bogaard (2004), we have adopted five criteria for identifying the use of dung fuel at each site.

1. Presence of charred dung in archaeological deposits (Miller 1984; 1998; Miller, Smart 1984; Charles 1998). Miller and Smart (1984: 18) describe fragments and ash as modern charred dung fuel by-products. The ash has less diagnostic value as both dung fuel and other fuel sources can burn to ash, but the fragments are diagnostic. They describe them as friable amorphous masses of fine-grained matrix with inclusions such as charred stems, chaff and seeds. Charred sheep/goat pellets have been noted at archae-

ological sites such as Çatalhöyük containing seeds which could then be unequivocally linked to burnt animal dung (Bogaard et al. 2013). This is however problematic for the Aşvan sites, as the presence of dung was not noted during excavation, and it was not found in the floated material. Unequivocal evidence for dung fuel use is not present.

2. Proportion of seed to charcoal (Miller 1984; 1998). On the principle that dung-fuel residues will have a lower proportion of charcoal (Miller 1998: 246), Miller proposed establishing a ratio of seed to charcoal weight in grams, arguing that lower ratios (i.e. greater charcoal weight than seed weight) would indicate that more wood was being used and there was a reduced chance that dung fuel was present; a high ratio would increase the likelihood that dung fuel was being used on site (Miller 1984; 1998). She also took the precaution of focusing on weed seeds alone, in order to prevent the ratios being influenced by cooking accidents and plants brought to the site by humans for economic purposes.

3. Biology and ecology of non-crop species (Charles 1998; Charles, Bogaard 2004). Charles (1998: 114) notes that not all weedy species are eaten by animals and that some species may be brought to site by people for other functions or by other activities, such as for kindling or in crop-processing waste. He suggests that, instead of assuming all weeds were brought to a site in dung, it is essential to explore the growing conditions of the non-crop elements. For example, fruiting time could help determine whether a non-crop element was brought in with a harvest or not, while defensive mechanisms such as spikes, awns or chemicals might preclude it from being eaten by animals. Charles (1998) therefore suggests grouping weeds by winter, early summer and late summer flowering/fruiting time, and their palatability at time of fruiting. Charles and Bogaard (2004: 97) divide the weeds into: early weeds, that flower/fruit up to and including but not after the harvest month, which could accordingly represent arable weeds harvested with the cereal crop; intermediate weeds, which flower/fruit slightly before and slightly after the harvest time and could also have been harvested with a cereal crop; and late weeds, which do not begin flowering/fruiting until the harvest month (May in the case of their site, Jeitun) or later and were unlikely to have been harvested in fruit along with the dominant crop. This division, however, is problematic. If the weed has the potential to flower/fruit in the harvest month then it could potentially be harvested along with the crop, even if the flowering/fruiting time continues beyond the harvest season. For this reason, only weeds that begin flowering/fruiting after harvest (July for the Aşvan region) are considered as 'late' in this work, while weeds that have the potential to be harvested in fruit alongside the cereals are considered as intermediate or early, based on the criteria above (see appendix 2).

The ecology of the weeds is based on the collecting notes made by Hillman, Pat Ball and Nicholas Bean and Peter Symmons during their botanical surveys of the Aşvan region during the excavations. These surveys were not systematic, but should serve to denote whether or not a weed was present in fields and therefore whether it could have been a potential arable weed or not. Where the weeds were not noted in the Aşvan botanical surveys, this data (since *Flora of Turkey* – Davies 1966–1985; Davies et al.1988; Güner 2001 – does not provide the relevant ecological information) was compared with the detailed weed ecologies published in *Flora of Iraq* (Townsend, Guest 1966–1985), the closest region available for comparison. This work has also been consulted for information about the palatability of weeds to animals. The presence of unpalatable weeds can only be used to rule out their likely origin in dung fuel, not to show that dung fuel was not present. A high proportion of unpalatable weeds in an assemblage would imply that they did not mainly derive from dung fuel, as these weeds could not have been consumed by animals and must have come from other sources such as harvesting. A high proportion of palatable weeds, however, does not prove the presence of dung fuel. This would be compatible with assemblages from arable fields, for example, but could also derive from multiple sources, including crop-processing waste and/or dung fuel.

4. Behaviour of non-crop seeds in relation to crop processing (Charles 1998; Charles, Bogaard 2004). The sample composition of weed seeds within the primary crop assemblage (grain, chaff, etc.) can be used to indicate whether the assemblage derives from crop processing or whether it may have resulted from other sources.

5. Relative proportion of crop species and plant parts (Charles 1998; Charles, Bogaard 2004). It is also important to explore whether the mixing of crop species resulted from their being grown as a maslin, a mixture of grain types, or resulted from post-harvest mixing for fodder (Charles, Bogaard 2004). Charles (1998) has argued that maslin crops only occur if the processes applied to the different crops are similar, so, for example, a hulled and free-threshing wheat would not be grown as a maslin. Exploring the proportion of crop species to plant parts allows this problem to be investigated by considering whether the grain and chaff are consistent with a single origin in crop processing.

These five factors have an important part to play in assessing the impact of dung fuel on the preservation of the Aşvan macrobotanical remains and have implications for the analysis of plant use by human populations.

4.2.4. Site-formation processes

Plant materials may move around a settlement in different ways and, as is essential for their survival in the archaeological record, become carbonised. An appreciation of this is important for two reasons. First, plant assemblages may be mixed during these movements; for example, crops from different fields may be collected in one grain store or middens may contain accumulated refuse from different locations. Second, there will be a correlation between different archaeological contexts – areas of different function – and the plant materials deposited therein. A storeroom may contain primary products, while a midden has by-products used as fuel or burnt as refuse. The extent to which such a correlation occurs at Aşvan will be explored. The stratigraphy and the interrelationships of both soil and architectural features were carefully recorded at the Aşvan sites, and thus provide a good primary framework for exploring and analysing the nature of the archaeobotanical deposits that accumulated as the sites were formed. However, the processes of site formation on all four sites produced relatively few primary contexts, in the form of working floors, well-defined waste middens or single-usage rubbish pits. Most of the soil units and deposits derive from the degradation and collapse of mudbrick housing, the gradual accumulation of wind-blown soil and from other forms of erosion, which produced fills of mixed origin, or from pits that were filled and refilled on several occasions. In interpreting such secondary or indeterminate archaeological contexts, it is often necessary (following Hillman 1981; 1984a; 1984b; 1985; Fuller et al. 2014) to make inferences about the history of an archaeobotanical assemblage from its composition. This can be illustrated in the case of another east Anatolian excavation, at Tille Höyük, where the composition of the archaeobotanical samples makes it possible to see that storage samples were redeposited in pits, while burnt storage areas contained by-products as well as primary products (Nesbitt 2016).

4.2.5. Ratios and proportions

As tools to investigate these problems, a range of ratios and proportions has been calculated for each sample, following principles set out in Miller 1988; Hillman 1981; 1984a; 1984b; Jones 1983a; 1983b; 1984.

Cereal straw nodes to grains ratio: calculated as the number of culm nodes and basal nodes in relation to wheat, barley and rye grains. Culm nodes are not identifiable at species level so the total number of culm nodes is divided by the total number of wheat, barley and rye grains. The basal node of the cereal ear is not included in this ratio as it is part of the ear rather than the straw. High values for this ratio indicate cereal by-products from early processing stages.

Density: calculated as the gram weight of charcoal and seeds (charred material) in one litre of soil processed by flotation. Some archaeobotanists have calculated density as cm^3/litre (for example Colledge 2001a), others as seeds per litre of sediment (for example Weber 2003). Soil volumes were recorded in the Aşvan excavation notebooks in 18 litre *tenekes* (containers), although figures were not recorded for some flotation samples. Samples that were not floated (usually very rich in charred material) are indicated on the scoresheets. As with all figures in this report (see section 4.3), the densities must be treated with caution. It is likely that in some cases more charred material was recovered than has been scored. Density is of interest as a guide to the circumstances of deposition – high density suggests more intensive activity and a less disturbed soil unit (Colledge 2001b: 97; Weber 2003).

Seed to charcoal ratio: calculated as the weight of seeds (all non-charcoal items) relative to the weight of charcoal. This figure is not directly comparable to that calculated by Miller (1998: 246) as Miller's material was collected in a 2mm mesh whereas everything from the Aşvan sites was collected in a 1mm mesh.

Glume bases to grains ratio (after Valamoti 2004; Van der Veen 1992): this ratio is specific to different cereal species, as the number of grains in a spikelet varies. Emmer spikelets (with the exception of the terminal spikelet) contain two grains (a ratio of 2:2), while the one-grained variety of einkorn which occurred at Aşvan contains only one grain (a ratio of 2:1). This difference could theoretically be handled by sorting the hulled wheat chaff and grain to species level and calculating separate ratios. However, chaff could only be identified to this level in a small number of the Aşvan samples. In order to create a ratio calculated for all samples containing hulled wheats, einkorn and emmer chaff are assumed to have been present in the same proportion as grain. Before calculating the ratio, the number of einkorn grains was multiplied by two (thus giving them the same ratio to glume bases as the emmer grains: 2:2) and this figure was added to the emmer grain total to provide a total grain number. The ratio (expressed as a R^2 value) was calculated by dividing the glume bases by this total hulled grain number (glume bases:emmer + [einkorn × 2]). This ensures that in an intact sample the ratio of spikelet forks to grains would be expressed by the value 1. A value of much less than 1 implies a sample with less chaff, such as a storage sample of dehusked and clean grain; a value much in excess of 1 would point in the direction of a processing by-product, probably from an earlier stage of crop processing, or unclean, stored product.

Rachis segments to grain: this ratio is similar to that devised for the glume bases but is applied to free-threshing cereals (free-threshing wheat, barley, rye). The expected ratio in an unprocessed crop will vary according to species, as different cereals have different numbers of grains attached to a rachis segment. The ratios are 1:1 in two-row barley, 1:2 in wheats (as in the crop-processing models from the 1960s at Aşvan) and 1:3 in six-row barley.

Weeds to crop seeds: this measure of proportion refers to wild seeds but excludes those that were potentially wild-harvested foods. The crops in question are the primary product (for example grain, pulse, oilseed) rather than by-products like chaff. The purpose of this ratio is to separate products from by-products (Van der Veen 1992: 82).

Relative proportions: hulled wheat (as % of wheat grain), naked wheat (as % of naked grain), crop seed (as % of all seeds), cereal chaff (as % of all cereal elements) and weed seeds (as % of all seeds).

4.3. Site-by-site analysis

4.3.1. Çayboyu

4.3.1.1. Sample definition. The abundant plant resources at Çayboyu are potentially an important resource for interpreting the function of the excavated areas in the small trench ($4m^2$). As the site produced such copious samples it was not possible to analyse them all. Two samples (where possible) were chosen from each of the excavator's sub-phases for analysis; all the samples that were not analysed were similar to the rest in being very rich in cereals and chaff.

The degree of similarity between the deposits is obviously of special interest in view of the uncertainty as to the length of occupation represented by the 6m excavated. Table 16 shows the key ratios (see section 4.2.5) for each sample. Although individual ratios are sometimes similar, at least some ratios vary considerably between each sample. Most samples can therefore the treated as independent. However, three groups within table 16 do show potential similarity and merit further discussion.

The first group consists of samples 4 and 40 (from contexts 10.7 and 10.8). These two samples are similar in most ratios; sample 4, however, lacks *Lolium* while sample 40 contains 112 *Lolium* grains. Proportions of most other weed seeds are similar, but in view of the abundance of *Lolium* in sample 40, the samples 40 and 4 have been

Sample	*Density (charred material per litre soil)*	*Culm to grain*	*Glume bases to grain*	*Rachis to grain*	*Weed to crop*	*% crop (all seeds)*	*% weeds (all seeds)*	*% hulled wheat (all wheat)*	*% naked wheat (all cereals)*	*% cereal chaff (all cereal items)*
1	0.06	0.003	3.11	0.007	0.22	82.1	17.7	74.2	16.9	62.4
2	0.22	0.005	3.679	0.003	0.51	66.1	33.8	81.9	15.4	72.7
3	0.18	0	10.05	0.002	0.55	64.1	35.4	75.7	18.5	85.5
5	0.13	0.001	1.935	0.006	0.11	89.9	9.9	95.7	3.8	63.4
4	0.09	0.002	7.439	0	0.18	84.7	15.1	68	26.7	81.4
40	0.14	0.005	3.951	0.002	0.39	71.8	28.1	79.6	17.2	73.8
7	0.54	0	0.619	0	0.01	99.1	0.9	65.8	27.5	27
8	N/A	0	0.048	0	0	100	0	70.8	10.9	1.4
12 (seed layer)	N/A	0	0.257	0	0	99.7	0.3	71.6	11.4	7.4
14 (seed layer)	0.2	0	0.189	0	0.01	99.2	0.8	70.1	14.4	6.6
13	0.25	0.001	0.319	0	0.01	99.1	0.9	67.1	17.8	11.5
20	0.36	0	1.687	0	0.01	98.7	1.3	68.6	8.8	26.8
15	0.18	0	1.959	0	0.03	97.1	2.7	65.7	20.5	45.1
16	0.21	0.007	5.559	0	0.13	88.4	11.6	72.8	23.2	80.8
18	0.1	0	15.462	0.029	0.21	80.5	17	16.5	55.9	63.4
27	0.13	0.009	2.177	0.004	0.02	90.4	2.1	81.5	6.9	44.2
22	0.25	0.027	1.889	0	0.06	94.4	5.4	68.5	21.2	47.4
23	0.61	0.026	4.75	0.007	0.13	88.5	11.2	42.7	38.5	58.2
24	0.18	0.025	0.5	0	0.07	93.5	6.5	72.7	15	18.4
32	0.02	0.018	11.605	0.012	0.4	71.5	28.5	33.7	55.3	79.6

Table 16. Ratios at Çayboyu.

treated separately. The second group consists of samples 8 (context 10.9), 12 (10.13), 13 (10.15) and 14 (10.14). This group is of particular interest because it spans the seeds layer, indicated on the trench section (fig. 5), including samples 12 (10.13) and 14 (10.14). The distinctive features of the four samples are the high density of charred material (samples 8, certainly, and 12, probably, did not require flotation), the very low weed to crop proportions of 0.01–0.03, consistently high proportions of hulled wheat and low proportions of cereal chaff. Samples 8 (10.9), 12 (10.13), 13 (10.15) and 14 (10.14) formed the most homogeneous group at the site. The charcoal in these batches could have been included from various sources, either being introduced post-charring or during the charring event, if, for instance, a wooden structure or container held the significant quantity of burnt grain. However, without more information on the nature of the contexts this is only speculation. The weed flora of the four seed-layer samples is so scanty as to be of no help in judging their similarity. Sample 8 was not floated and is virtually pure charred material; it also contains no weed seeds. One possibility is that this represents part of the original deposit; the other three samples incorporate this together with weed seeds that derived from other depositional events. In any case, given the great similarity between the four samples, they were treated as one for site quantification. Sample 20 (context 10.6) and sample 15 (context 10.17), collected from below the seed layer, contain markedly more chaff but fewer weeds than the other samples from the column. In light of this and the archaeological evidence that at least some of these samples resulted from separate deposition events, these samples are treated as independent.

4.3.1.2. Crop processing. A tri-plot (fig. 57) shows three groups: a grain-rich group, a chaff-rich group and a less distinct, intermediate group with just two samples. None of the samples show large proportions of weeds (all weed proportions were less than 12%, with only two samples having more than 7.8% weeds relative to the proportion of chaff and grain). This is also reflected in the weed to field crop (fig. 58) and weed to cereal grain ratios (fig. 59), which showed that in all cases there was more grain than weed seeds.

Four of the grain-rich group (grain proportions over 88%) on the tri-plot correspond with the seed layer (samples 12 and 14) and samples 8 and 20. This suggests

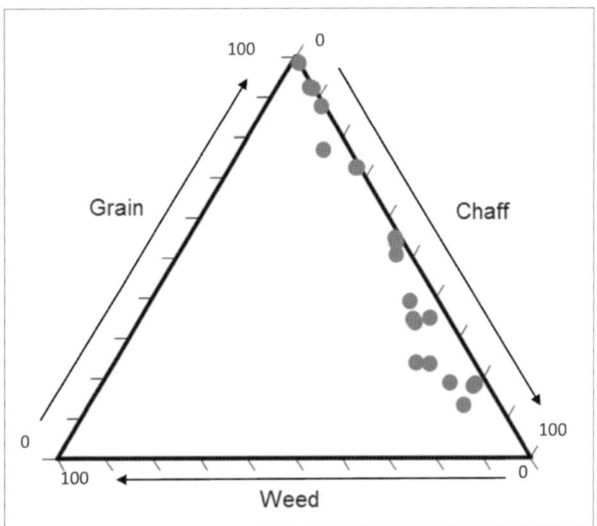

Fig. 57. Çayboyu crop-processing tri-plot, showing the relative proportion of cereal grain, chaff and weed.

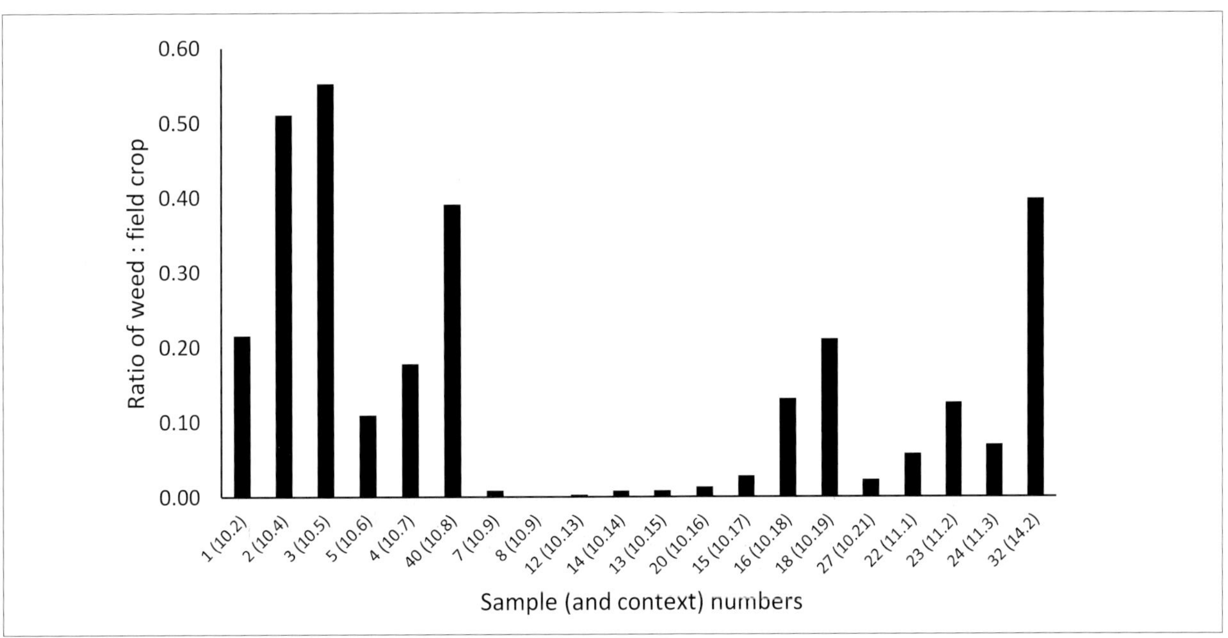

Fig. 58. Ratio of weed to field crop at Çayboyu.

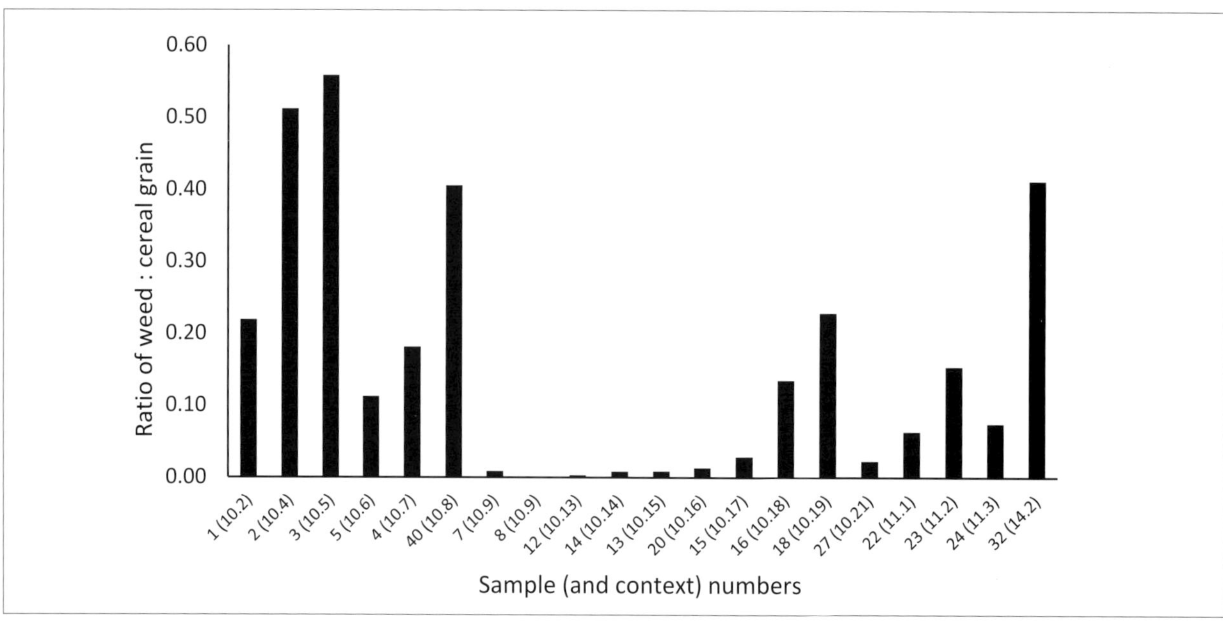

Fig. 59. Ratio of weed to cereal grain at Çayboyu.

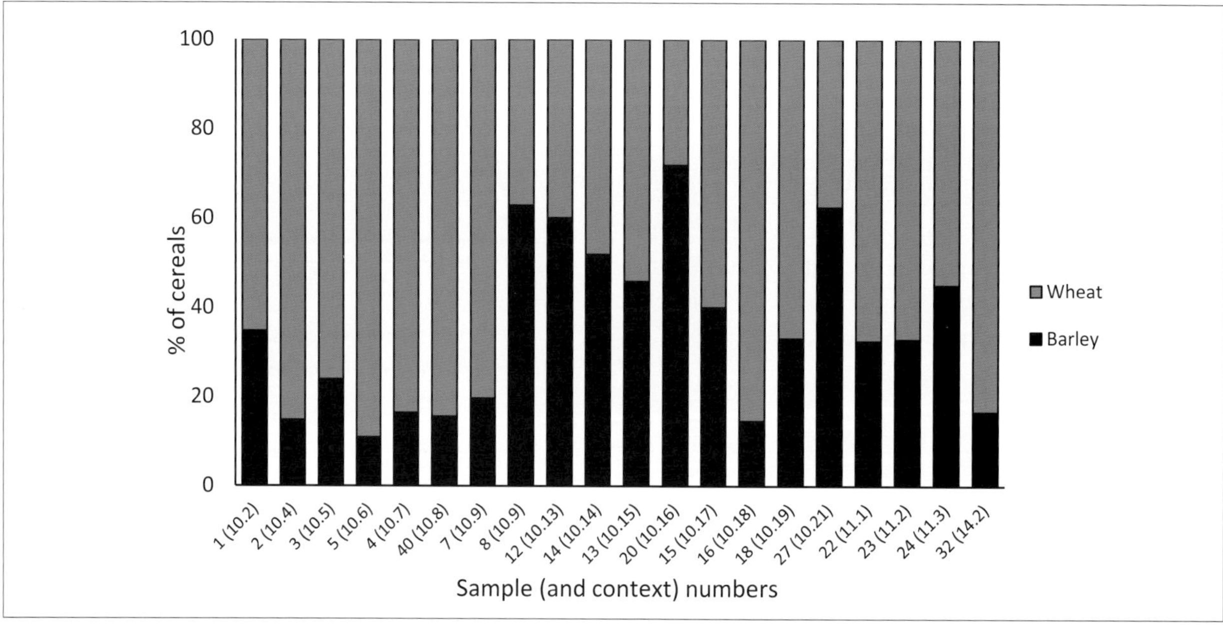

Fig. 60. Proportions of wheat and barley at Çayboyu.

that they comprise a cleaned product, or almost cleaned product, perhaps stored with some element of the chaff. There is no evidence of damage to the grains consistent with disposal of spoilt grain or the effect of extreme heat, which might have destroyed larger proportions of chaff, and there was no evidence for in situ burning in any sample. However, the picture of the individual samples is complicated as in all cases they contain a mixture of grain types. Sample 8 contains the largest proportion of grain (98.8%): 63% barley, 37% wheat, of which 71% is hulled (mostly emmer, but some einkorn as well) and 29% free-threshing durum (figs 60 and 61). The only chaff present, however, was not from barley but took the form of glume bases from hulled wheat, forming a proportion of 0.05 to the grain (fig. 62). This small quantity of glume bases appears more likely to be the result of incomplete cleaning of the wheat crop and poor processing rather than the remnants of whole spikelets, and therefore an indication of early-stage processing. The low chaff proportion of sample 8 seems typical of a storage sample. This is consistent with the absence of other chaff types and the absence of weeds. The sample did not contain any other field crops.

Samples 12 and 14 are marginally barley dominated (fig. 60) and the wheat is mostly hulled (fig. 61), as in sample 8. Some chaff is again present in both samples, and sample 14 also contains a single culm node as well as the small number of glume bases. The low chaff counts result in low proportions of chaff to grain, as in sample 8, suggesting that this was a stored, hulled wheat product, not processing waste mixed in with a clean barley and free-threshing wheat product. Unlike sample 8, however, weeds were present, albeit in low proportions relative to grain. These were mainly small, free, heavy seeds, typically the outcome of fine sieving, a late processing stage. Given the extremely low proportion of weeds and these late-stage indicators, these weeds are best interpreted as the few that slipped through the processing stages. Both samples had a low weed to field crop and weed to cereal ratio, indicating that the charred, clean barley/free-threshing wheat product and hulled wheat storage product were mixed with general waste from other sources.

Sample 13 is slightly different. Grain formed the main proportion of the assemblage at 87.8%, but unlike the other three samples the main cereal is wheat at 54% (67% hulled wheat, mostly emmer with einkorn, and 33% durum) with 46% barley. This sample has a slightly higher proportion

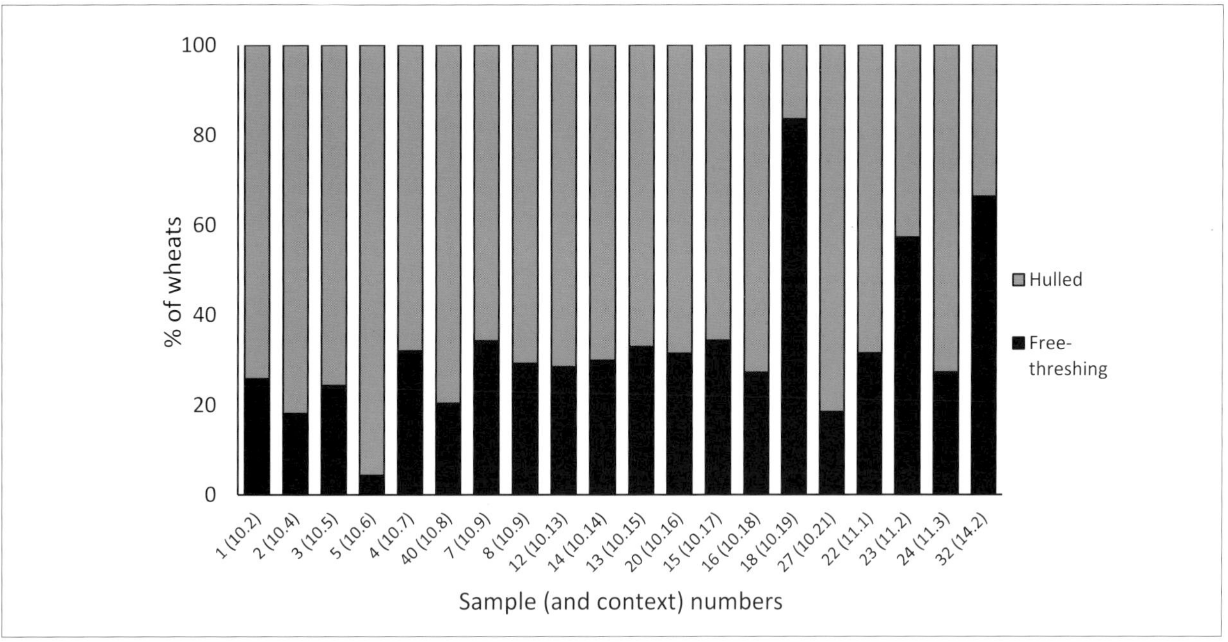

Fig. 61. Proportions of hulled and free-threshing wheat at Çayboyu.

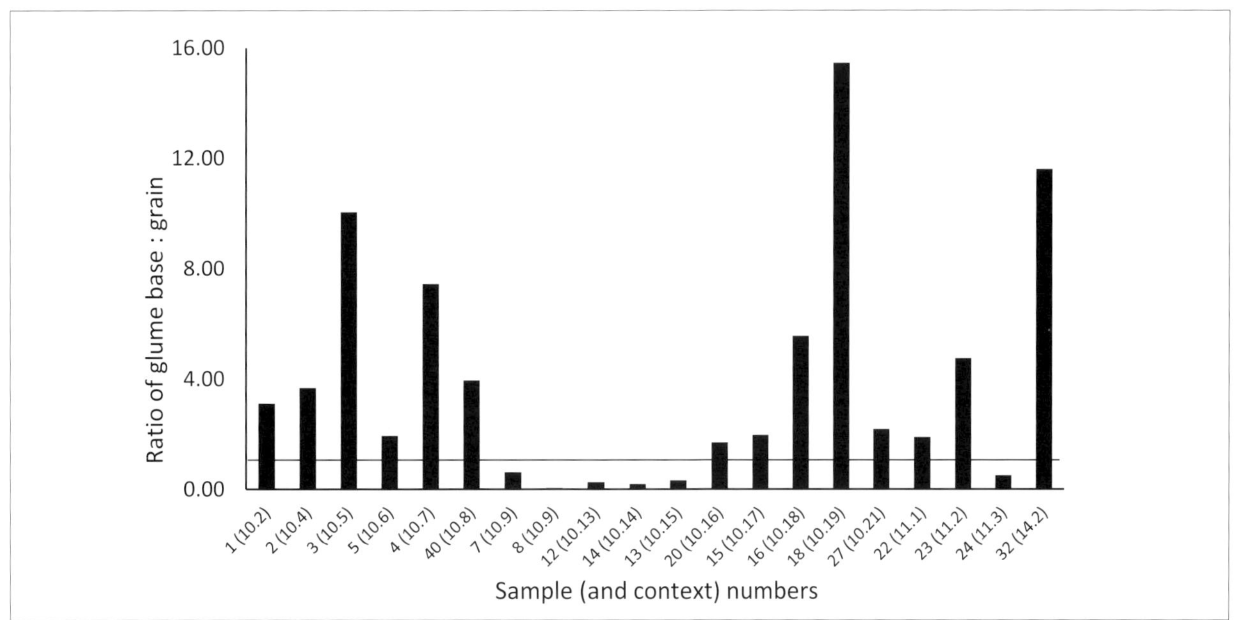

Fig. 62. Ratio of glume base to grain at Çayboyu. The line indicates the threshold of 1 (see section 4.2.5).

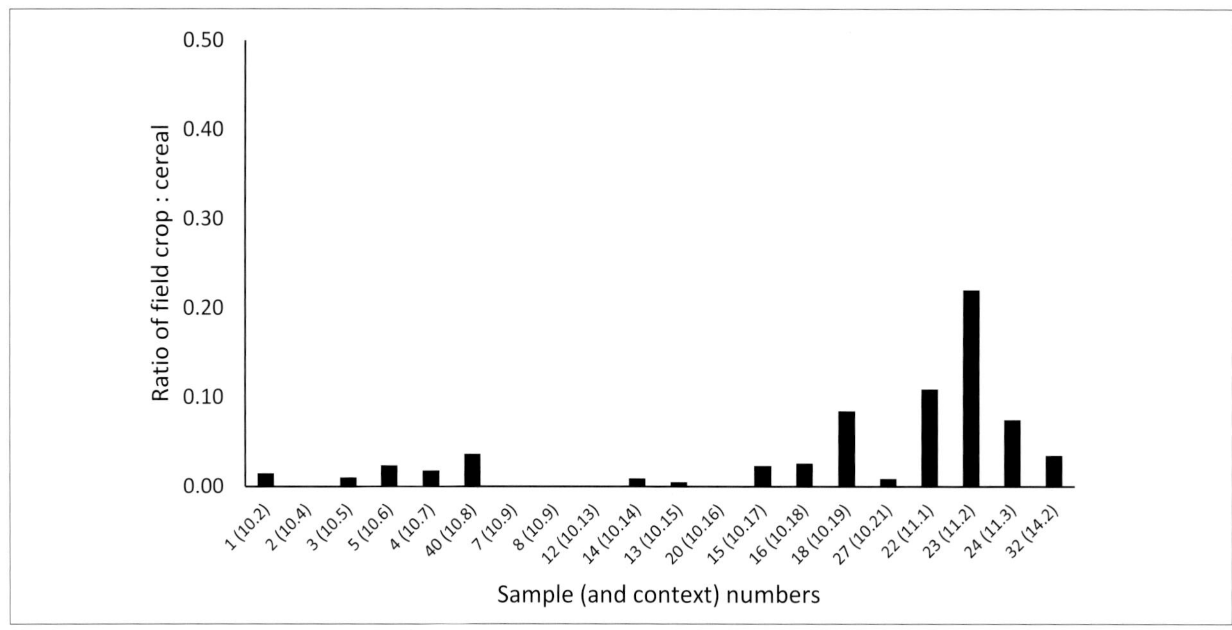

Fig. 63. Ratio of field crop to cereal at Çayboyu.

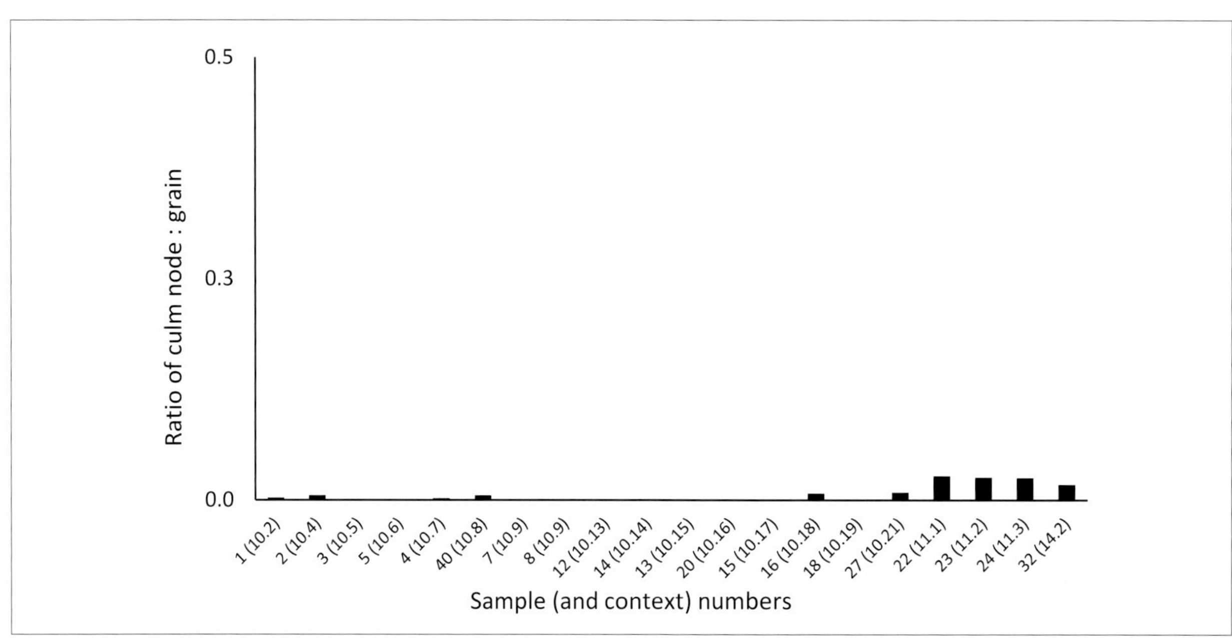

Fig. 64. Ratio of culm node to grain at Çayboyu.

of chaff, at 11.5%, and contained seven culm nodes. However, these create only a 0.001 proportion of culm to grain (fig. 64), which does not suggest early processing stages, and the culm nodes may be the result of wind-blown contamination or are connected with other activities such as bedding, construction or use as fuel. Some rachis fragments were also present, four from *Triticum durum*, but this also creates a low proportion of rachis to grain (0.0005) (fig. 65). A higher proportion of glume to grain is noted (0.32), but this is also a low figure, suggesting that this seed layer also derived from stored grain (fig. 62). Like the other three seed-layer samples, there is only a small proportion of weeds (0.8%) relative to grain and chaff, producing matching weed to field crop and weed to cereal proportions of 0.01 (figs 58 and 59). Eighteen species of weed were identified. Most of the weeds are small, free and heavy or big, free and heavy, indicative of fine-sieved or hand-sorted waste. Sample 13 also has a low proportion of field crops to cereals (0.0049), resulting from the presence of a few *Lens culinaris*, *Pisum sativum*, *Vicia ervilia*, *Pistacia* and flax seeds, similar to samples 12 and 14 (fig. 63).

The small quantities of chaff and weed in these grain-rich deposits are characteristic of storage samples. However, the mixing of three cereal types, the presence of some glume bases, including some non-cereal crops in three of the samples, and the size and repetition of the assemblages are not consistent with a stored product. This raises questions as to how to interpret the seed layers. How did so much grain come to be charred in successive large layers? How did hulled and free-threshing cereals get mixed when their processing requirements are so different? There is a further problem in explaining how some chaff was still present in the hulled grain. Are these characteristics consistent with a mixed grain store, ready for consumption, or are two different crops represented at different stages of storage, and if so why? The limited scope of the excavation at Çayboyu makes it impossible to resolve these issues. The trench was only 2m × 2m in size, with virtually no architecture visible. The successive destruction and collapse of storage structures belonging to buildings, with cleaned crops being stored on the roof, might be an explanation for why so much grain came to be burnt, and this could also account for the inclusion of other waste elements like the pulses. But it seems unlikely that such an event would have been repeated accidentally four times to produce four seed layers. Burning could of course be deliberate, perhaps echoing 'house closing' activities better documented in southeastern Europe and western Anatolia (cf. Twiss et al. 2008), but the activities that created these dense grain-rich assemblages remain enigmatic.

Turning to the other Çayboyu samples (ÇB 10.2, 10.4, 10.5, 10.6, 10.7, 10.8, 10.16, 10.17, 10.18, 10.19, 10.21, 11.1, 11.2, 14.2), the chaff-rich batches can be divided into upper and lower samples (i.e. those above and below the seed layer), although they are very similar to one another in composition. There is little culm present (fig. 64), which suggests they are not from early-processing stages. The ratio of rachis to grain is also low (fig. 65). What distinguishes these samples from the seed layer however is the ratio of glume to grain, between 1.93 and 15.46 (fig. 62). This is above the threshold value of 1 (see section 4.2.5), and therefore suggests that these samples contain processing by-products. This is important because, unlike the majority of the seed-layer samples, the upper-layer samples are dominated by wheat (fig. 60), of which 68–96%, consisting mainly of emmer with some einkorn, was hulled (fig. 61). The weed proportions for the upper samples are between 3.3–12.3%, relatively higher than in the seed layer, as are the weed to field crop and weed to cereal proportions (0.11–0.55 and 0.11–0.56; figs 58 and 59). Although not close to Çayboyu sample 1 (10.2), which might be expected for a by-product (Van der Veen 1992), these are relatively high ratios, and the range of species is also greater. Although some of the weed species, for example *Centaurea*, might potentially indicate earlier processing stages, such light seeds are not common and the majority of species were more probably waste resulting from fine sieving (small free heavy seeds such as *Stipa*) or hand sorting (large free heavy seeds such as *Aegilops*; see appendix 1). The high proportion of chaff and of hulled wheat, the high glume base to grain ratio and the large number of small free heavy weeds suggest that the upper-level samples 1–5 and 40 are formed of some fine-sieved or, less likely, coarse-sieved by-product, with some charred clean free-threshing grain included in them. We need to

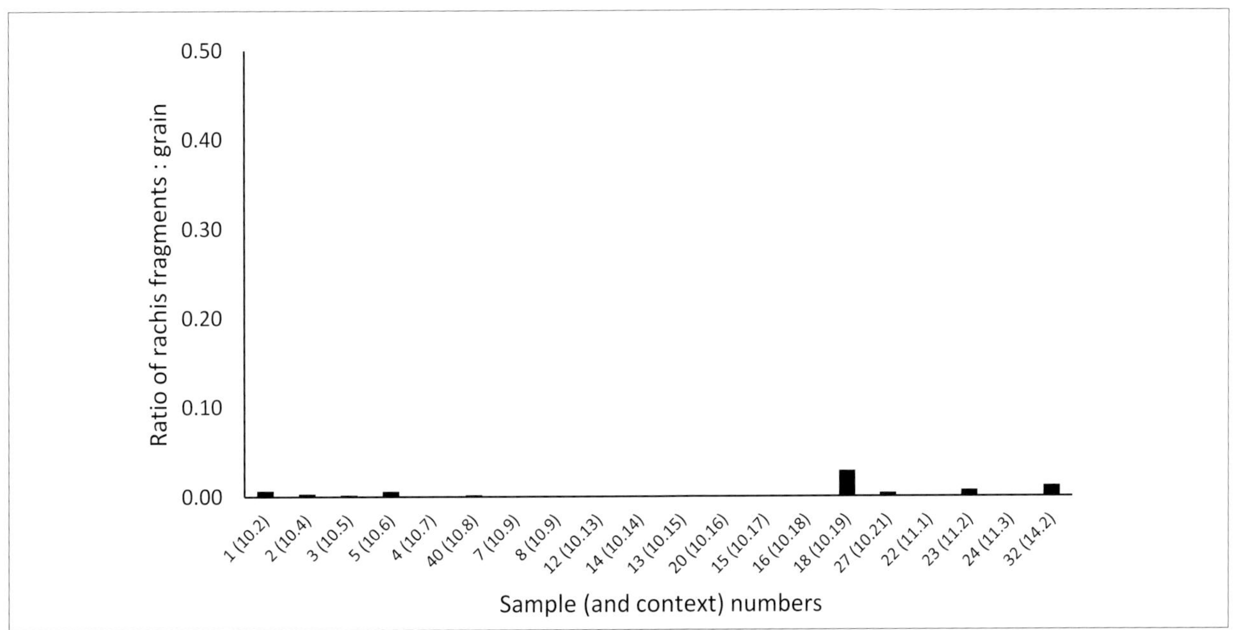

Fig. 65. Ratio of rachis fragments to free-threshing cereal grain at Çayboyu.

consider how the hulled and free-threshing grain types came to be mixed. All samples have some field crops mixed in with the cereal elements, although in low proportions. This suggests that these samples contain general as well as fine-sieved waste, including charred flax, lentils and a range of other pulses and fruits (see appendix 1).

Three samples have relatively higher proportions of grain (around 70%): samples 7, 20 and 24. There are similarities and differences between them. As with the other Çayboyu samples, there is a mix of cereal types (fig. 60) and a low incidence of culm nodes and rachis fragments (figs 64 and 65). The value derived from the glume to grain ratio, however, varies between the samples. For sample 7 it is 0.62 and for sample 24 it is 0.50, which may indicate that this was a semi-clean product rather than a by-product of crop processing. For sample 20 the higher figure of 1.69 suggests that this is a by-product of crop processing (fig. 62). The proportion of weeds varies. Like the seed layer, samples 7 and 20 have low proportions of weeds (0.6% and 1.0% respectively), while 24 is closer to the other samples (5.8%), and this corresponds with the weed to field crop and weed to cereal ratios (figs 58 and 59). The range of weed types, however, is very similar to the other Çayboyu samples, with mainly small free heavy weeds like *Stipa*, which would be consistent with fine sieving. Sample 7 contains a little flax and *Celtis*, and sample 24 contains a few specimens of *Lens culinaris*. In these three samples the low ratio of glume to grain, the lack of other chaff and the mixing of grain species suggest that these are similar to the seed layer. They remain difficult to explain.

The Çayboyu samples are particularly puzzling because of the significant proportions of hulled barley, hulled wheat and free-threshing wheat present in all samples, including the concentrated material in the seed layer. It is not likely that these were grown together since they have different maturation times and different processing requirements. It is also difficult to imagine them being stored together as they have different culinary properties. As such, explaining these samples in terms of crop processing is complex and it is hard to locate them in the sequence of cereal processing or to make a convincing suggestion about how the samples were formed. What can be noted, however, is that the mixing of the grains and the nearly clean hulled wheat is not random, nor did it occur in small quantities, but instead was a consistent and potentially large-scale activity that occurred throughout the occupation of the site.

4.3.1.3. Dung fuel. No dung fragments were found in the hand-sorted or floated samples (see section 4.2.3), and the presence of dung was not recorded during excavation. As such, no definitive evidence for dung fuel use is present at the site. Following Miller's formula it can be seen that the proportions of seed weight to charcoal weight are low in the majority of cases (Miller 1984; 1998; Miller, Marston 2012), and this would be an argument against the regular use of dung as a fuel (fig. 66).

The exceptions are the weight ratios of the seed layer. This could be a consequence of hand sorting which led to less effective charcoal collection (although sample 13 has significant charcoal weights) or suggest that these samples have high figures for grain, which have distorted the seed weight. Samples 7 and 20 also have higher ratios and may have been affected by the large quantity of grain present.

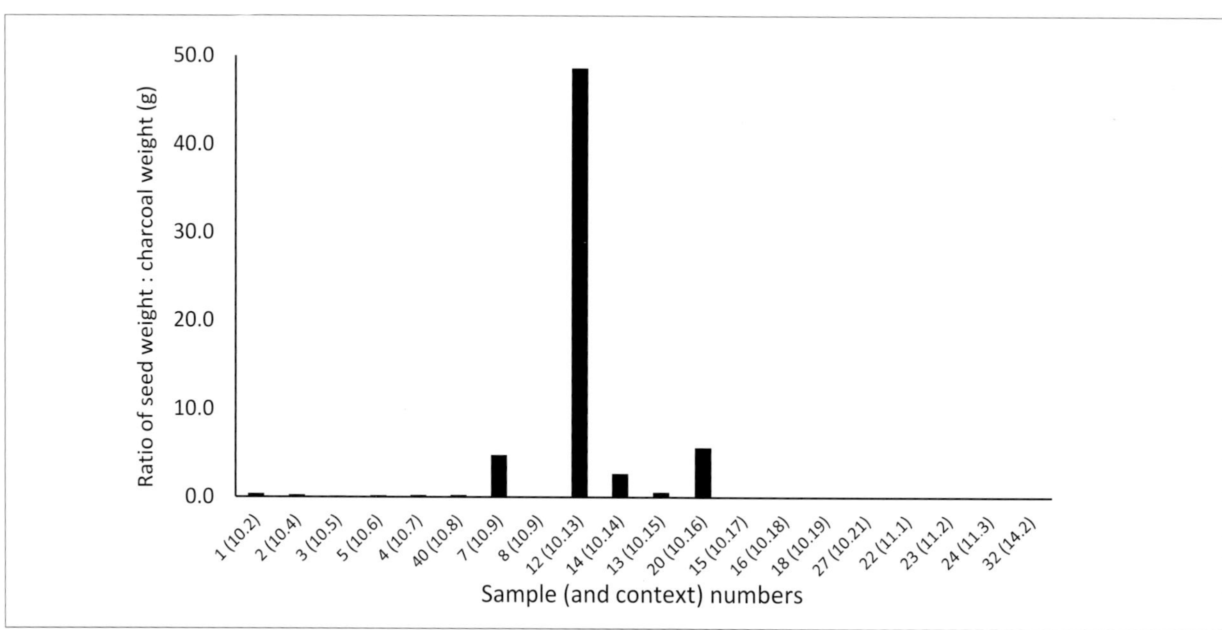

Fig. 66. Ratio of weight of seeds to weight of charcoal (g) at Çayboyu.

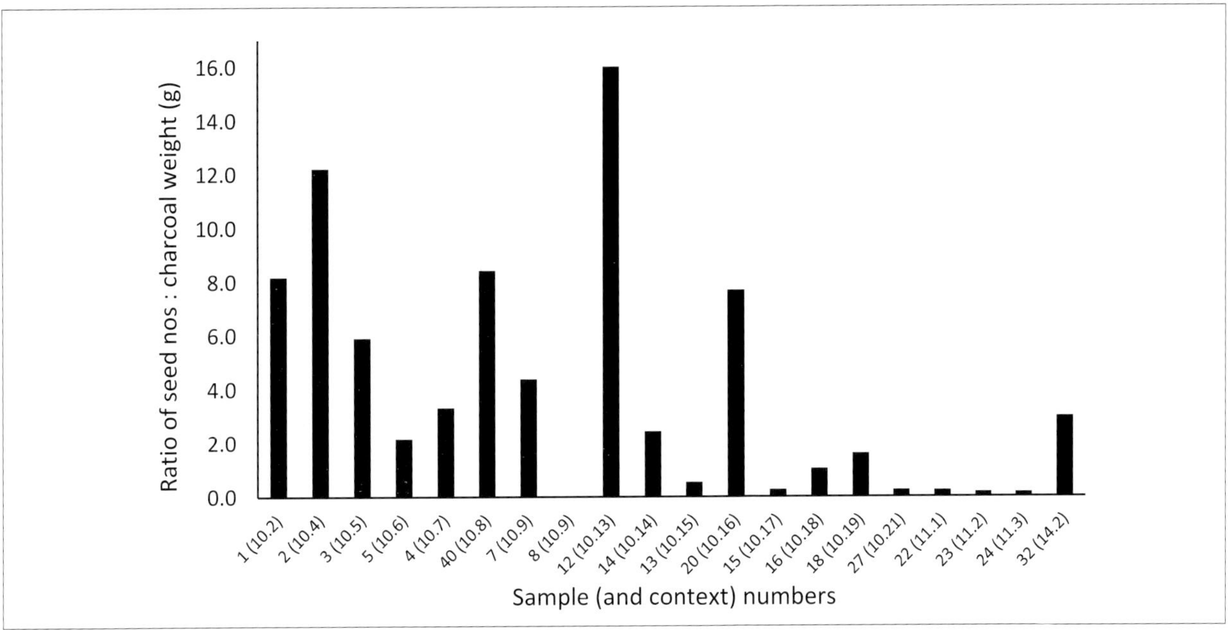

Fig. 67. Ratio of number of weed seeds to weight of charcoal (g) at Çayboyu.

The pattern regarding the ratios of weed numbers to charcoal weight is more complex (fig. 67). In the seed layer the seed to charcoal ratio of sample 12 is relatively high, which again could be a result of the hand collection of the charcoal residue. Looking at the flotation samples from the lower and upper phases, it can be suggested that there is a pattern of decreased wood use over time relative to the number of weed seeds appearing in the assemblage. Similar reductions in wood use are suggested for Miller's test site of Gritille (Miller 1998), although this is accompanied by increased seed weight relative to decreased charcoal weight. Since George Willcox's charcoal analysis shows that wood was abundant at this period at Çayboyu, it seems unlikely that the change between the lower and upper phases in the ratio of weed seed to charcoal weight was due to a decline in the availability of wood (Willcox 1974). A change in fuel choice is theoretically possible, but, as Charles (1998) has pointed out, in most societies wood is generally preferred over dung because of its superior burning qualities. An overall change in fuel use between phases based on generic choice seems unlikely. Without more contextual information about what activities were taking place at the site (for example pottery manufacture, metal smelting, food preparation) and an opportunity to compare fuel use across the site this remains an unexplained but interesting pattern.

Looking at the behaviour and ecology of the weed types present (following Charles 1998; Charles, Bogaard 2004), the change in seed numbers relative to charcoal weight over time does not suggest the increasing use of dung for fuel. The majority of weeds that could be identified at species/genus level flower/fruit in the harvest month of July (see appendix 2). Two species are defined as 'early' according to the criteria of Charles and Bogaard (2004): *Euclidium syriacum* and *Bellevalia*; the former was indeed noted flowering at Aşvan in June (see appendix 2). Charles and Bogaard's (2004) model suggests that these could have been collected after fruiting late during the harvest and were indeed weeds found on arable land. Two other species are defined as late: *Ajuga* and *Thalictrum*. These late-fruiting species could not have been collected as part of the harvest. However, neither formed a significant part of the weed assemblage in any of the samples to which they belong (*Ajuga* has a ubiquity of 27.78% and forms between 0.05% and 7.41% of the weeds, while *Thalictrum* has a ubiquity of 33.33% and forms between 0.05% and 2.13% of the weeds). Ecologically, the weed assemblage as a whole came from a wide range of potential habitats. However, most of the weed species noted in the Aşvan surveys (or in *Flora of Iraq*: Townsend, Guest 1966–1985) were found in or at the edge of crop fields. Five species do not fit this pattern: *Bolboschoenus glaucus, Echinochloa*, *Geum*, *Taeniatherum* and *Thalictrum*. These non-arable weeds are all associated with wet conditions such as wadis, riversides, irrigation ditches and canals. Their presence, as well as the consistent and ubiquitous presence of *Stipa*, are discussed in chapter 5.7. *Stipa*, a tough grass, grows in waste ground and on rocky slopes, but is unpalatable to animals and can be classified with other unpalatable weeds (fig. 68), making it unlikely to have been part of dung fuel. It was either collected for a specific purpose or it might have been associated with the cultivation of crops on rocky slopes (see chapter 5.7).

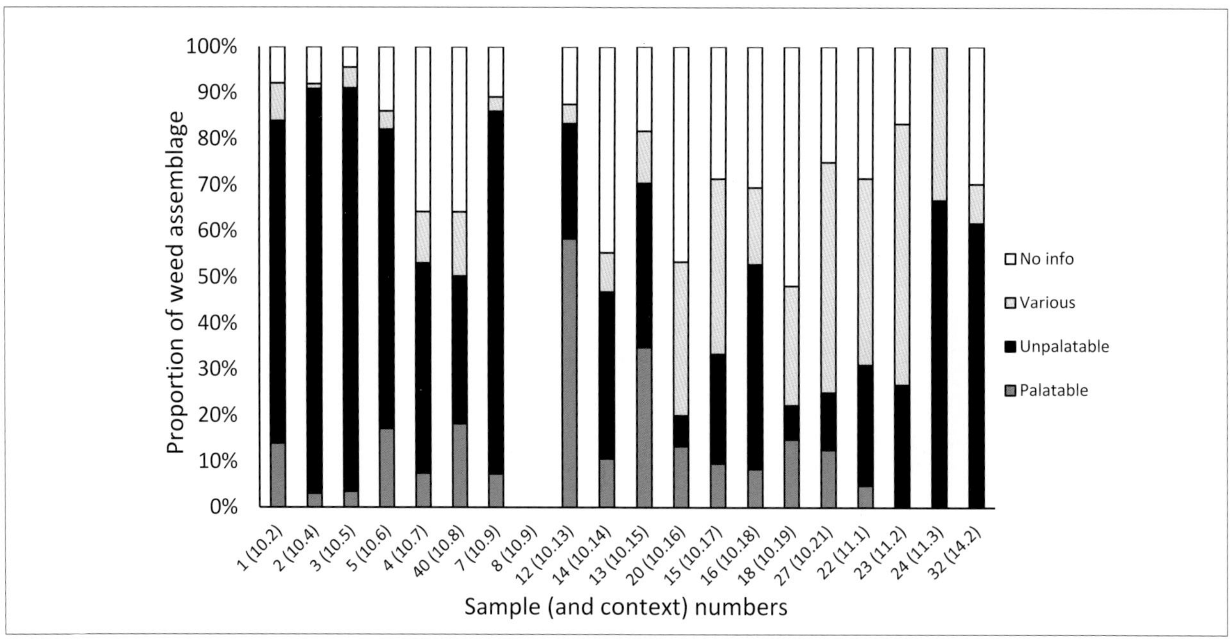

Fig. 68. Proportions of weeds based on palatability to animals at Çayboyu (data from Townsend, Guest 1966–1985).

Figure 68 presents the proportions of the weeds present at Çayboyu which could have been eaten at the time of fruiting by animals, either when grazing or foddering, those that would have been unpalatable at fruiting time and those for which no information has been listed. A large number of weed genera include a range of palatable and unpalatable species and are variably classifiable, although no information is available about the palatability of several species (Townsend, Guest 1966–1985). However, in general at Çayboyu unpalatable weeds outnumber palatable weeds, and this supports the view that the weed assemblage did not derive mainly from dung fuel. This pattern is confirmed by the figures for the two most ubiquitous unpalatable and palatable weeds. Proportionately more *Stipa* was found in all contexts than Trifolieae, except in samples 10 and 13 where equal proportions are noted. The proportionately higher presence of unpalatable weeds suggests that the majority of carbonised weed seeds at the site did not derive from dung fuel, although such weeds might also have been added to dung fuel to aid combustion.

No sample from the Aşvan sites appears to derive from the processing of a single crop. Charles (1998: 119) looked at the nature of the cereal component at Abu Salabikh and argues that the inclusion of chaff from barley and glume wheat was not suited to human consumption practices, since carbonised chaff in these quantities is not found in cooking and chaff is not mixed with barley for human consumption. These samples do not therefore represent maslin cropping. However, at Çayboyu the phenomenon that requires explanation is not the inclusion of two different processing stages, but the mixing of two different product types, hulled and free-threshing grains. As Charles (1998) notes, these would not be grown as maslin crops because of the different processing requirements. However, in the case of the seed layer, these were clean products which could have been deliberately mixed at the point of storage. The large quantity of grains, the low proportion of chaff and weeds, and the absence of any signs that the grain had been masticated (see Valamoti, Charles 2005) indicate decisively that the seed-layer samples do not derive from dung fuel. The upper- and lower-phase samples, with higher proportions of chaff, especially derived from glume wheat rather than free-threshing grains, could potentially be interpreted as derived from dung fuel, but, unlike at Abu Salabikh, these samples contain mixed hulled wheats, which dominate most samples, and free-threshing grain. The presence of glume bases is not surprising given that there is evidence that the samples had been fine sieved. This fine-sieved waste, however, must have been carbonised in order to survive, and in order for this to occur it must have either been swept into the fire or incorporated into dung fuel. Although the ratio of weed-seed numbers to charcoal weight in the upper-phase samples needs to be taken into account, the low ratio of seed weight to charcoal weight, the low number and ubiquity of non-arable weeds and the abundance of wood resources available at Çayboyu (Willcox 1974) make the former interpretation more convincing.

4.3.1.4. Site-formation processes. The small excavation area obviously limited the possibilities of interpreting the architectural remains at Çayboyu (Aksoy, Diamant 1973). The lower part of the trench (phase I) contained two distinct stone walls, ash and carbon lenses, mudbrick tumble and substantial traces of burning in phase Ib. It is not known with which samples this burning was associated as the key to the shading of the site section is incomplete (the only key to section shading is in Helms 1972: pl. 38), but it is likely to be the area of dark shading associated with samples 16 and 18.

The seed layer that divides the upper and lower parts of the trench rests on, and was also covered by, hard brown clay that contained minimal archaeological material. These layers might have resulted from deliberate levelling by the site's inhabitants, mudbrick debris eroding off the site (the trench was at its edge) or from the stream in the adjoining wadi, which had buried nearly half the trench under the current-day ground surface. In any case, the seed layer appears to result from relatively rapid deposition of material at a time when this part of the settlement was not in use.

The upper part of the trench (phase II) lacked clear architectural features. Lenses of ash and carbonised material were found with fragmentary floors. A saddle quern was found on a bed of carbonised wood – evidence which suggests a destructive fire, rather than cooking or waste disposal.

The Çayboyu trench thus showed three ways which could have produced charred material deposits: waste disposal, revealed by the many ash lenses; the use of a hearth, presumably for cooking; and a destructive fire, leading to the in situ burning of a saddle quern. Both a quern and its wooden seating would be valuable objects and unlikely to have been burnt on purpose. However, ash lenses dominated this trench and this fits well with the evidence from the samples: they are dominated by the by-products of fine sieving, which were charred when used as fuel and then discarded.

The most distinctive stratigraphical feature of the site is the dense deposit of seeds sandwiched between layers of sterile brown clay which appears about 3m below ground level in the western section (see chapter 1, fig. 5). The relative uniformity and the high seed density noted in all four samples (8, 12, 14 and 13) suggest that they were deposited rapidly around the same time, although sample 8 was collected about 50cm above the main seed concentration and sample 13 probably just below it. The excavators also noted that the seed layer extended for several metres beyond the excavated trench and was visible in the section cut by the stream on the eastern side of the mound. The deposit was accordingly substantial and covered a wide area. It is possible that the deposit resulted from clearing up after a destructive fire, leading to the carbonisation of a substantial cache of nearly pure stored grain, but this remains a speculative hypothesis.

In the rest of the Çayboyu samples it seems likely that the charred botanical material found in the ash lenses and the hearth feature resulted from burnt by-products of fine sieving, and this is also suggested by the sample composition. Although the proportions of the cereal grain, weeds and chaff vary between the samples, it is striking that other field crops, and wild food remains, are present in very low quantities. Taking the seeds of field crops, but excluding chaff, cereal grain accounts for at least 96% of field-crop seed in 16 samples. In only four samples there are significant admixtures of non-cereals; in one case (24) the sample size is very low and in the other three (18, 22, 23) the admixture is in the form of lentils. These three samples come from adjoining contexts, and it is therefore possible that the lentils derive from a one-off deposition.

The low density of plant material, and its lack of diversity, has two implications. First, it seems unlikely that such similar samples, in crop and weed composition, could continue to be deposited in exactly the same way, in the same part of the site unless they resulted from very similar processes. Second, this assemblage seems to have originated in a repeated, standardised activity, for example the cleaning out of hearths or ovens in which fine-sieved by-products were regularly charred.

4.3.2. Taşkun Mevkii

4.3.2.1. Sample definition. Table 17 shows the main ratios of samples taken from Taşkun Mevkii, trench J11. Five of the samples are very similar in composition, dominated by free-threshing wheat with small admixtures of emmer and hulled barley grain. It is difficult to draw inferences from the different proportional representation of seeds, because the samples are all small, ranging from 27 to 233 items. However, barley forms 24% and 36% of the grain in samples 501.23 and 502.12, compared with 3% to 15% in the samples from area 503.

Samples 503.14, 503.15 and 503.16 are all described in the excavator's notebook as being from a 'layer with burnt sherds on top'. The three samples were treated as one for the purposes of quantification. Sample 502.7 is very different in content to the others and clearly distinct, but contains only 28 seeds.

The six samples from trench K10c contain a strikingly similar range of species and fall into two clearly separate groups that relate to their archaeological context: (1) 101.24 (pot contents), dominated by hulled barley, and (2) 103.6 and 103.7 (context unknown), dominated by free-threshing wheat.

The hand-collected sample 101.24 is almost is almost pure barley, with just 94 weed seeds in more than 10,000 barley grains. In contrast, the flotation sample from the same context contains 10% wheat grain and a much wider range of weed seeds. The sample encompasses four deposits: (1) 101.23: barley, emmer, very little einkorn and distinct from 101.24 (flotation sample); (2) 101.24 (hand

Sample (TM)	*Density (charred material per litre soil)*	*Culm to grain*	*Glume bases to grain*	*Rachis to grain*	*Weed to crop*	*% crop (all seeds)*	*% weeds (all seeds)*	*% hulled wheat (all wheat)*	*% naked wheat (all cereals)*	*% cereal chaff (all cereal items)*
501.23	0.03	0	0	0	0.35	73.3	25.7	15.1	64.3	0
502.7	0.01	0	0	0	0.33	75	25	50	25	0
502.12	0	0	0	0	0.06	94.5	5.5	12.1	56.9	0
503.14	0.03	0	0	0	0	100	0	1.3	94.8	0
503.15	0.03	0	0	0	0	100	0	12.1	75.7	0
503.16	0.04	0	N/A	0	0	100	0	0	90.2	0
101.23	N/A	0.002	0.085	0	0.43	69.9	29.9	17.8	4	0.4
101.24	N/A	0	N/A	0	0.01	99.1	0.9	0	0	0
101.24	N/A	0	0.765	0	0.12	89.5	10.5	68.8	3	8.5
101.25	N/A	0.003	0.1	0	1.28	43.9	56.1	38.5	0.3	0.4
103.6	0.17	0	0.117	0.001	0.21	82.4	17.1	3	81.9	0.6
103.7	0.3	0.007	0.051	0	0.11	89.1	10.2	27.5	51.8	2.7

Table 17. Ratios at Taşkun Mevkii.

collected): pure barley in the jar; (3) 101.24 (flotation sample): emmer wheat and other wheats; (4) 101.25: nearly pure barley, similar to 101.24 (flotation sample), but with very abundant *Lolium* grains.

Sample 103.6 (free-threshing wheat) is broadly similar to 103.7, if we assume some uneven mixing in the grain store. The two samples are treated as one.

4.3.2.2. Crop processing. Unlike Çayboyu, the tri-plot for Taşkun Mevkii (fig. 69) suggests low chaff and variable weed proportions. Three groups can be identified: five samples are grain rich; two are half-grain, half-weed; and two are three-quarters grain, one-quarter weeds. Samples 502.7 and 101.25 are half-grain, half-weed, while sample 101.24 (flotation sample) has 7.7% chaff, relatively higher than the other samples, but still much lower than the proportion of grain in the sample. For the majority of samples which contain a high proportion of grain relative to weeds and chaff, the cereal remains should be interpreted as primary products.

The grain-rich samples are the combined samples 502.12 and 503.14–16, and the combined samples 101.24 (hand collected), 101.24 (flotation) and 103.6–7. Sample 503.14–16 is 100% grain, and came from soil units which contained burnt pot sherds. A *Cicer arietinum* seed is the single contaminant. There is some variability in the grain species of the grain-rich samples (fig. 70). The majority contain a predominance of wheat in proportions between 65% and 92%, most of it free-threshing (fig. 71), but samples 101.24 (hand collected) and 101.24 (flotation) are mainly barley, and came from a pot, an almost pure store of barley. Sample 101.23 is also mainly barley. Only three of these grain-rich samples contain chaff: 101.24 (flotation) is 7.7% chaff. This sample shows the advantage of flotation over hand sorting, as the hand-sorted sample from 101.24 includes no chaff, although it came from the same pot. 103.6–7 is 1.3% chaff and 501.23 is 0.3% chaff. In all cases this is mainly glume in low ratios (fig. 72), although sample 101.24 (flotation) contains two pieces of culm (fig. 72) and three pieces of rachis (ratio of 0.0002;

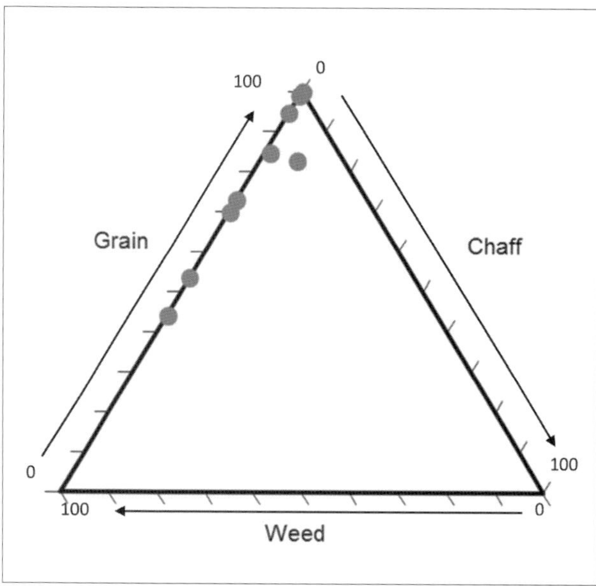

Fig. 69. Taşkun Mevkii crop processing tri-plot, showing the relative proportions of cereal grain, chaff and weeds.

fig. 73), and has a glume to grain value of 0.77, relatively higher than the rest of the Taşkun Mevkii samples. However, the value is still below the threshold of 1 and this assemblage should still be interpreted as a product rather than as a by-product (fig. 74). The weed proportion of the grain-rich samples varies between 0.0% and 27.1%, but the ratios of weed to field crop and weed to cereals (figs 75 and 76) are low, a fact which also supports the conclusion that these samples represent products rather than by-products. Twenty-four weed species are noted but none is common to all samples and 11 are unique to individual samples. Thirteen of these are small free heavy seeds, probably the result of fine sieving, and three are large free and heavy, probably the result of hand sorting. The low number of weed seeds may be due to contamination by other sources, or the seeds may have slipped through the processing stages. Six species cannot be assigned. Based on the high proportion of grain, the low ratios of chaff types and weeds, and the late-stage weed types, it seems likely that these samples represent stored products, containing weeds that passed through the processing stage and would need to be removed during the

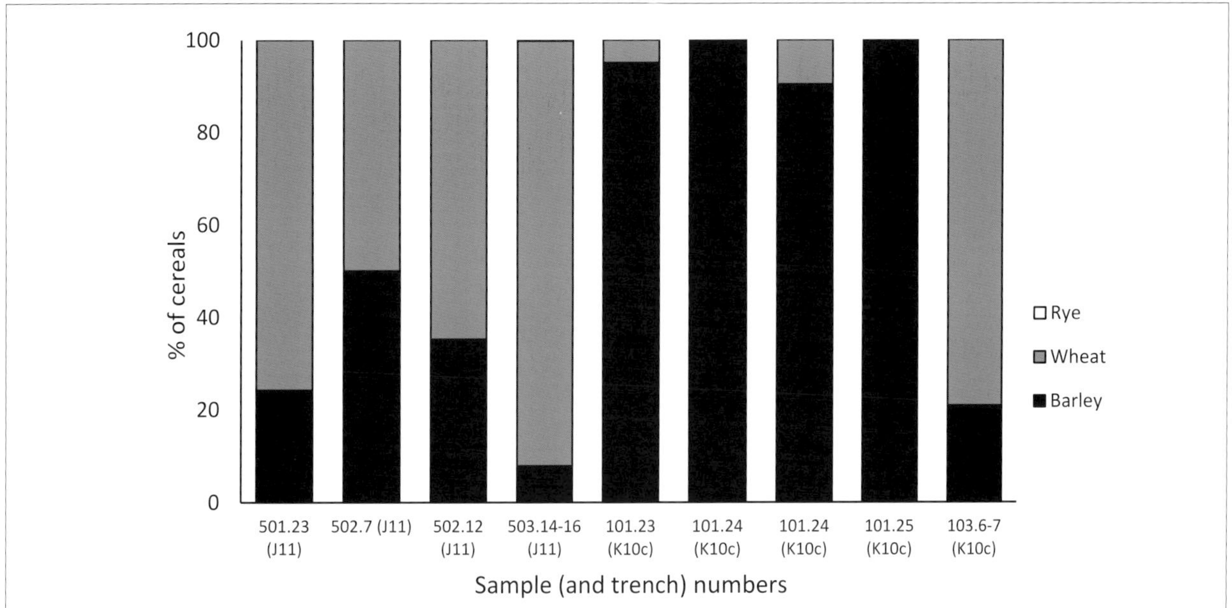

Fig. 70. Proportions of cereal grain species at Taşkun Mevkii.

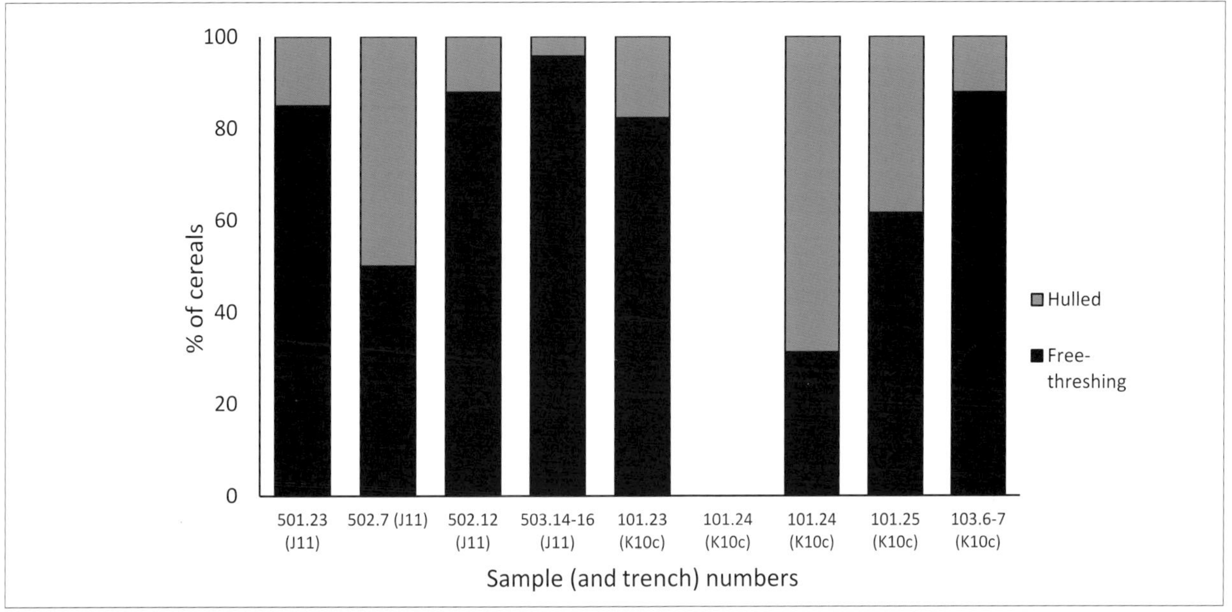

Fig. 71. Proportions of hulled and free-threshing wheat at Taşkun Mevkii.

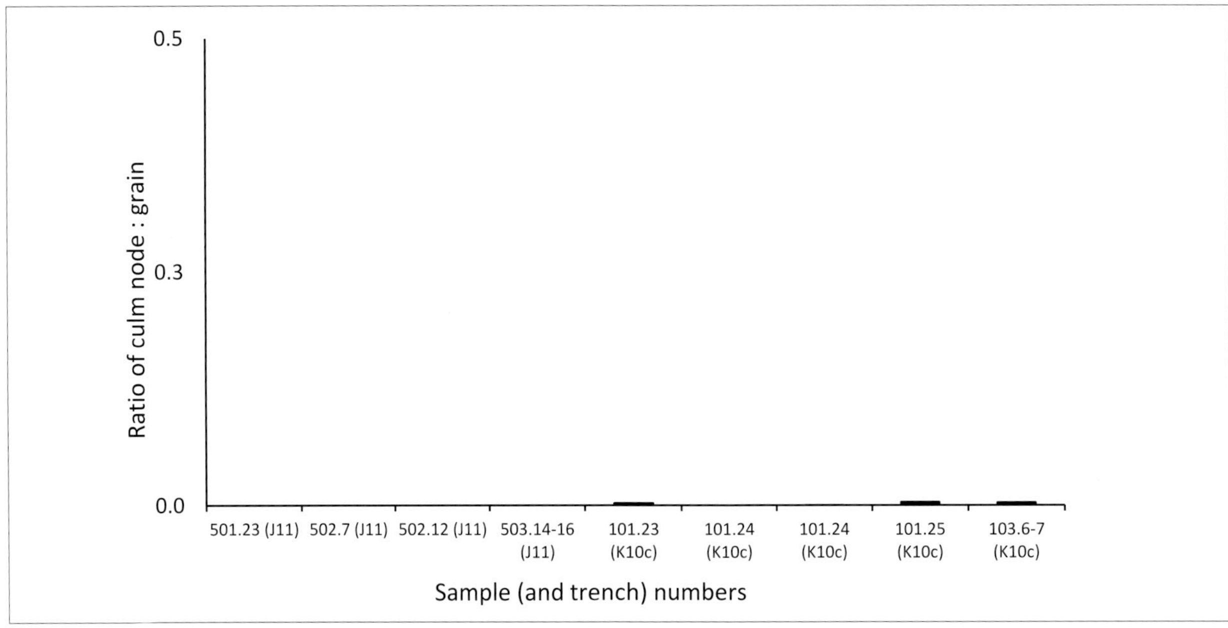

Fig. 72. Ratio of culm node to grain at Taşkun Mevkii.

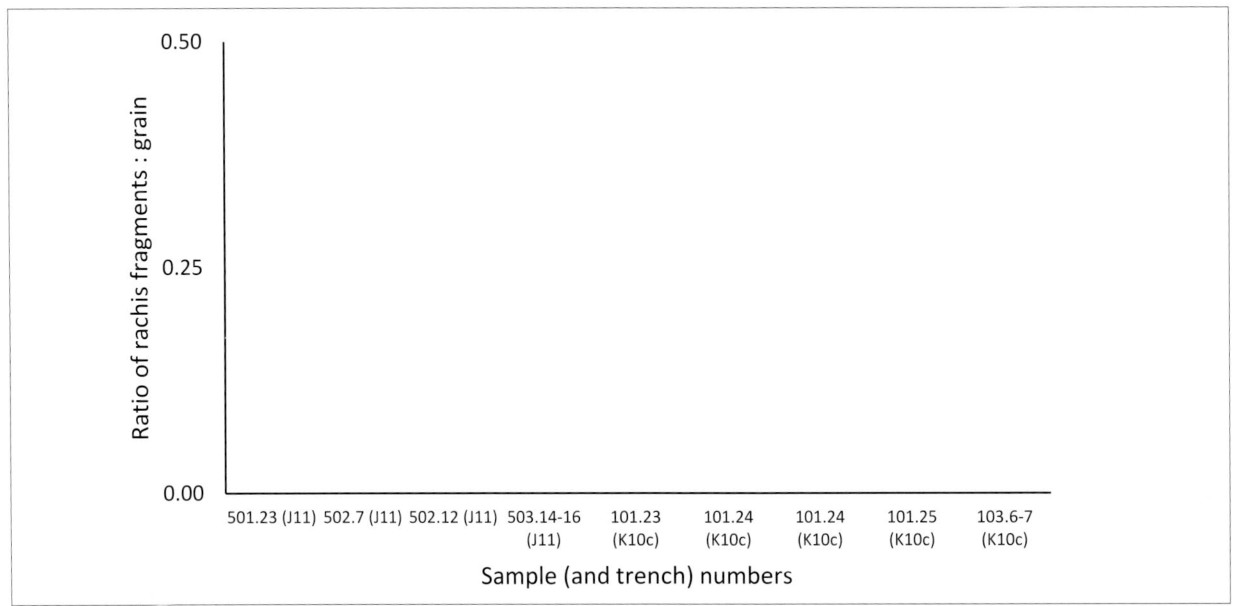

Fig. 73. Ratio of rachis fragments to free-threshing grain at Taşkun Mevkii.

final processing stages before consumption. All these samples had low levels of field crops present. The hand-recovered sample from 101.24 contains no field crops, although this is not the case with the floated sample from the same context. The low number of field crops relative to cereals suggests that a small amount of general waste was incorporated into the assemblages alongside the mostly clean cereal product. Based on the context information, the general cleanliness of the grain and the presence of a small amount of other non-grain material, these samples are interpreted as coming from domestic storage contexts. They were carbonised when burning occurred on the site, and the samples appear alongside a 'background noise' of daily cooking accidents and waste disposal.

Two samples – 502.7 (from a pithos) and 101.25 (from a destruction layer) – are noticeable on the tri-plot as they have almost equal proportions of grain and weed (fig. 69). In the case of 502.7, the results may be skewed by the low density of material. Sample 502.7 is half-barley and half-wheat, while 101.25 is 99.6% barley (figs 70 and 71). Chaff proportions are almost zero; there is none in 502.7 and only 0.2% in 101.25 (figs 72–74), and this suggests that the grain was clean of chaff and not stored in spikelet form. The proportions of weeds are 46.7% and 56% respectively. Sample 502.7 has a weed to field crop ratio of 0.33 and a weed to cereal ratio of 0.88; sample 101.25 has a value of 1.28 (weed to field crop and cereal). The high ratio of sample 101.25 is typical of crop-processing waste, but this sample also contains a large number of grains (5,833 in total; see appendix 1), which suggests that it may represent something other than waste. There are several possible explanations for sample 101.25, the potential destruction layer. Given the high proportion of grain, the low proportion of chaff and the presence of fine-sieving weeds, it may have been a barley product stored after fine sieving, in which the majority of rachis elements were removed as large joined segments rather than separated smaller fragments. Alternatively, the low chaff and high weed proportions may be due to differential survival (Boardman, Jones 1990). The weeds that are present are tough and often siliceous, and thus had a better chance of preservation when they were charred than the more fragile chaff. Sample 502.7 has only 28 seeds, of which 13 are *Vitis vinifera*, possibly associated with the pithos in which they were found; the remaining 14 seeds are probably background contamination from the surrounding excavation fill rather than from the primary contents of the pithos. Their number is too small to interpret.

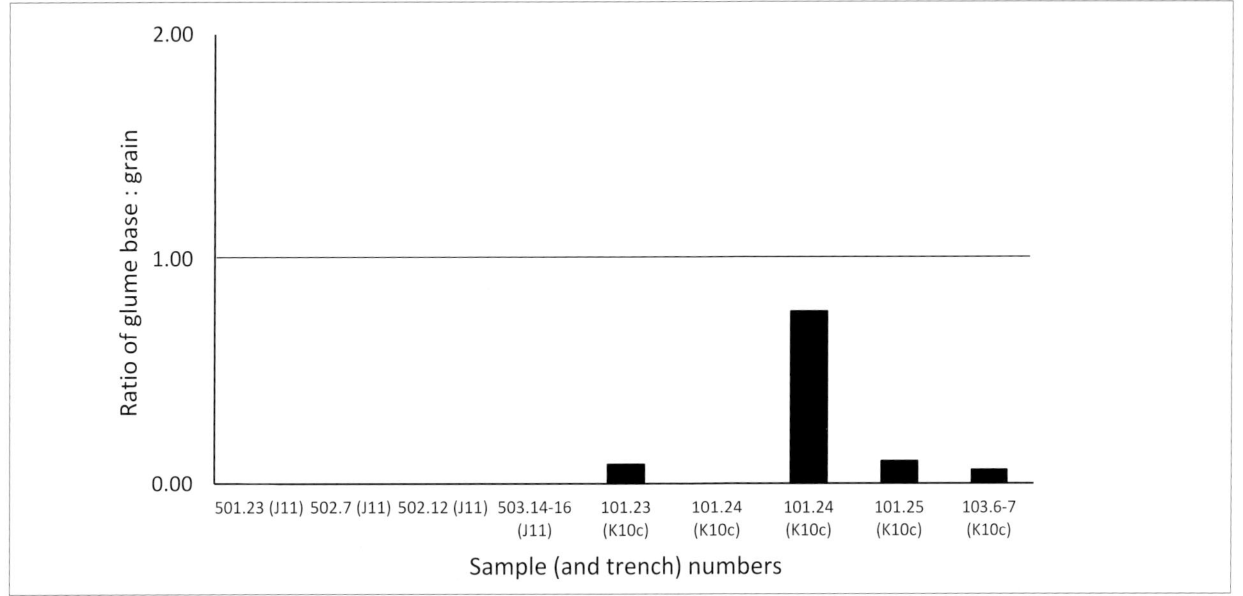

Fig. 74. Ratio of glume base to grain at Taşkun Mevkii. The line indicates the threshold of 1 (see section 4.2.5).

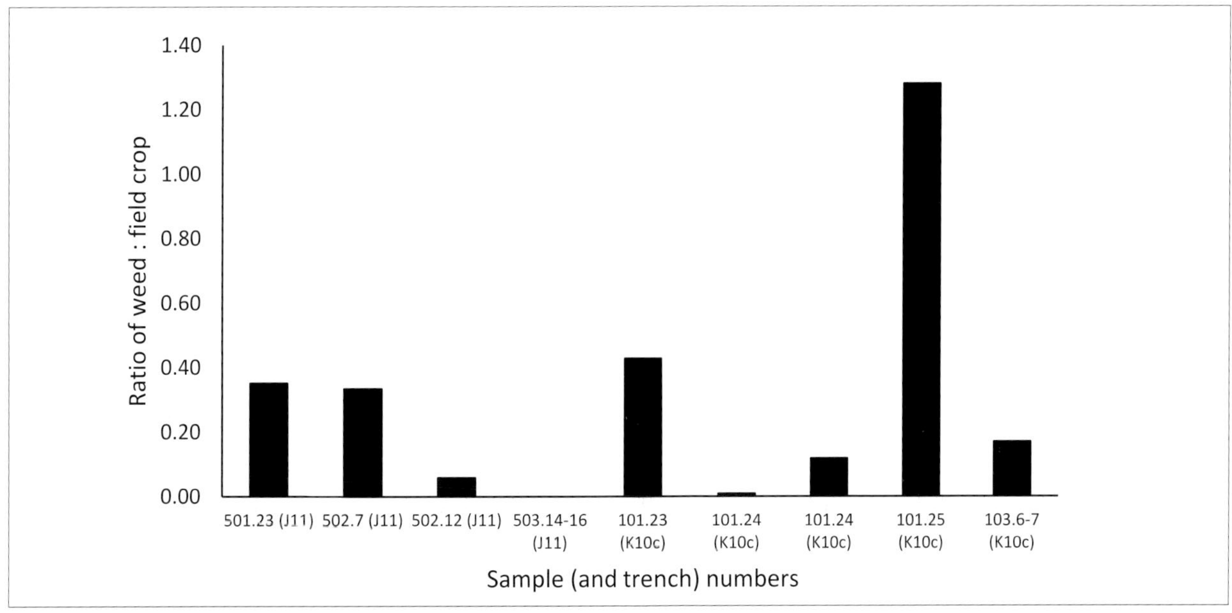

Fig. 75. Ratio of weed to field crop at Taşkun Mevkii.

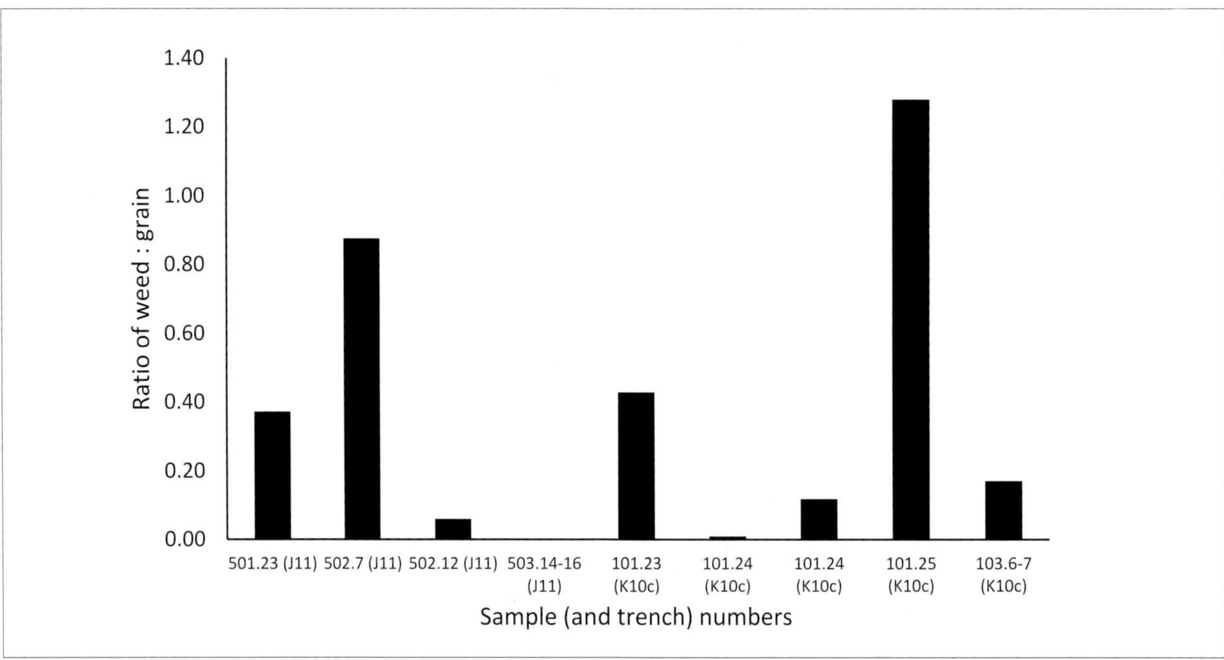

Fig. 76. Ratio of weed to cereal grain at Taşkun Mevkii.

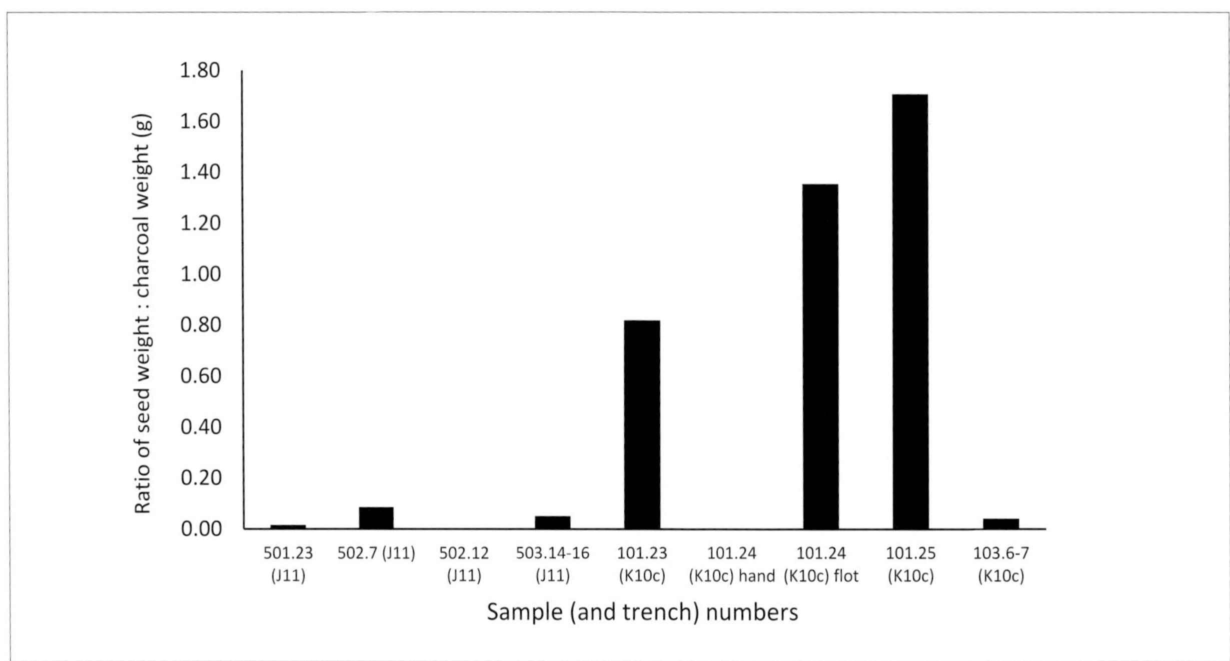

Fig. 77. Ratio of weight of seeds to weight of charcoal (g) at Taşkun Mevkii.

4.3.2.3. Dung fuel. As at Çayboyu, no dung was found in the samples from Taşkun Mevkii. The ratio of seed weight to charcoal weight is also low, suggesting more use of wood and less seed burning (fig. 77).

A slightly greater ratio of seed weight to charcoal weight is observed in samples 101.24 (flotation) and 101.25. These might potentially have derived from dung used as fuel or from the combustion of seed-rich materials, caused by activities such as cooking accidents or the burning of the waste products of crop processing. Samples 502.12 and 101.24 (hand collected) have values of 0, and this can be explained by the fact that these two samples were hand-sorted rather than floated, and no charcoal was collected. When sample 101.24 (hand collected) is compared with the material floated from the same sample (101.23), it is evident that charcoal was indeed present originally. The bar chart comparing weed-seed numbers to charcoal weight shows that sample 101.25 contains a high ratio of seeds relative to the weight of charcoal (fig. 78).

The weeds identified are all likely to have flowered or fruited before or during the harvest month (although no information is available on *Lallemantia*), and, as at Çayboyu, might have come from a wide range of habitats. With three exceptions all the seeds could have come from arable weeds. *Carex*, which forms 0.18% of the assemblage in sample 103.6–7 (combined), was not found among arable weeds during the Aşvan botanical surveys. This genus contains a range of species with variable palatability, and it is difficult to assess how likely these specimens were to have been included in dung fuel. *Carex* occurs in a range of damp environments such as riversides, wadis, swamps, on verges and trackways, in gorges and at cliff bases. *Bolboshoenus glaucus* is also found in a range of damp and even saline environments, including canals, irrigation ditches, riversides and swamps, but no palatability information is recorded in *Flora of Iran* (Townsend, Guest 1966–1985). It is unlikely that *Stipa*, as already discussed, would have been eaten by cattle and sheep/goats. Unlike at Çayboyu, *Stipa* was not ubiquitous at Taşkun Mevkii. This could be explained by a greater use of dung for fuel or by changes in agricultural strategy

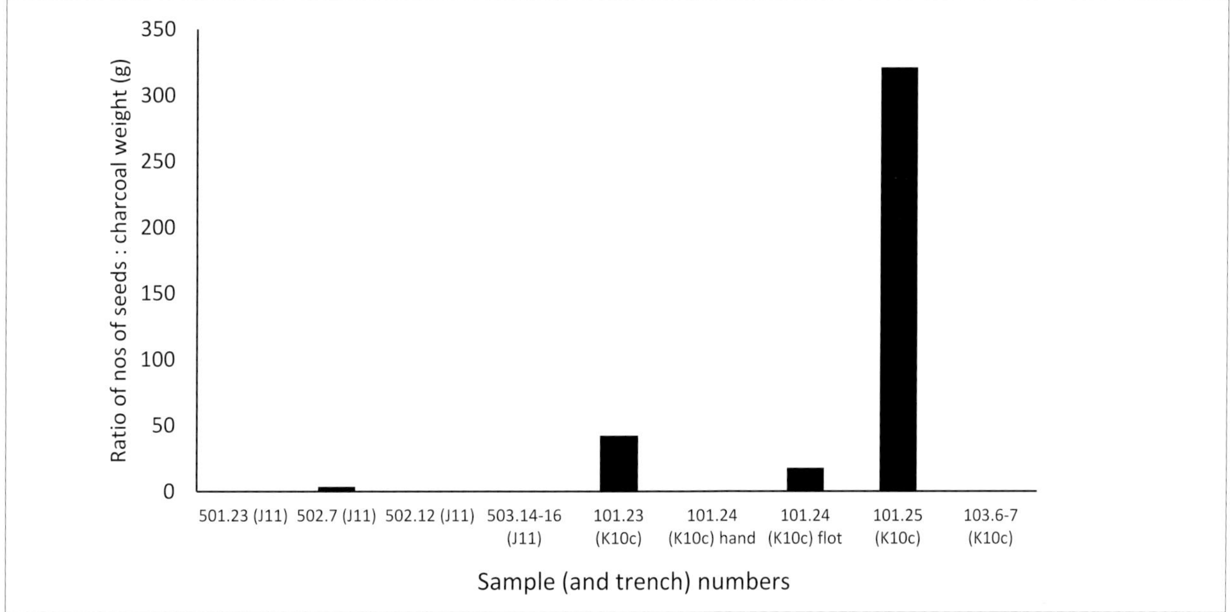

Fig. 78. Ratio of number of weed seeds to weight of charcoal (g) at Taşkun Mevkii.

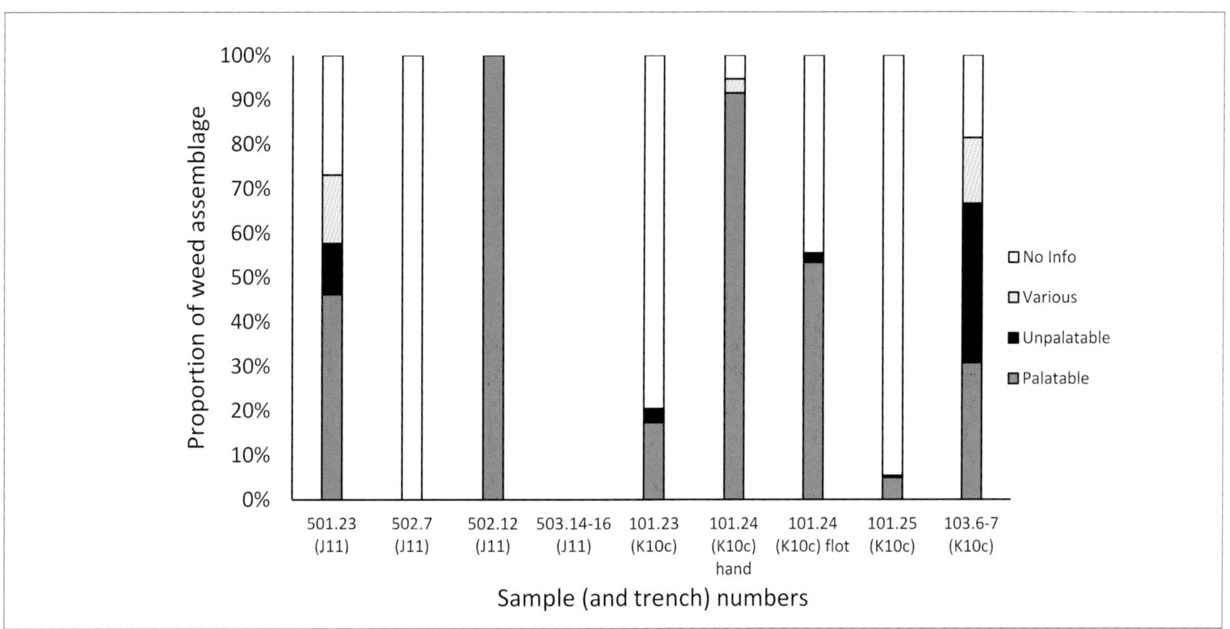

Fig. 79. Proportions of weeds based on palatability to animals at Taşkun Mevkii (data from Townsend, Guest 1966–1985).

(see chapter 5.7). Figure 79 provides information about the proportions of palatable, unpalatable, variable and unknown characteristics of the weed assemblage at Taşkun Mevkii.

The assemblage from Taşkun Mevkii contains proportionately more palatable than unpalatable weed species than that from Çayboyu. This is illustrated by the proportions of the most ubiquitous palatable and unpalatable species, *Lolium persicum* and *Stipa*. In all but one context where *Lolium persicum* and *Stipa* are present, there is a higher proportion of the more palatable *Lolium persicum*. Although not all weeds may have arrived at the site through animal consumption, a greater proportion of weeds in the Taşkun Mevkii samples are likely to have originated from a dung-fuel source.

The high proportion of grain, the mixing of grain types, the absence of chaff, the small proportion of weeds and the high wood charcoal proportions in the majority of samples from Taşkun Mevkii do not, however, support a dung-fuel interpretation. The high number of grains found in the 101-series samples, which came from a destruction phase, and the presence of associated weeds, suggest that these are the remnants of crop processing or derived from other contexts such as the use of this material for bedding or for building materials, rather than from dung fuel. Although it may have contributed to the overall picture, the use of dung fuel is not likely to be the explanation for the occurrence of the weeds that occur in some of the Taşkun Mevkii contexts.

4.3.2.4. Site-formation processes. The presence of stored crop samples is entirely consistent with their preservation in the burnt phase 3 of Taşkun Mevkii (chapter 1.3.4.3, fig. 6).

The grain-filled jar found in structure 1, a single-roomed wattle-and-daub building, is probably represented by sample 101.24. The other 101 samples must also derive from structure 1, which contained a plastered hearth and a basalt quern. The samples from J11 must derive from structure 3, a mudbrick house containing a hearth. In other words, the Taşkun Mevkii samples come from storage in a domestic context, where cooking accidents and waste disposal formed the regular background to life.

4.3.3. Aşvan Kale and Taşkun Kale

4.3.3.1. Sample definition: Early Bronze Age. All the Early Bronze Age samples from Aşvan Kale came from featureless archaeological soil, termed 'fill' by the excavators. They were recovered from the step trench which was excavated in 1969 to establish the prehistoric settlement sequence on the mound and contained few or no architectural features. Plans are not available for the contexts that contained plant remains. The ratios are shown in table 18.

In the 1200 series of samples from trench G2b, sample 1204.11 is distinguished by its high weed content (95% of items). The other six samples in the 1200 series had very similar contents (barley, free-threshing wheat), in similar proportions in five samples but with free-threshing wheat dominant in 1204.1. Although detailed archaeological contexts are not available for 1204.1a, 1204.2, 1204.3,

Context	*Density (charred material per litre soil)*	*Culm to grain*	*Rachis to grain*	*Weed to crop*	*% crop seed (all seeds)*	*% weeds (all seeds)*	*% naked wheat (all cereals)*	*% cereal chaff (all cereal items)*
1204.1 (1)	N/A	0	0	0.41	70.4	29.1	80.5	0
1204.1a (2)	N/A	0	0	0.14	84.8	12.1	25	0
1204.2 (3)	N/A	0	0	0.12	89.2	10.8	25	0
1204.3 (4)	N/A	0	0	0.05	94.1	4.7	29.2	0
1204.10 (11)	N/A	0	0.019	0.07	93.5	6.5	35.2	1.82
1204.11 (12)	N/A	N/A	N/A	N/A	0	100	N/A	100
1204.12 (13)	N/A	0	0	0.01	99	1	38.8	0
1015.3	N/A	0	0	0	99.9	0.1	99.5	0
1016.1	N/A	0	0	0	100	0	99.9	0
1016.5	N/A	0	0	0	100	0	99	0
1016.6	N/A	0	0	0	100	0	99.2	0
1017.2	N/A	0	0	0	100	0	98.9	0

Table 18. Ratios at Aşvan Kale for the Early Bronze Age II/III.

Sample	*Density (charred material per litre soil)*	*Culm to grain*	*Rachis to grain*	*Weed to crop*	*% crop seed (all seeds)*	*% weeds (all seeds)*	*% naked wheat (all cereals)*	*% cereal chaff (all cereal items)*
507.15	N/A	0	0	0	100	0	16.7	0
508.4	N/A	0	0	0.13	88.7	11.3	43	0

Table 19. Ratios at Aşvan Kale for the Late Bronze Age.

1204.10 and 1204.12, the drawing of the southern section of trench G2b suggests that a series running from 1204.1 to 1204.12 probably encompassed at least 2m of excavation, suggesting that these samples should be treated as independent of one another (Sagona 1994: fig. 13).

The samples of trench G3b can be distinguished from those of G2b by the predominance of free-threshing wheat and the near absence of barley. The samples strikingly lack other crops or weeds. The sample series for G3b runs from 1015.3 to 1017.2, suggesting a reasonable diversity of contexts.

Part of the explanation for the difference in sample composition derives from differences in preservation and recovery. The G2b samples were all floated; those from G3b were collected by hand sampling from the trench. Although densities cannot be calculated for the G2b samples, the small quantities of seed and abundant charcoal point to low-density material dispersed in soil. In trench G3b the samples are of fair size (1–10g) with very little charcoal. It is therefore likely that these samples derive from burnt stores. Without further archaeological evidence, it is impossible to say whether these samples derive from one burnt store or many; evidence of in situ burning is not mentioned in the brief excavation report of this trench (Sagona 1994: 9–11). Here they are treated as independent, but of limited value for quantification, as they simply represent some snapshots of stored crops.

Late Bronze Age. Both Late Bronze Age samples from Aşvan Kale came from Pit 7. Sample 508.4 contains free-threshing wheat, hulled barley and bitter vetch seeds, while sample 507.15 is dominated by hulled wheat, with a small presence of free-threshing wheat. The samples were distinct in composition and treated as independent (table 19).

Hellenistic. Most samples from the Hellenistic burnt level at Aşvan Kale are clearly independent: each is dominated by one crop, a typical sign of burnt stores, and is the only sample of that crop from a given room. It is a major advantage for the interpretation of the Hellenistic burnt area that the samples can be assigned to rooms, and thus are known to be independent of one another.

Some samples from the same room are similar in composition (table 20) and required further examination.

Room I, samples 12.12 and 12.14: two samples of hulled barley, one (12.14) with a scarce admixture of weeds and other crops. However, sample 12.12 is larger (239 items; 59 in 12.12), so this could just be an effect of sampling. Given their near adjacent context numbers, these are treated as one sample.

Room III, 606.6 (15) and 606.6 (38): two pure samples of chickpeas, which are treated as one sample.

Room V, 807.6, 807.14 and 809.1: three samples of hulled barley, with a small admixture of free-threshing wheat. Sample 807.14 comes from flotation and includes bitter vetch, grape pips and a large number of *Galium* seeds. If the three samples are connected, as the context numbers suggest, then all three probably derive from a single deposit of hulled barley, with a minor component of free-threshing wheat. Samples 807.14 and 807.6 may also contain part of a separate deposit of bitter vetch, as a minor component. The grape pips and *Galium* in the flotation sample might derive from another in situ sample or, more likely, from the general soil matrix, in view of the abundant charcoal and presence of weeds. Sample 807.14 is treated as an independent sample because of its different taphonomic history, while 807.6 and 809.1 are united.

Room VIII, 1506.1 and 1506.3: two flotation samples dominated by hulled barley, but incorporating different suites of weed seeds from the soil matrix; these are treated independently.

Room VIII, 1507.23 and 1507.27 (7): two samples with a shared, distinctive composition dominated by *Panicum* millet, hulled barley and free-threshing wheat. The hand-collected sample (1507.27 (7)) contains fewer weed seeds than the flotation sample (0.1% versus 0.7%), again suggesting that the weed seed component comes from the soil matrix and is not associated with the stored deposit. The millet, with its much smaller grain and different harvest season to wheat and barley, is likely to derive from what was originally a separate deposit. The two samples have been combined for quantification.

Room VIII, 1507.27 (34) and 1507.27 (35): two samples of free-threshing wheat (conceivably the source of the free-threshing wheat in the 1507 samples discussed above). The millet grains probably derive from the same source as for samples 1507.23 and 1507.27 (7)). The two samples are treated as one.

Context	Density (charred material per litre soil)	Culm to grain	Rachis to grain	Weed to crop	% crop seed (all seeds)	% weeds (all seeds)	% naked wheat (all cereals)	% cereal chaff (all cereal items)
12.12	N/A	0	0	0	100	0	3.4	0
12.14	N/A	0	0	0.03	96.7	3.3	0.9	0
111.4	N/A	0	0	0.01	99.1	0.9	20.2	0
602.24	N/A	0	0	0.02	98.4	1.6	0.8	0
602.25	N/A	0	0	0	100	0	75	0
606.6 (MN 1)	N/A	N/A	N/A	0.03	97.5	2.5	N/A	N/A
606.6 (MN 2)	N/A	0	0	0.01	99.4	0.6	97.7	0
606.6 (7)	N/A	N/A	N/A	N/A	0	0	N/A	N/A
606.6 (15)	N/A	N/A	N/A	0	100	0	N/A	N/A
606.6 (38)	N/A	N/A	N/A	0	100	0	N/A	N/A
606.15 (19)	N/A	N/A	N/A	0	100	0	0	N/A
606.15 (21)	N/A	N/A	N/A	0	100	0	N/A	N/A
728.14	N/A	0	0	0	99.8	0.2	0.5	0
726.26	N/A	0	0	0	100	0	71.4	0
726.27 (6)	N/A	N/A	N/A	0	99.6	0.4	N/A	N/A
729.18	N/A	0	0	0	100	0	2	0
807.6	N/A	0	0	0	100	0	23.7	0
809.1 (2)	N/A	0	0	0	98.6	0	33.3	0
807.14	N/A	0	0	1.41	41.5	58.3	28.7	0
1506.1	0.71	0	0	0.5	66.7	33.3	4.5	0
1506.3	N/A	0	0	2.4	29.4	70.6	0	0
1507.23	N/A	0	0.001	0	99.9	0.1	0.8	0.004
1507.27 (7)	N/A	0	0	0.01	99.3	0.7	83	0
1507.27 (34)	N/A	0	0	0	100	0	86.7	0
1507.27 (35)	N/A	0	0	0	100	0	82.5	0
1713.1 (24)	N/A	0	0	0.11	90.3	9.7	0	0

Table 20. Ratios at Aşvan Kale for the Hellenistic period.

Roman. The two Roman samples are very different in composition. Sample 1601.60 is dominated by lentils and peas, while sample 1806.4 is dominated by millets (table 21).

Medieval (including Taşkun Kale). Four groups of samples from the Medieval period were assessed (table 22).

Trench H3c, Pit 2: the origin of sample 606.4 is uncertain, although it is known that it came from a pit. Its composition is strikingly similar to that of 603.13, from Pit 2 in the same trench. Both are dominated by *Vicia ervilia*. These are treated as one sample.

H3d, 712.7 and 712.8: these two samples have a very similar composition of barley grains. Both are from fill and are treated as one sample.

H3d, Pit 1: a series of eight samples was collected from 714.8 (714.8 MN 1, 4, 2, 3, 190, 191, 273; 714.10). It is not known how these relate to each other stratigraphically. Seven samples are dominated by bitter vetch; of these, two are nearly pure samples (714.8 MN 1 and 4). One sample contains a few weed seeds. The five samples with substantial quantities of bitter vetch also contain significant proportions of hulled barley and free-threshing wheat. As discussed below (in section 4.3.3.2), the crop-processing status of the Pit 1 samples shows that these were primary products. In this case, the material is best interpreted as two samples, one of bitter vetch and one of hulled barley, which became mixed with one another. For purposes of quantification 714.8 (MN2 and MN3) are treated as one sample, 714.8 (MN1, MN4, MN191) and 714.10 as another. The isolated occurrence of chickpeas in MN191 may be the result of admixture from a pure chickpea sample.

H4cd, Pit 7: two flotation samples (1501.13 and 1501.15), both dominated by free-threshing wheat, but one of which, 1501.15, containing grape pips and hackberries. They are treated as separate.

Context	*Density (charred material per litre soil)*	*Culm to grain*	*Rachis to grain*	*Weed to crop*	*% crop seed (all seeds)*	*% weeds (all seeds)*	*% naked wheat (all cereals)*	*% cereal chaff (all cereal items)*
1601.6	N/A	0	0	0.19	84.2	15.8	50	0
1806.4 (6)	N/A	0	0	0.18	84.5	15.5	11.5	0

Table 21. Ratios at Aşvan Kale for the Roman period.

Context	*Density (charred material per litre soil)*	*Culm to grain*	*Rachis to grain*	*Weed to crop*	*% crop seed (all seeds)*	*% weeds (all seeds)*	*% naked wheat (all cereals)*	*% cereal chaff (all cereal items)*
1501.3	N/A	0	0	0	53	0.2	51.2	0
1502.4 (2)	N/A	0	0	0.03	96.3	3.2	98.3	0
603.13	N/A	0	0	0	99.7	0.3	33.3	0
606.4	N/A	0	0	0	100	0	72.7	0
712.7	N/A	0	0	0	100	0	28.9	0
712.8	N/A	0	0	0	100	0	37.5	0
714.8 (MN 1)	N/A	0	0	0.01	98.7	1.3	22.5	0
714.8 (MN 4)	N/A	0	0	0	99.8	0.2	15.7	0
714.10	N/A	0	0	0.02	98.5	1.5	42.9	0
714.8 (MN 2)	N/A	N/A	N/A	0	100	0	N/A	0
714.8 (MN 3)	N/A	0	0	0.01	99	1	0	0
714.8 (MN 190)	N/A	N/A	N/A	13	7.1	92.9	N/A	0
714.8 (MN 191)	N/A	0	0	0.11	90	10	10.7	0
714.8 (MN 273)	N/A	0.235	0.353	0.11	88.2	9.8	11.8	37
1501.8 (14)	N/A	0	0	0.01	99.4	0.6	53.1	0
1501.13	N/A	0	0	0	83.3	0	82.9	0
1501.15	N/A	0	0	0.04	90.2	3.9	69.1	0
1503.3 (4)	N/A	0	0	0	98.8	0	95.7	0
910.22 (1)	N/A	N/A	N/A	N/A	0	0	N/A	0
3101.40 (1)	N/A	0	0	0	100	0	98.6	0
1902.4	N/A	N/A	N/A	0	100	0	N/A	0
TK 703.11 (1)	0.14	0.067	0.067	0.48	67.7	32.3	80	11.76
TK 605.5 (1)	1.57	0	0	0.62	61.7	38.3	0	0
TK 201.15	N/A	0	0	0.01	98.7	1.3	0	0

Table 22. Ratios at Aşvan Kale and Taşkun Kale for the Medieval period.

4.3.3.2. Crop processing. The disappearance of hulled wheat from the Early Bronze Age II onwards is marked by the absence of glume bases, which had hitherto served as a useful marker of the by-products of fine sieving in non-storage assemblages. As most of the samples from Aşvan Kale and Taşkun Kale contain no more than a trace of free-threshing rachis segments, weeds are more important for interpretative purposes, as potential indicators of production stages like coarse sieving and fine sieving.

Four samples from the tri-plot (fig. 80), all containing chaff, stand out as unusual, with the rest lying along the grain-weed line. Sample 714.8 (MN 273) from Medieval II is 31.3% chaff. The other three samples contain between 0.3–7.4% chaff. The rest of the samples have no chaff at all. The proportions of cereal types are shown in figure 81, the ratio of culm to grain in figure 82, the ratio of rachis fragments to grain in figure 83, the ratio of weeds to field crops in figure 84 and the ratio of weeds to cereals in figure 85.

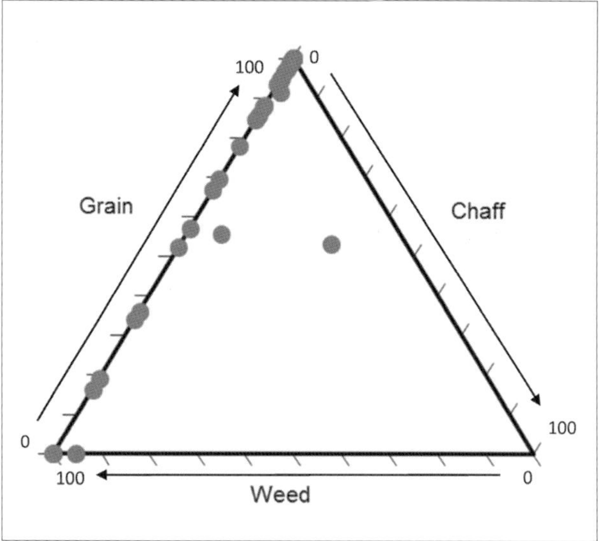

Fig. 80. Aşvan Kale and Taşkun Kale (all periods) crop processing tri-plot, showing the relative proportion of cereal grain, chaff and weeds. Samples have been combined where appropriate (see section 4.3.3.1).

Early Bronze Age II. All samples except one – sample 1204.11 (12) – are grain-rich. The samples contain either barley or wheat (fig. 81), with no millet or rye present. All but one of these grain-rich samples contain no chaff. No culm nodes are present in 1204.10 (11), the only sample containing chaff (fig. 82), and the rachis to grain ratio of 0.02 (fig. 83) is a result of one piece of *Triticum durum* rachis being present, suggesting that the assemblage is not the by-product of an early processing stage. The proportion of weeds varies between 0% and 30.6%, and the values of weed to field crop and weed to cereal vary between 0 and 0.14 (figs 84 and 85). All have similar weed types: eight species in total, of which four are small free and heavy, one large free and heavy, and two or three are unclassified. Sample 1204.1 (1) has one small free light weed which could indicate winnowing but is more likely a consequence of contamination from another source, especially given that the weed assemblage comprises a large number of *Galium* seeds (37 compared with 118 cereal seeds). This high number of *Galium* compared with the number of grains, the lack of chaff and the low number of seeds of other weed species suggests that the *Galium* may have been incorporated separately from another source. This is plausible in a fill context which is likely to have been composed as a result of multiple activities rather than as an individual deposit. Based on the low ratio of weed seeds to grain and the later-stage indicators from the weed types, it is suggested that these grain-rich samples show mixed product rather than processing waste. All these samples, with the exception of 1015.3–1016.6 (combined) which have no field crops, have low ratios of field crop to cereal, suggesting some general waste was mixed into the assemblages alongside the mixed grain product. Given the small amount of field crops mixed into the cereal product these samples could also derive from cooking waste.

Sample 1204.11 (12) differs because it contains no grain, but some chaff and lots of weeds. The chaff proportion (4.5%) is formed of nine pieces of *Triticum durum* rachis. The weeds (95.5% of the sample) are from seven species, but the majority of these are very small and diverse, and cannot be identified to genus level. This sample, which does not contain any field crops, could be fine-sieving waste but could equally have come from a range of other sources such as dung fuel, bedding and foddering.

Late Bronze Age. Like the majority of the Early Bronze Age samples, the two Late Bronze Age pit samples are grain-rich. The hand-picked sample 507.15 is 100% grain, made up of 83.3% barley and 16.7% wheat; 508.4 is 84.7% grain (57% barley and 43% wheat; fig. 81) and 15.3% weeds. The value of weed to field crop is 0.13 and that of weed to cereal is 0.18 (figs 84 and 85). These are low values and therefore suggest product rather than by-product. The species also suggest late-stage processing: three small free heavy weeds, one large free heavy weed and three unassigned. The combination of grain-rich, low weed to crop ratios and late-stage weeds suggests a stored product rather than a by-product assemblage. Sample 507.1 had no field crops, while 508.4 had low ratios of field crop to cereal, suggesting some general waste is incorporated into the assemblage. The mix of cereal product and field crops could also indicate cooking waste.

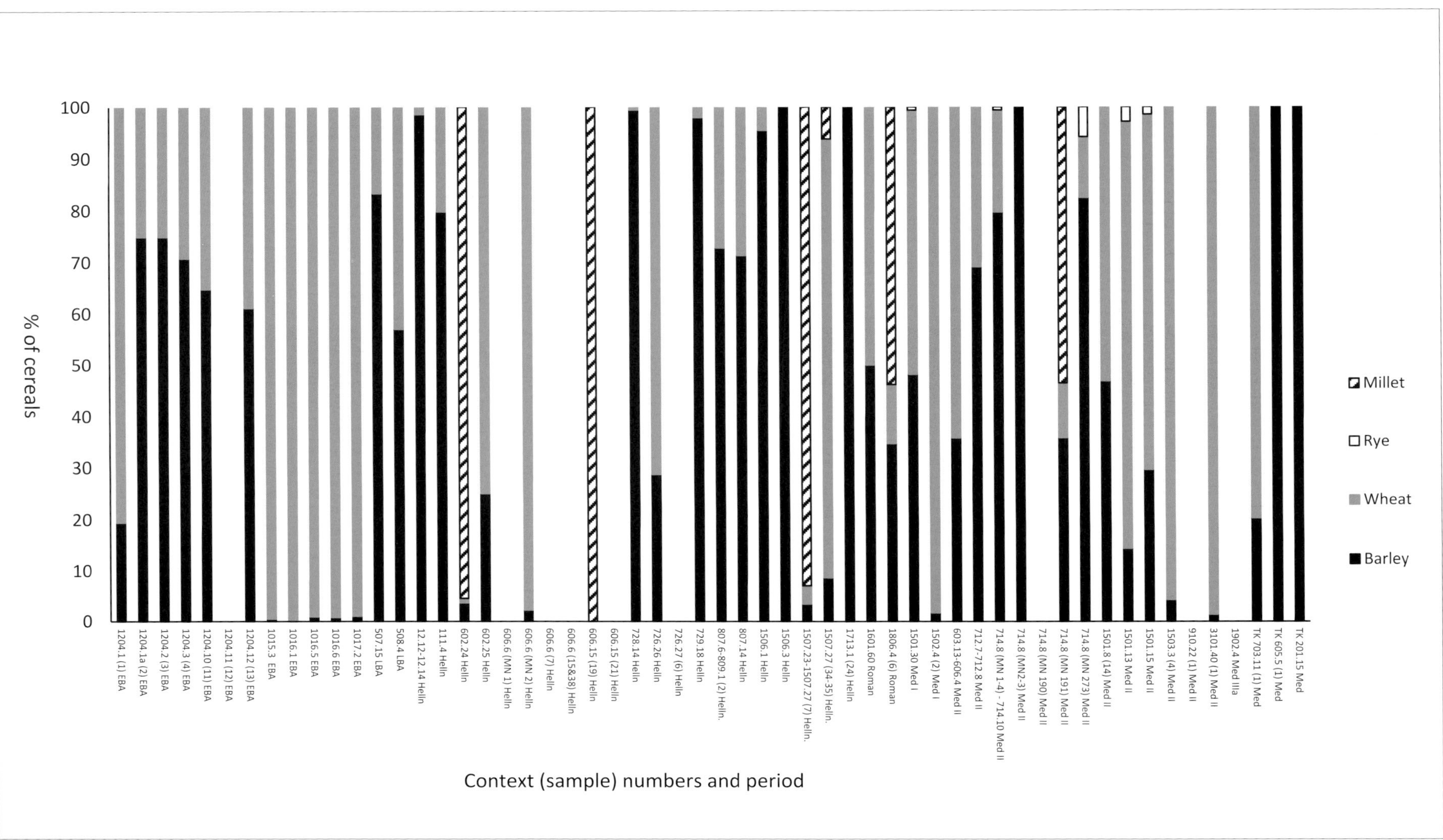

Fig. 81. Proportions of cereal grain species at Aşvan Kale and Taşkun Kale (all periods).

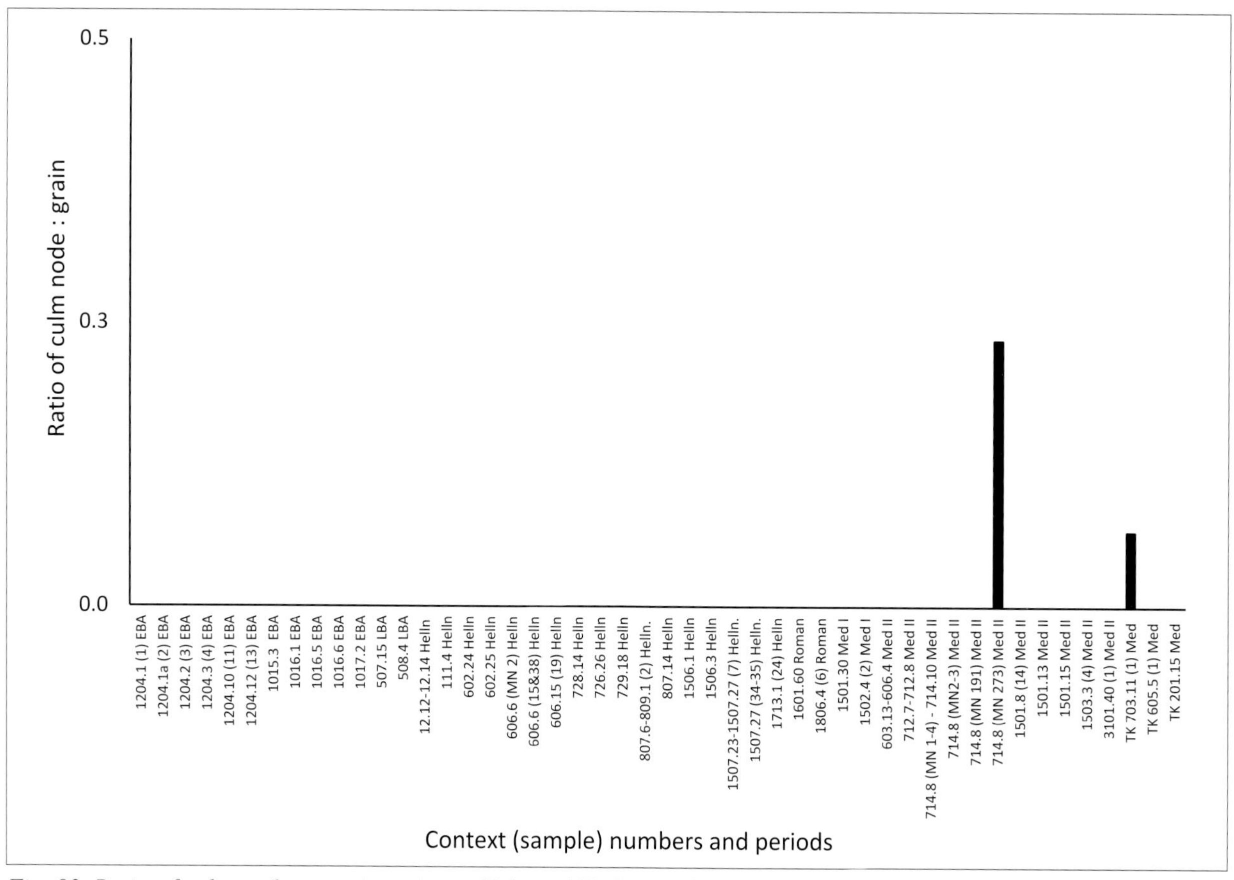

Fig. 82. Ratio of culm node to grain at Aşvan Kale and Taşkun Kale (all periods).

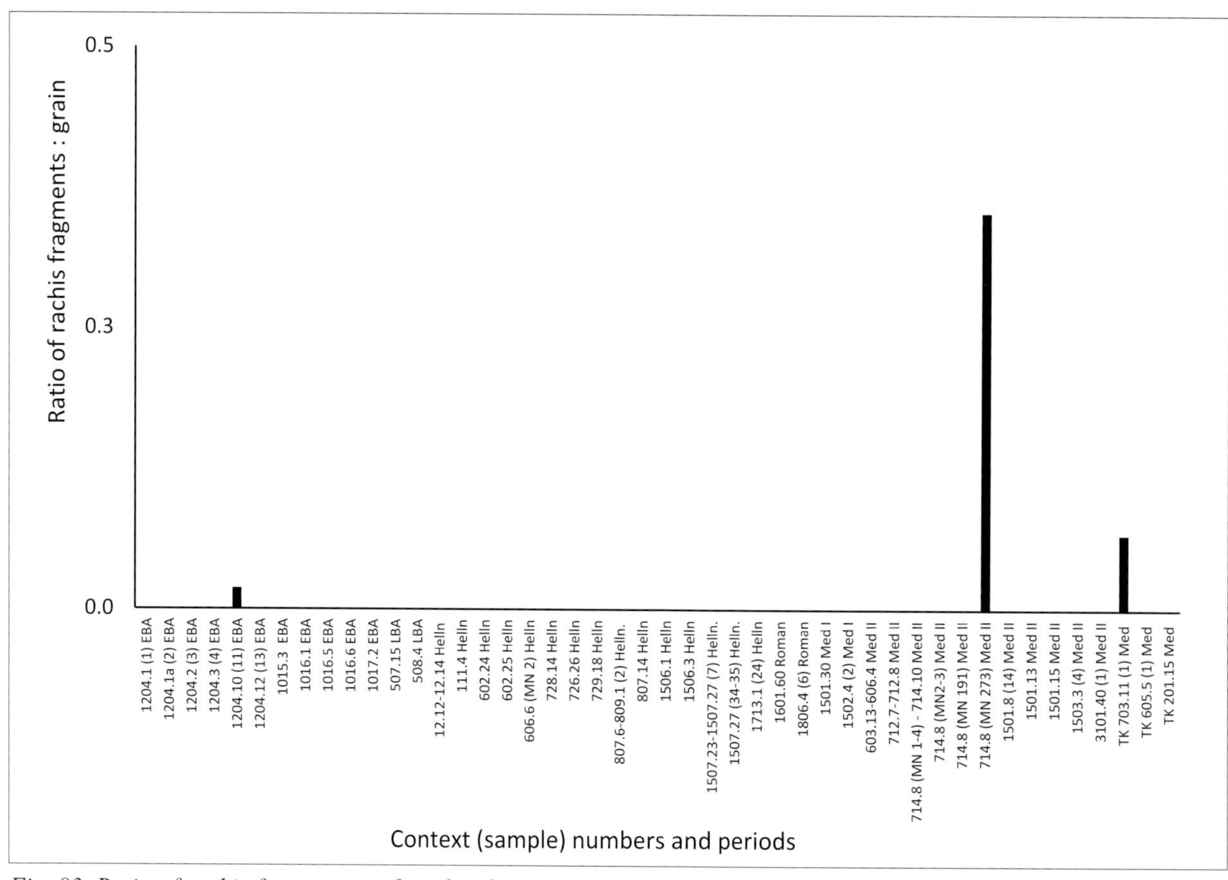

Fig. 83. Ratio of rachis fragments to free-threshing grain at Aşvan Kale and Taşkun Kale (all periods).

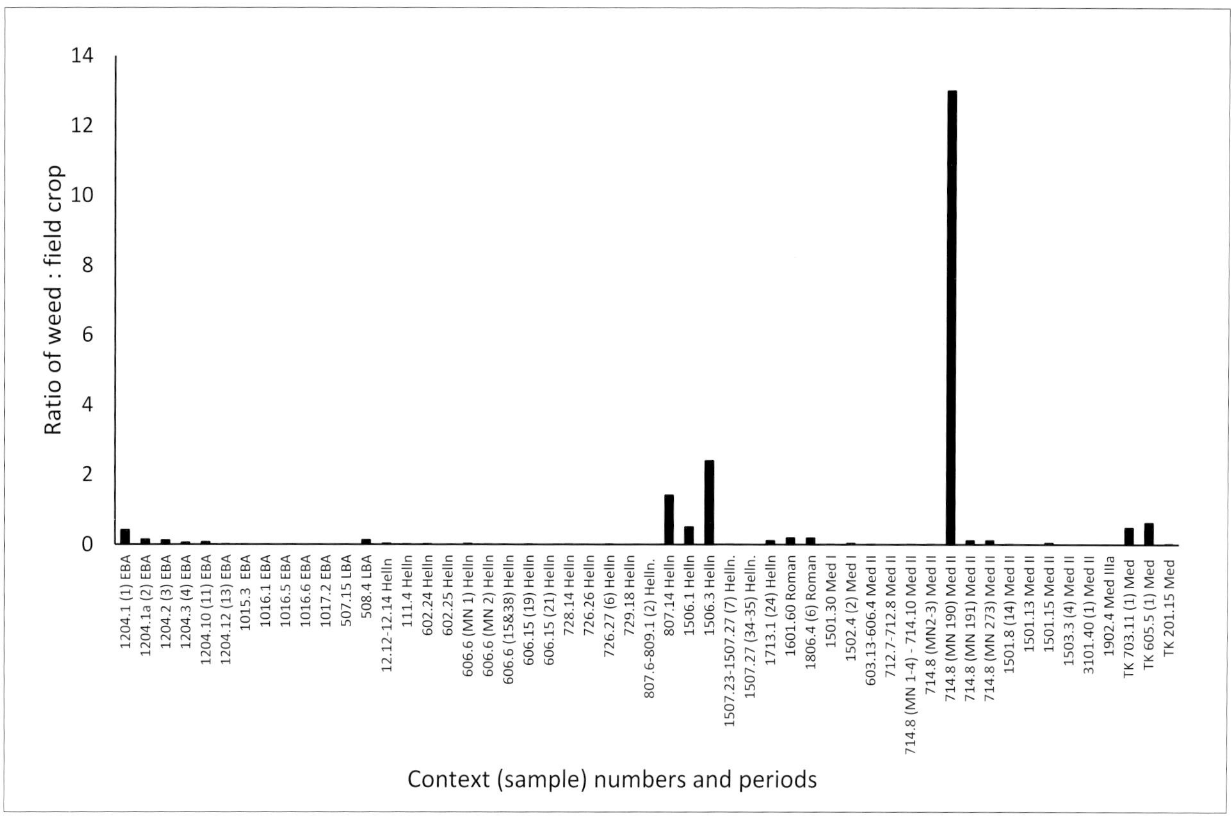

Fig. 84. Ratio of weed to field crop at Aşvan Kale and Taşkun Kale (all periods).

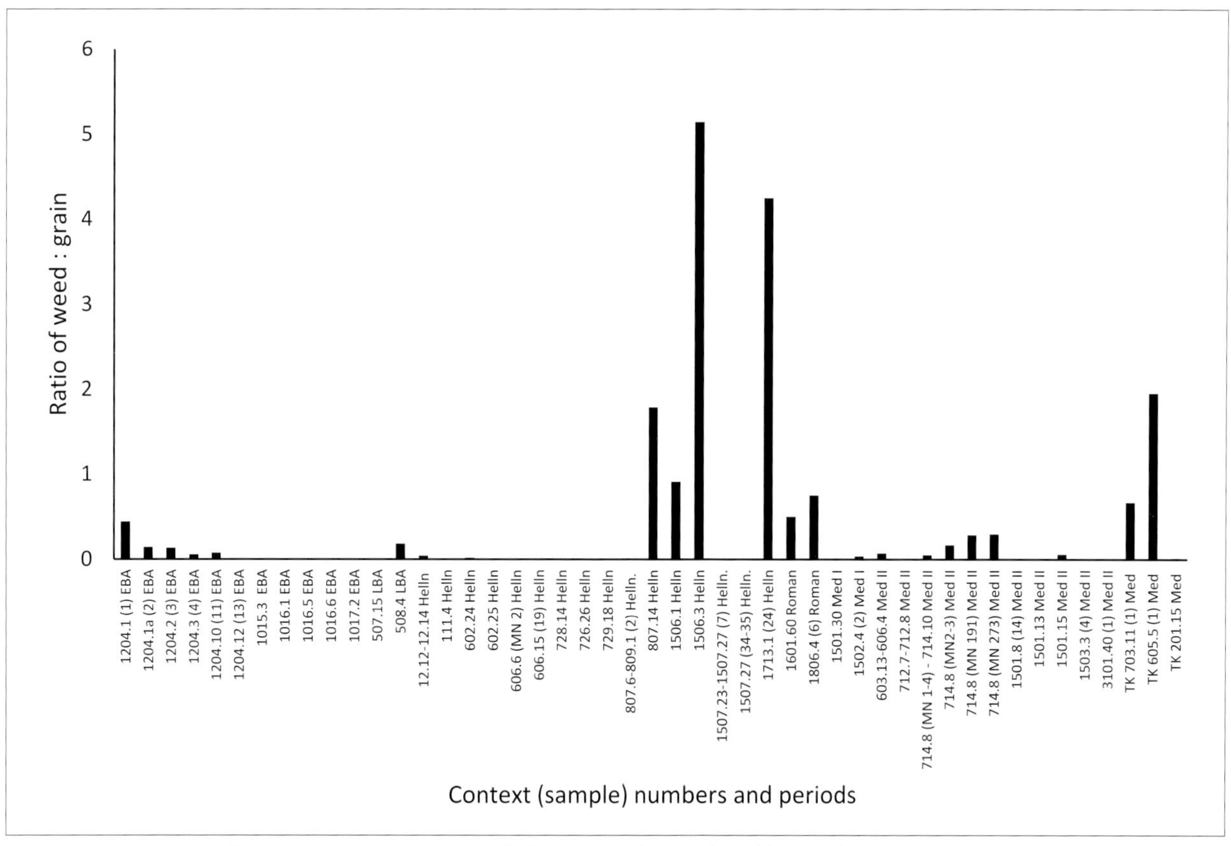

Fig. 85. Ratio of weed to cereal grain at Aşvan Kale and Taşkun Kale (all periods).

Hellenistic. Sample 606.6 (15–38) (combined) and 606.15 (21) has no cereals, chaff or weeds present. Sample 606.6 (15–38) is pure *Cicer arietinum*, while 606.15 (21) has ten fragments of *Amygdalus communis*.

The other samples can be divided into three groups: grain-rich, weed-rich and two samples that are half grain/weed. Sample 1507.23–27 (combined) contains nine pieces of *Hordeum vulgare* rachis, but, since there is a large number of grains, this calculates to a <0.0% chaff proportion relative to the grain and weeds. The rest of the samples have no chaff.

The majority of samples are grain-rich, with proportions of grain between 97.3 and 100%. However, the proportion of cereal species is variable (fig. 81). Three samples have high proportions of millet (606.24 is 95.4% millet with some barley and a little wheat; 1507.23–27 (combined) is 93% millet with some barley and little wheat; while 606.15 is all millet). The rest of the samples are either barley or wheat dominated (71.4–99.5%) with millet only present in one context. There is no rye (fig. 81). As millet is harvested later in summer than wheat and barley, the admixtures suggest either post-harvest mixing or post-depositional contamination (Nesbitt, Summers 1988). Of the 21 Hellenistic samples, only three show the presence of mixing between harvest seasons, a relatively rare occurrence. In these few contexts the admixed cereal(s) are found only in small proportions. Given the nature of the formation process (a destruction event), it seems probable that these admixed cereals represent contamination as a result of contingent background circumstances rather than deliberate intentional mixing. This could be cereal waste that was mixed through processes such as the collapse of storage containers onto fill deposits or floors, or the mixing of storage containers in the same room, as suggested for samples 1507.27 (34–35) and 1507.23–27.

The weed proportions in the grain-rich samples are between 0 and 2.7%, resulting in weed to field crop and weed to cereal ratios of 0–0.03 (figs 84 and 85). Only one weed species is shared across the samples and this could not be assigned. The other weeds are a mix of small free and heavy, and large free and heavy, or unassigned. Based on the grain-rich nature of the samples, the lack of chaff, which suggests a lack of early processing waste, the low proportions of weeds and the late-stage characteristics these samples are best interpreted as stored products. The majority of samples had low field crop to cereal values (below 0.17) suggesting that they include small amounts of general waste in addition to the charred product. The mix of cereal product and field crop might also be cooking waste. However, two samples stand out. Sample 602.25 has a value of 14.5 because of a large number of *Vicia ervilia* seeds (with no other field crops present). A hanging bag containing *Vicia* product might have been charred and fallen during the destruction and consequently incorporated in the destroyed floor debris. The large number of *Nigella* seeds from 606.15 (19), which create a value of 16.61 field crops to cereal, can also be explained as a stored batch of this seed which was incorporated into the assemblage alongside the cereal product during the destruction event.

The weed-rich Hellenistic samples are 606.6 (MN1), 726.27 (6), 1713.1 (24) and 1506.3. Two of these samples do not have any grains in them and the other two (1506.3 and 1713.1 (24)) have 16.3% and 19% respectively; in both cases only barley (fig. 81). In the two samples without grains, 606.6 (MN1) and 726.27 (6), the weed to field crop proportions are low (fig. 84). The latter sample has a very large quantity of flax compared with only ten Poaceae seeds. Sample 606.6 (MN 1) is a near pure sample of chickpea accompanied by a few weeds, which could not be assessed for their size, aerodynamic or weight properties. In sample 1506.3, 83.7% of weeds had a weed to field crop value of 2.4 and a weed to cereal value of 5.14. This sample was probably a crop-processing by-product or formed of cooking waste/refuse. There are three small free and heavy weeds, one large free and heavy weed, and two unassigned. The sample has a relatively high proportion of mixed species field crops to cereals value (1.14), suggesting that some general waste was incorporated into the assemblage. Sample 1713.1 (24) is 81% weeds, with a weed to field crop value of 0.11, but a weed to cereal value of 4.25, based on a small number of grains. The weeds are three species of small free and heavy, with one large free and heavy type, and three unassigned. This may be a by-product of later-stage processing, mixed with a large quantity of another field crop (*Vicia ervilia*), which generated a very high value of field crop to cereal (38.50) for this sample. Unlike the grain-free samples, this is not a 'pure' cache, as lentils, peas and grape were also found, suggesting some general waste was incorporated into the assemblage along with the crop-processing waste.

The two final samples are roughly half-grain, half-weed. Sample 1506.1 is 52.4% grain, of which 95.5% is barley and the rest is wheat. The weed proportion (47.6%) gives a weed to field crop value of 0.5, but a weed to cereal value of 0.91, which is close to 1 and therefore could indicate that this sample is formed of processing by-product. Only five species of weed were noted, of which three are small free and heavy; the other two are unclassified. These may have been late-stage processing weeds. Some general waste is incorporated (field crop to cereal ratio of 0.82) in the form of peas, grapes and pistachio. Sample 807.14 has slightly higher weed proportions: 64.1% compared with 35.9% grain. The grain is 71.3% barley and 28.7% wheat. The value of weed to field crop is 1.41 and that of weed to cereal is 1.79, suggesting, again, that this sample is composed of processing waste with some general field crop waste incorporated, although not in a high value relative to the cereal waste (0.27). The weeds are dominated by *Galium*, along with one species of small free and heavy weed, two types of large free and heavy weeds, and four other unclassified weeds. The high number of *Galium* weeds might have been incorporated from another source, as for sample 1204.1 (1) of the Early Bronze Age. The high ratio of weed to crop, the inclusion of other field crops and the large number of one particular weed relative to the low numbers of the other weed types suggest that this sample is a mix of product, general waste and crop-processing by-product. The absence of chaff and the presence of weeds associated with fine sieving and hand-sorting is appropriate for late-stage processing. The mix of cereal product and field crops could also indicate cooking waste.

Roman. The two Roman samples, 1601.6 and 1806.4, are similar to one another in that they have roughly even proportions of grain and weed, without chaff present. In the case of 1601.6 the density of material is generally low. Sample 1806.4 is more diverse both in crop (cereal and field crops) and weeds. The cereal proportion is 57.1%, of which 34.6% is barley, 11.5% wheat and 53.8% millet (fig. 81). As for the Hellenistic samples, this mixing of millet and wheat and barley must have occurred post-harvest. The sample came from a fill, a generic build of material, and therefore the mixing could have been deliberate or accidental, part of storage, cooking or refuse deposition. The weeds (42.9%) have a value in relation to field crops of 0.18 and to cereals of 0.75 (figs 84 and 85). This is below 1, and could therefore suggest that these were primary products, but is higher than most other samples (for example the majority of Hellenistic samples) and it might be argued that the sample includes some processing by-product. The weeds are mainly small free and heavy, with two unclassified. The mixing of cereals and a large number of *Vitis* seeds via a separate route (ratio 3.10) is similar to the Hellenistic sample 807.14. It can therefore be best interpreted as a primary product mixed with general refuse or cooking waste mixed with crop-processing by-product.

Medieval (including Taşkun Kale). Two of the Medieval samples from Aşvan Kale have no cereal elements: 910.22 (1) and 1902.4; 910.22 (1) also contains no field crops. Sample 1902.4 is a sample of cotton seeds associated with 1,200g of charcoal, without weeds, suggesting a clean, stored product.

Except for one weed-rich sample – 714.8 (MN 190) – all the samples are grain-rich. Two are less dominated by either weeds or grain – 714.8 (MN 191) and TK 605.5 (1) – and two are chaff-rich: 714.8 (MN 273) and TK 703.11 (1).

The grain-rich samples contain 85.7–100% grain. These are mainly either wheat or barley dominant, with a couple that are half/half, some accompanied by a little rye (fig. 81). The weed proportions vary between 0 and 6.7%, providing weed to field crop values of 0–0.3 and weed to cereal value of 0–0.17 (figs 84 and 85), suggesting that these samples represent product rather than by-product. The few weeds in the samples are from later processing stages (appendix 1). The majority of samples have low proportions of field crops (with values in relation to cereals of up to 0.4), suggesting some waste product inclusion or that these samples represent mixed cooking accidents with a bias towards cereals, as may be seen in many of the samples from the Aşvan sites across all periods. Three samples have large inclusions of *Vicia ervilia* – 603.13–606.4, 714.8 (MN1–4), 714.8 (MN2–3) – which could suggest that are cached product which entered the assemblage through different routes. Sample 1501.30 has large numbers of both *Vitis vinifera* and *Celtis*. This mixture of species may indicate the presence of multiple products from several routes or be the result of cooking accidents incorporated into fills alongside clean cereal product. Sample 712.7–8 (combined) also stands out as unusual as it has no field crops, chaff or weeds, only grain. This suggests a completely clean cereal product. However, these two samples, combined, were hand-sorted, and this may account for the lack of small elements like chaff and weeds. The pithos, TK 201.15, contained an almost pure barley sample, with chaff component, and only minor admixtures of a single lentil and grape pip, which are interpreted as contamination post-deposition, and a small number of *Galium* and indeterminate weeds, the remnants of crop processing. This almost completely clean barley sample can be interpreted as a cleaned, stored product in an intact, in situ context.

The two samples with both grain and weeds –714.8 (MN 191) and TK 605.5 (1) – have different assemblages. While 714.8 (MN 191) is made up of millet and barley with a little wheat, TK 605.5 (1) is all barley. The weeds are also different: TK 605.5 (1) has a diverse range while 714.8 (MN 191) has only *Galium*. The presence of a single weed species could imply that this came from another source. Both samples contain other crops, including a range of pulses. TK 605.5 (1) is interpreted as either cooking waste or the charring of a pure barley product mixed with general refuse. Sample 714.8 (MN 191) is interpreted as refuse disposal from multiple sources.

The two samples containing chaff are, as pointed out at the start of this section, unusual for this period and site. 714.8 (MN 273) came from a pit which contained several other samples explored above while TK 703.11 (1) came from a *tandir*. Sample 714.8 (MN 273) is a very small sample and is 53.1% grain, mainly barley with wheat and a little rye (fig. 81). The chaff proportion is formed of four pieces of culm, creating a value of 0.235, and from six rachis pieces giving a value of 0.35, both of which may not be a result of early-stage processing on site but may have been derived from another source: from contemporary contamination, from passing through the processing stages or from the mixture of processing waste with a clean product. The 15.6% weed proportion gives a weed to field crop value of 0.11 and a weed to cereal value of 0.29, again suggesting a clean product mixed with small amounts of processing waste. One of the weed species is small free and heavy, and one is unassigned. This sample also contains field crops in a value in relation to cereals of 1.65, suggesting that this sample represents general waste such as cooking debris.

The majority of samples from the Medieval period, therefore, seem to be derived from primary products or cooking accidents, with a couple of samples representing products mixed with other waste and processing by-products.

4.3.3.3. Dung fuel. As at the other two sites, no dung was noted in the samples from Aşvan Kale or Taşkun Kale for any period. On-site conditions, as observed by the excavators, were not favourable for the preservation of dung in any recognisable form, and we assume that both raw dung as well as dung cakes would have disintegrated rapidly and been absorbed into the surrounding soil matrix. The ratio of seed weight to charcoal weight (g) is shown in figure 86; figure 87 presents the ratio of weed seed numbers to charcoal weight (g); and the palatability of weeds is detailed in figure 88.

Little or no charcoal was collected from the majority of samples at Aşvan Kale and Taşkun Kale. The charcoal to seed ratios that are detailed in figure 86 relate to floated samples from Early Bronze Age levels (1015.3, 1016.1, 1016.6, 1017.20) and to one of the Hellenistic samples (728.14) with a few seeds and charcoal fragments,which was hand-sorted. The other seed to charcoal ratios of the samples in figures 86 and 87 have not been calculated and we have interpreted them all as crop products (see section 4.3.3.2).

The proportions of weed seeds is very similar across all periods. All weeds potentially flowered or fruited at the time of harvest in July, and all except the low proportions of *Bolboschoenus glaucus* (in one sample) and variable proportions of *Stipa* (found in two samples), occurring in Early Bronze Age II/III levels, and *Setaria* (one sample), occurring in the Hellenistic period, were found in arable fields in the course of the Aşvan botanical surveys.

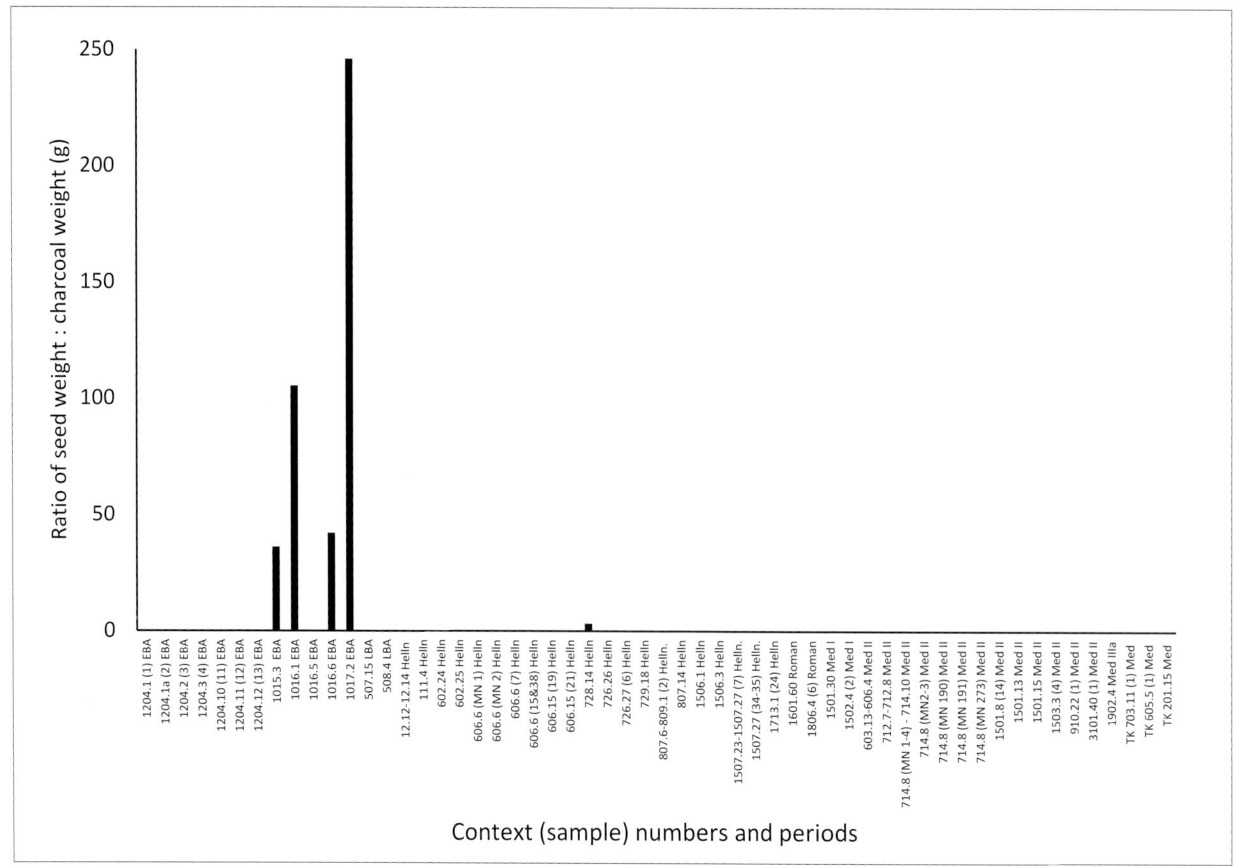

Fig. 86. Ratio of weight of seeds to weight of charcoal (g) at Aşvan Kale and Taşkun Kale (all periods).

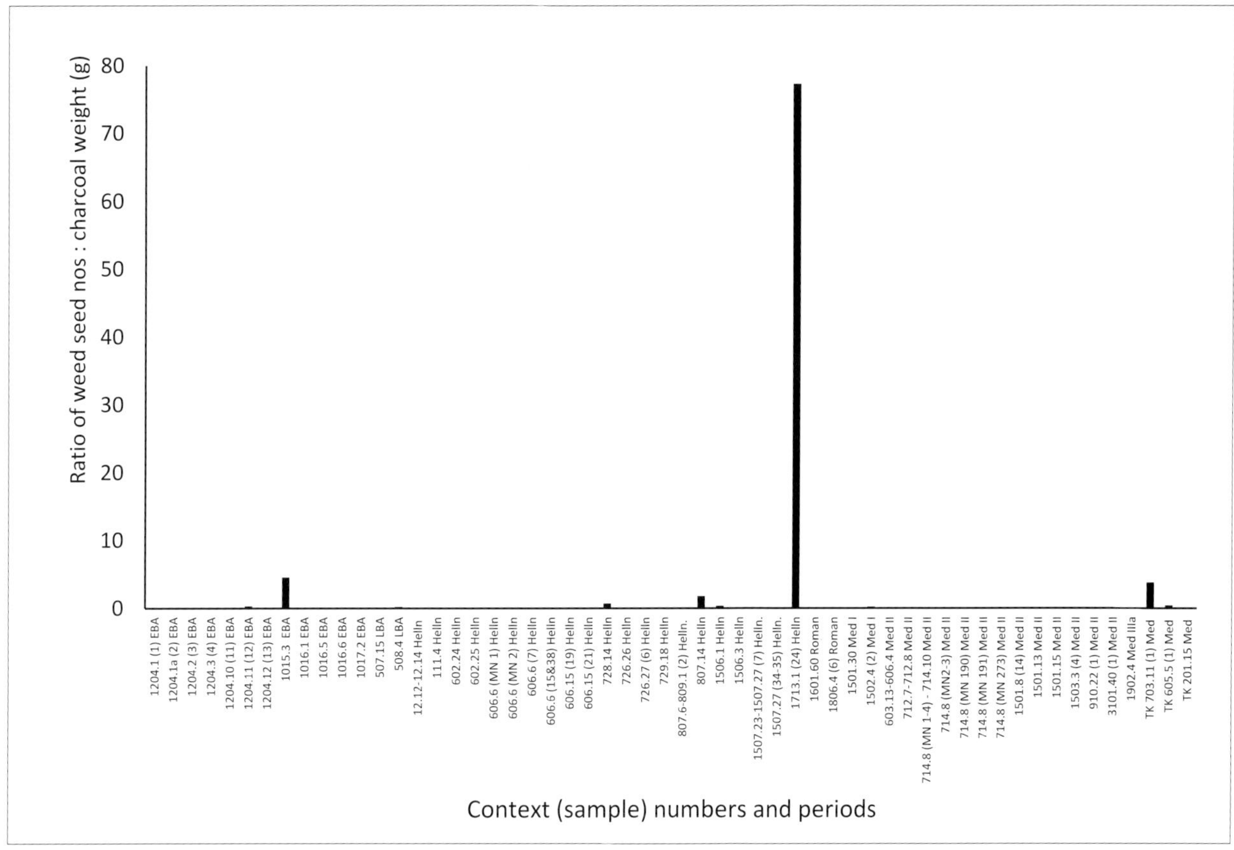

Fig. 87. Ratio of number of weed seeds to the weight of charcoal (g) at Aşvan Kale and Taşkun Kale (all periods).

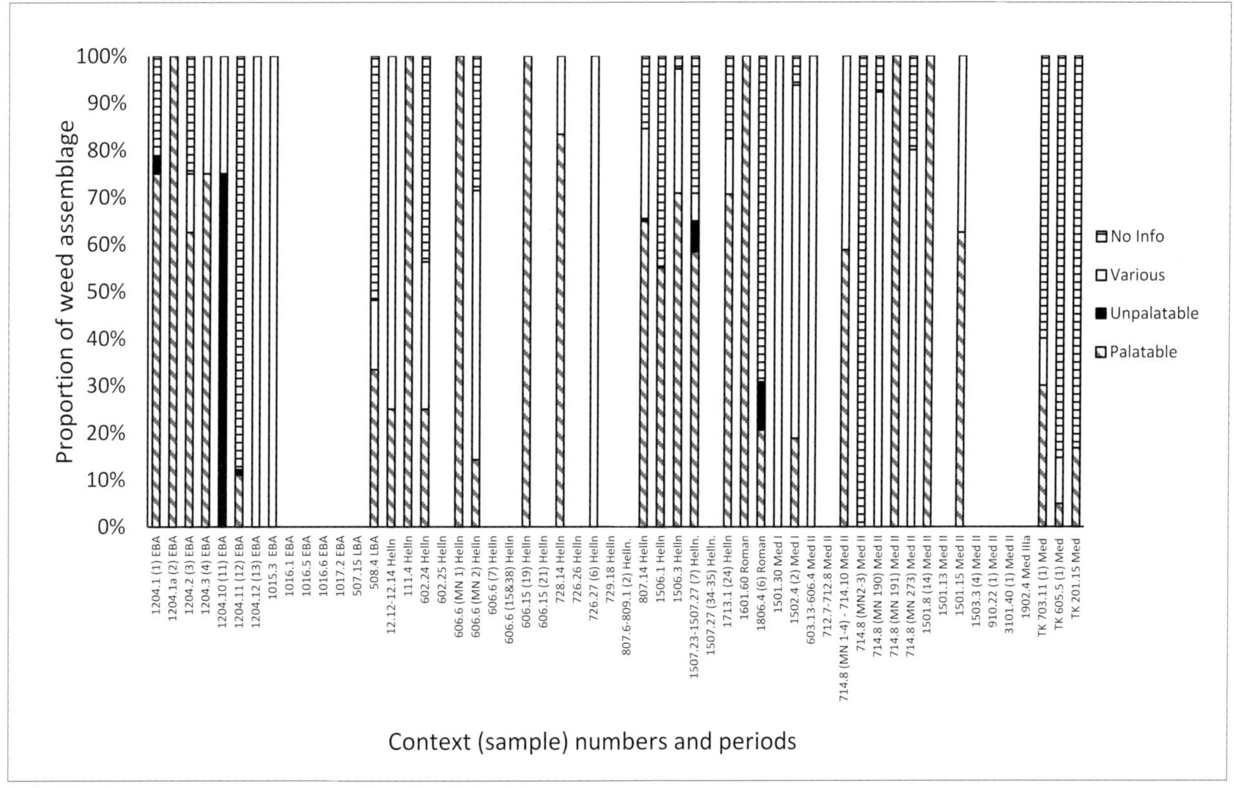

Fig. 88. Proportion of weeds based on palatability to animals at Aşvan Kale and Taşkun Kale (all periods).

Bolboschoenus glaucus grows in wet places such as riversides, wadis and swampy areas, *Stipa* grows on rocky slopes and *Setaria* was found in village gardens, rocky outcrops, ditches, irrigation canals, waste ground and wet areas like wadis, riverside banks and above the floodplain in the botanical surveys. The majority of samples containing weeds which could be rated for palatability (fig. 88) are interpreted as species commonly consumed by animals as fodder or whilst grazing (Townsend, Guest 1966–1985). There is, therefore, no evidence to suggest that dung fuel was not present at the sites, but no positive evidence for it.

Most of the samples found outside the Hellenistic destruction levels have been interpreted for all periods as cooking waste or as part of a crop-processing process. Dung fuel could account for the weeds in cooking waste assemblages, if the ashes were scraped into the fill along with the cooking waste. For the Hellenistic period the majority of samples are related to the destruction level and represent a wider range of activities, including product storage. It is unlikely that these included dung fuel, which was normally stored outside the house.

4.3.3.4. Site-formation processes: Early Bronze Age and Late Bronze Age. The samples from mudbrick debris in the small exploratory trenches at the edge of the Aşvan mound were mainly crop-rich samples that can be classified as products. The presence of the occasional grape pip and pulses suggests these samples may have originated through regular but low-level casual hearth cleaning or cooking activities. Weed content is well below that at Çayboyu, suggesting that these plant remains do not result from the regular burning of crop by-products. One sample – 1204.11 – may be the result of a different kind of deposition event, such as waste from crop processing.

Hellenistic. The late Hellenistic level at Aşvan Kale was not only well defined in terms of its architecture and functionality, but also presented a better condition of material preservation than any other part of the Aşvan sites. It is useful to restate the main information about this context to aid the interpretation of the botanical remains.

> On the top of Aşvan Kale there was a building complex of the late Hellenistic period, second to first centuries BC, which had been destroyed by fire, precisely, to judge by the dating of the coins of the Aşvan hoard, in 66 BC. Finds included a rich assortment of fine and coarse pottery, bronze vessels (a bowl, part of a water pitcher, scale pans, and the hinges of a wooden chest), and a wooden loom, apart from the 48 coins of the hoard and three more silver drachms which may have been the contents of a purse. A two-storey range of rooms, three of which included clay bread ovens or cooking stoves, ran along the north side, and served as the main living quarters for the inhabitants. A single-storey annexe of two rooms, probably designed to house animals or for storage, projected to make an L-shape beside an open courtyard. This was the house of a well-off local family, occupying the top of the mound which would have inevitably been the focus of a village settlement (Mitchell 1998: 92–93).

The Hellenistic burnt level, from this house, produced the kind of samples that might be expected: pure deposits, usually of one crop or of several crops that might have been cultivated and harvested during a single season. Some samples definitely result from a mixing of in situ deposits during burning or during excavation, and some samples that were floated incorporate material from the general soil matrix.

Two of the samples (1506.1 and 1506.3) have a notably different composition. It is possible that these are the remains of mixed refuse that may have been kept ready to be thrown on a fire. However, it is perhaps more likely that these derive from general refuse in the large volume of soil matrix that was floated for these samples.

An odd feature of the in situ material is the small size of the samples. Usually burnt domestic areas yield bins or pots full of burnt stores. These samples appear not to be associated with any containers; if they were stored in bags this might partly explain why only a little material survived the fire. Stores, however, might have been low at the time of the destruction, especially if the inhabitants were besieged there for several days. Alternatively, foodstuffs may have been stored on a larger scale elsewhere on the site.

Roman. The one Roman sample large enough to be really useful (1806.4) is from a pit and is (in contrast to the Medieval 714.8) very diverse and typical of general refuse disposal. The small number of samples recovered is not surprising, as the architectural context has been interpreted as a religious structure not domestic housing (Mitchell 1980: 41–45; 1998: 93). Although the paving levels of the courtyard outside the main structure produced large quantities of broken animal bone, perhaps from ritual or festive meals and sacrifices, there was little sign of carbonised botanical residues.

Medieval I. The two Medieval samples, from a pit and from fill, show once again that such refuse-type samples from Aşvan Kale are less diverse and less weedy than might be expected. Sample 1502.4 is a more-or-less pure sample of free-threshing wheat, although it also contains a lot of wood charcoal; 1501.30 is made up of wheat and barley grain, grape pips and hackberries. Very few weed seeds are present. It is unlikely that the grain, hackberry and grape were deposited as a single by-product or via the accidental charring of a product. The hackberry and grape pips were probably discarded as refuse; the grain as the result of accidental charring. In each case the lack of diversity in the sample argues for a food consumption/preparation event, as slower accumulation of refuse would have led to greater diversity in the samples.

Medieval II. 'The top of the mound [at Aşvan Kale] contained a large building divided into five chambers, which were identified as workshops, a cistern, a mass of pits and three identifiable pottery kilns used for the production of glazed pottery' (Mitchell 1998: 94; cf. Mitchell 1980: 49–53). The Medieval II samples mainly come from refuse pits inside workshops and close to the pottery kilns. The pits and fill mainly contain pure, product-type assemblages of crop seeds or pure samples of refuse such as hackberries or grape pips. As in the Medieval I samples, most appear to originate from rapid, possibly one-off deposition events. This is reflected in the fact that most samples were sufficiently concentrated as to be visible to excavators and were hand collected. The same applies to the *tandir* (oven), which contained 350 grains of barley and wheat and abundant charcoal, but little else. When a deposit of unmilled but carbonised wheat and barley grains is found in or next to a *tandir*, in an area of workshops etc., a rational explanation would be that this grain had been intended for making a sort of gruel or porridge, but was destroyed in a cooking accident. Porridge of this type was a regularly feature of the rural diet in western Turkey in the Roman period, and was doubtless much more widespread than the written sources suggest (Mitchell 2015: 290). A hint as to other processes that may have led to the deposition of isolated deposits of plant remains is the occurrence of an oak gall in one of the Medieval pits (3101.24), identical to those found in the Hellenistic burnt area (see chapter 3.8.5).

Sample 703.11 at Taşkun Kale is a *tandir* fill, found in the rooms to the west of the church, and sample 605.5 is from a pit in Room 33 of the fort. Both samples are diverse in content, and are probably examples of routine rubbish disposal. Sample 201.15 is from a pithos in Room 8, and, unsurprisingly, holds a pure sample of barley as well as wood charcoal.

4.4. Comparison of the four sites

In making comparisons between the sites it is essential to take account of the variation in collection strategies. Sixteen out of the 20 contexts from the very limited excavation at Çayboyu were collected by flotation. In contrast, only a third of the Aşvan Kale samples (21 out of 62 uncombined contexts, see section 4.3.3.1) were floated. This provides one explanation for the larger numbers of weeds that were noted at Çayboyu. The differential methods of collection affect the interpretation of all the assemblages.

It is nevertheless clear that a variety of sample formation processes shaped the archaeobotanical assemblages of the four sites, and also accounts for differences within the sites themselves. Çayboyu represents two kinds of activities: rapid deposition that may have resulted from repeated site destruction by catastrophic fires, as shown by the seed layer, and repetitive domestic refuse disposal activities, such as oven cleaning, which occurred in the upper and lower phases. Taşkun Mevkii on the whole shows an assemblage which reflects product storage, with some evidence for cooking waste and crop processing, or for the use of dung fuel. The burning of stored products could relate to the widespread burnt level of phase 3 at the site. Apart from the Hellenistic destruction layers at Aşvan, which present a snap-shot of domestic activities in situ, the assemblages from Aşvan Kale and Taşkun Kale tend in general to be related to cooking waste and the storage of discrete products in modest quantities.

5. Plant husbandry and use

5.1. Introduction

Having explored the pathways to preservation in the previous chapter, there are several questions that can be asked of the archaeobotanical dataset at Aşvan. One way to approach this would be to establish hypotheses and seek to demonstrate exactly how plants were used. This is a challenging objective as it relies on multiple linked assumptions about the way in which plants might have been exploited in the past. It would require detailed ethnographic observations on the full range of uses for each species, and an examination of how these potential uses affected their chances of preservation on an archaeological site. It was beyond the scope of the Aşvan project to carry out such a comprehensive archaeobotanical investigation, attempting to reconstruct every process that plants went through or every function for which a plant was gathered or produced. As a less ambitious objective, an important aim of this chapter is to consider which plants were potentially used as food, fuel, fodder, construction materials or were collected for other purposes, for instance to serve as drugs or medicines. It has also been an objective to explore changes in plant use over time, particularly the range of crops cultivated and their manner of cultivation. These questions can then be linked to bigger issues such as the intensity and centralisation of the settlement occupation, questions of productivity and reliability of production, changes in contact with other regions and other forms of farming like pastoralism. This chapter will explore the issues of plant husbandry and use over time with these broader issues in mind.

5.2. Approaches

5.2.1. Comparative quantification

The quantification of archaeobotanical remains is an essential step in the analysis of any assemblage. The nature of archaeobotanical assemblages, coming as they do from unevenly sized samples and a range of depositional and preservational conditions, necessitates standardisation to allow for comparisons to be made without biasing the data towards the larger or better-preserved samples in which the greater number of seeds are found (Miller 1988). By standardising the data, it becomes possible to compare assemblages and even individual samples with other archaeobotanical datasets, thus making inter-site and inter-project comparisons possible. However, there is no single methodology for the quantification of archaeobotanical remains (see papers in Hastorf, Popper 1988). Indeed, Deborah Pearsall (1989) and Virginia Popper (1988) have argued that quantification techniques must be chosen based on the nature of the materials analysed and the questions asked of them. In this research, three quantification methodologies were chosen.

Quantity. Comparing the quantities (also known as absolute counts) of different species in a sample or group of samples must obviously be undertaken with great caution (Popper 1988: 60). Samples may be of greatly differing size according to preservation conditions or sampling strategy. For example, a single sample that is rich in barley will skew the overall results in favour of that species. However, within a sample, careful comparison of the abundance of different species, expressed as either the absolute number or as a percentage, will lead to suggestions as to which of the crop components might have been consciously planted and which less common species might be inadvertent or tolerated contaminants. At phase or site level, however, quantity is a handy at-a-glance indicator of abundance but nothing more. Quantification of absolute counts of cereals has been carried out using grain rather than chaff, because counting chaff would have resulted in multiple counts for single items (cereal spikelets produce both grain and chaff) and because chaff for free-threshing cereals is more fragile and much rarer than that of hulled cereals.

Species dominance. Species dominance is most often used as a measure by archaeobotanists working with burnt stores which consist of relatively pure deposits of single species (Jones et al. 1986), but can also be applied to flotation samples. In principle, the more widely a plant is cultivated or harvested, the more likely it is that it will dominate a sample. One species can sometimes be identified in a sample as the intended component of a cultivated or gathered harvest. However, dominance of a species is most likely to occur in a relatively unmixed storage sample or as processing by-product; species dominance in very mixed samples, if it occurs, may be due to chance. More than one species may be present, as for example in the production of maslin crops, the risk-aversion strategy of planting more than one species together in a planned mixture (Van der Veen 1995), or where post-harvest mixing occurs during crop processing or storage. Additionally, this measure depends on a representative range of samples being found. If the number of samples is small, or from a limited area within a settlement, chance may lead to species being under- or over-represented. Nonetheless, species dominance represents a refinement over absolute quantity and is a measure that can be compared with ubiquity. Species dominance is not a useful measure for weeds since many weed species grow in most fields, while most crop fields are dominated by one or two crop taxa. Species dominance has been assessed in the simplest possible way, with the most abundant plant species (crop or useful wild plant) recorded. It was decided that a strategy of selecting two dominant species when two were especially abundant in a sample, would be too complex. Dominance has been calculated as the percentage of samples in which that species was the dominant species.

Ubiquity (presence analysis). This widely used measure is based on the number of samples in which a species occurs, expressed as a percentage of the total number of samples (Popper 1988: 60–64). As with species dominance, its usefulness depends on careful delimitation of samples, so that one sample represents one deposit. Its main weakness is that a markedly less abundant species that is more likely to be preserved, or which grows as a minor admixture in an important crop, may be as ubiquitous as a dominant crop. Einkorn wheat, an invariably minor component of emmer crops at Aşvan, is an example of the latter.

5.2.2. Defining plant uses

In this chapter plant species have been assigned to one of three categories: crops, useful wild plants and weeds. The distinction between these categories, which has been applied in the scoresheets and throughout this volume, is fundamental to the interpretation of the plant remains.

For this purpose, crops are here defined as cultivated, domesticated plants. This category includes both those plants deliberately tended and crop plants that were accidentally tended when they occurred as minor admixtures. The species that make up the Near Eastern crop complex are well-documented (Zohary et al. 2012). The only ambiguity at Aşvan concerns the possible oil crops *Lallemantia* sp. in the Early Bronze Age I and *Carthamus* spp. in the Hellenistic period. Particular attention was given to oil seeds as the argument has been made that a wider range of oilseeds was cultivated or gathered in the past and therefore these should not be overlooked (Jones, Valamoti 2005; Fairbairn et al. 2007). Only three *Carthamus* seeds were found and one of *Lallemantia* spp. was recovered in the Early Bronze Age I level at Taşkun Mevkii. In this study both have been classified as weeds.

Weeds are here defined as wild plants that were not deliberately collected and may have occurred as weeds of crop fields or as components of wild vegetation such as forage plants. These are two very different habitats, but as most of the wild plants found as Aşvan occur in both of them, it is not possible to make a clear distinction between crop weeds and other plants. In practice, as discussed in chapter 3, most of the wild plants which occur in the Aşvan samples are probably derived from field weeds.

The category of useful wild plants refers to those deliberately collected by people living at Aşvan, and comprises the wild fruits of hackberry (*Celtis* spp.), hawthorn (*Crataegus* spp.), terebinth (*Pistacia* spp.), wild plum (*Prunus* spp.), oak gall (*Quercus* spp.) and wild grape (*Vitis sylvestris*). Two factors define this group: ethnobotanical evidence for their use (except in the case of wild grape) and their habit as trees or climbers, which rules out their occurrence as field weeds in the sense defined above.

It is recognised that the application of these definitions runs the risk of obscuring the function of plants that are on the borders between definitions, for example 'weed' plants that are deliberately harvested for their seed. However, setting aside the wild tree fruits, current-day ethnobotanical evidence from the Near East shows that seed is very sparsely harvested from wild plants; rather, it is the leaves and roots that are most important. For example, Füsun Ertuğ's (2000) study of a village in central Anatolia found that over 300 species of wild plant were used, but, excluding the trees, there were very few cases of the seed or fruit being used. There is, of course, ethnographic evidence that seeds of non-woody plants have been used in Turkish agricultural communities, as in the case of oil extraction from field weeds such as *Cephalaria syriaca* (Yazıcıoğlu et al. 1978), and archaeobotanical evidence of harvesting of wild seeds, again for oil, at Çatalhöyük (Fairbairn et al. 2007). Nonetheless, this is uncommon, and positive evidence is required, for example in the form of unusual occurrence patterns such as caches, to show that the presence of non-woody plant seeds in the archaeobotanical record represents their use rather than their inclusion through other pathways such as crop processing or dung fuel.

This point is worth emphasising, as many plants, including many here classified as weeds, have recorded uses in the ethnobotanical record (Rivera Núñez et al. 2011a; 2011b). It is common practice among archaeobotanists to imply that all plants found at a site were used for all purposes for which there is an ethnographic record. However, the parts of the plant most commonly used as medicine or food were the leaves, and use usually involved the consumption of relatively small quantities, in a short time period. We are unlikely to find remains of such use in the archaeological record, which is of course strongly biased to material that survives in carbonised form after combustion. Furthermore, commonly used wild plants such as spring greens are young plants, without mature seed. An archaeobotanical find of a seed from one of these plants is thus not evidence that it had been used.

5.2.3. Explaining mixed samples

In some samples, mainly those derived from burnt storage areas such as the pithos from Taşkun Mevkii and a couple of pure samples from the Hellenistic kitchen at Aşvan Kale, a single crop or useful wild plant was found, a pure and isolated sample. Obviously these were grown or collected as one species and the status of these plants is straightforward – these were deliberately chosen as independent crops or useful wild plants.

The problem arises in mixed samples of crops which could have various explanations: (1) the deliberate cultivation of mixed species, maslin cropping, as has been observed in Greece (Jones, Halstead 1995); (2) a tolerated admixture or weed in a crop, such as rye in wheat (Hillman 1978); (3) deliberate mixing after harvest, for instance in cookery; (4) refuse disposal through human action, for instance hearth sweepings or cooking accidents; or (5) dispersal and mixing through site formation processes, including the movement, both natural and human, of soil matrix across the site. Two approaches help to disentangle these possible causes. One is to look at the ecology of the crops. Can they be grown together? Millet and wheat, for example, cannot grow together, and it is very doubtful whether barley and wheat would be grown together in this region. In cases where such admixtures are found, it is reasonable to assume that this occurred either as the outcome of deliberate post-harvest mixing or during refuse disposal. Another line of enquiry is then to examine the find context and to ask whether the mixtures occur in intact deposits or in disturbed and floated deposits? Intact deposits that are relatively pure can be explained through the usual processes of moving processed crops from the threshing floor to the storage or use areas. Weeds can be explained as originating from the field or as being introduced by post-harvest handling. Semi-intact samples found in close proximity to pure samples may indicate that mixing occurred during the destruction event that led to their preservation as a charred sample. Mixed samples without pure samples nearby, such as the Early Bronze Age grab samples containing no weed seeds and two cereals that are unlikely to have been grown together, are best explained by a similar process. The very mixed, very diverse samples that are typically found from flotation are very likely formed from multiple events.

5.3. Cereals

Late Chalcolithic

In the Çayboyu samples all three measures (quantity, dominance, ubiquity) point to hulled barley and emmer wheat as equally important species (fig. 89). Although emmer shows slightly higher values in these measures, the difference is trivial.

Barley is present in greater quantities in the earlier phase of Çayboyu; emmer is more abundant in the later phase. The weakness of ubiquity as a measure of importance is demonstrated by the case of einkorn wheat, present in 80% of Late Chalcolithic samples (n = 20), compared with emmer and hulled barley at 100%. This minor difference in ubiquity contrasts with the figures for abundance (proportion of the cereal assemblage): einkorn forms 4.8% of the cereal grain in this period, compared to over 36% each for emmer and hulled barley (fig. 90). A similar but less marked contrast

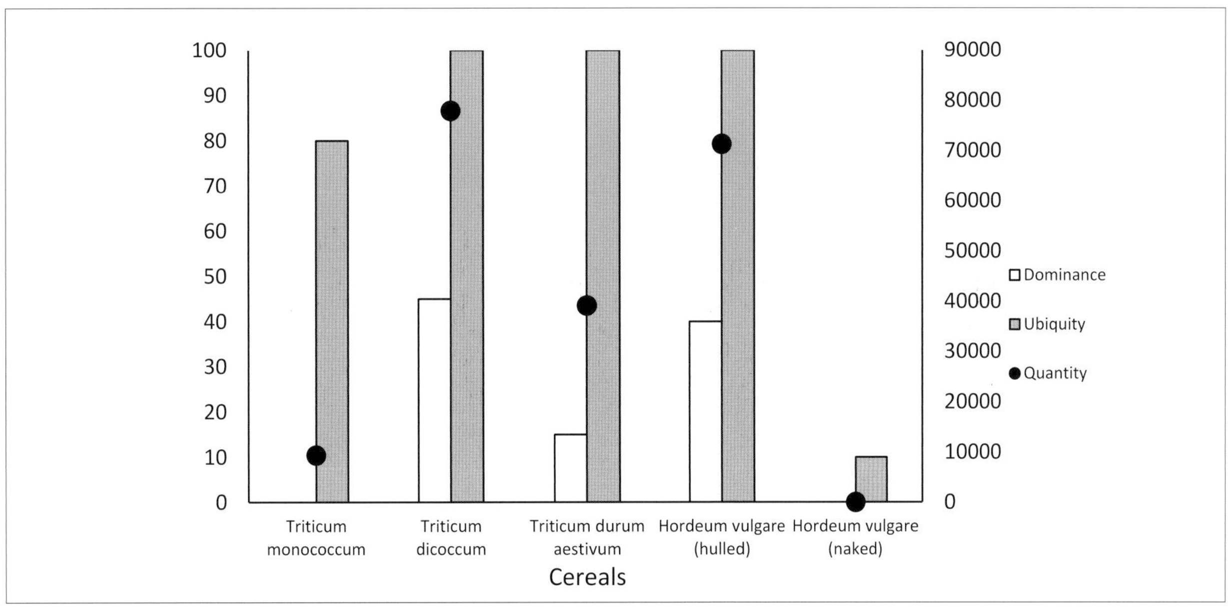

Fig. 89. Quantity, dominance and ubiquity of cereals at Çayboyu (whole site). The left axis shows the number of contexts containing species and also the relative dominance of species as a percentage of the contexts analysed (n = 20), while the right axis shows the number of seeds of each species for the quantity value.

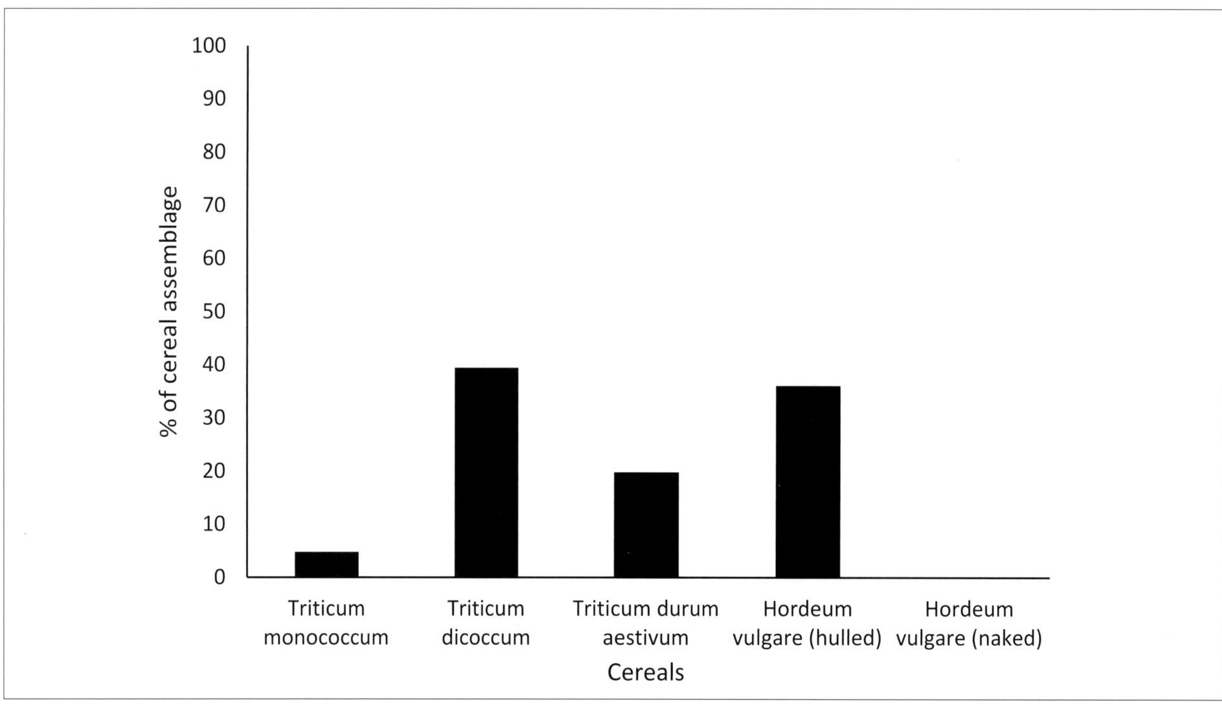

Fig. 90. Proportions of the cereal assemblage at Çayboyu.

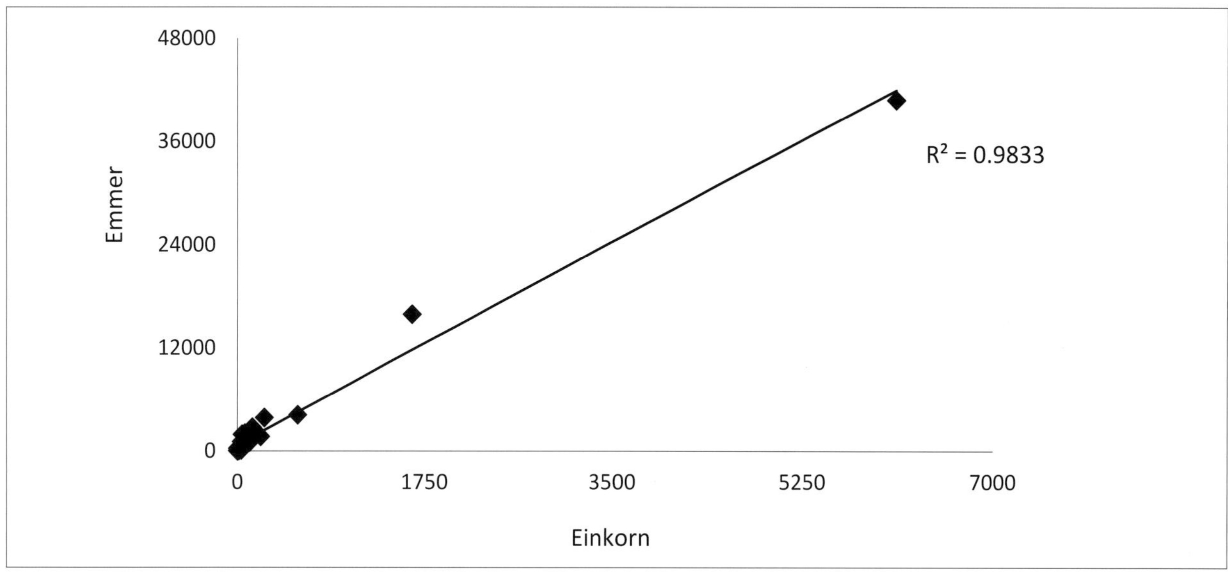

Fig. 91. Comparison of the quantity of emmer and einkorn wheat at Çayboyu with a linear regression line to determine the correlation.

arises for free-threshing wheat, which has a ubiquity of 100% and forms only 19.8% of the grain (fig. 90).

High ubiquity and low abundance could result if einkorn grew as a minor component of emmer; it would then be present in most samples containing emmer (high ubiquity), but at low abundance. This hypothesis has been tested by comparing the quantities of einkorn to those of emmer, barley and free-threshing wheat. Comparison of the three wheat species to each other resulted in R^2 values exceeding 0.98, evidence of a very close correlation (figs 91–93).

On the other hand, comparison of emmer and einkorn abundance to barley produced R^2 figures of 0.46 and 0.36 respectively (figs 94 and 95). These results suggest that einkorn, emmer and free-threshing wheat were cultivated together in fairly consistent proportions and that hulled barley was cultivated separately.

Considering the wheat element of the assemblages in more detail, free-threshing wheat dominates three samples (18, 23, 32), suggesting that it could be considered as a crop in its own right during this period. However, these three samples are part of the set of seven samples taken from the deepest part of the trench which contained very few wheat grains compared with samples from the top of the trench. The taphonomic analysis of chapter 4.3.1.2 suggests that these samples may not be representative of what was actually harvested and instead may be by-products of fine sieving. In the remaining samples, emmer dominates at 57–79% of the wheat grain component, with free-threshing wheat and some einkorn (absent in four samples) forming the rest of the wheat assemblage.

In summary, the Çayboyu samples may represent cereal production that was made up of about half hulled barley and half emmer wheat. Einkorn wheat was probably only cultivated as an admixture with emmer. The evidence for separate cultivation of free-threshing wheat is uncertain, although three samples suggest that it may have been a possibility. A few grains of naked barley are present, very likely a tolerated admixture of hulled barley.

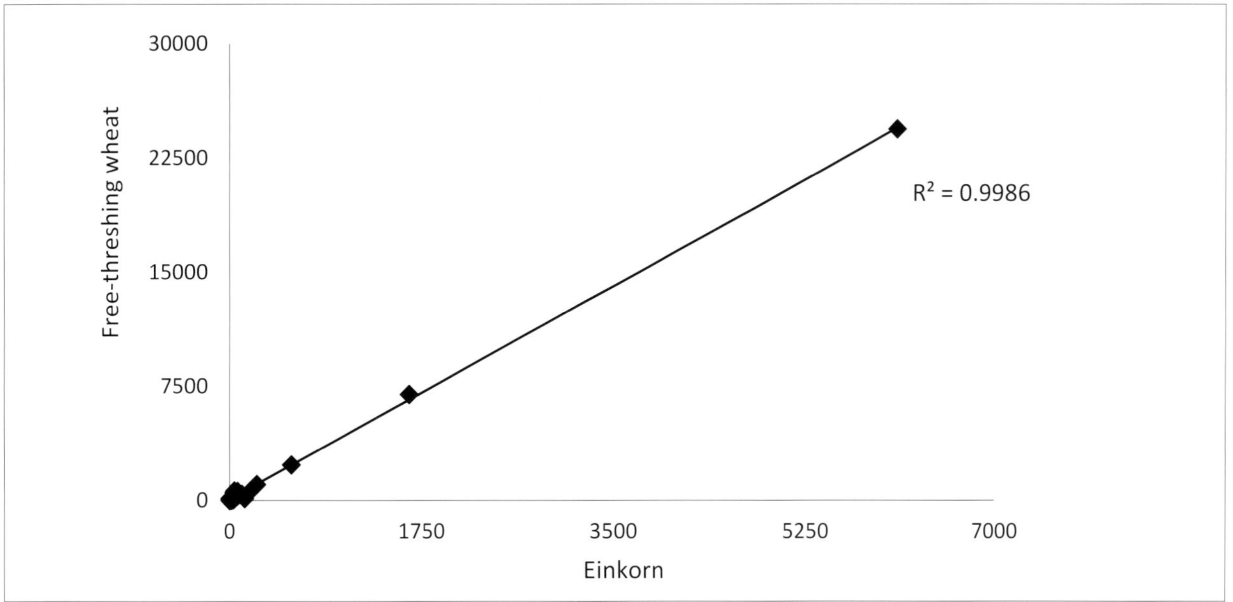

Fig. 92. Comparison of the quantity of free-threshing wheat and einkorn at Çayboyu with a linear regression line to determine the correlation.

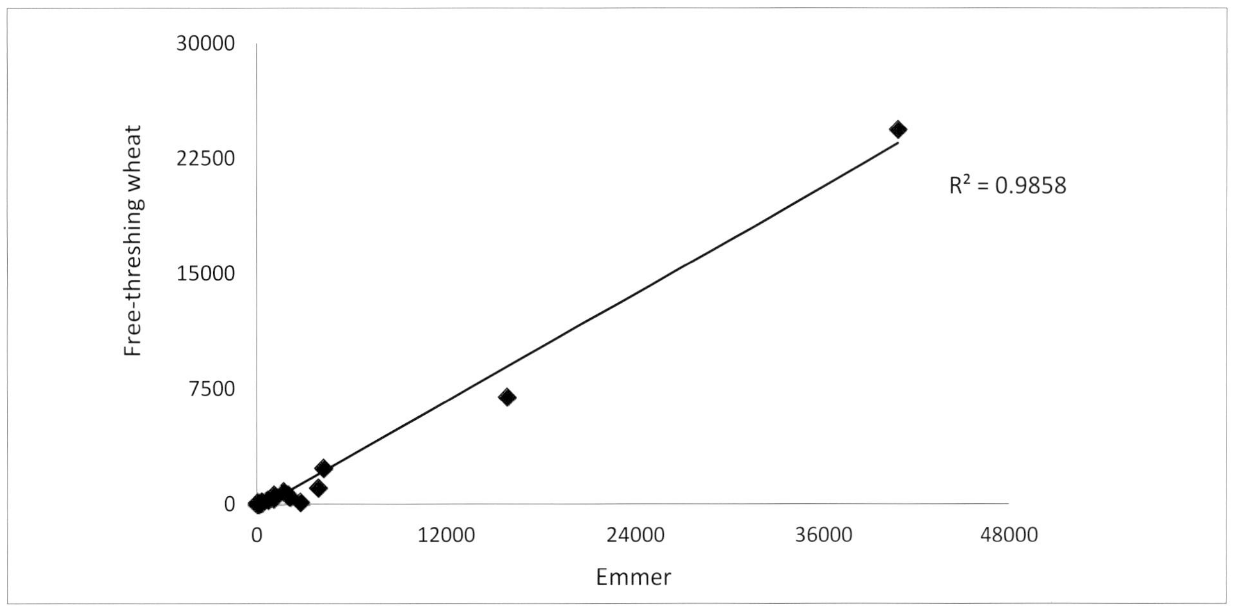

Fig. 93. Comparison of the quantity of free-threshing wheat and emmer at Çayboyu with a linear regression line to determine the correlation.

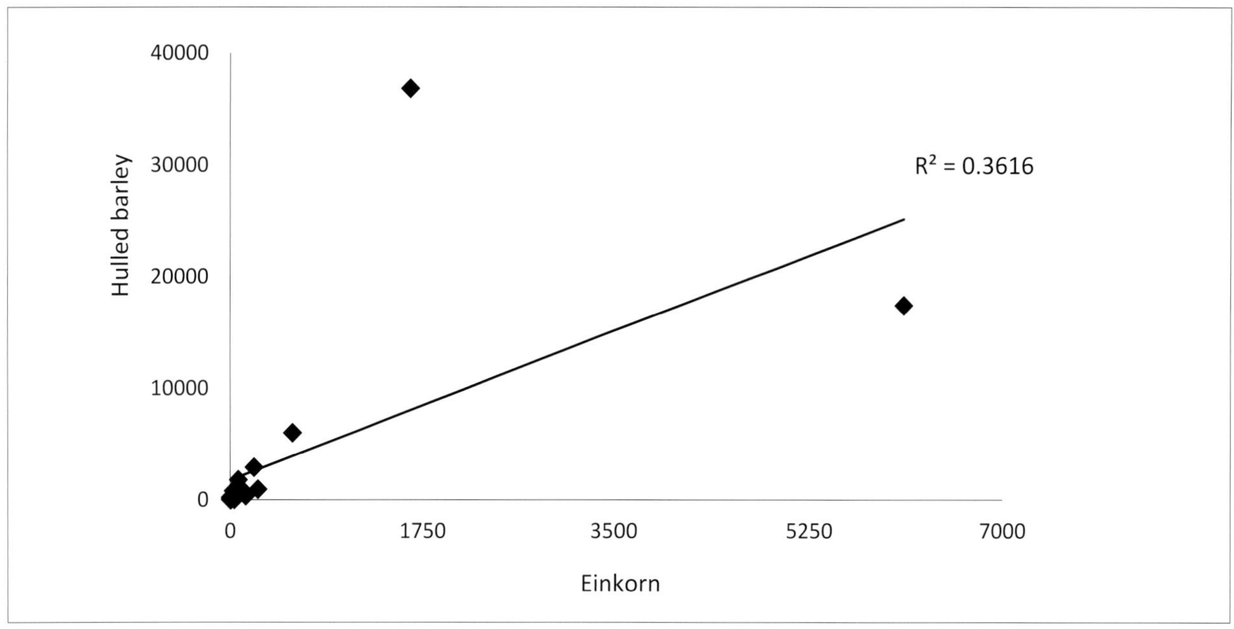

Fig. 94. Comparison of the quantity of hulled barley and einkorn at Çayboyu with a linear regression line to determine the correlation.

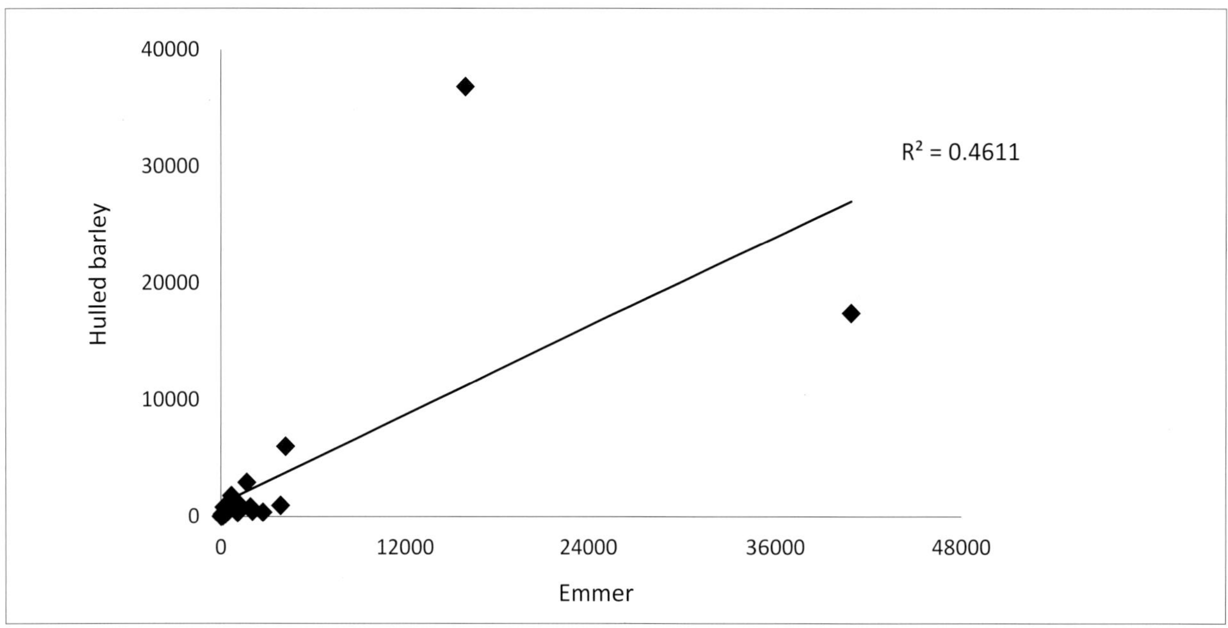

Fig. 95. Comparison of the quantity of hulled barley and emmer at Çayboyu with a linear regression line to determine the correlation.

Early Bronze Age I

Of the nine Taşkun Mevkii samples, five are dominated by hulled barley and four by free-threshing wheat (fig. 96). One sample has a very small quantity of grain in it and this sample has more hulled barley than wheat, but, given the scarcity of the botanic material collected and the small number of samples, it is difficult to draw conclusions about the nature of plant use from the taphonomy of this assemblage.

Hulled barley is much more abundant than any other cereal at the site: 47,241 grains in total (fig. 96). This is accounted for by the series of four large samples (101.23 to 101.25; see chapter 4.3.2.2). Smaller quantities of emmer and einkorn are present: 1,638 and 246 grains respectively across all samples. Most of the emmer grains are in one sample (101.24 flotation), which is dominated by barley. If this is part of the same barley deposition event as the other 101 samples, which are virtually devoid of

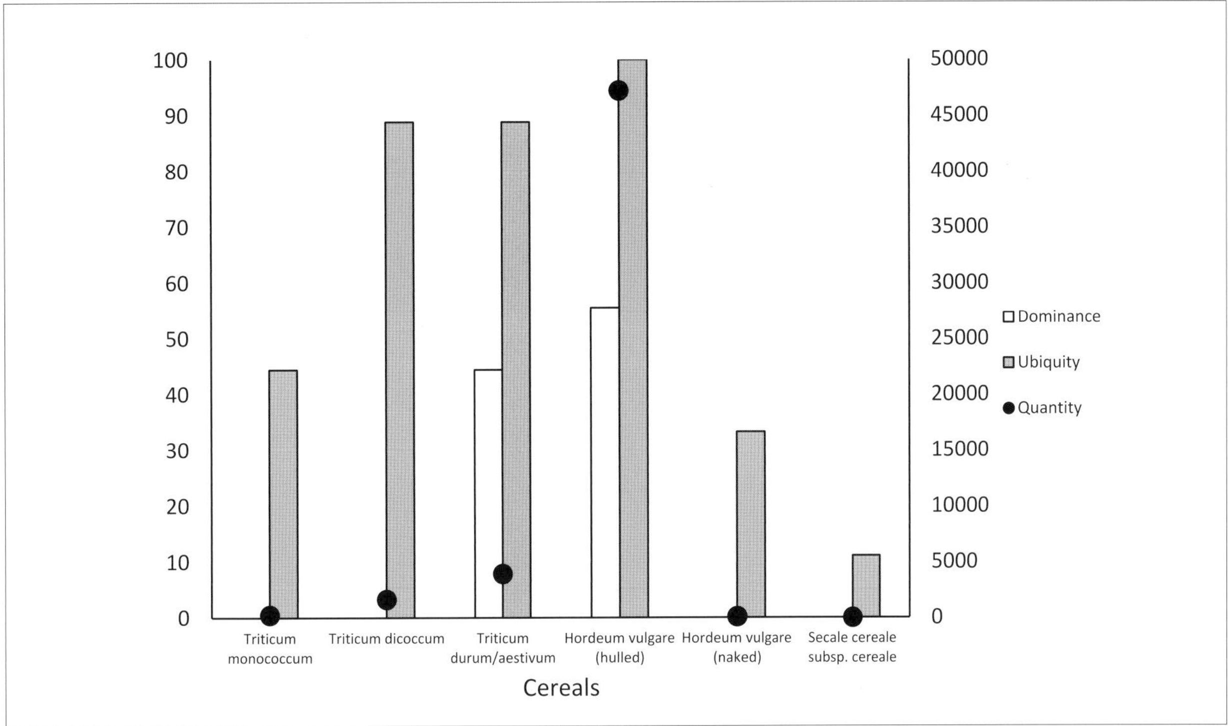

Fig. 96. Quantity, dominance and ubiquity of cereals at Taşkun Mevkii (whole site). The left axis shows the number of contexts containing species and the relative dominance of species as a percentage of the contexts analysed (n = 9), while the right axis shows the number of seeds of each species for the quantity value.

wheat, then the wheat grains in this sample derive from a separate origin or event. If that is the case, then the relative proportions of wheat grain point to an emmer crop with significant admixture of free-threshing wheat and einkorn. Einkorn is of lower ubiquity in this period (44%) than in the Late Chalcolithic, doubtless because emmer was uncommon. Einkorn is absent (or nearly absent) from three of the larger free-threshing wheat samples, suggesting that, although emmer may have grown as a weed within free-threshing wheat, einkorn did not.

The small number of independent samples from Taşkun Mevkii limits the conclusions that can be drawn about the use of cereals in the Early Bronze Age I period at the Aşvan sites. The two dominant cereals (not necessarily grown in equal amounts) were hulled barley and free-threshing wheat; emmer was a minor component of free-threshing wheat crops and may have been grown independently; einkorn still lingered as a weed in emmer but was less abundant. A single grain of domesticated rye is present; the large deposit(s) of hulled barley contain a small amount of naked barley (samples 101.24 flotation, 101.25, 103.6).

Early Bronze Age II/III and Late Bronze Age

The 12 samples from Aşvan Kale Early Bronze Age II/III are dominated by only two cereals – hulled barley and free-threshing wheat – in roughly equal ubiquity and dominance, although there are more grains of free-threshing wheat than barley overall (fig. 97).

No grains of einkorn, emmer, naked barley or rye were found. The proportions of cereals in this period appear to represent the culmination of the reduction in quantity of hulled wheats observed in the previous period (fig. 98).

The low number of samples from the Late Bronze Age (n = 2) means that interpretation is limited, but it can be observed that their composition is similar to that of the Early Bronze Age II/III samples (fig. 99), with only hulled barley and free-threshing wheat present, although hulled barley appears to dominate both samples.

Hellenistic and Roman

The 21 Hellenistic samples from Aşvan Kale in the burnt level mainly comprise hulled barley, which dominates 42%, and free-threshing wheat, which dominates 19% of the samples. The two cereals have similar ubiquities (71% and 61% respectively; see fig. 100), raising the question of whether free-threshing wheat was more abundant than its sample dominance suggests.

However, free-threshing wheat occurs frequently in hulled barley stores, and may have resulted from post-harvest mixing. This is supported by the occurrence of free-threshing wheat as the main component of four samples, suggesting that it was grown as an independent crop.

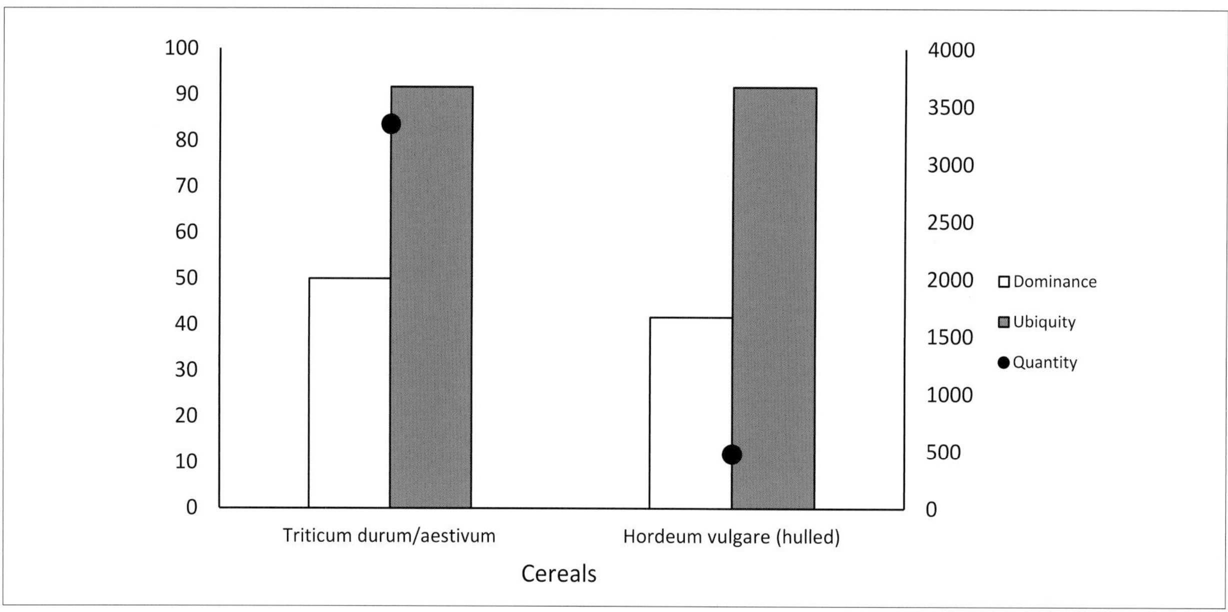

Fig. 97. Quantity, dominance and ubiquity of cereals at Aşvan Kale in the Early Bronze Age II/III. The left axis shows the number of contexts containing species and also the relative dominance of species as a percentage of the contexts analysed (n = 12), while the right axis shows the number of seeds of each species for the quantity value.

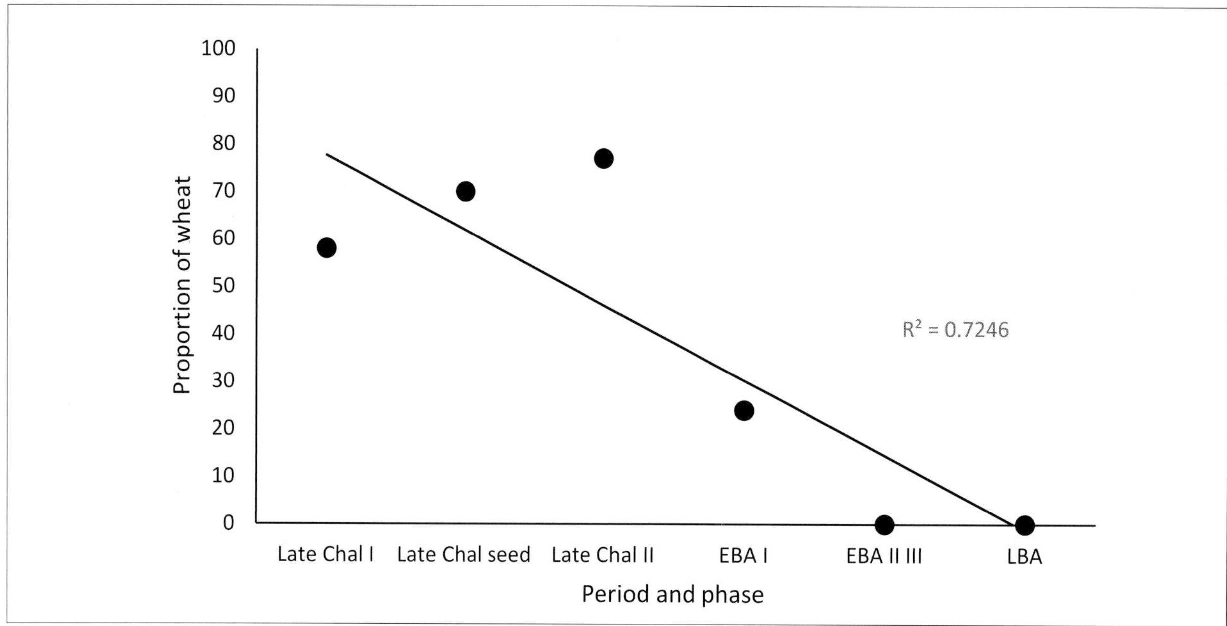

Fig. 98. Hulled wheats as a proportion of all wheats by period and phase, showing linear regression line. A strong negative correlation is indicated by the R^2 value of 0.7.

The Hellenistic period saw the first appearance of both common and foxtail millet (see Nesbitt, Summers 1988). The very different harvest time of millet, in late summer, compared with barley and wheat, which were harvested in July, means that, when millet occurs mixed with one of the large-grained cereals, this must have resulted from post-harvest mixing. Admixtures of millet and wheat and barley occurred in only one wheat-dominated context and in two of the millet-dominated contexts (see chapter 4.3.3.2), and these have been interpreted as showing contexts contaminated during or after the charring event rather than deliberate post-harvest actions.

Accepting this assumption, and taking the millet component alone, common millet is dominant in two samples (606.24 and 1507.23–24), foxtail millet in one (606.15 [19]), and they are more or less equal in abundance in 606.24. Their ubiquity is similar: 19% and 14% respectively. Overall, the evidence suggests that both foxtail millet and broomcorn millet were cultivated as independent crops, and the samples include more-or-less exclusive batches of both millets. However, in view of the small number of samples in which millet is present, it is not possible to say if one species was more important than the other.

Overall, hulled barley was the dominant and arguably the most important cereal in this period, followed by free-threshing wheat and then by common and foxtail millet. All four cereals were cultivated independently.

The two Roman samples contain free-threshing wheat and barley, and *Setaria italica*, but the small sample number makes it is impossible to draw further conclusions. The millet, as discussed in chapter 4.3.3.2, was probably mixed with the early harvest cereals as part of waste

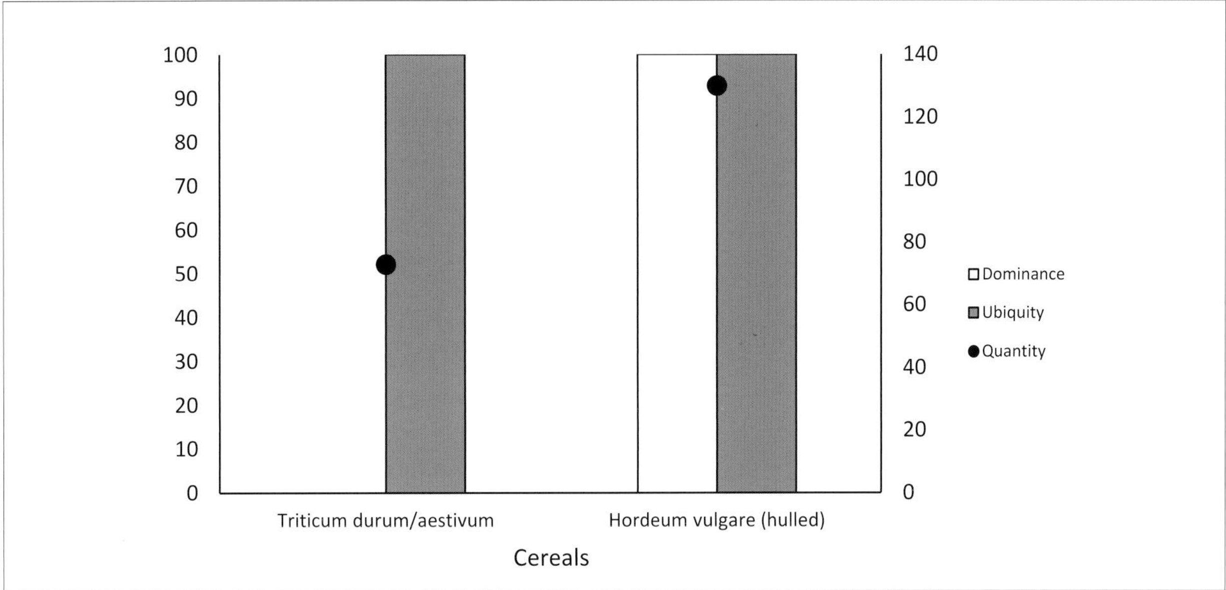

Fig. 99. Quantity, dominance and ubiquity of cereals at Aşvan Kale in the Late Bronze Age. The left axis shows the number of contexts containing species and also the relative dominance of species as a percentage of the contexts analysed (n = 2), while the right axis shows the number of seeds of each species for the quantity value.

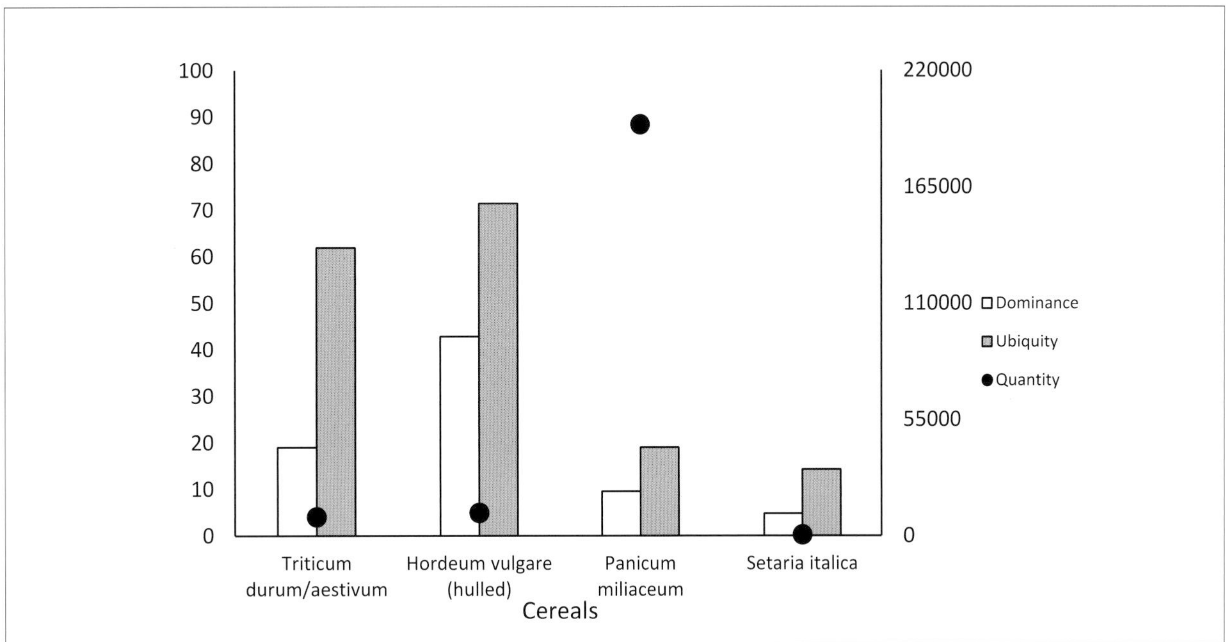

Fig. 100. Quantity, dominance and ubiquity of cereals at Aşvan Kale in the Hellenistic period. The left axis shows the number of contexts containing species and also the relative dominance of species as a percentage of the contexts analysed (n = 21), while the right axis shows the number of seeds of each species for the quantity value.

disposal. Interestingly, the cereals are not the dominant crops in either sample in their period, but this may be due to poor preservation or to low sample numbers.

Medieval

Free-threshing wheat dominates 47% and hulled barley 32% of the 19 samples (fig. 101).

The ubiquity of the two cereals is very similar: 68% free-threshing wheat and 79% hulled barley, though the less-dominant species has the higher ubiquity. Barley (1,677 grains) is more abundant than wheat (1,235 grains), but this is accounted for by the exceptionally large find of 905 barley grains in a single pithos (TK 201.15). Overall, the lack of correlation between dominance and ubiquity suggests that, if free-threshing wheat was more important than barley, it was not by a huge margin and that both barley and free-threshing wheat were equally important cereals in the Medieval period.

Three other cereals are noted. One grain of naked barley is found in one sample (TK 201.15). This is probably a weed of the almost pure hulled-barley crop held in the pithos. Rye is also found in five samples from Aşvan Kale, giving it a low ubiquity (26%). The quantities are low (between one and two grains in each case), and it is never a dominant element of the samples. It is therefore unlikely to have been a crop, and was probably a weed of the other cereals. *Panicum miliaceum* is found in context 714.8 (MN191), a fill from pit 1 that is interpreted as refuse disposal.

Summary of cereal use

Figure 102 shows the patterns in the changing proportions of cereals over time at the Aşvan sites.

The most obvious trend in cereal use across the Aşvan sites is the disappearance of hulled wheat, which occurred between the Late Chalcolithic period, when emmer and (hulled) barley dominated the cereal assemblage, and the Early Bronze Age II/III, when hulled wheats were entirely absent. The role of hulled wheats in the Early Bronze Age I is less clear because of the low sample numbers from Taşkun Mevkii, and because it is unclear how independent the nine samples are. Measured by ubiquity in these samples, emmer is present in 89% of samples, but has low abundance, at 1,638 grains compared with 47,241 barley grains. A shift is also evident in the types of wheat used, from emmer, which was nearly twice as abundant as free-threshing wheat in the Late Chalcolithic, to free-threshing wheat, present twice as abundantly as emmer in the Early Bronze Age. While it is possible that emmer was still cultivated independently in the Early Bronze Age, it is likely to have been a much less important crop.

From the Early Bronze Age I to the Medieval period, hulled barley and free-threshing wheat were more or less equally important. The only major change was the appearance of foxtail and broomcorn millet, possibly as two distinct crops, in the Hellenistic period. The geographical writer Strabo reports that millet and sorghum were present in the Pontic region of northeastern Anatolia in the late

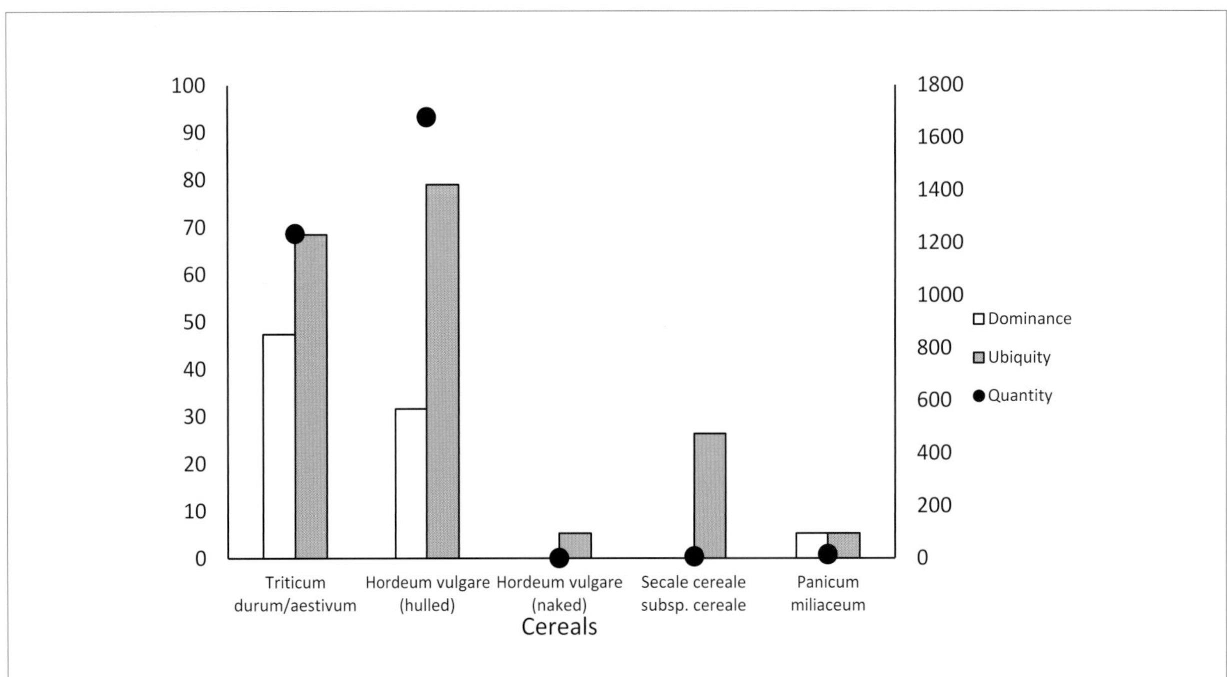

Fig. 101. Quantity, dominance and ubiquity of cereals at Aşvan Kale and Taşkun Kale in the Medieval period. The left axis shows the number of contexts containing species and also the relative dominance of species as a percentage of the contexts analysed (n = 19), while the right axis shows the number of seeds of each species for the quantity value.

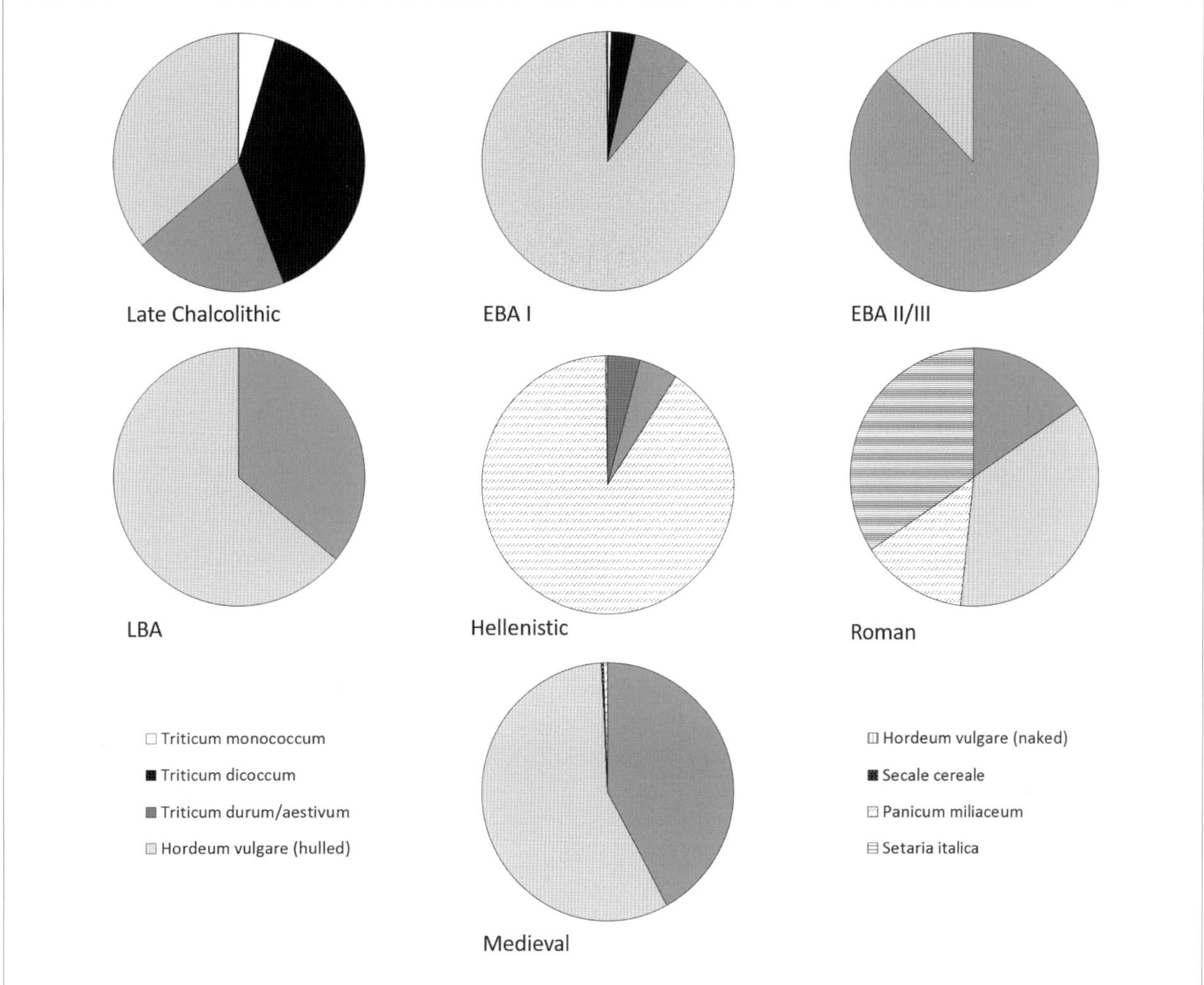

Fig. 102. Pie charts of cereal proportions by period at the Aşvan sites.

Hellenistic period (Strabo 13.3.15; Mitchell 2015: 286). Millet was relatively uncommon, suggesting it were not grown on the same scale as wheat and barley, but its presence represents an investment in summer cropping, increasing yields and productivity (Nesbitt, Summers 1988). A few grains of naked barley and rye in its domesticated large-grained form are present in samples of several periods, but in such low numbers they probably represent inadvertent admixtures to other crops.

5.4. Pulses

At the Aşvan sites there are fewer pulses than cereals in almost all cases. This general rule has also been noted across the Near East throughout the Bronze Age by Simone Riehl (2012) in her synthesis of Near Eastern archaeobotanical data. It has been argued that pulses are often less common than cereals at sites because they are less likely to be charred (Fuller 2000; Fuller, Harvey 2006). The seeds are easy to extract from pods, meaning fewer seeds will accompany the by-product fractions of legume seed processing, and the pod fragments are light and less likely to survive charring. At the same time, it is likely that there were far fewer pulse seeds present in settlements. Cereals are usually the dominant staple in ethnographic examples in the Near East and Anatolia. Gordon Hillman's work at Aşvan itself shows that about 78.5% of the calorific value of the 1970s village diet was derived from bread consumption (Hillman 1973b: 229, see appendix 5; cf. Weinstein 1973). Pulses yield far fewer seeds than cereals, meaning that, even if significant quantities were grown, the number of seeds would be disproportionately low compared with cereal grains. It is therefore difficult to compare the importance of cereals to pulse crops, but perfectly possible to compare pulses with one another (for example Fuller 2000; Fuller, Harvey 2006).

Late Chalcolithic

Three pulses were noted in the Late Chalcolithic material from Çayboyu: lentil, pea and bitter vetch (fig. 103). None is the dominant crop at the site in any sample, although lentil is noted in 80% of them. Lentils are found in greatest abundance (276 seeds), followed by peas (181 seeds) and

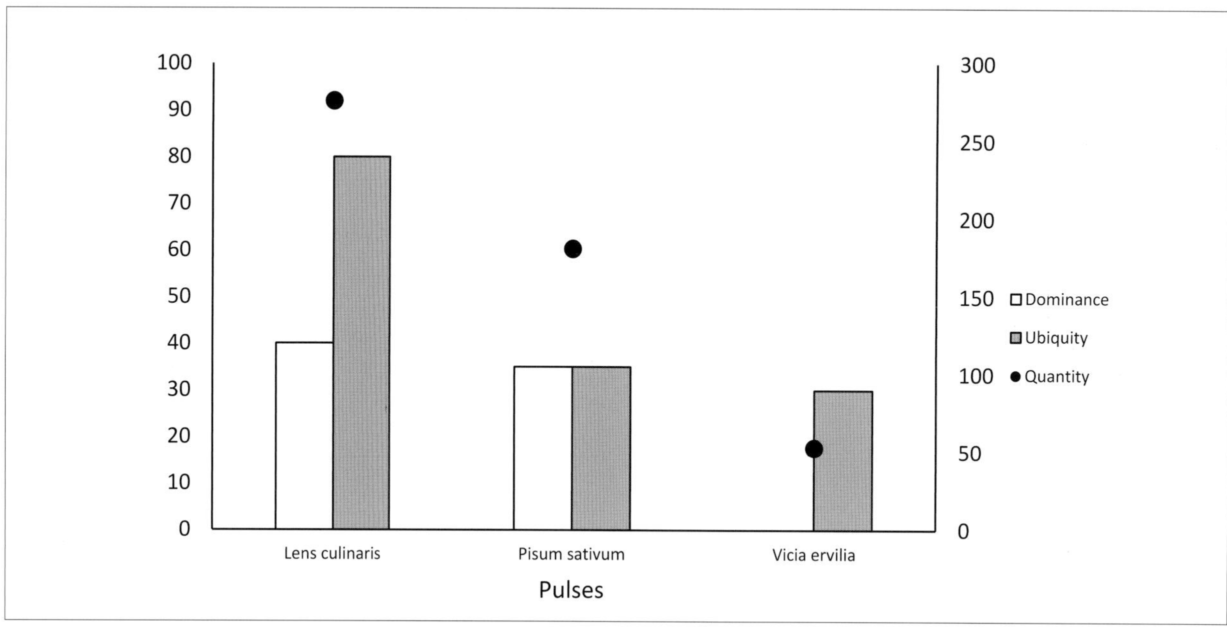

Fig. 103. Quantity, dominance (of pulses only) and ubiquity of pulses at Çayboyu in the Late Chalcolithic. The left axis shows the number of contexts containing species and also the relative dominance of pulses as a percentage of the contexts analysed (n = 20), while the right axis shows the number of seeds of each species for the quantity value.

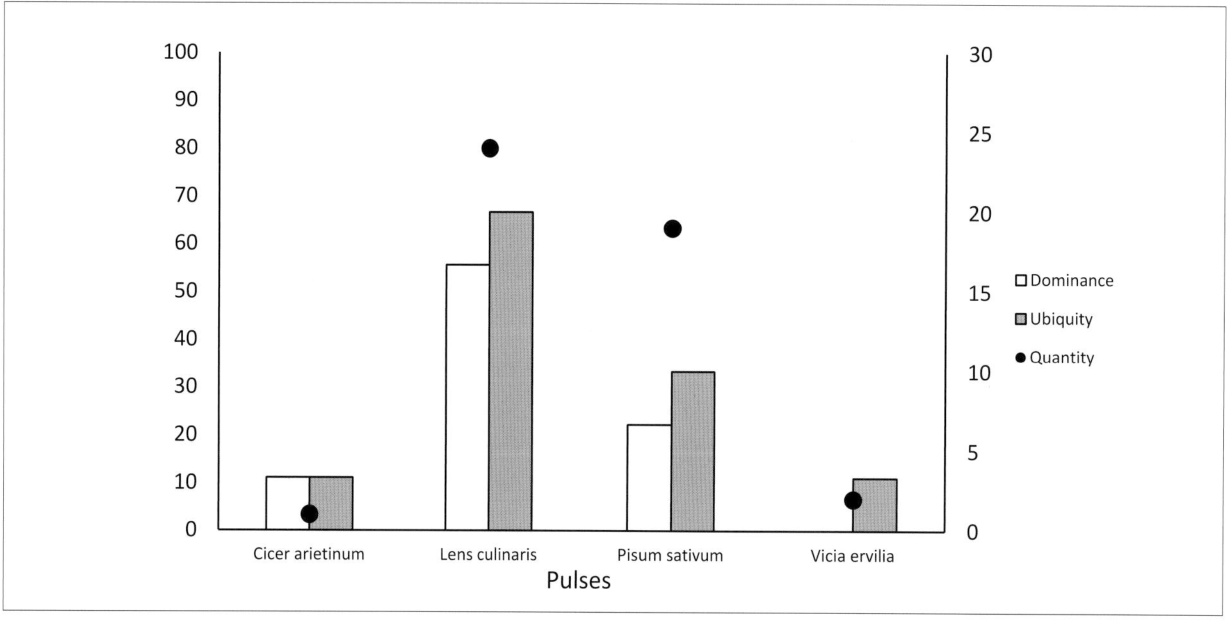

Fig. 104. Quantity, dominance (of pulses only) and ubiquity of pulses at Taşkun Mevkii in the Early Bronze Age I. The left axis shows the number of contexts containing species and also the relative dominance of pulses as a percentage of the contexts analysed (n = 9), while the right axis shows the number of seeds of each species for the quantity value.

bitter vetch (53 seeds), which had similar, low ubiquity (35% and 30% of samples respectively). None of these are pure caches, but found mixed with cereals, which suggests either mixing during cooking or post-charring, as they are processed differently from cereals (Fuller 2000; Fuller, Harvey, 2006). This provides more evidence against the use of maslins, since these mixtures are common but must have occurred post-harvest.

Early Bronze Age I

A new pulse was added to the suite in the Early Bronze Age I – chickpea – although only one seed has been found (fig. 104). In general, the ubiquity and abundance of pulses declined in this period compared with the preceding Late Chalcolithic, but this may be a result of different sampling or preservation pathways between the two sites. Lentils remained the most abundant pulse, followed by pea, then bitter vetch, as in the Late Chalcolithic, although the ubiquity of lentils (67%) and bitter vetch (11%) decreased, while that of pea did not (33%). Again, none of these are pure caches, suggesting either mixing during cooking or post-charring (Fuller 2000; Fuller, Harvey 2006).

Early Bronze Age II/III and Late Bronze Age

The range of pulses declines in the Early Bronze Age II/III samples compared with the earlier periods; only lentils and bitter vetch are noted (fig. 105). Again, these are not dominant crops, but, as noted in the introduction to section 5.4, this could be explained by the taphonomy or by differential yields and uses of crops. Of the two Early Bronze Age II/III pulses, lentil is present in greatest abundance (14 seeds across 33% of samples), while only one bitter vetch seed was noted. These were found mixed with other crops including cereals.

This decline in the range of pulses is also seen in the Late Bronze Age samples, although again the low sample number must be highlighted (n = 2). Sixty one seeds of bitter vetch were found mixed with cereals and other crops in the sample from 508.4.

Hellenistic and Roman

The Hellenistic period saw an increase in the presence and abundance of pulses in the samples from the Aşvan sites. All four pulses are present (chickpea, lentil, pea and bitter vetch; fig. 106). Unusually for the Aşvan sites, pea is found in the lowest quantity (15 seeds) compared with chickpea (57 seeds), but is slightly more ubiquitous (10% of samples) than chickpea (5%). Chickpea, however, occurs in a single pure sample – 606.6 (15–38) – in the burnt layer, which confirms that it was grown as an independent crop. Chickpea is the dominant pulse in 5% of samples. Lentils and bitter vetch are the most abundant pulses (260 lentil seeds and 251 bitter vetch) found in similar ubiquity (lentil in 52% of samples and bitter vetch in 43%), although bitter vetch is the dominant pulse in 29% of samples. Lentils and bitter vetch then appear to have been the most important pulses, although pure samples of chickpea suggest that this independent crop may have also played a role that may be masked by different storage or use practices.

The low sample number (n = 2) in the Roman period limits the potential for analysis. Lentils and peas are found in similar abundance, dominance and ubiquity (four seeds, equally dominant pulse in one sample, 50% ubiquity), with bitter vetch found in half the abundance but similar ubiquity.

Medieval

Unlike at other periods, the measures of abundance and dominance suggest that bitter vetch was more important in the Medieval period than lentils (fig. 107). A total of 3,084 seeds were found, and bitter vetch is the dominant pulse in 31% of samples. Only 28 lentils, 18 chickpeas and two peas were found. However, looking at the ubiquity measures, although chickpea and pea have low ubiquities in keeping with their low abundances, the figures for lentil and bitter vetch are similar (52% and 42% respectively). Looking at the contexts of the bitter vetch, it can be noted

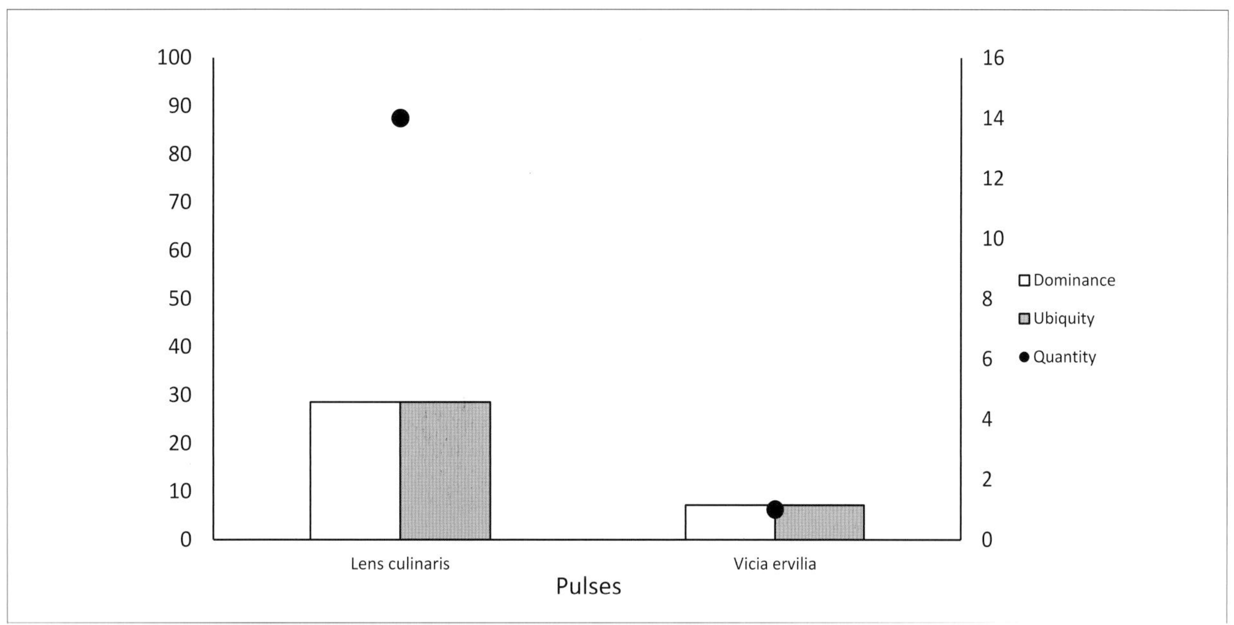

Fig. 105. Quantity, dominance (of pulses only) and ubiquity of pulses at Aşvan Kale in the Early Bronze Age II/III. The left axis shows the number of contexts containing species and also the relative dominance of pulses as a percentage of the contexts analysed (n = 14), while the right axis shows the number of seeds of each species for the quantity value.

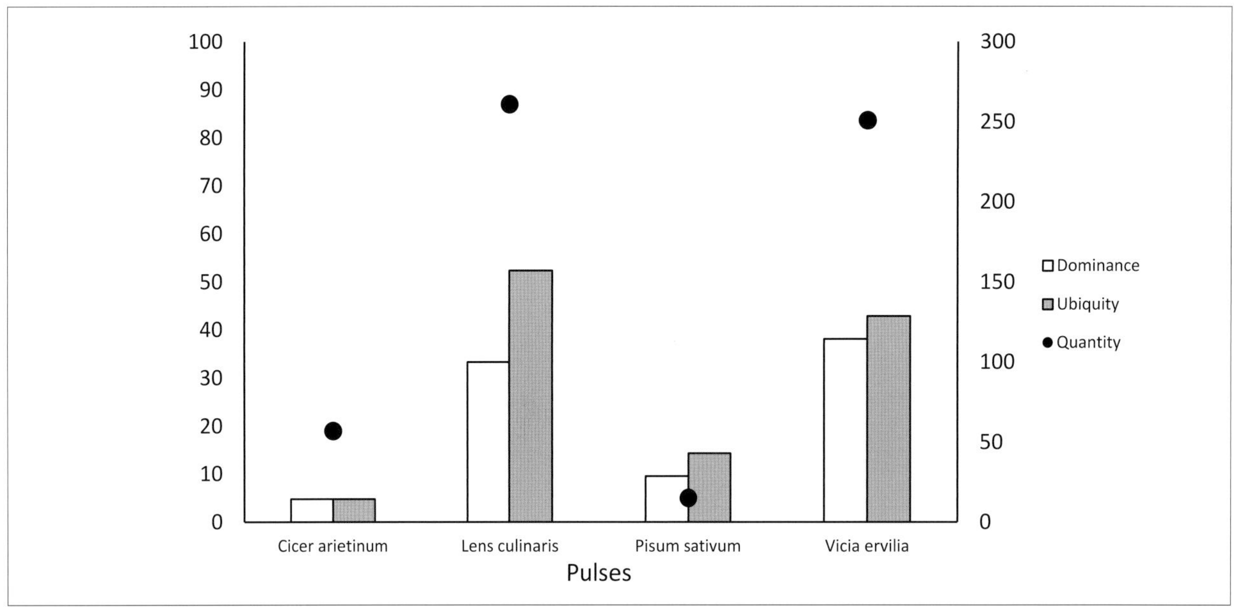

Fig. 106. Quantity, dominance (of pulses only) and ubiquity of pulses at Aşvan Kale in the Hellenistic period. The left axis shows the number of contexts containing species and also the relative dominance of pulses as a percentage of the contexts analysed (n = 21), while the right axis shows the number of seeds of each species for the quantity value.

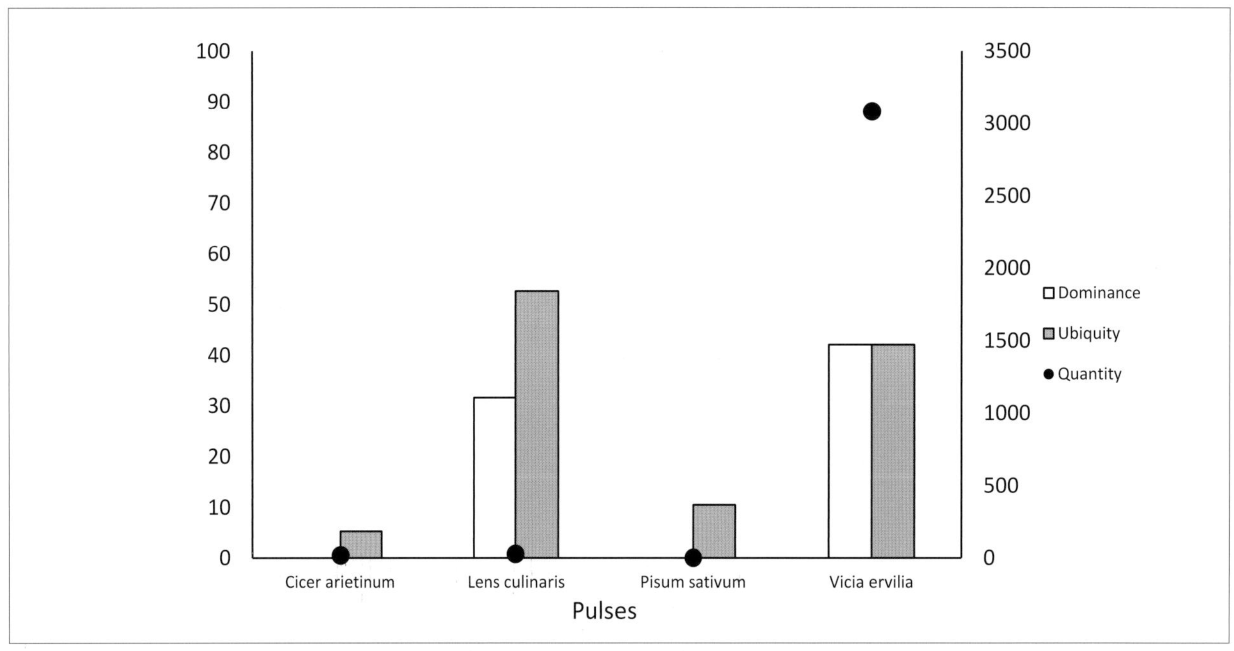

Fig. 107. Quantity, dominance (of pulses only) and ubiquity of pulses at Aşvan Kale and Taşkun Kale in the Medieval period. The left axis shows the number of contexts containing species and also the relative dominance of pulses as a percentage of the contexts analysed (n = 19), while the right axis shows the number of seeds of each species for the quantity value.

that the high abundance is due to an exceptionally abundant pure find in a pit (714.8 MN2–3) and two large but mixed finds: one in the same pit (714.8 MN 1–4) and one in another pit (603.13–606.4). Perhaps different taphonomic pathways, such as different processing methods or the use of these plants for fodder, might explain why there were larger quantities of bitter vetch than lentils in this period.

Summary of pulse use

Lentil and bitter vetch therefore appear to have dominated pulse production at the Aşvan sites. Peas are consistently present in the samples but the low frequency suggests that they were less important than lentils and bitter vetch. Chickpeas occur occasionally. In all periods with a good sample size (i.e. excluding the Late Bronze Age and Roman periods, for which n = 2) lentils had the highest ubiquities. They would have had the highest abundance but for the unusual deposition of bitter vetch in the Medieval pit 714.8. In the earlier periods (Late Chalcolithic to Early Bronze Age II/III) bitter vetch played a lesser role to the second pulse, pea. Pea is found in high abundance in the Late Chalcolithic samples but declines over time. In the Hellenistic and Medieval periods, bitter vetch appears to have grown more important as a crop, shown by the similarly high, if not the higher, abundance and ubiquity to lentils.

5.5. Oilseed and fibre crops

As with the other crops outlined above, the different paths to preservation faced by oil and fibre crops means that comparisons with pulses and cereals are difficult to make, but comparisons within this group are more rigorous. It is interesting therefore that the patterns for oilseed and fibre crops are somewhat erratic. This could be a result of either differing importance over time or erratic paths to preservation, as, especially in the case of fibre crops, the charring of these seeds is not likely to have been a regular event. Day-to-day contact with fire is less likely both for fibre and for oil seeds. At the same time, oilseed and fibre seeds are more fragile and less likely to survive charring.

Cotton was a late introduction to the sites. Although a single seed was found in a Hellenistic period sample, which could be intrusive or a chance survival, it is not present in significant numbers until the samples of the Medieval period, where it is found in 37% of contexts (a relatively high ubiquity compared with other oilseed/fibre crops); because of a single pure context (AK 1902.4) it has a dominance of 6%. This single clean context, devoid of any other crop or weed seed, confirms that it was cultivated as a pure crop in this period rather than being introduced, for example as a contaminant in raw cotton fibres.

For an important oilseed, flax appears surprisingly erratic, although less so if it were being used primarily for fibre. Flax, also called linseed, is present in the Late Chalcolithic samples as the only oil/fibre crop, and is found in over 50% of contexts, always mixed with other crop types. It is also found at Taşkun Mevkii in the Early Bronze Age I material, in much smaller abundance and ubiquity, and as a pure crop in high abundance and therefore as the dominant crop in one context from the Hellenistic period at Aşvan Kale. This clean stored crop suggests that it was being cultivated alone as a pure crop in this period. It appears again in a single Medieval context at Taşkun Kale; this is a mixed context in which it is the dominant crop.

Black cumin (*Nigella sativa*) was present in the Hellenistic period. It is dominant in one sample and with high abundance and low ubiquity similar to flax. The *Lallemantia* and *Carthamus* seeds are considered most likely to be wild taxa (section 5.2.2).

5.6. Fruit and useful wild plants

There are similar issues in comparing fruits with pulses and oilseed/fibre crops. They have different taphonomic pathways from other crops and are not, therefore, directly comparable. Two domesticated fruits are noted from the Aşvan sites: almond and grape. It has been noted that the growing of domestic fruit trees is very different from that of other crops because of the different scale of investment (Zohary et al. 2012: 114). Instead of short-term returns from annuals like cereals, or from annuals/perennials like pulses and oilseed/fibre crops, fruit trees require long-term land allocation and provide delayed returns. As such, their exploitation is an example of a different form of agricultural strategy.

Useful wild plants are defined as wild plants deliberately collected for human use, but the Aşvan archaeological assemblages are restricted to carbonised woody tree products, specifically fruit seeds and nut shells. Tree crops are not collected in the same way as cultivars and therefore may end up on site in different proportions. We can approach the question of the role of fruits and nuts at the Aşvan sites over time by assessing their abundance, dominance and ubiquity.

Beginning with the domesticated fruits, the use of almond appears limited to the Hellenistic period. Ten nuts were found in a single context – AK 606.15 (21) – interpreted as a kitchen. This is a unique cache, in which almond is the dominant crop. As the pitted shells of domesticated almond are robust and distinctive, and regularly discarded as waste, the uniqueness of this find tends to suggest that almond was not commonly consumed. If it had been widespread, we would expect identifiable traces to appear in other contexts.

Compared with other fruit and nuts, domesticated grape pips (fig. 108) were both abundant and found in relatively high ubiquity in the Early Bronze Age I material. Grapes are the dominant crop in one of these contexts at Taşkun Mevkii, but is mixed with other crop types including cereals, suggesting post-processing mixing. Grape is present in high ubiquity (42%) in the Early Bronze Age II/III, is found in one of the Late Bronze Age samples and in the Hellenistic (48%). It is found in high abundance in one of the Roman samples, in which it is the dominant crop. Two hundred and thirty five seeds were recovered from Medieval samples, and this shows that grapes were relatively abundant compared to other fruits and the pips have an ubiquity of 57%. The consistently high ubiquity levels for all these periods suggest that there was regular use and consumption of grapes from Early Bronze Age I onwards.

The relatively high abundance of domesticated grape can be compared with that for wild grape from the Late Chalcolithic period (fig. 108). Seeds were found from this

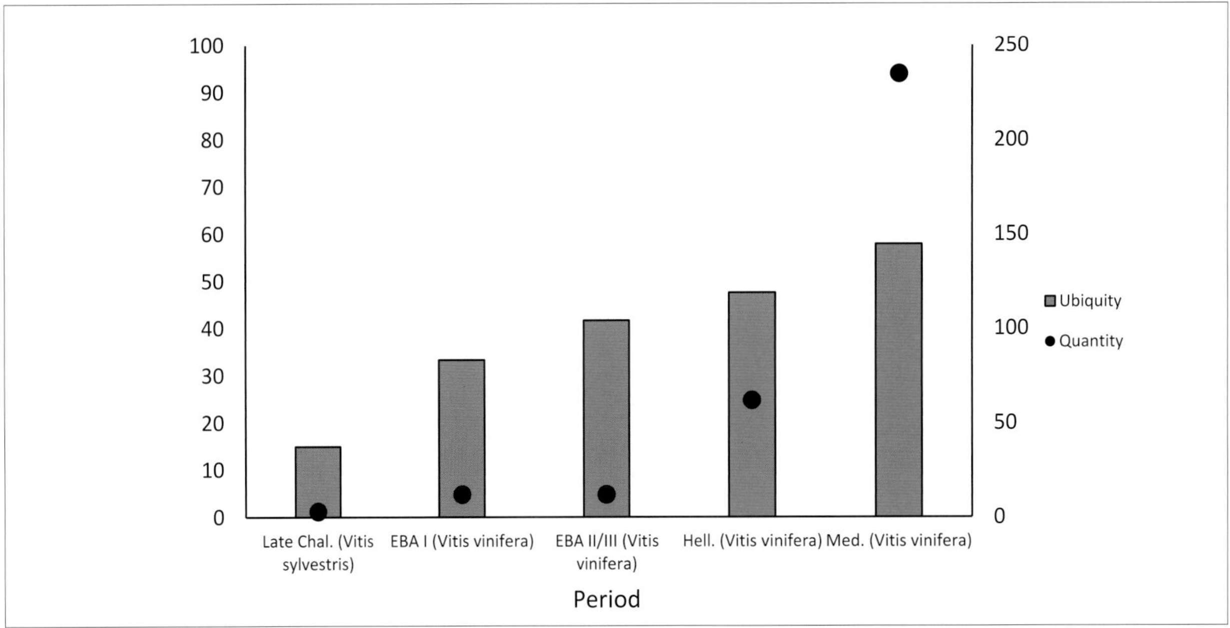

Fig. 108. Quantity and ubiquity of grape by period. The left axis shows the number of contexts containing species as a percentage of the contexts analysed, while the right axis shows the number of seeds of each species for the quantity value.

period in only low abundance (three seeds) and low ubiquity (15%). This suggests that wild grapes were subsequently replaced by domesticated grapes, which were then used more intensively than the wild species. Another wild plant that, with the exception of a single Hellenistic find, appears mainly in the Late Chalcolithic samples is wild plum. Although this appeares with relatively high ubiquity (40% of Late Chalcolithic samples), it was found in low abundance. Hawthorn shows a similar pattern, being present in the Late Chalcolithic samples (15% ubiquity, low abundance) and also in Early Bronze Age II/III samples in low ubiquity and abundance, but not in other periods.

Hackberry and terebinth, however, show different trends. Both are noted in the Late Chalcolithic (although in different abundance and ubiquities) and Early Bronze Age II/III samples, in which their abundance and ubiquity are both low. Terebinth is also found in the Hellenistic period samples in low abundance and ubiquity, and both are noted in the Medieval material, although hackberry is found in notably higher abundance and relatively higher ubiquity (473 seeds in 32% of contexts) and was also the dominant crop in two samples: AK1501.3, which is not a pure cache but contains other crops including cereals, and AK910.22(1), a pure cache of hackberry, devoid of other crops and weeds. The cache of this wild crop is interesting as it suggests that these seeds were deliberately gathered and stored.

The other wild harvested plant to be identified is oak gall. Oak galls, as discussed in chapter 3.8.5, are formed by wasp larva. A large number of these (81) is noted at Aşvan Kale in the destruction level of the Hellenistic house. Their survival is attributed to unusual natural preservation in that level: the burning of rooms in situ. Oak galls, which are not edible, could have been used in tanning leather (Procter 1914; Coles 1973; Van Driel-Murray 2000), but this seems an unlikely use for this cache, which was small and found in a domestic context. Medicinal use is more likely. The galls of *Quercus infectoria* Olivier (which grow abundantly in the Elazığ region, as subspecies *boissieri*) are still widely used in the Near East as an astringent in folk medicine, including treatment of diarrhoea (Rivera Núñez et al. 2011b: 426).

As far as the small numbers allow us to judge, there is very little patterning to much of the fruit and nut consumption in terms of use or change in use over time. It can, however, be noted that terebinth and hackberry were consumed throughout the occupation of the site and that wild grapes were replaced by domesticated grapes after the Late Chalcolithic.

5.7. Weeds

The analysis of weeds has always been a priority for archaeobotanists, who recognise their high potential for understanding past agricultural strategies, crop-processing methods and the seasonality of cropping, irrigation, harvesting, foddering, grazing and herding. They also contribute to building a picture of the past environmental setting. However, it is an important limitation of archaeological samples that seeds often cannot be determined to species or even to genus level. Moreover, the ecological range of plants can be very flexible. While some are specific to their ecological niche, others can live in a broad range of habitats. A brief exploration of the most prevalent weeds in each period will be undertaken by analysing their quantity, dominance and ubiquity, as well as by exploring some of the general patterns related to one of the most debated topics in archaeology: water management.

One pattern that is immediately clear is that the later period samples have a lower number of weeds and a lower number of weed species compared with those from earlier periods (fig. 109). The lower diversity of weeds in the later periods could have a sampling explanation. The lower weed incidence in later periods may be a consequence of the recovery strategy at Aşvan Kale and Taşkun Kale, which involved less flotation than at Çayboyu and Taşkun Mevkii.

Figure 110 shows the relationship between the percentage of samples floated and the number of weed species collected. From this it can be seen that there is a strong positive correlation (R^2 value of 0.55) between the number of samples that were floated and the number of

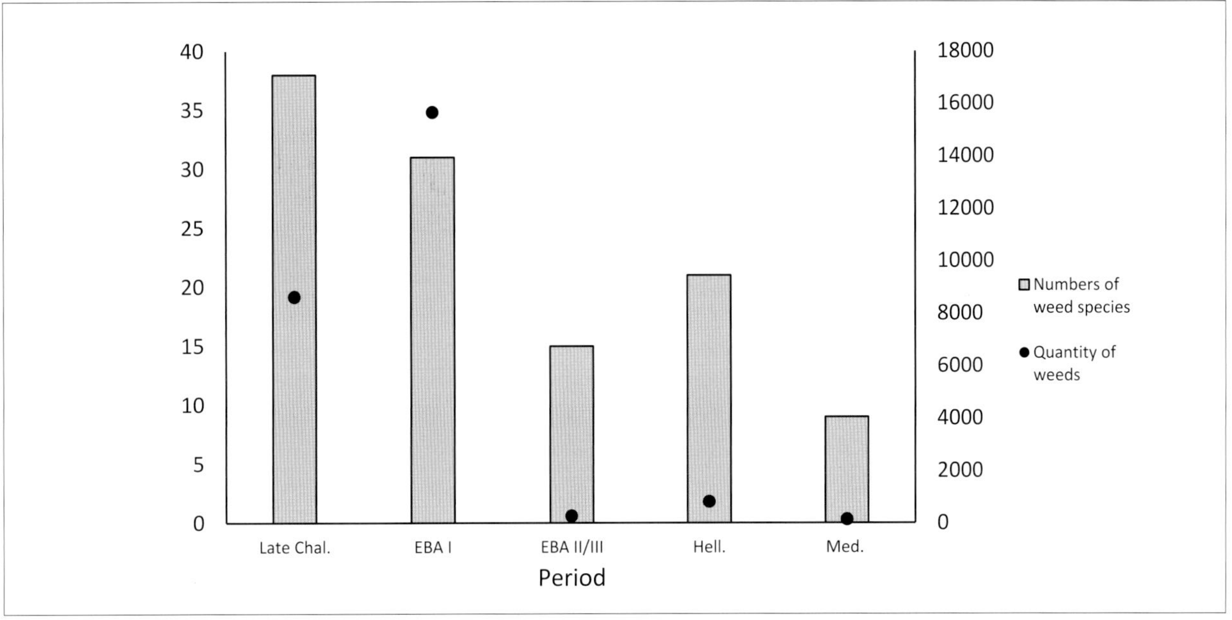

Fig. 109. Quantity of weeds and number of weed species by period at the Aşvan sites. The left axis shows the number of weed species and the right axis shows the quantity of weeds.

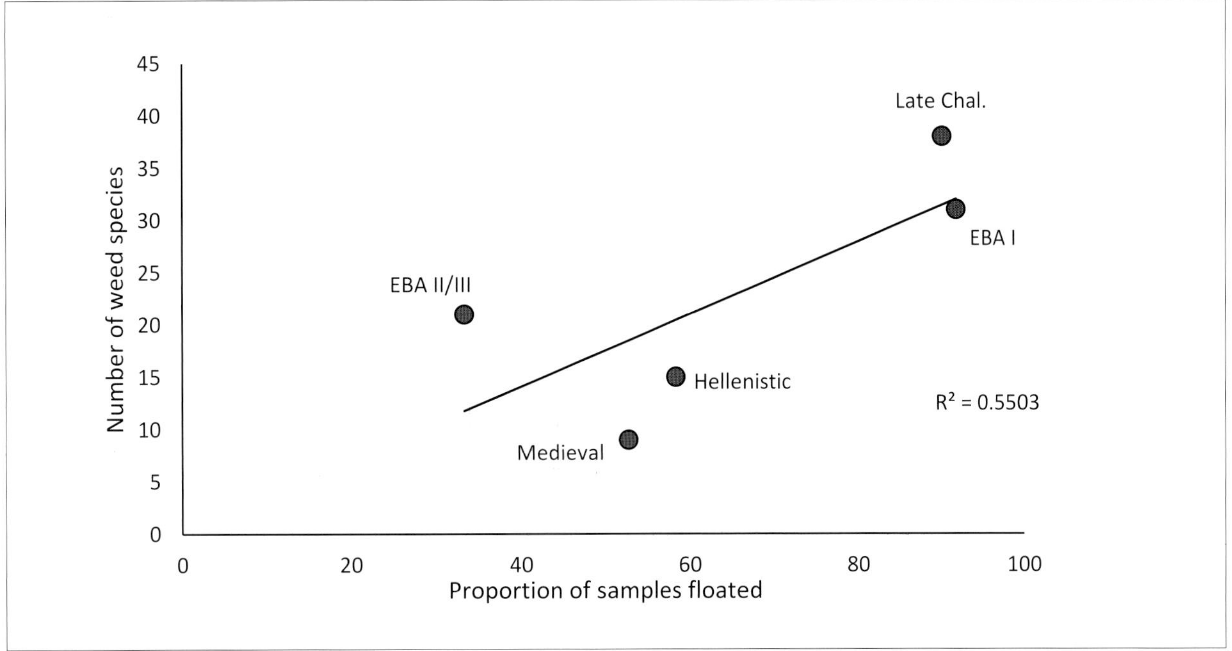

Fig. 110. Impact of sampling method on weed diversity recovered. The linear regression line shows the correlation between the proportion of floated samples and the number of weed species.

weed species that were observed. This has implications for the analysis of all the Aşvan Kale/Taşkun Kale weeds: the assemblage as a whole is not necessarily fully representative of what was present in the soil during excavation and may have been biased by different sampling strategies.

Late Chalcolithic

Figure 111 illustrates the ubiquity, dominance and quantity of all weeds from Çayboyu, and shows that, aside from the ubiquitous indeterminate weeds, the most dominant, commonly found weed with the greatest abundance is *Stipa*.

As noted in chapter 4.2.1.3, it is unexpected to find *Stipa* in such quantities in agricultural samples given that it is not a weed of arable fields nor is it commonly eaten by animals during its flowering/fruiting season As *Stipa* was not being brought to site by animals, it must have been brought by human action. Why was *Stipa* present on the site in such quantity? Hillman (2000) notes that *Stipa* was present at the epi-Palaeolithic site of Abu Hureyra and may have been gathered deliberately as a human food. Large numbers of *Stipa* awns and grains found in pits at farming sites in Europe, such as Vliněves in the Czech Republic (2300–1600 BC; Bienick, Pokorný 2005) and Kujawy in Poland (5400–4000 BC; Bienick 2002), have been interpreted as evidence that it was used either for food or to protect grain stored in pits by sterilisation or for decoration. At Çayboyu, however, although the lemma and palea are not adherent in *Stipa* and therefore could have been destroyed in charring, it is striking that none of the *Stipa* grains is still in its rigid lemma or palea and no floret bases were found. The strongest argument against these being processed as a food source at Çayboyu is that there is no evidence for *Stipa* being used in this way at agricultural sites in the Near East. Seeds recovered at such sites have been interpreted as weeds, which were mixed with large proportions of domesticated cereals and other seeds. It is therefore argued here that *Stipa* occurred as a weed of a cereal crop and was not gathered as a food in itself. There remains a possibility that *Stipa* was deliberately added to storage pits to protect grain from pests and to sterilise the pits, as has been suggested for the site at Vliněves (Bienick, Pokorný 2005). However, its presence throughout the samples at Çayboyu, including fill contexts, suggests rather that *Stipa* was simply gathered as part of a harvest. Why, then, was it part of the harvest in the first place? According to the observations made during the Aşvan survey and for the *Flora of Iraq* (Townsend, Guest 1966–1985), *Stipa* is not a weed associated with arable land, but is noted mainly on slopes and in steppic environ-

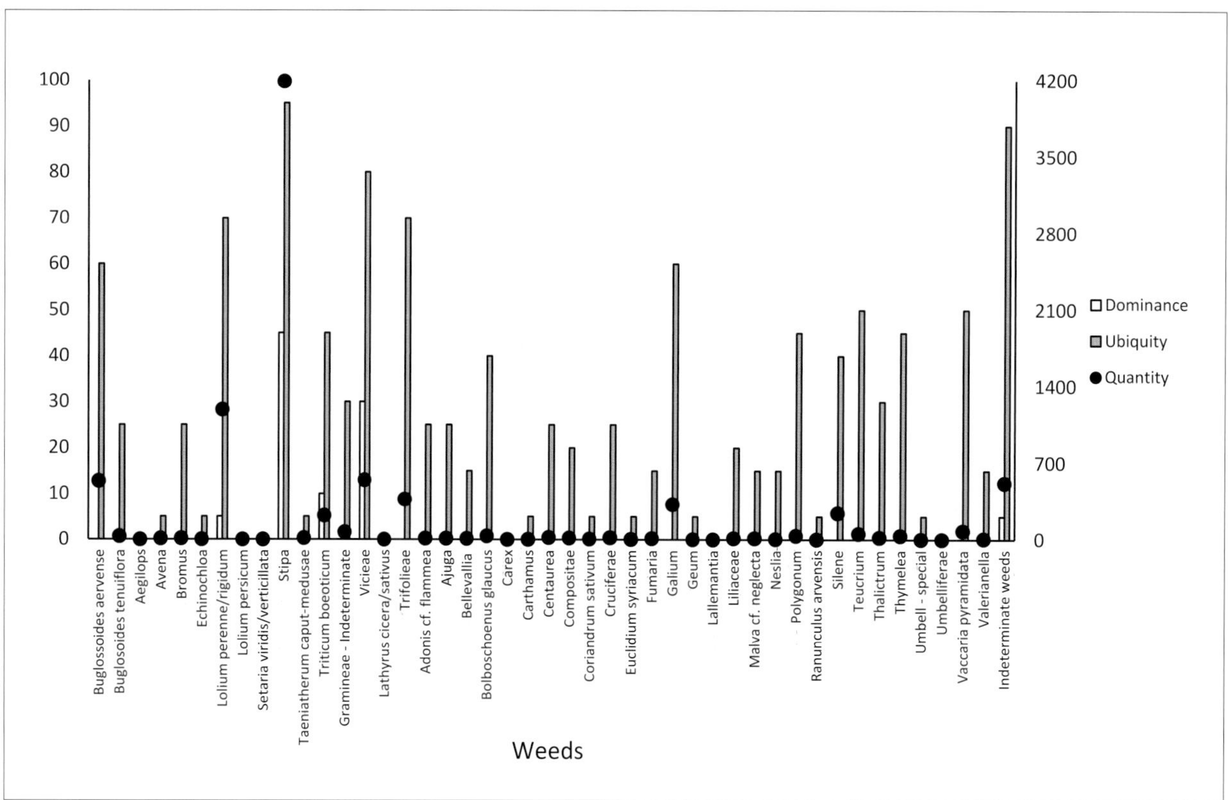

Fig. 111. Quantity, dominance and ubiquity of weeds at Çayboyu. The left axis shows the number of contexts containing species and also the relative dominance of species as a percentage of the contexts analysed (n = 20), while the right axis shows the number of seeds of each species for the quantity value.

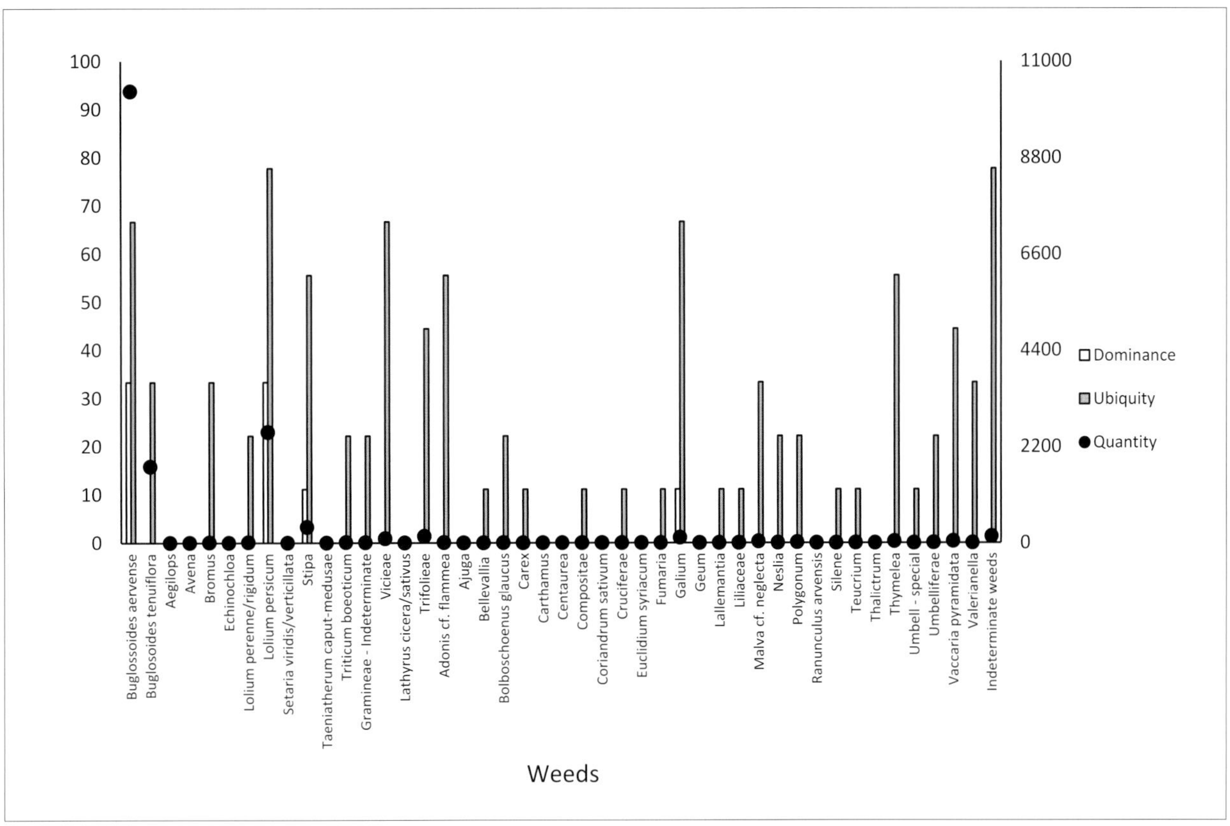

Fig. 112. Quantity, dominance and ubiquity of weeds at Taşkun Mevkii in the Early Bronze Age I. The left axis shows the number of contexts containing species and also the relative dominance of species as a percentage of the contexts analysed (n = 9), while the right axis shows the number of seeds of each species for the quantity value.

ments. This suggests that, during this period, agricultural fields were relatively newly established or were expanding into previously uncultivated areas. Indeed, *Stipa* is not the only species noted from Çayboyu that can be found in rocky slopes; *Avena*, *Bromus*, *Taeniatherum*, Fabeae, Trifolieae, *Carthamus*, *Centaurea*, Asteraceae, *Galium*, *Ranunculus arvensis*, *Thymelaea* and Apiaceae were also noted on slopes as well as in other habitats during the Aşvan botanical surveys.

Early Bronze Age I

Two weeds share similarly high dominance and ubiquity: *Buglossoides arvense* and *Lolium persicum* (fig. 112). However, *Buglossoides arvense* is present in greater abundance, due in part to two contexts: 101.23 and 101.25 (7).

Buglossoides arvense is unlikely to be highly palatable, as the plant is covered in bristles, but *Lolium persicum* is noted as a common grazing and even fodder species in *Flora of Iran* (Townsend, Guest 1966–1985). The reduced role of *Stipa* is also noticeable in Early Bronze Age I compared with the Late Chalcolithic. Although still fairly ubiquitous, it has much lower dominance and quantity in comparison with *Buglossoides arvense* and *Lolium persicum*. These two weeds are not associated with slopes and were commonly found on arable fields during the Aşvan botanical surveys. This suggests that agriculture had 'normalised' as it changed over time.

Early Bronze Age II/III and Late Bronze Age

The indeterminate weed abundance in Early Bronze Age II/III was raised by a single context – 1204.11 (12) – with a large number of small, diverse unidentified weeds (fig. 113). Otherwise, the most abundant, ubiquitous and dominant weed in the samples is *Galium*. This is also the most abundant weed in the one Late Bronze Age context which contained weeds (508.4). *Galium* is a common weed, found in a wide range of ecological contexts, although, as Naomi Miller (2010) notes, it can be an indicator of disturbance and overgrazing as well as typical of arable fields, where it was noted during the Aşvan botanical surveys. One of the species of *Galium*, *G. verum*, listed in *Flora of Turkey* as a possible species for the Aşvan region, is also noted in *Flora of Iraq* (Townsend, Guest 1966–1985) as having several properties that might make it attractive for human use. It can be used to curdle milk for cheese-making and to create purple dye, and has diuretic properties useful in the

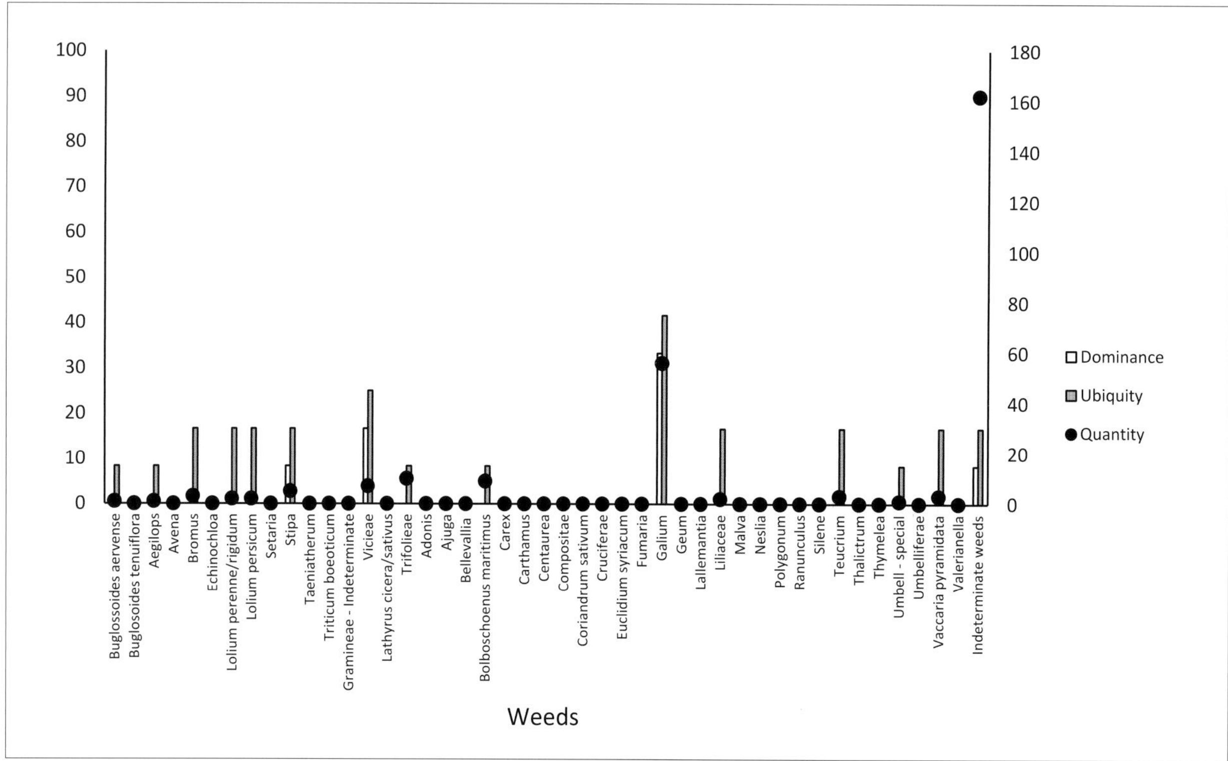

Fig. 113. Quantity, dominance and ubiquity of weeds at Aşvan Kale in the Early Bronze Age II/III. The left axis shows the number of contexts containing species and also the relative dominance of species as a percentage of the contexts analysed (n = 12), while the right axis shows the number of seeds of each species for the quantity values.

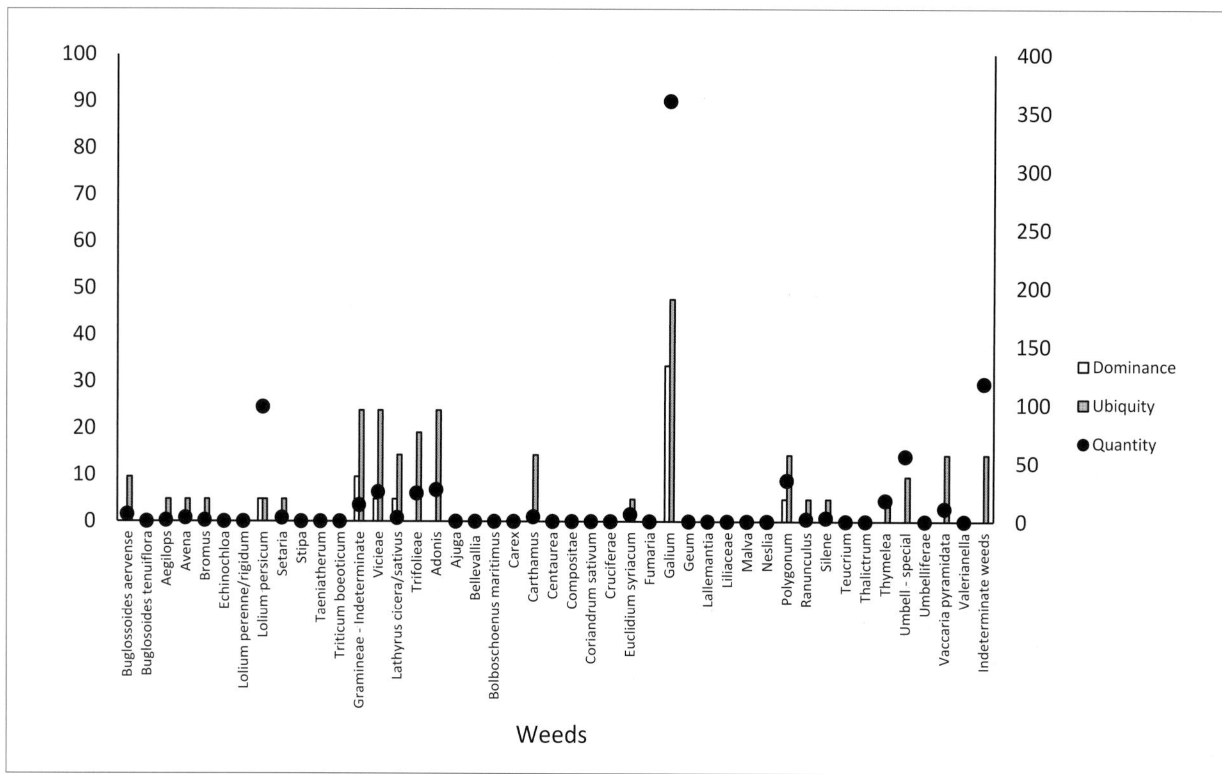

Fig. 114. Quantity, dominance and ubiquity of weeds at Aşvan Kale in the Hellenistic period. The left axis shows the number of contexts containing species and also the relative dominance of species as a percentage of the contexts analysed (n = 21), while the right axis shows the number of seeds of each species for the quantity values.

treatment of urinary infections. These properties come not from the seed but from the leaves or roots, and thus do not help to explain the charring of large numbers of seeds. Similarly, the *Galium* at Aşvan in Early Bronze Age II/III and Late Bronze Age samples was not found in a cache in any contexts and was also found alongside other weeds, suggesting that it was not being gathered for a specific purpose and instead had been brought in as part of the harvest. The high numbers might also suggest that the land was very disturbed, as *Galium* is a disturbance marker (Miller 2010).

Hellenistic and Roman

In the Hellenistic period samples *Galium* continues to be the most prevalent weed by all three measures, and this suggests that there was a high level of soil disturbance (Miller 2010).

The two Roman contexts have different weed assemblages, and it is notable that the most abundant weed in sample 1806.4 is *Bolboschoenus glaucus*. This weed prefers wet conditions such as riversides, canals, wadis and swamps (Aşvan botanical survey, see appendix 3). However, this single context cannot be used to extrapolate patterns for the entire site.

Medieval

Figure 115 shows that the quantity of indeterminate weeds in the Taşkun Kale samples is high, but they do not occur in the Aşvan Kale samples from this period, suggesting that the data may be influenced by the recovery procedures or may result from problems of species identification. The most prevalent weed by all three measures is *Vicieae*, followed closely by *Galium*. *Vicieae*, as a legume, has the potential to be a fodder crop (Townsend, Guest 1966–1985) and might indicate some reliance on herding compared with farming; but caution is needed in interpreting the low numbers of weeds found in the Medieval levels.

Change over time

The change in the prevalence of *Stipa* between the Late Chalcolithic and Early Bronze Age I is noted above. *Stipa* declined from being the most abundant species according to all three measures (quantity, dominance and ubiquity) to similar ubiquity but lower quantity and dominance than *Buglossoides arvense* and *Lolium persicum* in the Early Bronze Age I levels at Taşkun Mevkii. There may have been a change in the location of arable fields between the earlier and later periods, with a decline in the use of slopes

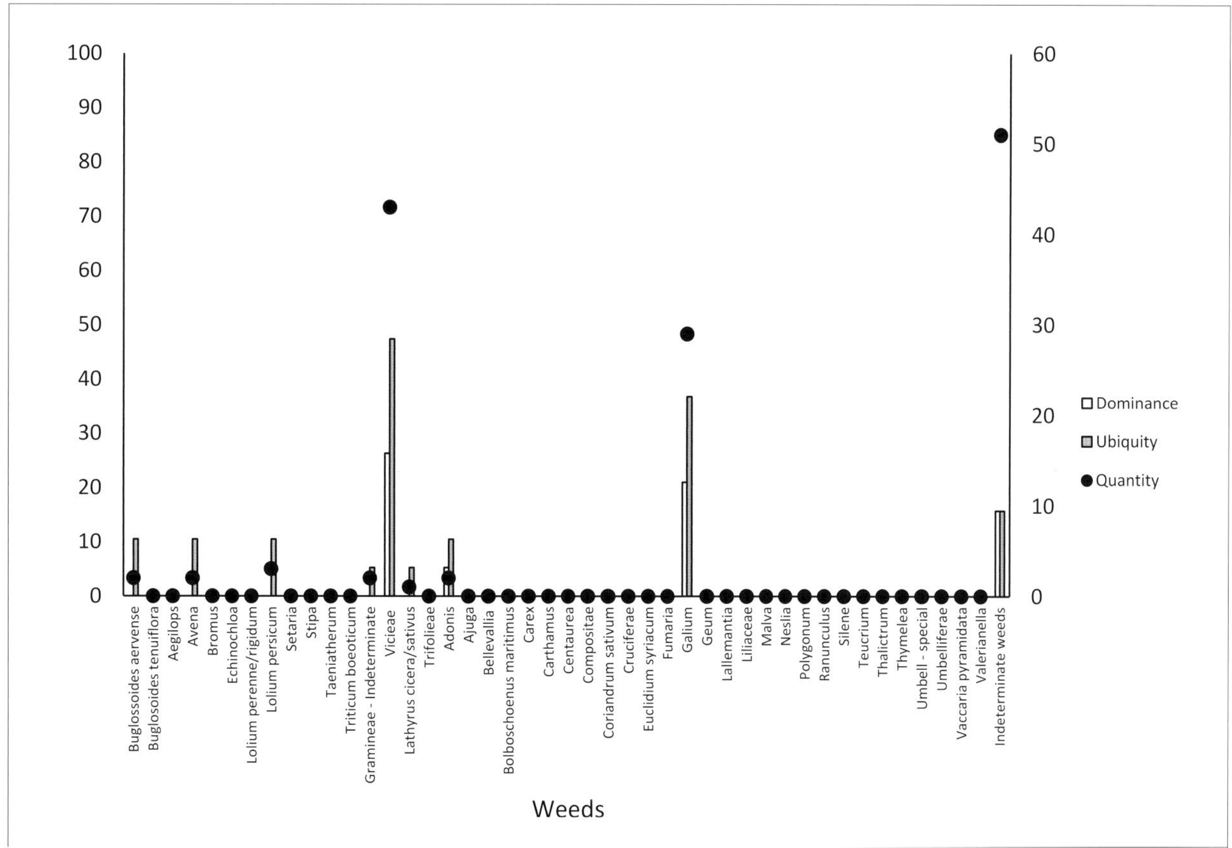

Fig. 115. Quantity, dominance and ubiquity of weeds at Aşvan Kale and Taşkun Kale in the Medieval period. The left axis shows the number of contexts containing species and also the relative dominance of species as a percentage of the contexts analysed (n = 19), while the right axis shows the number of seeds of each species for the quantity values.

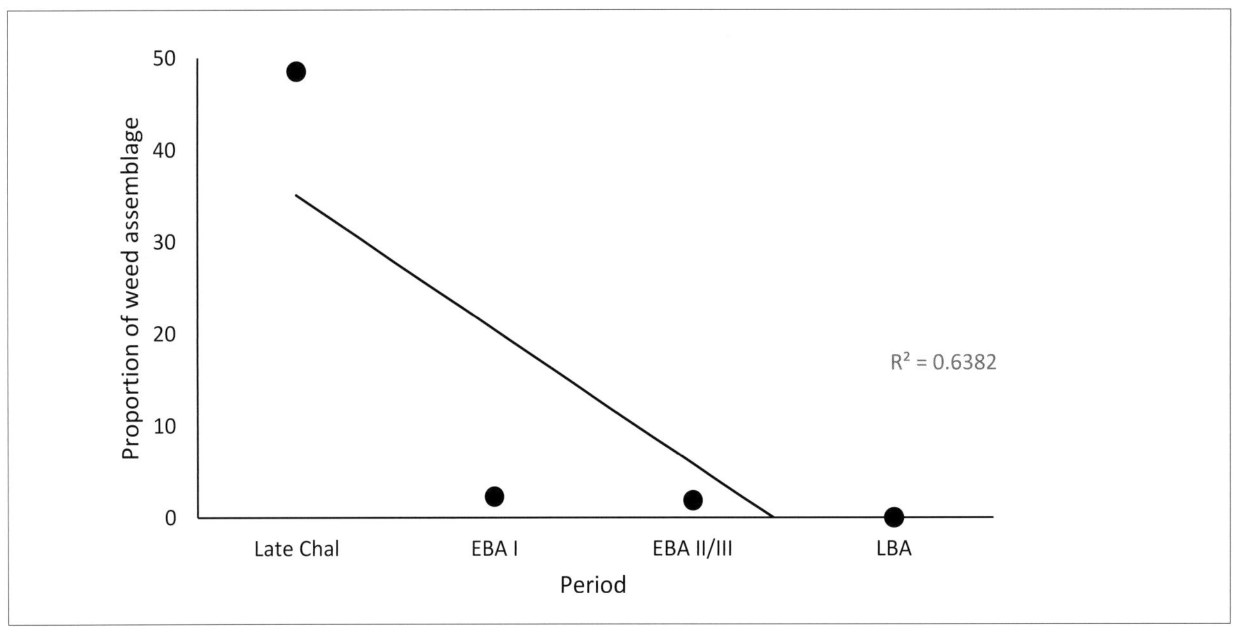

Fig. 116. Stipa *as a proportion of all weeds by period, showing linear regression line. Strong negative correlation is indicated by the R^2 value of 0.6.*

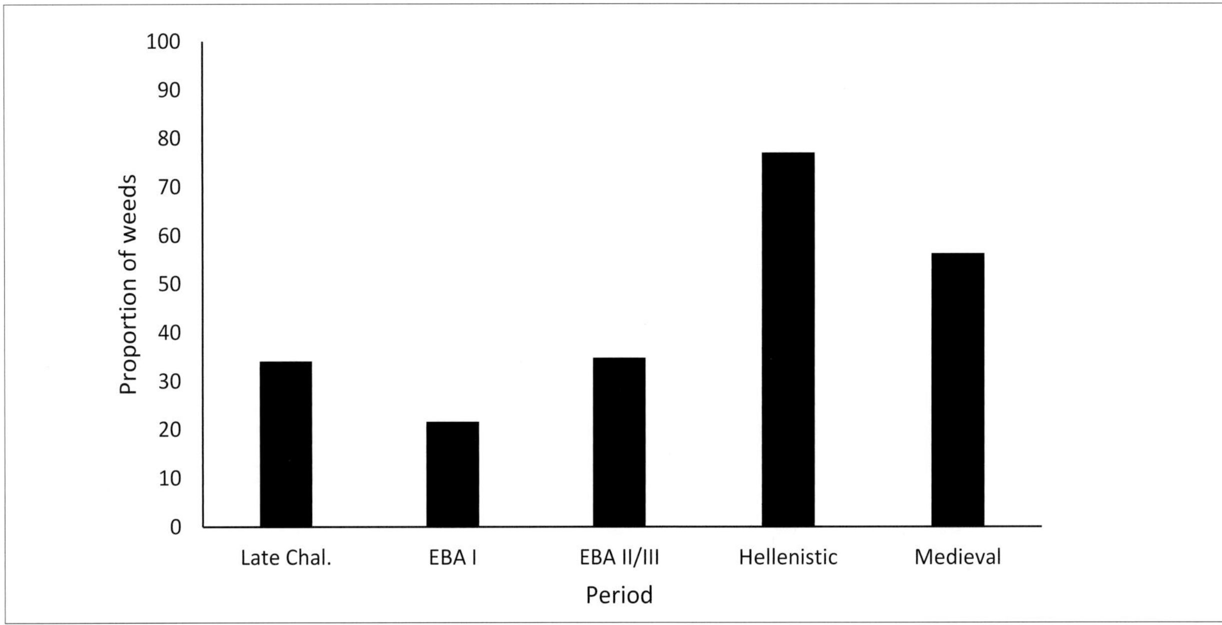

Fig. 117. Proportion of wet-habitat weeds by period (from irrigated fields, irrigation canals and ditches according to the Aşvan botanical surveys; see appendix 3).

or, as suggested above, the figures could indicate that the number of 'naturally' occurring weeds declined and they were replaced by those more commonly associated with arable fields. This would suggest that during Early Bronze Age I a typical arable weed flora was well established. Indeed, to judge from the occurrence of *Stipa* across the sites, the proportion of *Stipa* in the samples declined over time (fig. 116) with a strongly correlated linear trend (R^2 value 0.6). Allowing for the fact that the absence of *Stipa* in the Late Bronze Age may be explained by the small number of samples from this period, this may represent a normalising of the expansion of agricultural land that began in the Late Chalcolithic period. Over time, as slope areas were taken over for agricultural purposes, the proportion of *Stipa* was reduced and replaced by agricultural weeds.

Galium was an especially prevalent weed in the later period, replacing *Stipa* as the dominant species. *Galium* is commonly found in areas of high soil disturbance, and Miller (2010) has suggested that the proportion of *Galium* can be used as an indicator of the dependence on farming or even the intensity of farming. The proportion of *Galium* in the weed assemblage is highest in the Hellenistic period, but this observation relies on a number of other factors, such as preservation bias across sites and periods, and differential preservation between species. Not all weeds survive charring in the same fashion, and highly siliceous weeds survive better than others.

The incidence of *Buglossoides arvense* raises an interesting issue since the plants only grow to the low height of 15–20cm. As Lucie Martin (2015) points out, the inclusion of the seeds of such a low-growing plant in a cereal assemblage shows that harvesting involved low sickle cuts. This demonstrates an aspect of harvesting technology and the way in which crops were collected, but also implies that the full range of weeds was collected during the harvest, which would have consequences for post-harvest crop processing. *Buglossoides arvense* is present at all periods except the Late Bronze Age, when its absence is likely simply due to the small sample size.

Is there evidence for irrigation or water management? The answer provided from botanical records is complicated, as many wet-loving species will also be found in non-irrigated areas such as riverbanks, uncultivated swampy patches and floodplains. Using a similar approach to Miller (2010), an exploration of the proportions of weeds associated with irrigation was undertaken. Only weed species identified during the Aşvan botanical surveys as growing in irrigated fields, ditches and canals were included in this study as they are known to be associated with specifically irrigated conditions in this region (see appendix 3). Figure 117 suggests that there was a peak in wet-habitat plants in the Hellenistic period. This could indicate an increase in agricultural intensity in this period, perhaps relating to the exploitation of the later summer crops of millet, which would have had to be irrigated (Miller 2010). Alternatively, this could also be related to natural changes in water availability, a topic to be explored further in chapter 6.4.

The caveat to the pattern suggested in figure 117 is that these archaeobotanical samples have been subjected to numerous transformations from the processes of harvesting, charring and sampling (see chapter 4.1) and therefore do not necessarily represent the full field suite of wet-habitant weeds. However, they should provide a relative indication of changing water availability and input. This can then be compared with the climatic models which are discussed in chapter 6.

6. Evidence for climate change

6.1. Reconstructing climate change

The modelling of information about past climates in Anatolian Turkey is for the most part based on proxy data provided by pollen, geomorphology, lake salinity levels and oxygen isotopes. These, however, are not themselves direct evidence for climate change and often reflect other factors. Pollen, for instance, provides indications of the extent and nature of local vegetation cover, but climate is only one of the factors which determines this. Naomi Miller (1997) has noted that in the post-Bronze Age period other factors became more important as human actions such as agricultural intensification and resulting deforestation can mask the impact of climatic change in proxies. Models accordingly need to be interpreted with caution. The issue of time-scale is also crucial. Proxy climatic data and archaeological data are often collected at different resolutions and dated with different degrees of precision and by different criteria. Comparing archaeological and climate data can be complicated.

Even without these issues, understanding climate in eastern Anatolia between ca 4000 BC and AD 1500 is problematic because of the sparse records. Apart from the attention that has been given to specific events in prehistory, most notably the 8.2kya episode, a rapid cooling in the northern hemisphere that occurred around 6200 BC, there has been little focused research into the climate history of eastern Anatolia, and the small amount of data available is often stretched geographically to create larger models with a wide general application. The most comprehensive data-set from near the Aşvan sites is from Lake Van, the fourth largest terminal lake in the world (Lemcke, Sturm 1997; Wick et al. 2003). This lake is highly sensitive to climate changes. It sits approximately 350km east of the Aşvan sites in the transitional zone between two vegetation types: the high plateau steppe of northeastern Anatolia and the Kurdo-Zagrosian oak steppe-forest (Wick et al. 2003) that also characterises the Keban region (Zohary 1973). Any alterations in the position of the jet stream affect the lake's salinity and water levels, as well as the vegetation around it (Wick et al. 2003). The other data-sets that have been cited in building models for the eastern Anatolian region are those from Eski Acıgöl, approximately 400km west of Aşvan (Roberts et al. 2001), and the Pasinler Basin, approximately 300km northeast of Aşvan (Collins et al. 2005). There are also data-sets from Jebel al Aqra in southern Turkey (Casana 2008) and the Soreq Cave in Israel (Bar-Matthews et al. 1998). Several studies offer a pan-Anatolian or eastern Mediterranean perspective (Fairbridge et al. 1997; Collins et al. 2005; Beach, Luzzadder-Beach 2008; Dusar et al. 2011). Thus no data-sets are available for the immediate vicinity of the Aşvan sites. Furthermore, the available studies of the most relevant comparable data, partly as a result of their divergent geographical scope, do not necessarily provide a coherent or continuous chronology and rely on different proxy evidence, collection methods and research approaches, and use divergent dating methodologies.

6.2. Climatic models for the Aşvan study area

During the last Ice Age, at around 17,000 BP, temperatures and precipitation dropped to a low level (Dusar et al. 2011; Wick et al. 2003) and much of the Near East and Anatolia was covered in steppe. Lucia Wick and colleagues (2003) note the presence of steppe plants such as Chenopodiaceae (*Artemisia* sp.) and Apiaceae (*Ferula* sp., *Bunium* sp., *Pimpinella* sp.) at Lake Van. After 14,000BP there was a general period of warming and increased precipitation (Dusar et al. 2011; Wick et al. 2003), except for a period between 12,600 and 10,450 BP, during which the oxygen isotopes, Mg/Ca and pollen at Lake Van provide evidence for cold arid conditions (Lemcke, Sturm 1997; Wick et al. 2003). This should be equated with the Younger Dryas, the so-called Big Freeze. This period is distinguished by the presence of steppic plants such as *Ephedra* and Chenopodiaceae, typical of treeless deserts, and open steppe plants like Asteraceae (for example *Centaurea* sp., *Cousinia* sp.), Liliaceae (*Eremurus* sp., *Tulipa* sp.) and *Polygonum arviculare.* Around 10,450 BP there was a rapid shift back to warmer and wetter conditions (Lemcke, Sturm 1997; Wick et al. 2003). This warmer, wetter period was accompanied by the sporadic but increasing presence of deciduous trees, including *Quercus* sp., *Pistacia* sp. and *Salix* sp. (Wick et al. 2003), an increase in Poaceae and more frequent *Acer* sp. and *Amygdalus* sp., but also by a decrease in Chenopodiaceae, *Ferula* sp. and *Ephedra* (which also suggests improved soil quality) and an expansion of *Pistacia* sp. at Lake Van (Van Zeist, Bottema 1991; Wick et al. 2003). Timothy Beach and Sheryl Luzzadder-Beach (2008), in their more general summary of climate conditions in southern Anatolia, also note an increase in *Pinus* sp., *Quercus* sp., *Cedrus* sp. and *Juniperus* sp.

The difficulties involved in separating the human from climatic impact on vegetation has led to different opinions about the extent of climate change during the Holocene period and its effects on vegetation and agriculture in Anatolia and the Near East. According to the evidence from Lake Van, the most notable feature in the regional climate history of the early to mid Holocene was the Climatic Optimum, ca 6200–4000 BP, which roughly corresponds to the local Late Chalcolithic to Early Bronze Age II periods at the Aşvan sites (Wick et al. 2003). The indications for this climatic optimum are based on oxygen isotopes, Mg/Ca and pollen from Lake Van. Other summaries suggest that there were fluctuations at the broader level across Anatolia. Rhodes Fairbridge and colleagues (1997), for example, note warmer conditions between 3250 and 2900 BC in Anatolia generally. The more localised records from Lake Van and the Pasinler Basin (Wick et al. 2003; Collins et al. 2005) also suggest that this period was warm and wet with optimum soil conditions. This period witnessed the maximum extension of forest-steppe at Lake Van and Eski Acıgöl (Wick et al. 2003; Roberts et al. 2011), as well as the presence of deciduous oak and pistachio (Wick et al. 2003) and evidence for clearance (Beach, Luzadder-Beach 2008), which is also implied by the presence of *Pinus* sp. (Roberts et al. 2011).

The onset of drier conditions at the end of the Climatic Optimum, the so-called 4.2kya episode, is the climatic event that requires most discussion in relation to the four Aşvan sites. This transition has attracted attention from archaeologists seeking explanations for the widespread collapse in settlement density in the Near East and elsewhere after the 4.2kya event. It has been suggested that drier conditions led to agricultural failures and the collapse of existing socio-political organisation in an area which extended across the Indus Valley, Egypt and the Near East (see, for example, the papers in Dalfes et al. 1997). Both the causes and the extent of this change in the climate, and the synchronicity and extent of societal collapse, are matters for debate. The oxygen isotopes at Lake Van (Lemcke, Sturm 1997; Wick et al. 2003) and in the lake palaeohydrology of the Dead Sea (Migowski et al. 2006) suggest a sudden aridification. Wick and colleagues (2003) suggest that this would have resulted in drier conditions in spring, the cereal growing season. The various climatic proxy records provide little clarity about the length of this arid episode, and suggestions have included: a start date of 4200 BP (Migoswki et al. 2006); a range of 4100–3040 BP (Lemcke, Strum 1997), which would cover the Early Bronze Age III to Iron Age; or between the Early Bronze Age III and the Hellenistic period (4100–2100 BP) (Wick et al. 2003).

The subsequent picture is more complex. Two studies have concluded that there was a continental climate after Early Bronze Age III at Pasinler, and that from the Middle Bronze Age to the Iron Age conditions again were generally wetter (Roberts et al. 2011; Fairbridge et al. 1997). Catastrophic events, such as the eruptions of Thera ca 1650 BC and Hekla ca 1159 BC in the Aegean area, may have had a short-term impact on the regional climate area, and the latter eruption has been linked to the end of the Mediterranean Late Bronze Age (Neumann, Parpola 1987; Kuniholm 1990). Human impact on land-use is observable in the Lake Van pollen records from the Middle Bronze Age onwards, and this includes the spread of plantain, *Plantago lanceolata*, which may have accompanied agricultural developments in the Iron Age (Wick et al. 2003). Beach and Luzadder-Beach (2008) summarise the impact of human activity on southern Anatolia and the eastern Mediterranean region as leading to an increase of *Olea* sp. (olive), *Juglans* sp. (walnut) and *Pistacia* sp. (pistachio), and a decline in *Pinus* sp., *Cedrus* sp. and *Juniperus* sp. Bert Dusar and colleagues (2011) note increases in cereals, olive, walnut, *Tamarix* sp. and *Vitis* sp. (grape), as well as indications of disturbance shown by the occurrence of *Rumex* sp., *Plantago* sp. and *Artemisia* sp. Soil erosion evidence has been cited to argue for a brief phase of extreme precipitation at Jebel al Aqra during the Hellenistic period (Casana 2008), but this is not reflected in other records, which instead suggest a more variable rainfall situation and minor oscillations between wet and dry conditions during a period in which temperatures were in general similar to those of the present day (Reale, Dirmeyer 2000; Wick et al. 2003; Dusar et al. 2011).

More recent events have affected the Aşvan region. One is a general decline in anthropic signatures seen in the eastern Mediterranean at the end of what has been called the Beyşehir Occupation Phase (BOP; running from ca 1000 BC to ca AD 670). Dusar and colleagues (2011, citing Kaniewski et al. 2007 and England et al. 2008), argue that this was accompanied by the development of secondary *Pinus* sp. woodland, and that agriculture was not re-established on a similar scale to that of the Beyşehir Occupation Phase until ca AD 1100. This re-establishment of agriculture may coincide with a period of warming, which has been suggested for the period ca AD 900–1300 in the Near East (for example Reale, Dirmeyer 2000; Dusar et al. 2011), but no consensus has been reached on this. Evidence for a period of increased rainfall between AD 1000–1800 has also been noted from sites including the Soreq Cave in Israel, the Jebel al Aqra region and the Pasinler Basin (for example Bar-Matthews et al. 1998; Collins et al. 2005; Casana 2008; Dusar et al. 2011), although Wick and colleagues (2003) do not note this from Lake Van, and comment only on the intensification of agriculture in the pollen record at this period. Oreste Reale and Paul Dirmeyer (2000) have also postulated that the Little Ice Age, ca AD 1500–1800, would have affected eastern Anatolia.

In essence then, there is evidence for some climatic events in the Holocene period that may have affected the sites, and these include the shift from the Climatic Optimum through the 4.2kya episode to the milder continental conditions that followed. The impact of these was minor compared with the impact of the last Ice Age which occurred during the Late Glacial period. Despite some indications of variations in the extent of cultivation and types of agricultural practice, there is little consensus on the impact of climate change in the later historical periods.

6.3. Charcoal evidence for fuel use and vegetation change

George Willcox's study of the charcoal finds from the Aşvan excavations did not investigate the archaeological context of the samples. Species were scored on the basis of the percentage of samples (i.e. ubiquity) that occurred during any given period at the four sites (Willcox 1974).

For the Chalcolithic period and Early Bronze Age oak (*Quercus* sp.) is present in 100% and Salicaceae (poplar and willow) in about 20% of the samples. Shrubby plants like Ulmaceae (probably *Celtis* sp. – hackberry) occurred in 50% of the Chalcolithic and about 15% of the Early Bronze Age samples. *Pistacia* sp. (terebinth) only occurs in the Chalcolithic material, with *Juniperus* sp. also present, but only in fewer than 5% of samples. Oak, *Pistacia* and juniper woodland also appear to have been exploited for fuel and timber in the Late Chalcolithic and Early Bronze Age periods.

As few classical samples were available, Willcox amalgamated the Hellenistic and Roman results. Oak occurs in about 50%, Salicaceae in about 60%, juniper in 20% and Ulmaceae in 30% of the 41 samples. Willcox deduced from the increase in Salicaeae that poplars, which might have provided roof beams for buildings, were being deliberately planted or protected, and that their growth was helped by irrigation. Without this they risked extinction, given the limited extent of their riverine habitat (Willcox 1974).

For the early Medieval period oak makes up 80% of the 54 samples, with Salicaceae and *Juniperus* also present. For the late Medieval material the incidence of oak decreases to 40% and *Pinus* sp. evidently became important at this time. Willcox suggests that the pine in these late Medieval samples had probably been imported for use as roof timbers from the Pontic region to the north of Aşvan. At the same time, there was an increase in *Juniperus* sp., which may represent its expansion into cleared forest, before it became extinct between the late Medieval period and the present day.

Rarer tree species in the classical-period samples included spiny shrubs such as *Lycium* sp., *Rubus* sp. and *Paliurus spina-christi*. These are resistant to grazing and could thus expand into deforested areas. They would have been more widely collected for fuel once the spineless, more easily collectable species were no longer growing in the area (Willcox 1974).

The evidence points clearly to large-scale deforestation by human agency at some period after the Early Bronze Age. In view of the high level of settlement in the Late Bronze Age and Roman period there is no need to invoke climate change as an explanation. There is also historical evidence for large-scale exploitation of wood in the 19th century for use in the mines at Keban, which would have exhausted much of any tree cover that remained.

Charcoal remains have also been studied at Arslantepe, where the large temple in the Late Uruk phase VIA (3350–3000 BC) was destroyed by fire. The charcoal of many structural timbers has been preserved (Sadori et al. 2008). The dominant species were alder (*Alnus* sp.), pine (*Pinus* sp.), juniper (*Juniperus* sp.) and poplar (*Populus* sp.). All of these trees were tall and straight, and thus suitable for building purposes. The near absence of species such as oak cannot in itself be regarded as significant for environmental reconstruction.

Subsequent investigation of a much wider range of charcoal samples from Arslantepe has found evidence of change through time (Masi et al. 2011). The summary results indicate a predominance of wet environment species such as alder, poplar and ash in the Late Uruk period (Arslantepe VIA) and Early Bronze Age III (phase VID), and of woody steppe species such as oak in Early Bronze Age I–II (phases VIB1 –VIC). A switch to wet-loving species in the last part of the Early Bronze Age would not necessarily contradict the results from Aşvan, where the long gap in samples after the Early Bronze Age makes it impossible to date the decline in oak use. This could have occurred at the end of the Early Bronze Age. The results from the Late Uruk period at Arslantepe VIA are not consistent with those from Aşvan. However, it is likely that the massive burning in Arslantepe level VIA has led to over-representation of wood used for structural timbers in these samples, and that this evidence is not necessarily representative of the overall incidence of these trees in the wider landscape. It is necessary to take the contexts of these samples into account when making comparisons with timber use on other sites.

Robert Whallon and Sönmez Kantman (1969) suggest that the wealth and number of occupied sites and the hierarchy of the Altınova region might have been based on metal production and on the export of timber, which could be floated down the Euphrates to Mesopotamia. Metal smelting is highly plausible as the area is rich in copper, iron, lead and silver. Wood exports are possible, but the evidence is tenuous. Whallon and Kantman (1969) note that the eastern Taurus mountains, potentially including the Elazığ region, are referred to in Sumerian accounts as the 'wild cypress mountain' (Rowton 1967), and that cypress was exported to Sumer, resulting in deforestation during the Early Bronze Age. This specific hypothesis is implausible. No cypress (*Cupressus sempervirens*) is recorded in the Aşvan charcoal or at other sites in the region. It is a rare tree in Turkey, restricted to Mediterranean habitats, and has not been found even in the more protected woodland areas of east-central Anatolia. However, the Sumerian term *ha-šu-úr*, previously translated as cypress, may have the more general meaning of 'tree', and the reference may be less specific than previously thought.

6.4. Correlating archaeobotany and climate

The proxy evidence provided by pollen for climate change has been affected by human activity, and this necessarily occupies an even larger place in the discussion of archaeobotanical indicators of climate change (Hillman 1991; Van Zeist 1993; Riehl 2009; 2012). Carbonised seeds from archaeological sites are not a direct proxy for environmental reconstruction as they result from human actions such as crop processing (Hillman 1991; Van Zeist 1993; Riehl 2009). However, as Simone Riehl (2009) has stated, it is for this reason that charred plant remains present an opportunity to explore human decision making in the face of climatic change. Riehl has examined the impact of mid-Holocene climatic events on the archaeobotanical remains from Near Eastern sites and her work has important implications for the current study (Riehl 2009; 2012). On the basis that 'agricultural decision making is based on variable and complex relationships of environmental conditions and change, economic interests, political goals and cultural preferences', she argues that the political and economic background to agricultural practices may be heavily influenced or determined by environmental stress factors such as drought, while human political and economic interests play a larger role in determining the agricultural system under stable environmental conditions (Riehl 2009: 96). In an arid or semi-arid region such as the Near East, and in the Aşvan case, where the rainfall was on average below 400mm per year, water is one of the key stress factors, and a plant species' susceptibility to drought will play an important role in decisions about whether to cultivate it or not (Riehl 2009). Other factors in arid or semi-arid regions include a plant's tolerance of saline soils, its speed of growth (also a factor in drought tolerance) and its yield in response to water stress (Riehl 2009: table 1). Riehl clarifies these assumptions about the interplay between humans and climate, noting that 'there is no general straightforwardness in the relationship between climate change and local economic development', and that other factors such as the overall economic environment of production and consumption, agricultural specialisation, 'innovation capacity' (see Van der Leeuw 2009) and social preferences can also play a role (Riehl 2012: 113). Overall Riehl's analysis of the impact of climate change, and especially the 4.2kya episode, on Near Eastern agriculture deals with the presence or absence, ubiquity and proportion of crops at 138 sites in the Near East over the Early Bronze Age to Iron Age, and concludes that there are notable shared broad-scale patterns of change related to the 4.2kya episode, but that these are variable and influenced by economic interests and climatic conditions at the local scale. Riehl argues that the abandonment of emmer wheat, a drought-resistant crop, was not due to aridification but was caused by economic concerns about yield and labour investment. In addition, the westward shift in the cultivation of grass pea across the region in the Middle Bronze Age is seen to relate to the extent of local water availability during the aridification period (Riehl 2009; 2012).

6.5. Aşvan plant remains

The species suite noted from the Aşvan sites is very similar to that noted by Simone Riehl and Mark Nesbitt in their discussions of agricultural responses to climatic changes in the Near East from the Early Bronze Age to the Iron Age and Hellenistic period (Riehl, Nesbitt 2003; Riehl 2009; 2012). The crop patterns at the Aşvan sites are situated on luvic calcisols in a semi-arid area of similar rainfall potential (200–400mm per year) to that of the Near Eastern sites. As such, they would be expected to conform to the models presented in Riehl 2009 and 2012, and Riehl and Nesbitt 2003. In the light of this hypothesis we will examine the appearance, disappearance and frequency (quantity, dominance and ubiquity, see chapter 5.2.1) of crops by period at the Aşvan sites, looking for patterns that may correlate to the climatic models described in section 6.2.

6.5.1. Drought-resistant crops

Of all the species considered by Riehl which are found at the Aşvan sites, barley is the most drought- and saline-tolerant species. Barley is also one of the dominant crops at the Aşvan sites in all periods (chapter 5.3), with little change over time in its use relative to other crops.

Free-threshing wheat was also present. There was a marked change in the use of free-threshing wheat between the Late Chalcolithic period at Çayboyu and the Early Bronze Age I period at Taşkun Mevkii, when it went from being a minor cereal to reaching similar levels of dominance and ubiquity to barley, although it was less abundant than barley (figs 99 and 106). For subsequent periods it was found in comparable ubiquity, dominance and quantity to barley, suggesting it was an equally important crop after Early Bronze Age I. Free-threshing wheats are less tolerant of drought but still considered as a generally drought-resistant crop (Riehl 2009). As noted in chapter 3.4.1.2, it is impossible to distinguish the type of free-threshing wheat based on the grains alone. Tetraploid wheats are in fact more drought-tolerant than hexaploid ones (Riehl 2009), but as only seven pieces of free-threshing chaff identifiable at ploidy level were recovered from the Aşvan sites (the majority are hexaploid), this line of enquiry could not be followed up. Because there is little change over time in the ubiquity, dominance and quantity of free-threshing wheat in the samples it seems that its use remained relatively constant in the Late Chalcolithic and Early Bronze Age periods.

Hulled wheat, emmer, appears in the Late Chalcolithic contexts at Çayboyu in equal quantity, ubiquity and dominance to barley, but it is rare and found only in small quantities in the Early Bronze Age I samples from Taşkun Mevkii, suggesting a change in its importance between these periods (figs 99 and 106). It is not present in the Early Bronze Age II/III samples from Aşvan Kale and does not reappear in later samples (fig. 108). This is interesting, as emmer is regarded as a drought-tolerant (Nesbitt, Samuel 1996; Riehl 2009) and possibly a saline-tolerant crop (Hunshal et al. 1990), although this final point has been questioned (see Nesbitt, Samuel 1996). Emmer also tolerates poor soil quality (Riehl 2009). Other than the cereals, the most notable drought-tolerant crop is bitter vetch (*Vicia ervilia*). This pulse is not the most ubiquitous of the legumes in the Late Chalcolithic or Early Bronze Age I samples, but increases in proportion after the Early Bronze Age II/III to become as common as lentils. Although drought-tolerant, this pulse is toxic and requires special processing to make it palatable (Riehl 2009).

6.5.2. Drought-susceptible and less tolerant crops

Unlike its hulled relative, einkorn wheat is extremely susceptible to drought (Oleinikova 1976), and Riehl describes it as one of the crops 'least likely to be grown in a period of increasing aridity' (Riehl 2009: 104). However, einkorn is not present as a major crop in samples from any period at the Aşvan sites (figs 99 and 106). According to the charred samples that were excavated and analysed (fig 108), it occurred in small quantities and low ubiquity in the Late Chalcolithic and Early Bronze Age I, and by Early Bronze Age II/III had ceased being used at the sites.

The millets *Panicum miliaceum* and *Setaria italica* appear in the Hellenistic period samples (fig. 116), probably as a consequence of the introduction of summer cropping (Nesbitt, Summers 1988), but were not found in large quantities, dominance or ubiquity. This suggests that they were not a staple part of the diet but may have been a supplementary feature of the agricultural production system. Miller (2010) has argued that, although millet is often considered to be drought-tolerant, as a summer crop under the dry seasonal conditions in Anatolia it would require irrigation to supplement the low rainfall. The results of the analysis of wet-habitat weeds indicate that the greatest incidence of this weed assemblage occurred in the Hellenistic period, and this may indicate that some form of irrigation had been introduced (fig. 127; see chapter 5.7).

By all three measures the most commonly identified pulse is lentil. This pulse has a moderate stress tolerance (Riehl 2009), but experiments have suggested that the yield drops in arid conditions (Erskine, El 1993). However, the ubiquity and use of lentils do not appear to have changed much between periods at the Aşvan sites. This is not the case with garden peas. *Pisum sativum* has moderate to low drought tolerance but high to moderate salinity tolerance (Riehl 2009), and yields react to soil moisture. Unlike lentils there is a pattern of decline after the Early Bronze Age in all three frequency measures (ubiquity, quantity and dominance) at the Aşvan sites. Chickpea does not appear to have played a major role in any period.

Domesticated grapes occur at Aşvan from Early Bronze Age I. Grapes require soil moisture and fairly high rainfall (ca 500–1200mm) in the growing season (February to July), and therefore probably benefitted from supplemental irrigation (Riehl 2009), even if this was not an obligatory requirement. Cotton was a Medieval arrival at the Aşvan sites, and requires a significant amount of water to grow (Riehl 2009). Flax also needs abundant water (Riehl 2009). It was not a major crop in any period, but is found in greatest quantity in the Chalcolithic samples.

6.6. Aşvan in context

6.6.1. Regional

Riehl's models show a pattern similar to that outlined for the Aşvan sites across the Near East. Barley was the main crop in all periods between the Early Bronze Age and Iron Age. She also observes the decline and disappearance of emmer across the whole of Syria during the Early Bronze

Age, noting some regional variation; emmer is better represented in the southern Levant, while free-threshing wheats were favoured in northern Mesopotamia. By the Middle Bronze Age emmer had disappeared except from two upper Khabur sites. Free-threshing wheats show a different pattern in that they decreased between the Early and Late Bronze Age in all regions except the southern Levant, and increased again in the Iron Age, a period during which there was a uniform pattern of wheat use, favouring free-threshing wheat. Bitter vetch increased in ubiquity in the Middle Bronze Age and remained stable in all regions except the southern Levant. As at the Aşvan sites, lentils were the most widespread crop in all periods across the Near East, but, unlike at the Aşvan sites, there was a decline in ubiquity in the Middle Bronze Age, and also a shift in use towards the Mediterranean coast between the Middle and Late Bronze Age (Riehl 2009; 2012). In the Iron Age this crop returned to similar use patterns as in the Early Bronze Age. The use of garden peas declined in the Middle Bronze Age, and their cultivation shifted westwards, but recovered slightly in the Iron Age. As at the Aşvan sites, einkorn and flax exploitation virtually died out in the Near East after the Middle Bronze Age. Flax, however, recovered in the southern Levant in the Iron Age (Riehl 2009). Grape shows a decline in ubiquity in the Middle Bronze but an increase in the Late Bronze and Iron Ages. Riehl's (2009; 2012) models then show similar patterns to that from the Aşvan sites, and her Near Eastern trends can be extrapolated to eastern Anatolia on the basis of the Aşvan data; but there are local variations and temporal distributions, for instance, between the northern and southern Levant (Riehl 2009).

Riehl and Nesbitt (2003) have also explored Iron Age cropping patterns across the Aegean region, Anatolia and the Near East. While there is little observed change in the major cereal crops, they note that millets became more common across the Near East in this period. This development can already be observed in areas flanking the Near East such as Greece and Iran in the Middle Bronze Age (Nesbitt, Summers 1988; Nesbitt 2016), but becomes marked in the Iron Age (Riehl, Nesbitt 2003). A few millet seeds have been noted from Middle Bronze Age Sos Höyük (Longford et al. 2009) and Late Bronze Age Kilise Tepe (Colledge 2001b; Nesbitt, Summers 1988), respectively in northeastern and south-central Turkey, and more have been found at Iron Age Tille Höyük on the middle Euphrates (Nesbitt, Summers 1988). There seems to be a similar evolution in the cultivation of sesame, another summer crop, as well as almond and grape. Riehl and Nesbitt accordingly characterise the Iron Age as a period of agricultural diversification in the Near East (Riehl, Nesbitt 2003). The general pattern is demonstrated at Aşvan by the appearance of millets in the Hellenistic period.

6.6.2. Climatic

The climatic models discussed in section 6.2 suggest there should be a shift at the Aşvan sites from a more mixed assemblage in the Late Chalcolithic and Early Bronze Age I and II periods, before the 4.2kya event, towards a more drought-tolerant assemblage during the more arid period of Early Bronze Age III, with a possible return towards a more diverse assemblage at a later date in the Hellenistic period. The picture is more complicated in later periods, but proxy indicators, which have been applied to analysing prehistoric climate change, have recently been identified and interpreted as evidence that periods of warmer and/or wetter climate may have been responsible for agricultural intensification from the Byzantine period and led to a more varied agricultural strategy.

There are some changes in the pattern of cultivation in the earlier periods that have a bearing on climatic modelling. The first is the transformation of wheat cultivation between the Chalcolithic and the Early Bronze Age. During this period hulled wheats, mainly emmer but also the minor cereal, einkorn, disappeared and were replaced by free-threshing wheat. This is surprising during a period which has been linked with the onset of drier conditions, given that emmer is more tolerant of drought than free-threshing wheats. It has been argued (Nesbitt, Samuel 1996; Riehl, Nesbitt 2003; Riehl 2009; 2012) that the driver of this change was not climate change, but economic preference. Three explanations have been proposed for the disappearance of emmer and einkorn: change in production aims (i.e. yield and demand), change in use, resulting from different dietary or culinary choices, and cultural preferences. Riehl sums up the first argument surrounding the abandonment of hulled wheats as 'explained best by reference to its economic properties, such as time-consuming processing in comparison with free-threshing wheat, making it less attractive as a staple food compared with other cereals' (Riehl 2009: 111). It has been suggested (Nesbitt, Samuel 1996) that, regardless of the climatic events, there was economic pressure across the Near East for increased productivity which resulted in a shift from cultivating the harder-to-process hulled wheats to the easier free-threshing varieties. However, at Aşvan there is no indication of the higher population or increased centralisation that might have led to significant changes in agricultural production. In fact, survey evidence suggests that population density decreased in the Kura-Araxes phase of Early Bronze Age I. There is, then, little data to explain why farmers chose to grow – or not to grow – emmer and einkorn wheat. In general, the disappearance of these crops during the Bronze Age and Iron Age in the Near East suggests they lost favour as populations grew and settlement centralisation increased. But there is no obvious reason why small-scale farmers (such as those in the Kura-Araxes cultural area, which extended to the Aşvan sites) would drop these species. Dietary preferences are hard to detect in the archaeological record, and investigation of this line of enquiry would require a study of food-processing technology and pottery uses that is outside the scope of the current study.

Nevertheless, archaeological evidence supports the explanation that the change was driven by cultural preference. The introduction of free-threshing wheats coincides with the transition at Aşvan between the Late Chalcolithic and Kura-Araxes cultures. According to a preliminary analysis, the Kura-Araxes Late Chalcolithic levels at Sos Höyük in the Pasinler Valley of eastern Anatolia are dominated by barley and free-threshing wheat (Longford et al. 2009). The preference for free-threshing wheat may be part of this cultural shift rather than a development linked to wider Near Eastern patterns. Full study of the plant remains from Sos Höyük and other Kura-Araxes sites may elucidate this further. The disappearance of hulled wheats, in particular emmer, cannot be related to climatic events; it appears to be the outcome of regional economic or cultural decisions.

There is little evidence at Aşvan to support arguments for climate change in the later periods. The staples of barley and free-threshing wheat had been well-established since Early Bronze Age I when the main cropping system was settled: barley and free-threshing wheat formed the basis, accompanied by lentils and bitter vetch, with all other cultivars except the summer crops being incidental additions. Summer crops of millet, made possible by irrigation, were introduced in the Hellenistic period. The appearance of millet is evidence for a more diverse cropping strategy and intensification based on irrigation, part of a process which occurred across the Near East during the Iron Age and subsequent periods (Nesbitt, Summers 1988; Riehl, Nesbitt 2003; Riehl 2009; 2012; Miller 2010).

The introduction of new summer crops in the Iron Age across the Near East and in Anatolia, including cumin (see chapters 3.7.3 and 5.5) and almond (chapter 3.6.2), could have coincided with the continued aridity noted at Lake Van (Lemcke, Sturm 1997; Wick et al. 2003) but not with the increased precipitation noted in the Pasinler Basin (Roberts et al. 2011). This is a classic example of the difficulty in correlating archaeological and palaeoenvironmental datasets.

The range and diversity of other crops grown at Aşvan continued as before, and there were no further significant additions until the appearance of cotton in the Medieval period, another summer crop that probably depended on irrigation (Riehl 2009; Miller 2010). It might be expected that cotton would have appeared alongside millet, but only a single cotton seed has been found in the Hellenistic samples, possibly the result of contamination, and it was not until the Medieval period that cotton was exploited as a main fibre and oil crop (chapter 5.5). Figure 127 shows a large proportion of wet-habitat weeds relative to total weed numbers, indicating that there may have been some irrigation in the Medieval period, although perhaps on a smaller scale than in the Hellenistic period. This statement however needs to be taken with some caution given the taphonomic differences between the periods (see chapter 4.1, 4.4).

One example that might support the theory of climatic impact on agricultural production at the Aşvan sites is the change in pulses, which can also be seen across the Near East (Riehl 2009). Pulses are particularly susceptible to changes in water availability because it affects their yields or restricts where they can grow. At Aşvan there was a decrease in garden pea, a particularly drought-susceptible crop, and an increase in drought-tolerant bitter vetch during Early Bronze Age II/III, roughly at the time of the 4.2kya event. This pattern is also noted in Riehl's study of the Near East and she argues that 'decreasing mean annual rainfall is the best explanation' (Riehl 2009: 111).

6.7. Conclusions

The relationship between climatic change and the Aşvan agricultural strategy is unsurprisingly neither simple nor clear cut. The relationship between people and climate is complicated (Butzer 1982; McIntosh et al. 2000; Rosen 2007), and, to quote Riehl, 'there is an almost unmanageable amount of literature on environmental psychology and cultural ecology studying the influence of the environment on human perception' (Riehl 2012: 118). Arlene Rosen has argued that not everyone reacts to climate change or will even perceive it in the same way within a culture because 'there are several different dimensions of environmental perception' (Rosen 2007: 8). At the same time, a range of factors, including the regularity with which periods of drought occur, the level of agricultural specialisation and technological innovations, affects the ways in which populations react to the environment (Riehl 2012). This complexity is seen in the impact of the 4.2kya episode on the Aşvan sites and the Near East more generally. Although climatic change might be a reason for the change in the species of pulses grown, the shift from emmer to free-threshing wheat is not so easily explicable, and may instead be related to issues of cultural preference, crop processing and yield. The question becomes more complicated after the Bronze Age, not least because of the time gaps between the Aşvan sites. It has been suggested (Riehl, Nesbitt 2003;

Riehl 2009) that the Iron Age was a particularly important period in the Near East as it shows evidence for 'enrichment in food production' (Riehl 2009: 112) and diversification in the form of summer production (Riehl, Nesbitt 2003). Riehl and Nesbitt have argued that while some palaeo-environmental proxies suggest continuing arid conditions, the introduction of water-demanding species in this period shows the importance of irrigation to the agricultural strategies of the Near East.

In the later periods, while agricultural strategies at the Aşvan sites still relied heavily on drought-tolerant species such as barley and free-threshing wheat, irrigation technology enabled the introduction of more summer crops. An awareness of rainfall variability and the recurrent risk of hard drought conditions were major factors that shaped the agricultural choices of the peoples of the Aşvan sites. The combination of technological innovation and a well-adapted strategy following the 4.2kya episode seems to have resulted in a resilient agricultural system, which was subject to relatively little change in the Byzantine and Medieval periods, and was not seriously affected by contemporary climatic events.

7. The archaeobotany of Aşvan in context

7.1. Aşvan in a regional context

7.1.1. The Keban-Malatya region

The most complete study of economic change between the Late Chalcolithic and Early Bronze Age in the Keban-Malatya region relates to the site of Arslantepe (Frangipane 2010; Restelli et al. 2010). Archaeobotanical data have been used to compare the centralised and Uruk-influenced Late Chalcolithic phase VI A and the Early Bronze Age village of phase VI B2 at Arslantepe. Cereal production during both periods was dominated by hulled barley: six-row in VI A and two-row in VI B2. Wheat was the second most dominant crop in both periods, consisting mainly of emmer, with some einkorn and a small proportion of free-threshing wheat. This suggests that, unlike at the Aşvan sites, there was no shift towards free-threshing wheats at Arslantepe between the Late Chalcolithic and Early Bronze Age I. The argument is complicated, however, by the low incidence of seeds found in phase VI B1 at Arslantepe (3000–2900 BC). This phase is archaeologically comparable to the settlement at Taşkun Mevkii, as both belonged to the Kura-Axes cultural sphere, evidenced by the use of red-burnished pottery and circular wattle-and-daub houses. However, the decline in the use of hulled wheats seen at Taşkun Mevkii becomes apparent only in Early Bronze Age II/III at Arslantepe in the assemblages of phase VI C, which are dominated by barley with a little free-threshing wheat, (although it must be noted this comes from a single room and could therefore indicate a specialised storage area), and phase VI D, which is dominated by free-threshing wheat, with minor components of barley and emmer present. The sites of Korucutepe, Tepecik (Van Zeist and Bakker-Heeres in Van Loon 1975: 225–57) and Tille (Nesbitt 2016) also show a reduction in the use of hulled wheat, so that by the Middle Bronze and Iron Ages there are only trace amounts of this crop in southeastern Turkey. The Early Bronze Age is the crucial period of transition from hulled to free-threshing wheats. At the Aşvan sites the relatively small number of samples (albeit containing large numbers of grains) from Early Bronze Age I Taşkun Mevkii point to the main shift taking place at the beginning of the Early Bronze Age. This observation is subject to the cautionary note that there was an interval of up to 1,000 years between the Late Chalcolithic settlement at Çayboyu and that at Taşkun Mevkii, and, accordingly, the chronology of the change is not fixed precisely. This shift is not found at the site of Sos Höyük (Longford et al. 2009), where free-threshing wheats occur from the earliest period at the site, the Late Chalcolithic. In their preliminary conclusions Catherine Longford and her colleagues argue that the shift instead 'may have occurred earlier in the north-eastern highlands of Anatolia than in the rest of the region. This could be because this region in the Late Chalcolithic was part of the Early Transcaucasian cultural complex' (Longford et al. 2009: 126). However, if the change to free-threshing wheats at Aşvan occurred during the early part of the 1,000-year gap that separates Çayboyu from Early Bronze Age I Taşkun Mevkii, then it might have been nearly contemporary with their introduction at Sos Höyük.

The most securely established change at Arslantepe is that from six-row barley in phase VI A to two-row barley which dominates VI B2 and VI C. Francesca Restelli has argued that this represents either a change in the function of the crop, from fodder to human food source, or, given the greater water requirements of six-row barley, a decline in the practice of crop irrigation (Restelli et al. 2010: 116). However, these interpretations remain hypotheses. Apart from two batches from Taşkun Mevkii, all the samples from the Aşvan sites, regardless of period, contain two-row barley, and this is also the pattern at Korucutepe (Van Zeist and Bakker-Heeres in Van Loon 1975: 225–57). The Sos Höyük preliminary data show a dominance of hulled barley in the Late Chalcolithic, Middle Bronze Age and Iron Age (Longford et al. 2003), although there is uncertainty whether this was the two- or six-row type. The samples do not suggest that barley was being used as a fodder at the Aşvan sites, and the ethnographic evidence does not favour an interpretation of foddering. These observations support Restelli's interpretation of the two-row barley at Arslantepe as a human food source. There is also little change in the animal bone assemblage at Arslantepe to indicate changes in husbandry between the Late Chalcolithic and Early Bronze Age. In both periods sheep and goat account for about 70–75% of the individuals, followed by cattle at about 20% (Bartosiewicz 2010; Palumbi 2010). Furthermore, Laura Sadori and her colleagues (2006) state that there is no evidence for beer-making at Arslantepe in the form of germinated caryopses or other ingredients, another similarity to the Aşvan sites.

This raises the question of the extent to which the Kura-Araxes culture found in the first part of the Early Bronze Age was a pastoralist society. The relatively large amounts of grain found at Early Bronze Age I Taşkun Mevkii, associated with wattle-and-daub houses and pottery that are clearly of Kura-Araxes tradition, point to a society carrying out agriculture with a broad diversity of crop types – cereals, pulses, grapes and flax – which were capable of supporting a sedentary population. Zooarchaeological evidence from Late Chalcolithic sites like Sos Höyük and Early Bronze Age sites like Arslantepe shows that both large and small settlements derived their meat and wool mainly from sheep or goats and also from herded cattle; thus distinguishing between farming and pastoralist sites might not be possible on the basis of their animal-bone spectra. Pastoralist management of animals would not have been very different from the animal husbandry practised by settled farmers. In both cases herding of animals involves travelling away from the village in search of the best pasture lands. In other words, the combination of archaeobotanical evidence from the Aşvan sites and the Early Bronze Age zooarchaeological evidence from Arslantepe points to a typical village economy of the period, dependent on cereals, sheep, goat and cattle. The construction of relatively flimsy wattle-and-daub buildings is likely to be a matter of cultural preference rather than evidence that farmers were not sedentary.

Foxtail and broomcorn millets, as discussed in chapter 5.3, were introduced to the Aşvan sites in the Hellenistic period. A few millet grains have been found in Iron Age deposits at Sos Höyük (Longford et al. 2003) and a large number of foxtail millets are noted in by Mark Nesbitt and Geoff Summers (1988) at the site of Tille Höyük in the Iron Age (ca 607 BC). Little discussion of these beyond their identification criteria has been made with regards to their role in the agricultural development of the Keban region. Naomi Miller (2010) has discussed millet cultivation as part of a summer cropping and irrigation system at the Iron Age Anatolian site of Gordion, and this appears to be one of the agricultural innovations that spread across Anatolia and the Aegean during the Iron Age (Riehl, Nesbitt 2003). Large quantities of broomcorn and foxtail millet, along with hulled barley, have been recovered from storage jars at the Urartian fortress site of Ayanis in the Van region, datable to the mid seventh century BC. Smaller quantities of rye and bread wheat (*triticum aestivum*) have also been attested in small quantities. Tuğba Solmaz and Emel Dönmez, the archaeobotanists responsible for this report, also conclude that millet was introduced to the region, perhaps from China, in the Middle or Late Bronze Age, or the Iron Age (Solmaz, Dönmez 2013).

Pulse use is often overlooked in archaeobotanical reports, which generally focus on staple cereal crops and on cereal processing (Fuller 2000; Fuller, Harvey 2006). It is interesting therefore to note the differences between the Aşvan sites and Arslantepe with regards to the use of chickpeas. Although lentils and peas are present in the samples of the early periods of both sites (Late Chalcolithic to Early Bronze Age II/III), chickpea appears to have played a significant role at Arslantepe, as evidenced by the detailed study of room A607 (Sadori et al. 2006). However, only a single chickpea seed has been noted at Taşkun Mevkii and none at all in the contemporary period at Aşvan Kale. Cultivation here was certainly not on the scale suggested by the Arslantepe finds. Instead, the dominant pulse in the Early Bronze Age II/III at the Aşvan sites was lentils. Korucutepe produced a similar range of pulses to those found at Arslantepe (Van Zeist and Bakker-Heeres in Van Loon 1975) and only a single lentil was recorded in the Iron Age levels at Sos Höyük (Longford et al. 2003). These sites reveal a different agricultural focus or different taphonomic pathways to those found at Aşvan. A range of pulse choices was available across the region. The episodic occurrence of oilseeds and fibre seeds at the Aşvan sites is mirrored at other sites in the region, including the burnt stores of flax or linseed at Tille Hoyuk (Nesbitt 2016).

The grape pips at Aşvan may contribute valuable new evidence for the development of viticulture. *Vitis sylvestris* has a widespread distribution across the Near East and Anatolia. The measurements of grape pips from the Late Chalcolithic and Early Bronze Age II at Arslantepe have been interpreted as indicating that there was a mix of wild and cultivated types in both periods (Belisario et al. 1994). Subsequently, Sadori and colleagues suggested that the domestication may have occurred locally at Arslantepe, but that the site lies outside the natural range of wild grape (Sadori et al. 2006). This observation, however, is counterintuitive, as one would expect to encounter a wild progenitor at the location where a crop is domesticated. Miller has also made the suggestion, based on the modern distribution of wild grape, that domestication occurred in Anatolia (Miller 2008: fig. 2). Given Gordon Hillman's observation of wild grapes not far north of Aşvan, on the road to Çemişgezek, and the occurrence of what may be wild grapes at Chalcolithic Çayboyu, we suspect that wild grapes were growing in this part of Turkey, probably in larger quantities prior to extensive riverside cultivation. Seed remains of *Vitis* sp. have been recorded at Kurban Höyük in the southeast of Turkey for the Late Chalcolithic period and increased in frequency in the Middle and Late Bronze Age, as can be observed at Arslantepe (Miller 2008).

The Aşvan sites belong to a mosaic of sites that does not necessarily show a single pattern of plant exploitation across the region. Broad patterns, however, such as the change over time towards free-threshing wheat, the mixed wheat-barley economy and the suite of pulses are common to them all. This picture fits well with trends that can be followed at the broader, Near Eastern scale.

7.1.2. The wider region

Despite the region-by-region and even site-by-site variation of crop choices at the fine scales of proportion, ubiquity and dominance which are noted by Simone Riehl across the Near East (Riehl 2009; 2012), there are many similarities between the Aşvan sites and the overall Near Eastern patterns, especially regarding the shifts in the use of wheat types, the overall range of pulses and the use of oilseed and fibre crops and fruit.

R.N.L.B. Hubbard's survey of Near Eastern sites showed that the decline in the ubiquity of emmer wheat began around 3000 BC in Anatolia and around 2000 BC in the Levant and Mesopotamia (Hubbard 1980). It has to be noted, however, that few Chalcolithic sites in Anatolia had been studied at the time of Hubbard's research. Riehl has shown that emmer was present in high ubiquity but low proportions in the Early Bronze Age in southeastern Anatolia and Syria, but that it was largely absent by the Middle Bronze Age. Emmer was present in both high ubiquity and proportion in the southern Levant (modern Israel and Jordan) in the Early Bronze Age, but also declined in the Middle Bronze Age. The proportions of wheat and barley suggest these two crops were equally important. This general pattern of declining hulled-wheat use by the Middle Bronze Age occurred earlier at the Aşvan sites, where it should be linked not with the 4.2kya episode but with other factors such as cultural preferences, yield requirements or the organisation of crop processing. In the Aegean and western and central Anatolia hulled wheats remained important in the Iron Age (Riehl, Nesbitt 2003; Valamoti 2004), with einkorn usually more abundant than emmer. At Gordion, for example, einkorn was present in high ubiquity in the Iron Age (Miller 2010). Here it may have been introduced by Phrygian migrants from southeastern Europe rather than as a consequence of continuous cultivation from earlier prehistoric times (Miller 2010: 43). Emmer was present in low proportions at Kilese Tepe in southeastern Turkey throughout the site's history (Bending 2007). The decline of hulled wheats by the beginning of the Early Bronze Age and their replacement by free-threshing wheat may therefore be particular to eastern Anatolia and northern Syria.

The Iron Age has been characterised as period of change in the Near East, one of the biggest of which was the introduction of summer cropping (Nesbitt, Samuel 1988; Riehl, Nesbitt 2003; Riehl 2009; 2012), particularly the cultivation of millet. Although millets have been noted from numerous sites at much earlier periods (see, for example, the synthesis by Hunt et al. 2008), their domesticated status and use as a cultivar before the Iron Age has been in question, either because of identification issues or because of the paucity of finds (Nesbitt, Samuel 1988; Hunt et al. 2008). It has been noted (Nesbitt, Samuel 1988) that millets were absent from Anatolia until the Iron Age, although they were present in the middle of the first half of the second millennium BC in Iran and in the Late Bronze Age in Greece (Valamoti 2013). They were not established as a major crop across the Near East until the middle of the Iron Age. Riehl and Mark Nesbitt (2003) suggest that this spread was part of a larger pattern, marked also by the introduction of crops such as sesame and *Vicia faba,* as well as other crops such as almonds, which spread from the flanking regions across the Near East and Anatolia and may be an outcome of the widening trade networks of the Iron Age. The Iron Age levels at the Aşvan sites were not excavated, but during the Hellenistic period there was a diversification and intensification of agricultural strategy. Without evidence from the intermediate periods of the Late Bronze Age and Iron Age it is impossible to decide whether this was the continuation of a long-term pattern which started in an earlier period or a later development for this region. The patterns of cultivation observable in the Hellenistic period continue into the Medieval period at the Aşvan sites. This offers general support for Riehl and Nesbitt's (2003) suggestion that the 'Islamic Agricultural Revolution' was part of a much more complex transformation of agricultural practices that started as far back as the Iron Age (see Watson 1983; Decker 2009).

The sites of Gordion in north-central Anatolia (Miller 2010) and Gritille in the southeast (Miller 1998) provide comparative material for the Hellenistic and Medieval periods at the Aşvan sites. Despite differences in the approach to the interpretation of the archaeobotanical data from a theoretical standpoint (including the assumption that the majority of archaeobotanical remains resulted from dung fuel – see chapter 4.2.3), several broad similarities can be established between these later occupation sites.

The agricultural strategy at Gordion was well established by the Hellenistic period: barley and free-threshing wheat dominated, with lentils and bitter vetch, and some millet also being present. Rice was introduced during the Medieval period. Based on the ratios of wild seeds to cereals, the balance between pastoral and farming activities may have varied, with the Hellenistic period seeing less farming and more pastoral activity than the previous period, and more reliance on steppe and woodland. The weed seeds contain fewer indications of irrigation and the quantity of millet and cash crops decreased. This de-intensification is very different from the situation at Aşvan in the same period. However, after the introduction of rice cultivation and increased irrigation in the Medieval period, the archaeobotanical and zooarchaeological evidence at Gordion indicates an overall intensification of both pastoral and arable activities, rather than a shift from pastoralism to farming (Miller 2010). Although a similar suite of crops is present at both Gordion and the Aşvan sites, the actions relating to them are potentially different. More work on the animal bones from the Aşvan sites, to consider issues such as kill-off patterns, may help to resolve this and other questions relating to the balance between pastoral and agricultural activity at Aşvan.

The crop range at Gritille resembles that at the Aşvan sites, including wheat, barley, lentils, peas, bitter vetch, vetchling and faba bean alongside a range of fruits and fibres, with rice and millets also present in the Medieval period. Miller (1998) has suggested that there was again a period of pastoral focus during the late 12th century, before a return to intensive agriculture during the 13th century. This pastoralism was not, however, linked with a decline in agricultural intensity, since, as at Gordion, the production of cotton and rice alongside large quantities of wheat suggests that irrigation was practised (Miller 1998).

Somewhat different patterns of exploitation can be observed at these three contemporary sites, although there are broad similarities in the range of crops cultivated. At Aşvan there was an apparent intensification in agriculture in the Hellenistic period (a process which might have begun during the preceding Iron Age) and this continued into the Medieval period. At Gordion there was a decline in agricultural activity in the Hellenistic period, and the local economy had a more pastoral focus. This trend was reversed in the Medieval period with the reintroduction of irrigation and new summer crops. At Gritille there was a shift to a more mixed but still potentially intensive strategy in the Muslim 12th century and a return to a pattern based on arable farming in the 13th century, similar to the pre-Islamic strategy. These differences are an indication of the complexity of cultural factors in the Classical and Medieval periods. It is unlikely that a single social event, the arrival of Islam, led to a wholesale diversification of agricultural strategies (Watson 1983; Samuel 2001; Riehl, Nesbitt 2003; Decker 2009). More research, considering archaeobotanical data from a wider range of sites across Anatolia, is therefore needed to test the hypotheses about the supposed 'Islamic Agricultural Revolution'.

7.2. Avenues for future research

In very brief summary, the work on the Aşvan sites has established that the main cereal cultivars in the Chalcolithic period (ca 4000 BC) were hulled barley and emmer wheat in equal proportions, with some einkorn present. In the Early Bronze Age I (from ca 3500 BC) free- threshing wheat largely replaced emmer (and einkorn), but hulled barley now dominated. In Early Bronze Age II and III and the Late Bronze Age free-threshing wheats achieved parity with hulled barley. This appears also to have been the case in the Hellenistic and Roman periods, by which time the summer crops of broomcorn and foxtail millet had been introduced to the region. In the Medieval period free-threshing wheats came to predominate over hulled barley, as they did in the modern period. Pulses were part of the food crop from the Early Bronze Age and became more important in Hellenistic and Roman times (chapter 5.4). Climate change does not seem to have had important implications for the choice of crops grown at Aşvan (chapter 6.6.1). The more drought-resistant hulled wheats (emmer, einkorn) were replaced by free-threshing wheats in the Early Bronze Age despite the occurrence of a period of high aridity (the 4.2kya episode), and this should be explained by cultural and economic, not climatic factors. In the later historical periods, after the introduction of millet, a summer crop which required irrigation, the choice of cultivars remained relatively stable and there are no clear-cut indications of substantive climate change through the Hellenistic, Roman and Medieval periods, as hypothesised in a recent survey (Haldon et al. 2014).

The analysis in this volume has left several questions open and certain aspects of the evidence unexplored.

There is scope for a closer analysis of the Hellenistic levels at Aşvan Kale, by relating the exact find-spots of the botanical material to the layout of the kitchen area. This might tell us about the use of space within a kitchen area with regards to storage, food preparation, cooking and consumption practices, and might help in the interpretation of some of the wild taxa, such as the oak gall and *Galium*, whose functions are unexplained.

Potentially, a more fine-grained phase analysis of the botanical material from the Medieval layers at Aşvan Kale and Taşkun Kale might throw light on the impact of religious change on agricultural practice, as this period saw the introduction both of Christianity and Islam to the Aşvan community, as well as shifts in the balance between these two groups. However, the possibilities are limited by the absence of primary find contexts that can be closely tied to the cultural and economic activities of specific groups within the population.

The weed data could be further refined and analysed, by using statistical methods such as correspondence analysis or discriminant analysis to look in more detail at both crop processing and agricultural strategies. For example, the analysis of the weed data could be expanded upon through the use of autecological, phytosociological or FIBS (functional identification of botanical surveys) approaches (following, for example, Hillman 1991; Küster 1991; Van der Veen 1992; Charles et al. 1997; Bogaard et al. 1998; 1999, Jones et al. 2000b; 2010). This would enable closer study of manuring, weeding, ploughing and crop-rotation practices.

The archaeobotanical data need to be integrated with other agricultural proxies, in particular the animal bones, so as to make possible a study of the relationship between farming and herding practices. This may be particularly valuable for the Early Bronze Age I levels of Taşkun Mevkii, as well as for the Hellenistic to Medieval period, and raises questions about farming intensification, herding and pastoralism, and economic diversification.

The last of these future objectives is probably the one most likely to be realised, and may be achieved when the animal bone assemblages from the Aşvan excavations have been fully analysed and published, a project which is currently under way. Further detailed study of the excavation notebooks from Aşvan Kale and Taşkun Kale, which are available for consultation at the British Institute at Ankara, in the light of the botanical data published in this volume, may bring further clarity to the first two questions. Intensive work on the weed data could potentially refine the analysis of the agricultural strategies, although the scarcity of well-defined find contexts reflecting the life-cycle of crop processing at Aşvan sets a limit to the possibilities.

No archaeological report can ever be final and definitive. It is clear that the Aşvan excavations and archaeobotany in the Near East would be ill served by further delays to this publication. We hope, rather, that this monograph will encourage the current generation of field workers and archaeobotanical specialists active in the region to build on the results from Aşvan and this study, and to extend their researches into a field that is still seriously under-researched, especially with regard to the later historical periods.

Appendix 1.
Botanical find contexts at the Aşvan sites

This appendix contains a complete list of the find contexts of the botanical samples recovered from the four Aşvan sites and the seed counts that were recorded in these samples. The information is presented in a standard format, although not all categories of information were obtained for or are relevant to every sample.

The tables are organised as follows:

Site: ÇB = Çayboyu; TM = Taşkun Mevkii; AK= Aşvan Kale; TK = Taşkun Kale.

Period: LC = Late Chalcolithic (late fifth millennium BC); EBA I = Early Bronze Age I (3000–2800 BC); EBA II–III = Early Bronze Age II–III (2800–2300 BC); LB = Late Bronze Age (late second to early first millennium BC); Helln. = Hellenistic (first century BC); Roman (? first century AD); Med I = Medieval I (11th century AD); Med II = Medieval II (12th to 13th century AD); Med III = Medieval III (14th century AD).

Context: the stratigraphical find location of the sample; more precisely, the numbered soil deposit identified by the excavator on site. The context code is made up of two parts: a three- or four-digit number (originally termed the page number), which was assigned to a particular area of the trench, and a decimal number, recording individual soil units in depositional sequence (e.g. 1902.4).

Sample: the sample numbers assigned when the material was recovered from the trench. Numbers after the letters MN were assigned by Mark Nesbitt to batches during the analysis of the botanical material.

Year: year of excavation (1969–1972).

Trench: the 10 × 10m trench identified by the numbering and lettering of the site excavation grids, for example M10, R11, or H4c/d. The letters a, b, c, d identify 5 × 5m quadrants of 10 × 10m trenches. The grids for each of the four sites are separate from one another.

Room: room number of an excavated building (this applies only to the Hellenistic level at Aşvan Kale).

Context type: pit; *tandır* (bread oven); destr. = destruction level, etc. Indeterminate contexts ('fill') are usually not specified.

Site phase: chronological phase within the site, as determined by the excavator.

>2.8mm: indicates whether and in what proportion the 0.28mm fraction was subsampled.

>0.7mm: indicates whether and in what proportion the 0.7mm fraction was subsampled.

Charcoal (g): weight of charcoal in grams. Where possible, the total weight of seed and charcoal in the sample has been given; where the charcoal could not be found, or might be incomplete, a question mark is given instead.

Seeds (g): weight of carbonised seeds in grams.

Volume floated (litres): the volume of earth from the soil unit from which botanical material was recovered by flotation. The number of litres of soil, which was collected in rectangular metal containers (*teneke*) each holding 20 litres, has been given where this information is available. F = entire sample floated; N = volume not recorded.

Merged samples: samples from the same or adjacent soil units which were merged for the purpose of analysis.

Classification: material recovered as a flotation sample (FS) or by hand collection (P).

All counts have been multiplied up to give the appropriate figure for 100% of each sample (see chapter 2.4 for discussion).

	Site	**ÇB**	**ÇB**	**ÇB**	**ÇB**	**ÇB**	**ÇB**	**ÇB**	**ÇB**
	Period	**LC**	**LC**	**LC**	**LC**	**LC**	**LC**	**LC**	**LC**
	Context	10.2	10.4	10.5	10.6	10.7	10.8	10.9	10.9
	Sample	1	2	3	5	4	40	7	8
	Year	1970	1970	1970	1970	1970	1970	1970	1970
	Trench	M11	M11	M11	M11	M11	M11	M11	M11
	Room								
	Context type								
	Period	LC	LC	LC	LC	LC	LC	LC	LC
	Site phase	IIc	IIb	IIb	IIb	IIb	IIa	IIa	IIa
	>2.8mm	100	100	100	100	100	100	25	25
	>0.7mm	100	100	100	100	22	0	0	25
	Charcoal (g)	63	128	324	175.33	108.47	295.1	175.76	0
	Seeds (g)	25	33	46	34.05	23.87	70.1	835.88	26.48
	Volume floated (litres)	1,404	720	2,070	1,674	1,440	2,700	1,890	N
	Merged samples								
	tenekes	78	40	115	93	80	150	105	N
	Classification	FS	FS	FS	FS	FS	FS	FS	P
DOMESTICATED CEREALS									
Triticum monococcum	grain	114	70	43	140	37	251	6,106	73
Triticum dicoccum	grain	1,028	2,056	1,929	2,736	1,092	3,874	40,835	680
Triticum durum/aestivum	grain	398	470	633	129	531	1,054	24,396	311
Triticum monococcum/dicoccum	glume bases	3,906	8,080	20,250	5,835	8,674	17,288	32,812	40
Triticum durum/aestivum	rachis segment	7	3	3	0	0	0	0	0
Hordeum vulgare (hulled)	grain	818	450	818	369	326	956	17,417	1,800
Hordeum vulgare (naked)	grain	0	0	0	0	0	0	0	0
Hordeum vulgare (hulled)	rachis segment	1	0	0	3	0	4	20	0
Hordeum/Triticum	sub-basal rachis*	1	1	0	0	0	0	0	0
Hordeum/Triticum	culm node or culm base	6	16	0	2	4	32	8	0
Secale cereale subsp. *cereale*	grain	0	0	0	0	0	0	0	0
Secale cereale subsp. *cereale*	rachis segment	0	0	0	0	0	0	0	0
Panicum miliaceum	grain	0	0	0	0	0	0	0	0
Setaria italica	grain	0	0	0	0	0	0	0	0
DOMESTICATED PULSES									
Cicer arietinum	seed	0	0	0	0	0	0	0	0
Lens culinaris	seed	9	0	22	8	5	85	0	0
Pisum sativum	seed	0	0	4	64	19	0	0	0
Vicia ervilia	seed	0	0	3	0	0	12	0	0
DOMESTICATED FRUITS									
Amygdalus communis	fruit	0	0	0	0	0	0	0	0
Vitis vinifera	seed	0	0	0	0	0	0	0	0
OTHER CROPS									
Linum usitatissimum		26	3	6	8	12	128	8	0
Gossypium arboreum/herbaceum		0	0	0	0	0	0	0	0
Nigella sativa		0	0	0	0	0	0	0	0
USEFUL WILD PLANTS									
Celtis		0	0	0	0	2	0	4	0
Crataegus		1	0	6	0	0	0	0	0
Pistacia	nutlet	2	4	13	1	1	4	0	0
Prunus	stone	0	1	1	1	1	1	0	0
Quercus	galls	0	0	0	0	0	0	0	0
Vitis sylvestris	seed	1	0	0	1	0	0	0	0

*or culm/spike node

	Site	ÇB	ÇB	ÇB	ÇB	ÇB	ÇB	ÇB	ÇB
	Period	**LC**	**LC**	**LC**	**LC**	**LC**	**LC**	**LC**	**LC**
	Context	10.2	10.4	10.5	10.6	10.7	10.8	10.9	10.9
	Sample	1	2	3	5	4	40	7	8
WILD PLANTS									
Boraginaceae									
Buglossoides aervense	seed	11	12	33	7	57	408	0	0
Buglosoides tenuiflora	seed	0	1	4	1	3	20	0	0
Leguminosae									
Fabeae (Vicieae)		40	10	76	6	38	294	0	0
Lathyrus cicera/sativus		0	0	0	0	0	0	0	0
Trifolieae		38	24	9	3	12	236	20	0
Poaceae									
Aegilops	grain	88	208	221	28	88	224	144	0
Aegilops	spikelet fork	1	1	5	8	0	8	4	0
Avena	grain	0	0	0	0	0	0	8	0
Bromus	grain	0	2	0	0	0	4	0	0
Echinochloa	grain	0	1	0	0	0	0	0	0
Lolium	grain	4	0	0	13	0	112	4	0
Setaria	grain	0	0	0	0	0	0	0	0
Stipa	grain	269	1,149	1,449	204	74	457	458	0
Taeniatherum	grain	0	0	0	0	0	0	12	0
Taeniatherum	chaff	0	0	0	0	0	0	0	0
Triticum boeoticum	grain	11	0	4	57	4	8	12	0
Poaceae - Indeterminate	grain	0	3	0	0	0	24	24	0
Other families									
Adonis		1	0	0	0	1	4	0	0
Ajuga		0	0	1	0	1	0	0	0
Apiaceae		0	0	0	0	0	0	0	0
Asteraceae		0	1	3	2	0	0	0	0
Bolboschoenus glaucus		2	5	1	4	3	8	0	0
Brassicaceae		2	0	2	6	0	4	0	0
Carex		0	0	0	0	0	0	0	0
Carthamus		1	0	0	0	0	0	0	0
Centaurea		1	0	3	2	1	12	0	0
Coriandrum sativum		0	0	0	0	0	0	0	0
Euclidium syriacum		0	3	0	0	0	0	0	0
Fumaria		0	0	0	6	1	0	0	0
Galium		17	17	52	5	10	200	4	0
Geum		0	0	0	0	0	0	0	0
Lallemantia		0	0	0	0	0	0	0	0
Liliaceae		0	3	3	1	0	4	0	0
Malva		6	0	0	0	0	4	0	0
Neslia		0	2	0	1	1	0	0	0
Polygonum		0	0	2	0	2	20	0	0
Ranunculus		0	0	0	0	0	0	0	0
Silene		11	44	15	2	9	140	20	0
Teucrium		0	3	0	2	4	20	4	0
Thalictrum		4	4	1	4	0	4	0	0
Thymelea		0	11	3	1	2	4	0	0
Vaccaria pyramidata		3	5	1	4	0	20	32	0
Valerianella		0	0	0	0	0	0	0	0
Indeterminate weeds		7	50	28	20	49	256	28	0
TOTAL		6,835	12,713	25,647	9,684	11,064	26,184	122,380	2,904
TOTAL seeds		2,913	4,612	5,389	3,836	2,386	8,852	89,536	2,864

	Site	**ÇB**	**ÇB**	**ÇB**	**ÇB**	**ÇB**	**ÇB**	**ÇB**	**ÇB**
	Period	**LC**	**LC**	**LC**	**LC**	**LC**	**LC**	**LC**	**LC**
	Context	10.13	10.14	10.15	10.16	10.17	10.18	10.19	10.21
	Sample	12	14	13	20	15	16	18	27
	Year	1971	1971	1971	1971	1971	1971	1971	1971
	Trench	M11	M11	M11	M11	M11	M11	M11	M11
	Room								
	Context type								
	Period	LC	LC	LC	LC	LC	LC	LC	LC
	Site phase	Seed layer	Seed layer	Ib	Ib	Ib	Ib	Ib	Ib
	>2.8mm	12.5	100	100	100	100	100	100	100
	>0.7mm	12.5	100	100	100	0	100	100	100
	Charcoal (g)	12	19.27	213.57	1.95	321.87	34.26	16.72	31.75
	Seeds (g)	583.6	51.7	122.87	10.97	29.96	2.87	1.3	3.43
	Volume floated (litres)	?	360	1,350	36	1,926	180	180	270
	Merged samples								
	tenekes	?N (47)	20	75	2	107	10	10	15
	Classification	P	P	P	FS	FS	FS	FS	FS
DOMESTICATED CEREALS									
Triticum monococcum	grain	1,637	217	564	27	73	36	0	18
Triticum dicoccum	grain	15,895	1,687	4,201	189	1,081	130	13	88
Triticum durum/aestivum	grain	6,971	812	2,339	99	602	62	66	24
Triticum monococcum/dicoccum	glume bases	4,936	400	1,699	410	2,404	1,123	201	270
Triticum durum/aestivum	rachis segment	0	0	4	0	0	0	2	1
Hordeum vulgare (hulled)	grain	36,832	2,926	6,014	806	1,174	39	39	216
Hordeum vulgare (naked)	grain	0	1	6	0	0	0	0	0
Hordeum vulgare (hulled)	rachis segment	0	0	0	0	0	0	1	0
Hordeum/Triticum	sub-basal rachis*	0	0	2	0	0	0	0	0
Hordeum/Triticum	culm node or culm base	0	1	7	0	0	2	0	3
Secale cereale subsp. *cereale*	grain	0	0	0	0	0	0	0	0
Secale cereale subsp. *cereale*	rachis segment	0	0	0	0	0	0	0	0
Panicum miliaceum	grain	0	0	0	0	0	0	0	0
Setaria italica	grain	0	0	0	0	0	0	0	0
DOMESTICATED PULSES									
Cicer arietinum	seed	0	0	0	0	0	0	0	0
Lens culinaris	seed	16	2	9	0	17	7	9	1
Pisum sativum	seed	0	27	36	0	28	0	0	0
Vicia ervilia	seed	0	0	2	0	0	0	1	2
DOMESTICATED FRUITS									
Amygdalus communis	fruit	0	0	0	0	0	0	0	0
Vitis vinifera	seed	0	0	0	0	0	0	0	0
OTHER CROPS									
Linum usitatissimum		0	24	17	0	24	0	0	0
Gossypium arboreum/herbaceum		0	0	0	0	0	0	0	0
Nigella sativa		0	0	0	0	0	0	0	0
USEFUL WILD PLANTS									
Celtis		0	0	0	0	0	0	0	0
Crataegus		0	0	0	0	0	0	2	0
Pistacia	nutlet	0	0	1	0	4	0	1	1
Prunus	stone	0	0	0	0	1	0	1	1
Quercus	galls	0	0	0	0	0	0	0	0
Vitis sylvestris	seed	0	1	0	0	0	0	0	0

*or culm/spike node

	Site	ÇB	ÇB	ÇB	ÇB	ÇB	ÇB	ÇB	ÇB
	Period	**LC**	**LC**	**LC**	**LC**	**LC**	**LC**	**LC**	**LC**
	Context	10.13	10.14	10.15	10.16	10.17	10.18	10.19	10.21
	Sample	12	14	13	20	15	16	18	27
WILD PLANTS									
Boraginaceae									
Buglossoides aervense	seed	0	1	2	1	0	1	1	0
Buglosoides tenuiflora	seed	0	0	0	0	0	0	0	0
Leguminosae									
Fabeae (Vicieae)		0	0	10	4	16	6	7	4
Lathyrus cicera/sativus		0	0	0	0	0	0	0	0
Trifolieae		8	2	11	1	0	1	2	0
Poaceae									
Aegilops	grain	0	10	21	0	0	0	0	0
Aegilops	spikelet fork	8	0	0	0	0	0	0	1
Avena	grain	0	0	0	0	0	0	0	0
Bromus	grain	0	0	0	1	0	1	0	1
Echinochloa	grain	0	0	0	0	0	0	0	0
Lolium	grain	8	1	0	0	8	1	0	0
Setaria	grain	0	0	0	0	0	0	0	0
Stipa	grain	32	5	15	1	12	14	2	1
Taeniatherum	grain	0	0	0	0	0	0	0	0
Taeniatherum	chaff	0	0	0	0	0	0	0	0
Triticum boeoticum	grain	96	2	25	0	0	0	0	0
Poaceae - Indeterminate	grain	0	0	0	0	12	0	0	0
Other families									
Adonis		0	0	0	0	0	0	2	0
Ajuga		0	0	0	0	4	1	2	0
Apiaceae		0	0	1	0	0	0	0	0
Asteraceae		8	0	0	0	0	0	0	0
Bolboschoenus glaucus		0	0	0	0	4	0	4	0
Brassicaceae		0	3	0	0	0	0	0	0
Carex		0	0	0	0	0	0	0	0
Carthamus		0	0	0	0	0	0	0	0
Centaurea		0	0	0	0	0	0	0	0
Coriandrum sativum		0	5	0	0	0	0	0	0
Euclidium syriacum		0	0	0	0	0	0	0	0
Fumaria		0	0	3	0	0	0	0	0
Galium		8	1	3	0	4	0	0	0
Geum		0	0	1	0	0	0	0	0
Lallemantia		0	0	0	0	0	0	0	0
Liliaceae		0	0	0	0	0	0	0	0
Malva		0	0	1	0	0	0	0	0
Neslia		0	0	0	0	0	0	0	0
Polygonum		0	1	2	1	4	0	0	0
Ranunculus		0	0	1	0	0	0	0	0
Silene		0	0	0	0	0	0	0	0
Teucrium		0	0	1	4	12	2	1	0
Thalictrum		0	1	0	0	0	0	0	0
Thymelea		8	1	3	0	0	1	0	0
Vaccaria pyramidata		8	1	2	0	0	2	0	0
Valerianella		0	0	1	0	4	1	0	0
Indeterminate weeds		16	13	12	2	4	5	6	2
TOTAL		66,487	6,145	15,016	1,546	5,492	1,435	363	634
TOTAL seeds		61,543	5,744	13,304	1,136	3,088	310	159	359

	Site	ÇB	ÇB	ÇB	ÇB	TM	TM	TM	TM
	Period	LC	LC	LC	LC				
	Context	11.1	11.2	11.3	14.2	501.23	502.7	502.12	503.14
	Sample	22	23	24	32	7	1	3	4
	Year	1971	1971	1971	1971	1971	1971	1971	1971
	Trench	M11	M11	M11	M11	J11	J11	J11	J11
	Room								
	Context type						Pithos	Floor	Burnt sherds
	Period	LC	LC	LC	LC				
	Site phase	Ib	Ib	Ib	Ia				
	>2.8mm	100	100	100	100	100	100	100	100
	>0.7mm	100	100	100	100	100	100	100	100
	Charcoal (g)	175.38	173.25	18.64	15.72	40.33	1.88	0	18.75
	Seeds (g)	6.96	2.41	0.4	1.45	0.63	0.16	0.93	1.88
	Volume floated (litres)	720	288	108	792	1,386	144	900	666
	Merged samples								*
	tenekes	40	16	6	44	77	8	50	37
	Classification	FS	FS	FS	FS			P	P
DOMESTICATED CEREALS									
Triticum monococcum	grain	0	0	0	6	1	0	0	0
Triticum dicoccum	grain	305	56	16	26	7	2	8	3
Triticum durum/aestivum	grain	140	75	6	63	45	2	58	220
Triticum monococcum/dicoccum	glume bases	576	266	8	441	0	0	0	0
Triticum durum/aestivum	rachis segment	0	1	0	1	0	0	0	0
Hordeum vulgare (hulled)	grain	214	64	18	19	17	4	36	8
Hordeum vulgare (naked)	grain	0	0	0	0	0	0	0	0
Hordeum vulgare (hulled)	rachis segment	0	0	0	0	0	0	0	0
Hordeum/Triticum	sub-basal rachis*	0	0	0	0	0	0	0	0
Hordeum/Triticum	culm node or culm base	18	5	1	2	0	0	0	0
Secale cereale subsp. *cereale*	grain	0	0	0	0	0	0	0	1
Secale cereale subsp. *cereale*	rachis segment	0	0	0	0	0	0	0	0
Panicum miliaceum	grain	0	0	0	0	0	0	0	0
Setaria italica	grain	0	0	0	0	0	0	0	0
DOMESTICATED PULSES									
Cicer arietinum	seed	0	0	0	0	0	0	0	1
Lens culinaris	seed	52	30	3	1	4	0	1	0
Pisum sativum	seed	0	0	0	3	0	0	0	0
Vicia ervilia	seed	20	13	0	0	0	0	0	0
DOMESTICATED FRUITS									
Amygdalus communis	fruit	0	0	0	0	0	0	0	0
Vitis vinifera	seed	0	0	0	0	0	13	0	0
OTHER CROPS									
Linum usitatissimum		0	0	0	0	0	0	0	0
Gossypium arboreum/herbaceum		0	0	0	0	0	0	0	0
Nigella sativa		0	0	0	0	0	0	0	0
USEFUL WILD PLANTS									
Celtis		0	0	0	0	0	0	0	0
Crataegus		0	0	0	0	0	0	0	0
Pistacia	nutlet	1	1	0	0	1	0	0	0
Prunus	stone	0	0	0	0	0	0	0	0
Quercus	galls	0	0	0	0	0	0	0	0
Vitis sylvestris	seed	0	0	0	0	0	0	0	0

*or culm/spike node

	Site	ÇB	ÇB	ÇB	ÇB	TM	TM	TM	TM
	Period	**LC**	**LC**	**LC**	**LC**				
	Context	11.1	11.2	11.3	14.2	501.23	502.7	502.12	503.14
	Sample	22	23	24	32	7	1	3	4
WILD PLANTS									
Boraginaceae									
Buglossoides aervense	seed	0	0	0	1	1	5	0	0
Buglosoides tenuiflora	seed	0	0	0	0	0	0	0	0
Leguminosae									
Fabeae (Vicieae)		15	14	1	3	2	0	0	0
Lathyrus cicera/sativus		0	0	0	0	0	0	0	0
Trifolieae		1	0	0	0	0	0	0	0
Poaceae									
Aegilops	grain	0	0	0	3	1	0	0	0
Aegilops	spikelet fork	0	0	0	0	0	0	0	0
Avena	grain	0	0	0	0	0	0	0	0
Bromus	grain	0	0	0	0	0	0	0	0
Echinochloa	grain	0	0	0	0	0	0	0	0
Lolium	grain	0	1	0	0	2	0	4	0
Setaria	grain	0	0	0	0	0	0	0	0
Stipa	grain	11	7	2	26	1	0	0	0
Taeniatherum	grain	0	0	0	0	0	0	0	0
Taeniatherum	chaff	0	0	0	0	0	0	0	0
Triticum boeoticum	grain	0	0	0	0	0	0	0	0
Poaceae - Indeterminate	grain	1	1	0	1	0	0	0	0
Other families									
Adonis		1	0	0	0	0	1	0	0
Ajuga		0	0	0	0	0	0	0	0
Apiaceae		0	0	0	0	2	0	0	0
Asteraceae		0	0	0	0	0	0	0	0
Bolboschoenus glaucus		0	0	0	0	0	0	0	0
Brassicaceae		0	0	0	0	0	0	0	0
Carex		0	0	0	0	0	0	0	0
Carthamus		0	0	0	0	0	0	0	0
Centaurea		0	0	0	0	0	0	0	0
Coriandrum sativum		0	0	0	0	0	0	0	0
Euclidium syriacum		0	0	0	0	0	0	0	0
Fumaria		0	0	0	0	0	0	0	0
Galium		1	0	0	0	8	0	2	0
Geum		0	0	0	0	0	0	0	0
Lallemantia		0	0	0	0	0	0	0	0
Liliaceae		0	0	0	0	0	0	0	0
Malva		0	0	0	0	2	0	0	0
Neslia		0	0	0	0	0	0	0	0
Polygonum		1	2	0	0	0	0	0	0
Ranunculus		0	0	0	0	0	0	0	0
Silene		0	1	0	0	0	0	0	0
Teucrium		0	0	0	0	0	0	0	0
Thalictrum		0	0	0	0	0	0	0	0
Thymelea		0	0	0	0	1	0	0	0
Vaccaria pyramidata		0	0	0	0	0	0	0	0
Valerianella		0	0	0	0	0	0	0	0
Indeterminate weeds		11	4	0	13	6	1	0	0
TOTAL		1,368	541	55	609	101	28	109	233
TOTAL seeds		774	269	46	165	101	28	109	233

	Site	**TM**	**TM**	**TM**	**TM**	**TM**	**TM**	**TM**	**TM**
	Period								
	Context	503.15	503.16	101.23	101.24	101.24	101.25	103.6	103.7
	Sample	5	6	–	3 (hand)	3 (flot)	7	1	2
	Year	1971	1971	1970	1970	1970	1970	1970	1970
	Trench	J11	J11	K10c	K10c	K10c	K10c	K10c	K10c
	Room								
	Context type	Burnt sherds	Burnt sherds	Destr.?	Pot	Pot	Destr.?		
	Period								
	Site phase			3	3	3	3	3	3
	>2.8mm	100	100	25	6.25	100	25	100	100
	>0.7mm	100	100	25	6.25	100	25	100	0
	Charcoal (g)	37.5	18.75	118.27	0	142.25	23.26	147.12	577.88
	Seeds (g)	1.17	0.76	96.89	86.54	192.71	39.73	17.71	12.43
	Volume floated (litres)	1,458	486	F	N	F	F	990	1,944
	Merged samples	*	*					*	*
	tenekes	81	27					55	108
	Classification			P	P	FS	P	P	
DOMESTICATED CEREALS									
Triticum monococcum	grain	0	0	5	0	236	0	4	0
Triticum dicoccum	grain	15	0	97	0	1,178	10	45	273
Triticum durum/aestivum	grain	109	74	471	0	642	16	1,598	718
Triticum monococcum/dicoccum	glume bases	0	0	17	0	1,984	2	11	28
Triticum durum/aestivum	rachis segment	0	0	3	0	0	0	0	0
Hordeum vulgare (hulled)	grain	20	8	11,069	10,336	19,254	5,791	304	394
Hordeum vulgare (naked)	grain	0	0	3	0	72	16	0	0
Hordeum vulgare (hulled)	rachis segment	0	0	0	0	3	1	1	0
Hordeum/Triticum	sub-basal rachis*	0	0	0	0	0	0	0	0
Hordeum/Triticum	culm node or culm base	0	0	29	0	2	20	0	10
Secale cereale subsp. *cereale*	grain	0	0	0	0	0	0	0	0
Secale cereale subsp. *cereale*	rachis segment	0	0	0	0	0	0	0	0
Panicum miliaceum	grain	0	0	0	0	0	0	0	0
Setaria italica	grain	0	0	0	0	0	0	0	0
DOMESTICATED PULSES									
Cicer arietinum	seed	0	0	0	0	0	0	0	0
Lens culinaris	seed	0	0	2	0	5	0	3	9
Pisum sativum	seed	0	0	2	0	15	0	0	2
Vicia ervilia	seed	0	0	0	0	0	0	0	2
DOMESTICATED FRUITS									
Amygdalus communis	fruit	0	0	0	0	0	0	0	0
Vitis vinifera	seed	0	0	2	0	0	0	0	3
OTHER CROPS									
Linum usitatissimum		0	0	1	0	0	0	0	0
Gossypium arboreum/herbaceum		0	0	0	0	0	0	0	0
Nigella sativa		0	0	0	0	0	0	0	0
USEFUL WILD PLANTS									
Celtis		0	0	0	0	0	0	0	0
Crataegus		0	0	0	0	0	0	0	0
Pistacia	nutlet	0	0	24	0	0	0	11	11
Prunus	stone	0	0	0	0	0	0	0	0
Quercus	galls	0	0	0	0	0	0	0	0
Vitis sylvestris	seed	0	0	0	0	0	0	0	0

*or culm/spike node

Appendix 1: Botanical find contexts at the Aşvan sites

	Site	TM	TM	TM	TM	TM	TM	TM	TM
	Period								
	Context	503.15	503.16	101.23	101.24	101.24	101.25	103.6	103.7
	Sample	5	6	-	3 (hand)	3 (flot)	7	1	2
WILD PLANTS									
Boraginaceae									
Buglossoides aervense	seed	0	0	3,344	0	905	6,041	5	12
Buglosoides tenuiflora	seed	0	0	564	0	180	995	0	0
Leguminosae									
Fabeae (Vicieae)		0	0	5	3	4	15	50	19
Lathyrus cicera/sativus		0	0	0	0	0	0	0	0
Trifolieae		0	0	66	0	7	4	40	32
Poaceae									
Aegilops	grain	0	0	0	0	12	0	0	0
Aegilops	spikelet fork	0	0	1	0	0	0	0	0
Avena	grain	0	0	0	0	0	0	0	0
Bromus	grain	0	0	2	0	1	0	2	2
Echinochloa	grain	0	0	0	0	0	0	0	0
Lolium	grain	0	0	739	80	1,294	344	38	28
Setaria	grain	0	0	0	0	0	0	0	0
Stipa	grain	0	0	139	0	31	10	138	38
Taeniatherum	grain	0	0	0	0	0	0	0	0
Taeniatherum	chaff	0	0	0	0	0	0	0	0
Triticum boeoticum	grain	0	0	0	0	6	0	4	2
Poaceae - Indeterminate	grain	0	0	0	0	0	3	3	2
Other families									
Adonis		0	0	1	2	1	4	0	0
Ajuga		0	0	0	0	0	0	0	0
Apiaceae		0	0	1	0	4	0	0	0
Asteraceae		0	0	1	0	0	0	0	0
Bolboschoenus glaucus		0	0	2	0	0	0	1	2
Brassicaceae		0	0	1	0	0	0	0	0
Carex		0	0	0	0	0	0	1	0
Carthamus		0	0	0	0	0	0	0	0
Centaurea		0	0	0	0	0	0	0	0
Coriandrum sativum		0	0	0	0	0	0	0	0
Euclidium syriacum		0	0	0	0	0	0	0	0
Fumaria		0	0	1	0	0	0	0	0
Galium		0	0	51	6	34	18	0	0
Geum		0	0	0	0	0	0	0	0
Lallemantia		0	0	0	0	0	0	1	0
Liliaceae		0	0	1	0	0	0	0	0
Malva		0	0	4	0	0	0	22	4
Neslia		0	0	2	0	3	0	0	0
Polygonum		0	0	6	0	0	0	5	4
Ranunculus		0	0	0	0	0	0	0	0
Silene		0	0	0	0	1	0	0	0
Teucrium		0	0	0	0	0	0	3	0
Thalictrum		0	0	0	0	0	0	0	0
Thymelea		0	0	3	0	2	4	15	12
Vaccaria pyramidata		0	0	13	0	19	8	2	0
Valerianella		0	0	1	0	1	0	1	0
Indeterminate weeds		0	0	38	3	9	16	75	4
TOTAL		144	82	16,711	10,430	25,905	13,318	2,383	1,611
TOTAL seeds		144	82	16,661	10,430	23,916	13,295	2,371	1,573

	Site	AK	AK	AK	AK	AK	AK	AK	AK
	Period	**EBA**	**EBA**	**EBA**	**EBA**	**EBA**	**EBA**	**EBA**	**EBA**
	Context	1204.1	1204.1a	1204.2	1204.3	1204.10	1204.11	1204.12	1015.3
	Sample	1	2	3	4	11	12	13	
	Year	1970	1970	1970	1970	1970	1970	1970	1969
	Trench	G2b	G2b	G2b	G2b	G2b	G2b	G2b	G3b
	Room	Step trench	Step trench	Step trench	Step trench	Step trench	Step trench	Step trench	
	Context type	Fill	Fill	Fill	Fill	Fill	Fill	Fill	Fill
	Period	EBA	EBA	EBA	EBA	EBA	EBA	EBA	EBA
	Site phase								
	>2.8mm	100	100	100	100	100	100	100	100
	>0.7mm	100	100	100	100	100	100	100	100
	Charcoal (g)	525	?	?	?	?	600	487.5	0.22
	Seeds (g)	0.89	0.19	0.46	0.82	0.45	1.29	3.88	7.93
	Volume floated (litres)	F	F	F	F	F	F	F	N
	Merged samples								
	tenekes								
	Classification	P	P	P	P	P		P	P
DOMESTICATED CEREALS									
Triticum monococcum	grain	0	0	0	0	0	0	0	0
Triticum dicoccum	grain	0	0	0	0	0	0	0	0
Triticum durum/aestivum	grain	95	7	15	21	19	0	179	786
Triticum monococcum/dicoccum	glume bases	0	0	0	0	0	0	0	0
Triticum durum/aestivum	rachis segment	0	0	0	0	1	0	0	0
Hordeum vulgare (hulled)	grain	23	21	45	51	35	0	282	4
Hordeum vulgare (naked)	grain	0	0	0	0	0	0	0	0
Hordeum vulgare (hulled)	rachis segment	0	0	0	0	0	9	0	0
Hordeum/Triticum	sub-basal rachis*	0	0	0	0	0	0	0	0
Hordeum/Triticum	culm node or culm base	0	0	0	0	0	0	0	0
Secale cereale subsp. *cereale*	grain	0	0	0	0	0	0	0	0
Secale cereale subsp. *cereale*	rachis segment	0	0	0	0	0	0	0	0
Panicum miliaceum	grain	0	0	0	0	0	0	0	0
Setaria italica	grain	0	0	0	0	0	0	0	0
DOMESTICATED PULSES									
Cicer arietinum	seed	0	0	0	0	0	0	0	0
Lens culinaris	seed	5	0	4	1	4	0	0	0
Pisum sativum	seed	0	0	0	0	0	0	0	0
Vicia ervilia	seed	0	0	0	0	0	0	1	0
DOMESTICATED FRUITS									
Amygdalus communis	fruit	0	0	0	0	0	0	0	0
Vitis vinifera	seed	3	0	2	7	0	0	11	0
OTHER CROPS									
Linum usitatissimum		0	0	0	0	0	0	0	0
Gossypium arboreum/herbaceum		0	0	0	0	0	0	0	0
Nigella sativa		0	0	0	0	0	0	0	0
USEFUL WILD PLANTS									
Celtis		1	1	0	0	0	0	0	0
Crataegus		0	0	0	1	0	0	0	0
Pistacia	nutlet	0	0	0	0	0	0	0	0
Prunus	stone	0	0	0	0	0	0	0	0
Quercus	galls	0	0	0	0	0	0	0	0
Vitis sylvestris	seed	0	0	0	0	0	0	0	0

*or culm/spike node

	Site	**AK**	**AK**	**AK**	**AK**	**AK**	**AK**	**AK**	**AK**
	Period	**EBA**	**EBA**	**EBA**	**EBA**	**EBA**	**EBA**	**EBA**	**EBA**
	Context	1204.1	1204.1a	1204.2	1204.3	1204.10	1204.11	1204.12	1015.3
	Sample	1	2	3	4	11	12	13	
WILD PLANTS									
Boraginaceae									
Buglossoides aervense	seed	0	0	1	0	0	0	0	0
Buglosoides tenuiflora	seed	0	0	0	0	0	0	0	0
Leguminosae									
Fabeae (Vicieae)		0	0	0	0	1	0	5	1
Lathyrus cicera/sativus		0	0	0	0	0	0	0	0
Trifolieae		0	0	0	0	0	10	0	0
Poaceae									
Aegilops	grain	0	0	0	0	0	0	0	0
Aegilops	spikelet fork	0	0	0	0	0	0	0	0
Avena	grain	0	0	0	0	0	0	0	0
Bromus	grain	1	0	0	0	0	2	0	0
Echinochloa	grain	0	0	0	0	0	0	0	0
Lolium	grain	1	0	1	0	0	3	0	0
Setaria	grain	0	0	0	0	0	0	0	0
Stipa	grain	2	0	0	0	3	0	0	0
Taeniatherum	grain	0	0	0	0	0	0	0	0
Taeniatherum	chaff	0	0	0	0	0	0	0	0
Triticum boeoticum	grain	0	0	0	0	0	0	0	0
Poaceae - Indeterminate	grain	0	0	0	0	0	0	0	0
Other families									
Adonis		0	0	0	0	0	0	0	0
Ajuga		0	0	0	0	0	0	0	0
Apiaceae		0	0	1	0	0	0	0	0
Asteraceae		0	0	0	0	0	0	0	0
Bolboschoenus glaucus		0	0	0	0	0	9	0	0
Brassicaceae		0	0	0	0	0	0	0	0
Carex		0	0	0	0	0	0	0	0
Carthamus		0	0	0	0	0	0	0	0
Centaurea		0	0	0	0	0	0	0	0
Coriandrum sativum		0	0	0	0	0	0	0	0
Euclidium syriacum		0	0	0	0	0	0	0	0
Fumaria		0	0	0	0	0	0	0	0
Galium		37	4	4	3	0	8	0	0
Geum		0	0	0	0	0	0	0	0
Lallemantia		0	0	0	0	0	0	0	0
Liliaceae		1	0	0	1	0	0	0	0
Malva		0	0	0	0	0	0	0	0
Neslia		0	0	0	0	0	0	0	0
Polygonum		0	0	0	0	0	0	0	0
Ranunculus		0	0	0	0	0	0	0	0
Silene		0	0	0	0	0	0	0	0
Teucrium		1	0	0	0	0	2	0	0
Thalictrum		0	0	0	0	0	0	0	0
Thymelea		0	0	0	0	0	0	0	0
Vaccaria pyramidata		2	0	1	0	0	0	0	0
Valerianella		0	0	0	0	0	0	0	0
Indeterminate weeds		7	0	0	0	0	155	0	0
TOTAL		179	33	74	85	63	198	478	791
TOTAL seeds		179	33	74	85	62	189	478	791

	Site	**AK**	**AK**	**AK**	**AK**	**AK**	**AK**	**AK**	**AK**
	Period	**EBA**	**EBA**	**EBA**	**EBA**	**LBA**	**LBA**	**Helln**	**Helln**
	Context	1016.1	1016.5	1016.6	1017.2	507.15	508.4	12.12	12.14
	Sample								
	Year	1969	1969	1969	1969	1969	1969	1969	1969
	Trench	G3b	G3b	G3b	G3b	G3d	G3d	G4a	G4a
	Room							I	I
	Context type	Fill	Fill	Fill	Fill	Pit 7	Pit 7	Destr.	Destr.
	Period	EBA	EBA	EBA	EBA	LBA	LBA	Helln	Helln
	Site phase								
	>2.8mm	100	100	100	100	100	100	100	100
	>0.7mm	100	100	100	100	100	100	100	100
	Charcoal (g)	0.07	0	0.12	0.04	0	127.5	0	0
	Seeds (g)	7.37	0.95	5.04	9.84	0.54	1.31	0.58	2.6
	Volume floated (litres)	N	N	N	N	N	F	N	N
	Merged samples							*	*
	tenekes								
	Classification	P	P	P	P	P	P	P	
DOMESTICATED CEREALS									
Triticum monococcum	grain	0	0	0	0	0	0	0	0
Triticum dicoccum	grain	0	0	0	0	0	0	0	0
Triticum durum/aestivum	grain	703	104	490	925	9	64	2	2
Triticum monococcum/dicoccum	glume bases	0	0	0	0	0	0	0	0
Triticum durum/aestivum	rachis segment	0	0	0	0	0	0	0	0
Hordeum vulgare (hulled)	grain	1	1	4	10	45	85	56	225
Hordeum vulgare (naked)	grain	0	0	0	0	0	0	0	0
Hordeum vulgare (hulled)	rachis segment	0	0	0	0	0	0	0	0
Hordeum/Triticum	sub-basal rachis*	0	0	0	0	0	0	0	0
Hordeum/Triticum	culm node or culm base	0	0	0	0	0	0	0	0
Secale cereale subsp. *cereale*	grain	0	0	0	0	0	0	0	0
Secale cereale subsp. *cereale*	rachis segment	0	0	0	0	0	0	0	0
Panicum miliaceum	grain	0	0	0	0	0	0	0	0
Setaria italica	grain	0	0	0	0	0	0	0	0
DOMESTICATED PULSES									
Cicer arietinum	seed	0	0	0	0	0	0	0	0
Lens culinaris	seed	0	0	0	0	0	0	0	1
Pisum sativum	seed	0	0	0	0	0	0	0	0
Vicia ervilia	seed	0	0	0	0	0	61	1	1
DOMESTICATED FRUITS									
Amygdalus communis	fruit	0	0	0	0	0	0	0	0
Vitis vinifera	seed	0	0	0	1	0	1	0	2
OTHER CROPS									
Linum usitatissimum		0	0	0	0	0	0	0	0
Gossypium arboreum/herbaceum		0	0	0	0	0	0	0	0
Nigella sativa		0	0	0	0	0	0	0	0
USEFUL WILD PLANTS									
Celtis		0	0	0	0	0	0	0	0
Crataegus		0	0	0	0	0	0	0	0
Pistacia	nutlet	0	0	0	0	0	0	0	0
Prunus	stone	0	0	0	0	0	0	0	0
Quercus	galls	0	0	0	0	0	0	0	0
Vitis sylvestris	seed	0	0	0	0	0	0	0	0

*or culm/spike node

Appendix 1: Botanical find contexts at the Aşvan sites

	Site	AK	AK	AK	AK	AK	AK	AK	AK
	Period	**EBA**	**EBA**	**EBA**	**EBA**	**LBA**	**LBA**	**Helln**	**Helln**
	Context	1016.1	1016.5	1016.6	1017.2	507.15	508.4	12.12	12.14
	Sample								
WILD PLANTS									
Boraginaceae									
Buglossoides aervense	seed	0	0	0	0	0	0	0	0
Buglosoides tenuiflora	seed	0	0	0	0	0	0	0	0
Leguminosae									
Fabeae (Vicieae)		0	0	0	0	0	0	0	6
Lathyrus cicera/sativus		0	0	0	0	0	0	0	1
Trifolieae		0	0	0	0	0	0	0	0
Poaceae									
Aegilops	grain	0	0	0	0	0	0	0	0
Aegilops	spikelet fork	0	0	0	0	0	0	0	0
Avena	grain	0	0	0	0	0	0	0	0
Bromus	grain	0	0	0	0	0	0	0	0
Echinochloa	grain	0	0	0	0	0	0	0	0
Lolium	grain	0	0	0	0	0	4	0	0
Setaria	grain	0	0	0	0	0	0	0	0
Stipa	grain	0	0	0	0	0	0	0	0
Taeniatherum	grain	0	0	0	0	0	0	0	0
Taeniatherum	chaff	0	0	0	0	0	0	0	0
Triticum boeoticum	grain	0	0	0	0	0	0	0	0
Poaceae - Indeterminate	grain	0	0	0	0	0	0	0	0
Other families									
Adonis		0	0	0	0	0	1	0	0
Ajuga		0	0	0	0	0	0	0	0
Apiaceae		0	0	0	0	0	1	0	0
Asteraceae		0	0	0	0	0	0	0	0
Bolboschoenus glaucus		0	0	0	0	0	0	0	0
Brassicaceae		0	0	0	0	0	0	0	0
Carex		0	0	0	0	0	0	0	0
Carthamus		0	0	0	0	0	0	0	0
Centaurea		0	0	0	0	0	0	0	0
Coriandrum sativum		0	0	0	0	0	0	0	0
Euclidium syriacum		0	0	0	0	0	0	0	0
Fumaria		0	0	0	0	0	0	0	0
Galium		0	0	0	0	0	5	0	1
Geum		0	0	0	0	0	0	0	0
Lallemantia		0	0	0	0	0	0	0	0
Liliaceae		0	0	0	0	0	3	0	0
Malva		0	0	0	0	0	0	0	0
Neslia		0	0	0	0	0	0	0	0
Polygonum		0	0	0	0	0	0	0	0
Ranunculus		0	0	0	0	0	0	0	0
Silene		0	0	0	0	0	0	0	0
Teucrium		0	0	0	0	0	0	0	0
Thalictrum		0	0	0	0	0	0	0	0
Thymelea		0	0	0	0	0	0	0	0
Vaccaria pyramidata		0	0	0	0	0	3	0	0
Valerianella		0	0	0	0	0	0	0	0
Indeterminate weeds		0	0	0	0	0	10	0	0
TOTAL		704	105	494	936	54	238	59	239
TOTAL seeds		704	105	494	936	54	238	59	239

	Site	AK	AK	AK	AK	AK	AK	AK	AK
	Period	Helln	Helln	Helln	Helln	Helln	Helln	Helln	Helln
	Context	111.4	602.24	602.25	606.6	606.6	606.6	606.6	606.6
	Sample				MN 1	MN 2	7	15	38
	Year	1968	1969	1969	1969	1969	1969	1969	1969
	Trench	G4b	H3c	H3c	H3c	H3c	H3c	H3c	H3c
	Room	II	III	III	III	III	III	III	III
	Context type	*Tandır*	Destr.	Destr.	Destr.	Destr.	Destr.	Destr.	Destr.
	Period	Helln	Helln	Helln	Helln	Helln	Helln	Helln	Helln
	Site phase								
	>2.8mm	100	100	100	100	100	100	100	100
	>0.7mm	100	100	100	100	100	100	100	100
	Charcoal (g)	0	112.5	0	0	0	0		
	Seeds (g)	1.01	0.39	0.03	1.8cc	8.29	40.45		5cc
	Volume floated (litres)	N	N	N	N	N	N	N	N
	Merged samples							*	*
	tenekes								
	Classification	P	P	P	P	P	P	P	
DOMESTICATED CEREALS									
Triticum monococcum	grain	0	0	0	0	0	0	0	0
Triticum dicoccum	grain	0	0	0	0	0	0	0	0
Triticum durum/aestivum	grain	21	8	3	0	1,024	0	0	0
Triticum monococcum/dicoccum	glume bases	0	0	0	0	0	0	0	0
Triticum durum/aestivum	rachis segment	0	0	0	0	0	0	0	0
Hordeum vulgare (hulled)	grain	83	36	1	0	24	0	0	0
Hordeum vulgare (naked)	grain	0	0	0	0	0	0	0	0
Hordeum vulgare (hulled)	rachis segment	0	0	0	0	0	0	0	0
Hordeum/Triticum	sub-basal rachis*	0	0	0	0	0	0	0	0
Hordeum/Triticum	culm node or culm base	0	0	0	0	0	0	0	0
Secale cereale subsp. *cereale*	grain	0	0	0	0	0	0	0	0
Secale cereale subsp. *cereale*	rachis segment	0	0	0	0	0	0	0	0
Panicum miliaceum	grain	0	513	0	0	0	0	0	0
Setaria italica	grain	0	401	0	0	0	0	0	0
DOMESTICATED PULSES									
Cicer arietinum	seed	0	0	0	0	0	0	15	42
Lens culinaris	seed	1	0	0	79	164	0	0	0
Pisum sativum	seed	0	0	0	0	0	0	0	0
Vicia ervilia	seed	1	0	58	0	4	0	0	0
DOMESTICATED FRUITS									
Amygdalus communis	fruit	0	0	0	0	0	0	0	0
Vitis vinifera	seed	0	4	0	0	10	0	0	0
OTHER CROPS									
Linum usitatissimum		0	0	0	0	0	0	0	0
Gossypium arboreum/herbaceum		0	0	0	0	0	0	0	0
Nigella sativa		0	0	0	0	0	0	0	0
USEFUL WILD PLANTS									
Celtis		0	0	0	0	0	0	0	0
Crataegus		0	0	0	0	0	0	0	0
Pistacia	nutlet	0	0	0	0	0	0	0	0
Prunus	stone	0	0	0	0	0	0	0	0
Quercus	galls	0	0	0	0	0	81	0	0
Vitis sylvestris	seed	0	0	0	0	0	0	0	0

*or culm/spike node

	Site	AK	AK	AK	AK	AK	AK	AK	AK
	Period	Helln	Helln	Helln	Helln	Helln	Helln	Helln	Helln
	Context	111.4	602.24	602.25	606.6	606.6	606.6	606.6	606.6
	Sample				MN 1	MN 2	7	15	38
WILD PLANTS									
Boraginaceae									
Buglossoides aervense	seed	0	0	0	0	0	0	0	0
Buglosoides tenuiflora	seed	0	0	0	0	0	0	0	0
Leguminosae									
Fabeae (Vicieae)		0	0	0	0	3	0	0	0
Lathyrus cicera/sativus		1	0	0	0	0	0	0	0
Trifolieae		0	0	0	0	1	0	0	0
Poaceae									
Aegilops	grain	0	0	0	0	0	0	0	0
Aegilops	spikelet fork	0	0	0	0	0	0	0	0
Avena	grain	0	0	0	0	0	0	0	0
Bromus	grain	0	0	0	0	0	0	0	0
Echinochloa	grain	0	0	0	0	0	0	0	0
Lolium	grain	0	0	0	0	0	0	0	0
Setaria	grain	0	0	0	0	0	0	0	0
Stipa	grain	0	0	0	0	0	0	0	0
Taeniatherum	grain	0	0	0	0	0	0	0	0
Taeniatherum	chaff	0	0	0	0	0	0	0	0
Triticum boeoticum	grain	0	0	0	0	0	0	0	0
Poaceae - Indeterminate	grain	0	0	0	0	0	0	0	0
Other families									
Adonis		0	2	0	0	0	0	0	0
Ajuga		0	0	0	0	0	0	0	0
Apiaceae		0	0	0	0	1	0	0	0
Asteraceae		0	0	0	0	0	0	0	0
Bolboschoenus glaucus		0	0	0	0	0	0	0	0
Brassicaceae		0	0	0	0	0	0	0	0
Carex		0	0	0	0	0	0	0	0
Carthamus		0	0	0	0	2	0	0	0
Centaurea		0	0	0	0	0	0	0	0
Coriandrum sativum		0	0	0	0	0	0	0	0
Euclidium syriacum		0	0	0	0	0	0	0	0
Fumaria		0	0	0	0	0	0	0	0
Galium		0	4	0	2	0	0	0	0
Geum		0	0	0	0	0	0	0	0
Lallemantia		0	0	0	0	0	0	0	0
Liliaceae		0	0	0	0	0	0	0	0
Malva		0	0	0	0	0	0	0	0
Neslia		0	0	0	0	0	0	0	0
Polygonum		0	5	0	0	0	0	0	0
Ranunculus		0	0	0	0	0	0	0	0
Silene		0	0	0	0	0	0	0	0
Teucrium		0	0	0	0	0	0	0	0
Thalictrum		0	0	0	0	0	0	0	0
Thymelea		0	0	0	0	0	0	0	0
Vaccaria pyramidata		0	0	0	0	0	0	0	0
Valerianella		0	0	0	0	0	0	0	0
Indeterminate weeds		0	5	0	0	0	0	0	0
TOTAL		107	978	62	81	1,233	81	15	42
TOTAL seeds		107	978	62	81	1,233	81	15	42

	Site	AK	AK	AK	AK	AK	AK	AK	AK
	Period	**Helln**	**Helln**	**Helln**	**Helln**	**Helln**	**Helln**	**Helln**	**Helln**
	Context	606.15	606.15	728.14	726.26	726.27	729.18	807.6	809.1
	Sample	19	21			6			2
	Year	1969	1969	1969	1969	1969	1969	1969	1969
	Trench	H3c	H3c	H3d	H3d	H3d	H3d	I3c	I3c
	Room	III	III	III	IV	IV	IV	V	V
	Context type	Destr.	Destr.	Destr.	Destr.	Destr.	Destr.	Destr.	Destr.
	Period	Helln	Helln	Helln	Helln	Helln	Helln	Helln	Helln
	Site phase								
	>2.8mm	10	100	50	100	20	100	100	100
	>0.7mm	10	100	50	100	20	100	100	100
	Charcoal (g)			8.42		0	0		
	Seeds (g)		70cc	27.3	1.42	0.38	1.41	1.34	0.65
	Volume floated (litres)	N	N	N	N	N	N	N	N
	Merged samples							*	*
	tenekes								
	Classification	P	P	P	P	P	P	P	
DOMESTICATED CEREALS									
Triticum monococcum	grain	0	0	0	0	0	0	0	0
Triticum dicoccum	grain	0	0	0	0	0	0	0	0
Triticum durum/aestivum	grain	0	0	14	75	0	3	28	23
Triticum monococcum/dicoccum	glume bases	0	0	0	0	0	0	0	0
Triticum durum/aestivum	rachis segment	0	0	0	0	0	0	0	0
Hordeum vulgare (hulled)	grain	0	0	2,720	30	0	144	90	46
Hordeum vulgare (naked)	grain	0	0	0	0	0	0	0	0
Hordeum vulgare (hulled)	rachis segment	0	0	0	0	0	0	0	0
Hordeum/Triticum	sub-basal rachis*	0	0	0	0	0	0	0	0
Hordeum/Triticum	culm node or culm base	0	0	0	0	0	0	0	0
Secale cereale subsp. *cereale*	grain	0	0	0	0	0	0	0	0
Secale cereale subsp. *cereale*	rachis segment	0	0	0	0	0	0	0	0
Panicum miliaceum	grain	2	0	0	0	0	0	0	0
Setaria italica	grain	150	0	0	0	0	0	0	0
DOMESTICATED PULSES									
Cicer arietinum	seed	0	0	0	0	0	0	0	0
Lens culinaris	seed	0	0	1	1	0	1	2	0
Pisum sativum	seed	0	0	0	0	0	0	0	0
Vicia ervilia	seed	0	0	0	0	0	1	4	0
DOMESTICATED FRUITS									
Amygdalus communis	fruit	0	10	0	0	0	0	0	0
Vitis vinifera	seed	0	0	0	2	0	1	0	0
OTHER CROPS									
Linum usitatissimum		0	0	0	0	2,375	0	0	0
Gossypium arboreum/herbaceum		0	0	1	0	0	0	0	0
Nigella sativa		2,524	0	0	0	0	0	0	0
USEFUL WILD PLANTS									
Celtis		0	0	0	0	0	0	0	0
Crataegus		0	0	0	0	0	0	0	0
Pistacia	nutlet	0	0	0	0	0	0	0	0
Prunus	stone	0	0	0	0	0	0	0	1
Quercus	galls	0	0	0	0	0	0	0	0
Vitis sylvestris	seed	0	0	0	0	0	0	0	0

*or culm/spike node

	Site	AK	AK	AK	AK	AK	AK	AK	AK
	Period	Helln	Helln	Helln	Helln	Helln	Helln	Helln	Helln
	Context	606.15	606.15	728.14	726.26	726.27	729.18	807.6	809.1
	Sample	19	21			6			2
WILD PLANTS									
Boraginaceae									
Buglossoides aervense	seed	0	0	0	0	0	0	0	0
Buglosoides tenuiflora	seed	0	0	0	0	0	0	0	0
Leguminosae									
Fabeae (Vicieae)		0	0	0	0	0	0	0	0
Lathyrus cicera/sativus		0	0	0	0	0	0	0	0
Trifolieae		0	0	0	0	0	0	0	0
Poaceae									
Aegilops	grain	0	0	0	0	0	0	0	0
Aegilops	spikelet fork	0	0	0	0	0	0	0	0
Avena	grain	0	0	0	0	0	0	0	0
Bromus	grain	0	0	0	0	0	0	0	0
Echinochloa	grain	0	0	0	0	0	0	0	0
Lolium	grain	0	0	0	0	0	0	0	0
Setaria	grain	0	0	0	0	0	0	0	0
Stipa	grain	0	0	0	0	0	0	0	0
Taeniatherum	grain	0	0	0	0	0	0	0	0
Taeniatherum	chaff	0	0	1	0	0	0	0	0
Triticum boeoticum	grain	0	0	0	0	0	0	0	0
Poaceae - Indeterminate	grain	0	0	1	0	10	0	0	0
Other families									
Adonis		0	0	0	0	0	0	0	0
Ajuga		0	0	0	0	0	0	0	0
Apiaceae		0	0	0	0	0	0	0	0
Asteraceae		0	0	0	0	0	0	0	0
Bolboschoenus glaucus		0	0	0	0	0	0	0	0
Brassicaceae		0	0	0	0	0	0	0	0
Carex		0	0	0	0	0	0	0	0
Carthamus		0	0	0	0	0	0	0	0
Centaurea		0	0	0	0	0	0	0	0
Coriandrum sativum		0	0	0	0	0	0	0	0
Euclidium syriacum		0	0	0	0	0	0	0	0
Fumaria		0	0	0	0	0	0	0	0
Galium		1	0	5	0	0	0	0	0
Geum		0	0	0	0	0	0	0	0
Lallemantia		0	0	0	0	0	0	0	0
Liliaceae		0	0	0	0	0	0	0	0
Malva		0	0	0	0	0	0	0	0
Neslia		0	0	0	0	0	0	0	0
Polygonum		0	0	0	0	0	0	0	0
Ranunculus		0	0	0	0	0	0	0	0
Silene		0	0	0	0	0	0	0	0
Teucrium		0	0	0	0	0	0	0	0
Thalictrum		0	0	0	0	0	0	0	0
Thymelea		0	0	0	0	0	0	0	0
Vaccaria pyramidata		0	0	0	0	0	0	0	0
Valerianella		0	0	0	0	0	0	0	0
Indeterminate weeds		0	0	0	0	0	0	0	0
TOTAL		2,677	10	2,743	108	2,385	150	124	70
TOTAL seeds		2,677	10	2,742	108	2,385	150	124	70

	Site	AK	AK	AK	AK	AK	AK	AK	AK
	Period	Helln	Helln	Helln	Helln	Helln	Helln	Helln	Helln
	Context	807.14	1506.1	1506.3	1507.23	1507.27	1507.27	1507.27	1713.1
	Sample					7	34	35	24
	Year	1969	1971	1971	1972	1972	1972	1972	1972
	Trench	I3c	H4cd	H4cd	H4cd	H4cd	H4cd	H4cd	H5
	Room	V	VIII	VIII	VIII	VIII	VIII	VIII	Ct. yard
	Context type	Destr.	Destr.	Destr.	Destr.	Destr.	Destr.	Destr.	Destr.
	Period	Helln	Helln	Helln	Helln	Helln	Helln	Helln	Helln
	Site phase								
	>2.8mm	100	100	100	11	100	100	100	100
	>0.7mm	100	100	100	11	100	100	100	100
	Charcoal (g)	187.5	56.25	?	?	2.57	0	0	0.22
	Seeds (g)	1.43	0.22	0.09	181.11	55.59	1.22	0.69	0.04
	Volume floated (litres)	F	80	20	100	N	N	N	N
	Merged samples				*	*	*	*	
	tenekes		80lit	20lit	100lit				
	Classification				P		P		P
DOMESTICATED CEREALS									
Triticum monococcum	grain	0	0	0	0	0	0	0	0
Triticum dicoccum	grain	0	0	0	0	0	0	0	0
Triticum durum/aestivum	grain	54	1	0	1,533	5,910	137	80	0
Triticum monococcum/dicoccum	glume bases	0	0	0	0	0	0	0	0
Triticum durum/aestivum	rachis segment	0	0	0	0	0	0	0	0
Hordeum vulgare (hulled)	grain	134	21	14	6,663	562	5	17	4
Hordeum vulgare (naked)	grain	0	0	0	0	0	0	0	0
Hordeum vulgare (hulled)	rachis segment	0	0	0	9	0	0	0	0
Hordeum/Triticum	sub-basal rachis*	0	0	0	0	0	0	0	0
Hordeum/Triticum	culm node or culm base	0	0	0	0	0	0	0	0
Secale cereale subsp. *cereale*	grain	0	0	0	0	0	0	0	0
Secale cereale subsp. *cereale*	rachis segment	0	0	0	0	0	0	0	0
Panicum miliaceum	grain	0	0	0	193,344	649	16	0	0
Setaria italica	grain	0	0	0	8	1	0	0	0
DOMESTICATED PULSES									
Cicer arietinum	seed	0	0	0	0	0	0	0	0
Lens culinaris	seed	8	0	1	0	0	0	0	1
Pisum sativum	seed	0	9	0	0	4	0	0	2
Vicia ervilia	seed	29	0	2	0	0	0	0	150
DOMESTICATED FRUITS									
Amygdalus communis	fruit	0	0	0	0	0	0	0	0
Vitis vinifera	seed	13	8	13	6	2	0	0	1
OTHER CROPS									
Linum usitatissimum		1	0	0	0	0	0	0	0
Gossypium arboreum/herbaceum		0	0	0	0	0	0	0	0
Nigella sativa		0	1	0	0	0	0	0	0
USEFUL WILD PLANTS									
Celtis		0	0	0	0	0	0	0	0
Crataegus		0	0	0	0	0	0	0	0
Pistacia	nutlet	1	0	0	9	0	0	0	0
Prunus	stone	0	0	0	0	0	0	0	0
Quercus	galls	0	0	0	0	0	0	0	0
Vitis sylvestris	seed	0	0	0	0	0	0	0	0

*or culm/spike node

	Site	AK	AK	AK	AK	AK	AK	AK	AK
	Period	Helln	Helln	Helln	Helln	Helln	Helln	Helln	Helln
	Context	807.14	1506.1	1506.3	1507.23	1507.27	1507.27	1507.27	1713.1
	Sample					7	34	35	24
WILD PLANTS									
Boraginaceae									
Buglossoides aervense	seed	0	4	0	0	2	0	0	0
Buglosoides tenuiflora	seed	0	0	0	0	0	0	0	0
Leguminosae									
Fabeae (Vicieae)		8	0	0	6	1	0	0	1
Lathyrus cicera/sativus		0	0	1	0	0	0	0	0
Trifolieae		1	5	0	17	0	0	0	0
Poaceae									
Aegilops	grain	1	0	0	0	0	0	0	0
Aegilops	spikelet fork	0	0	0	0	0	0	0	0
Avena	grain	0	0	0	3	0	0	0	0
Bromus	grain	0	0	0	0	0	0	0	1
Echinochloa	grain	0	0	0	0	0	0	0	0
Lolium	grain	0	0	0	93	5	0	0	0
Setaria	grain	0	0	0	3	0	0	0	0
Stipa	grain	0	0	0	0	0	0	0	0
Taeniatherum	grain	0	0	0	0	0	0	0	0
Taeniatherum	chaff	0	0	1	0	0	0	0	0
Triticum boeoticum	grain	0	0	0	0	0	0	0	0
Poaceae - Indeterminate	grain	1	0	1	0	0	0	0	1
Other families									
Adonis		0	4	1	8	11	0	0	1
Ajuga		0	0	0	0	0	0	0	0
Apiaceae		55	0	0	0	0	0	0	0
Asteraceae		0	0	0	0	0	0	0	0
Bolboschoenus glaucus		0	0	0	0	0	0	0	0
Brassicaceae		0	0	0	0	0	0	0	0
Carex		0	0	0	0	0	0	0	0
Carthamus		0	0	1	0	0	0	0	1
Centaurea		0	0	0	0	0	0	0	0
Coriandrum sativum		0	0	0	0	0	0	0	0
Euclidium syriacum		0	0	0	6	0	0	0	0
Fumaria		0	0	0	0	0	0	0	0
Galium		216	6	50	36	28	0	0	11
Geum		0	0	0	0	0	0	0	0
Lallemantia		0	0	0	0	0	0	0	0
Liliaceae		0	0	0	0	0	0	0	0
Malva		0	0	0	0	0	0	0	0
Neslia		0	0	0	0	0	0	0	0
Polygonum		0	0	18	12	0	0	0	0
Ranunculus		2	0	0	0	0	0	0	0
Silene		0	0	0	3	0	0	0	0
Teucrium		0	0	0	0	0	0	0	0
Thalictrum		0	0	0	0	0	0	0	0
Thymelea		0	0	0	18	0	0	0	0
Vaccaria pyramidata		0	1	0	9	0	0	0	1
Valerianella		0	0	0	0	0	0	0	0
Indeterminate weeds		52	0	0	61	0	0	0	0
TOTAL		576	60	103	201,847	7,175	158	97	175
TOTAL seeds		576	60	102	201,838	7,175	158	97	175

	Site	AK	AK	AK	AK	AK	AK	AK	AK
	Period	**Roman**	**Roman**	**Med I**	**Med I**	**Med II**	**Med II**	**Med II**	**Med II**
	Context	1601.60	1806.4	1501.30	1502.4	603.13	606.4	712.7	712.8
	Sample		6		2				
	Year	1970	1971	1970	1970	1969		1969	1969
	Trench	I4cd	I5	H4cd	H4cd	H3c	H3c	H3d	H3d
	Room								
	Context type	Pit 7	Fill	Pit 7	Pit 2	Pit 2	Pit	Fill	Fill
	Period	Roman	Roman	Med I	Med I	Med II	Med II	Med II	Med II
	Site phase								
	>2.8mm	100	100	100	100	100	100	100	100
	>0.7mm	100	100	100	100	100	100	100	100
	Charcoal (g)	?	675	431.25	75	0	0		0
	Seeds (g)	0.05	0.21	1.6	4.22			1.6	0.46
	Volume floated (litres)	F	F	F	F	N	N	N	N
	Merged samples					*	*	*	*
	tenekes								
	Classification			P	P	P		P	
DOMESTICATED CEREALS									
Triticum monococcum	grain	0	0	0	0	0	0	0	0
Triticum dicoccum	grain	0	0	0	0	0	0	0	0
Triticum durum/aestivum	grain	3	6	84	458	1	8	44	18
Triticum monococcum/dicoccum	glume bases	0	0	0	0	0	0	0	0
Triticum durum/aestivum	rachis segment	0	0	0	0	0	0	0	0
Hordeum vulgare (hulled)	grain	3	18	79	8	2	3	108	30
Hordeum vulgare (naked)	grain	0	0	0	0	0	0	0	0
Hordeum vulgare (hulled)	rachis segment	0	0	0	0	0	0	0	0
Hordeum/Triticum	sub-basal rachis*	0	0	0	0	0	0	0	0
Hordeum/Triticum	culm node or culm base	0	0	0	0	0	0	0	0
Secale cereale subsp. *cereale*	grain	0	0	1	0	0	0	0	0
Secale cereale subsp. *cereale*	rachis segment	0	0	0	0	0	0	0	0
Panicum miliaceum	grain	0	8	0	0	0	0	0	0
Setaria italica	grain	0	20	0	0	0	0	0	0
DOMESTICATED PULSES									
Cicer arietinum	seed	0	0	0	0	0	0	0	0
Lens culinaris	seed	4	0	1	3	0	1	0	0
Pisum sativum	seed	4	0	0	1	0	0	0	0
Vicia ervilia	seed	2	0	1	3	314	476	0	0
DOMESTICATED FRUITS									
Amygdalus communis	fruit	0	0	0	0	0	0	0	0
Vitis vinifera	seed	0	161	173	2	1	2	0	0
OTHER CROPS									
Linum usitatissimum		0	0	0	0	0	0	0	0
Gossypium arboreum/herbaceum		0	0	0	0	0	0	0	0
Nigella sativa		0	0	0	0	0	0	0	0
USEFUL WILD PLANTS									
Celtis		0	0	300	2	0	0	0	0
Crataegus		0	0	0	0	0	0	0	0
Pistacia	nutlet	0	0	0	0	0	0	0	0
Prunus	stone	0	0	0	0	0	0	0	0
Quercus	galls	0	0	0	0	0	0	0	0
Vitis sylvestris	seed	0	0	0	0	0		0	0

*or culm/spike node

Appendix 1: Botanical find contexts at the Aşvan sites

	Site	AK	AK	AK	AK	AK	AK	AK	AK
	Period	Roman	Roman	Med I	Med I	Med II	Med II	Med II	Med II
	Context	1601.60	1806.4	1501.30	1502.4	603.13	606.4	712.7	712.8
	Sample		6		2				
WILD PLANTS									
Boraginaceae									
Buglossoides aervense	seed	0	1	0	1	0	0	0	0
Buglosoides tenuiflora	seed	0	0	0	0	0	0	0	0
Leguminosae									
Fabeae (Vicieae)		0	0	1	12	1	0	0	0
Lathyrus cicera/sativus		0	0	0	0	0	0	0	0
Trifolieae		0	8	0	0	0	0	0	0
Poaceae									
Aegilops	grain	0	0	0	0	0	0	0	0
Aegilops	spikelet fork	0	1	0	0	0	0	0	0
Avena	grain	0	0	0	1	0	0	0	0
Bromus	grain	0	0	0	0	0	0	0	0
Echinochloa	grain	0	0	0	0	0	0	0	0
Lolium	grain	0	0	0	1	0	0	0	0
Setaria	grain	0	4	0	0	0	0	0	0
Stipa	grain	0	0	0	0	0	0	0	0
Taeniatherum	grain	0	0	0	0	0	0	0	0
Taeniatherum	chaff	0	0	0	0	0	0	0	0
Triticum boeoticum	grain	0	0	0	0	0	0	0	0
Poaceae - Indeterminate	grain	0	0	0	0	0	0	0	0
Other families									
Adonis		0	2	0	0	0	0	0	0
Ajuga		0	0	0	0	0	0	0	0
Apiaceae		0	0	0	0	0	0	0	0
Asteraceae		0	0	0	0	0	0	0	0
Bolboschoenus glaucus		0	10	0	0	0	0	0	0
Brassicaceae		0	0	0	0	0	0	0	0
Carex		0	0	0	0	0	0	0	0
Carthamus		0	0	0	0	0	0	0	0
Centaurea		0	0	0	0	0	0	0	0
Coriandrum sativum		0	0	0	0	0	0	0	0
Euclidium syriacum		0	0	0	0	0	0	0	0
Fumaria		0	0	0	0	0	0	0	0
Galium		3	0	0	1	0	0	0	0
Geum		0	0	0	0	0	0	0	0
Lallemantia		0	0	0	0	0	0	0	0
Liliaceae		0	0	0	0	0	0	0	0
Malva		0	0	0	0	0	0	0	0
Neslia		0	0	0	0	0	0	0	0
Polygonum		0	0	0	0	0	0	0	0
Ranunculus		0	0	0	0	0	0	0	0
Silene		0	0	0	0	0	0	0	0
Teucrium		0	0	0	0	0	0	0	0
Thalictrum		0	0	0	0	0	0	0	0
Thymelea		0	0	0	0	0	0	0	0
Vaccaria pyramidata		0	0	0	0	0	0	0	0
Valerianella		0	0	0	0	0	0	0	0
Indeterminate weeds		0	14	0	0	0	0	0	0
TOTAL		19	253	640	493	319	490	152	48
TOTAL seeds		19	252	640	493	319	490	152	48

	Site	**AK**	**AK**	**AK**	**AK**	**AK**	**AK**	**AK**
	Period	**Med II**	**Med II**	**Med II**	**Med II**	**Med II**	**Med II**	**Med II**
	Context	714.8	714.8	714.10	714.8	714.8	714.8	714.8
	Sample	MN 1	MN 4		MN 2	MN 3	MN 190	MN 191
	Year	1969	1969	1969	1969	1969	1969	1969
	Trench	H3d	H3d	H3d	H3d	H3d	H3d	H3d
	Room							
	Context type	Pit 1	Pit 1	Pit 1	Pit 1	Pit 1	Pit 1	Pit 1
	Period	Med II	Med II	Med II	Med II	Med II	Med II	Med II
	Site phase							
	>2.8mm	100	100	100	100	100	100	100
	>0.7mm	100	100	100	100	100	100	100
	Charcoal (g)	0	0	0	0	0		0
	Seeds (g)	16.37	25.21	1.11	0.48	1.73		0.48
	Volume floated (litres)	N	N	N	N	N	N	N
	Merged samples	*	*	*	*	*		
	tenekes							
	Classification		P		P			P
DOMESTICATED CEREALS								
Triticum monococcum	grain	0	0	0	0	0	0	0
Triticum dicoccum	grain	0	0	0	0	0	0	0
Triticum durum/aestivum	grain	27	31	9	0	0	0	3
Triticum monococcum/dicoccum	glume bases	0	0	0	0	0	0	0
Triticum durum/aestivum	rachis segment	0	0	0	0	0	0	0
Hordeum vulgare (hulled)	grain	91	166	12	0	6	0	10
Hordeum vulgare (naked)	grain	0	0	0	0	0	0	0
Hordeum vulgare (hulled)	rachis segment	0	0	0	0	0	0	0
Hordeum/Triticum	sub-basal rachis*	0	0	0	0	0	0	0
Hordeum/Triticum	culm node or culm base	0	0	0	0	0	0	0
Secale cereale subsp. *cereale*	grain	2	0	0	0	0	0	0
Secale cereale subsp. *cereale*	rachis segment	0	0	0	0	0	0	0
Panicum miliaceum	grain	0	0	0	0	0	0	15
Setaria italica	grain	0	0	0	0	0	0	0
DOMESTICATED PULSES								
Cicer arietinum	seed	0	0	0	0	0	0	18
Lens culinaris	seed	2	4	0	0	0	0	2
Pisum sativum	seed	0	0	0	0	0	0	0
Vicia ervilia	seed	824	1,258	43	27	89	0	22
DOMESTICATED FRUITS								
Amygdalus communis	fruit	0	0	0	0	0	0	0
Vitis vinifera	seed	7	2	0	0	0	0	2
OTHER CROPS								
Linum usitatissimum		0	0	0	0	0	0	0
Gossypium arboreum/herbaceum		9	9	2	0	0	1	0
Nigella sativa		0	0	0	0	0	0	0
USEFUL WILD PLANTS								
Celtis		0	0	0	0	0	0	0
Crataegus		0	0	0	0	0	0	0
Pistacia	nutlet	0	0	0	0	0	0	0
Prunus	stone	0	0	0	0	0	0	0
Quercus	galls	0	0	0	0	0	0	0
Vitis sylvestris	seed	0	0	0	0	0	0	0

*or culm/spike node

	Site	AK	AK	AK	AK	AK	AK	AK
	Period	Med II	Med II	Med II	Med II	Med II	Med II	Med II
	Context	714.8	714.8	714.10	714.8	714.8	714.8	714.8
	Sample	MN 1	MN 4		MN 2	MN 3	MN 190	MN 191
WILD PLANTS								
Boraginaceae								
Buglossoides aervense	seed	0	0	0	0	0	1	0
Buglosoides tenuiflora	seed	0	0	0	0	0	0	0
Leguminosae								
Fabeae (Vicieae)		6	1	0	0	0	10	0
Lathyrus cicera/sativus		0	0	0	0	0	0	0
Trifolieae		0	0	0	0	0	0	0
Poaceae								
Aegilops	grain	0	0	0	0	0	0	0
Aegilops	spikelet fork	0	0	0	0	0	0	0
Avena	grain	0	0	0	0	0	0	0
Bromus	grain	0	0	0	0	0	0	0
Echinochloa	grain	0	0	0	0	0	0	0
Lolium	grain	0	0	0	0	0	0	0
Setaria	grain	0	0	0	0	0	0	0
Stipa	grain	0	0	0	0	0	0	0
Taeniatherum	grain	0	0	0	0	0	0	0
Taeniatherum	chaff	0	0	0	0	0	0	0
Triticum boeoticum	grain	0	0	0	0	0	0	0
Poaceae - Indeterminate	grain	0	0	0	0	0	2	0
Other families								
Adonis		0	0	0	0	1	0	0
Ajuga		0	0	0	0	0	0	0
Apiaceae		0	0	0	0	0	0	0
Asteraceae		0	0	0	0	0	0	0
Bolboschoenus glaucus		0	0	0	0	0	0	0
Brassicaceae		0	0	0	0	0	0	0
Carex		0	0	0	0	0	0	0
Carthamus		0	0	0	0	0	0	0
Centaurea		0	0	0	0	0	0	0
Coriandrum sativum		0	0	0	0	0	0	0
Euclidium syriacum		0	0	0	0	0	0	0
Fumaria		0	0	0	0	0	0	0
Galium		7	2	1	0	0	0	8
Geum		0	0	0	0	0	0	0
Lallemantia		0	0	0	0	0	0	0
Liliaceae		0	0	0	0	0	0	0
Malva		0	0	0	0	0	0	0
Neslia		0	0	0	0	0	0	0
Polygonum		0	0	0	0	0	0	0
Ranunculus		0	0	0	0	0	0	0
Silene		0	0	0	0	0	0	0
Teucrium		0	0	0	0	0	0	0
Thalictrum		0	0	0	0	0	0	0
Thymelea		0	0	0	0	0	0	0
Vaccaria pyramidata		0	0	0	0	0	0	0
Valerianella		0	0	0	0	0	0	0
Indeterminate weeds		0	0	0	0	0	0	0
TOTAL		975	1,473	67	27	96	14	80
TOTAL seeds		975	1,473	67	27	96	14	80

	Site	AK	AK	AK	AK	AK	AK	AK
	Period	**Med II**	**Med II**	**Med II**	**Med II**	**Med II**	**Med II**	**Med II**
	Context	714.8	1501.8	1501.13	1501.15	1503.3	910.22	3101.40
	Sample	MN 273	14			4	1	1
	Year	1969					1969	1972
	Trench	H3d	H4cd	H4cd	H4cd	H4cd	I4a	I6
	Room							
	Context type	Pit 1	*Tandır*	Pit 7	Pit 7	Pit 6	Pit 19	Pit 4
	Period	Med II	Med II	Med II	Med II	Med II	Med II	Med II
	Site phase							
	>2.8mm	100	100	100	100	100	100	100
	>0.7mm	100	100	100	100	100	100	100
	Charcoal (g)	0	600	56.25	525			?
	Seeds (g)	0.53	3.71	0.34	1.44	1.35		0.55
	Volume floated (litres)	N	F	F	F	F	N	N
	Merged samples							
	tenekes				F	F		N
	Classification		P	P	P	P	P	P
DOMESTICATED CEREALS								
Triticum monococcum	grain	0	0	0	0	0	0	0
Triticum dicoccum	grain	0	0	0	0	0	0	0
Triticum durum/aestivum	grain	2	187	29	96	156	0	70
Triticum monococcum/dicoccum	glume bases	0	0	0	0	0	0	0
Triticum durum/aestivum	rachis segment	4	0	0	0	0	0	0
Hordeum vulgare (hulled)	grain	14	165	5	41	7	0	1
Hordeum vulgare (naked)	grain	0	0	0	0	0	0	0
Hordeum vulgare (hulled)	rachis segment	0	0	0	0	0	0	0
Hordeum/Triticum	sub-basal rachis*	0	0	0	0	0	0	0
Hordeum/Triticum	culm node or culm base	4	0	0	0	0	0	0
Secale cereale subsp. *cereale*	grain	1	0	1	2	0	0	0
Secale cereale subsp. *cereale*	rachis segment	2	0	0	0	0	0	0
Panicum miliaceum	grain	0	0	0	0	0	0	0
Setaria italica	grain	0	0	0	0	0	0	0
DOMESTICATED PULSES								
Cicer arietinum	seed	0	0	0	0	0	0	0
Lens culinaris	seed	2	4	0	3	0	0	0
Pisum sativum	seed	0	0	0	1	0	0	0
Vicia ervilia	seed	24	0	0	0	0	0	0
DOMESTICATED FRUITS								
Amygdalus communis	fruit	0	0	0	0	0	0	0
Vitis vinifera	seed	1	0	0	41	0	0	1
OTHER CROPS								
Linum usitatissimum		0	0	0	0	0	0	0
Gossypium arboreum/herbaceum		1	0	0	0	0	0	0
Nigella sativa		0	0	0	0	0	0	0
USEFUL WILD PLANTS								
Celtis		0	0	7	12	2	150	0
Crataegus		0	0	0	0	0	0	0
Pistacia	nutlet	1	0	0	0	0	0	0
Prunus	stone	0	0	0	0	0	0	0
Quercus	galls	0	0	0	0	0	0	0
Vitis sylvestris	seed	0	0	0	0	0	0	0

*or culm/spike node

	Site	AK	AK	AK	AK	AK	AK	AK
	Period	**Med II**	**Med II**	**Med II**	**Med II**	**Med II**	**Med II**	**Med II**
	Context	714.8	1501.8	1501.13	1501.15	1503.3	910.22	3101.40
	Sample	MN 273	14			4	1	1
WILD PLANTS								
Boraginaceae								
Buglossoides aervense	seed	0	0	0	0	0	0	0
Buglosoides tenuiflora	seed	0	0	0	0	0	0	0
Leguminosae								
Fabeae (Vicieae)		4	0	0	3	0	0	0
Lathyrus cicera/sativus		0	0	0	0	0	0	0
Trifolieae		0	0	0	0	0	0	0
Poaceae								
Aegilops	grain	0	0	0	0	0	0	0
Aegilops	spikelet fork	0	0	0	0	0	0	0
Avena	grain	0	0	0	1	0	0	0
Bromus	grain	0	0	0	0	0	0	0
Echinochloa	grain	0	0	0	0	0	0	0
Lolium	grain	0	0	0	0	0	0	0
Setaria	grain	0	0	0	0	0	0	0
Stipa	grain	0	0	0	0	0	0	0
Taeniatherum	grain	0	0	0	0	0	0	0
Taeniatherum	chaff	0	0	0	0	0	0	0
Triticum boeoticum	grain	0	0	0	0	0	0	0
Poaceae - Indeterminate	grain	0	0	0	0	0	0	0
Other families								
Adonis		1	0	0	0	0	0	0
Ajuga		0	0	0	0	0	0	0
Apiaceae		0	0	0	0	0	0	0
Asteraceae		0	0	0	0	0	0	0
Bolboschoenus glaucus		0	0	0	0	0	0	0
Brassicaceae		0	0	0	0	0	0	0
Carex		0	0	0	0	0	0	0
Carthamus		0	0	0	0	0	0	0
Centaurea		0	0	0	0	0	0	0
Coriandrum sativum		0	0	0	0	0	0	0
Euclidium syriacum		0	0	0	0	0	0	0
Fumaria		0	0	0	0	0	0	0
Galium		0	2	0	4	0	0	0
Geum		0	0	0	0	0	0	0
Lallemantia		0	0	0	0	0	0	0
Liliaceae		0	0	0	0	0	0	0
Malva		0	0	0	0	0	0	0
Neslia		0	0	0	0	0	0	0
Polygonum		0	0	0	0	0	0	0
Ranunculus		0	0	0	0	0	0	0
Silene		0	0	0	0	0	0	0
Teucrium		0	0	0	0	0	0	0
Thalictrum		0	0	0	0	0	0	0
Thymelea		0	0	0	0	0	0	0
Vaccaria pyramidata		0	0	0	0	0	0	0
Valerianella		0	0	0	0	0	0	0
Indeterminate weeds		0	0	0	0	0	0	0
TOTAL		61	358	42	204	165	150	72
TOTAL seeds		51	358	42	204	165	150	72

	Site	**AK**	**TK**	**TK**	**TK**
	Period	**Med III**	**Med III**	**Med III**	**Med III**
	Context	1902.4	703.11	605.5	201.15
	Sample		1	1	
	Year	1971	1971	1971	1970
	Trench	G4cd	J22	R11	S11
	Room				
	Context type	Fill	*Tandır*	Pit 2	Pithos
	Period	Med IIIa	Med	Med	Med
	Site phase				
	>2.8mm	100	100	100	100
	>0.7mm	100	100	100	100
	Charcoal (g)	1200	2.63	93.75	222.75
	Seeds (g)	27cc	0.14	0.26	22.28
	Volume floated (litres)	100	20	60	F
	Merged samples				
	tenekes	100 lit	20lit	60lit	
	Classification	P			P
DOMESTICATED CEREALS					
Triticum monococcum	grain	0	0	0	0
Triticum dicoccum	grain	0	0	0	0
Triticum durum/aestivum	grain	0	12	0	0
Triticum monococcum/dicoccum	glume bases	0	0	0	0
Triticum durum/aestivum	rachis segment	0	1	0	0
Hordeum vulgare (hulled)	grain	0	3	21	905
Hordeum vulgare (naked)	grain	0	0	0	1
Hordeum vulgare (hulled)	rachis segment	0	0	0	0
Hordeum/Triticum	sub-basal rachis*	0	0	0	0
Hordeum/Triticum	culm node or culm base	0	1	0	0
Secale cereale subsp. *cereale*	grain	0	0	0	0
Secale cereale subsp. *cereale*	rachis segment	0	0	0	0
Panicum miliaceum	grain	0	0	0	0
Setaria italica	grain	0	0	0	0
DOMESTICATED PULSES					
Cicer arietinum	seed	0	0	0	0
Lens culinaris	seed	0	0	5	1
Pisum sativum	seed	0	0	0	0
Vicia ervilia	seed	0	3	0	0
DOMESTICATED FRUITS					
Amygdalus communis	fruit	0	0	0	0
Vitis vinifera	seed	0	1	1	1
OTHER CROPS					
Linum usitatissimum		0	0	38	0
Gossypium arboreum/herbaceum		342	2	1	0
Nigella sativa		0	0	0	0
USEFUL WILD PLANTS					
Celtis		0	0	0	0
Crataegus		0	0	0	0
Pistacia	nutlet	0	0	0	0
Prunus	stone	0	0	0	0
Quercus	galls	0	0	0	0
Vitis sylvestris	seed	0	0	0	0

*or culm/spike node

	Site	AK	TK	TK	TK
	Period	Med IIIa	Med	Med	Med
	Context	1902.4	703.11	605.5	201.15
	Sample		1	1	
WILD PLANTS					
Boraginaceae					
Buglossoides aervense	seed	0	0	0	0
Buglosoides tenuiflora	seed	0	0	0	0
Leguminosae					
Fabeae (Vicieae)		0	1	4	0
Lathyrus cicera/sativus		0	1	0	0
Trifolieae		0	0	0	0
Poaceae					
Aegilops	grain	0	0	0	0
Aegilops	spikelet fork	0	0	0	0
Avena	grain	0	0	0	0
Bromus	grain	0	0	0	0
Echinochloa	grain	0	0	0	0
Lolium	grain	0	2	0	0
Setaria	grain	0	0	0	0
Stipa	grain	0	0	0	0
Taeniatherum	grain	0	0	0	0
Taeniatherum	chaff	0	0	0	0
Triticum boeoticum	grain	0	0	0	0
Poaceae - Indeterminate	grain	0	0	0	0
Other families					
Adonis		0	0	0	0
Ajuga		0	0	0	0
Apiaceae		0	0	0	0
Asteraceae		0	0	0	0
Bolboschoenus glaucus		0	0	0	0
Brassicaceae		0	0	0	0
Carex		0	0	0	0
Carthamus		0	0	0	0
Centaurea		0	0	0	0
Coriandrum sativum		0	0	0	0
Euclidium syriacum		0	0	0	0
Fumaria		0	0	0	0
Galium		0	0	2	2
Geum		0	0	0	0
Lallemantia		0	0	0	0
Liliaceae		0	0	0	0
Malva		0	0	0	0
Neslia		0	0	0	0
Polygonum		0	0	0	0
Ranunculus		0	0	0	0
Silene		0	0	0	0
Teucrium		0	0	0	0
Thalictrum		0	0	0	0
Thymelea		0	0	0	0
Vaccaria pyramidata		0	0	0	0
Valerianella		0	0	0	0
Indeterminate weeds		0	6	35	10
TOTAL		342	26	107	920
TOTAL seeds		342	26	107	920

Appendix 2.
The flowering/fruiting periods of weeds

The following table details the flowering/fruiting periods of weeds in the vicinity of sites local to Aşvan, including Çemişgezek, and at Can Hasan in the southern Konya plain. This information is collated from unpublished field observation notes taken in the 1970s by Gordon Hillman (GCH), Peter Symmons (P. Symmons) and Pat Ball and Nicholas Bean (Ball & Bean). The notes are stored in the Aşvan archive at the British Institute at Ankara. FI = *Flora of Iraq* (http://www.kew.org/science-conservation/research-data/science-directory/projects/flora-iraq).

Species	*April*	*May*	*June*	*July*	*August*	*September*	*October*	*November*
Buglossoides arvensis			GCH (Can Hasan)		GCH (Aşvan)	GCH (Aşvan)		
Buglossoides tenuiflora			GCH (Can Hasan)		GCH (Aşvan)	GCH (Aşvan)		
Aegilops			GCH (Aşvan; Can Hasan)	GCH (Aşvan; Çemişgezek); P. Symmons (Aşvan)	GCH (Aşvan)	GCH (Aşvan; Çemişgezek)	GCH (Aşvan; Çemişgezek)	GCH (Can Hasan)
Avena			GCH (Can Hasan)	GCH (Aşvan); P. Symmons (Aşvan)	GCH (Aşvan); Ball & Bean (Aşvan)	GCH (Aşvan)		
Bromus			GCH (Aşvan; Can Hasan)	GCH (Aşvan); Ball & Bean (Aşvan)	GCH (Aşvan)	GCH (Aşvan)		
Echinochloa				Ball & Bean (Aşvan)	GCH (Aşvan); Ball & Bean (Aşvan); P. Symmons (Aşvan)	GCH (Aşvan)		
Lolium			GCH (Cemisgezeck)	GCH (Aşvan)	GCH (Aşvan); P. Symmons (Aşvan)	GCH (Aşvan)	GCH (Aşvan)	GCH (Can Hasan)
Setaria				P. Symmons (Aşvan)	GCH (Aşvan); Ball & Bean (Aşvan)	GCH (Aşvan)		
Stipa	GCH (SW coast Demre)			GCH (Aşvan)		GCH (Aşvan)		
Taeniatherum				GCH (Aşvan)	GCH (Aşvan)			
Triticum boeoticum			GCH (Can Hasan)	GCH (Aşvan)	GCH (Aşvan)	GCH (Aşvan; Çemişgezek)	GCH (Çemişgezek)	
Gramineae Indeterminate				GCH (Aşvan) – cf. *Festuca*; Ball & Bean (Aşvan)	GCH (Aşvan); Ball & Bean (Aşvan); P. Symmons (Aşvan)		GCH (Aşvan)	
Pea/wild pulse				Ball & Bean (Aşvan)		GCH (Aşvan)	GCH (Aşvan)	
Lathyrus cicera/sativus	GCH (SW coast Demre) – *Lathyrus* sp.		GCH (Çemişgezek)	Ball & Bean (Aşvan)			GCH (Aşvan)	

Species	*April*	*May*	*June*	*July*	*August*	*September*	*October*	*November*
Trifolieae	[GCH (SW coast Demre) – *Trifolium*]		GCH (Can Hasan) – *Medicago sativa*, *Melilotus*, *Trigonella*, *Galium verum*, *Trifolium*, *Triongella cerantiaca*	GCH (Aşvan) – *Trifolium*, *Medicago sativa*, *Medicago*, *Medicago radiata;* P. Symmons (Aşvan) – *Trigonella*; Ball & Bean (Aşvan) – *Trifolium*, *Hedysarum?*, *Medicago*, *Trifolium* nr. *repens*, *Medicago lupina*, *Trifolium* nr. *fragiferum*, *Trigonella*	GCH (Aşvan) – *Medicago*, *Trigonella*, *Medicago* cf. *lupina*, *Trifolium*, *Medicago* cf. *sativa*, *Medicago? facta*, *Trigonella* nr. *corniculata*, *Medicago arbiularis*, *Medicago? neapolitana*; Ball & Bean (Aşvan) – *Medicago*, *Trifolium*; P. Symonns (Aşvan) – *Medicago sativa*, *Trifolium*	GCH (Aşvan) – *Medicago*, *Trifolium*, *Trifolium arvense*, *Medicago radiata*, *Trigonella*, *Medicago sativa*	GCH (Can Hasan) – *Trigonella*, *Medicago sativa*	
Adonis			GCH (Can Hasan)		Ball & Bean (Aşvan)			
Ajuga						GCH (Aşvan)		
Bellevallia	FI (Can Hasan)	FI (Can Hasan)						
Bolboschoenus glaucus/ Scirpus		FI (Aşvan)	FI (Aşvan)	FI (Aşvan)	FI (Aşvan)			
Carex			GCH (Aşvan; Can Hasan)		GCH (Aşvan)	GCH (Aşvan)	GCH (Aşvan)	GCH (Can Hasan)
Carthamus			GCH (Aşvan); P. Symmons (Aşvan); Ball & Bean (Aşvan)					
Centaurea			GCH (Can Hasan)	GCH (Aşvan); P. Symmons (Aşvan); Ball & Bean (Aşvan)	GCH (Aşvan); P. Symmons (Aşvan)	GCH (Aşvan)		GCH (Can Hasan)
Compositae			GCH (Can Hasan)	Ball & Bean (Aşvan) – cf. *Cinoeceas*, *Helicarysum stoechas?*, *Circium*, *Chicorum intybus* (wild chicory), *Chamaemelum*, *Solidago*, *Filago*, *Condrilla juncea* cf., *Galacthes?*, *Artemesia*, cf. *Crepis*	GCH (Aşvan); Ball & Bean (Aşvan) – Comp. *Bidens*, Comp. nr. *Crysanthemum* (cultivar), Comp. nr. *Lalthca* (weed), Comp. nr. *Calendula* (weed); P. Symonns (Aşvan) – *Antheunis* cf. *arvensis*, cf. *Helichrysum*, cf. *Chrysanthemum parthenium*			GCH (Can Hasan)

Species	*April*	*May*	*June*	*July*	*August*	*September*	*October*	*November*
Coriandrum sativum				FI (Aşvan)				
Cruciferae				GCH (Aşvan); Ball & Bean (Aşvan) – *Alyssum*, *Sisymbrium*, *Aethlonema opposititi-folium?*, *Sterigmo-sperma*, cf. *Lepidum vesi-carium*, *Alyssum* cf. *strictum*, *Thlaspi*, *Silidus*	GCH (Aşvan); Ball & Bean (Aşvan) – Crucif. nr./cf. *Sysymbrium*, Alysssum sp.; P. Symmons (Aşvan) – *Sisymbrium loesii*, *Alyssum xanthocarpum*, cf. *Cochlearia* sp.	GCH (Aşvan)	GCH (Aşvan)	
Euclidium syriacum	FI (Aşvan)	FI (Aşvan)	FI (Aşvan)					
Fumaria			GCH (Can Hasan)					
Galium			GCH (Can Hasan)	GCH (Aşvan); P. Symmons (Aşvan); Ball & Bean (Aşvan)	GCH (Aşvan); P. Symmons (Aşvan); Ball & Bean (Aşvan)	GCH (Aşvan)		
Geum	FI (Aşvan)	FI (Aşvan)	FI (Aşvan)	FI (Aşvan)				
Lallemantia								
Liliaceae				Ball & Bean (Aşvan) – cf. *Allium* (onion)	Ball & Bean (Aşvan) – Liliaceae cf. *Polygonatum*; P. Symmons (Aşvan) – cf. *Asphodelus*		GCH (Aşvan)	
Malva				Ball & Bean (Aşvan)	GCH (Avsan); Ball & Bean (Aşvan)			
Neslia			GCH (Can Hasan)		GCH (Aşvan)			
Polygonum			GCH (Can Hasan)	GCH (Aşvan); Ball & Bean (Aşvan)	GCH (Aşvan); Ball & Bean (Aşvan); P. Symmons (Aşvan)	GCH (Aşvan)	GCH (Aşvan)	
Ranunculus			GCH (Can Hasan)	GCH (Aşvan)	GCH (Aşvan); P. Symmons (Aşvan)	GCH (Aşvan)	GCH (Aşvan)	
Silene				GCH (Aşvan); P. Symmons (Aşvan); Ball & Bean (Aşvan)	GCH (Aşvan); P. Symmons (Aşvan)	GCH (Aşvan)	GCH (Aşvan)	
Teucrium				P. Symmons (Aşvan)	GCH (Aşvan)	GCH (Aşvan)		GCH (Can Hasan)
Thalictrum					GCH (Aşvan)			

Species	*April*	*May*	*June*	*July*	*August*	*September*	*October*	*November*
Thymelea				P. Symmons (Aşvan); Ball & Bean (Aşvan)	GCH (Aşvan)	GCH (Aşvan)	GCH (Aşvan)	
Umbelliferae			GCH (Can Hasan)	GCH (Aşvan); P. Symmons (Aşvan); Ball & Bean (Aşvan) – nr. *Pastinaca*, *Daucus*	GCH (Aşvan); P. Symmons (Aşvan) – cf. *Orlaya* sp., *Scandix* sp.; Ball & Bean (Aşvan) – *Carum carvi* (caraway), *Daucus carota* (carrot)	GCH (Aşvan)	GCH (Çemişgezek)	
Vaccaria pyramidata			GCH (Can Hasan)	P. Symmons (Aşvan); Ball & Bean (Aşvan)	GCH (Aşvan)			
Valerianella				GCH (Aşvan)	GCH (Aşvan)			

Appendix 3.
Weed ecology data compiled from field observation notes taken in the 1970s

The following weed ecology data have been compiled from field observation notes (unpublished) taken in the 1970s by Gordon Hillman (G. Hillman), Peter Symmons (P. Symmons) and Pat Ball and Nicholas Bean (Ball & Bean). The notes are stored in the Aşvan archive at the British Institute at Ankara. The Aşvan botanical team did not collect specimens or record ecological data for some of these species, and in these cases we refer to the information about plant habitat provided by the *Flora of Iraq* (Townsend, Guest, 1966–1985).

Buglossoides arvensis and *tenuiflora*

Crop field edge (barley field in June and by roadside ditch in June) – G. Hillman at Can Hasan.

Rocky roadside verge (in June) – G. Hillman at Can Hasan.

Oak-covered rocky hillside (20% oak cover, limestone hills, lower slopes, at bottom edge of wood, grazed and trampled frequently, in August) – G. Hillman at Aşvan.

Oak-covered rocky slope (30% oak cover and dense ground cover, verge above vineyard wall in June) – G. Hillman at Can Hasan.

? Gully (north-facing gulley in conglomerate towards northern edge of rock outcrop near edge of village, washed by water from village, often flushed by village water and muck) – G. Hillman at Aşvan.

Riverbed/riverside (well-watered, rocky terrain, sandy in places, lush vegetation, loose limestone/dolomite, ca 60° slope, large rock outcrops interspersed with soil pockets/screelets, fast-moving water, moist crevices, surrounding plant cover, grassland with shallow soil and rock outcrops/pavement, in wet earth in August) – Ball & Bean at Aşvan.

Bank of Murat (sand shore, pebble beach, two zones – upper very colonised, lower less so, in September on lower sand-shore line, but poorly colonised) – G. Hillman at Aşvan.

Aegilops sp.

Crop field (barley edge overlying conglomerate thin pebbly soil in August, *Aegilops ovata* and *Aegilops speltoides* in very sandy, coarse pebbly pavement in August and as weeds in *H.distichum* fields alongside *Avena* in August) – G. Hillman at Aşvan; crop field (*Aegilops speltoides* – foot of limestone hill with frequent oak scrub and ploughed fields) – G. Hillman at Çemişgezek; crop field (*Aegilops* nr. *murtica* in July in harvested *T. aestivum* field) – P. Symmons at Aşvan; crop field (in unirrigated durum wheat fields in July) – Ball & Bean at Aşvan.

Crop field edge (harvested *Triticum durum* edge in road band between stubble and irrigation ditch/soil much deeper in August, coarse pebble pavement, possibly from underlying conglomerate, with very scanty soil and *Aegilops* cf. *speltoides* in July between *Crataegus* brushes with *Secale* [weedy rye], *T. boeoticum* and *Bromus*) – G. Hillman at Aşvan; crop field edge (edge of barley field in June, *Aegilops truncialis*, and *Aegilops* sp. in November) – G. Hillman at Can Hasan.

Grassy verge – G. Hillman at Aşvan; grassy verge (*Aegilops* cf. *cylindrica* in June between track and field of *T. durum*) – G. Hillman at Can Hasan.

Fallow (in August between irrigated maize fields, presumed irrigated in the previous season and furrowed, now dry with sparse weed cover, in the alluvial flats below the village immediately below a conglomerate and clay outcrop by the village) – G. Hillman at Aşvan.

Ditch field edge (in July) – Ball & Bean at Aşvan.

Waste ground (in July) – G. Hillman at Aşvan.

Rough grazing area (northwest edge of Aşvan village, for tethered donkeys and sheep, just below conglomerate cliff up to first gardens, trampled and heavily grazed, stony, dry soils, in August – G. Hillman at Aşvan.

Roadside (*Aegilops* nr. *speltoides* on dry sandy roadside bank beside irrigated maize field and ditch, no tree cover, dry loose sand in August and *Aegilops* sp. in September on trackside conglomerate of chalky soil) – G. Hillman at Aşvan.

Rubbish fill (covered with dung, *Aegilops speltoides* in August) – G. Hillman at Aşvan

Alluvial flats (*Aegilops* sp. and *Aegilops* [?very large *speltoides*?] on alluvial flats below Aşvan village, upper section immediately below conglomerate and clay outcrop by village with cultivated patch between irrigated maize, presumably irrigated earlier in season and furrowed but now dry) – G. Hillman at Aşvan.

Limestone hills (dry, stony surface with numerous rock outcrops, grazed, probably frequently, with cultivation nearby, in August) – G. Hillman at Aşvan; limestone hills (dry, stony surface with numerous rock outcrops, grazed, probably frequently, with cultivation nearby, stony rocky terraces high up on limestone hills with numerous patches of low oak scrub in September, *Aegilops columnaris* on stony rocky terraces high up on limestone hills with numerous patches of low oak scrub in September and *Aegilops speltoides* at foot of limestone hills with frequent patches of low oak scrub and ploughed fields in September) – G. Hillman at Çemişgezek.

Grassy hills (upper slopes, treeless/shrubless, frequently grazed by sheep, goats and cattle, *Aegilops* dominated, *Aegilops* nr. *speltoides* in September) – G. Hillman at Aşvan.

Northeast-facing slopes (loose surface, 30% cover, mainly marble, crystalline limestone, with occasional areas of grass, *Aegilops* cf. *murtica* and *Aegilops* sp. in July) – G. Hillman at Aşvan; northeast-facing slopes (loose surface, 30% cover, mainly marble, crystalline limestone, with occasional areas of grass, *Aegilops* nr. *speltoides* in October) – G. Hillman at Çemişgezek.

East-facing slopes (high, *Aegilops murtica* in July on hills to south of Aşvan with fields below them) – P. Symmons at Aşvan.

Wooded hills (limestone, north-facing, loose rocks and rock outcrops, steep near top, open woodland throughout upper part of hills, little grazed steppe in upper parts, frequent below, collections from 1,050m to top, which is at 1,250m, and from bottom of hill above fields, lower has sparse trees with grazing evident, *Aegilops* cf. *murtica* and *Aegilops* sp. at bottom of hill in July) – G. Hillman at Aşvan.

Dried out stream bed in wadi (*Aegilops* nr. *ovata* in loose dry sand and Aegilops nr. *speltoides*, both in August) – G. Hillman at Aşvan.

Scree slopes and promontories (large scree slopes of igneous extensive over limestone, steep, with boulders, thick with *Quercus* [scrub and tree] and einkorn, *Aegilops speltoides*, *linguistica* and *truncalis* in October) – G. Hillman at Çemişgezek.

Rocky soil (on level area below road with grassy cover, *Aegilops* nr. *truncalis* in June) – G. Hillman at Can Hasan.

Near river (*Aegilops ovata* and *Aegilops speltoides* in soil very sandy, coarse pebble pavement in soil very sandy, coarse pebble pavement) – G. Hillman at Aşvan.

River flats (dry wadi in July, and on dry river flat sands and gravel terraces in July) – Ball & Bean at Aşvan.

Riverside (narrow valley bottom, damp alluvium, shady, regular grazing, river wide and shallow, very swift, *Aegilops* cf. *speltoides* in July on shingle and sand besides Murat) – Ball & Bean at Aşvan.

Bank of Murat (sand shore, pebble beach, two zones, upper very colonised, lower less so, lightly grazed and trampled, well above the Xanthium on the shoreline, in September) – G. Hillman at Aşvan.

Above floodplain (steep banks, grazed lightly and trampled, *Aegilops* cf. *murtica* in September) – G. Hillman at Asvan.

Dense stand – G. Hillman at Aşvan.

Watered wadi (small watered wadi, grazed, trampled slope ca 50% cover, *Aegilops speltoides* in July) – G. Hillman at Aşvan.

Wadi slopes (west-facing, rocky, dry, dominated by *Aegilops*, steep banks of rock powder, *Aegilops* nr. *murtica* and *Aegilops* sp. in July) – G. Hillman at Aşvan.

Rocky gorge (in August, also *Aegilops* nr. *speltoides* and *Aegilops* nr. *murtica* in August) – G. Hillman at Aşvan; rocky gorge (rocky crevices and screes in August) – Ball & Bean at Aşvan.

Soil scree – G. Hillman at Aşvan.

Nests at side of ploughed fields (*Aegilops* nr. *speltoides* in October) – G. Hillman at Aşvan.

Avena sp.

Crop field (barley edge overlying conglomerate thin pebbly soil in August, harvested barley, *H. distichum*, weeds: *Aegilop speltoides*, *Avena*, *Secale cereale* in August and *Avena* sp. in July) – G. Hillman at Aşvan; crop field (*Avena sterilis* in June in cultivated barley on marl soil, and *Avena sterilis* in June in cultivated *Vicia ervilia* near road) – G. Hillman at Can Hasan; crop field (*Avena* sp. in July in harvested *T. aestivum*) – P. Symmons at Asvan.

Limestone hills (dry, stony surface with numerous rock outcrops, grazed, probably frequently, with cultivation nearby, *Avena sativa* top of low Eocene limestone hill in August) – G. Hillman at Aşvan.

East-facing slopes (high, in July on hills to south of Aşvan with fields below) – P. Symmons at Aşvan.

Wooded hills (limestone, north-facing, loose rocks and rock outcrops, steep near top, open woodland throughout upper part of hills, little grazed steppe in upper parts, frequent below, collections from 1,050m to top, which is at 1,250m, and from bottom of hill above fields, lower has sparse trees with grazing evident, on uppermost slopes, no seeds, in July and *Avena* sp. on bottom of hill in July) – G. Hillman at Aşvan.

Bank of Murat (sand shore, pebble beach, two zones, upper very colonised, lower less so, on lower sand shoreline, poorly colonised area, in September) – G. Hillman at Aşvan.

Where wadi opens to plains on rocky soil (in July) – G. Hillman at Aşvan.

Rocky gorge (in August) – G. Hillman at Aşvan; rocky gorge (above water level at 3–15m, rocky crevices, heavily eroded rock, sparsely covered with vegetation, very desiccated, arid conditions, *Avena fatua* in August in sandy crevices) – Ball & Bean at Aşvan.

Rocky crevice (with reasonable soil depth) – G. Hillman at Aşvan.

Bromus sp.

Crop field (*Bromus* nr. *mollis* as weed of *Vicia ervilia* by road, at margin of field adjacent to wheat field, in August) – G. Hillman at Aşvan; crop field (*Bromus* nr. *mollis* as weed of *Vicia ervilia* near road, in June) – G. Hillman at Can Hasan.

Crop field edge (*Bromus* nr. *mollis* as weed of wheat in August and general note that in July *Bromus* sp. is found between *Crateagus* brushes with *Secale* [weedy rye], *Aegilops* cf. *speltoides* and *T. boeoticum*) – G. Hillman at Aşvan.

Village gardens (crops and weeds present, mainly under irrigation regimes in close proximity of houses, in July) – Ball & Bean at Aşvan.

Ditch field edge (between cotton and maize and spinach fields, apparently recently used for irrigation, in July) – G. Hillman at Aşvan.

Rough grazing area (northwest edge of Aşvan village, for tethered donkeys and sheep, just below conglomerate cliff up to first gardens, trampled and heavily grazed, stony, dry soils, in August) – G. Hillman at Aşvan.

Grassy hills (upper slopes, treeless/shrubless, frequently grazed by sheep, goats and cattle, *Aegilops* dominated, in September) – G. Hillman at Aşvan.

Wooded hills (limestone, north-facing, loose rocks and rock outcrops, steep near top, open woodland throughout upper part of hills, little grazed steppe in upper parts, frequent below, collections from 1,050m to top, which is at 1,250m, and from bottom of hill above fields, lower has sparse trees with grazing evident, *Bromus* sp. at bottom of hill in July) – G. Hillman at Aşvan.

Rock outcrops (in August near village, frequently washed by water from village) – G. Hillman at Aşvan.

Gully (north-facing gulley in conglomerate towards northern edge of rock outcrop near edge of village, washed by water from village, often flushed by village water and muck, in August) – G. Hillman at Aşvan.

River flats (actually dried wadi, in July) – Ball & Bean at Aşvan.

Above floodplain (steep banks, grazed lightly and trampled, in September) – G. Hillman at Aşvan.

Wadi mud terrace (originally 200m back from river, 2m deep, dry sandy bottom, in September) – G. Hillman at Aşvan.

Wadi slopes (west-facing, rocky, dry, dominated by *Aegilops*, steep banks of rock powder, in July) – G. Hillman at Aşvan.

Rocky gorge (in August) – G. Hillman at Aşvan.

Soil scree – G. Hillman at Aşvan.

Echinochloa sp.

Grassy verge (in June) – G. Hillman at Can Hasan.

Village gardens (crops and weeds present, mainly under irrigation regimes in close proximity of houses, in July) – Ball & Bean at Aşvan.

Wet ditch (pavement with running water, *Echinochloa crus-galli*) – G. Hillman at Aşvan.

Irrigation canal (*Echinochloa crus-galli* in irrigation ditch, intermittent water flow leaving damp mud, thistles dominant but plants green in damp patch in August) – P. Symmons at Aşvan.

Riverbed/side (well-watered, rocky terrain, sandy in places, lush vegetation, loose limestone/dolomite, ca 60° slope, large rock outcrops interspersed with soil pockets/screelets, fast-moving water, moist crevices, surrounding plant cover grassland with shallow soil and rock outcrops/pavement, *Echinochloa crus-galli* in August in wet soil) – Ball & Bean at Aşvan.

Riverside (narrow valley bottom, damp alluvium, shady, regular grazing, river wide and shallow, very swift, *Echinochloa crus-galli* in August on wet bank) – P. Symmons at Aşvan.

Mudflats (*Echinochloa crus-galli* in September) – G. Hillman at Aşvan.

Wet mud shore (of river in August) – G. Hillman at Aşvan.

Wide gorge (flat-bottomed, occasional cliffs, broad gravel sweeps, summer river, occasional mud banks, poplar groves on northern edges, vegetation on gravel) – G. Hillman at Aşvan.

Lolium sp.

Crop field (*Lolium temulentum* in possibly irrigated fields in August) – G. Hillman at Aşvan.

Irrigated crop field (*Lolium temulentum* in possibly irrigated fields in July) – G. Hillman at Aşvan.

Crop field edge (in November) – G. Hillman at Can Hasan.

Grassy verge (in June) – G. Hillman at Can Hasan.

Rough grazing area (northwest edge Aşvan village, for tethered donkeys and sheep, just below conglomerate cliff up to first gardens, trampled and heavily grazed, stony, dry soils, *Lolium perenne* in August) – G. Hillman at Aşvan.

Irrigation canal (*Lolium perenne* in August) – G. Hillman at Aşvan; irrigation canal (*Lolium* sp. in August on bank at edge of irrigation ditch in shade) – P. Symmons at Aşvan.

Between summer and winter Murat river shoreline – G. Hillman at Aşvan.

Sand-gravel above pebble beach – G. Hillman at Aşvan.

Bank of Murat river (sand shore, pebble beach, two zones, upper very colonised, lower less so, on lower of sand shore lines, poorly colonised, in September) – G. Hillman at Aşvan.

Swampy area (near trackway with no free water, *Lolium* nr. *multiflorum* in June) – G. Hillman at Can Hasan.

Stream edge (*Lolium temulentum*) – G. Hillman at Aşvan.

40cm-deep soil between rocks (*Lolium temulentum*) – G. Hillman at Aşvan.

Nests at side of ploughed fields – G. Hillman at Aşvan.

Setaria sp.

Village gardens (crops and weeds, mainly under irrigation regimes in close proximity of houses, found in August growing as a weed in an irrigated patch) – Ball & Bean at Aşvan.

Rock outcrops (in August near village, frequently washed by water from village, under thistles) – G. Hillman at Aşvan.

Wayside ditch (in September) – G. Hillman at Aşvan.

Irrigation canal (in August on waste ground near canal and on banks of canal itself) – G. Hillman at Aşvan; irrigation canal (in July on bank at edge of irrigated sugarbeet field sloping down to unirrigated harvested *T. aestivum* field) – P. Symmons at Aşvan.

Waste ground – G. Hillman at Aşvan.

Canal banks – G. Hillman at Aşvan.

Riverbed/side (well-watered, rocky terrain, sandy in places, lush vegetation, loose limestone/dolomite, ca 60° slope, large rock outcrops interspersed with soil pockets/screelets, fast-moving water, moist crevices, surrounding plant cover grassland with shallow soil and rock outcrops/pavement, in August in wet soil) – Ball & Bean at Aşvan.

Above floodplains (steep banks, grazed lightly and trampled, in September) – G. Hillman at Aşvan.

Stipa sp.

Waste ground (rough ground around amphitheatre in April) – G. Hillman on the southwestern coast of Turkey at Demre.

Northeast-facing slopes (loose surface, 30% cover, mainly marble, crystalline limestone, with occasional areas of grass, *Stipa* cf. *pennata* in July) – G. Hillman at Aşvan.

Flat part of slopes (numerous granite outcrops, overlooking Murat river, lower area of slopes, rock powder/ground, barley colonised by plants, in September) – G. Hillman at Aşvan.

Wadi slopes (west-facing, rocky, dry, dominated by *Aegilops*, steep banks of rock powder, *Stipa* cf. *pennata* in July).

Taeniatherum sp.

Rock outcrops (cf. *Taeniatherum* in August near village, frequently washed by water from village, under grass) – G. Hillman at Aşvan.

Conglomerate outcrop – G. Hillman at Aşvan.

Riverside (narrow valley bottom, damp alluvium, shady, regular grazing, river wide and shallow, very swift, *Taeniatherum* above summer river level, dry, coarse, rocky, in August) – G. Hillman at Aşvan.

Wadi slopes (west-facing, rocky, dry, dominated by *Aegilops*, steep banks of rock powder, in July) – G. Hillman at Aşvan.

Drier patches (above summer river level, dry, coarse, rocky) – G. Hillman at Aşvan

Rocky gorge (in August) – G. Hillman at Aşvan.

Triticum boeoticum

Crop field – G. Hillman at Aşvan.

Crop field edge (in September and also weed of wheat field in August?) – G. Hillman at Aşvan.

Roadside (trackside conglomerate of chalky soil, in September) – G. Hillman at Aşvan.

Limestone hill (dry, stony surface with numerous rock outcrops, grazed, probably frequently, with cultivation nearby, stony/rocky terraces high up on limestone hills with numerous patches of low oak scrub, in September) – G. Hillman at Çemişgezek.

Scree slopes and promontories (large scree slopes of extensive igneous over limestone, steep, with boulders, thick with *Quercus*, scrub and tree, and Einkorn, in October) – G. Hillman at Çemişgezek.

Rocky soil (on level area below road, grassy cover, in June) – G. Hillman at Can Hasan.

Gramineae indeterminate

Waste ground (not *Echinochloa*, in July on heavily grazed, trampled areas on top of conglomerate, some dry ditches) – Ball & Bean at Aşvan.

Rock outcrops (cf. *Festuca*, in July) – G. Hillman at Aşvan.

Scree slopes and promontories (dry, powdery or gravel ridges with shade cover or no cover except at base, in August) – G. Hillman at Aşvan.

Riverbed/side (well-watered, rocky terrain, sandy in places, lush vegetation, loose limestone/dolomite, ca 60° slope, large rock outcrops interspersed with soil pockets/screelets, fast-moving water, moist crevices, surrounding plant cover grassland with shallow soil and rock outcrops/pavement, Gramineae in August on dry soil in wadi above water level) – Ball & Bean at Aşvan.

Riverside (narrow valley bottom, damp alluvium, shady, regular grazing, river wide and shallow, very swift, *Digiteria* and *Koeleria* in August on exposed ridge) – P. Symmons at Aşvan.

Drier patches – G. Hillman at Aşvan.
Nests at side of ploughed fields – G. Hillman at Aşvan.

Pea/wild pulse
Irrigated field (*Hedysarum*? in July) – Ball & Bean at Aşvan.
Waste ground – Ball & Bean at Aşvan.
Marble hills overlooking Murat river (legume, in October) – G. Hillman at Aşvan.
Irrigation canal (in July in shaded area) – Ball & Bean at Aşvan.
Above floodplains (steep banks, grazed lightly and trampled, legume, in September) – G. Hillman at Aşvan.
Nests at side of ploughed fields (legume, in October) – G. Hillman at Aşvan.

Lathyrus cicera/sativa
Crop field (*Lathyrus pseudo-cicera* in June in cultivated barley field on marl soil, and *Lathyrus* in June in cultivated *Vicia ervilia* near road) – G. Hillman at Can Hasan; crop field (as field weed in July) – Ball & Bean at Aşvan.
Second year fallow (dominated by *Galium*, *Aparene*, *Cephalaria* sp., weedy cereals and *Ranunculus arvensis*, *Lathyrus* in June in dry, cracked soil, ca 50% cover) – G. Hillman at Can Hasan.
Waste ground (*Lathyrus* sp. in rough ground around amphitheatre in April) – G. Hillman on the southwestern coast of Turkey at Demre.
Irrigation canal (or could be *Vicia*, in shaded area in July) – Ball & Bean at Aşvan.
Nests at side of ploughed fields (cf. *Lathyrus* in October) – G. Hillman at Aşvan.

Trifolieae
Crop field (*Medicago* in soil very sandy, coarse pebble pavement, in August, *Trigonella* in soil very sandy, coarse pebble pavement and on shallow pebbly soil overlying conglomerate, both in August, *Medicago* cf. *lupulina* in field of onions away from wadi but irrigated, densely overgrown with weeds especially-*Chenopodium*, next to woods, left to seed, therefore fallow?, in August, *Trigonella* in cultivated fields at base of limestone hills, overlying grit rock, in October, *Medicago* in cultivated fields at base of limestone hills, overlying grit rock, in October, *Trifolium* in cultivated fields at base of limestone hills, overlying grit rock, in August) – G. Hillman at Aşvan; crop fields (*Trigonella* in June in cultivated *Vicia ervilia* near road, *Medicago sativa* in June in cultivated *Vicia ervilia* near road, *Trigonella* in November on marl) – G. Hillman at Can Hasan; crop fields (*Trigonella* in July in harvested *T. aestivum*) – P. Symmons at Aşvan.
Irrigated field (*Medicago* cf. *lupulina* in field of onions away from wadi but irrigated, densely overgrown with weeds especially *Chenopodium*, in August, *Trifolium* in August in irrigated beat field/ditch margin, still damp) – G. Hillman at Aşvan; irrigated field (*Medicago* and *Trifolium* in July) – Ball & Bean at Aşvan.
Crop field edge (*Medicago* at *T. durum* field edge, *Trigonella* at edge of cultivated fields at base of limestone hills, overlying grit rock, *Medicago* at edge of cultivated fields at base of limestone hills, overlying grit rock, *Trifolium* at edge of cultivated fields at base of limestone hills, overlying grit rock) – G. Hillman at Aşvan; crop field edge (*Medicago sativa* in June at edge of neighbouring barley field) – G. Hillman at Can Hasan.
Grassy verge (*Medicago sativa* in June in dense grass, *Melilotus* in June) – G. Hillman at Can Hasan.
Fallow (*Medicago* cf. *lupulina* with lots of weeds, mostly *Chenopodium album*, in onion field left to fallow, 'left to seed') – G. Hillman at Aşvan.
Ditch field edge (*Trifolium* in dried-out ditch at edge of field, thin pebbly soil overlying conglomerate, possibly irrigation ditch, *Medicago sativa* between cotton and maize and spinach fields, apparently recently used for irrigation, in July) – G. Hillman at Aşvan.
Waste ground (*Trifolium* on rough ground around amphitheatre in April) – G. Hillman on southwestern coast of Turkey at Demre; waste ground (*Medicago* nr. *facta* in August) – G. Hillman at Aşvan; waste ground (*Trifolium* nr. *repens* in July on top of conglomerate outcrop and waste land leading down to gardens, heavily used path trampled by humans and beasts where sloping, *Medicago lupina* in July on heavily grazed, trampled areas on top of conglomerate, some dry ditches) – Ball & Bean at Aşvan.
Grazing area (below conglomerate cliff, *Medicago sativa* in September) – G. Hillman at Aşvan.
Rough grazing area (northwestern edge of Aşvan village, for tethered donkeys and sheep, just below conglomerate cliff up to first gardens, trampled and heavily grazed, stony, dry soils, *Trifolium* and *Medicago* cf. *sativa* in August) – G. Hillman at Aşvan.
Heavily grazed area (seasonally inundated, *Trifolium* cf. *fragiferum* in November) – G. Hillman at Can Hasan.
Alluvial flats (*Trigonella* nr. *corniculata*, *Medicago* and *Trigonella* on alluvial flats below Aşvan village, upper section immediately below conglomerate, and clay outcrop by village on cultivated patch between irrigated maize – presumably irrigated earlier in season – furrowed, but now dry with sparse cover of weeds only, in August) – G. Hillman at Aşvan.
Limestone hills (dry, stony surface with numerous rock outcrops, grazed, probably frequently, with cultivation nearby, *Medicago* nr. *noeana* in August) – G. Hillman at Aşvan.

Northeast-facing slopes (loose surface, 30% cover, mainly marble, crystalline limestone, with occasional areas of grass, *Medicago* in July) – G. Hillman at Aşvan.

East-facing slopes (high, cf. *Trigonella* in July on hills to south of Aşvan, with fields below) – P. Symmons at Aşvan.

Steppe on marl (very heavily grazed by sheep/angora flocks, *Trigonella* in November) – G. Hillman at Can Hasan.

Oak rocky hills (20% oak cover, limestone hills, upper slopes, cf. *Trigonella* in August) – G. Hillman at Aşvan.

Wooded hills (limestone, north-facing, loose rocks and rock outcrops, steep near top, open woodland throughout upper part of hills, little grazed steppe in upper parts, frequent below, collections from 1,050m to top, with maximum height of 1,250m, and from bottom of hill above fields – lower has sparse trees with grazing evident, *Medicago* sp. at bottom of hill in July) – G. Hillman at Aşvan.

Marble hills overlooking Murat river (in October) – G. Hillman at Aşvan.

Rock outcrops (*Trifolium* in July) – G. Hillman at Aşvan.

Irrigation canal (*Medicago sativa* in irrigation ditch, intermittent water flow leaving damp mud, thistles dominant but plants green in damp patch, in August) – P. Symmons at Aşvan; irrigation canal (*Medicago*, *Trifolium* nr. *repens* in July in shaded area, *Trifolium* nr. *fragiferum* in July in shaded ditch bottom, *Trigonella* in July in shaded area growing underneath a hedge) – Ball & Bean at Aşvan.

Cliff slip (area shaded by cliff slip above pebble beach, thick with grass and vegetation, *Trigonella* in September) – G. Hillman at Aşvan.

Rocky slope (numerous granite outcrops, overlooking Murat river, *Trifolium* sp. and *Trifolium arvense* in September) – G. Hillman at Aşvan.

Flat part of slopes (numerous granite outcrops, overlooking Murat river, lower area of slopes, rock powder/ground, barley colonised by plants, *Medicago* in September) – G. Hillman at Aşvan.

Near river (*Medicago* and *Trigonella* in soil very sandy, coarse pebble pavement) – G. Hillman at Aşvan.

River flats (*Trigonella* in July in sand and gravel river flats) – Ball & Bean at Aşvan.

Riverside (narrow valley bottom, damp alluvium, shady, regular grazing, river wide and shallow, very swift, *Trifolium* in August) – G. Hillman at Aşvan; riverside (narrow valley bottom, damp alluvium, shady, regular grazing, river wide and shallow, very swift, *Trifolium* in August) – P. Symmons at Aşvan; riverside (narrow valley bottom, damp alluvium, shady, regular grazing, river wide and shallow, very swift, *Medicago* in July in shingle/sand beside Murat river and *Trigonella* in July) – Ball & Bean at Aşvan.

Banks of Murat river (sand shore, pebble beach, two zones, upper very colonised, lower less so, *Trigonella* and *Medicago* on lower of sand shore lines, poorly colonised, in September and *Medicago* nr. *neapolitana* in August on soil banks at spring river level in dense vegetation in the damp) – G. Hillman at Aşvan.

Wadi (water freely available, *Trifolium* in July) – Ball & Bean at Aşvan.

Watered wadi (small watered wadi, grazed, trampled slope ca 50% cover, *Medicago* in July) – G. Hillman at Aşvan.

Rockier drier area above wadi (*Medicago* sp. and *Medicago radiata* in July) – G. Hillman at Aşvan.

Wadi slopes (west-facing, rocky, dry, dominated by *Aegilops*, steep banks of rock powder, *Trigonella* nr. *corniculata* and *Medicago* in July) – G. Hillman at Aşvan.

Spring (high on wadi slopes at Taşkun Mevkii, *Medicago radiata* in September) – G. Hillman at Aşvan.

Drier patches (*Trifolium*) – G. Hillman at Aşvan.

Rocky gorge (*Medicago* in August) – G. Hillman at Aşvan; rocky gorge (above water level at 3–15m, with rocky crevices, heavily eroded rock, sparsely covered with vegetation, very desiccated, arid conditions, *Medicago* in August in dry, sandy, rocky crevices and *Trifolium* in August on sand/rock slope) – Ball & Bean at Aşvan.

Soil scree (*Medicago*) – G. Hillman at Aşvan.

Rock ledges (*Medicago*) – G. Hillman at Aşvan.

Next to woods (*Medicago* cf. *lupulina* in field of onions away from wadi but irrigated, densely overgrown with weeds especially *Chenopodium*, next to woods, left to seed, therefore fallow possibly) – G. Hillman at Aşvan.

Nests at side of ploughed fields (*Medicago* in October) – G. Hillman at Aşvan.

Grassy valley (bottom of valley in clumps of *Quercus*/*Pistachia*, *Trigonella* in June and *Trifolium* in June) – G. Hillman at Can Hasan.

Wood valley (bottom of narrow, wooded valley in limestone, poplars and irrigated orchards and gardens at bottom, then oaks and scattered junipers on highest slopes, ample water despite no rains, *Medicago sativa* in November in wet, possibly irrigated meadow between stream and river) – G. Hillman at Can Hasan.

Adonis sp.

Crop field (in June in cultivated barley field in marl soil and also in June in cultivated *Vicia ervilia* near road) – G. Hillman at Can Hasan.

Crop field edge (in June on edge of neighbouring barley field) – G. Hillman at Can Hasan.

Grassy verge (in June on verge of track by wheat field) – G. Hillman at Can Hasan.

Ajuga sp.
Crop field edge (*Ajuga chamaepitys* in September on edge of ploughed barley field) – G. Hillman at Aşvan.
Riverbed/side (well-watered, rocky terrain, sandy in places, lush vegetation, loose limestone/dolomite, ca 60° slope, large rock outcrops interspersed with soil pockets/screelets, fast-moving water, moist crevices, surrounding plant cover grassland with shallow soil and rock outcrops/pavement, *Ajuga chamaepitys* in August in moist areas) – Ball & Bea at Aşvan.

Bellevallia sp.
Crop field – *Flora of Iraq*.
Grassy verge – *Flora of Iraq*.
Fallow – *Flora of Iraq*.
Swampy meadow – *Flora of Iraq*.
Orchard– *Flora of Iraq*.

Bolboschoenus glaucus/Scirpus sp.
Irrigation canal – *Flora of Iraq*.
Canal bank – *Flora of Iraq*.
Riverside – *Flora of Iraq*.
Swampy area – *Flora of Iraq*.
Saline area – *Flora of Iraq*.

Carex sp.
Grassy verge (*Carex ovalis* in June in dense grass) – G. Hillman at Can Hasan.
Occasional cliffs and screes (*Carex* cf. *acuta*) – G. Hillman at Aşvan.
Base of cliff face (*Carex* cf. *acuta*) – G. Hillman at Aşvan.
Half a metre above summer river level (*Carex* cf. *acuta*) – G. Hillman at Aşvan.
Bank of Murat river (where it flows through hills of igneous rock, in September) – G. Hillman at Aşvan.
River beach (wide, pebble/rock/boulder beach with boulders to edge of river, in September) – G. Hillman at Aşvan.
Small lake (still water, nearby ridge, *Carex* nr. *vesicaria* at water's edge with *Typha*) – G. Hillman at Aşvan.
Swamp, no free water (*Carex* nr. *hirsuta* in June near trackway, ground more or less firm) – G. Hillman at Aşvan.
Swamp area (near trackway, no free water, *Carex* nr. *hirsuta* in June) – G. Hillman at Can Hasan.
Seasonally swampy meadow (dry in summer and lightly grazed by cattle, but swampy in winter, in November) – G. Hillman at Can Hasan.
Wadi (water freely available, in October) – G. Hillman at Aşvan.
Swamp in wadi (at base of rock slope overlooking Murat river, *Carex* nr. *hirsuta* in September) – G. Hillman at Aşvan.
Near trackway (*Carex* nr. *hirsuta*) – G. Hillman at Aşvan.
Wide gorge (flat-bottomed, occasional cliffs, broad gravel sweeps, summer river, occasional mud banks, poplar groves on northern edges, vegetation on gravel, *Carex* nr. *acuta* in August) – G. Hillman at Aşvan.

Carthamus sp.
Crop field (*Carthamus* sp. in July in harvested *T. aestivum*) – P. Symmons at Aşvan; crop field (in July in very windswept barley fields) – Ball & Bean at Aşvan.
Northeast-facing slopes (loose surface, 30% cover, mainly marble, crystalline limestone, with occasional areas of grass, in July) – Ball & Bean at Aşvan.
East-facing slopes (high, in July in hills to south of Aşvan, fields below) – P. Symmons at Aşvan.
Wayside (nr. *Carthamus* sp. in July) – G. Hillman at Aşvan.

Centaurea sp.
Crop field (*Centaurea* cf. *cyanus* in June in cultivated barley field on marl soil) – G. Hillman at Can Hasan; crop field (cf. *Centaurea solstitialis* and cf. *Centaurea* sp. in harvested, unirrigated *T. aestivum* field in July) – P. Symmons at Aşvan; crop field (*Centaurea solstitialis* in July in unirrigated durum wheat fields) – Ball & Bean at Aşvan.
Irrigated fields (*Centaurea* sp., cf. *Centaurea spinosa* and *Centaurea solstitialis* in July) – Ball & Bean at Aşvan.
Crop field edge (*Centaurea* cf. *solstitialis* in October on conglomerate terraces at field margins) – G. Hillman at Aşvan.
Ditch field edge (*Centaurea* cf. *cyanus* between cotton and maize and spinach fields, apparently recently used for irrigation, in July) – G. Hillman at Aşvan.
Waste ground (*Centaurea solistitales* and *Centaurea* nr. *nibra* in July on heavily grazed, trampled areas on top of conglomerate, some dry ditches) – Ball & Bean at Aşvan.
Rough grazing (northwestern edge of Aşvan village, for tethered donkeys and sheep, just below conglomerate cliff up to first gardens, trampled and heavily grazed, stony, dry soils, *Centaurea* nr. *calcitrapa* and *Centaurea* nr. *solstitialis* in August) – G. Hillman at Aşvan.
Grassy hills (upper slopes, treeless/shrubless, frequently grazed by sheep, goats and cattle, *Aegilops* dominated, in September) – G. Hillman at Aşvan.
East-facing slopes (high, in July in hills to south of Aşvan, fields below) – P. Symmons at Aşvan.
Steppe on marl (very heavily grazed by sheep/angora flocks, in November) – G. Hillman at Can Hasan.
Wooded hills (limestone, north-facing, loose rocks and rock outcrops, steep near top, open woodland

throughout upper part of hills, little grazed steppe in upper parts, frequent below, collections from 1,050m to top, with maximum height of 1,250m, and from bottom of hill above fields, lower has sparse trees with grazing evident, *Centaurea* sp. on upper part of hill in July) – G. Hillman at Aşvan.

Base of rock outcrop (dominated by *Lepodium* sp., *Centaurea calcitrapa* in August) – G. Hillman at Aşvan.

Gully (nr. *Centaurea* sp. in August in north-facing gulley in conglomerate towards northern edge of rock outcrop near edge of village, washed by water from village, often flushed by village water and muck) – G. Hillman at Aşvan.

Irrigation canal (*Centaurea solsititialis* in irrigation ditch, intermittent water flow leaving damp mud, thistles dominant but plants green in damp patch in August) – P. Symmons at Aşvan.

Scree slopes and promontories (dry, powdery or gravel ridges with shade cover or no cover except at base, between pine trees, in August) – G. Hillman at Aşvan.

Riverside (narrow valley bottom, damp alluvium, shady, regular grazing, river wide and shallow, very swift, *Centaurea* cf. *conifera* in August under oak) – P. Symmons at Aşvan.

Compositae (Asteraceae)

Irrigated field (in July at field margin and in August in irrigated beat field in ditch margin, still damp) – G. Hillman at Aşvan; irrigated field (in July and *Solidago* sp. in July) – Ball & Bean at Aşvan.

Crop field edge (in July at irrigated field margin) – G. Hillman at Aşvan.

Grassy verge (in June) – G. Hillman at Can Hasan.

Village garden (crops and weeds, mainly under irrigation regimes in close proximity of houses, nr. *Chrysanthemum* sp. in August as a cultivar, cf. *Lalthca* sp. as weed of ditches in August, nr. *Calendula* sp. in August as weed and various plants as aesthetics in August) – Ball & Bean at Aşvan.

Waste ground (*Chamaemelum* sp. in July on top of conglomerate outcrop and waste land leading down to gardens, heavily used path trampled by humans and beasts where sloping, *Filago* sp. and cf. *Condrilla juncea* in July on heavily grazed, trampled areas on top of conglomerate, some dry ditches) – Ball & Bean at Aşvan.

Rubbish fill (covered in dung, in August) – G. Hillman at Aşvan.

Northeast-facing slopes (loose surface, 30% cover, mainly marble, crystalline limestone, with occasional areas of grass, cf. *Helicarysum stoechas* in July) – Ball & Bean at Aşvan.

Steppe on marl (very heavily grazed by sheep/angora flocks, in November) – G. Hillman at Can Hasan.

Wooded hills (limestone, north-facing, loose rocks and rock outcrops, steep near top, open woodland throughout upper part of hills, little grazed steppe in upper parts, frequent below, collections from 1,050m to top, with maximum height of 1,250m, and from bottom of hill above fields, lower has sparse trees with grazing evident, *Circium* sp. in July) – Ball & Bean at Aşvan.

Gully (cf. *Cinoeceas* in July in drainage gully) – Ball & Bean at Aşvan.

Irrigation canal (*Anthemis* cf. *arvensis* in irrigation ditch, intermittent water flow leaving damp mud, thistles dominant but plants green in damp patch, in August) – P. Symmons at Aşvan; irrigation canal (cf. *Galactites* sp. in July in shade, growing underneath a hedge) – Ball & Bean at Aşvan.

Riverbead/side (well-watered, rocky terrain, sandy in places, lush vegetation, loose limestone/dolomite, ca 60° slope, large rock outcrops interspersed with soil pockets/screelets, fast-moving water, moist crevices, surrounding plant cover grassland with shallow soil and rock outcrops/pavement, *Bidens* sp. in August in moist soil) – Ball & Bean at Aşvan.

River flats (*Artemesia* sp., *Solidago* sp. and *Silidus* sp. in July and cf. *Crepis* sp. in a dry wadi in July) – Ball & Bean at Aşvan.

Riverside (narrow valley bottom, damp alluvium, shady, regular grazing, river wide and shallow, very swift, cf. *Helichrysum* sp., cf. *Chrysanthemum parthenium* in August and various species on ridge) – P. Symmons at Aşvan; riverside (narrow valley bottom, damp alluvium, shady, regular grazing, river wide and shallow, very swift, arid and dry river terrace, in July) – Ball & Bean at Aşvan.

Wadi (water freely available, *Alyssum* sp. in July) – Ball & Bean at Aşvan.

Rocky gorge (in August) – G. Hillman at Aşvan.

Grassy valley (bottom of valley in clumps of *Quercus*/*Pistachia*, in June) – G. Hillman at Can Hasan.

Cruciferae

Crop field (probably *Sisymbrium* sp., in July in very windswept barley fields) – Ball & Bean at Aşvan.

Village gardens (crops and weeds, mainly under irrigation regimes in close proximity of houses, nr./cf. *Sisymbrium* sp. in August, *Malva parviflora* in July and various species in July) – Ball & Bean at Aşvan.

Waste ground (*Sisymbrium* sp. in July on top of conglomerate outcrop and waste land leading down to gardens, heavily used path trampled by humans and beasts where sloping, cf. *Aethlonema oppositifolium* in July

and *Erysimum* sp. in July in heavily grazed, trampled areas on top of conglomerate, some dry ditches) – Ball & Bean at Aşvan.
Roadside ditch (shallow, may have earlier been irrigation water ditch) – G. Hillman at Aşvan.
Dry limestone (in July) – G. Hillman at Aşvan.
Irrigation canal (*Sisymbrium loeselii* in irrigation ditch, intermittent water flow leaving damp mud, thistles dominant but plants green in damp patch, in August) – P. Symmons at Aşvan.
West-facing dry slope (in September) – G. Hillman at Aşvan.
Near river (gravel of river bend, water table just below surface, in August) – G. Hillman at Aşvan.
River flats (various species in July also in dry wadi in July, *Alyssum* sp. and cf. *Lepidum vesicarium* in July in dry wadi, *Sisymbrium* sp. in July on dry upper river terrace at margin of cultivation) – Ball & Bean at Aşvan.
Riverside (narrow valley bottom, damp alluvium, shady, regular grazing, river wide and shallow, very swift, cf. *Cochlearia* sp. in August on ridge) – P. Symmons at Aşvan; riverside (narrow valley bottom, damp alluvium, shady, regular grazing, river wide and shallow, very swift, *Alyssum* cf. *strictum* in July in dry river bank shingle and sand) – Ball & Bean at Aşvan.
Wadi gravel banks (where wadi starts to cross mud terraces, on otherwise barely colonised gravel, in September) – G. Hillman at Aşvan.
Mountain (*Alyssum* sp.) – Ball & Bean at Aşvan.

Euclidium syriacum
Ditch field edge – *Flora of Iraq*.
Waste ground – *Flora of Iraq*.
Dry limestone – *Flora of Iraq*.
Limestone hills (dry, stony surface with numerous rock outcrops, grazed, probably frequently, with cultivation nearby) – *Flora of Iraq*.
Irrigation canal – *Flora of Iraq*.
Mountain – *Flora of Iraq*.
Oak forest – *Flora of Iraq*.

Fumaria sp.
Crop field (in June in cultivated *Vicia ervilia* near road) – G. Hillman at Can Hasan.

Galium sp.
Crop field (in shallow pebbly soil overlying conglomerate, in August) – G. Hillman at Aşvan; crop field (*Galium* nr. *aparine* in June in cultivated barley field on marl soil; *Galium verum* in June in cultivated *Vicia ervilia* near road) – G. Hillman at Can Hasan; crop field (cf. *Galium nerum* and *Galium* sp. in July in harvested *T. aestivum*) – P. Symmons at Aşvan.
Irrigated field (*Galium* nr. *mollugo* in July) – Ball & Bean at Aşvan.
Crop field edge (*Galium verum* in June at edge of neighbouring barley field) – G. Hillman at Can Hasan; crop field edge (in July in harvested *T. aestivum*) – P. Symmons at Aşvan.
Grassy verge (*Galium verum* in June) – G. Hillman at Can Hasan.
Grazing area (below conglomerate cliff, *Galium* sp. in September) – G. Hillman at Aşvan.
East-facing slopes (high, *Galium verum* in July in hills to south of Aşvan with fields below) – P. Symmons at Aşvan.
Oak rocky hills (20% oak cover, limestone hills, upper slopes, *Galium* nr. *articulatum* in August) – G. Hillman at Aşvan.
Irrigation canal (bank at edge of irrigated beat field sloping down to unirrigated harvested *T. aestivum* field, in July, in irrigation ditch, intermittent water flow leaving damp mud, thistles dominant but plants green in damp patch, in August) – P. Symmons at Aşvan; irrigation canal (shaded area in July) – Ball & Bean at Aşvan.
Riverside (narrow valley bottom, damp alluvium, shady, regular grazing, river wide and shallow, very swift, in August, including near rocks) – P. Symmons at Aşvan.
Wadi (water freely available, in July) – G. Hillman at Aşvan.
Rocky gorge (in August) – G. Hillman at Aşvan; rocky gorge (above water level at 3–15m, rocky crevices, heavily eroded rock, sparsely covered with vegetation, very desiccated, arid conditions, cf. Galium in August in a sandy rock crevice) – Ball & Bean at Aşvan.
Rock ledges – G. Hillman at Aşvan.

Geum sp.
Damper and shadier areas – *Flora of Iraq*.
Irrigation canal – *Flora of Iraq*.
Canal banks – *Flora of Iraq*.
Wooded valley (bottom of narrow, wooded valley in limestone, poplars and irrigated orchards and gardens in bottom, then oaks and scattered junipers on highest slopes, with ample water despite no recent rains) – *Flora of Iraq*.
Orchard – *Flora of Iraq*.

Liliaceae
Crop field (in July, cf. *Allium* sp. as crop alongside cotton, tomatoes, maize and sorghum) – Ball & Bean at Aşvan.
Village gardens (crops and weeds, mainly under irrigation regimes in close proximity of houses, cf. *Polygonatum* sp. in August, as an aesthetic) – Ball & Bean at Aşvan.
Scree slopes (dry, powdery or gravel ridges with either shade cover or no cover except at base, top end of scree, in October) – G. Hillman at Aşvan.

Riverside (narrow valley bottom, damp alluvium, shady, regular grazing, river wide and shallow, very swift, cf. *Lilium* sp. in August, *Asphodelus* sp. in August near oak) – P. Symmons at Aşvan.

Rocky gorge (above water level at 3–15m, rocky crevices, heavily eroded rock, sparsely covered with vegetation, very desiccated, arid conditions, in August, 'wild onion' on sandy screes) – Ball & Bean at Aşvan.

Malva sp.

Irrigated field (in July) – Ball & Bean at Aşvan.

Village gardens (crops and weeds, mainly under irrigation regimes in close proximity of houses, in gardens and ditches in July, *Malva parviflora* in July) – Ball & Bean at Aşvan.

Waste ground (in July on top of conglomerate outcrop and waste land leading down to gardens, heavily used path trampled by humans and beasts where sloping) – Ball & Bean at Aşvan.

Rock outcrops (*Malva* sp. in August near village, frequently washed by water from village) – G. Hillman at Aşvan.

Damper and shadier areas (*Malva* sp. in August) – G. Hillman at Aşvan.

Irrigation canal (in shaded area in July, *Malva parviflora* in July in used irrigation ditch) – Ball & Bean at Aşvan.

Riverbed/side (well-watered, rocky terrain, sandy in places, lush vegetation, loose limestone/dolomite, ca 60° slope, large rock outcrops interspersed with soil pockets/screelets, fast-moving water, moist crevices, surrounding plant cover grassland with shallow soil and rock outcrops/pavement, Malvaceae in August growing alone, direct effects of water seen) – Ball & Bean at Aşvan.

Neslia sp.

Crop field (*Neslia apiculata* in June in cultivated barley field on marl soil) – G. Hillman at Can Hasan.

Oak rocky hills (20% oak cover, limestone hills, upper slopes, *Neslia* cf. *paniculata* in August) – G. Hillman at Aşvan.

Polygonum sp.

Crop field (Terra rosa soil, cultivated fields at base of hard-limestone ridges/hills, in part overlying grit rock, in August, *Polygonum* nr. *aviculare* in cultivated fields at base of limestone hills, overlying grit rock, in October, *Polygonum lapathifolum* in August on lower flats on slightly sandier, but exclusively rocked alluvium, cultivated field of melons) – G. Hillman at Aşvan; crop field (cf. *Polygonum* sp. and *Polygonum aviculare* in June in cultivated barley field on marl soil) – G. Hillman at Can Hasan.

Crop field edge (*Polygonum* nr. *aviculare* in September on shady field bank) – G. Hillman at Aşvan.

Grassy verge – G. Hillman at Aşvan; grassy verge (in June between a track and a field of *T. durum*) – G. Hillman at Can Hasan.

Fallow (*Polygonum* nr. *aviculare* in cultivated fields at base of limestone hills, overlying grit rock, presumably fields ploughed last season, and in October on northeast-facing slope of hard limestone ridge, upper cretaceous, steep slope with 60–70° angle, with large boulders, with cultivated fields at base of these hills with terra rosa soil in part overlying grit rocks, weed found in these fallow fields) – G. Hillman at Aşvan.

Roadside ditch (shallow, may have earlier been an irrigation water ditch, *Polygonum* nr. *aviculare* in October) – G. Hillman at Aşvan.

Rubbish fill (covered with dung, *Polygonum* nr. *aviculare* in August) – G. Hillman at Aşvan.

Alluvial flats (*Polygonum* nr. *aviculare* on alluvial flats below Aşvan village, upper section immediately below conglomerate and clay outcrop by village – cultivated patch between irrigated maize – presumably irrigated earlier in season, furrowed, dry at time of observation) – G. Hillman at Aşvan.

Gully (*Polygonum* nr. *aviculare* in August in north-facing gulley in conglomerate towards northern edge of rock outcrop near edge of village, washed by water from village, often flushed by village water and muck) – G. Hillman at Aşvan.

Locally abundant – G. Hillman at Aşvan.

Damper/shadier area (*Polygonum* sp. in August and in August on conglomerate outcrop) – G. Hillman at Aşvan.

Street ditch (regularly swamped with water, *Polygonum lapathifolium* in September) – G. Hillman at Aşvan.

Irrigation canal (*Polygonum* nr. *aviculare* in August) – G. Hillman at Aşvan; irrigation canal (*Polygonum aviculare* in irrigation ditch, intermittent water flow leaving damp mud, thistles dominant but plants green in damp patch, in August) – P. Symmons at Aşvan; irrigation canal (shaded, growing underneath a hedge in July) – Ball & Bean at Aşvan.

Riverbed/side (well-watered, rocky terrain, sandy in places, lush vegetation, loose limestone/dolomite, ca 60° slope, large rock outcrops interspersed with soil pockets/screelets, fast-moving water, moist crevices, surrounding plant cover grassland with shallow soil and rock outcrops/pavement, *Polygonum* cf. *persicaria* in August in wet earth) – Ball & Bean at Aşvan.

River flats (*Polygonum* cf. *persicaria*, *Polygonum* cf. *arenastrum* in July, *Polygonum aviculare* in wadi in July, *Polygonum* sp. in river flats and dry wadi in July) – Ball & Bean at Aşvan.

Wadi (water freely available, *Polygonum* nr. *aviculare* in July, *Polygonum* sp. in October) – G. Hillman at Aşvan.

Ranunculus sp.

Crop field (cultivated fields at base of limestone hills, overlying grit rock in October, *Ranunculus arvensis* in wheat field in July) – G. Hillman at Aşvan; crop field (*Ranunculus arvensis* in June in cultivated barley field on marl soil) – G. Hillman at Can Hasan.

Crop field edge (edge of cultivated fields at base of limestone hills, overlying grit rock) – G. Hillman at Aşvan.

Second-year fallow (dominated by *Galium aparene*, *Cephalaria* sp., weedy cereals and *Ranunculus arvensis*, in June in cracked dry soil with ca 50% cover) – G. Hillman at Can Hasan.

Rough grazing (northwestern edge of Aşvan village, for tethered donkeys and sheep, just below conglomerate cliff up to first gardens, trampled and heavily grazed, stony, dry soils, *Ranunculus* cf. *sprunerianus* in August) – G. Hillman at Aşvan.

East-facing slopes (high, *Ranunculus arvensis* in August) – G. Hillman at Aşvan; east-facing slopes (high, *Ranunculus argyreus* in July in hills to south of Aşvan with fields below) – P. Symmons at Aşvan.

Irrigation canal (*Ranunculus* cf. *cornutus* or *montanus* in irrigation ditch, intermittent water flow leaving damp mud, thistles dominant but plants green in damp patch, in August) – P. Symmons at Aşvan.

Riverside (narrow valley bottom, damp alluvium, shady, regular grazing, river wide and shallow, very swift, *Ranunculus* cf. *arvensis* in August) – G. Hillman at Aşvan.

Shallow stagnant water (bay behind shingle bank, *Ranunculus trichophyllus* in August) – P. Symmons at Aşvan.

Bank of Murat river (sand shore, pebble beach, two zones, upper very colonised, lower less so, *Ranunculus* cf. *arvensis* in September, lower of sand shore lines, poorly colonised) – G. Hillman at Aşvan.

Swampy area (near trackway, no free water) – G. Hillman at Can Hasan.

Drier patches (*Ranunculus* cf. *arvensis*) – G. Hillman at Aşvan.

Nests at side of ploughed fields – G. Hillman at Aşvan.

Silene sp.

Crop field (*Silene conoidea* in harvested, unirrigated *T. durum* field in July) – P. Symmons at Aşvan.

Irrigated field (field of sugarbeet in August, *Silene conoidea* in August in irrigated beat field/ditch margin, still damp) – G. Hillman at Aşvan.

Roadside ditch (shallow, may have previously been an irrigation water ditch, *Silene otites* and *Silene* cf. *Silene* sp. in August) – G. Hillman at Aşvan.

Rock outcrops (in July) – G. Hillman at Aşvan.

Gully (*Silene conoidea* in August in north-facing gulley in conglomerate towards northern edge of rock outcrop near edge of village, washed by water from village, often flushed by village water and muck) – G. Hillman at Aşvan.

Locally abundant (in August) – G. Hillman at Aşvan.

River flats (in July) – Ball & Bean at Aşvan.

Bank of Murat river (sand shore, pebble beach, two zones, upper very colonised, lower less so, found on poorly colonised lower sand shore line in September) – G. Hillman at Aşvan.

Summer stream banks (*Silene* nr. *subconica* in September) – G. Hillman at Aşvan.

Teucrium sp.

Crop field (*Teucrium polium* in July in harvested *T. aestivum*) – P. Symmons at Aşvan.

Crop field edge (*Teucrium polium* in July in harvested *T. aestivum*) – P. Symmons at Aşvan.

Steppe on marl (very heavily grazed by sheep/angora flocks, *Teucrium* cf. *polium* in November) – G. Hillman at Can Hasan.

Damper/shadier area (riverside shade under trees in August) – G. Hillman at Aşvan.

Irrigation canal (cf. *Teucrium polium* in July on bank at edge of irrigated beat field sloping down to unirrigated harvested *T. aestivum* field) – P. Symmons at Aşvan.

Riverside (narrow valley bottom, damp alluvium, shady, regular grazing, river wide and shallow, very swift, *Teucrium* cf. *polium*, above summer river level, dry, coarse, rocky) – G. Hillman at Aşvan.

Bank of Murat river (sand shore, pebble beach, two zones, upper very colonised, lower less so, found on poorly colonised lower sand shore line in September) – G. Hillman at Aşvan.

Swampy meadow (swampy area in low-lying wet meadow on marl, grazed but not heavily, *Teucrium* cf. *scordium* in November) – G. Hillman at Can Hasan.

Small wadi with swamp (all-year spring drawing water into plains, on limestone, in September) – G. Hillman at Aşvan.

Swamp in wadi (at base of rock slope overlooking Murat river, in September) – G. Hillman at Aşvan.

Drier patches (*Teucrium* cf. *polnium* above summer river level, dry, coarse, rocky) – G. Hillman at Aşvan.

Rocky gorge (*Teucrium* cf. *polnium* in August) – G. Hillman at Aşvan.

Large crevice (*Teucrium* cf. *polium*) – G. Hillman at Aşvan.

Thalictrum sp.
Riverside (narrow valley bottom, damp alluvium, shady, regular grazing, river wide and shallow, very swift, *Thalictrum* cf. *flavum* in August) – G. Hillman at Aşvan.
Drier patches (*Thalictrum* cf. *flavum*) – G. Hillman at Aşvan.

Thymelaea sp.
Crop field (*Thymelaea* cf. *passerina* in July in harvested *T. aestivum*) – P. Symmons at Aşvan.
Crop field edge (*Thymelaea* cf. *passerina* in August) – G. Hillman at Can Hasan.
Fallow (*Thymelaea* cf. *passerina* in August, in field on top of low hill of ploughed fallow) – G. Hillman at Aşvan.
Waste ground (Thymelaea passerina in July on heavily grazed, trampled areas on top of conglomerate, some dry ditches) – Ball & Bean at Aşvan.
East-facing slopes (high, *Thymelaea* cf. *passerina* in July on hills to south of Aşvan with fields below) – P. Symmons at Aşvan.
Mable hills overlooking Murat river (*Thymelaea* nr. *passerina* in October) – G. Hillman at Aşvan.
Near river (August in gravel of river bend, water table just below surface) – G. Hillman at Aşvan.

Umbelliferae (Apiaceae)
Crop field (in wheat field in July) – G. Hillman at Aşvan; crop field (in July in harvested *T. aestivum*) – P. Symmons at Aşvan.
Irrigated field (in July in irrigated field margin) – G. Hillman at Aşvan.
Village gardens (crops and weeds, mainly under irrigation regimes in close proximity of houses, various in July, caraway seen as plant dried in situ with erect bunches as a crop in August, *Daucus carota* as carrot crop in August) – Ball & Bean at Aşvan.
Ditch at field edge (between cotton and maize and spinach fields, apparently recently used for irrigation, in July) – G. Hillman at Aşvan.
Waste ground (nr. *Pastinaca* sp. in July on top of conglomerate outcrop and waste land leading down to gardens, heavily used path trampled by humans and beasts where sloping) – Ball & Bean at Aşvan.
Rough grazing area (northwestern edge of Aşvan village, for tethered donkeys and sheep, just below conglomerate cliff up to first gardens, trampled and heavily grazed, stony, dry soils, in August) – G. Hillman at Aşvan.
Roadside (on trackside conglomerate of chalky soil in September) – G. Hillman at Aşvan.
Limestone ridge (large boulders, cliffs, terra rossa soil between boulders, lightly grazed on gentler slopes) – G. Hillman at Aşvan.
Limestone hills (dry, stony surface with numerous rock outcrops, grazed, probably frequently, with cultivation nearby, in August) – G. Hillman at Aşvan.
East-facing slopes (high, in July on hills to the south of Aşvan, with fields below) – P. Symmons at Aşvan.
Oak rocky hills (20% oak cover, limestone hills, upper slopes, in August) – G. Hillman at Aşvan.
Wooded hills (limestone, north-facing, loose rocks and rock outcrops, steep near top, open woodland throughout upper part of hills, little grazed steppe in upper parts, frequent below, collections from 1,050m to top with maximum height of 1,250m, and from bottom of hill above fields, lower has sparse trees with grazing evident, in July) – Ball & Bean at Aşvan.
Irrigation canal (in October on bank overlooking irrigation canal) – G. Hillman at Çemişgezek; irrigation canal (cf. *Orlaya* sp. and *Scandiceae* sp. in irrigation ditch, intermittent water flow leaving damp mud, thistles dominant but plants green in damp patch, in August) – P. Symmons at Aşvan; irrigation canal (in July in shaded canal growing underneath hedge and in wet ground) – Ball & Bean at Aşvan.
River flats (in July in gravel and sand by river, *Daucus* in July in dry sand and gravel terrace by Murat river) – Ball & Bean at Aşvan.

Vaccaria pyramidata
Crop field (possibly irrigated field, coarse soil, well drained with gulley, in August) – G. Hillman at Aşvan; crop field (in June in cultivated barley field on marl soil) – G. Hillman at Can Hasan; crop field (harvested, unirrigated *T. durum* field, in July) – P. Symmons at Aşvan.
Irrigated field (possibly irrigated field, coarse soil, well-drained with gulley, in August) – G. Hillman at Aşvan.
Crop field edge (irrigated field margin, in July) – G. Hillman at Aşvan.
Grassy verge (swamped by dune cover, in June) – G. Hillman at Can Hasan.
Waste ground (heavily grazed, trampled areas on top of conglomerate, some dry ditches, in July) – Ball & Bean at Aşvan.
River flats (in July) – Ball & Bean at Aşvan.

Valerianella sp.
Crop field (in wheat field, in July) – G. Hillman at Aşvan.
Irrigated field (in August in irrigated beat field/ditch margin, still damp) – G. Hillman at Aşvan.

Appendix 4.

AGRICULTURAL RESOURCES AND SETTLEMENT IN THE AŞVAN REGION

By GORDON HILLMAN

Following Wagstaff's paper on physical geography and settlements, a brief expansion of the discussion of distribution of agricultural resources is in place. This topic provides the necessary background for studies conducted in the village itself[1] as well as for the following paper on "Agricultural productivity and past population potential at Aşvan".

My object here is firstly, to outline the spatial distribution of major land resources (this is achieved via Figs. 1 and 2), secondly to discuss a few of the factors which appear to have conditioned this distribution and, thirdly, to outline some problems involved in the location of ancient settlements relative to these land resources. Few conclusions can, however, be drawn until we have more data on sedimentation history (and thence ancient distribution of soils) in the region.

BACKGROUND

Baseline date

As a basis for estimating the likely limits of ancient agriculture in the Aşvan area, it was immediately evident that the modern (1970) distribution and productivity of cultivated land would be misleading. Tractors had been in use (by some families) for up to twenty years, with the result that large areas of grazing land had been brought under the malboard plough and the relative contributions of different crops altered completely. Crop yields had also greatly increased as a result of the application of chemical fertilizers. Admittedly, many farmers in 1970 still used entirely traditional forms of husbandry and equipment (except for the addition of chemical fertilizers), but our baseline was finally fixed at *c.* 1938 by the fact that detailed cadastral surveys of Aşvan territory had been compiled in that year, and the maps were available for our inspection. Further this 1938 baseline represented a time when farming technology throughout the village may well have been little different from that applied in the Aşvan region for several millennia and as such, provided us with the best information available on the likely limits of ancient husbandry in our area.

The 1938 Aşvan economy

This was sedentary, based on mixed farming. The only elements that could be regarded as in any way mobile were firstly, the groups of harvesters who lived out in the more remote fields in temporary shelters for up to a month during early summer and secondly, the shepherds who stayed out with their flocks for short periods during the warmer months.

A high level of agricultural productivity placed 1938 Aşvan well above the level of pure subsistence, a fact evident from the production of large surpluses and cash crops discussed in the following paper (pp. 225–240). Almost all families appear to have practised both crop and animal husbandry to varying degrees and

[1] See Hall, *et al.* and Weinstein in this volume.

to have been more than self-sufficient for both human foods and for the grain-feed necessary to maintain their often large animal holdings through the winter.

Up to 25 different types of field-crop were grown under various combinations of topography and soil-types, irrigation levels and rotation systems. The resulting pattern of husbandry and background resources was complex, particularly when one includes the different garden and orchard cultures,[2] timber plantations and various qualities of grazing land.

Spatial limits

Attention here (and in the following paper on population levels) is confined to the sort of "site territories"[3] likely to have been "habitually exploited" by sedentary economies based on our sites in the *Aşvan Bölgesi.* Such territories are assumed (in the absence of evidence either way) to have been limited to the areas covered by map 1 with the exception of Taşkun-based populations who may have habitually exploited areas up the Kuru Çay valley off the SE corner of the map. The territory exploited by 1938 Aşvan is indicated on the map, Fig. 1 by a heavy dotted line.

The maps

The first map, Fig. 1 shows the sites and modern settlements superimposed on the 1938 distribution of the most basic classes of land use[4] in the area, while on the second map, Fig. 2, the corresponding topography is indicated by 40 m. contours. The sources used in compiling the first map and the data referred to in the text, were the following:

(a) 1938 cadastral survey maps (1:4,000) of field and plot outlines.

(*b*) 1938 land ownership lists. These included crude land classifications for some areas.

(*c*) Collective interviews with groups of older villagers on what was grown where in the late 1930s and early 1940s. (The advantage of collective interviews was that data advanced by one farmer was subject to immediate correction by the others).

(*d*) Interviews with individual farmers on the present and past distribution of their own crops and the forms of management applied.

(*e*) Our own studies of present-day crop husbandry in the areas concerned.

SPATIAL DISTRIBUTION OF CULTIVABLE LAND

Distribution v.v. distance

Aşvan village itself provides the most useful example for considering this relationship here. Its valley-bottom location with a far from concentric distribution of exploitation territory is characteristic of many sites. The impossibility

[2] Over 40 different garden and orchard species were (and are) cultivated. These are listed in the appendix on pages 238–9.

[3] See Higgs and Vita-Finzi (1972, 30) for definitions of territory types.

[4] A meaningful classification of grazing land is impossible here because much of it came under the plough in the 1950s. While the villagers claim that much of this "potentially arable" grazing was better quality than any that now remains, we have no proof that this was universal.

of extending northwards (or westwards beyond Fatmalı village) doubtless conditioned the cultivation of areas at considerable distances from Aşvan in the SE of the territory. (This would only have occurred once population or taxation pressure necessitated the cultivation of extra land.)

The distance relationship is most clearly illustrated by quantitative analysis of the Aşvan catchment using the system advanced by Higgs and Vita-Finzi (1970 and 1972).[5]

Distance from Aşvan	% of each land type (unweighted)				
	Irrigable arable	Dry arable	Grazing, potentially arable	Other grazing	Unproductive (very approx.)
up to 1 km	77%	9%	–%	11%	3%
2	24	22	11	34	9
3	1	35	25	37	2
4	–	28	23	41	8
5	–	33	20	41	5
6	–	32	11	51	6
7	–	39	? 6	47	8

Note: these percentages are not weighted for decrease in productivity with distance. (But see "rotation systems" in following paper.)

FIG.3. Table showing analysis of 1938 Aşvan territory (figures are all approximate)

The southernmost, dry-cultivated lands belonging to 1938 Aşvan were well over two hours oxen-walk (6–7 km.) away from the village, while the easternmost cultivated land (in the "Tapanlı" unit) was three hours (well over 7 km.) away for a villager leading his oxen. Further, these sorts of distances were encountered by almost all villagers: the land holding of each was fragmented into *c.* 15 units which were evenly scattered over the territory.

The distances just quoted may appear to exceed the thresholds of economic practice in terms of energy balances. The mean distance between a villager's house and his fields in 1938 Aşvan worked out at *c.* 2·6 km. which is still uneconomic according to the figures quoted by Chisholm.[6] However, this problem was alleviated in the following ways:

(1) Irrigation agriculture, dry-land fallow systems and manure application were arranged such that there was a decrease in economic intensity (and thence labour input/unit area/year) with increased distance from the village.[7]

(*a*) The most labour-intensive of all systems of cultivation at Aşvan was the irrigated garden. These gardens were located either within the village[8] or around the village fringes (see map, Fig. 1).

[5] Although I have used site catchment analysis for a single territory here, it must be remembered that its great value is for the comparison of different site territories.

[6] Chisholm (1962, 66) suggests (for modern subsistence agriculture) that "at a distance of 1 km., the decline in net return is large enough to be significant as a factor adversely affecting the prosperity of the farming population . . ." and that ". . . at about 3–4 km., the costs of operation rise sufficiently to be oppressive and seriously detrimental . . .".

[7] The effect of variations in % fallow on overall mean production/unit area/year is discussed in the following paper.

[8] See Hall, *et al.* (p. 259, Fig. 9) for the 1970s arrangement of gardens and irrigation systems within the village.

(*b*) Field-scale irrigation husbandry represented the next level of labour intensity, though it must be realized here that a wide range of different irrigation frequencies and levels are involved. Field irrigation was largely confined to areas around the village (see Fig. 1) or, more likely, the village was deliberately placed within the largest irrigable area (see discussion below).

(*c*) Beyond the irrigated land came dry cultivation. Here, rotation systems[9] were arranged such that there was an increase in percentage fallow with increased distance from Aşvan: my data indicates an average of 25% fallow in any one year at "Köyönü" (less than 1 km. from Aşvan), 28–29% at "Karamanlar" and "Kızıl Toprak" (3–5½ km.), *c.*33% at "Mahkeme" (5–7 km.) and around 40% at Tapanlı (7 km. over uneven terrain).

(*d*) When manuring was practised, it appears to have been confined to areas near Aşvan village (presumably, to the irrigated land). Unless horse- or oxen-carts were used here (and the oxen, at least, would be busy ploughing at this time), the donkey-basket transport of dung would have made more distant manuring uneconomic.

(2) The villagers lived out in the fields in temporary shelters for about one month during the labour-intensive harvesting of more distant fields.

(3) Ploughing, sowing and harrowing presented a greater problem.

(*a*) In distant fields, the extra ploughing characteristic of many fields closer to Aşvan was omitted. Sowing and harrowing were then combined with a single ploughing and the total number of journeys involved thereby reduced to a minimum.

(*b*) In at least some families, horses instead of oxen were used for ploughing their more remote fields, again reducing travelling time.

(*c*) There were some buildings about two-thirds of the way out to the most remote fields east of Aşvan, and it has been suggested that these were used as overnight accommodation by villagers ploughing in the vicinity.

We can reasonably expect that practices of this sort have origins which substantially predate the 1930s, and we should perhaps allow for this in estimating areas exploitable from ancient settlements (see following paper).

Distribution v.v. topography and soils

The maps, Figs. 1 and 2, viewed together, give some idea of the relationship between topography and cultivation in pre-tractor days. In the crudest terms, only relatively flat land was cultivated (see Wagstaff, p. 208, for the gradients involved). This excluded, however, flat land on exposed hill-tops, except where the underlying rock appears to have been sufficiently soft to provide a reasonable depth of raw "soil" (rock powder) as, for example, on the hill called "Boz Toprak". Only since the arrival of the tractor has cultivation extended over most of the flattest hilltops, though never to the hard diorite hills in the E and SE of our area. (The possibilities offered by the tractor were combined, in the early 1950s with the impetus of particularly favourable wheat prices and an expanding Aşvan population.)

---

[9] For examples of rotation systems used in Aşvan, see the following paper, p. 227.

On the flatter land, the effects of variation in soil type appear to have manifested themselves in the range of crops grown and in variations in crop yield, rather than in the distribution of cultivation as a whole.

Distribution v.v. water-availability

Water appears to be the most universally limiting factor for crop husbandry in this area. Its availability to plants grown under dry cultivation is conditioned by such factors as soil composition, catchment effect of slopes and by aspect, so these factors will again tend to determine the distribution of cultivation. The farmers' response to this effect of aspect, for example, is clearly seen on some low hills in our area where cultivation extends considerably further up north-facing slopes than up corresponding, dryer, south-facing slopes.

Irrigation[10] can, of course, mitigate some of these effects, but the distribution of gravity-irrigation is again determined by topography as well as by the proximity of flowing water during spring and autumn.[11] These two factors automatically limit all large-scale irrigation to the Aşvan terraces.

There are, however, other areas where only one or else neither of these necessary conditions is fulfilled, but where either or both may have changed out of all recognition during the time span represented by our sites. An example here is the area by Taşkun Kale: plenty of water flows past the mound, but the present topography prevents its distribution (for irrigation) over more than a few dönüm (= 1,000 m.^{2}), (see Fig. 1). However, Wagstaff points out in the preceding paper that both the deeply cut-in stream and the long colluvial slopes which sweep down to this area from three sides may well be recent features: their development was presumably associated with increased run-off following deforestation and cultivation on the nearby hills. A less cut-in stream flowing over flatter terrain would certainly have permitted more extensive irrigation in this area than was practised in recent years, though the total area of irrigation could never have amounted to more than a fraction of that on the Aşvan terraces below.

LOCATION OF MODERN VILLAGES AND SITES IN RELATION TO THESE CULTIVABLE LANDS

Assuming relatively small changes in basic crop-husbandry resources, the modern villages and sites in the region are well situated for both extensive crop husbandry and for simultaneous pastoralism. The present-day villages of Ahurik and Fatmalı are conspicuous exceptions, and it is doubtless significant that the 1938 Ahurik economy was heavily biased towards pastoralism, which may well have been the case for Fatmalı as well. Fatmalı's present crop production is limited by the proximity of the Aşvan territorial boundary which embraces almost all the best arable land: Fatmalı may well have been founded relatively recently on land of little value to a pre-existent Aşvan, though probably before the *Aşvanlılar* pushed their cultivation up into the hills (see following paper).

---

[10]"Irrigation" here covers any systematic application of surface water on a field or garden scale. At the lowest levels, water is only applied once or twice during the whole growing season (as for some wheats).

[11]Autumn irrigation is less important here as a rule.

Aşvan and Çayboyu are situated towards the centre of what is now one of the largest areas of irrigable land in the lower Murat valley, namely on the fan of the Kuru Çay. Even if the past course of the Murat cut due west across the northern edge of Aşvan (and this is likely to have happened at least once during the occupation of the Aşvan terrace – Wagstaff, pers. comm.), the richest part of this irrigable land still remains. It is perhaps not irrelevant that the southernmost extension of the Aşvan boundary, whatever pressures may have stimulated this configuration, gives Aşvan complete control over the water of Kuru Çay, with the small areas of irrigable land upstream thrown into the bargain.

But to view this relationship the other way round, where on the basis of the distribution of cultiv*able* land (or at later stages, irrig*able* land) would we expect ancient settlements to have been located? The attractions of any one area will have changed with time and two phases are considered here:

(1) *Initial penetration of crop-husbandry into the area*

The factors likely to have affected the farmers' choice of location will have included the following:

(*a*) *Forest cover:* Forest clearing would quite likely have been unavoidable in the extension of cultivation in any part of the area except, perhaps, on the drier, south-facing slopes.[12]

(*b*) *Soils:* The initial selection of areas for growing crops would doubtless have depended, secondly, on the distribution of farmable soils, and this is likely to have changed considerably in the intervening period (Wagstaff, pp. 211–2). Examples here are the now fertile soils offered by the alluvial fan and by the adjacent colluvial slopes overlying the Aşvan terraces. The fan probably accumulated from material eroded from around the "upland basin" following deforestation and cultivation in that area, and the colluvial slopes from similar processes on the hills behind Aşvan. The same probably applies to the huge sweep of colluvium over the "upland basin" itself.

It may well be, therefore, that soils (and other factors) involved in favouring extension of arable farming were initially more amenable in the "upland basin", and that agricultural settlements only occurred on the Aşvan terraces after soil erosion (following deforestation and cultivation) in – and possibly below – the "upland basin" had deposited the richer soils characteristic of the Aşvan terraces today. The distribution of known sites in the area appears to support this, (the earliest occurs in the "upland basin", see French, p. 77). However, French and

---

[12] There is a scatter of trees – unrelated to the position of springs or streams – throughout the Aşvan territory. The species concerned are invariably either spiny and/or produce edible fruits (e.g. *Celtis*, *Elaeagnus*, *Crataegus*), and it is these very categories which tend to survive deforestation (if any trees survive at all). It therefore appears that most of this area is not only *capable* of supporting forest, but actually did so in the past. Certainly, it is evident from the Aşvan plant remains that trees such as *Pistacia eurycarpa* were accessible to the Aşvan villagers during classical times, though the nearest live specimens that I know of now are near Çemişgezek (23 km. away). The dominant in the few forest remnants in the area is *Quercus pubescens*, and it is quite likely that this and other oaks once covered much of our area.

That there was once abundant forest in the sub-province as a whole is verified by nineteenth century records. Cuinet (1892, ii, 334) comments that the needs of the silver mines at Keban had destroyed all the forests of the sanjak of Kharput-Mezre. (This sanjak includes the *Aşvan Bölgesi*).

Wagstaff point out that these presumed recent deposits may well have obscured certain sites in the area, rendering distribution of the remaining sites potentially misleading.

(*c*) *Irrigability:* Under present conditions, the attractions of irrigation agriculture in the Aşvan terraces make them the obvious first choice for occupation, but before suggesting that the early agriculturalists responded to this attraction we have to assume firstly, that irrigation technology and its effects were familiar to the farmers concerned, secondly, that suitable soils were present on the terraces, thirdly, that pressures for increased food production were sufficient to mobilize the farming group(s) into being prepared to expend the extra energy involved in this considerably more labour-intensive form of cultivation and fourthly, that there were no political, strategic or disease[13] factors persuading them to the contrary.

Similar attractions elsewhere in the Aşvan region do not exist: the likely extent of irrigable land up the Kuru Çay Valley and in the "upland basin" would almost certainly have been minimal compared to the enormous potential of the Aşvan terraces. It must also be remembered that it would have been uneconomic (in terms of energy expended in travelling) to place a settlement far away from irrigated land, if this land made a substantial contribution to the settlement's economy: irrigation agriculture is always more labour-intensive than its dry-land equivalent.

In general, the attractions of irrigation are considerable. The most extreme example of the possibilities offered by irrigation is barley yield: irrigated 2-row barley in 1938 Aşvan could regularly produce six times[14] (and 6-row barley over twelve times) more than its dry-land equivalent in the same area. Striking differences are also met in most other crops.

Occupation of the Aşvan terraces would, therefore, have been logical for irrigation agriculture (if, indeed, the advantages of irrigation were appreciated or required), but problems of tree-clearing or the absence of suitable soils may, in any case, have dictated against the selection of these terraces during the earliest phase of agricultural extension in the region.

(2) *Later extension of cultivation within the Aşvan region*

Here, I assume that cultivable soils were distributed over at least part of their present area, and that irrigation technology was both familiar and necessary to meet the food needs of expanding populations.

At this point,[15] occupation could be expected wherever irrigation agriculture was possible over areas greater than, say, 200 dönüm. The Aşvan terrace must have stood out as the richest location in the lower Murat Valley, with secondary locations at Han, Engüzek and Taşkun area. (Although the possibility of extensive irrigation at Taşkun seems improbable, there is the attraction of what is now one of the richest springs in the region). The area of cultivable land in the "upland

---

[13] Malaria may have dissuaded against a valley-bottom location like the Aşvan terraces (see Angel, 1972).

[14] This is a mean for several years and allows for fallow years in the rotation sequences on dry-cultivated land.

[15] No dates are suggested here. We may be in a position to fix time correlates when we have examined more of the relevant remains from the sites.

basin" would have allowed (as now) for several settlements of moderate size. (See following paper on population levels.)

If these speculations are reasonable, then there are sites missing for certain periods at some of these locations. Most conspicuous is the absence of any known Late Bronze Age site on the Aşvan terraces, and French and Wagstaff point out that it is not impossible that such a site exists (or existed) somewhere beneath the Kuru Çay fan. The same explanation may apply to the apparent absence of a Neolithic site on these terraces, though complete absence would not be surprising here if some of the situations suggested above actually existed in Neolithic times.

The point which emerges most clearly from this paper is that few conclusions can be drawn until firstly, more is known about sedimentation history during the occupation span of the sites in our area and secondly, until we have assembled all our archaeological data pertaining to past agricultural practices.

BIBLIOGRAPHY

ANGEL, J. L., 1972. "Ecology and population in the Eastern Mediterranean", *World Archaeology* 4, 88–105.

CHISHOLM, M., 1962. *Rural settlement and land use*, London.

CUINET, V., 1892. *La Turquie d'Asie. Géographie Administrative. Vol. 2*, Paris.

HIGGS, E. S. and VITA-FINZI, C., 1970. "Prehistoric economy in the Mount Carmel area of Palestine: site catchment analysis", *PPS.*, 36, 1–37.

——— 1972. "Prehistoric economies: a territorial approach", in Higgs, E. S. ed. *Papers in economic prehistory*, Cambridge.

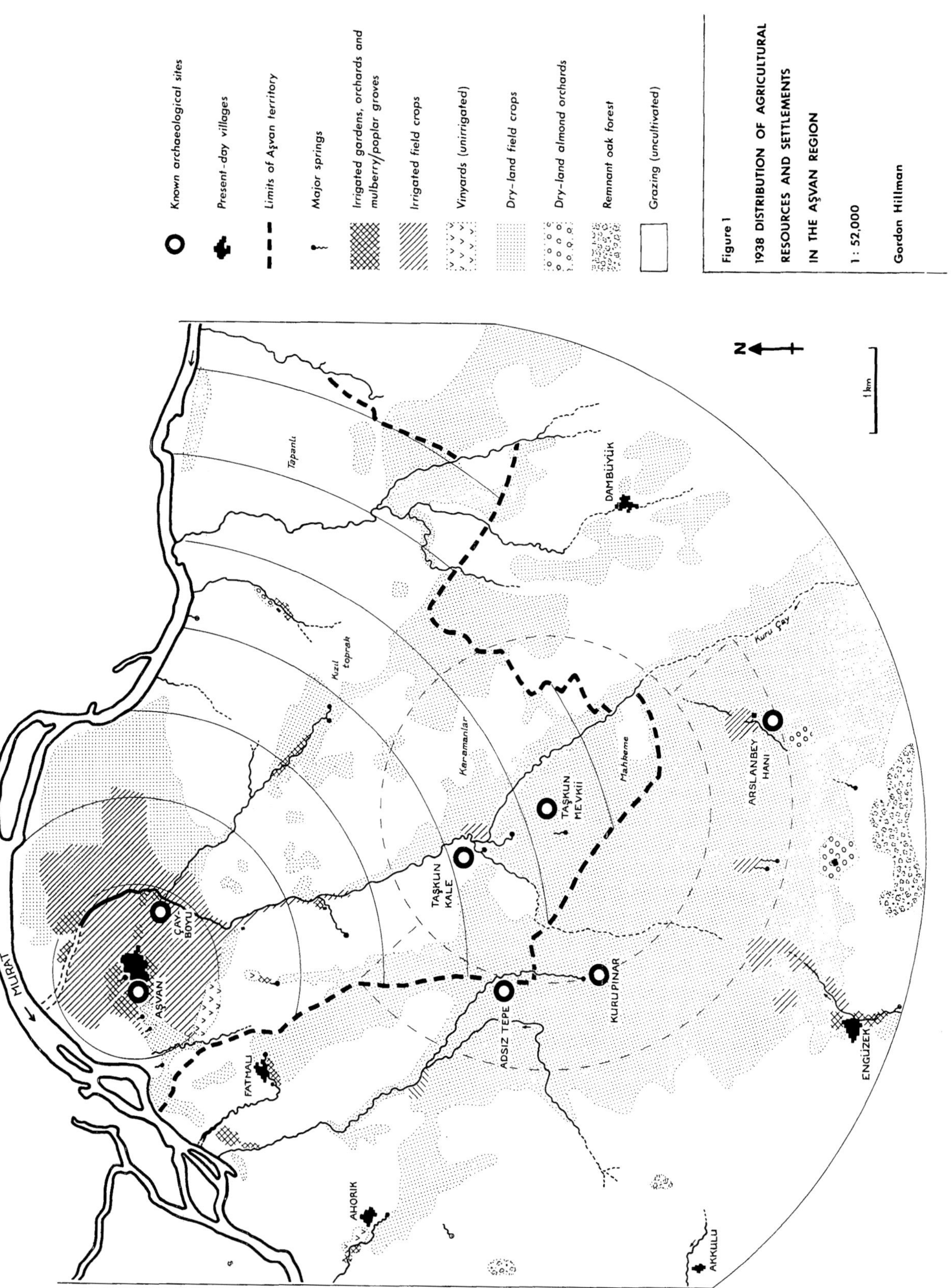

Figure 1
1938 DISTRIBUTION OF AGRICULTURAL RESOURCES AND SETTLEMENTS IN THE AŞVAN REGION
1 : 52,000
Gordon Hillman

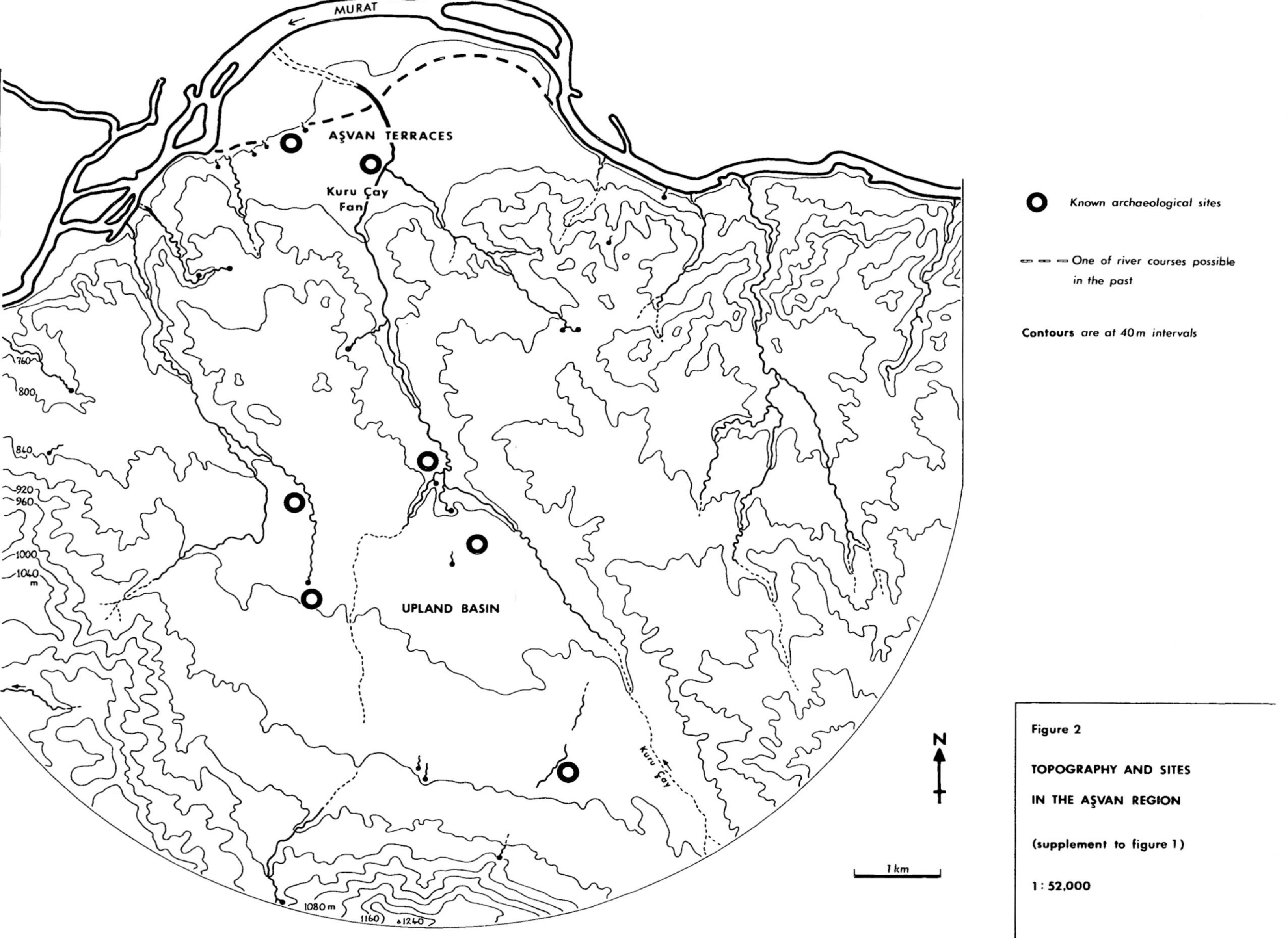

Figure 2
TOPOGRAPHY AND SITES IN THE AŞVAN REGION
(supplement to figure 1)
1: 52,000

Appendix 5.

AGRICULTURAL PRODUCTIVITY AND PAST POPULATION POTENTIAL AT AŞVAN

An exercise in the calculation of carrying capacities

By GORDON HILLMAN

This paper is not a discussion of archaeological evidence for past population levels in our area, nor of likely sequences of change in population through time. Instead, it is a set of estimations of upper levels of population that would have been possible at recent and ancient agricultural[1] settlements in the Aşvan region, assuming certain combinations of territory, land management systems and levels of productivity. This contrasts, therefore, with the approach more frequently adopted in estimating past population levels which uses settlement size and structural remains.

The points in time at which these hypothetical situations (with their corresponding population levels) were likely actually to have existed in the Aşvan region are not considered in detail here. We may be in a position to fix time correlates in some cases once we have more data on local erosion and sedimentation history[2] and once we have assembled all data arising from the site materials, in particular the data from the very large quantities of plant and animal remains.[3]

The object here, then, is to provide some coarse parameters applicable in assessing past population levels at sites in the Aşvan territory (see Fig. 1 of preceding paper). These parameters offer, perhaps, a crude guide for similarly situated sites in other regions as well. What follows is largely a breakdown of the agricultural productivity and population level in pre-tractor Aşvan (during the late 1930s and early 1940s). From this base line situation, I have then calculated the sort of population levels possible in the past if one postulates major changes in agricultural systems or territorial limits.

QUESTIONS OF CAUSE AND EFFECT

The population levels suggested in this paper were calculated in respect of stated levels of agricultural productivity and territorial limits. This approach could be taken to imply, perhaps, that factors such as productivity were tacitly assumed to operate as independent variables, actively imposing upper limits on population growth at all times. Certainly, it is possible to conceive of extreme situations where population expansion would be limited in this way. (See Angel, 1972, for some of the mechanisms involved here.) However, Boserup (1965) has presented a persuasive case for population changes themselves being treated as the most independent of the variables involved.

In this "chicken and egg" situation, I am inevitably forced to work backwards from what may be effects to their likely causes. As an archaeo-botanist, my

[1] These calculations are not relevant to more sophisticated economies or to technologies which existed prior to the adoption of the drawn plough.

[2] Wagstaff (this vol., pp. 198–215) intends to continue his research on this topic during the coming (1973) season.

[3] See Payne (in this vol., pp. 206–303) "Kill-off patterns in sheep and goats: the mandibles from Aşvan Kale".

particular class of archaeological remains is not likely to provide me with data directly indicative of population levels, but it *is* likely to indicate any implementation of intensification practices like irrigation[4] (assuming that relevant deposits were discovered in the course of excavation). I have, therefore, approached population levels via stated husbandry situations whose development might well have resulted from earlier population or taxation pressures, but as I have calculated the *maximum*[5] population that each closed system could be expected to maintain, it makes little difference which is the chicken and which the egg.

THE BASE-LINE SITUATION: 1940 AŞVAN

Primary data

1940 was selected as our base-line firstly, because detailed cadastral maps of the Aşvan territory had been compiled by then and were available for our inspection and secondly, because the more dramatic agricultural changes did not occur in the Aşvan region until well after this date. (The most important changes were those which followed the introduction of chemical fertilizers and modern farm machinery.)

The data collected in Aşvan village included sowing rates and yield ratios[6] for each major crop type at each of the customary levels of irrigation. These data were collected in respect of each of the thirty units of the Aşvan territory where the family being interviewed held land. Interviews with the eight sample families were supplemented by collective interviews conducted with some of the older male villagers. Estimates of basic food requirements per family were procured from similar sources, though not all the farmers concerned felt able to quantify with any accuracy here. One problem relating to all these data was the tendency of individuals to "weight" their estimates one way or the other. Only internal cross-checks and the results of collective interviews revealed the likely extent of weighting, and attempts at compensating for its effect on my mean values relied on a measure of intuition based, in turn, on some acquaintance with the farmers concerned. The measure of error in these figures is therefore very uncertain, and I have not included estimates of variance. However, the compounded error in some of the derived data which follow may be considerable.

The major field-crops and some of their yields are listed in Appendixes 1 and 2 (pp. 237–9) together with a list of the 40-odd minor domestic species grown at Aşvan. The most important crops were wheat and barley: the mean gross yield[7] for dry-cultivated soft wheat was 63 kg./dönüm,[8] for hard wheat under

[4] I am currently working on the possibility of using the range of weed seed types present in samples of plant remains as a means of recognizing past husbandry practices like irrigation.

[5] Use of *maximum* levels implies, in each case, a situation where the "needs" of the population were satisfied and no more: that is, the resources immediately available in that situation were fully utilized and any further population increase would have demanded some change in the system as a whole, quite likely a change involving economic intensification. ("Needs" as used here may, of course, include accustomed luxuries.)

[6] I worked in terms of sowing rates and yield ratios because the villagers were not accustomed to thinking in terms of yields/unit area.

[7] Gross yield in this case is the yield before removal of next year's seed, but after winnowing and coarse sieving.

[8] 1 dönüm = 1,000 m.^{2} = 1/10 hectare = *c.* 1/4 acre.

low-intensity irrigation 110 kg./dönüm, for dry-cultivated two-rowed barley 41 kg./dönüm, and for the same barley under low-intensity irrigation 115 kg./dönüm. The Aşvan yields fall well within the lower range of mean yields quoted for this sub-province (Köy İşleri Bakanlığı 1966, 150–1) but fall well below the means for Turkey as a whole (Christiansen-Weniger 1970, 86, and the Ministry of Agriculture of the Republic of Turkey 1968, 45).

It is perhaps worth putting these Aşvan yields into the broader context of traditional agriculture in other areas. Zohary (1969, 56) quotes yields of 50–150 kg./dönüm for indigenous Palestine barleys and hard wheats under dry-land "wooden-plough agriculture", while Webley (1970, 175) quotes 44 and 75 kg./dönüm[9] for "cereals" on two different soil types at Tell Gezer (Palestine) under dry cultivation with 350 mm. rainfall.

The rotation systems varied considerably in different parts of the Aşvan territory: the villagers were quite specific about which system could be applied where. In the case of irrigated land, it was necessary for the farmers to synchronize their rotation sequences in any one area so that crops requiring similar levels and frequencies of irrigation were grown in the same year. A few, typical rotation sequences are shown in Fig. 1. Many permutations along these lines were possible, especially when extra crops such as chick-peas or lentils were incorporated into the sequence. Fallow years on irrigated land were rare, as were two-year fallows on dry land, and I know of no case of multicropping.

Year	Dry fields			Irrigated fields[10]	
1	soft wheat	soft wheat	soft wheat	hard wheat	hard wheat
2	fallow	fallow	fallow	sorghum	cotton
3	soft wheat	barley (2-row)	barley (2-row)	barley (2 or 6-row)	barley or wheat
4		fallow	bitter vetch	common vetch	common vetch
5		oats	soft wheat	hard wheat	hard wheat
6		fallow	fallow	melons or squashes (+ some sunflower and maize)	
7		soft wheat	barley (2-row)	barley (2 or 6-row)	
8			grass pea	cotton	
9			soft wheat	hard wheat	

FIG.1. Some sample rotation systems.

In general, percentage fallow increased with distance from Aşvan village. Fallow-free, irrigation husbandry (and probably any manuring) was limited to the first 1·5 km. or so (see preceding article and Fig. 1, p. 218). Beyond this zone, dry-land fallow increased from *c.* 25% at 1·5 km. from Aşvan, to around 40% at 7+ km. from Aşvan, and this was closely paralleled by a corresponding decrease in gross production/unit area/year.

[9] For these figures, I have assumed that Webley's "quintal" is equivalent to 100 kg. of grain, rather than the other standards of 112 pounds or 104 pounds.

[10] Lentils, chickpeas, grass peas and soft wheat were occasionally irrigated. Conversely, the local forms of hard wheat and 6-row barley were occasionally sown on dry land. Dry cultivation of water melons is frequent on certain soils, but not standard in the area as a whole.

It is perhaps worth noting that the decline in gross production/unit area with increased distance from Aşvan village was smaller than that suggested by the distance-weighting factors adopted by Higgs and Vita-Finzi (1970, 28) in their analysis of Palestinian site catchments. Overall *net* energy production/unit area/year (i.e. net calorie yield/unit area/year *minus* the energy expended in husbandry operations and in travelling to the area concerned) will inevitably have decreased more abruptly with distance from Aşvan. But on the other hand, the *Aşvanlılar* had systems for reducing the amount of energy expended in this way (see preceding paper, pp. 219–220).

Base-line population level

The population of Aşvan village in 1940 was approximately 440, comprising some 80 families[11] with an average of 5·5 persons per family[12] (including children). The corresponding population density for the Aşvan territory was nearly 12 persons/km.^{2}. By comparison, the rural population density of the neighbouring sub-province of Keban was 13·3/km.^{2} in 1962, and of the Elâzığ province as a whole 22·5/km.^{2} (Köy İşleri Bakanlığı 1966, 28). At the end of the last century, however, the rural population density of the sub-province of "Keban-Ma'aden" appears to have been somewhat higher at *c.* 16/km.^{2} (Cuinet 1892, 367 and map p. 315).

Human foods in 1940 Aşvan

The crops grown at Aşvan are listed together with their uses in Appendixes 1 and 2 (pp. 237–9). The animal food-producers included sheep, goat and cow.

Food production per family or individual per year is based – in the case of the major crops – on village means for net production in each item. In the case of animal products, the figure is derived from estimates made by Payne (pers. comm.). "Other foods" includes a range of minor food plants and animal products which, though they contributed little to calorie intake,[13] were doubtless important both in providing necessary nutrients outside carbohydrates and proteins and in flavouring otherwise dull fare. (See Fig. 2 below).

Calorie intake is estimated at *c.* 3,100 calories per person per day. This figure is based on estimates of food "necessary for a family of five or six persons" given by the villagers, and seems to tally with other data available. Consumption of animal products was, it seems, greater than that met with at the present time[14]

---

[11] This figure is based on 1938 land-ownership lists.

[12] 5·5 persons/family is a little above the highest mean value (5·2) for any other section of this province (Köy İşleri Bakanlığı 1966, derived from tables 10 and 29).

[13] Of these minor foods, the most important calorie-contributors were eggs. But even allowing for an average family holding of five chickens, which is well above the average for this province (Köy İşleri Bakanlığı 1966, 60–1) and for each of these chickens laying a medium-sized egg every day of the year (impossible), then the percentage contribution to total calorie production is still only 1%.

Of the minor plant foods, concentrated grape-juice (*pekmez*) was perhaps the most important calorie-contributor, but this again was relatively insignificant.

[14] This apparent decrease is presumably related to the drastic reduction in animal holdings which occurred during the past 20 years following the arrival of the tractor and the shift to greater wheat production.

but even so, 80% of the calories consumed appear to have been derived from wheat products alone. (The equivalent of *c.* 320 kg. of unmilled wheat was eaten/person[16] /year.)

	Wheats[15] (unmilled)	Grain legumes	Meat & milk products	Other foods
kg. produced/family/year	2,126 kg.	110 kg.		small amounts
kg. produced/person/year[16]	386 kg.	20 kg.		,,
% contribution to total calorie production[17]	78·5%	3·5%	16%	2%

FIG.2. Table showing food production (village means).

It is not surprising in a relatively opulent village like Aşvan that the apparent calorie intake/person/day is greater than the figure of 2,650 calories quoted by the US Department of Agriculture (1960) as the mean quantity consumed/-person/day in present-day Turkey. Any such estimate will, of course, disguise considerable variation, e.g. Buck (1937) noted a range between 1,000 and 4,000 calories consumed/person/day in some Chinese villages.

Food requirements. A further comparison can be made with the theoretical mean minimum calorie requirement of a medium-sized man engaged in physical work for *c.* 8 hours/day in a seasonally cold climate. FAO (1957) estimated this minimum requirement at *c.* 2,500 calories/person/day which may be an over-estimate for the Aşvan situation where little work appears to be done during the winter months.

Production of animal feed in 1940

The long, harsh winters of the Aşvan region made winter feed for animals essential. These grain feeds were heavily supplemented with both wheat and legume straw (together with lucerne hay on the rare occasions that this crop was grown). Estimates given by the villagers for the feed requirements of the different animals (Payne, pers. comm.) enable us to convert the feed production figures

	Barley	Sorghum	Oats	Maize	Vetches
kg. produced/family/year	1706 kg.	90	563	43	863

(For the uses of each product, see Appendixes 1 and 2)
FIG.3.

[15]The wheat production figures are based on grain which had been coarse-sieved to remove the worst of the weed seeds and other contaminants, but which had not been milled to remove the bran. "Even the poorest subsistence economies find wheat bran indigestible and mill off 10%" (Clark and Haswell, 1967, 67).

[16]5·5 persons/family includes children, so that production (and consumption) per *adult* would have been greater than the figures given.

[17]The calorific values used here (in cal/g.) were as follows: wheat 3·15, grain-legumes 2·7, fatty meat 3·5, milk and milk products 0·8 cal/g. of milk. (Medical Research Council 1960.) (The estimate for milk is higher than figures for cow milk to allow for the richer milk of sheep and goat.)

into the maximum animal holding possible for the average family: one possible combination would be *c.* 42 sheep and goat, 2 milk cows, 2 draught oxen and 1 horse (plus a donkey[18] or so and some chickens[19]). Flock size here greatly exceeds the villagers' own estimates for pre-tractor times (Payne, pers. comm.): this discrepancy represents a considerable surplus of barley feeds (see below).

Cash products

Cotton and silk were produced, it seems, almost entirely for sale outside the village. (Whether they were first spun, dyed and woven in Aşvan itself, I do not know.) Silk production at Aşvan has since ceased altogether, though the beginning of the decline in this sub-province appears to date back to the end of the last century (Cuinet 1892, 331). Apart from cotton and silk, saleable surpluses existed for most agricultural products (see below).

Land holdings

See Appendix 3 (p. 239) for the village means of the amount of land of each class held per family.

CORRECTED BASE-LINE SITUATION: ALLOWANCE FOR CROP-FAILURE

The 1940 production figures (above) exceed consumption estimates and theoretical calorie requirements by a healthy margin. However, it became apparent that the villagers' estimates of yield ratios (which form the basis of the preceding figures for production) represented average to moderately good years only. The *Aşvanlılar* claimed to suffer "bad harvests" one year in four or five together with very occasional "near failures" on dry lands. These yield reductions, they said, were due to the autumn and/or spring rains[20] arriving too late, with meagre winter snowfall presumably aggravating the situation. This frequency of poor harvests appears to correspond crudely with the 1 year in 4·9 when total annual precipitation fell below 350 mm., as indicated in the Elâzığ precipitation figures for the past 43 years (see Wagstaff, Fig. 5, p. 202). Other causes of crop failure, e.g. large-scale disease of cereals, appear to have accounted for smaller and less predictable losses.

The effects of drought extended to irrigated crops, as well as to those under dry-cultivation: not only may irrigation water itself be reduced (presumably with varying delays), but this water only supplies a fraction of the needs of some of the low-intensity irrigation crops like hard wheat (*Triticum durum*). (The latter would be given only a few doses per season.)

[18] The villagers made no special allowance for winter feed for donkeys: almost any fodder was deemed sufficient (Payne, pers. comm.). The only notable attempt at persuading a donkey to live on air was apparently a failure (Tales of Nasrettin Hoja).

[19] Chickens were fed on weed seeds mostly sieved out of grain crops during the first round of sieving, while grain weights quoted here are *post* primary sieving.

[20] The wheats (both hard and soft) were generally autumn-sown (early October), while barley and the legumes were mostly spring-sown (early March).

The villagers were able to mitigate these effects, if only fractionally, so long as ample irrigation water was still running. Firstly, they administered extra irrigation to crops like hard wheat. Secondly, dry-cultivated fields adjacent to irrigated areas (e.g. at the east end of the gently-sloped Aşvan terraces) were irrigable if small extensions to the existing water-channel systems were dug. (The already complex system of irrigation timings must then have become highly involved.)

The correction factors

The necessary correction factors could not be calculated from the crude, village estimate of the frequency of bad harvests. I have, therefore, used data on levels and frequencies of low yields in Anatolia as a whole since 1928, as provided by Christiansen-Weniger (1970, 86) and the Ministry of Agriculture of Turkey (1968, 45).[21] (These data include any reductions due to disease, insect or bird damage, as well as those due to reduced water availability.) Their figures suggest a reduction in yield which, spread evenly over all other years, would have amounted to an annual loss of 9%. For the Aşvan area, this is probably an overestimate.

	Frequency	% reduction in yield	Equivalent mean % reduction/year (= correction factor)
"bad harvest"	1 yr. in 4	30%	5·75%[22] } 9%
"near failure"	1 yr. in 17	55%	3.24%

FIG.4. Derivation of correction factor for bad harvests

Firstly, it appears that Aşvan yields in "bad" years were not as severely reduced as mean yields for Turkey as a whole. (It is on the latter that the figure of 9% is based.) Secondly, the percentage of the total area under irrigation at Aşvan is higher than for Turkey in general, and drought effects have, therefore, a better chance of being moderated. This exaggerated yield-reduction is, however, used throughout the calculations which follow.

COMMENTS ON THE 1940 BASE-LINE PRODUCTIVITY LEVELS

Substantial surpluses of most foodstuffs were produced by Aşvan village during normal and good years. Much of this surplus appears to have provided for dry years when harvests were bad. But, even having allowed for this, surpluses were still well in excess of both theoretical minimum food requirements and the villagers' far-from-Spartan consumption estimates. Examples here are the corrected annual production figures for wheats and edible legumes. Assuming the 1940 Aşvan dietary balance, production of wheats and legumes exceeded

[21]In estimating % reductions in yields during bad years from these data, I have attempted to eliminate the effects of more recent use of chemical fertilizers in extending the upper end of the frequency-distributions for yield levels.

[22]These figures allow for the 1 year in 17 with "near failure" coinciding with one of the "bad harvest" years.

consumption estimates by 11% and 12% and theoretical minimum requirements by 36% and 28% respectively.

In the animal feeds, a substantial barley surplus was produced. It is, in any case, possible to regard the massive production of meat and milk as something of a luxury, especially when so much land was devoted to growing winter feed for the animals concerned.

Any surplus must, of course, be measured against the cost of the minimum acceptable requirement for those clothing materials, metal utensils and tools which had to be purchased outside the home. There were no taxes imposed on farmers at this time, and the surpluses of the 1940s appear to have exceeded these purchase requirements by a healthy margin. The consequent accumulation of cash is evident from the rapid purchase of expensive agricultural machinery (admittedly with some state aid) twenty years ago.

The Aşvan economy was not, therefore, one of mere subsistence.[23] The annual allocation of 400 dönüm of the best irrigated land on the Kuru Çay fan to a cash crop like cotton indicates, in itself, absence of any fear of food shortages. It may also be significant that the village appears to have been able to support three families of craftsmen (two carpenters and one blacksmith). However, it is possible that the families concerned held their own land and met much of their own food requirement. Perhaps the neatest indicator of the high level of productivity at 1940 Aşvan is the economic wheat equivalent[24] of approx. 2,400 kg./person/year. (For comparison, the mean for Turkey in 1960 was 788 kg. and for the Near East as a whole *c.* 620 kg./person/year, Clark and Haswell 1967, 72.)

This level of productivity was achieved using traditional forms of husbandry and equipment which may well have existed in this area for several millennia. In addition, most of the major crops grown at Aşvan are those well known to be natives of SW Asia. Not surprisingly, these classes of crop have some antiquity in the Aşvan area itself: a cursory examination of the plant remains from the sites indicates that wheats,[25] barleys and legumes like bitter vetch have been conspicuous crops in our area at least since the Early Bronze Age.

EARLIER POPULATION LEVELS

Maximum levels for an Aşvan-based population using territories and husbandry systems of the 1940 type

These estimates are based on production figures corrected for years of bad harvest as indicated above. Cultivation of cash crops and surplus barley has,

[23]This situation is not unusual in dry areas of Turkey. Christiansen-Weniger (1970, 86) points out that "... in Trockengebieten ... in normalen und guten Jahren, der Ertrag den Eigenverbrauch der Bauern erheblich übersteigt ...".

[24]Economic wheat equivalent is the measure of real product most easily used in communities where grain is the major commodity. Other products are converted into grain equivalents at the rate at which they exchange against wheat in local markets (Clark and Haswell 1967, 224). I have had to use 1970 prices here.

[25]The sequence starts with emmer and ends up with free-threshing wheats.

however, been eliminated.[26] Firstly, with consumption at the levels estimated for 1940, overall production was in excess of needs by *c.* 23%.[27] On this basis, maximum possible population would have been *c.* 98 families (*c.* 544 persons). Secondly, with consumption at the levels of the theoretical minimum requirement of 2,500 calories/day (but with the 1940 balance between the major classes of food consumed), maximum population could have been *c.* 118 families (*c.* 655 persons). The corresponding population densities for the Aşvan territory as a whole would have been 14·5 and 17·5 persons/km.^{2} respectively.

Using these population maximums as a base-line, it is now possible to consider the likely effect on population level of entirely different husbandry systems and territorial limits. However, the sequence of arrival in our area not only of each of the major domestic species, but also of the drawn plough, wheeled transport, shortened fallows and effective irrigation is unknown. It is difficult, therefore, to suggest combinations of these factors which were likely to have co-existed in the past: I have taken only a few extreme possibilities to serve as bases for population estimates. These estimates can, I hope, provide crude guidelines for our deliberations once the analysis of the site materials reveals evidence for ancient forms of husbandry practised in the Aşvan area.

It must, however, be remembered that these estimates cannot necessarily be regarded as relevant to the earliest phases of agricultural extension into the Aşvan area on account of the present uncertainty surrounding the extent of cultivable soils at that time. (See preceding paper, pp. 222–3 and Wagstaff, pp. 211–2.)

In the following sections, husbandry systems and territories differ from the above base-line situation only as stated in the respective headings. All other aspects remain unchanged. Population levels are all calculated on the basis of food consumption at the rather generous level estimated for 1940, and *not* at the theoretical minimum. (The latter would permit a population level *c.* 20% higher than that calculated in each case.)

Without any major food-producing animals

The diet here is reduced essentially to wheat and pulse products, with minor contributions by other foodstuffs.[13]

Odum (1963, 39–40) points out that "... more men can survive on a square mile if they function as primary rather than secondary consumers". Use of all cultivated land to produce wheat and legumes for direct human consumption (together with a relatively small area to grow winter-feed for draught animals) is, therefore, the most obvious way of maximising the Aşvan carrying capacity. On the other hand, the 2,580 dönüm of land used to grow winter feed for sheep, goats and cows provided only up to three months worth of their annual food requirement. The remainder was largely derived from pastures confined to hilly terrain where it was not in the villagers' interest to attempt cultivation in any case (not, at least, until the arrival of the tractor).

[26] The land involved in the production of cash crops, of the barley surplus of 34% and of the saleable surplus of two minor crops (grapes and water melons) was re-allocated (in calculation) to land of the respective classes being used to grow all other crops.

[27] Calculated as Σ [(% excess production of food A) × (% contribution of food A to total Aşvan calorie production)] + [same for food B] + etc.

The balance of this situation is that the huge gain in calories from the extra wheat and edible pulse products would have greatly outweighed the loss of calories normally supplied by animal products: the result is a nett increase in calorie production of 36% over the corresponding base-line figure. With total consumption at the 1940 level of 3,100 calories/person/day and with consumption of legumes relative to wheats increased from 1:20 to 1:10,[28] maximum population could have been *c.* 740 persons in *c.* 135 families. The corresponding population density within the Aşvan territory would then have been 20 people/km.^{2}

With animals on year-round grazing

Here I have assumed an improbable situation in which winters were so mild that specially-grown winter feed for food-producing animals could be eliminated. (Some special feed for draught animals would presumably still be necessary.) Under these conditions, it would have been possible to maintain a population over 50% larger than the base-line maximum, namely *c.* 810 people in *c.* 147 families. The corresponding population density would have been *c.* 22 people/km.^{2}

This is probably an over-estimate, as the quality of grazing in even the mildest Anatolian winter would presumably fall below the value of grain feeds, and reductions in milk production would follow.

Without irrigation

Here, the maximum levels for Aşvan-based populations drop more than 20% below those maintainable within the 1940-type system. This figure is based on the replacement of yields under irrigation by their nearest dry-land equivalent, though manuring of fields within a *c.* 1·5 km. radius of Aşvan village has been arbitrarily assumed to reduce this drop in yield by a mean factor of 10% for all crops in this zone. The corresponding population maximum would have been 436 people in 79 families (at the rather generous 1940 consumption levels). (Without manuring, the figures are 425 and 77 respectively.)

It is not known when irrigation agriculture was first adopted in the Aşvan region, but means of recognizing its effects in samples of plant remains from our sites may soon be available (see following paper, pp. 241–244).

With territorial boundary at 4·5 km. radius from Aşvan village

This radius brings the southern boundary up to the edge of the "upland basin" (see maps, p. 218). Without exploitation of the more distant dry-lands, total calorie output drops almost 22% below the base-line maximum. The corresponding maximum population under these conditions would have been *c.* 425 persons in *c.* 77 families (for 1940 food-consumption levels), with the population density for this reduced territory considerably higher at 18·8/km.^{2}

With cultivation limited to the Aşvan terraces

(a) *With irrigation*

Under these circumstances, it would have been possible to maintain a

---

[28] I have presumed that, with animal-derived foods largely reduced to eggs and poultry, the villagers would feel inclined to increase the ratio of consumption of legumes v.v. wheat.

population level at *c.* 60% of the maximum estimated for the 1940 type of situation, namely, *c.* 320 persons in *c.* 57 families. This reduction is small compared to the total loss of cultivated land involved, and reflects the concentration on the terraces of all the more intensive forms of husbandry.

(b) *Without irrigation*

The figures here are again based on the replacement of yields under irrigation by their nearest dry-land equivalent and assumes the same response to manuring as before. The corresponding figures here are 245 people in 36 families and a population density of 6·5 people/km.^{2}

Such situations are not unlikely in the past. Substantial pressure from, say, population increases would have been required before the *Aşvanlılar* extended cultivation into the dry hills behind the village: it is necessary to travel over 2 km. beyond the terrace limits and up into the hills before reaching any sizeable area of cultivable land. (Arable land belonging to Fatmalı village is, however, somewhat closer, which suggests that Fatmalı was established before the *Aşvanlılar* started cultivating hill territory.) This sort of situation is, of course, not uncommon for valley-bottom settlements.

With cultivation limited to the terraces and without food-producing animals

Here, the boundary for all forms of exploitation is set at the terrace limits. Irrigation at the 1940 levels is assumed.

The loss of calories from animal-derived food is more than offset by the gain in calories from the extra wheat and pulse products grown on land released from animal feed production. A population level considerably higher than in the equivalent situation with animals (above) is possible therefore (*c.* 448 people in *c.* 81 families) but this is still 18% below the base-line maximum. The corresponding population density would have been *c.* 56 people/km.^{2} This very high density reflects intensive exploitation of the small territory assumed in this section.

With the Murat flowing E to W across the foot of Aşvan village

The River Murat is quite likely to have occupied this sort of position at least once during the occupation of the terrace sites (Wagstaff, pers. comm.). Assuming the course indicated by dotted lines on Fig. 2, (p. 218), much of the zone of intensive husbandry would have been lost, with a consequent 12% reduction in the production of human foodstuffs. Corresponding population levels would have been 480 people in 87 families.

Application of more intensive forms of crop husbandry on the remaining land and/or cultivation of new land would have been unavoidable had this loss of land ever occurred when population level was already at a maximum. Customary levels of consumption (in its broadest sense) could not otherwise have been maintained.

Maximum levels for Taşkun Mevkii-based populations within agricultural systems of the 1940 Aşvan type

Taşkun Mevkii was well placed for the simultaneous pursuit of both dry-land arable farming and pastoralism (see maps, p. 218). However, this statement assumes, firstly, that the distribution of cultivable soils in the "upland basin" at the time of occupation was similar to that at present, secondly, that woodland did not cover too much of the Taşkun territory and, thirdly, that the territories of neighbouring settlements did not restrict the south-westerly spread of Taşkun Mevkii's cultivation.

Irrigation agriculture could not have been practised on a scale in any way comparable to 1940 Aşvan. The areas over which irrigation was physically feasible may, however, have been greater than at present (see preceding paper). Either way, garden scale irrigation would have been feasible had the villagers known of, or required this labour-intensive form of husbandry.

The physical situation of 1940 was adopted as the base-line here (in the absence of any other) together with the 1940 Aşvan balance between the major classes of food consumed. I have adopted two limits for cultivation (see Fig. 1, p. 218), the first an incomplete circle at 2 km., the second a 180° arc to the SW of the site at 3 km. This pattern permits easy access to grazing lands to the NE of Taşkun Mevkii, though I have set no precise limits on grazing here.[29]

(a) *With cultivation up to 2 km.*

Here, the mean house-to-field distance (assuming randomly scattered holdings) would have been *c.* 1·5 km. which, according to Chisholm (1962, 66), is already beyond the bounds of economic practice. This distance is, however, far less than the 2·5 km. travelled by the average *Aşvanlı* in 1940 (see preceding paper). The crop-husbandry exploitation territory is spatially more compact than the Aşvan dry-lands, a fact that should have allowed for greater economic intensification (in terms of shortened fallows and manuring) had population pressure demanded this. Under such conditions, the maximum population level would have been *c.* 88 families (*c.* 485 people).

(b) *With cultivation up to 3 km.*

The mean house-to-field distance of *c.* 2 km. is still less than the equivalent distance at 1940 Aşvan. A less intensive form of husbandry must be assumed for the extra arc of land between 2 and 3 km., but even so, a considerably larger population would have been possible here, with the maximum at around 155 families (over 850 people) if food consumption were maintained at the 1940 Aşvan level. Still further increases may theoretically have been possible, though rather improbable.

Slightly lower population levels would have been possible for agricultural settlements at Taşkun Kale and the site by Han (Arslanbey Hanı) and a rather higher level at Kurupınar. Similar husbandry systems at Engüzek would not have been able to support such large populations, and extensive forest clearance would certainly have been involved in the early stages of settlement here.

Farming of the "upland basin" by several settlements simultaneously may well have a long history. The area available for husbandry conducted by any one of them would, therefore, have been limited by the boundaries of the others.[30]

---

[29]The limits adopted here for size of animal holdings are those imposed by the amount of land available for growing winter feed: this I have calculated as the same proportion of 1940 Aşvan lands devoted to the same crop types.

[30]Any suggestion as to the territory likely to have been available to any one site in the "upland basin" can be little more than speculation in view of the possible existence of sites buried beneath the broad sweep of supposedly recent colluvium here.

This limitation would have been minimised by positioning the settlements around the edge of the basin, a pattern which would also ease access to grazing land outside the basin. Once earlier population pressures had motivated some intensification of the husbandry systems employed under these circumstances, the upland basin could probably have supported a population of at least 1,200. The population density for the territory (including grazing) exploited by this population would have been approximately 20/km.^{2}. It must, however, be stressed here that water supply anywhere in this upland basin appears to be far less reliable than that down at Aşvan. This factor (even in the absence of any irrigation technology in the area) may well have favoured Aşvan as the major settlement of this region, despite the agricultural potential of the "upland basin".

Further situations which were likely to have existed in ancient times could doubtless have been included here. This did not seem justified either in terms of the level of accuracy possible or (in the case of pre-plough technologies) in terms of the available reference studies. If, however, these crude guides can assist in the understanding of the sites in the Aşvan region and similar areas elsewhere, then the primary purpose of this study is fulfilled.

APPENDIX 1. Major (and some minor) field crops and their yields in 1940 Aşvan.
(The examples of yields and sowing rates are in each case means for 8 sample families. Yields under dry cultivation are for non-manured fields only. 1 dönüm = 1,000 m^2 = 1/10 hectare = *c.* 1/4 acre.)

Crop type		Use of product	Management type	Gross yield /dönüm	Sowing rate /dönüm
Triticum aestivum	soft wheat	bread	dry cult.	63 kg.	9·2 kg.
T. durum	hard wheat	bread or *bulgur*	irrigated	110	12
Hordeum sativum	hulled, 2-row barley	sheep or goat feed	dry cult.	41	5
,,	,,	,,	irrigated	115	13
,,	hulled, 6-row barley	,,	irrigated	250	15
Avena sativa	oats	horses (+ s/g)	dry cult.	97	12
Sorghum vulgare	sorghum				
Panicum miliaceum	common millet	,,	irrigated	80+	?3
Vicia sativa	common vetch	oxen (+ cows)	irrigated	150	17
V. ervilia	bitter vetch	,,	dry cult.	70	7
Lathyrus sativus	grass pea	milk cows	dry cult.	90	7
,,	,,	,,	irrigated	165	15
Lens esculentus	lentil	human food	dry cult.	40	7
,,	,,	,,	irrigated	132	13·5
Cicer arietinum	chick pea	,,	dry cult.	25	3
Phaseolus vulgaris	kidney bean	,,	irrigated	120	*c.* 10
Zea mays	maize	cows etc. (& humans)	irrigated	65	?

APPENDIX 2. Minor crops grown at Aşvan: their names, origins and uses.
(The reputed origins are based on Schiemann (1932) and several other authors.)

Crop names			Reputed origins	Uses
Latin	English	Turkish		
FIELD CROPS				
Vitis vinifera	vine	üzüm	SW Asia	fresh fruit & "pekmez"[13]
Gossypium herbaceum	cotton	pamuk	S Asia	fibre
Citrullus vulgaris	water melon	karpuz	Kalahari	usual
Sesamum indicum	sesame	susam	Africa (? + S Asia)	bread additive (+ some oil)
SMALL-SCALE FIELD OR GARDEN CROPS				
Cucumis melo (2 varieties)	cantaloupe melon	kavun	Africa or near East	usual
Cucurbita pepo	courgette	dolma kabağı	America	fresh fruit and edible seeds
,,	pumpkin	bal kabağı	,,	,,
,,	squash	kara kabak	,,	,,
,,	,,	sarı kabak	,,	,,
Medicago sativa	lucerne	yonca	SW Asia	fodder
Trigonella foenum-graecum	fenugreek	boy	? SW Asia	fodder for animals & grain for treating *pastırma* (meat)
Phaseolus vulgaris	kidney bean	kuru fasulye	America	seeds cooked
,,	haricot bean	,,	,,	,,
OTHER GARDEN CROPS				
Dolichis lablab	hyacinth bean		S Asia	seeds cooked
Vicia faba	broad bean	bakla	? Medit.	cooked as seeds or as young pods
Pisum sativum	pea	bezelye	? Near East	seeds cooked
Cannabis sativa	hemp, etc.	kendir	S Asia	seeds roasted
Cucumis sativus	cucumber	salatalık or hıyar	S Asia	salads
Lycopersicon esculentum	tomato	domates	America	,,
Capsicum annuum	sweet pepper	dolma biberi	America	salads & cooking
C. frutescens	hot pepper	sivri biber	,,	,, ,,
,,	chilli	çuşka biberi	,,	cayenne pepper
Solanum melanogena	aubergine	patlıcan	S Asia	cooked
Solanum tuberosum	potato	patates	America	,,
Petroselinum crispum var. *tuberosum*	celeriac	kereviz	?	,,
Daucus carota	carrot	havuç	? Asia	,, or raw
Raphanus sativus (several varieties)	radish	turp	? Near East	salads
Allium cepa	onion	soğan	Central Asia	usual
A. sativum	garlik	sarmısak	,,	,,
Amaranthus chlorostachys	an amaranth	?	America	as a spinach
Portulaca olearacea ssp. *sativa*	purslane	semiz otu	? SW Asia	,, ,, or as a salad plant
Petroselinum hortense	–	maydanoz	? Medit.	salads
Nigella sativa	black cumin	çöre otu	SW Asia	flavouring in bread or cheese
	–	irahan	? SW Asia	flavouring meat
Mentha sp.	mint	nane	?	herb
Lawsonia inermis	henna	kına	S Asia	dyeing skin & hair
Lagenaria vulgaris	water gourd	su kabağı	S Asia, E Africa (and America)	carrying water
ORCHARD AND TIMBER TREES				
Cydonia vulgaris	quince	ayva	W Asia	usual
Pyrus communis (several vars.)	pears	armut	SW Asia	,,
Prunus persica	peach	şeftali	China	,,
P. armenaica	apricot	kayısı	E & C Asia	,,
P. dulcis	almond	badem	SW Asia	,,

P. cerasus	morello cherry	vişne	,,	
P. avium	sweet cherry	kiraz	,,	,,
P. domestica (several varieties)	plums	erik	,,	,,
Punica granatum	pomegranate	nar	C & SW Asia	fresh fruit, etc.
Morus alba	white mulberry	beyaz dut	Asia	silk, fruit & timber
M. nigra	red mulberry	kırmızı dut	W Asia	fruit and timber
Juglans regia	walnut	ceviz	C & SW Asia	nuts and dye from outer flesh
Elaeagnus angustifloia	oleaster	iğde	SW Asia	sugary fruit, timber for ploughs & hedge shrub
Populus spp.	poplars	kavak	Asia & Europe	heavy timber
Salix spp.	willow	söğüt	?	light timber (from polarding)

APPENDIX 3. Total land-holding per family (village means).

For production of human foods – field crops – dry cult.		55·0* dönüm
– irrigated		6·6
– gardens/orchards (irrig.)		2·0
– vineyards (dry cult.)		2·3
For animal feeds – dry cultivated		40·0*
– irrigated		10·0
Timber for building & tools (irrigated)		0·8
Cash crops – cotton (,,)		5·0
– silk mulberry (,,)		0·5
	total	122 dönüm/family (= 12·2 hectares)

(grazing land is common village property)
*Only *c.* 65% of this dry land is cultivated in any one year.

BIBLIOGRAPHY

ANGEL, J. L., 1972. "Ecology and population in the eastern Mediterranean", *World Archaeology* 4, 88–105.

BOSERUP, E., 1965. *The conditions of agricultural growth*, Chicago.

BUCK, J. L., 1937. *Land utilization in China, Vol. III, Statistics*, as cited by Clark and Haswell 1967.

CHISHOLM, M., 1962. *Rural settlement and land use*, London.

CHRISTIANSEN-WENIGER, D. F., 1970. *Ackerbauformen im Mittelmeerraum und Nahen Osten dargestellt am Beispeil der Türkei*, Frankfurt am Main.

CLARK, C. and HASWELL, M., 1967. *The economics of subsistence agriculture*, London.

CUINET, V., 1892. *La Turquie d'Asie. Géographie Administrative, Vol. 2*, Paris.

FOOD AND AGRICULTURE ORGANIZATION (U.N.), 1957. *Nutritional studies: Calorie requirements* No. 15.

HIGGS, E. S. and VITA-FINZI, C., 1970. "Prehistoric economy in the Mount Carmel area of Palestine: Site catchment analysis", *PPS* 36, 1–37.

1972. "Prehistoric economies: a territorial approach", in Higgs, E. S. ed. *Papers in Economic Prehistory*, Cambridge.

KÖY İŞLERİ BAKANLIĞI, 1966. *Köy Envanter Etüdlerine Göre: Elazığ*. K.İ.B. Yayinlari: 44, Konya.

MEDICAL RESEARCH COUNCIL, 1960. *The Composition of Foods*, London.

MINISTRY OF AGRICULTURE OF THE REPUBLIC OF TURKEY, 1968. *Trends in Turkish Agriculture. Graphics and statistics 1938–66*, Ministry of Agriculture Planning and Research Organization Publication No. 31, Ankara.

ODUM, E. P., 1963. *Ecology*, New York.

SCHIEMANN, E., 1932. *Entstehung der Kulturpflanzen* (Vol. III of *Handbuch der Vererbungswissenschaft*), Berlin.

U.S. DEPT. OF AGRICULTURE, 1960/1. *Food balances in foreign countries*, U.S.D.A. FAS-M 108, II.

YUDKIN, J., 1969. "Archaeology and the nutritionist", in Ucko, P. J. and Dimbleby, G. W. eds. *The domestication and exploitation of plant and animals*, London.

WEBLEY, D., 1972. "Soils and site location in prehistoric Palestine", in Higgs, E. S. ed. *Papers in economic prehistory*, Cambridge.

ZOHARY, D., 1969. "The progenitors of wheat and barley in relation to agricultural dispersal in the Old World", in Ucko, P. J. and Dimbleby, G. W. eds. *The domestication and exploitation of plant and animals*, London.

Appendix 6.

CROP HUSBANDRY AND FOOD PRODUCTION: MODERN BASIS FOR THE INTERPRETATION OF PLANT REMAINS

By GORDON HILLMAN

The full analysis of the initial and most exhaustive of our studies of present-day agriculture at Aşvan could not be completed in time for the present volume. It seemed relevant, however, to present a brief outline of some of the principles involved and the data collected.

Samples of vegetable remains represent a body of information which is concerned (in part, at least) with human manipulations of plant resources. These plants may have functioned as foods, fuels, building-timber, tools, dyes, drugs, cosmetics or as decorations. The compounded information may, further, suggest certain forms of ancient economy, though quantification of the data at a level representative of the settlement as a whole is rarely possible. Any such inferences can, however, only exist within the realms of one's own familiarity with equivalent modern situations (or, less consistently, historical situations). If our deductions here are to be repeatable, our present-day (or historical) models must be defined: it is not sufficient to have hazy analogues lurking in the data banks of our subconscious.

A. THE ARCHAEOLOGICAL SITUATION

Given an adequate reference collection of seeds and woods, the species-composition of a sample of plant remains can generally be determined. For agricultural economies, we are then faced with the interpretation of these identifications firstly, in terms of crop husbandry practices (e.g. use of irrigation), secondly, in terms of processing sequences applied to the harvested crops and, thirdly, in terms of the uses to which these plant products were put. Crudely, the question we are asking is – what does a particular sample of plant remains represent in terms of human activities?

It is reasonable to expect that the husbandry and processing sequences which were applied to specific crops affected the composition of the resulting products. The use which was originally intended for these products will, further, not only have influenced their composition, but will have determined the sort of village context in which they were deposited. The relationship between (a) the composition of archaeological samples of such products and (b) human activities, may therefore be direct, or may be indirectly indicated via the stratigraphic association of the parent deposit with some structure that can be identified in terms of human functions. (See Dennell, 1972, for some examples from archaeological contexts here.)

The problem, however, is to relate this sample composition to human activities without resort to an excess of untestable intuition. See Figs. 1 and 2.

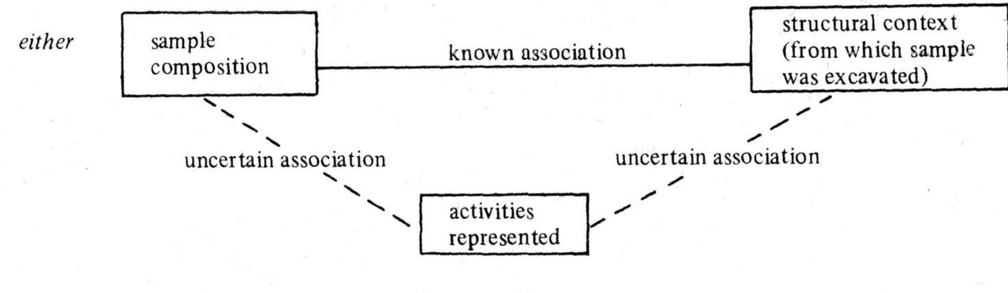

FIG.1.

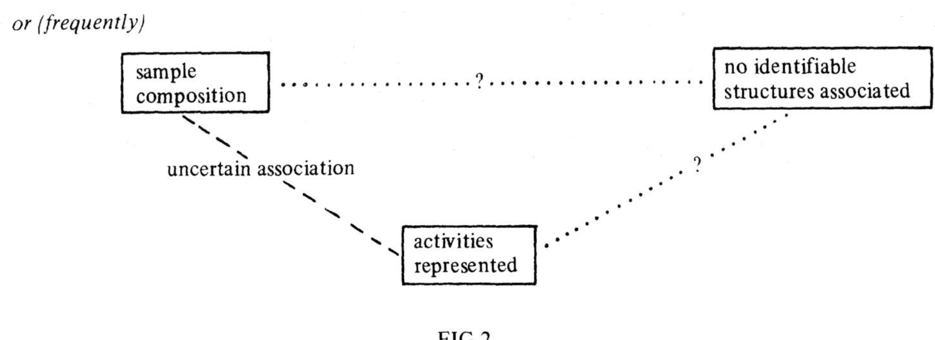

FIG.2.

B. THE MODERN SITUATION

Within a functioning, agricultural settlement, samples of products and by-products can be taken at each step of defined, crop-processing sequences performed, in turn, in defined village contexts. For each sample, information can also be gathered on the types of husbandry which were applied in the production of that particular batch of grain. The composition of these samples can subsequently be determined (given an adequate reference collection of weed seeds), thereby providing us with the set of associations indicated in Fig. 3.

If there proves to be significant correlation between variation in sample composition and, say crop processing stage, then we have a defined base for interpreting samples of plant remains (of similar composition) in terms of equivalent processes. At the very least, the basis of our reasoning is clear and as such, more easily tested by others. Further, if the distribution of these processes and their products shows significant association with specific context types, then

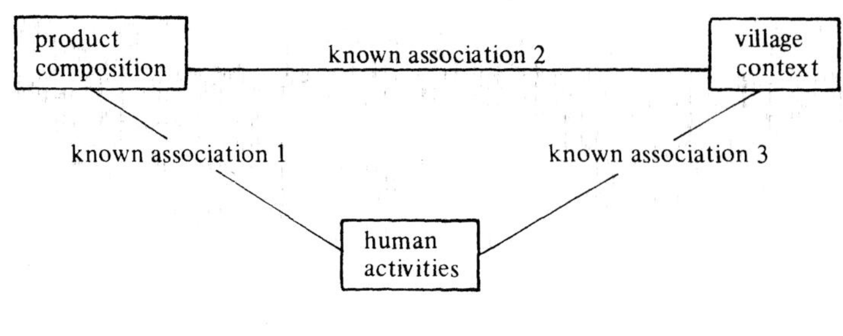

FIG.3.

we have additional grounds for suggesting the range of human activities which is represented by archaeological samples of similar composition and derived from similar structural contexts.

AŞVAN: DATA COLLECTED

Starting in 1970, we undertook a programme of sample and data collection as outlined under "modern situation" above.

Association 1 (see Fig. 3)

Over 110 samples of 2 kg. were selected from set stages of the traditional, grain-processing sequences being applied to the various crops grown by Aşvan village. (See App. 1, p. 237, for a list of the crops involved here.) Every sample was accompanied by data concerning the husbandry practices utilized in producing that specific batch of grain, in particular, data on those practices likely to have affected composition of the product. (The sort of husbandry factors relevant here included intensity of irrigation, manuring, existence of fallow in the preceding year, cereal harvesting methods and cutting heights and the form of threshing applied.) The intended use(s) of the product was also noted in each case.[1]

During the first season, we concentrated primarily on collecting samples which could be used to test apparent correlations between product-composition and variations in irrigation intensity, harvesting height and sieving practices.[2] In the subsequent two seasons, we are able to sample for most of the remaining aspects, though a few gaps still exist.

In the case of the wheats, well over thirty different classes of product were generated by the major processing sequences applied to threshed crops within the village. (Somewhat similar sequences were applied to most other grain crops.) Many of these products were then subjected to secondary sequences of manipulations, and recycling of certain components was common. The more complex tangles of this sort were not sampled as there was little hope of unravelling – or even recognizing – equivalent situations in archaeological contexts. Despite this, a rather complex sampling-framework was unavoidable.

Sample composition is defined here firstly, in terms of the frequencies (per unit kg. of grain) of each of the weed seed contaminants (well over fifty different species are present in some samples) and secondly, in terms of the frequency-distribution of grain-size of the crop itself. As the first step here, all samples were crudely sorted by a team of Aşvan village girls (under our supervision), and most were size-graded using test sieves. (Final sorting and identification of these samples is currently in progress at Ankara.)

Association 2 (product composition v.v. village context)

Food-storage contexts received sampling priority here firstly, because storage

---

[1] I should like here, to thank Miss Behin Aksoy for patiently translating for me during this first season when I was without any Turkish. (Well over an hour was spent in interviewing each farmer concerned in this study.)

[2] Several forms of goat-gut sieve were used at different stages of grain-processing and we sampled in respect of each of them.

products have a good chance of being represented among plant remains and secondly, because storage contexts are very easily sampled. Oven- and hearth-contents (post-firing) were our next priority and a few samples were collected. Their relevance here is that anything which survives burning represents (by virtue of having become carbonized) a class of material that is capable of surviving in archaeological contexts (in dryer climates, at least). Time did not permit work in this section to progress very far, though further contexts, such as middens, may well be sampled (via water sieving) this season (1973).

Association 3 (activities v.v. contexts)

The levels of association of human activities (particularly subsistence activities) with structurally definable contexts have been studied by Hall *et al.* and by Weinstein (see pp. 245–269 and 271–6 in this volume).

Effort is at present being concentrated on the analysis of "association 1" (see Fig. 3) as this is where data are most complete. If there is, in fact, any significant correlation between product composition and major husbandry- or processing-practices like irrigation and grain-sieving, then the number and distribution of my samples should enable me to demonstrate this correlation in repeatable terms, terms which are then usable in the interpretation of samples of plant remains of similar composition.

BIBLIOGRAPHY

DENNELL, R. W., 1972. "The interpretation of plant remains: Bulgaria", in Higgs, E. S. (ed.) *Papers in economic prehistory*, Cambridge.

Bibliography

1968 Summer Work (Middle East Technical University Keban Project Publications 1,1). Ankara, Middle East Technical University 1970

Akkermans, P.M.M.G., Schwartz, G.M. 2003: *The Archaeology of Syria*. Cambridge, Cambridge University Press

Aksoy, B., Diamant, S. 1973: 'Çayboyu' *Anatolian Studies* 23: 97–108. http://dx.doi.org/10.2307/3642532

Aschenbrenner, S.E., Cooke, S.R.B. 1978: 'Screening and gravity concentration: recovery of small-scale remains' in G. Rapp, S.E. Aschenbrenner (eds), *Excavations at Nichoria in S.W. Greece*. Minneapolis, University of Minnesota Press: 156–65

Baird, D. 2004: 'Settlement expansion on the Konya plain, Anatolia: 5th–7th centuries A.D.' in H. Bowden, L. Lavan, C. Machado (eds), *Recent Research in the Late Antique Countryside*. Leiden, Brill: 219–46. http://dx.doi.org/10.1163/22134522-90000026

Balossi-Restelli, F. 2012: 'The beginning of the Late Chalcolithic occupation at Arslantepe, Malatya', in C. Marro (ed.), *After the Ubaid: Interpreting Change from the Caucasus to Mesopotamia at the Dawn of Urban Civilization (4500–3500 BC)*. Paris, De Boccard: 235–69

Bar-Matthews, M., Ayalon, A., Kaufman, A. 1998: 'Middle to Late Holocene (6500 yr. period) palaeoclimate in the eastern Mediterranean region from stable isotopic composition of speleothems from Soreq Cave, Israel' in A. Issar, N. Brown (eds), *Water, Environment and Society in Times of Climate Change*. Dordrecht/Boston/London, Kluwer Academic Publishers: 203–14. http://dx.doi.org/10.1007/978-94-017-3659-6_9

Bartosiewicz, L. 2010: 'Herding in period VI A. Development and changes from period VII' in M. Frangipane (ed.), *Economic Centralisation in Formative States. The Archaeological Reconstruction of the Economic System in Fourth Millennium Arslantepe*. Rome, Studi di Prehistoria Orientale: 119–48

Beach, T.P., Luzzadder-Beach, S. 2008: 'Geoarchaeology and aggradation around Kinet Höyük, an archaeological mound in the eastern Mediterranean, Turkey' *Geomorphology* 101: 416–28. http://dx.doi.org/10.1016/j.geomorph.2007.04.025

Belisario, M.V., Follieri, M., Sadori, L. 1994: 'Nuovi dati archeobotanici sulla coltivazione di *Vitis vinifera L.* ad Arslantepe (Malatya, Turchia)' in L. Milano (ed.), *Drinking in Ancient Societies. History and Culture of Drinks in the Ancient Near East*. Padova, Sargon: 77–90

Bending, J. 2007: 'The archaeobotanical assemblages' in N. Postgate, D. Thomas (eds), *Excavations at Kilise Tepe, 1994–1998: From Bronze Age to Byzantine in Western Cilicia*. Cambridge, British Institute at Ankara/McDonald Institute for Archaeological Research, University of Cambridge: 583–95

Bieniek, A. 2002: 'Archaeobotanical analysis of some early Neolithic settlements in the Kujawy region, central Poland, with potential plant gathering activities emphasised' *Vegetation History and Archaeobotany* 11: 33–40. http://dx.doi.org/10.1007/s003340200004

Bieniek, A., Pokorný, P. 2005: 'A new find of macrofossils of feather grass (Stipa) in an Early Bronze Age storage pit at Vliněves, Czech Republic: local implications and possible interpretation in a central European context' *Vegetation History and Archaeobotany* 14: 295–302. http://dx.doi.org/10.1007/s00334-005-0076-9

Boardman, S., Jones, G.E.M. 1990: 'Experiments on the effects of charring on cereal plant components' *Journal of Archaeological Science* 17: 1–12. http://dx.doi.org/10.1016/0305-4403(90)90012-T

Bogaard, A.C, Charles, M., Livarda, A., Ergun, M., Filipovic, D., Jones, G. 2013: 'The archaeobotany of mid–later Neolithic occupation levels at Çatalhöyük' in I. Hodder (ed.), *Humans and Landscapes of Çatalhöyük: Reports from the 2000–2008 Seasons*. London/Los Angeles, British Institute at Ankara /Cotsen Institute of Archaeology, University of California: 93–128

Bogaard, A.C., Hodgson, J.G., Wilson, P.J., Band, S.R. 1998: 'An index of weed size for assessing the productivity of ancient crop fields' *Vegetation History and Archaeobotany* 7: 17–23. http://dx.doi.org/10.1007/BF01393414

Bogaard, A.C., Palmer, C., Jones, G., Charles, M., Hodgson, J.G. 1999: 'A FIBS approach to the use of weed ecology for archaeobotanical recognition of crop rotation' *Journal of Archaeological Science* 26: 1211–24. http://dx.doi.org/10.1006/jasc.1998.0364

Braidwood, R.J., Çambel, H., Lawrence, B., Redman, C.L., Stewart, R.B. 1974: 'Beginnings of village-farming communities in southeastern Turkey – 1972' *Proceedings of the National Academy of Sciences of the United States of America* 71.2: 568–72. http://dx.doi.org/10.1073/pnas.71.2.568

Bryce, T.R. 1999: *The Kingdom of the Hittites*. Oxford, Oxford University Press

Burney, C.A. 1966: 'A first season of excavations at the Urartian citadel of Kayalıdere' *Anatolian Studies* 16: 55–111. http://dx.doi.org/10.2307/3642479

Butzer, K.W. 1982: *Archaeology as Human Ecology: Method and Theory for a Contextual Approach*. Cambridge, Cambridge University Press. http://dx.doi.org/10.1017/CBO9780511558245

Casana, J. 2008: 'Mediterranean valleys revisited: linking soil erosion, land use and climate variability in the northern Levant' *Geomorphology* 101: 429–42. http://dx.doi.org/10.1016/j.geomorph.2007.04.031

Charles, M. 1998: 'Fodder from dung: the recognition and interpretation of dung-derived plant material from archaeological sites' *Environmental Archaeology* 1: 111–22. http://dx.doi.org/10.1179/env.1996.1.1.111

Charles, M., Bogaard, A.C. 2004: 'Identifying livestock diet from charred plant remains: a Neolithic case study from southern Turkmenistan' in J. Davis, M. Fabis, I. Mainland, M. Richards, R. Thomas (eds), *Diet and Health in Past Animal Populations: Current Research and Future Directions*. Oxford, Oxbow Books: 93–103

Charles, M., Jones, G., Hodgson, J.G. 1997: 'FIBS in archaeobotany: functional interpretation of weed floras in relation to husbandry practices' *Journal of Archaeological Science* 24: 1151–61. http://dx.doi.org/10.1006/jasc.1997.0194

Coles, J. 1973: *Archaeology by Experiment*. London, Routledge

Colledge, S. 2001a: *Plant Exploitation on Epipalaeolithic and Early Neolithic sites in the Levant*. Oxford, British Archaeological Reports

— 2001b: 'Final report on the archaeobotanical analyses' in R.J. Matthews, N. Postgate (eds), *Contextual Analysis of the Use of Space at Two Near Eastern Bronze Age Sites*. http://archaeologydataservice.ac.uk/archives/view/TellBrak/

Collins, P.E.F., Rust, D.J., Salih Bayraktutan, M., Turner, S.D. 2005: 'Fluvial stratigraphy and palaeoenvironments in the Pasinler Basin, eastern Turkey' *Quaternary International* 140–41: 121–34. http://dx.doi.org/10.1016/j.quaint.2005.05.016

Conti, A.M., Persiani, C. 1993: 'When worlds collide. Cultural developments in eastern Anatolia in the Early Bronze Age' in M. Frangipane, H. Hauptmann, M. Liverani, P. Matthiae, M. Mellink (eds), Between the Rivers and Over the Mountains (Archaeologica Anatolica et Mesopotamica Alba Palmieri Dedicata). Rome, Universita di Roma 'La Sapienza': 361–413

Dadandi, M.Y., Kökdil, G., İlçim, A., Özbilgin, B. 2009: 'Seed macro- and micro-morphology of the selected nigella (*Ranunculaceae*) taxa from Turkey and their systematic significance' *Biologia* 64: 261–70. http://dx.doi.org/10.2478/s11756-009-0030-x

Dalfes, H.N., Kulka, G., Weiss, H. (eds) 1997: *Climate Change in the Third Milllennium BC: Its Impact on Old World Social Systems*. Berlin, Springer

Davis, E.M., Wesolowsky, A.B. 1975: 'The Izum: a simple water separation device' *Journal of Field Archaeology* 2: 271–73

Davis, P. 1965–1985: *Flora of Turkey* 1–9. Edinburgh, Edinburgh University Press

Davis, P., Miller, R., Tan, K. 1988: *Flora of Turkey* 10. Edinburgh, Edinburgh University Press

De Moulins, D. 1997: *Agricultural Changes at Euphrates and Steppe Sites in the mid-8th to the 6th Millennium B.C.* Oxford, British Archaeological Reports

Decker, M. 2009: 'Plants and progress: rethinking the Islamic agricultural revolution' *Journal of World History* 20.2: 187–206. https://doi.org/10.1353/jwh.0.0058

Diamant, S. 1974: 'Çayboyu' in *METU Keban Project 1971 Activities*. Ankara, Middle East Technical University: 48–49

— 1979: 'A short history of archaeological sieving at Franchthi Cave, Greece' *Journal of Field Archaeology* 6: 203–17. http://dx.doi.org/10.1179/009346979791489366

Doomed by the Dam. A survey of the monuments threatened by the creation of the Keban dam flood area. Elazığ 18–29 October 1966. Faculty of Architecture, Department of Restoration, Middle East Technical University, Ankara 1967

Dusar, B., Verstraeten, G., Notebaert, B., Bakker, J. 2011: 'Holocene environmental change and its impact on sediment dynamics in the eastern Mediterranean' *Earth-Science Reviews* 108: 137–57. http://dx.doi.org/10.1016/j.earscirev.2011.06.006

England, A., Eastwood, W.J., Roberts, N., Turner, R., Haldon, J.F. 2008: 'Historical landscape change in Cappadocia (central Turkey): a palaeoecological investigation of annually laminated sediments from Nar Lake' *The Holocene* 18: 1229–45. http://dx.doi.org/10.1177/0959683608096598

Erskine, W., El, A.F. 1993: 'Rainfall and temperature effects of lentil (*Lens culinaris*) seed yield in Mediterranean environments' *Journal of Agricultural Science* 121: 347–54. http://dx.doi.org/10.1017/S0021859600085543

Ertuğ, F. 2000: 'An ethnobotanical study in central Anatolia (Turkey)' *Economic Botany* 54: 155–82. http://dx.doi.org/10.1007/BF02907820

Fairbridge, R., Erol, O., Karaca, M., Yilmaz, Y. 1997: 'Background to mid-holocene climate change in Anatolia and adjacent regions' in H.N. Dalfes, G. Kulka, H. Weiss (eds), *Third Millennium BC Climate Change and Old World Collapse* (NATO ASI Series. Global Environmental Change 49). Berlin, Springer: 595–610

Fairbairn, A.S., Martinoli, D., Butler, A., Hillman, G.C. 2007: 'Wild plant seed storage at Neolithic Çatalhöyük, Turkey' *Vegetation History and Archaeobotany* 16: 467–79. http://dx.doi.org/10.1007/s00334-006-0069-3

Fairbairn, A.S., Weiss, E. (eds) 2009: *From Foragers to Farmers: Papers in Honour of Gordon C. Hillman*. Oxford, Oxbow Books

Frangipane, M. 2000: 'The Late Chalcolithic/EB I sequence at Arslantepe. Chronological and cultural remarks from a frontier site' in C. Marro, H. Hauptmann (eds), *Chronologies des pays du Caucase et de l'Euphrate aux IVe et IIIe millénaires*. Paris, Institut français d'études anatoliennes d'Istanbul: 439–71

— 2001: 'Centralization processes in Greater Mesopotamia. Uruk "expansion" as the climax of systemic interactions among areas of the Greater Mesopotamian region' in M. Rothman (ed.), *Uruk Mesopotamia and its Neighbors. Cross-cultural Interactions in the Era of State Formation*. Santa Fe, School for Advanced Research Press: 307–47

— 2003: 'Developments in fourth millennium public architecture in the Malatya plain: from simple tripartite to complex and bipartite pattern' in H. Hauptman, M. Ozdogan (eds), *From Primary Villages to Cities: Essays in Honour of Ufuk Esin*. Istanbul, Arkeoloji ve Sanat Yayınevi: 147–69

— 2010: 'Politics, economy and political economy in early centralised societies. Theoretical debate and archaeological evidence' in Frangipane, M. (ed.), *Economic Centralisation in Formative States. The Archaeological Reconstruction of the Economic System in Fourth Millennium Arslantepe*. Rome, Studi di Prehistoria Orientale: 11–22

— 2011: 'Arslantepe-Malatya: a prehistoric and early historic center in eastern Anatolia' in G. McMahon, S. Steadman (eds), *The Oxford Handbook of Ancient Anatolia (10,000–323 BCE)*. Oxford, Oxford University Press

— 2012: 'The collapse of the 4th millennium centralised system at Arslantepe and the far-reaching changes in third millennium societies' *Origini* 34: 237–60

French, D.H. 1970: '1968 Aşvan excavations. Preliminary report' in *1968 Summer Work* (Middle East Technical University Keban Project Publications 1,1). Ankara, Middle East Technical University: 53–60

— 1971a: '1969 Aşvan excavations' in *1969 Summer Work* (Middle East Technical University Keban Project Publications 1,2). Ankara, Middle East Technical University: 21–37

— 1971b: 'An experiment in water-sieving' *Anatolian Studies* 21: 59–64. http://dx.doi.org/10.2307/3642629

— 1972: 'Aşvan excavations 1970' in *METU Keban Project 1970 Activities*. Ankara, Middle East Technical University: 53–60

— (ed.) 1973a: 'Aşvan 1968–1972: an interim report' *Anatolian Studies* 23: 71–307. http://dx.doi.org/10.1017/S0066154600003550

— 1973b: 'Aşvan 1968–1972: the excavations' in D.H. French (ed.), 'Aşvan 1968–1972' *Anatolian Studies* 23: 73–91. http://dx.doi.org/10.2307/3642530

— 1973c: 'Asvan Project' in D.H. French (ed.), 'Aşvan 1968–1972' *Anatolian Studies* 23: 191–96. https://doi.org/10.2307/3642539

French, D.H., Hillman, G.C., Payne, S., Payne, R.J. 1972: 'Excavations at Can Hasan III, 1969–1970' in E.S. Higgs (ed.), *Papers in Economic Prehistory*. Cambridge, Cambridge University Press: 181–90

Fuller, D.Q. 2000: *The Emergence of Agricultural Societies in South India: Botanical and Archaeological Perspectives*. PhD thesis, University of Cambridge

Fuller, D.Q., Harvey, E.L. 2006: 'The archaeobotany of Indian pulses: identification, processing and evidence for cultivation' *Environmental Archaeology* 11: 219–46. http://dx.doi.org/10.1179/174963106x123232

Fuller, D.Q., Stevens, C.J., McClatchie, M. 2014: 'Routine activities, tertiary refuse and labour organisation: social inferences from everyday archaeobotany' in M. Madella, C. Lancelotti, M. Savard (eds), *Ancient Plants and People, Contemporary Trends in Archaeology*. Tucson, University of Arizona Press: 174–217

Goddard, J., Nesbitt, M. 1997: 'Why draw seeds? Illustrating archaeobotany' in S. Goddard (ed.), *Graphic Archaeology* 1997: 13–21

Gökgöl, M. 1935: *Türkiye Buğdayları (Die Türkischen Weizen)* 1. Istanbul, Tan Matbaası

— 1939: *Türkiye Buğdayları (Die Türkischen Weizen)* 2. Istanbul, Tan Matbaası

— 1941: 'Über die Genzentrentheorie und den Ursprung der Weizen' *Zeitschrift für Pflanzenzüchtung* 23: 526–78
— 1955: *Buğdayların Tasnıf Anahtarı*. Istanbul, Ziraat Vekaleti Yayın
Griffin, E.A. 1980: 'The Middle and Late Bronze Age pottery' in M.N. van Loon (ed.), *Korucutepe* 3. *Final Report on the Excavations of the Universities of Chicago, California (Los Angeles) and Amsterdam in the Keban Reservoir, Eastern Anatolia, 1968–1970*. Amsterdam, North-Holland Publishing Co.: 3–110
Güner, A. 2001: *Flora of Turkey* 11. Edinburgh, Edinburgh University Press
Haldon J., Roberts, N., Izdebski, A., Fleitmann, D., McCormick, M., Cassis, M., Doonan, O., Eastwood, W., Elton, H., Ladstätter, S., Manning, J., Newhard, J., Nicoll, K., Telelis, I., Xoplaki, E. 2014: 'The climate and environment of Byzantine Anatolia: integrating science, history, and archaeology' *Journal of Interdisciplinary History* 45: 113–61. http://dx.doi.org/10.1162/JINH_a_00682
Hall, G., McBride, S., Riddell, A. 1973: 'Architectural study' in D.H. French (ed.), 'Aşvan 1968–1972' *Anatolian Studies* 2: 245–69. http://dx.doi.org/10.2307/3642544
Hansen, J.M. 1991: *The Palaeoethnobotany of Franchthi Cave*. Bloomington, Indiana University Press
Harlan, J.R., Zohary, D. 1966: 'Distribution of wild wheats and barley' *Science* 153: 1074–80. http://dx.doi.org/10.1126/science.153.3740.1074
Hastorf, C.A. 1996: 'Botanical archive report 1996' in *Çatalhöyük 1996 Archive Report*. http://www.catalhoyuk.com/archive_reports/1996
— 1999: 'Recent research in palaeoethnobotany' *Journal of Archaeological Research* 1: 55–103. http://dx.doi.org/10.1007/BF02446085
Hastorf, C.A., Popper, V.S. (eds) 1988: *Current Palaeoethnobotany: Analytical Methods and Cultural Interpretations of Archaeological Plant Remains*. Chicago, Chicago University Press
Heiss, A.G., Kropf, M., Sontag, S., Weber, A. 2011: 'Seed morphology of *Nigella* sp. (Ranunculaceae): identification, diagnostic traits, and their potential phylogenetic relevance' *International Journal of Plant Sciences* 172: 267–84. http://dx.doi.org/10.1086/657676
Helbaek, H. 1952: 'Spelt (*Triticum spelta L.*) in Bronze Age Denmark' *Acta Archaeologica* (Copenhagen) 23: 97–107
— 1970: 'The plant husbandry of Hacılar' in J. Mellart (ed.), *Excavations at Hacilar* 1. Edinburgh, Edinburgh University Press: 189–244
Helms, S. 1972: 'Taşkun Mevkii (N 52/1)' in *METU Keban Project 1970 Activities*. Ankara, Middle East Technical University: 60–62
Heun, M., Schäfer-Pregl, R., Klawan, D., Castagna, R., Accerbi, M., Borghi, B., Salamini, F. 1997: 'Site of einkorn wheat domestication identified by DNA fingerprinting' *Science* 278: 1312–14. http://dx.doi.org/10.1126/science.278.5341.1312
Hillman, G.C. 1973a: 'Agricultural resources and settlement in the Aşvan region' *Anatolian Studies* 23: 217–24 (= appendix 4 in this volume). http://dx.doi.org/10.2307/3642541
— 1973b: 'Agricultural productivity and past population potential at Aşvan' *Anatolian Studies* 23: 225–40 (= appendix 5 in this volume). http://dx.doi.org/10.2307/3642542
— 1973c: 'Crop husbandry and food production: modern models for the interpretation of plant remains' *Anatolian Studies* 23: 241–44 (= appendix 6 in this volume). http://dx.doi.org/10.2307/3642543
— 1978: 'On the origins of domestic rye – *Secale cereale*: the finds from aceramic Can Hasan III in Turkey' *Anatolian Studies* 28: 157–74. http://dx.doi.org/10.2307/3642748
— 1981: 'Reconstructing crop husbandry practices from charred remains of crops' in R. Mercer (ed.), *Farming Practice in British Prehistory*. Edinburgh, Edinburgh University Press: 123–61
— 1984a: 'Interpretation of archaeological plant remains: the application of ethnographic models from Turkey' in W. Van Zeist, W.A. Casparie (eds), *Plants and Ancient Man – Studies in Paleaoethnobotany*. Rotterdam, Balkema: 1–41
— 1984b: 'Traditional husbandry and processing of archaic cereals in modern times: part I, the glume-wheats' *Bulletin on Sumerian Agriculture* 1: 114–52
— 1985: 'Traditional husbandry and processing of archaic cereals in modern times: part II, the free-threshing wheats' *Bulletin on Sumerian Agriculture* 2: 1–31
— 1991: 'Phytosociology and ancient weed floras: taking account of taphonomy and changes in cultivation methods' in D.R. Harris (ed.), *Modelling Ecological Changes: Perspectives from Neoecology, Palaeoecology and Environmental Ecology*. London, Institute of Archaeology, University College London: 27–40
— 2000: 'The plant food economy of Abu Hureyra 1 and 2' in A.M.T. Moore, G.C. Hillman, A.J. Legge (eds), *Village on the Euphrates. From Foraging to Farming at Abu Hureyra*. Oxford, Oxford University Press: 327–98

— 2001 'Archaeology, Percival, and the problems of identifying wheat remains' in P.D.S. Caligari, P.E. Brandham (eds), *Wheat Taxonomy: The Legacy of John Percival* (Linnean Special Issue 3). London, Linnean Society: 27–36

Hillman, G.C., Mason, S., de Moulins, D., Nesbitt, M. 1996: 'Identification of archaeological remains of wheat, the 1992 London workshop' *Circea* 12: 195–209

Hjelmquist, H. 1970: 'Some carbonised seeds and fruits from the necropolis of Salamis' in V. Karageorghis (ed.), *Salamis* 4. *Excavations in the Necropolis of Salamis* II. Nicosia: Department of Antiquities: 329–35

Hole, F., Flannery, K.V., Neely, J. 1969: *Prehistory and Human Ecology of the Deh Luran Plain: An Early Village Sequence from Khuzistan, Iran*. Ann Arbor, Museum of Anthropological Archaeology

Hopf, M. 1983: 'Jericho plant remains' in K.M. Kenyon, T.A. Holland (eds), *Excavations at Jericho* 5. London, British School of Archaeology in Jerusalem: 576–621

Hubbard, R.N.L.B. 1980: 'Development of agriculture in Europe and the Near East: evidence from quantitative studies' *Economic Botany* 34: 51–67. http://dx.doi.org/10.1007/BF02859554

Hubbard, R.N.L.B., Clapham, A. 1992: 'Quantifying macroscopic plant remains' *Review of Palaeobotany and Palynology* 73: 117–32. http://dx.doi.org/10.1016/0034-6667(92)90050-Q

Hunshal, C.S., Balikai, R.B., Viswanath, D.P. 1990: '*Triticum dicoccum* – its performance in comparison with barley under salinity' *Journal of Maharashtra Agricultural Universities* 15: 376–77

Hunt, H.V., Vander Linden, M., Liu, X., Motuzaite-Matuzeviciute, G., Colledge, S., Jones, M.K. 2008: 'Millets across Eurasia: chronology and context of early records of the genera *Panicum* and *Setaria* from archaeological sites in the Old World' *Vegetation History and Archaeobotany* 17: 5–18. http://dx.doi.org/10.1007/s00334-008-0187-1

Jacomet, S. 1987: *Prähistorische Getreidefunde*. Basel, Botanisches Institut der Universität

— 2006: *Identification of Cereal Remains from Archaeological Sites* (2nd edition). Basel, IPAS

Janushevitch, Z.V., Nikolaenko, G.M., Kuzminova, N. 1985: 'La viticulture à Chersonèse de Tauride aux IVe–IIe s. av. n. è. d'après les recherches archéologiques et paléoethnobotaniques' *Revue Archéologique*: 115–22

Johnson, B.L. 1975: 'Identification of the apparent B-genome donor of wheat' *Canadian Journal of Genetics and Cytology* 17.1: 21–39. http://dx.doi.org/10.1139/g75-004

Jones, G.E.M. 1983a: 'The ethnoarchaeology of crop processing: seeds of a middle-range methodology' *Archaeological Review from Cambridge* 2: 17–26

— 1983b: *The Use of Ethnographic and Ecological Models in the Interpretation of Archaeological Plant Remains: Case Studies from Greece*. PhD thesis, University of Cambridge

— 1984: 'Interpretation of archaeological plant remains: ethnographic models from Greece' in W. Van Zeist, W.A. Casparie (eds), *Plants and Ancient Man – Studies in Paleaoethnobotany*. Rotterdam, Balkema: 43–61

— 1987: 'A statistical approach to the archaeological identification of crop processing' *Journal of Archaeological Science* 14: 311–23. http://dx.doi.org/10.1016/0305-4403(87)90019-7

Jones, G.E.M., Wardle, K., Halstead, P., Wardle, D. 1986: 'Crop storage at Assiros' *Scientific American* 254: 96–103. http://dx.doi.org/10.1038/scientificamerican0386-96

Jones, G.E.M., Halstead, P. 1995: 'Maslins, mixtures and monocrops: on the interpretation of archaeobotanical crop samples of heterogeneous composition' *Journal of Archaeological Science* 22: 103–14. http://dx.doi.org/10.1016/S0305-4403(95)80168-5

Jones, G.E.M., Valamoti, S.M., Charles, M. 2000a: 'Early crop diversity: a "new" glume wheat from northern Greece' *Vegetation History and Archaeobotany* 9: 133–46. http://dx.doi.org/10.1007/BF01299798

Jones, G.E.M., Bogaard, A.C., Charles, M., Hodgson, J.G. 2000b: 'Distinguishing the effects of agricultural practices relating to fertility and disturbance: a functional ecological approach in archaeobotany' *Journal of Archaeological Science* 27: 1073–84. http://dx.doi.org/10.1006/jasc.1999.0543

Jones, G.E.M., Valamoti, S.M. 2005: '*Lallemantia*, an imported or introduced oil plant in Bronze Age northern Greece' *Vegetation History and Archaeobotany* 14: 571–77. http://dx.doi.org/10.1007/s00334-005-0004-z

Jones, G.E.M., Charles, M., Bogaard, A.C., Hodgson, J.G. 2010: 'Crops and weeds: the role of weed functional ecology in the identification of crop husbandry methods' *Journal of Archaeological Science* 37: 70–77. http://dx.doi.org/10.1016/j.jas.2009.08.017

Jørgensen, G. 1979: 'A new contribution concerning the cultivation of spelt, *triticum spelta L.*, in prehistoric Denmark' in U. Körber-Grohne (ed.), *Festschrift Maria Hopf zum 65. Geburtstag*. Cologne, Rheinland-Verlag: 135–45

Kaniewski, D., Paulissen, E., De Laet, V., Dossche, K., Waelkens, M. 2007: 'A high resolution Late Holocene landscape ecological history inferred from an intramontane basin in the western Taurus mountains, Turkey' *Quaternary Science Reviews* 26: 2201–18. http://dx.doi.org/10.1016/j.quascirev.2007.04.015

Kelly-Buccellati, M. 1979: 'The outer Fertile Crescent culture: north-eastern connections of Syria and Palestine in the third millennium B.C.' *Ugarit-Forschungen* 11: 413–30

Kiguradze, T. 2003: 'On the origins of the Kura-Araxes cultural complex' in A.T. Smith, K.S. Rubinson (eds), *Archaeology in the Borderlands: Investigations in Caucasia and Beyond.* Los Angeles, Cotsen Institute of Archaeology, University of California: 38–94

Kilian, B., Ozkan, H., Walther, A., Kohl, J., Dagan, T., Salamini, F., Martin, W. 2007: 'Molecular diversity at 18 loci in 321 wild and 92 domesticate lines reveal no reduction of nucleotide diversity during *Triticum monococcum* (Einkorn) domestication: implications for the origin of agriculture' *Molecular Biology and Evolution* 24: 2657–68. http://dx.doi.org/10.1093/molbev/msm192

Körber-Grohne, U., Piening, U. 1980: 'Microstructure of the surfaces of carbonized and non-carbonized grains of cereals as observed in scanning electron and light microscopes as an additional aid in determining prehistoric findings' *Flora* 170: 189–228

Köroğlu, K. 2003: 'The transition from Bronze Age to Iron Age in eastern Anatolia' in B. Fischer, H. Genz, É. Jean, K. Köroglu (eds), *From Bronze to Iron Ages in Anatolia and its Neighbouring Regions.* Istanbul, Türk Eskiçağ Bilimleri Enstitüsü: 231–44

Kosina, R. 1980: 'Statistical analysis of the grain morphology of the present and fossil cereals' *Acta Societatis Botanicorum Poloniae* 49: 321–37. http://dx.doi.org/10.5586/asbp.1980.028

Kroll, H. 1979: 'Kulturpflanzen aus Dimini' in U. Körber-Grohne (ed.), *Festschrift Maria Hopf zum 65. Geburtstag.* Cologne, Rheinland-Verlag: 173–89

— 1983: 'Kastanas, die Pflanzenfunde: Ausgrabungen in einem Siedlungshügel der Bronze- und Eisenzeit Makedoniens 1975–1979' in B. Hänsel (ed.), *Prähistorische Archäologie in Südosteuropa.* Berlin, Spiess Verlag: 1–176

— 1999: 'Vor- und fruhgeschichtliche Weinreben – wild oder angebaut?' *Trierer Zeitschrift* 62: 151–53

Kuniholm, P.I. 1990: 'The archaeological record: evidence and non-evidence for climatic change' in S.K. Runcorn, J.-C. Pecker (eds), *The Earth's Climate and Variability of the Sun Over Recent Millennia.* London, Royal Society: 645–55

Küster, H. 1991: 'Phytosociology and archaeobotany' in D. Harris, K.D. Thomas (eds), *Modelling Ecological Changes: Perspectives from Neoecology, Palaeoecology and Environmental Ecology.* London, Institute of Archaeology, University College London: 17–26

Kuzucuoğlu, C., Marro, C. (eds) 2007: *Sociétés humaines et changement climatique à la fin du troisième millénaire: une crise a-t-elle eu lieu en Haute Mésopotamie*? Paris, De Boccard

Lancelotti, C. 2010: *Fueling Harappan Hearths: Human-Environment Interactions as Revealed by Fuel Exploitation and Use.* PhD thesis, University of Cambridge

Lemcke, G., Sturm, M. 1997: 'δ^{18}o and trace element measurements as proxy for the reconstruction of climate changes at lake Van (Turkey): preliminary results' in H.N. Dalfes, G. Kulka, H. Weiss (eds), *Third Millennium BC Climate Change and Old World Collapse* (NATO ASI Series. Global Environmental Change 49). Berlin, Springer: 653–78. http://dx.doi.org/10.1007/978-3-642-60616-8_29

Limp, W.F. 1974: 'Water separation and flotation processes' *Journal of Field Archaeology* 2: 119–23

Longford, C., Drinnan, A., Sagona, A.G. 2009: 'Archaeobotany of Sos Höyük, northeast Turkey' in A. Fairburn, S. O'Connor, B. Marwick (eds), *New Directions in Archaeological Science.* Canberra, Australian National University E Press: 121–36

Luo, M.C., Yang, Z.L., You, F.M., Kawahara, T., Waines, J.G., Dvorak, J. 2007: 'The structure of wild and domesticated emmer wheat populations, gene flow between them, and the site of emmer domestication' *Theoretical and Applied Genetics* 114: 947–59. http://dx.doi.org/10.1007/s00122-006-0474-0

Macqueen, J.G. 1986: *The Hittites, and their Contemporaries in Asia Minor.* London, Thames and Hudson

Marinova, E., Riehl, S. 2009: 'Carthamus species in the ancient Near East and south-east Europe: archaeobotanical evidence for their distribution and use as a source of oil' *Vegetation History and Archaeobotany* 18: 341–49. http://dx.doi.org/10.1007/s00334-009-0212-z

Marro, C. 1997: *La culture du Haut-Euphrate au Bronze Ancien. Essai d'interprétation à partir de la céramique peinte de Keban (Turquie).* Paris, Institut français d'études anatoliennes d'Istanbul

— 2005: 'Cultural duality in eastern Anatolia in late prehistory. The examples of the Araxes Basin in the Late Chalcolithic and the Upper Euphrates in the Early Bronze Age' *Archäologische Mitteilungen aus Iran und Turan* 37: 27–34

Marston, J.M., Miller, N.F. 2014: 'Intensive agriculture and land-use at Gordium, central Turkey' *Vegetation History and Archaeobotany* 23: 761–73. http://dx.doi.org/10.1007/s00334-014-0467-x

Martin, L. 2015: 'Plant economy and territory exploitation in the Alps during the Neolithic (5000–4200 cal bc): first results of archaeobotanical studies in the Valais (Switzerland)' *Vegetation History and Archaeobotany* 24: 63–73. http://dx.doi.org/10.1007/s00334-014-0490-y

Martinoli, D., Nesbitt, M. 2003: 'Plant stores at Pottery Neolithic Höyücek, southwest Turkey' *Anatolian Studies* 53: 17–32. http://dx.doi.org/10.2307/3643085

Masi, A., Sadori, L., Sabato, D. 2011: 'Environmental and social changes recorded in the charcoal remains of Arslantepe (Anatolia) from 3350 to 2000 years BC' in E. Badal, Y. Carrión, E. Grau, M. Macías, M. Ntinou (eds), *5th International Meeting of Charcoal Analysis*. Valencia, Sagvntvm Extra: 93–94

Mason, S., Nesbitt, M. 2009: 'Acorns as food in southeast Turkey: implications for past subsistence in southwest Asia' in A.S. Fairbairn, E. Weiss (eds), *From Foragers to Farmers: Papers in Honour of Gordon C. Hillman*. Oxford, Oxbow Books: 71–85

McIntosh, R.J., Tainter, J.A., McIntosh, S.K. 2000: 'Climate, history and human action' in R.J. McIntosh, J.A. Tainter, S.K. McIntosh (eds), *The Way the Wind Blows*. New York, Columbia University Press: 1–44

McNicoll, A.W. 1973: 'The Aşvan hoard: coins of two Cappadocian monarchs' in D.H. French (ed.), 'Aşvan 1968–1972' *Anatolian Studies* 23: 181–86. http://dx.doi.org/10.2307/3642537

— 1983: *Taşkun Kale: Keban Rescue Excavations, Eastern Anatolia*. London, British Institute of Archaeology at Ankara

Megaloudi, F. 2006: *Plants and Diet in Greece from Neolithic to Classic Periods: The Archaeobotanical Remains*. Oxford, Archaeopress

Migowski, C., Stein, M., Prasad, S., Negendank, J.F.W., Agnon, A. 2006: 'Holocene climate variability and cultural evolution in the Near East from the Dead Sea sedimentary record' *Quaternary Research* 66: 421–31. http://dx.doi.org/10.1016/j.yqres.2006.06.010

Miksicek, C.H. 1987: 'Formation processes of the archaeobotanical record' *Advances in Archaeological Method and Theory* 10: 211–47. http://dx.doi.org/10.1016/B978-0-12-003110-8.50007-4

Miller, N.F. 1984: 'The use of dung as fuel: an ethnographic example and an archaeological application' *Paleórient* 10: 71–79. http://dx.doi.org/10.3406/paleo.1984.941

— 1988: 'Ratios in palaeoethnobotanical analysis' in C.A. Hastorf, V.S. Popper (eds), *Current Palaeoethnobotany: Analytical Methods and Cultural Interpretations of Archaeological Plant Remains*. Chicago, Chicago University Press: 72–85

— 1991: 'The Near East' in W. Van Zeist, K. Wasylikowa, K.-E. Behre (eds), *Progress in Old World Palaeoethnobotany: A Retrospective View on the Occasion of 20 Years of the International Working Group for Palaeoethnobotany*. Rotterdam, Balkema: 133–57

— 1997: 'The macrobotanical evidence for vegetation in the Near East c. 18000/16000 BC to 4000 BC' *Paléorient* 23: 197–207. http://dx.doi.org/10.3406/paleo.1997.4661

— 1998: 'Patterns of agriculture and land use in medieval Gritille' in S. Redford (ed.), *The Archaeology of the Frontier in the Medieval Near East: Excavations at Gritille, Turkey*. Philadelphia, University of Pennsylvania Museum of Archaeology and Anthropology: 211–52

— 2008: 'Sweeter than wine? The use of the grape in early western Asia' *Antiquity* 82: 937–46. http://dx.doi.org/10.1017/S0003598X00097696

— 2010: *Botanical Aspects of Environment and Economy at Gordion, Turkey*. Philadelphia, University of Pennsylvania Museum of Archaeology and Anthropology

Miller, N.F., Marston, J.M. 2012: 'Archaeological fuel remains as indicators of ancient west Asian agropastoral and land-use systems' *Journal of Arid Environments* 86: 97–103. https://doi.org/10.1016/j.jaridenv.2011.11.021

Miller, N.F., Smart, T.L. 1984: 'Intentional burning of dung as fuel: a mechanism for the incorporation of charred seeds into the archaeological record' *Journal of Ethnobiology* 4: 15–28

Mitchell, S. 1980: *Aşvan Kale. The Hellenistic, Roman and Medieval Sites*. London, British Institute of Archaeology at Ankara

— 1993: *Anatolia. Land, Men, and Gods in Asia Minor* 1: *The Celts and the Impact of Roman Rule*. Oxford, Oxford University Press

— 1998: 'The Aşvan Project' in R. Matthews (ed.), *Anatolian Archaeology. Fifty Years' Work by the British Institute of Archaeology at Ankara*. London, British Institute of Archaeology at Ankara: 85–100

— 2015: 'Food, culture and environment in ancient Asia Minor' in J. Wilkins, R. Nadeau (eds), *A Companion to Food in the Ancient World*. Oxford, Wiley-Blackwell: 285–95

Mitchell, S., Katsari, C. (eds) 2005: *Patterns in the Economy of Roman Asia Minor*. Swansea, Classical Press of Wales

Mitford, T.B. 2017: *East of Asia Minor. Rome's Hidden Frontier*. Oxford, Oxford University Press

Müller, U. 2005: 'Norşuntepe and Lidar Höyük. Two examples for cultural change during the Early Iron Age' in A. Çilingiroglu, G. Darbyshire (eds), *Anatolian Iron Ages* 5. London, British Institute at Ankara: 107–14

Negrul, A.M. 1960: 'Archaeological findings of grape seeds' *Soviet Archaeology* 1: 111–19

Nesbitt, M. 1993: 'Ancient crop husbandry at Kaman-Kalehöyük: 1991 archaeobotanical report' in T. Mikasa (ed.), *Essays on Anatolian Archaeology* (Bulletin of the Middle Eastern Culture Center in Japan 7). Wiesbaden: Harrassowitz: 75–97

— 2006: *Identification Guide for Near Eastern Grass Seeds*. London, Institute of Archaeology, University College London

— 2016: 'Iron Age agriculture at Tille Höyük' in S. Blaylock (ed.), *Tille Hoyuk* 3.2. *The Iron Age: Pottery, Objects and Conclusions*. London, British Institute at Ankara: 369–94

Nesbitt, M., Samuel, D. 1996: 'From staple crop to extinction? The archaeology and history of the hulled wheats' in S. Padulosi, K. Hammer, J. Heller (eds), *Hulled Wheats*. Rome, International Plant Genetic Resources Institute: 41–100

Nesbitt, M., Summers, G.D. 1988: 'Some recent discoveries of millet (*Panicum miliaceum L.* and *Setaria italica (L.) P. Beauv.*) at excavations in Turkey and Iran' *Anatolian Studies* 38: 85–97. http://dx.doi.org/10.2307/3642844

Neumann, J., Parpola, S. 1987: 'Climatic change and the eleventh–tenth-century eclipse of Assyria and Babylonia' *Journal of Near Eastern Studies* 46: 161–82. http://dx.doi.org/10.1086/373244

Oleinikova, T.V. 1976: 'Water-holding capacity and drought resistance of wheat species and cultivars' *Trudy po Prikladnoi Botanike, Genetike i Seletskii* 57: 46–58

Özdoğan, M. 1977: *Aşagı Fırat Havzası. 1977 Yüzey Arastırmaları*. Istanbul, Middle East Technical University, Lower Euphrates Project Publications

— 2004: 'The Neolithic and the highlands of eastern Anatolia' in A.G. Sagona (ed.), *A View from the Highlands: Archaeological Studies in Honour of Charles Burney*. Leuven, Peeters: 23–34

Özkan, H., Brandolini, A., Schäfer-Pregl, R., Salamini, F. 2002: 'AFLP analysis of a collection of tetraploid wheats indicates the origin of emmer and hard wheat domestication in southeast Turkey' *Molecular Biology and Evolution* 19: 1797–801. http://dx.doi.org/10.1093/oxfordjournals.molbev.a004002

Palumbi, G. 2003: 'Red-black pottery: eastern Anatolian and Transcaucasian relationships around the mid-fourth millennium BC' *Ancient Near Eastern Studies* 40: 80–134. http://dx.doi.org/10.2143/ANES.40.0.562935

— 2010: 'Pastoral models and centralised animal husbandry. The case of Arslantepe' in M. Frangipane (ed.), *Economic Centralisation in Formative States. The Archaeological Reconstruction of the Economic System in 4th Millennium Arslantepe*. Rome, Studi di Prehistoria Orientale: 149–66

Payne, S. 1972: 'Partial recovery and sample bias: the results of some sieving experiments' in E.S. Higgs (ed.), *Papers in Economic Prehistory*. Cambridge, Cambridge University Press: 49–64

— 1973: 'Kill-off patterns in sheep and goats: the mandibles from Aşvan Kale' in D.H. French (ed.), 'Aşvan 1968–1972' *Anatolian Studies* 23: 281–303. http://dx.doi.org/10.2307/3642547

Pearsall, D.M. 1988: 'Interpreting the meaning of macro remains abundance: the impact of source and context' in C.A. Hastorf, V.S. Popper (eds), *Current Palaeoethnobotany: Analytical Methods and Cultural Interpretations of Archaeological Plant Remains*. Chicago, Chicago University Press: 97–118

— 1989: *Palaeoethnobotany: A Handbook of Procedures*. San Diego, Academic Press

— 2000: *Paleoethnobotany: A Handbook of Procedures* (2nd edition). New York, Academic Press

Peña-Chocarro, L. 1999: *Prehistoric Agriculture in Southern Spain during the Neolthic and Bronze Age: The Application of Ethnographic Models*. Oxford, Archaeopress

Popper, V.S. 1988: 'Selecting quantitative measures in palaeoethnobotany' in C.A. Hastorf, V.S. Popper (eds), *Current Palaeoethnobotany: Analytical Methods and Cultural Interpretations of Archaeological Plant Remains*. Chicago, Chicago University Press: 53–71

Procter, H.R. 1914: *The Making of Leather*. Cambridge, Cambridge University Press

Reale, O., Dirmeyer, P. 2000: 'Modeling the effects of vegetation on Mediterranean climate during the Roman classical period part I: climate history and model sensitivity' *Global and Planetary Change* 25: 163–84. http://dx.doi.org/10.1016/S0921-8181(00)00002-3

Reddy, S.N. 1997: 'If the threshing floor could speak: integration of agriculture and pastoralism during the Late Harappan in Gujarat, India' *Journal of Anthropological Archaeology* 16: 162–87. http://dx.doi.org/10.1006/jaar.1997.0308

— 2003: *Discerning Palates of the Past: An Ethnoarchaeological Study of Crop Cultivation and Plant usage in India*. Ann Arbor, International Monographs in Prehistory

Redford, S. 1998: *The Archaeology of the Frontier in the Medieval Near East: Excavations at Gritille, Turkey*. Philadelphia, University Museum Publications, University of Pennsylvania

Renfrew, J.M. 1970: 'Carbonised seeds and fruits from the necropolis of Salamis' in V. Karageorghis (ed.), *Salamis* 4. *Excavations in the Necropolis of Salamis* II. Nicosia, Department of Antiquities: 318–28

— 1973: *Palaeoethnobotany: The Prehistoric Food Plants of the Near East and Europe*. New York, Columbia University Press

Restelli, F.B., Sadori, L., Masi, A. 2010: 'Agriculture at Arslantepe at the end of the IV millennium BC. Did the centralised political institutions have an influence on farming practices?' in M. Frangipane (ed.), *Economic Centralisation in Formative States. The Archaeological Reconstruction of the Economic System in 4th Millennium Arslantepe*. Rome, Studi di Prehistoria Orientale: 103–18

Riehl, S. 1999: *Bronze Age Environment and Economy in the Troad: The Archaeobotany of Kumtepe and Troy*. Tübingen, Mo Vince

— 2009: 'Archaeobotanical evidence for the interrelationship of agricultural decision-making and climate change in the ancient Near East' *Quaternary International* 197: 93–114. http://dx.doi.org/10.1016/j.quaint.2007.08.005

— 2012: 'Variability in ancient Near Eastern environmental and agricultural development' *Journal of Arid Environments* 86: 113–21. http://dx.doi.org/10.1016/j.jaridenv.2011.09.014

Riehl, S., Nesbitt, M. 2003: 'Crops and cultivation in the Iron Age Near East: change or continuity?' in B. Fischer, H. Genz, É. Jean, K. Köroğlu (eds), *Identifing Changes: The Transition from Bronze to Iron Ages in Anatolia and its Neighbouring Regions*. Istanbul, Türk Eskiçağ Bilimleri Enstitüsü: 301–12

Rivera Núñez, R., Matilla Séiquer, G., Obón de Castro, C., Alcaraz Ariza, F. 2011a: *Plants and Humans in the Near East and the Caucasus* 1. *The Landscapes. The Plants: Ferns and Gymnosperms*. Murcia, Ediciones de la Unverisdad de Murcia

— 2011b: *Plants and Humans in the Near East and the Caucasus* 2. *The Plants: Angiosperms*. Murcia, Ediciones de la Unverisdad de Murcia

Robert, L. 1961: 'Lettres byzantines 2. Le combustible de Synnada' *Journal des Savants*: 115–166; reprinted in *Opera Minora Selecta* VII. Amsterdam 1990: 19–49

Roberts, N., Eastwood, W.J., Kuzucuoglu, C., Fiorentino, G., Caracuta, V. 2011: 'Climatic, vegetation and cultural change in the eastern Mediterranean during the mid-Holocene environmental transition' *The Holocene* 21: 147–62. http://dx.doi.org/10.1177/0959683610386819

Roberts, N., Reed, J.M., Leng, M.J., Kuzucuoğlu, C., Fontugne, M., Bertaux, J., Woldring, H., Bottema, S., Black, S., Hunt, E., Karabiyikoglu, M. 2001: 'The tempo of Holocene climatic change in the eastern Mediterranean region: new high-resolution crater-lake sediment data from central Turkey' *The Holocene* 11: 721–36. http://dx.doi.org/10.1191/09596830195744

Rosen, A.M. 2007: *Civilizing Climate: Social Responses to Climate Change in the Ancient Near East*. Lanham, Altamira Press

Rothman, M.S. 2003: 'Ripples in the stream: Transcaucasia-Anatolian interaction in the Murat/Euphrates Basin at the beginning of the third millennium BC' in A.T. Smith, K.S. Rubinson (eds), *Archaeology in the Borderlands: Investigations in Caucasia and Beyond*. Los Angeles, Cotsen Institute of Archaeology, University of California: 95–110

Rowton, M.B. 1967: 'The woodlands of ancient western Asia' *Journal of Near Eastern Studies* 26: 261–77. http://dx.doi.org/10.1086/371919

Russell, H.F. 1980: *Pre-Classical Pottery of Eastern Anatolia*. Oxford, British Institute of Archaeology at Ankara

Sadori, L., Susanna, F., Persiani, C. 2006: 'Archaeobotanical data and crop storage evidence from an Early Bronze Age 2 burnt house at Arslantepe, Malatya, Turkey' *Vegetation History and Archaeobotany* 15: 205–15. http://dx.doi.org/10.1007/s00334-005-0029-3

Sadori, L., Susanna, F., Restelli, F.B. 2008: 'Collapsed beams and wooden remains from a 3200 BC temple and palace at Arslantepe (Malatya, Turkey)' in G. Fiorentino, D. Magri (eds), *Charcoals from the Past: Cultural and Palaeoenvironmental Implications*. Oxford, British Archaeological Reports: 237–50

Sagona, A.G. (ed.) 1994: *The Aşvan Sites* 3. *Keban Rescue Excavations, Eastern Anatolia. The Early Bronze Age*. London, British Institute of Archaeology at Ankara

Sagona, A.G., Sagona, C. 2000: 'Excavations at Sos Hüyük 1998–2000: fifth preliminary report' *Ancient Near Eastern Studies* 37: 56–127. https://doi.org/10.2143/ANES.37.0.1082

Samuel, D. 2001: 'Archaeobotanical evidence and analysis' in S. Berthier (ed.), *Peuplement rural et aménagements hydroagricoles dans la moyenne vallée de l'Euphrate fin VIIe–XIXe siècle*. Damascus, Institut français d'études arabes de Damas: 343–481

Salih, B., Sipahi, T., Oybak-Dönmez, E. 2009: 'Ancient nigella seeds from Boyalı Höyük in north-central Turkey' *Journal of Ethnopharmacology* 124: 416–20. http://dx.doi.org/10.1016/j.jep.2009.05.039

Schiemann, E. 1948: *Weizen, Roggen, Gerste. Systematik, Geschichte, und Verwendung*. Jena, Fischer

Smith, A.T., Rubinson, K.S. (eds) 2003: *Archaeology in the Borderlands. Investigations in Caucasia and Beyond*. Los Angeles, Cotsen Institute

Solmaz, T., Dönmez, E. 2013: 'Archaeobotanical studies at the Urartian site of Ayanis, Van province, eastern Turkey' *Turkish Journal of Botany* 37: 282–96

Stevens, C.J. 2003: 'An investigation of agricultural consumption and production models for prehistoric and Roman Britain' *Environmental Archaeology* 8: 61–76. http://dx.doi.org/10.1179/env.2003.8.1.61

Stummer, A. 1911: 'Zur Urgeschichte der Rebe und des Weinbaues' *Mitteilungen der Anthropologischen Gesellschaft in Wien* 41: 283–96

TAY Project 1998–: *The Archaeological Settlements of Turkey*. http://www.tayproject.org/

Toll, M.S. 1988: 'Flotation sampling: problems and some solutions, with examples from the American southwest' in C.A. Hastorf, V.S. Popper (eds), *Current Palaeoethnobotany: Analytical Methods and Cultural Interpretations of Archaeological Plant Remains*. Chicago, Chicago University Press: 36–52

Tosun, O. 1953: *Türkiye Buğdaylarının Standardızasyonu Üzerinde Araştırmaları*. Ankara, Ankara Üniversitesi Ziraat Fakültesi Yayını

Townsend, C.C., Guest, E. (eds) 1966–1985: *Flora of Iraq*. Baghdad, Ministry of Agriculture and Agrarian Reform

Twiss, K.C., Bogaard, A., Bogdan, D., Carter, T., Charles, M.P., Farid, S., Russell, N., Stevanović, M., Yalman, E.N., Yeomans, L. 2008: 'Arson or accident? The burning of a Neolithic house at Çatalhöyük, Turkey' *Journal of Field Archaeology* 33: 41–57

Valamoti, S.M. 2004: *Plants and People in Late Neolithic and Early Bronze Age Northern Greece: An Archaeobotanical Investigation*. Oxford, Archaeopress

— 2009: 'Plant food ingredients and "recipes" from prehistoric Greece: the archaeobotanical evidence' in J.P. Morel, A.M. Mercuri (eds), *Plants and Culture. Seeds of the Cultural Heritage of Europe*. Bari, Centro Europeo per i Beni Culturali Ravello: 25–38

— 2013: 'Millet, the late comer: on the tracks of *Panicum miliaceum* in prehistoric Greece' *Archaeological and Anthropological Sciences* 8.1: 51–63. http://dx.doi.org/10.1007/s12520-013-0152-5

Valamoti, S.M., Charles, M. 2005: 'Distinguishing food from fodder through the study of charred plant remains: an experimental approach to dung-derived chaff' *Vegetation History and Archaeobotany* 14: 528–33. http://dx.doi.org/10.1007/s00334-005-0090-y

Van Driel-Murray, C. 2000: 'Leatherwork and skin products' in P.T. Nicholson, I. Shaw (eds), *Ancient Egyptian Materials and Technology*. Cambridge, Cambridge University Press: 304–06

Van der Leeuw, S. 2009: 'The long-term evolution of social organization' in D. Lane, D. Pumain, S. van der Leeuw, G. West (eds), *Complexity Perspectives in Innovation and Social Change*. Berlin, Springer: 85–116

Van der Veen, M. 1992: *Crop Husbandry Regimes: An Archaeobotanical Study of Farming in Northern England 1000 BC – AD 500*. Sheffield, University of Sheffield Archaeological Monographs

— 1995: 'The identification of maslin crops' in H. Kroll, R. Pasternak (eds), *Res Archaeobotanicae. International Workgroup for Palaeoethnobotany: Proceedings of the 9th Symposium, Kiel 1992*. Kiel, Oetker-Voges: 335–43

Van der Veen, M., Fieller, N. 1982: 'Sampling seeds' *Journal of Archaeological Science* 9: 287–98. http://dx.doi.org/10.1016/0305-4403(82)90024-3

Van Loon, M.N. (ed.) 1975: *Korucutepe* 1. *Final Report on the Excavations of the Universities of Chicago, California (Los Angeles) and Amsterdam in the Keban Reservoir, Eastern Anatolia 1968–1970*. Amsterdam, North-Holland Publishing Co

— 1980: 'Conclusion' in M.N. van Loon (ed.), *Korucutepe* 3. *Final Report on the Excavations of the Universities of Chicago, California (Los Angeles) and Amsterdam in the Keban Reservoir, Eastern Anatolia, 1968–1970*. Amsterdam, North-Holland Publishing Co: 271–77

Van Zeist, W. 1968: 'Studies of modem and Holocene pollen precipitation in south-east Turkey' *Palaeohistoria* 14: 19–40

— 1968–1970: 'Prehistoric and early historic food plants in the Netherlands' *Palaeohistoria* 14: 41–173

— 1972: 'Palaeobotanical results in the 1970 season at Çayönü, Turkey' *Helinium* 12: 3–19

— 1993: 'Archaeobotanical evidence of the Bronze Age field weed flora of northern Syria' in C. Brombacher, S. Jacomet, J.N. Haas (eds), *Dissertationes Botanicae; The Zoller Festschrift: Contributions to the Philosophy and History of the Natural Sciences, Evolution and Systematics, Ecology and Morphology, Geobotany, Pollen Analysis, and Archaeobotany*. Stuttgart, Cramer: 499–511

Van Zeist, W., Bakker-Heeres, J.A.H. 1982: 'Archaeobotanical studies in the Levant 1. Neolithic sites in the Damascus basin: Aswad, Ghoraifé, Ramad' *Palaeohistoria* 24: 165–256

— 1984a: 'Archaeobotanical studies in the Levant 2. Neolithic and Halaf levels at Ras Shamra' *Palaeohistoria* 26: 151–70

— 1984b: 'Archaeobotanical studies in the Levant 3. Late Palaeolithic Mureybit' *Palaeohistoria* 26: 171–99

— 1985: 'Archaeobotanical studies in the Levant 4. Bronze Age sites on the north Syrian Euphrates' *Palaeohistoria* 27: 247–316

Van Zeist, W., Bottema, S. 1971: 'Plant husbandry in Early Neolithic Nea Nikomedeia, Greece' *Acta Botanica Neerlandica* 20: 524–38. http://dx.doi.org/10.1111/j.1438-8677.1971.tb00736.x

— 1991: *Late Quaternary Vegetation of the Near East*. Wiesbaden, Reichert

Van Zeist, W., Casparie, W.A. 1984: *Plants and Ancient Man: Studies in Palaeoethnobotany. Proceedings of the Sixth Symposium of the International Work Group for Palaeoethnobotany, Groningen 1983*. Boston/Rotterdam, Balkema

Viklund, K. 1998: *Cereals, Weeds and Crop Processing in Iron Age Sweden*. Umeaa, Department of Archaeology, University of Umeaa

Wagstaff, J.M. 1973: 'Physical geography and settlements' in D.H. French (ed.), 'Aşvan 1968–1972' *Anatolian Studies* 23: 197–215. http://dx.doi.org/10.2307/3642540

Watson, A.M. 1983: *Agricultural Innovation in the Early Islamic World. The Diffusion of Crops and Farming Techniques, 700–1100*. Cambridge, Cambridge University Press

Watson, P.J. 1976: 'In pursuit of prehistoric subsistence: a comparative account of some contemporary flotation techniques' *Mid-Continental Journal of Archaeology* 1: 77–100

Weaver, M.E. 1971: 'A new water separation process for soil from archaeological excavations' *Anatolian Studies* 21: 65–68. http://dx.doi.org/10.2307/3642630

Weber, S.A. 2003: 'Archaeobotany at Harappa: indications for change' in S.A. Weber, W.R. Belcher (eds), *Indus Ethnobiology: New Perspectives from the Field*. Lanham, Lexington Books: 175–98

Weinstein, M.W. 1973: 'Household structures and activities' in D.H. French (ed.), 'Aşvan 1968–1972' *Anatolian Studies* 23: 271–76. http://dx.doi.org/10.2307/3642545

Whallon, R. 1979: *An Archaeological Survey of the Keban Reservoir Area of East-Central Turkey*. Ann Arbor, Museum of Anthropological Archaeology

Whallon, R., Kantman, S. 1969: 'Early Bronze Age development in the Keban reservoir, east-central Turkey' *Current Anthropology* 10: 128–33. http://dx.doi.org/10.1086/201015

Whittow, M. 2003: 'Decline and fall? Studying long-term change in the east' in L. Lavan W. Bowden (eds), *Theory and Practice in Late Antique Archaeology*. Leiden, Brill: 404–23

Wick, L., Lemcke, G., Sturm, M. 2003: 'Evidence of Lateglacial and Holocene climatic change and human impact in eastern Anatolia: high-resolution pollen, charcoal, isotopic and geochemical records from the laminated sediments of Lake Van, Turkey' *The Holocene* 13: 665–75. http://dx.doi.org/10.1191/0959683603hl653rp

Wilkinson, T.J. 1990: *Town and Country in Southeastern Anatolia* 1. *Settlement and Land Use at Kurban Höyük and Other Sites in the Lower Karababa Basin*. Chicago, Oriental Institute of the University of Chicago

Willcox, G. 1974: 'A history of deforestation as indicated by charcoal analysis of four sites in eastern Anatolia' *Anatolian Studies* 24: 117–33. http://dx.doi.org/10.2307/3642603

— 2009: 'Gordon Hillman's pioneering influence on Near Eastern archaeobotany, a personal appraisal' in A.S. Fairbairn, E. Weiss (eds), *From Foragers to Farmers: Papers in Honour of Gordon C. Hillman*. Oxford, Oxbow Books: 15–18

Williams, D. 1973a: 'Modern agricultural technology in Aşvan' in D.H. French (ed.), 'Aşvan 1968–1972' *Anatolian Studies* 23: 277–79. http://dx.doi.org/10.2307/3642546

Williams, D. 1973b: 'Flotation at Siraf' *Antiquity* 47: 288–92. http://dx.doi.org/10.1017/S0003598X00039132

Winn, M.M. 1980: 'The Early Iron Age pottery' in Van Loon (ed.), *Korucutepe* 3. *Final Report on the Excavations of the Universities of Chicago, California (Los Angeles) and Amsterdam in the Keban Reservoir, Eastern Anatolia, 1968–1970*. Amsterdam, North-Holland Publishing Co: 155–75

Wollstonecroft, M.M., Hroudová, Z., Hillman, G.C., Fuller, D.Q. 2011: 'Bolboschoenus glaucus (Lam.) S. G. Smith, a new species in the flora of the ancient Near East' *Vegetation History and Archaeobotany* 20: 459–70. http://dx.doi.org/10.1007/s00334-011-0305-3

Yazıcıoğlu, T., Karaali, A., Gökçen, J. 1978: '*Cephalaria syriaca* seed oil' *Journal of the American Oil Chemists Society* 55: 412–15. http://dx.doi.org/10.1007/BF02911903

Zhukovsky, P. 1933: *La Turquie Agricole.* Leningrad, Selkhozgiz

Zohary, D., Hopf, M., Weiss, E. 2012: *Domestication of Plants in the Old World: The Origin and Spread of Domesticated Plants in Southwest Asia, Europe, and the Mediterranean Basin* (4th edition). Oxford, Oxford University Press. http://dx.doi.org/10.1093/acprof:osobl/9780199549061.001.0001

Zohary, M. 1973: *Geobotanical Foundations of the Middle East.* Sttutgart/Amsterdam, Fischer/Sweets and Zeitlinger